WEIMAR

Other Books by Michael H. Kater

Das "Ahnenerbe" der SS, 1935–1945: Ein Beitrag zur Kulturpolitik des Dritten Reiches (Deutsche Verlags-Anstalt, 1974)

Studentenschaft und Rechtsradikalismus in Deutschland, 1918–1933: Eine sozialgeschichtliche Studie zur Bildungskrise in der Weimarer Republik (Hoffmann & Campe, 1975)

The Nazi Party: A Social Profile of Members and Leaders, 1919–1945 (Harvard University Press, 1983)

Doctors under Hitler (University of North Carolina Press, 1989)

Different Drummers: Jazz in the Culture of Nazi Germany (Oxford University Press, 1992)

The Twisted Muse: Musicians and their Music in the Third Reich (Oxford University Press, 1997)

Composers of the Nazi Era: Eight Portraits (Oxford University Press, 2000)

Hitler Youth (Harvard University Press, 2004)

Never Sang for Hitler: The Life and Times of Lotte Lehmann, 1888–1976 (Cambridge University Press, 2008)

WEIMAR

FROM ENLIGHTENMENT TO THE PRESENT

MICHAEL H. KATER

YALE UNIVERSITY PRESS
NEW HAVEN AND LONDON

For information about this and other Yale University Press publications, please contact:
U.S. Office: sales.press@yale.edu   www.yalebooks.com
Europe Office: sales@yaleup.co.uk   www.yalebooks.co.uk

Set in Adobe Caslon Pro by IDSUK (DataConnection) Ltd
Printed in Great Britain by TJ International Ltd, Padstow, Cornwall

Library of Congress Cataloging-in-Publication Data

Kater, Michael H., 1937-
    Weimar : from Enlightenment to the present / Michael H. Kater.
      pages cm
    Includes bibliographical references and index.
    ISBN 978-0-300-17056-6 (cloth : alkaline paper)
1. Weimar (Thuringia, Germany)—History.   2. Weimar (Thuringia,
Germany)—Intellectual life.   3. Weimar (Thuringia, Germany)—Politics
and government.   4. Social change—Germany—Weimar
(Thuringia)—History.   I. Title.
    DD901.W4K38 2014
    943'.2241—dc23
                                                        2014019000

A catalogue record for this book is available from the British Library.

10 9 8 7 6 5 4 3 2 1

For Jonah

Contents

Illustrations

Prologue

My initial reason for studying the history of Weimar was very personal. One of my direct ancestors was a member of the circle of savants surrounding Dowager Duchess Anna Amalia and her son, Duke Karl August, and he is among the men populating the first chapter. When I was growing up in Germany during and after World War II, there was always much talk about him in my grandparents' home, and so my interest in Weimar was piqued from the time I was a youngster. I did not get to see the town until the end of the 1960s, when as a young academic from Canada I came to visit it along with several other East German cities. I was depressed by the run-down scenery with large Communist posters covering walls and fences, and did not have occasion to search for my relative's grave. The dreadful sights of nearby Buchenwald camp further decreased my interest in him, but at the same time induced me to think harder about Weimar as an ancestral heritage. My next chance to inspect the town came in the early 1990s, when my friend and colleague, Göttingen resident Adelheid von Saldern, invited my wife and myself to Weimar on a day trip. I remember eating a modest lunch in a fish restaurant near the Herder Church, in what I now recognize as the well-restored house of Karoline Jagemann, Karl August's chief mistress. (This fish restaurant still exists, but it has changed its ambience under the cold-bright fluorescent cathode lights now manda-tory in the city.) I admired the famous Lucas Cranach painting in the Herder Church. Schillerstrasse, today in a pedestrian zone, was full of plastic Trabant cars. I also remember standing in front of an imposing, if dilapidated, façade near the Ilm river on the edge of town; the doors seemed bolted shut; later I saw them again as the reconstituted entrance to the Goethe and Schiller Archive. In Buchenwald, one could finally reflect on evidence of a post-May 1945 Soviet presence, of which, naturally, there had not been a whisper to me from the Communist functionary guides twenty-five years earlier. They had been more interested in pointing out where Communist leader Ernst Thälmann had been shot by the SS and had shown me shrunken inmates' heads.

A scholarly interest in Weimar flared up, bolstered by my not always dormant private motives, after I had read David Clay Large's history of Berlin (2000), the exemplary chronicle of a commune. At the turn of the last century, I had become more interested in German culture in connection with my project on opera singer Lotte Lehmann, even though her culture, apart from her operatic training and repertoire, was really more of Austria and the United States. Before that, I had completed studies of the German music scene under the Nazis. As I was reading Large's book, I became more consciously aware that what for decades had been called "Weimar Culture" was, in reality, "Berlin Culture" and that "Weimar Germany" (1919–33) historically had very little to do with the town of Weimar itself. It had of course been the seminal book by Peter Gay, *Weimar Culture* (1968), which had, not intentionally I hope, helped to foster that confusion. With the notable exception of the original Bauhaus from 1919 to 1925, there was precious little emanating from Weimar that determined what turned out to be the predominant culture of the German republic: men like Max Reinhardt, Thomas Mann, Arnold Schoenberg, Bertolt Brecht, Erwin Piscator, Kurt Weill, and the Expressionist painters were connected to Berlin or Vienna rather than Weimar. The Weimar National Assembly, which gave the republic its name, was housed in Weimar's local theater for little more than half a year, before it relocated to Berlin.

When I returned to Weimar in 2007, and revisited it in the next few years, to find out what the town was really like and how over the centuries it connected to the rest of Germany, its culture, politics, society, and economy, I was not sure whether it was a prism through which to view the whole of Germany, or whether it had developed along a local *Sonderweg*. Researching and writing my book, I found evidence of both, but no pattern of consistency. Often Weimar seemed to be in isolation from the rest of the country (as when it hosted the eighteenth-century Muses' Court); at other times it was the epitome of trends in Germany, as at the time of Hitler's Buchenwald. I have come to no conclusion built on a theory, or on which to build a theory. At the same time the uniqueness of the town was undeniable – atmosphere, buildings, feeling, cuisine, landscape, lingual dialect, sight, sound, and physical touch – as it had appeared to citizens and visitors over many decades. Quaint Weimar was always seductively attractive, with ordinariness and ugliness often hidden.

Weimar's atmosphere, apart from any politics and the everyday business of – what today has become, in large parts, commodified – culture, comes through uncannily in the second book that influenced me toward writing a modern history: Thomas Steinfeld's *Weimar* (1998). One can hear the rustling of the tree leaves near the Ilm as one reads that book. More of a factual history, also published around this time, was Peter Merseburger's spirited *Mythos Weimar*, a great inspiration, although unfortunately it concentrated more on the early phase of the town's past than on the latter and now is due for some serious factual revisions.

The large scope of the research before me demanded that I seek help of an institutional, financial and interpersonal nature. For the finances I am in debt – once again – to York University and the Social Sciences and Humanities Research Council of Canada in Ottawa, for generous help over three years. The same goes for the Alexander von Humboldt-Stiftung in Bonn, whose Konrad-Adenauer Research Award in Germany I have received, and in which capacity I was reinvited. Here Gerhard A. Ritter, the Munich emeritus historian, acted as my sponsor for the third time. Local institutional assistance was provided by Weimar's Bauhaus-Universität, which afforded me temporary guest status, helping me overcome logistic hurdles. I especially thank Professor Gerd Zimmermann, the rector, and Dr. Christiane Wolf of the university's Archiv der Moderne. Dr. Wolf introduced me to the relevant libraries and archives, most importantly the Anna Amalia Library's imposingly modern new users' room. She and her husband Michael repeatedly demonstrated hospitality and friendship at their Weimar home. At the library, Petra Schneider kindly and patiently provided the many large-formatted newspaper volumes I perused. At the Thüringisches Hauptstaatsarchiv Weimar Dr. Bernhard Post and Dr. Frank Boblenz were of help, and at the town archive Dr. Jens Riederer. I could approach them with detailed questions, even from Canada. I gladly acknowledge having received valuable tips and assistance from Professor Karl Schawelka of the Bauhaus-Universität and Anne Feuchter-Schawelka, as well as Dr. Holm Kirsten of Gedenkstätte Buchenwald. In addition, I have to thank Dr. Bernd Ufer, Rosemarie Spath, and Jana Braunholz for helping with accommodation. Also in Weimar and Jena, I owe much to Dr. Justus H. Ulbricht and his wife, the publisher Christine Jäger, for generous hospitality, books, and advice. At the University of Jena, it was my colleague Norbert Frei who, together with Dr. Sybille Steinbacher, invited me to a dedicated symposium in October of 2009, at which I could air first impressions and receive valuable feedback.

In Garmisch-Partenkirchen at the Richard Strauss-Institut, Dr. Christian Wolf and Dr. Jürgen May allowed me to examine papers from the composer's Weimar period, from 1889 to 1894, none of which had yet been published. In Kiel in October 2008, long-time friends Professor Hartmut Lehmann and Dr. Silke Lehmann, formerly of Washington, DC, and Göttingen, provided a weekend of culture and recreation which afforded opportunities for discussion and reflection. They have my gratitude.

Research in Canada was supported substantially by the combined efforts of York University librarians Mary Lehane, Gladys Fung, Sandra Snell, and Samantha McWilliams. Often, they helped me in the capacity of research assistants, beyond the call of duty for librarians. I cannot thank them enough.

I have asked colleagues and friends to read parts of chapters or, indeed, whole chapters, for comment and criticism. In this regard I owe a primary debt to Hans Rudolf Vaget, an internationally known expert on Goethe, Wagner, and Thomas Mann, who aided me in a variety of ways. Constructive criticism also came from William E. Seidelman, Peter Loewenberg, Pamela M. Potter, Jonathan Petropoulos, and Herman Schornstein. I like to think that they all saved me from several potential embarrassments.

And finally, at Yale University Press in London, it was my editor Heather McCallum who administered inspirational advice even before I signed with her. Her expert assistance and moral support throughout research and writing have never wavered. I was very fortunate to have her by my side. If I have made mistakes, neither she nor anyone else can share the blame.

Michael H. Kater

Abbreviations

AEG	Allgemeine Elektrizitätsgesellschaft
BDM	Bund Deutscher Mädel
BM	*Berliner Morgenpost* (Berlin)
BMW	Bayrische Motoren-Werke
BZ	*Berliner Zeitung* (Berlin)
CDU	Christlich Demokratische Union
DAW	Deutsche Ausrüstungswerke
DDP	Deutsche Demokratische Partei
DM	Deutsche Mark
DNT	Deutsches Nationaltheater
DNVP	Deutsch-Nationale Volkspartei
DR	*Das Reich* (Berlin)
DS	*Der Spiegel* (Hamburg)
DW	*Die Welt* (Hamburg)
DZ	*Die Zeit* (Hamburg)
ELG	Einkaufs- und Liefergenossenschaften
FAZ	*Frankfurter Allgemeine Zeitung* (Frankfurt am Main)
FDGB	Freier Deutscher Gewerksschaftsbund
FDJ	Freie Deutsche Jugend
FDP	Freie Demokratische Partei Deutschlands
FR	*Frankfurter Rundschau* (Frankfurt am Main)
FRG	Federal Republic of Germany
GDR	German Democratic Republic (DDR)
HA	*Hamburger Abendblatt* (Hamburg)
HAB	Hochschule für Architektur und Bauwesen
HJ	Hitler-Jugend
HKG	*Historisch-Kritische Gesamtausgabe*

HO	Handelsorganisation
IBKD	Internationales Komitee Buchenwald-Dora und Kommandos
KfdK	Kampfbund für deutsche Kultur
KPD	Kommunistische Partei Deutschlands
KV	Köchel-Verzeichnis
LDPD	Liberaldemokratische Partei Deutschlands
LPG	Landwirtschaftliche Produktionsgenossenschaften
NATO	North Atlantic Treaty Organization
NDPD	Nationaldemokratische Partei Deutschlands
NDR	Norddeutscher Rundfunk
NFG	Nationale Forschungs- und Gedenkstätten der klassischen deutschen Literatur in Weimar
NKVD	Narodny kommissariat vnutrennikh del
NS	Nationalsozialistisch
NSDAP	Nationalsozialistische Deutsche Arbeiterpartei
NSKG	Nationalsozialistische Kulturgemeinde
NYRB	*New York Review of Books* (New York)
NYT	*New York Times* (New York)
Ossi	*Ostdeutscher*
PDS	Partei des Demokratischen Sozialismus
POW	Prisoner of war
RM	Reichsmark
SA	Sturm-Abteilungen
SAP	Sozialistische Arbeiterpartei
SED	Sozialistische Einheitspartei Deutschlands
SMAD	Sowjetische Militäradministration in Deutschland
SMATh	Sowjetische Militäradministration in Thüringen
SPD	Sozialdemokratische Partei Deutschlands
SS	Schutzstaffel
SS-RuSHA	SS-Rasse- und Siedlungshauptamt
Stasi	Staatssicherheit
SZ	*Süddeutsche Zeitung* (Munich)
TAZ	*Thüringer Allgemeine Zeitung* (Weimar)
TB	Tuberculosis
TLZ	*Thüringische Landeszeitung* (Weimar)
TOB	Thüringer Ordnungsbund
USPD	Unabhängige Sozialdemokratische Partei Deutschlands
VB	*Völkischer Beobachter* (Munich/Berlin)
Vopo	Volkspolizei
Wessi	*Westdeutscher*
WS	*Welt am Sonntag* (Hamburg)

CHAPTER 1

---◆---

A Weimar Golden Age
1770 to 1832

ON FEBRUARY 15, 1770, IN THE TOWN OF WEIMAR, THE MUNICIPAL council chose Johann Michael Heintze, one of three candidates, to be the new rector of the Wilhelm-Ernst Gymnasium. Weimar was the capital of one of four independent Saxon duchies, in an area now called Thuringia, in the center of Germany. The Wilhelm-Ernst Gymnasium was the only upper school in the realm, and one that taught classical languages. The fifty-three-year-old Heintze had experience as deputy director of the Gymnasium in North German Lüneburg. He had studied Greek, Latin, and Hebrew in Leipzig and Göttingen, and as a teacher had been so popular that several students followed him to Weimar. Even the famous Weimar-born medical scholar Christoph Wilhelm Hufeland would later remember him in his autobiography.[1] Dowager Duchess Anna Amalia of Saxe-Weimar-Eisenach, who was raised a princess of Braunschweig-Wolfenbüttel, immediately approved the appointment. In attempting to reform the duchy's school system, in particular the curriculum of the Gymnasium next to the Town Church of St. Peter and Paul, it is likely that she herself had suggested Heintze as one to be trusted with this important job, because Lüneburg was close to Wolfenbüttel. At his inauguration in June Heintze was introduced in Latin. He himself answered with a speech, "De vera auctoris classici notione."[2] When he passed away twenty years later, his personal friend and superior, Superintendent Johann Gottfried Herder, called Heintze's former students fortunate. For "a true Roman" had taught them Latin, a man whom Gotthold Ephraim Lessing nonetheless had once praised for his brilliant command of the German language.[3]

A reformation of the Weimar Gymnasium was meant to spearhead reforms in the entire educational system of the duchy, and hence Heintze was called upon as both an administrator and a teacher. Conditions were not good. Next to Heintze, there were only seven other teachers (still, this Gymnasium had a much larger faculty than comparable German schools), who were both lazy and unsystematic in their work.[4] Subjects of instruction were ill-defined. Many students practiced absenteeism; some left the school before graduation to enter the nearby University of Jena. Students were forced to wear school uniforms that some could not afford and which grew shabby; others were cheated by duchy officials out of the meal tickets that had been the Gymnasium's privilege for decades.[5]

Heintze, an indefatigably conscientious educator, tried for years to bring about changes, enthusiastically backed by Herder when he arrived in the fall of 1776. But neither he nor Herder could make a difference: the school situation in Weimar, as in the entire duchy, remained dismal.[6] Heintze may have been compensated for this failure by the company he was able to keep; next to Herder he socialized with Christoph Martin Wieland, who arrived in 1772, and Johann Wolfgang Goethe, who came three years later.[7] His staff member Johann Musäus was a well-respected author of fairy tales. Thus he became part of a small circle of highly educated bureaucrats and politicians, joined by educated members of the nobility, most of them in the service of the court. All were supportive of and active in culture, knowledge, and science. Heintze's own specialties were classical literature, philosophy, and history; he was known for his published disquisitions in these fields and had translated Plato and Cicero into German.[8]

Heintze shared the humanism and interest in the classics of Wieland, who arrived in Weimar from nearby Erfurt University in September 1772, after Duchess Anna Amalia had hired him as educator to her oldest son, Dauphin Karl August. The ever-artistic Anna Amalia was aware of Wieland's writings, such as his most recent, the novel *History of Agathon*. Alongside Klopstock, Lessing, and Gellert, this thirty-nine-year-old professor of philosophy was already one of the best-known authors in Germany. Madame de Staël later compared him to Voltaire, with whom Wieland, son of a Swabian clergyman, shared religious skepticism. His lightness of style even in German reminded her of the French manner.[9] Wieland came to Weimar after Anna Amalia had read his new work, *The Golden Mirror*, in which pedagogical ideas were aired. This made the duchess consider him as tutor for her fifteen-year-old son Karl August, whose current tutor, Count Johann Eustach von Görtz, she mistrusted. It was possible, she feared, that Görtz would influence her son in the direction of a palace revolution, with the aim of dethroning her. Wieland was to act as a counterweight.[10]

Although the poet was not averse to educating the young prince, what he really wanted was to have time for his own writings, unfettered by a university curriculum. Originally, he had eyed not the small Weimar platform but the imperial court in Vienna, as did most of the poets in the Holy Roman Empire. But after accepting Weimar he became good friends with Görtz. Being paid around 600 taler annually with a life pension attached (Heintze was earning around 350 taler), Wieland was able to write an opera, *Alceste*, with music by the court composer Anton Schweitzer, which was performed by Anna Amalia's lay theater troupe in May 1773, and successfully repeated on the Weimar stage.[11] Today it is regarded as the first true German opera. As expected, Wieland put in regular appearances at the Weimar court, dining there several times a month; he educated the prince in history and law, and still had time for his own work.[12] Already well entrenched in the classical tradition, he authored, in poetic form, *Oberon* in 1780; at the same time he devoted himself to the German idiom and started producing a journal, *Der Teutsche Merkur*. It sought contributions from the likes of Hufeland, who published an article on Mesmer's magnetism there in 1785.[13]

With Wieland's appointment Anna Amalia had followed, for the second time, a strategy by which she would attract to her court men of culture and of letters without the outlay of large funds possessed by a prominent Maecenas of the Renaissance. As the niece of Frederick the Great of Prussia and reared at a sophisticated paternal court she was deeply immersed in culture herself.[14] Hence she offered these men posts in the administration of her realm, and as salaried officials they would entertain her on the side – an educated coterie as permanent fixture.[15] The third time this approach was tried was in 1775 when her son, now the reigning duke and barely of age, expressed his intention to sign up the young Frankfurt lawyer Johann Wolfgang Goethe.

Goethe was born on August 28, 1749. With his play *Götz von Berlichingen* (1773), a historical drama influenced by Shakespeare, he achieved fame all over Germany; with his novel *Die Leiden des jungen Werther* (1774), in which a young man kills himself over unrequited love, European fame. It became a cult book. Everywhere young men were dressing in the Werther style: yellow vest and trousers, complemented by a blue frock and brown boots.[16] In that sense, Goethe was the creator of modern popular culture, long before the Beatles. Others committed copycat suicides, with the *Werther* book placed on their body. In describing this greatest of German writers, who was also an artist, a stage director, a landscape architect, a mine administrator and a politician, superlatives abound. About 3,000 drawings by him are extant, and his works and letters amount to 138 volumes. In the words of Nicholas Boyle, so far his most authoritative biographer, "he had a natural affinity with the rhythms of the German language and throughout his life produced, unpredictably, but with dreamlike facility, lyric poems of unique form and character." His two-part drama *Faust* constitutes the greatest long poem of recent European literature, inspiring numerous further treatments of the theme.[17] Madame de Staël has written that in himself alone he united "all that distinguishes German genius: and no one besides is so remarkable for a peculiar species of imagination which neither Italians, English, or French, have ever attained."[18] The young Wilhelm von Humboldt was overwhelmed by *Werther*: he read it through the night until he finished in the morning.[19] Friedrich Nietzsche placed Goethe above all other Germans, but his view that Goethe was beyond envy was erroneous.[20] Karl Jaspers credits him as a giant of "world literature," who conjured "the unity of mankind."[21]

Goethe came from a patrician family of recent upward mobility; his father was a Frankfurt municipal councillor independently wealthy enough to lead a comfortable rentier's life.[22] Goethe studied law in Leipzig and Strasbourg and attained a comparatively modest licentiate, although soon everybody would call him "Doctor Goethe." He knew of Wieland, whose *Alceste* in 1773 he publicly blamed for having falsified the image of Greek gods.[23] Goethe, a handsome young man and popular with the ladies, was nevertheless unhappy with his likely future as a lawyer in Frankfurt, felt stifled in his literary creativity, and was looking for alternatives.[24] In 1774 he met both Prince Karl August of Weimar and his younger brother Constantin, who were in the area for French education, accompanied by the latter's mentor, Carl Ludwig von Knebel. This retired major wished to meet with Goethe because of the Wieland controversy. Goethe and Knebel became fast friends and he also took to the crown prince. Back in Weimar Knebel, a literary man of Anna Amalia's liking, beat the drum for Goethe, who was persuaded to move to Weimar in November 1775 as guest of the new duke. Just married to Princess Luise of Hesse-Darmstadt, Karl August was then a mere eighteen years old, whereas Goethe was twenty-six.[25] Could the multi-talented Goethe not serve in the duchy's administration as well as be the cultured friend of Knebel, Karl August, and Anna Amalia?

One may ask not only why Goethe went to Weimar, but also why he stayed there, for many years, when he could easily have moved on. For 1775–76, bored with Frankfurt and with himself, and having been acquainted with several young women without committing himself, Goethe felt that Weimar seemed just the right place for a young man with his particular talents. He displayed great ambition, was nothing less than arrogant, and wanted to exert influence over people, hoping for rapid promotion. Weimar was geographically in the middle of Germany, roughly equidistant from Frankfurt and Leipzig on the east–west axis, and from Berlin and Munich to the north and south. As a town it was much smaller than any of the dominant four, and the principality itself was manageable. Goethe could stir up events here in a manner that was not possible in a larger place where he would not be able to stand out.[26] He could avail himself of friendship with a duke young enough to be malleable, who stood to grant him a significant position in the administration and a commensurate salary. Indeed, in June 1776 Goethe received the title of legation councillor and a seat on the three-member Secret Council headed by the much older Prime Minister Baron Jakob Friedrich von Fritsch, after his objections had been neutralized – especially by Anna Amalia who was, as always, interested in good government.[27] Goethe's pay was to be 1,200 taler, twice the money Wieland earned. There was the closeness of a university – at Jena, some ten miles to the east.[28] And then there were the interpersonal factors. Wieland, whom he had criticized earlier, enthusiastically welcomed his arrival, calling Goethe "a wonderful human being," whom it was necessary to be introduced to "face to face."[29] Goethe would be called upon by Karl August to join him and a few select friends in their capers, on the hunt and in the hamlets chasing village beauties, to say nothing of keeping company with polite society at court. Finally, a few days after his arrival in Weimar, Goethe met a woman seven years his senior, very attractive and with an inquisitive intellect. Baroness Charlotte von Stein had an indifferent husband, the equestrian marshal at court, and Goethe would remain inordinately attached to her for years.[30]

Before Goethe made his name in Weimar as a policy-maker, he acquired a questionable reputation as a prankster, always in the company of his friend, the duke. Trading on his reputation as a famous author, he took liberties in his behavior, knowing that the duke would approve and even encourage him. He bristled with self-confidence. The ladies of high society would gush over him, insofar as they had read his romantic novel *Werther*, but also for his handsomeness. Young men would strive to wear the "Werther Costume," that suggestive combination of blue, brown, and yellow; in some cases Karl August even insisted on the outfit. This was in the aura of German post-"Storm and Stress" (*Sturm und Drang*) that had spawned Goethe's earliest writings, and it elicited activities on the borderline of insanity but nonetheless termed *Geniestreiche*, or hits of genius. These included skinny-dipping, riding roughshod over the crops of unsuspecting peasants, staying out at night and drinking recklessly, as well as cavorting with lasses in the field or at village festivities.[31] As a practical joke Goethe and Karl August would stand in the central market square for hours and crack whips, to the annoyance of the vendors and pedestrians.[32] One of the worst of such mindless activities occurred when the two men decided to visit the house of the young entrepreneur Friedrich Justin Bertuch, who had just got married. The duke, declaring Bertuch's new home appointments petit-bourgeois, ripped pages from a book and punctured the new wallpaper with a dagger. Goethe stood by sheepishly yet obviously embarrassed, and when the rampage was over he apologized to the devastated young wife, acknowledging to her that she was having "a tough beginning." Bertuch himself fell gravely ill, but in the end recovered.[33]

Altogether, on the part of Goethe, this demonstrated immaturity rather than a balanced personality. Goethe therefore stood to benefit from the wisdom and experience of the next man to arrive at the court of Weimar, who was five years older. The young law student had met Johann Gottfried Herder 1770 in Strasbourg, where Herder underwent an eye operation. Herder became head preacher at the Bückeburg court in North Germany, where he was unhappy, because his talents were underutilized and the pay was meager. This theologian, a native of East Prussia, resembled Goethe in his plethora of interests; Wieland knew of him and so did Heintze, and when Karl August asked Goethe to find a replacement for the recently deceased superintendent, Goethe suggested Herder. Since a call to a professorship in Göttingen did not materialize, Herder began his new employment in Weimar in October 1776, being paid the same as Goethe.[34] Although he would principally be active in church supervision, he was to oversee the reform of the school system as well. Herder embarked on both tasks, proving himself a charismatic preacher and attempting to introduce teachers' seminaries.[35] But as the polymath that he was, he tried to have time left over for his other interests: writing essays in universal history and literary criticism, collecting folk songs (he would publish a collection in 1778–79), and authoring treatises in philosophy. He worked on a law of humanity, a criticism of his one-time Königsberg teacher Immanuel Kant, and he published a series of *Humanitätsbriefe* well into the 1790s.[36] He emphasized the concept of the *Volk* and championed everything German – although, like Wieland and Goethe, he acknowledged the importance of classical ideas. As a person, Herder stood out: not only because of his deep piety, sharp wit and exquisite learnedness, but also for his charm, concern for others (he became a caring friend of Duchess Luise), and unconventional manners. There was much that was incongruous in his character; for example he would generally chide pupils who went to the theater because the young actresses they sought there he regarded as little better than whores, yet he himself enjoyed stage plays when he thought they were of quality.[37] He was a moody hypochondriac and considered himself increasingly isolated, especially as he found that his writings met with little response, except from his old admirer Wieland, at least at first.[38]

Other figures were instrumental in what has usually been described as Weimar's "Muses' Court" after 1770: most with daytime jobs. Some were professionals such as the court physicians Dr. Hufeland, Christoph Wilhelm's father, and Dr. Wilhelm Ernst Huschke, others professors at the Gymnasium like Heintze's successor Karl August Böttiger. There were musicians, and there were courtiers, such as Knebel and the barons Einsiedel and Seckendorff. Friedrich Hildebrand von Einsiedel was a poet, trans-lator, and composer, but primarily a virtuoso cellist. He played in the ducal lay orchestras, and for opera and theater.[39] So did Siegmund von Seckendorff, a former officer under Frederick the Great, who could add piano and violin to his friend's cello.[40]

In cultural and intellectual intercourse, Goethe, Herder, and Einsiedel revolved around Anna Amalia and Karl August, but less as patrons than as state employers. Anna Amalia had begun her regency of the duchy one year after the death of her husband Ernst August in 1758, carrying with her and expanding on the tradition of culture she inherited from Wolfenbüttel. In that sense, then and later, as Walter Bruford has emphasized, the court at Weimar was not essentially different from courts at Mannheim, Mainz, or Gotha, the last-mentioned being another of the Saxon dukedoms.[41] Anna Amalia was particularly interested in music, and she hosted several of the itinerant opera companies that made the rounds of the European courts. She herself played the piano and some flute, though not as proficiently as her maternal uncle Frederick, and she tried her hand at composing. Of special interest to her were books, which she started collecting in a court library.[42] Theater was also important and the quality was high; touring companies performed works by Voltaire, Lessing, and Klopstock.[43] The example of Johann Michael Heintze illustrates how she cared for impor-tant institutions such as schools, the state church, which was Lutheran, and the university at Jena; and she turned to public welfare and the improve-ment of the health system.[44] In 1774 the theater burned down, but, undaunted, she continued staging plays in new quarters. After Karl August had assumed the reins in 1775, she held her own court and organized private productions in three modest palaces, the Wittumspalais in town, and Ettersburg and Tiefurt just outside. Irregularly and informally, the talents who were attracted to Weimar one by one kept her company, singly or in small groups, but an organized, institutionalized Muses' Court this was not.[45]

If Duchess Anna Amalia had demonstrated enlightened despotism in the manner of her Prussian uncle and, to an extent, Josef II of Austria, her son all but continued the practice. As a younger, hot-blooded, potentate, his reckless personal behavior belied the interest he had in the collective well-being of his subjects, which again places him squarely beside Frederick, Saxony's Elector Friedrich August III, or Baden's Margrave Karl Friedrich. But as Goethe found out through camaraderie, his tastes were coarse; field sports, a small if decorative army, parks, palaces, and especially young women, always occupied his mind. Being unhappily married to Luise of Hesse-Darmstadt, he took mistresses, often more than one: the Countess Jeanette von Werthern, the British Weimar resident Emilie Gore, and probably the mysterious actress Corona Schröter. Later he would woo the actress Karoline Jagemann, sire four children with her and grant her a noble title.[46] He loved the dance, and drinking and parties, roughing it up outside and traveling, even when his health was not the strongest.[47] But although he was of course the picture of an absolute monarch, his ears were not closed to talk of reform, and in the arts and literature he was increasingly well versed. Like his mother, he had read *Werther* before Goethe's arrival, and Goethe's counsel was just as important to him as it was to her.[48] Goethe shaped him gently and carefully, not only in the natural sciences with which he later impressed Alexander von Humboldt, but also in humanities.[49] Humane ideas preoccupied Karl August perhaps even more lastingly than they did the patrician Goethe, as the example of the child murderess Johanna Catharina Höhn was soon to show.

Goethe, Schiller and their Circles

Goethe was the catalyst for what in his very own lifetime became the Golden Age of Weimar, that Athens on the Ilm river, as it was increasingly called in the nineteenth century. Goethe and his fellow savants would propel to fame a small town in central Germany which hitherto had been noted only for the repeated visits of Martin Luther and as the short-term residence of Luther's friend, the painter Lucas Cranach, in the sixteenth century, as well as the musicianship of J. S. Bach in the early eighteenth century.[50]

As for Goethe himself, in the first decade of his career in the dukedom he put in an impressive performance as administrator, although his literary output lagged. Just as his superiors had expected, he excelled in politics. As the junior of the three-member privy council that governed the duchy, he attended one or two meetings a week. Altogether, from June 1776 to

February 1786, he was at over 600 sessions.[51] Commensurate with his performance, his rise was spectacular: from legation councillor he was promoted to secret councillor in 1779, having served instrumentally on various special commissions in a role that today would be that of a minister of state. His peak year was 1782: he was ennobled as Johann Wolfgang *von* Goethe and assumed de facto administration of finances.[52] It meant that he was shouldered with the not inconsiderable burden of putting the fiscal house in order. This was no easy matter, for since Anna Amalia's regency (and aided by the turmoil of the Seven Years War, 1756–63), in the cameral economic style of the time, expenditures of the court and the state had not been separate. Moreover, the costs of keeping court had taken up the bulk of the duchy's entire financial obligations. Already when Karl August assumed office in September 1775, he faced a sovereign deficit economy, which was not helped by events such as the fire in the castle area in the center of town during 1774.[53] Goethe, who had a shrewd sense of economy, tried as best he could, but ultimately without success, to improve this situation as he did with others, such as when he attempted to revitalize the copper and silver mines at nearby Ilmenau.[54] His underlying state philosophy was that of the benevolent absolute rulers of the time, while more progressive concepts of the Enlightenment increasingly tempered older, more traditional, notions of governance. In this he was joined by his intelligent duke, and he certainly had the blessing of the reform-minded Anna Amalia. But his was still an absolutist state, and it was far removed from any notions of democracy, as was Goethe personally.[55] Goethe still endorsed, participated in and even initiated some surprisingly unenlightened practices, such as suppressing regional peasants' rebellions, selling prison inmates to England for battle against American revolutionaries, and infiltrating the University of Jena's faculty and student body with spies.[56]

Goethe surprisingly stopped his gubernatorial activities by moving to Italy in September 1786 for almost two years, without even Karl August's permission. In retrospect, one can identify three reasons for this. One, he had grown tired of whatever his relationship with Charlotte von Stein had been and wanted to cool it down. Second, the sheer weight of his official duties was bearing down on him to the point of collapse. Third, and related to this, he had had no energy and time to be culturally creative – not least, to satisfy his ambitions as a visual artist.[57]

Indeed, since his arrival in Weimar Goethe had hardly written anything significant after *Werther*. With difficulty he completed his new play *Iphigenie auf Tauris*, the first version of which, in prose, was premiered in 1779. It was part of a loosely organized series in which the court expected all of its vaunted literati to participate as a matter of routine, and this was Goethe's – albeit high-quality – contribution.[58] In 1782 he finally completed the second book of what would later become known as his novel *Wilhelm Meister*. Apart from that, he wrote poems and playlets, again for court festivities or as part of his correspondence with Frau von Stein. Other duties for the court included taking part in lay theater, both as actor and director (here some of his less important, earlier, plays were performed), in which capacity he also hired a professional, the enchanting Corona Schröter, away from Leipzig, but these activities decreased in importance over time, especially because in 1783 the full-time troupe of Giuseppe Bellomo was installed.[59]

After returning to Weimar from Italy, Goethe largely withdrew from the administration of state, although he still intervened in matters he deemed important. He did not surrender his active involvement in the Ilmenau mining business and continued to control the affairs of Jena University. Culture in general demanded more of his attention: Anna Amalia's library, a modest drawing school, and his own new studies in color theory, botany, and anatomy.[60] He also rekindled his old love of the stage. With Bellomo's company gone in April 1791, Karl August appointed Goethe to the directorship of a ducal court theater. Here the privy councillor ordered his own plays to be performed, but also those of the very popular local playwright August Kotzebue, as well as *Die Räuber* and *Don Carlos*, dramas by a new and, in everybody's judgment quite sensational, author Goethe had had occasion to watch for a number of years now, by the name of Friedrich Schiller.[61]

Schiller was the first man of letters of note who arrived in Weimar not because he was being summoned to assume an office by the ruling powers, but of his own volition. Weimar's significance in this so-called Golden Age was precisely that it was able to make a name for itself first because a duke or duchess had had the brilliant foresight to invite to their township experts in education, politics, or administration who also functioned as originators and brokers of culture; then, when those personalities were anchored within the town walls, they in turn attracted men of similar caliber. Friedrich Schiller, too, arrived in Weimar with the intention of finding inspiration for his creative work from the likes of Wieland and Goethe (whom he had once seen as a visitor in his home town along with Duke Karl August); at the same time he wanted to find respectable, and permanent, employment.[62]

Unlike Goethe, Schiller was born into poverty, on November 10, 1759, in the small town of Marbach near Stuttgart (Swabia). His father was an army medic serving under the Duke Karl Eugen of Württemberg, who governed his territory in despotic fashion. The young Schiller came to resent him, especially since the duke, instead of allowing him to become a poet, pressed him into the service of a military physician himself. Punished several times for disobedience – Schiller had wielded his pen and temporarily deserted his army unit – the budding writer fled to Mannheim in early 1782, where his drama *Die Räuber* had been accepted for its premier performance, with the famous August Wilhelm Iffland in the leading role as Franz Moor.[63] Like *Werther* ten years earlier, this became an instant success and a source of annoyance for Goethe, not only because he was jealous but also because its main plot was redolent of revolt against authority. The latter aspect equally bothered Duke Karl August, whom Schiller met at Christmas 1784 at the court of Darmstadt. Schiller read to him from his unfinished play *Don Carlos*, whereupon he received the nominal title of a Weimar councillor, which suggested to him that the grass was much greener over there. It was an influential lady friend who had recommended him to the Darmstadt court; Schiller, tall with reddish-blond hair, a prominent nose, and a self-assured yet charming manner, was immediately attractive to women (he had almost been late for his *Räuber* debut because of a romp with a waitress). It was through yet another young woman, Charlotte von Kalb, married into one of Weimar's leading political clans, that Schiller finally found his way into town. Everyone in Weimar assumed at the time, probably correctly, that he was her lover, and predictably she facilitated his first important meetings with Weimar notables.[64]

After reaching Weimar on July 21, 1787, Schiller expected to find Goethe and Karl August there, but was disappointed that the privy councillor was in Italy indefinitely and the ruler just out traveling.[65] The differences and commonalities between Schiller and Goethe at that time are telling: ten years younger, Schiller was certainly as ambitious as Goethe had been twelve years earlier but not nearly as established. He had to try much harder, since Goethe had been *called* to visit, even though Schiller's fame at that time was not far from Goethe's then. In any event, Schiller went to see the fellow Swabian Wieland, with whom he got along quite well at first, owing not least to Wieland's kindly disposition. Although the older poet, like Goethe, disliked *Die Räuber*, he invited his colleague to collaborate on the *Teutsche Merkur*.[66] This became a problem, however, because Schiller was busy with his own journal projects, currently *Thalia* and later *Die Horen*, for publishing journals was one of his pursuits. The *Merkur* had lost subscribers lately. Hence there was rivalry from the outset, which later turned into mutual indifference and even animosity.[67] Next Schiller tried

Herder, with whom he had a less complicated relationship, eventually inviting him successfully to contribute to his *Horen*, until Schiller discovered the philosophy of Kant, whom Herder abhorred.[68]

Since Schiller did not receive a job offer, from the court or elsewhere, he remained stuck with making his money as a writer and editor for journals, and as a playwright – he cleared approximately 100 taler a year. Eventually he received a sinecure of 1,000 taler annually from the Danish minister of state Prinz Friedrich Christian von Augustenburg and his fellow politician Count Ernst Heinrich von Schimmelmann, who were admirers of Schiller's works.[69] Schiller's writings were now concerned with history. He had already studied much history for his drama *Don Carlos*, and by 1788, arising from this, he was concentrating on the rebellion of the oppressed Dutch provinces of Spain. Although this work would remain fragmentary, by September 1790 he had completed the first two of five volumes about the Thirty Years War (1618–48), which crystallized his – soon to be famous – drama *Wallenstein*.[70] Goethe, who since his return to Weimar in June 1788 had been painfully aware that Schiller was living just three houses away from his own (it certainly took some gall for Schiller to be so obtrusive), probably wanted to remove the younger rival when he had him appointed associate professor of history at Jena in December. Even without ulterior motives, however, Goethe knew what he was doing, for he wanted to polish the tarnished image of Jena's academy, which had declined as the duchy's only temple of higher learning. Schiller accepted in the hope of earning a steady income, realizing too late that this was merely an honorific position netting him only attendance fees. Since his reputation preceded him, the auditorium was packed when he held his inaugural lecture in May 1789, on the uses of universal history, but thereafter his students decreased in number. By this time Schiller had moved to Jena and out of Goethe's sight.[71]

With a good eye for opportunity and conscious of his successes with women, Schiller married Charlotte von Lengefeld in 1790, who came from another aristocratic Weimar-area family, actually having had a choice between Charlotte and her older, more sophisticated and vivacious, sister Caroline. (There is consensus today that he really loved Caroline, but thought Charlotte more pliable. Caroline was also still married, yet ready to divorce for Friedrich.)[72] "In spirit and in character he is an extremely interesting person," noted Wilhelm von Humboldt, who was temporarily making his home in Jena at this time, "and the poet in him is everywhere shining through."[73] Alas, only a year later Schiller was showing early symptoms of tuberculosis; the progressive illness delayed or prevented much of his future work.[74]

Apart from his tenuous livelihood and insidious disease, Goethe remained Schiller's main problem. The older man kept avoiding him, and when they finally met in nearby Rudolstadt in September 1788, at a party of the Lengefelds, their small talk led nowhere. By this time Schiller was well known, whereas the national memory of Goethe, who had been out of the sight of Germans for nearly two years, had sunk dramatically. In letters to his closest friends, Schiller admitted to a love–hate for Goethe; he saw him as a prude, "whom one should make a child, to humble her before the world."[75]

It took six more years for this relationship to reverse. But when it did, "a collaborative association was born, of superior effectiveness."[76] It marked the highlight, it defined the very essence of Weimar's Golden Age. Weimar was never, ever the same when this was over.

It is not clear what prompted Schiller to overcome his reticence, but on June 13, 1794, he wrote a letter to Goethe, inviting him to participate in the publication of *Die Horen*, a journal to discuss important issues but not, *expressis verbis*, politics. Instead, it would be "anything that can be treated with taste and in a philosophical spirit, philosophical problems as well as historical and poetic treatises." Those were the subjects that interested Schiller at the time. The fact that Goethe consented makes more sense, for he was still in the process of reinventing himself and could use such a medium as an important platform for new literary output. Among other thinkers who gave the nod to Schiller were Wilhelm von Humboldt and his younger brother Alexander, Johann Gottlieb Fichte (who was then teaching at Jena), Herder, and August Wilhelm Schlegel; even Kant agreed at first – a virtual *Who's Who* of fertile minds. The journal was to be produced by Schiller and Goethe's publisher Johann Friedrich Cotta in an edition of 1,500, and the royalties would be generous.[77]

The deletion of politics was meant to avoid personal rancor and preclude censorship, for political questions of the day would inevitably touch on matters of the French Revolution, which already was in its fifth year and by now had led to the death of the King of the French and a regime of human abuse. There was a double irony in this because in so many ways allusions to the revolution were to be unavoidable, no matter what the prescription, and Goethe and Schiller both had very decided opinions on it already. As an enlightened conservative Goethe had always condemned it, whereas Schiller had been a qualified champion until the outbreak of the Reign of Terror and the decapitation of Louis XVI, in January 1793.[78] Wieland and Herder were also for it, as they were for all of mankind's freedom and happiness, until the onset of the worst excesses.[79]

Thus the path had been cleared for Schiller and Goethe finally to get to know each other better. This was helped along by a meeting the two of them had in Jena on July 20, 1794, after some scholar had given a public talk about a botanical subject at the university. In retrospect Goethe maintained in 1817 that after the lecture he and Schiller happened to be exiting the building next to each other, but it is much more likely that Schiller sought to sidle up to Goethe on purpose because of Goethe's positive response to *Die Horen*. On the other hand, it is equally possible that Goethe sought Schiller's proximity in order to continue using him as his new medium. In any case, they met, and on the way to Schiller's house they continued their discourse about the nature of the archetypal plant. It was carried further once they were inside, and what resulted was the realization on both sides that although they had much in common aesthetically and philosophically, it was clear that Schiller was a metaphysically inclined idealist who, influenced by Kant, claimed that the archetypal plant could be nothing more than an idea. But Goethe contradicted Schiller, "explaining the archetypal plant as his 'experience' and sketching it with a few strokes." The incongruous results of this conversation fascinated both men and made them realize that a dialogue could be set in motion here that would foster their creativity in future.[80]

Without much ado, they now got their project, *Die Horen*, under way. Things went well at first, for Cotta secured 2,000 subscribers. In a section entitled "Epistles" Schiller and Goethe engaged in some interesting intellectual banter, Fichte published an article regarding "the genuine interest for truth," and Goethe produced his "Roman Elegies." Men like the older Humboldt, Herder, and the Jena historian Karl Ludwig Woltmann contributed, although Kant reneged on his promise. Perhaps the most important piece was a two-part dissertation by Schiller, "About Naïve and Sentimentalist Poetry," in 1795 and 1796. Here he categorized genres of poetry and types of poets. Underlying this was a discourse with Goethe, whom he defined as a "naïve" poet, whereas he, Schiller, was the "sentimentalist." Schiller wanted the gap to narrow, and Goethe seems to have given him hope that this was quite foreseeable.[81]

Die Horen survived only for three years, because it had too much against it (with the obvious exception that Schiller and Goethe did draw closer). Some, like the Kiel philosophy professor Wilhelm F.A. Mackensen, thought it too self-referential: mostly the same people wrote in it, always critiquing each other. But the in-group was small. When Fichte supplied a second article in 1795, Schiller as the editor in chief rejected it because it contradicted something he himself was just preparing for publication. Friedrich Schlegel was never admitted, whereas his older brother August Wilhelm was.[82] The quality of contributions began to suffer and, with a strong hint at events in France, the politically neutral stance was criticized. Wieland's much-longer-established *Merkur* was mentioned as an infinitely more balanced alternative, and Schiller's philosophical discussions were attacked as lightweight. Already in its second year *Die Horen*'s editor was losing interest, not least because even Goethe showed signs of withdrawal.[83]

But he and Schiller continued to work together on a collection of distichs, *Xenien*, which, perhaps as a vengeful reprise, was meant to sting their colleagues. *Xenien* was conceived to attack groups, trends, and personalities that Goethe and Schiller poured scorn on. Theirs was the most progressive point of view. One characteristically conspirational specialty of the new approach was the individual anonymity of the two authors, designed to keep the readers guessing which one of them had written. The idea was as brilliant as it was wicked, and for both reasons this immediately drew readers. "With *Xenien*," writes Schiller's biographer Sigrid Damm, "both men demonstrated their friendship, for the first time, in the literary public realm." Indeed, the "xenien" were satyrical attacks, often *ad personam*, against philistinism, provincialism, conservatism, mediocrity, and dilettantism. They targeted popular authors such as Kotzebue and religious bigots like Matthias Claudius and even Goethe's old Swiss friend Johann Caspar Lavater. German Jacobins who favored revolution on home soil were derided, early Romantics such as Friedrich Schlegel confronted. Wieland, who already had to bear *Die Horen* and now voiced objections, was ridiculed as a "virgin." *Xenien* began in January 1796, and when it ended nine months later there were 900 pieces. Goethe and Schiller amused themselves, as readers were guessing that the more acidic pieces had flowed from Schiller's pen. If anything these literary escapades fortified the two men's friendship.[84] Beyond those publicist efforts, Goethe and Schiller cooperated extensively after 1794, so that Schiller moved back from Jena to Weimar in December 1799. For example, Goethe helped Schiller in the conceptualization of his new extended drama *Wallenstein*, instructing him, among other things, in the basics of astrology, which had played such a predominant role in that general's life. Schiller in turn read and commented on parts of Goethe's new novel *Wilhelm Meisters Lehrjahre* and also *Faust*, which Goethe would labor over till the end of his life. Goethe later credited Schiller with having returned to him the gift of creativity, but since the older writer, with his notorious sense of self-importance, sometimes liked to overstate his case, we may take this assertion with a grain of salt. Schiller certainly never ceased in his devoutly reverential attitude towards the man. In 1797 both poets began composing what would become world-famous ballads, such as Schiller's *Der Ring des Polykrates* and Goethe's *Die Braut von Korinth*. They often discussed issues until the small hours, and Goethe had to be careful not to strain Schiller's health, for his tuberculosis was steadily worsening.[85]

Of particular significance was the two men's collaboration in matters of the theater. Here Goethe had the practical experience of a stage director, while Schiller had so far specialized in writing plays. As with the literature of the day, both men wanted to improve the standard of plays being performed and, while they were at it, the overall quality of acting. They had the advantage of Goethe's appointment, since 1791, as court theater director, and his ability to hire professional actors. With women there was always a risk because the consummate philanderer Karl August might take a fancy to one and choose her as his mistress. He did this on two known occasions (if not on three, with Corona Schröter earlier), once when he favored Luise Rudorf and impregnated her, so that Knebel was prevailed upon to marry her. Hence Rudorf, a fine actress, disappeared from the stage.[86] The other instance was more serious, when Karl August chose the voluptuous Karoline Jagemann, a native Weimarer, after the twenty-year-old had returned from professional training at the Mannheim stage in 1797. Since the duke in his capacity of employer had the right of censorship, in 1801 he prevented Schiller's *Jungfrau von Orleans* from being premiered in Weimar because Jagemann was earmarked for the title role, and Karl August thought (after the pattern of Voltaire's ribald *Pucelle*) that her honor would be compromised. Instead, Schiller had the play premiered in Leipzig.[87]

Goethe and Schiller's attempt at reform went a long way to being successful; mediocre pieces by the likes of Kotzebue and Iffland were purged from the program and, whenever possible, replaced by the poets' own. Hence Goethe's *Egmont*, as adapted for the stage by Schiller, was performed in 1796. Schiller's *Piccolomini* of the *Wallenstein* drama series in April 1799 became a huge success, and from Weimar it conquered Germany. The same happened with his *Wilhelm Tell* five years later: first the spectacular world premiere in Weimar, and a few months later sensational accolades in Berlin and on from there. For good reason, then, Goethe made Schiller his co-director of the stage. Schiller was, to all intents and purposes, the more popular of the two, as observed at work or in public.[88] Young actor Eduard Genast, later one of the mainstays of the Weimar theater, has left us impressions from around 1800, when Schiller, already nationally famous, mixed easily with actors and everyone around him, charming them with his quaint Swabian dialect and direct approach.

Goethe, on the other hand, appeared "proud like a king, his head raised high, nodding graciously whenever acknowledging a greeting."[89]

With Goethe and Schiller, individually or as a team constituting a natural core, Weimar's literati, artists, and more alert members of the nobility interacted with and revolved around each other. The result was the formation of a Court of Muses in the widest sense. Anna Amalia and Karl August, who had not intended those developments in precisely the fashion in which they transpired, were instrumental to the functioning of this circle, to the extent of their interest and how they cared to get involved on any given day. Frequently they were themselves in the center of inter-cultural events because of their granting of venues and their role as finan-ciers. But theirs was a random patronage, idealistic as much as materialistic. There existed, after all, four or five different courts between mother and son alone, not counting the separate residence of Duchess Luise – a storey in her husband's palais. One can say that Goethe's expansive house on the Frauenplan, loaned in 1782 and owned in 1792, was an extension of this loosely organized network, and perhaps Wieland's and Herder's houses also, albeit with their economic leverage noticeably curtailed. By 1800 Weimar had gained a widespread reputation as home of the Muses, attracting ever more visitors, several of whom stayed on.[90]

As for the intellectual exchange, the so-called Wednesday Society meetings – which had been held under Anna Amalia's auspices mostly at her Weimar Wittumspalais in the late 1770s and 1780s and to which everybody who counted in town came – were in the early 1790s replaced by gatherings of a Friday Society. These were moved, after interruptions, from a Weimar palace to Goethe's private quarters; attendance was rather selec-tive and the proceedings formal. Luminaries such as Herder, Hufeland, the Gymnasium director Böttiger, and Goethe himself would give learned papers, followed by discussion. Members of the ducal family were invited but Anna Amalia, whose chief interest was always music, attended only rarely, and eventually stayed away.[91] By 1801 there was yet a third institu-tionalized get-together, a *cour d'amour*, also in Goethe's house, and with him and Schiller as hosts. Only fourteen select personalities were invited, for dinner after the theater. This was the stiffest affair yet, in keeping with Goethe's growing pomposity, which Thomas Mann so brilliantly caricatured in his novel *Lotte in Weimar*.[92]

But Herder too had his tea parties, and Wieland entertained local and foreign visitors on his estate in Ossmannstedt, outside of town.[93] Visitors included not only the Humboldt brothers and some early Romantics like Schelling and the Schlegels, but also royalty from nearby principalities, such as Prinz August von Gotha, who once came with the French abbé Guillaume Raynal, a leader of the Enlightenment.[94] The most celebrated yet idiosyncratic visitor undoubtedly was Baroness Germaine de Staël who, because of Schiller's height, in 1803 mistook him for a general, still she did not warm as quickly to the overpowering Goethe. She harmonized best with the congenial Wieland, who was from the age of Voltaire she herself was so familiar with. Weimar had been a must-see town on her list of places in Germany to visit.[95]

Population, Economy, and Society

In the second half of the eighteenth century and into the early nineteenth, Weimar numbered approximately 6,000 people and was growing, with about 100,000 living in the entire duchy.[96] Weimar was an agricultural town structurally broken only by the requisite institutions for a ruling court – palaces, administrative buildings, princely stables. In height they and two churches – Jacobi and St. Peter and Paul's (the Town and later Herder Church) – towered over rows of small, cramped houses decked with incendiary shingles. There are many first impressions of Weimar, some recorded by famous people. Herder called it a "cross between a village and a court-city," Schiller a "village," Madame de Staël "a large castle."[97] There were trade shops and stalls; peasants from the surrounding countryside brought produce to market. Many peasants also lived in Weimar, keeping cows and sheep and pigs which were let out to pasture in the morning and driven back at night. Dung heaps were nestled next to house walls. Although almost every family lived in a house, these were very small, damp, cold, and uncomfortable, and prone to fires. Sanitary conditions were dismal, with open sewers, and chamber pots being emptied from windows over pedestrians' heads after sundown. Small streams and ponds were uncovered, contaminated, and unclean, constantly foul-smelling. Only gradually did the rulers pass ordinances to change this, to cover eyesores and prohibit abuses. But narrow, crooked, manure-soiled streets continued to be unpaved and unsafe, and always unlit at night. The lightning fire of 1774 in the middle of town, during which a worker lost his life, destroyed both the ducal palace Wilhelmsburg and the court theater and made the heart of town look ghastly. Jena University students would invade some evenings for binge-drinking in cheap taverns, riding in on haggard mares and causing a ruckus.[98]

However, to keep this in perspective, one has to ask how Weimar compared to other German places of similar proportions, and even to larger cities like Frankfurt and Berlin. In size, Weimar was typically medium, somewhat smaller than Heidelberg, Darmstadt, or Göttingen. Worms was smaller, at 5,000, Mannheim three times its size, Leipzig more than four times, Frankfurt more than five times, and Dresden ten times. The university towns of Jena and Marburg as well as Wolfenbüttel, Anna Amalia's birthplace, were all smaller.[99]

Nor were the town's conditions uniquely bad or uncomfortable. Darmstadt too was characterized by tradesmen and farmers who sustained its main economy. Frankfurt had no public garbage removal system until 1775, and in Berlin it was criminals who did what street-cleaning there was, although pigs within its city walls had been prohibited since 1681. Berlin had an advanced sewer system only in 1870. One town in the vicinity of Weimar which positively stood out was Gotha; head of a neighboring duchy, it was almost twice as large, airy and well-kept.[100]

From medieval times, historic Weimar was contained within square walls, its four main gates protecting rulers and citizens. In Goethe's years, the walls were already crumbling and the gates becoming relics. Goethe's stately house after 1782, one of a kind, was near the Frauentor on the Frauenplan; it dated from 1709. (In place of the old Frauentor a fine restaurant stands today, Café Frauentor. As one feasts on Thuringian dumplings and goose one has a marvelous view of the poet's residence). The old town was a square then, with the court buildings in the middle, some adjacent to markets. Steps away from the ducal residence, Anna Amalia's library (the former Green Castle) and the town hall were two restaurant-inns which would make history: one was the Elephant, which also figures in Mann's *Lotte in Weimar*, the other Der Erbprinz, almost next to it, where Schiller first lodged on arrival. Next to Goethe's home, and not far from Schiller's first, there was the less exclusive Weisse Schwan, a tavern Goethe frequented and still serving his alleged favorites today. In the Golden Age one could easily criss-cross the town on foot, if street grime would allow it; those few percent of citizens who were not peasants, tradesmen or retail merchants went by carriage. The Gymnasium of Heintze and Böttiger lay next to the main square on the Pottery Market (today named Herderplatz); it was next to St. Peter and Paul's, and Herder's house was close-by. Schiller later lived on the Esplanade (Schillerstrasse), halfway between Goethe's and Herder's houses, and Wieland's house was not far. These were not cumbersome distances to negotiate for the poets and thinkers of this small town on the Ilm, a rivulet passing by the palaces; they could visit each other easily, and appearances at court were quickly managed. More laborious were the trips to Anna Amalia's castles of Ettersburg, several miles to the north, and Tiefurt, equally far to the east, but carriages were usually at hand.[101]

The duchy in general, and Weimar in particular, was economically poor. A famine hit the town from 1770 to 1772; tuberculosis and the pox compounded poverty in the 1790s.[102] Weimar's agricultural base was threadbare, with no outstanding crop, such as wine in Heidelberg or Würzburg – towns vaguely comparable to Weimar in size.[103] Worms near Heidelberg, somewhat smaller, was poorer, having fallen from greater heights and now producing only corn, rape oil, and wine, and not sufficiently for export.[104] In Weimar's hinterland, the feudal open-field system, which was inefficient, could only slowly be got rid of, because it meant the elimination of sheep-farming, and sheep's wool was needed for the textile shops of nearby Apolda. As a consequence, insufficient crops were produced for human consumption, as well as inadequate feedstuff for cattle. The reform-minded Karl August attempted to encourage modern farming methods, but was hampered by traditional manor rights favoring the outlying estate owners, and himself played havoc with the fields by chasing over them with his hunting packs. Fertilizer shortage was chronic, the peasants themselves were overtaxed, abused for the hunts, and possessed no extra capital to invest in homestead improvement.[105]

The Apolda stocking weavers supported the most significant economic enterprise in the entire duchy, predicated on an interdependence with the region's sheep farmers. But this industry was bedeviled by short-sighted planning, curtailed transport, and the vagaries of supply and demand. If in one year, 1779, there was overproduction, after a steady rise in the number of looms, resulting in a surfeit but still not plentiful for export, in most years there was not enough wool for the mills. In the 1780s and '90s Apolda's weavers sank into poverty, a situation which is said to have troubled Minister Goethe, although, if that is true, he was not able to avert it.[106] And he could do equally little about the mainly state-owned copper and silver mines at Ilmenau, whose operations had been suspended after flooding in 1739. Yet even before that disaster, the mines had not been cost-effective. More money was poured into the venture in the following decades, with the court investing the majority. After a mine rupture in 1796 Goethe wasted all of his time in Ilmenau on resurrecting an enterprise that was technically rickety and economically not viable.[107]

Artisans toiled in Weimar, and some worked in the outlying villages, producing wares for home consumption – whatever the local market could bear – but no surplus or a specialty for export. In town, they often had no effective displays, only stalls. Since 1653 every October, a three-day festive onion market was held in the town center, where some extra money could be made by incoming farmers and, perhaps, local artisans. Earning little, many of them had to look for second jobs, usually as farmhands in the country; others took to begging, stealing, and violating aristocratic hunt and fishing restrictions.[108] And even if farmers, weavers, miners, and handicraftsmen had generated something original for export, they would have faced hurdles in getting their wares out of Weimar and the dukedom. The Ilm was too small a river for shipping – very unlike the Neckar at Heidelberg or the Main of Würzburg, to say nothing of Frankfurt's artery. The main land traffic went through Buttelstedt ten miles to the north of Weimar, where the post-and-coach monopoly had its nearest branch. So for national trade and commerce, Weimar was at the end of the world, even though for its needs as a town and a court, it lacked self-sufficiency.[109]

The court constituted by far the largest single industry in town, and although it continued to subsist on a deficit economy, it was always the largest employer. There was in fact overemployment, for instance in the army; Weimar had been a garrison town since 1753. Nevertheless, Goethe once succeeded in reducing the size of the infantry from as many as 500 to 250 men. He also cut down on the grossly overblown expenditures in court and princely stables, lowering the annual budget from 59,000 to 30,000 taler. But these were only drops in the bucket, for expenses for other items bypassed these treasuries – inevitably, since court and private funds often were mixed – what with the consumption of luxury items such as genuine Raphael sketches having to be bought for the court at the Leipzig Fair and all manner of foodstuffs ferried to the princely tables! But when surrounding municipalities needed firefighting equipment, the money was not there. All told, systematic infrastructure financing did not exist.[110]

The second-largest source of employment in town was a socio-economic phenomenon, unique for its time not just in Weimar but in all of Germany; however, it could make little difference to the overall demographic picture. As a young man, the native Weimarer Friedrich Justin Bertuch founded Weimar's first modern industrial compound, based on mercantilist principles. Bertuch had initially assisted Wieland with the publication of his *Teutsche Merkur*, but soon struck out on his own, creating a fashion journal, and from there branching out with a publishing company, an artificial-flower factory employing hundreds, and banking. His aim was to connect Weimar's modest commerce to the rest of Germany and to the world, and he himself eventually became well known beyond Weimar's narrow confines. But, on the cusp of modern capitalism, Bertuch was hampered by outmoded guild rules, by a complex system of tolls and tariffs, and by the sheer personal envy of his fellow citizens. Goethe, who was two years younger, had only contempt for him, because Bertuch too was ambitious as an author and editor. Still, this did not prevent the privy councillor from availing himself of Bertuch's services when expedient. In this case Schiller, too, showed arrogance. Although he benefited frequently from the entrepreneur's personal advice, he scoffed at him after Bertuch had suggested some kind of loose commercial partnership – in publishing. "The man deludes himself that we are on common ground," Schiller sneered, "yet I will not quite break off with him." After all, the poet of German Idealism thought that Bertuch could be of use to him in difficult times.[111]

The weavers of stockings in the pre-capitalist cottage industry of Apolda and, where there were remnants, of Weimar itself, constituted a preindustrial proletariat that existed below subsistence level.[112] They earned well below 100 taler a year, a fraction of the salary of Privy Councillor Goethe.[113] Unskilled miners in Ilmenau, many peasants, and untrained farmhands tended to earn even less, living in desolate poverty.[114] Despite assurances by recent Goethe apologists that he was sympathetic to such a plight, his sympathy was merely rhetorical.[115] Evidence shows that this foe of the French Revolution was unable to aid the miners and that he helped in the repression of economically straitened farmers.[116] He also treated his own servants in a miserly fashion, keeping their wages abysmally low.[117]

Well over one half of the population in and around Weimar belonged to this preindustrial proletariat during the decades of the Golden Age. Not quite a third may be counted as part of the better-off artisanal, merchant, and lower-professional stratum, earning between 100 and 400 taler annually. An upper layer of seasoned professionals, wealthy rentiers, and lower nobility made between 400 and 1,000 taler, and the elite comprised merely 2 percent, with more than 1,000 taler a year. Those top people were mostly at court, whereas the resident geniuses such as Wieland and Schiller straddled social classes – sometimes, like Schiller, in steady upward mobility. Schoolteachers were often at 100 taler – their impoverishment was proverbial – and Jena professors rarely above 300. When Hufeland was still employed by the court as a young physician, he earned no more than 100 taler, and only 200 more when teaching at the university.[118]

This second and third stratum of burghers was growing, to make up what later was called the *Mittelstand*, or middle class.[119] In classical Weimar, the divisions between the second stratum and the lower class on the one hand, and the third stratum and the upper class on the other were rigid (more so for the first-mentioned). At court, only members of the fourth and highest stratum were permitted, and the theater auditorium was divided between the right side, where the titled nobility took seats, and the left side, where burghers could sit – unlike the nobles, they had to pay for admission.[120] This seemingly insignificant example shows how important it was even for the idealistic thinkers of Weimar to constantly move up. Before long, there was pressure on Schiller and then also on Herder to obtain standing in the nobility (as Goethe had done early, effortlessly): both excused their self-serving quests, Schiller with the argument that his originally aristocratic wife needed it (she never lost her haughtiness), Herder with economic reasoning.[121] Wieland abstained but, not coincidentally, he was the most enthusiastic and enduring supporter of the French Revolution.

As far as women of all strata were concerned, they were expected to get married or stay with their relatives. Women from the best families could enter abbeys or perform services at court in exchange for room and board; those of the proletariat worked as maids. It was through the function of maids, unmarried women without means, and wealthy matriarchs that more details about Goethe's personality, and in particular his attitude toward society, can be revealed here. There was, for example, his role in the execution of child murderess Johanna Catharina Höhn, from the village of Tannroda, outside Weimar. On April 11, 1783, this twenty-three-year-old maid serving in a Weimar mill killed her newborn baby boy with the knife she had used to cut the umbilical cord. She was later arrested, tried for murder and found guilty. The case eventually came before the Privy Council on which Goethe was serving, along with Baron von Fritsch and a third member. It was supposed to advise Duke Karl August in the matter of the penalty: should Höhn be condemned to death or could the penalty be commuted to life imprisonment? Indeed, could she even receive a pardon? Von Fritsch was for mercy, whereas the third member, a known conservative, pleaded for the death penalty. Karl August leaned toward mercy as well; as an enlightened ruler he had in fact been looking for such an opportunity to set a precedent. Goethe's therefore was the decisive vote. He, who knew the intentions of his master well, asked for a week's delay and then pronounced in favor of the death sentence. On November 28 Johanna was beheaded in a public square, near the Erfurt Gate.[122]

These proceedings throw light not only on the liberal-leaning Karl August, but, in contrast, also on his conservative minister Goethe. Goethe's vote against Höhn is today surprising especially in view of his treatment of Margarethe in his original version of *Faust*, then already written: she suffers a similar fate, yet one that Goethe, the poet, sorely deplores. He sees in Margarethe the innocent victim of cruel conditions she cannot control; mitigating circumstances should have called for her life to be spared.[123] In parallel, these circumstances could again have been observed in Höhn's case. Like Margarethe, she had been seduced by a man, in this case presumably a farmhand (whom she would not name, but perhaps it was the miller himself), who had left her in the lurch. She had killed her child because the miller couple she worked for had not observed their duty, namely to look after her as a member of the family, even with child, which was called for by the post-feudal agrarian constitution at that time.[124] She had clearly acted out of desperation, in panic, not knowing how she could fend for herself and the child, especially once she lost her job. She had, after all, shown her pregnant belly to the miller's wife beforehand, obviously in a gesture seeking help. Hers had not therefore been an act of murder, but of manslaughter, at the most. And she had confessed. At the time of her deed and subsequent trial she could not have known that the government was already contemplating reforms and that hers could be a test case toward such progress. But Goethe knew, and Goethe clearly voted against this progress, and hence against what he had professed as an idealistic young man and, certainly, against women. To put it more succinctly, he voted against lower-class women, albeit legally correctly, for as the trained jurist that he was he acted in accordance with the code. Yet morally his decision was objectionable, as the thinker and writer whose calling it was to teach lessons in humanity – one of the classical ideals.[125]

Goethe's own sexuality is still not fully clarified, the less so, as one cannot tie it to a social-class system. He did not have normal heterosexual intercourse until he was in Italy at the age of thirty-nine. It may have been with a young Roman widow called Faustina whom he was sexually attracted to and who received financial compensation for her services. Alternatively, it could have been with several young Italian women (in which case "Faustina" would serve merely as a cipher).[126] For Goethe, "Faustina" served the purpose of a "sex clinic."[127] In any event, after his return to Weimar in 1788 Goethe met Christiane Vulpius, the daughter of a pauperized family, whose archivist father had died of drink. She was toiling in Bertuch's artificial-flower shop, when Goethe fell instantly in love with her and took her home, to his garden house near the Ilm river, as his mistress. A son, August, was born to them in 1789.[128]

These relationships, with women below his own social station, are juxtaposed to Goethe's professed love of the married Baroness Charlotte von Stein, who was his intimate from 1776 to 1786. An intimate, however, whom he knew carnally only up to a strictly defined physical limit, probably kisses on the mouth.[129] If Goethe wished to preserve his virginity in the close company of a highborn lady, the corollary is that he valued full sexual relations only with the lower classes. If sex constituted an act of defilement (rather than of romantic affection or for the sake of procreation), it was a measure of social estimation as applied to or withheld from women clearly identifiable as of lower, middle or upper class. But these are idle conjectures, especially in light of the fact that Goethe really did desire Frau von Stein. Did she desire him? So far, we have no conclusive explanation of why their love was never sexually consummated.

The Theory and Practice of Classical Harmony

Weimar's men of genius adhered to the classical ideal of ancient Rome and especially Greece, which suggested to them harmony and humanity and, for Goethe and Schiller in their mature years of cooperation, an escape from the real, imperfect, world. They had taken their cue from Johann Joachim Winckelmann, the son of a shoemaker, who was murdered in Trieste in June 1768 by his male lover, an impoverished cook. Supported by a modest Saxon pension, Winckelmann had become enthralled by Rome and with it the Greek concept of beauty. In Italy he savored antiquarian treasures and in 1755 published his *Reflections*, which hugely influenced the German intellectuals. He became the foremost art expert of his time.[130] His impact on Goethe throughout the poet's life cannot be overestimated; Goethe was impressed by this scholar's unrelenting quest. As much as Winckelmann roamed around in all fields of knowledge, wrote Goethe admiringly, "sooner or later he always returned to antiquity, especially Greek antiquity, with which he felt so akin and with which he would unite in his best days in such a fortuitous manner."[131]

In the Golden Age, visitors to Weimar would invariably take their leave with a profound impression of the resident geniuses' affinity with the values of the classics.[132] They could understand why these writers themselves were beginning to compare Weimar on the Ilm with the Athens of antiquity, although an occasional ironic undertone may have escaped them. Some of the learned denizens sensed early on that this would be conducive to the formation of myths, which would beget further myths, until there was no end.[133]

But the manifestations of such an infatuation with the classics were omnipresent, as it intensified over the decades. Heintze had been beholden to the teaching of Greek and Latin in his Gymnasium classes; his family members spoke those languages at the dinner table.[134] Wieland translated Horace and published poems in honor of "Olympia" in his *Teutsche Merkur*. In a letter of 1785, he waxed enthusiastic over the "light Greek spirit," in which his colleague Herder managed his translations into German from the writings of antiquity.[135] In Herder's quest for classic harmony and universal humanity, a "return to the measure and norms of antique life" could be best fulfilled by the Greeks.[136]

In his youth Goethe had wanted to study the classics in Göttingen and was early drawn to Rome. As early as 1773 he published a fragment, *Prometheus*, in which he developed a blueprint for enlightened government.[137] He was ultimately attracted to Weimar because in size and structure it resembled the historic polis of the Greeks – transparent and overseeable, humanely adaptable to man. He himself wanted to become Greek-like not only through his travels south, but also by putting Greek characters like his own Iphigenie on the stage, encouraging his actors to study antiquity and, like Wieland and Herder, delving into classical poets' writings such as Homer's *Iliad*.[138]

In conjunction with Schiller after 1794 these efforts centered more exclusively on the cultural and less on the political; officially, Goethe had put his political career behind him. Schiller, who initially had shared Goethe's idealistic view of the polis, preferred to entertain aesthetic notions and, influenced by Kant, questions of morality. He fastened on Greek tragedy. For both the age of antiquity became, increasingly, a refuge from the disorderly cosmos in which they lived (and on which they could wreak little change); high education (*Bildung*), aesthetics, and art were the ideal. This elitist, escapist, attitude became especially apparent in 1801, after Goethe and Schiller had begun their exclusive gatherings in Goethe's house. Greek subjects of discussion predominated.[139]

But if the "classical" ideal today evokes balance, harmony, and humanity, those were sometimes absent from the world the denizens of the Golden Age of Weimar inhabited. This is shown by the friction between Goethe and Schiller from before 1787, and then a rivalry that lasted beyond their first year of cooperation, 1794. *Die Horen* and, even more so, *Xenien*, targeting philistines, although justified, sowed discord. Goethe's growing haughtiness as a political mandarin and social patrician both belied the aura of caring, understanding, compassion, and love he had conjured up in works such as *Werther* or *Iphigenie*. Wieland's vanity was in constant conflict with the righteousness of a Herder, where, in addition, an ironic disregard for religion clashed with an almost bigoted Lutheran piety. The enlightened rulers Anna Amalia and Karl August attracted and attached brilliant minds to their courts, but more by happenstance and at random and, latterly, without their own doing (as with Schiller). Those very courts were in administrative insecurity, financial indebtedness, and bereft of vision for remedies, with or without a Goethe. Traditional social etiquette determined interaction at the courts and its extensions like the theater, despite the occasional gracious laxity allowed for by the duchess at her sole discretion. Moreover, the social and economic rift between rulers and courtiers and their invited genius guests on the one hand, and the general population of Weimar on the other, was too deep to be bridgeable. To be sure, much of that was a function of its times and there were places, such as Schiller's home court in Württemberg, where matters were much worse, but the type of personal contempt Karl August showed for the young entrepreneur Bertuch (whose furnishings he demolished) or the suffering class of peasants (whose fields he needlessly ravished) spoke not of humanity, but callousness.

Specific examples further illustrate the lack of harmonious balance and the absence of human concern for individual members of the community – prime classical values – at least until the death of Schiller, that great champion of people's liberties, in 1805. The savants may have been close to court – at least that was their intention, even Schiller's, who had more difficulty than others. But, despite what they said in their plays or novels, they were not close to ordinary people, who made up the great majority of Weimar's population. Nor did they really care what the people thought, except at the beginning of Karl August's rule, when he and Goethe conjured up artificial bucolic scenarios where, at village festivals, the duke could seduce a maid or two and Goethe looked on with amusement. Athens in Weimar on the Ilm was really only about the few hundred, mostly men, of privilege; the common folk lived next to them without any sense of comprehension, more often materially disadvantaged.[140]

Goethe, like his friends, disdained August Kotzebue, the author of merely popular plays, while at the same time he had no scruples performing them, precisely because they were so popular and filled the till. Kotzebue came from an established Weimar family and grew up with Hufeland; he had been on the amateur stage with Goethe as a boy. After Goethe had prevented the young lawyer from receiving an administrative position at court, Kotzebue moved to Russia. Later he was banished to Siberia but then was exonerated by the tsar. Kotzebue returned to Weimar with a title and much compensation money, and continued his success as a writer. Goethe, however, still did not deem him worthy of recognition and excluded him from the *cour d'amour* at his house in 1802. The privy councillor maintained that Weimar was like Japan: next to the worldly court there was a spiritual court, and that would forever be closed to a Kotzebue.[141] This judgment may have been premature, for in 1811 Ludwig van Beethoven used Kotzebue's play *Ruins of Athens* (the classical theme here is notable) to compose incidental music. Kotzebue himself ended tragically. In 1818 he moved to Mannheim, only to be stabbed to death there by a fanatical Jena student of theology a year later. The student, who was duly beheaded, had suspected Kotzebue of being a Russian spy in the service of the post-Napoleonic Metternich system of Europe-wide police control.[142]

Yet another author who fared badly at Goethe's hands was Herder, even though he was a pillar of the literary establishment. The fault was not Goethe's alone because, although really ill with liver and eye afflictions, Herder was a hypochondriac, always dissatisfied and blaming others, lonely, and prone to depression. That Herder would never get used to Heintze's successor Karl August Böttiger, whose never-ending garrulousness got on his nerves, was not the worst of it.[143] His initially irenic relationship with Wieland soon became uneasy because each imagined himself as leading a school of thought – Wieland one of skeptics and Herder one of the God-fearing. Caroline Herder in particular detested Wieland. There was friction with Schiller not merely because of their differences over Kant but also because Herder begrudged Schiller his eventual closeness to Goethe and growing critical acclaim. Herder's relations with Karl August remained fractious because the duke overburdened him with work in a hopelessly morose administration, in the school system as in the churches, all for what Herder considered insufficient pay. Herder actually never liked Weimar and was occasionally tempted to consider a university post in Jena or once again Göttingen, which had interested him already when he was in Bückeburg.[144]

At the beginning of his stay in Weimar in 1776 Herder was still friends with Goethe, and they remained friendly off and on until crisis separated them in the mid-1790s. As irksome as it was for Herder to have Goethe rule above him as a councillor, Goethe had no choice in exercising censorship of Herder's sermons because this formally absolutist state still required it. For his part, Goethe sought to be as benign and tactful as possible, yet this rankled with Herder.[145] The French Revolution of 1789 put a dent into the formerly close friendship when the two men found themselves on opposite sides.[146] By 1795 *Die Horen* and then *Xenien* were appearing, with the latter also taking aim at Herder. By now Johann Gottfried and Caroline Herder wanted Goethe to intervene with Karl August on behalf of scholarships for their children, of whom eventually they had eight. At first Goethe reacted scathingly, but in the end came through. When the Herders were already totally isolated, the superintendent of religion began to criticize Goethe's (and Schiller's) frivolity in his writings – Goethe above all was fond of priapisms. Herder died embittered in December of 1803, after he and Goethe had exchanged one last round of barbs.[147]

The classical idea of harmony suffered further as reflected by the fate of Christiane Vulpius, Goethe's partner. There was discord all around her, ever since Goethe had met her in the park on the Ilm during July 1788, as she was delivering a note from her underemployed brother Christian August, a writer of romance novelettes. Goethe tried to find a situation for him and took the twenty-three-year-old in as his mistress and housekeeper. As events unfolded, he himself contributed to the complications that developed, mainly by exacerbating her unfortunate status of social ostracism.[148]

The girl came from an impoverished, downtrodden family; some ancestors had been pastors and jurists, her father a low-grade state archivist. She had to help support the family, including a sister, by working for Bertuch, so moving in with Goethe meant an immediate economic benefit to her. She was a bit on the heavy side; actress Karoline Jagemann described her as "a very pretty, friendly, industrious girl, with a fresh face, round like an apple and with burning black eyes, and since she liked to laugh, her somewhat upturned cherry-red lips showed two rows of beautiful white teeth, with dark-brown luscious curls adorning her forehead and shoulders."[149]

Christiane's moving in with Goethe and the illegitimate birth of their son gave rise not only to all manner of vicious gossip among the townspeople regarding the privy councillor, usually perceived as haughty, but even more so about his lover. The most cutting judgments came from men and women who were close to Goethe, who were at the core of the classical community stylized as a Muses' Court. The prudish Herder couple, despite better knowledge, condemned Christiane as a "whore," and Böttiger named her "Vulpia," in sarcastic allusion to the Latin term for female genitalia, an injurious sobriquet in fact which soon was on everyone's lips, in learned and cultured Weimar.[150] Weimar worthies started noticing that Christiane was putting on weight and, not entirely unjustly, blamed this on a hankering for wine. One who relished repeating this particular charge was Charlotte von Stein, Goethe's ex-lady friend, for whom Vulpius was a natural enemy. Stein was on intimate terms with Charlotte Schiller, who adored the older woman, having once wanted to be, like her, a lady-in-waiting. There was no end to Frau Schiller's guffawing about poor Christiane. Even as Friedrich Schiller drew closer to his idol Goethe, he decried his spiritual friend's choice of women and marital arrangement; never did he convey greetings or remember himself to Christiane. Even the duke thought he had to punish Goethe for this breach of convention, by taking his (loaned) house on the Frauenplan from him for the duration of three years. Duchess Luise complained when little August was carried outside for fresh air, in a place where he would offend her eyes.[151]

The End of Classical Weimar

Historians as well as experts on German literature agree that with Friedrich von Schiller's death of complications from tuberculosis in 1805 the classical period of Weimar came to an end. Wieland died in 1813 and from then until his own death in 1832, Goethe was the sole representative of the Golden Age.[152]

He certainly also was, always, the most important. Even circumstances beyond his control, such as intermittent lags in creativity, Schiller's or his own problems with health, or the protracted insults he had to suffer because of his union with Christiane Vulpius, could not change that. Neither could political circumstances, such as the reverberations of the French Revolution in German lands. But with the rise of Napoleon Bonaparte and his physical presence in Weimar in the fall of 1806 this could have changed, had Goethe come to harm in any way. His by now beloved home town of Weimar, however, did have to suffer.

In the course of Napoleon's campaign against the Holy Roman Empire with the arch-duchy of Austria at its core and Prussia, with whom several German states were allied, the duchy of Saxe-Weimar-Eisenach had sided with Prussia. By July 1806 Napoleon had forged the Confederation of the Rhine, a union of pro-French German states with himself as "Protector." In August Napoleon exerted enough pressure on Emperor Franz II to surrender the Holy Roman Imperial crown, but Franz had already declared himself Emperor of Austria two years earlier. Karl August was at that time a Prussian general, and had joined 700 Weimar sharpshooters with Prussian units outside of Weimar. Anna Amalia, too, had left for Kassel, so that Duchess Luise was alone in the residential castle. By early October, Prussian troops could be seen in Weimar, and Prussian generals were staying in the castle, as French-led armies were advancing perilously close, from the East.[153]

Those generals left in time for Jena to take part in the defense of the area, as Napoleon attacked on the morning of October 14. His marshals had managed during the night to drag heavy artillery to the top of an embankment so that soldiers under French command could fire their cannons right into the advancing Prussians below. The Battle of Jena and nearby Auerstedt turned into a disaster for the soldiers of the Prussian-led alliance, who were fleeing in disarray, many passing screaming through Weimar's market square. They were followed closely by French soldiers, a lot of whom impressed Weimar's citizens as ferocious, because they were unkempt, wore dirty sack-like cloth, and carried large spoons on their three-cornered hats. During that day and on the 15th, they raped the

women, plundered houses, destroyed the interiors, and capriciously laid
fires. Had the wind changed, Weimar would have been obliterated in a
firestorm. As it turned out, many burghers were able to save themselves by
lying low and prudently hosting hungry invaders, as did Johanna
Schopenhauer, a well-off widow who with her daughter Adele had moved
into town from Danzig in the spring. Goethe on the Frauenplan withdrew
to rooms upstairs; he had expected to host a French general. As the great
man was accosted by dangerous spoon men, Christiane bravely threw
herself in front of him, possibly saving his life. The troops caused only a
little damage to his home, and thereafter Marshal Jean Lannes, one of
Napoleon's bravest, protected him. Others were not so lucky. Christiane's
brother, the writer, lost virtually everything and Melchior Kraus, teacher at
the drawing school, was roughed up so badly that he died three weeks later.
Altogether, no more than twenty houses had been left standing completely
untouched; several of Weimar's burghers were ruined.[154]

Meanwhile on October 15 Napoleon entered the castle intending to
stay for a couple of days, but found only Duchess Luise, who was with
Charlotte von Schiller. The emperor was chagrined because Karl August
had not joined his Confederation, and demanded an explanation. Luise
bravely tried to explain why her husband had been impelled to be with the
Prussians – it had been out of loyalty toward his Prussian relatives, and was
that not an honorable motive? Weimar's fate now hung in the balance for,
bereft of a Holy Roman Empire and not part of the Rhenish union, its
duchy was all on its own. As he had done with Electoral Hesse, Napoleon
could have decided that the small duchy be joined to another state (to make
it part of his Confederation).[155] But he granted Weimar a short respite,
knowing that Luise's sister was married to Margrave Karl Friedrich of
Baden, a staunch Confederation supporter, and that her daughter-in-law
Maria Pavlovna, wife of the crown prince Carl Friedrich, was a sister of
Tsar Alexander I, whom Napoleon courted. (Both Carl Friedrich and his
wife were also away at this time.) In December Karl August along with the
other three Saxon duchies did join the Rhenish alliance. He had to pay
expensive reparations and contribute Weimar troops to Napoleon's army,
who would later fight and die in Tyrol, Spain, and on the infamous Russian
campaign.[156]

Goethe reacted to all this with an equanimity that few could compre-
hend, but which illustrated once again not only that he was a highly independent thinker but also that he followed a logic which was idiosyncratically
elitist. First, he decided to legally wed Christiane, in gratitude for her having
risked her life for him. The ceremony took place in the Jakob Church on

October 19 and immediately became the butt of jokes in Weimar circles high and low.[157] Second, he resolved to express his respect to Napoleon – in a manner that would be visible to all but might also generate some rewards for himself. Goethe, summoned by Karl August, in October 1808 met with the emperor in nearby Erfurt (which, being Prussian since 1802, was French-dominated after 1806 and had joined the Confederation). Napoleon was holding court there in his capacity of Protector and received Goethe on October 2, 1808, during breakfast. According to Gustav Seibt's meticulous research, Goethe stayed for approximately half an hour. Napoleon conversed with him first about theater and literature, including Goethe's *Werther*, and then about the poet's personal circumstances and his relationship to the Weimar court. The emperor's admiring judgment of Goethe was: "Vous êtes un homme." It was obvious that the emperor had read *Werther*, and Goethe was frankly delighted. Wieland met Napoleon there on October 10, and both Wieland and Goethe later were awarded the Cross of the French Legion of Honor. Goethe proceeded to wear his proudly for "mein Kaiser," as he was now wont to say.[158] Why was Goethe so enamored of Napoleon? As Peter Merseburger has suggested, Goethe hated anarchy, he recognized in Napoleon a new, dynamic force that had done away with the excrescences of the Revolution and was promising to create something new, something orderly in Europe, an alternative to the corrupt Ancien Régime or the moribund structures of the Holy Roman Empire which, as Goethe also knew, had long been overdue.[159]

In the following years Karl August had to seek a balanced policy, as Prussia was pushing his little dukedom against France, with whom he was allied through the Confederation. This he managed astonishingly well until October 1813, when Prussia, Austria, and Russia defeated Napoleon decisively at Leipzig. At this point the strategically astute duke decided to change front again, siding with the anti-Napoleonic forces and eventually gaining for himself a seat at the Congress of Vienna, where he was elevated to the status of grand duke. After territorial redivisions, his dukedom was doubled in size. That he was not punished for his wavering must have been due to his Russian relations, who were looking out for him. At Vienna in 1914–15, a new federation of sovereign German states called the Deutsche Bund was now increased from the 36 members of Napoleon's Confederation of the Rhine to (eventually) 39, including three Free Cities. Saxe-Weimar-Eisenach was a fully independent member, albeit, like the others, nominally under Austrian control.[160]

One of the mandates handed by Prince Metternich to the German states now organized in the Deutsche Bund was constitutional reform, and

Karl August was the first potentate to realize it. His chief motive stemmed not so much from a desire for democracy as from the need to accommodate the newly won territories. Hence it now became possible to send elected representatives to a Landtag (legislative assembly): manor owners, burghers, and peasants with property. They received a say in tax policy and financial administration, and all new laws had to be approved by them. Law courts were now to be completely independent. Perhaps the most important reform was the introduction of press freedom. Even though there was henceforth little opposition to the ruler's policies and in practice he retained virtually all of his prerogatives, the conservative Goethe was less than excited about the new measures.[161]

These innovations of 1814–15 were followed in 1823 by new regulations concerning the residency of Jews, who had not yet been declared the equal of Christian burghers. There were thirty-six of them in Weimar in 1814, and sprinklings in other places, the most prominent being Jacob Elkan, who acted as a supplier of textiles to the court, and Gabriel Ulman, who was its arms broker. As was common at most German courts, they lived and worked under the special protection of the ruler, usually paying a defined tax. Because of the land gains after 1814, the entire grand duchy thereafter was home to 1,200 Jews. While no new arrivals from outside were tolerated, those in the duchy now gained occupational freedom, their religious congregations were officially recognized and government-regulated, Gymnasien and universities were opened to them, and marriage between Jews and Christians was permitted. This last measure once again was too much for Goethe, who asked if Weimar "in all areas" had to be a pioneer of the grotesque. Whereas Goethe did not hate the Jews, he was not, and had never been, a champion of them, either.[162]

The grand duchy in 1816 had grown to nearly 200,000 inhabitants, with Weimar itself almost 8,000 strong. By the time of the pro-Jewish decrees Weimar supported a population of over 9,000, increasing to over 10,000 around the time of Goethe's death.[163] Economically and socially, however, little had progressed. Goethe, who was not even a full-time administrator any more, now received 3,100 taler a year and hence was the richest employee. By contrast housemaids, small retailers, gendarmes, messengers, and choir members, to say nothing of many small pensioners, still lived on under 100 taler.[164] Bertuch continued to be the richest man in town, and his businesses flourished in various ways. Enthusiastically enlightened as he was, he could take advantage of the many new ideas emanating from the Industrial Revolution, whose aura was drifting eastward from British shores. On the banks of the Ilm, whoever was earning any decent money was, more often than not, working for the court. Weimar became, ever more, a court and rentier town, with shops of small dimensions and vestiges of agricultural activity. In the countryside, it was still not uncommon for a cow rather than a horse to do the ploughing, and even farmers' wives had to pull the hoe. But the cattle-feed situation had improved, and new staples were being farmed, such as potatoes. More meat and milk were being consumed by everyone, an indication that on the whole the standard of living was improving, however gradually.[165]

There was a political regime change in 1828 which benefitted Weimar socioeconomically, because of the beneficence of the new ruler's wife. On Karl August's death in June of that year his son Carl Friedrich succeeded him, and while he himself, if well-intentioned, was mentally slow, his Russian-born wife Maria Pavlovna had a keen intellect paired with a social conscience. Since she had arrived in Weimar very rich, she was able to put much of her own money to communal use, founding a savings bank, furthering adult education and training, and looking after orphans. Of long-term significance was the money she invested in the care of trees and parks, for this both aided employment and helped Weimar's growing image as the green heart in the green-forested center of Germany.[166] This drew more and more visitors, who also wanted to see Goethe, and the monuments of the classics.

The monuments of the classics? Indeed, Weimar had already begun to memorialize itself; it had started the process of becoming a living museum. Goethe himself did much to encourage this, because he knew he would be at the center of such cultification. He was only too painfully aware that since Schiller's death cultural institutions and intellectual intercourse in the town had been wilting – one reason why he was able to return to his own explorations in natural science and literary activity with renewed vigor, having suffered creative inertia upon Schiller's passing.[167]

There were accomplishments in culture, at the court and in the town of Weimar and even in Goethe's house, when he invited musicians such as the young Felix Mendelssohn from Berlin, from 1821 on. Yet many of these were substandard; the peaks of perfection in the classical Golden Age were not even close. In the music scene a number of undistinguished conductors and choirmasters were signed on, but their attempts at orchestral quality were hampered by insufficiently trained musicians who were demoralized by meager pay. Often the children of musicians and military bandsmen joined in, which hardly improved the music. In 1819 Johann Nepomuk Hummel was hired as court music director; he had been the last pupil of Mozart and was a friend of Beethoven. He was reputed to be the leading pianist of his time and was able to attract, as guest soloists, such international stars as the violinist Niccolò Paganini and soprano Wilhelmine Schröder-Devrient, but often lesser artists. In opera, the bassist Karl Stromeyer and Karl August's mistress Karoline Jagemann determined repertoire and quality of performances. Since Jagemann, despite her increasing age and rounded figure, would not let go of key roles on the stage, most operas presented, such as the works of Mozart, Rossini, and Weber, were less than satisfactory.[168]

In theater, Goethe continued his directorship, after the turmoil of Weimar's fall, in December 1806 unperturbed, but he was beginning to be opposed by a clique of artists around Stromeyer and Jagemann. In 1816, after artists supporting him had left for Berlin, Goethe found himself almost completely isolated. When in 1817 a poodle was scheduled to play a role on stage in a new French comedy, the poet was mortified. After his ultimatum went unheeded, he handed in his resignation as director to the grand duke who, under Jagemann's influence, accepted it. Goethe never entered the Weimar stage again.[169] From there things went downhill fast. "Our theater is getting worse every day," lamented Johanna Schopenhauer in December 1821, adding that Goethe's motto had become "after me, the deluge," and even the grand duke had withdrawn interest.[170] Five years later she complained about insignificant translations of French plays being featured on the stage, and two years after that, under a bevy of mediocre directors, she had given the theater up for good.[171]

In place of high-quality opera and theater Weimar embarked on carnivalesque activities, which were meant as homage to the vaunted culture of yesteryear. In 1809 a youthful "Genius of Weimar" walked in front of classically attired girls in a festive procession, carrying in their baskets objects from the works of geniuses, such as Wilhelm Tell's apple or Herder's palm leaves, to be presented to Duchess Luise. In 1813 celebratory pageants (*lebende Bilder*) were staged, groups of humans modeling classicist scenes, such as Apollo surrounded by the Muses, replete with fauns, nymphs, and a river god. Weimar culture was degenerating into kitsch, and Goethe even lent a hand to some of this.[172]

It was a partial contribution to the ongoing memorialization of classical Weimar, from which he would handily profit. He turned his own residence into a museum not only by virtue of the visitors he deigned to receive there, but also by the *jours fixes*, on which he lectured on color theory or geology or showed his art collection.[173] When Anna Amalia died in April 1807 he offered to write eulogies, to preserve Weimar properly in the chronicles of the dynasties and with that, preserve himself.[174] By 1809 he had begun to compose his autobiography, *Aus meinem Leben: Dichtung und Wahrheit*.[175]

Maria Pavlovna became a regular visitor to his "museum," and in October 1821 she surprised Goethe with a monument to himself in the so-called Princess Garden in nearby Jena.[176] In 1825 the inception of Karl August's reign was celebrated, no less than the golden service anniversary of Minister Goethe. Two years later Schiller's remains were ceremoniously transferred to the princely crypt.[177] Goethe himself commented on such historiciza-tion, as in 1814, when he admitted to thematizing his life and mirroring himself historically. In December 1831, a few months before his death, he wrote to Wilhelm Humboldt that "I appear to myself to be ever more historical."[178]

Probably one of the most positive aspects of the Weimar period from 1805 to 1832 was that Goethe was able to complete what he had started as a thinker and poet and what in combination with the earlier achievements went a long way in defining the Golden Age. Hence Goethe finished the first part of *Faust*, and the second was ready in manuscript form shortly before he died. *Aus meinem Leben: Dichtung und Wahrheit* was an ongoing project of the last decades in his life, presenting, in four parts, the history of his youth until his move from Frankfurt. He had also published the final version of his *Wilhelm Meister* novel, *Wilhelm Meisters Wanderjahre*, by 1829.[179] As an old man he embarked on new projects too, such as the *West-Östlicher Divan*, poems based on the work of the Persian bard Hafez.

In addition, his exploits in natural science were remarkable, adding to his lifetime and posthumous fame as the foremost of the Weimar savants. Already he had discovered the human intermaxillary bone, in 1784, inde-pendently of others before him; the existence of this bone in the human skull proved man's biological relationship to mammals – a pre-Darwinian feat! Now, his geological examinations became manifestly legendary as his collection of rock samples was increasing. Those had undoubtedly been inspired by his preoccupation with the Ilmenau mining venture.[180] Still, even while he was alive, the most serious criticism was reserved for his theory of colors, which, fully published in 1810, went squarely against Sir Isaac Newton. Goethe did not use mathematical tools as Newton had done, which is why to this day he is said to have been ascientific. Yet as sagacious a scientist as Nobel laureate Werner Heisenberg has attested that his color theory was "of multiple consequence in art, physiology, and aesthetics."[181]

Keeping busy with his work and being looked after well by Christiane until her death in 1816, Goethe did not socialize much in his final years. His circle of friends decreased; among the remaining ones was the trusted Johanna Schopenhauer, whose regular salon he would frequent, especially as she found it in her heart to tolerate Christiane, with Goethe usually sitting in a corner by himself and sketching. He gave the occasional formal dinner and graciously received visitors, some of them renowned. Goethe as a municipal tourist attraction is mentioned as early as 1830. The Olympian was becoming a fixture of Weimar in its process of ossification.[182]

There were crisis points in his development toward old age. Like Herder, he was something of a hypochondriac, always fearing illness. He had nasty altercations with Wieland, his only rival in town until 1813. And as Goethe got older, he was becoming more argumentative and generally hard to bear. To contradict him was unwise, for he was always in the right.[183] He treated former friends strangely, including Charlotte von Schiller, whom he had treasured as a young girl and whose children he should have supported financially. Yet from her he sought to withhold royalties from the publication of his correspondence with her husband Friedrich.[184] Eyebrows were raised when Goethe, through influence in high places, had his son August exempted from war service in 1813, although August had volunteered for the front.[185] And he showed opportunism when after Napoleon's Leipzig defeat in that year he tried to obtain an Austrian order, so he could dispense with the French one the emperor had given him.[186] Eventually Goethe possessed at least four major medals he could wear on every occasion just as the situation called for: the Austrian and the French orders, a Russian and the arch-ducal Weimar one as well.

Goethe's greatest personal crisis happened when Christiane died; he always reached the limit of his composure when death was near him. She had been suffering from kidney failure for some time and expired in great pain on June 6, 1816. Goethe chose not to be with her when she died, claiming to be sick himself, and he did not attend her funeral, as he had not attended Schiller's.[187] He himself passed away on March 22, 1832, of natural causes. He was eighty-two. With him died the German classic age and the most substantial part of the town of Weimar.

By way of a reprise: with all its unevenness and inconsistencies, the period in Weimar from 1770 to 1832 justly bears the name "Golden Age." It was unique in the history of civilization in that four geniuses simultaneously converged on a hitherto unknown little town and elevated it to great heights. That this town, surrounded by a small but manageable principality, should have been ruled by enlightened and empathetic monarchs lent added impetus. Together the four men, who were inspired by ideals of classical antiquity, made original literary, philosophical, linguistic, and natural-scientific contributions that had the potential for revolutionizing conventional modes of human interaction. The fact that Goethe towered over his three consociates, their work and their legacies, till 1832, as the most astute and the longest-living, lends the entire phenomenon of classical Weimar a special significance.

Nonetheless, despite its Golden Age nimbus, Weimar possessed, from the beginnings of its rise to greatness, weaknesses that may have made it appear more human in the eyes even of contemporary chroniclers. Its economic infrastructure was more tenuous than that of other German towns of comparable size, while the social divide was as gaping. Whereas the intellectual and artistic output of its savants was stellar and set records internationally, interpersonal relationships between those savants were often inharmonious. Further, Weimar was top-heavy with an artificially pumped up princely administration and, apart from the foreign-born thinkers, a mass of undistinguished denizens underneath. This socio-political structure the French invasion under Napoleon could not change, and possibly exacerbated. Within both segments – the bureaucracy and the governed – lay the seeds of political reaction which, if strong enough, could reduce Weimar to banality and ordinariness. This was the case once the great men had vanished and Weimar faced challenges in regaining the pinnacle of its classical achievements. It was to become one of the leading themes of its subsequent history.

CHAPTER 2

—◆—

Promising the Silver Age
1832 to 1861

ON THE DAY GOETHE DIED IN MARCH 1832, KARL VON STEIN, SON OF Goethe's old friend Charlotte von Stein, remarked that Weimar would now descend into the vacuum whence it had once risen.[1] These were prophetic words. The decline of Weimar had of course begun years before, but it continued after Goethe's death without any hope of reversal until the late 1840s. Contemporaries would now get into the habit of speaking of "Weimar's still life" and of the "great town of the dead." It became a living museum, a temple, the center of a memorial culture deferring to its former spiritual and artistic heroes.[2]

After the physical disappearance of Wieland, Herder, Schiller, and Goethe, acts of memorialization and devotion assumed the place of forward-looking creation. In particular, smaller figures filled the space Goethe had once occupied. There was his long-time secretary Johann Peter Eckermann, who had written down many of the aging poet's thoughts and preserved them for posterity. Originally uneducated, the University of Jena upon Goethe's nomination had bestowed an honorary doctorate on him. Now Dr. Eckermann was sharing his house with his beloved birds; it stank of bird droppings and he himself was laughed at for looking like a bird, adorned in a travel coat and wearing a cylindrical hat, both of which he was said to never remove, even in his cramped dwelling. Eckermann was surrounded by younger contemporaries of Goethe, who had been hangers-on rather than original minds, such as the philologist Friedrich Wilhelm Riemer, the painter Friedrich Preller, or the art critic Ludwig Schorn.[3] They assisted the rulers at the Weimar court, Grand Duke Carl Friedrich and his wife Maria Pavlovna, in establishing the commemorative aura which would manifest itself later in the century in the erection of a Schiller museum in 1846 and a Herder statue in 1850.[4] Two men who were reluctant to join in this, although they were certainly principals of that circle, were Goethe's grandsons. The bachelors Wolfgang and Walther, sons of August who had died of alcoholism even before Goethe, were shy and sickly and they lived, withdrawn, in attics of Goethe's splendid mansion, in a pious fear of desecrating it. Walther had studied music with Felix Mendelssohn in Leipzig, but to no effect, while Wolfgang possessed a doctorate in law from Heidelberg.[5] Goethe's house was accessible to reverent visitors as long as Ottilie von Goethe, the poet's temperamentally unstable daughter-in-law, lived in it, but after she had moved to Vienna it was eventually closed to any but the ducal family and the grandsons.[6]

In culture, the decline was showing on the stage, at musical perform-ances, and in the realm of science and scholarship. Ever since Goethe had been released from the directorship of the court theater in 1817, produc-tions had been going downhill. Actors of prodigious potential like Karoline Jagemann and Eduard Genast as well as lesser ones monopolized roles. Thus they prevented young talent from rising up and encouraged the repetitive staging of well-worn standards which they could play in their sleep, not excluding Goethe's and Schiller's own. But plays à la mode authored by August von Kotzebue and Zacharias Werner met more ideally with the average dull taste of the Weimar public. Theater directors with aristocratic titles such as Baron Karl Emil von Spiegel typically came from a military or courtier background, yet possessed neither education nor cultural finesse.[7] Under these conditions, originality and innovation remained absent from the Weimar stage, a situation by no means unique in German lands, although during the 1830s and '40s visitors to Weimar expected something of quality from this vaunted town of geniuses.[8]

Opera and concert suffered from similar insufficiencies. Maria Pavlovna, like Dowager Duchess Anna Amalia earlier, was an impressive pianist, and musical performance under Johann Nepomuk Hummel, whom she had hired as music director because of his pianistic skills, was satisfactory; however, he died in 1837. Star virtuosos passed through Weimar in the 1830s and '40s as they passed through other German towns: the likes of Swedish soprano Jenny Lind and twelve-year-old Russian pianist Anton Rubinstein. The youthful pianists Clara Schumann and Franz Liszt put in appearances as guests of the ducal family in the 1840s. But Hummel's successor André Hippolyte Chelard, once a violinist at the Paris Opéra, was a dismal failure as conductor, and lazy to boot.[9] Unlike Hummel, he was not paid out of the embarrassed Maria Pavlovna's private funds, but haphazardly funded elsewhere. The classical repertoire, even when accept-able, tended to be interspersed with cheap, popular acts, such as when

Sophie and Isabella Dulcken from London performed a "concerto" for piano and accordion in 1844.[10]

Grand Duchess Maria Pavlovna, but not her indolent husband Carl Friedrich, sought to reconstitute the intellectual life that had once sparkled at the Weimar courts as early as 1833, by attracting men of arts, letters, and the sciences. Perhaps this was due to a certain inquisitiveness about the human condition, possibly acquired as a child, after she had become aware, from an adjoining room, of the murder of her father Tsar Paul I, strangled by disgruntled generals. Paul's successor was Tsar Alexander I, Maria Pavlovna's brother, who was succeeded by his brother Nicholas I in 1825.[11]

In the manner of Anna Amalia, Maria Pavlovna wished to attract great minds to "Literary Evenings" at the courts of Belvedere Castle just outside Weimar and the palais inside town, inviting professors from Jena or guests traveling through. The topics ranged from Francis of Assisi to the evolving theses of Charles Darwin, and some well-known scientists, among them Alexander von Humboldt, actually came. But the University of Jena had been losing its lustre even before 1800, one of the reasons being miserable pay, so in Weimar's orbit only comparatively minor scholars could offer lectures on subjects from the natural sciences, art, and politics. These included Karl Wilhelm Göttling, a professor of philology, and Karl von Hase, a theologian. Maria Pavlovna was somewhat pedantic about those events; she wanted Weimar's educated classes to attend, ordered them to take notes and checked those after lectures and discussion in person, thinking all the while that she had conjured up the "Muses' Court," as it was then imagined to have existed.[12]

One participant who followed these proceedings keenly by the late 1830s was Carl Alexander, Maria Pavlovna's son, who was born in June 1818 and had sat on Goethe's knees. In January 1842 his father Carl Friedrich allowed him to use Ettersburg Castle north of Weimar, where Anna Amalia had staged many events, for his own cultural purposes. Essentially, Carl Alexander continued his mother's practice of holding soirées, but on a more systematic basis, inviting a fixed, select circle of writers and artists to this summer retreat in regular fashion. The prince and his Dutch wife Sophie (they were married October 1842) hosted locals like Eckermann and the writer Amalie Winter, but also out-of-towners who, he hoped, would settle permanently in Weimar in the way that Goethe and Herder had. Among these were the Danish poet Hans Christian Andersen, who would read from his fairy tales, and the globetrotter and park designer Prince Hermann Ludwig von Pückler. The Bohemian Moritz Hartmann passed through, who had translated Turgenev and Perrault and now recited poems (Carl Alexander had met him in Paris in 1845), and also Berthold Auerbach, the Jewish philosopher, a translator of Spinoza persecuted elsewhere in Germany for his democratic views. There were a good many aristocratic ladies from Weimar there, including Winter, who was using a pen name: the countesses Beust and von Redern, Frau von Plötz and Baroness Caroline Egloffstein.

After European revolutions and proclamations of freedom but also in an era of Metternichian police surveillance, this more or less tightly defined group saw itself as progressive. It continued to discuss bold modern ideas, as had the many Weimar groups before, it tried to overcome certain time-honored limits of convention set by the nobility through its own informal social intermingling, and it discussed liberal notions of emancipation, that of classes, women, and Jews, yet without actually emancipating them. It claimed to be able to ignore class barriers. There were bucolic moments when the circle mixed with the simple village folk around Ettersburg, just as Goethe and Karl August had done. Much of this was pretense. It is significant that French remained paramount as the medium of communication, the etiquette of the Weimar courts was still observed, and bourgeois women such as the Jewish writer Fanny Lewald, who corresponded at length with Carl Alexander on many subjects, were excluded from the gatherings.[13]

In the imagined tradition of both Karl August and Goethe, Carl Alexander saw the renaissance of Weimar and its culture as his personal mandate, both before and after his ascent to the throne as grand duke on August 28, 1853, Goethe's 104th birthday. As one contemporary writer trenchantly observed, he wished to wreak a complete change in Weimar's cultural situation, which had deteriorated "to the level of triviality."[14] In one sense Carl Alexander belonged to a group of independent German princes trying to prove themselves in the role of Maecenas to aid the development and spread of new bourgeois art forms; among them were the rulers of Hesse-Darmstadt, Bavaria, and Prussia.[15] What was unique for Weimar was that here Carl Alexander was leading a state that had already made significant strides in those areas and had recently lost its way.

The affable Weimar prince was a physically attractive man and not without interest for women: blond, tall, and slender, with a sensitive face, ascetic bearing, and impeccable self-control. He was used to rising at daybreak and always showed moderation in food and drink. Not of the most hardy constitution, he tried to steel himself by going outside in every weather, even when this meant joining the hunt, which he actually disliked.[16] Of above-average intelligence, he possessed some artistic talents, for example in drawing and painting; he knew something about literature and the theater, about which he liked to converse, but very little about music, about which he conversed much.[17] He thought he owed such demeanor to Goethe's memory. But when he was at his wits' end, sentimentality usually ruled.[18] His aesthetic conception was classical, the Greek belief in the ideal fit of beauty and goodness. Conversely, anything that did not immediately instill him with a sense of harmony, was always bad. In art and culture, he looked for change rather than revolution; evolution would be progressive and inoffensive, as he fancied Goethe to have understood it. In all, he adhered to a simplistic, naïve world-view that brooked no manifestations of radicalism, a world-view the more complicated of the contemporaries he wanted to surround himself with had trouble empathizing with. Nor could many agree with him that art and culture had to have a moral, didactic purpose and must reach the largest number of people possible.[19]

The awareness of his intellectual and artistic insecurity reinforced mannerisms such as stilted speech laden with difficult expressions, often interspersed with French, his mother tongue. Using precious idioms and bold figures of speech, he made, as Richard Wagner once noticed, strange observations that he took for original analyses, making a fool of himself, and the cognoscenti wary.[20] His deep Lutheran piety he shared with his wife Sophie, who spent a lifetime financing charitable works from her private purse.[21] It led him to take an extraordinary interest in the restoration of Luther's onetime hideaway, the Wartburg Castle in Eisenach to the west of Weimar, but rendered him bigoted and spoilt for any kind of humor.[22] His last resorts were courtly etiquette, the French language, perfect manners and composure, and the observance of social hierarchy – so that Weimar's theater throughout the nineteenth century remained divided into partitions, with the nobility on the right and the burghers on the left. Carl Alexander had many opportunities to change this antiquated arrangement during his long reign, but never chose to do so – this was but a mirror of his inner self: a warm and well-meaning monarch at first sight, who accepted some, and a cold elitist, who rejected many.[23] Carl Alexander's discriminative aloofness throughout his life prevented him from being the universally loved ruler he always wanted to be. In his closer circle of friends, he came across as a gifted amateur, a fickle gentleman who wished to please all, to be liked by all, yet in reality not wishing to cross certain lines in his mind and heart. And also not wanting to cross others' lines. In the end people thought they could sway him, only to be left in the lurch.[24]

Carl Alexander's stratagem to make Weimar great again was to attract important personalities to the town, as his forebears had done. Those would then attract others, as Goethe had attracted Herder. However, the problem was that this prince was either not able or not willing to offer the people he sought a properly anchored position, with corresponding remuneration. Hence many came, lured by Carl Alexander's promises, but just as many left again, even if a handful did stay for a decade or longer. Why the prince, who subsequently was the grand duke for almost a half-century, behaved in this unreliable manner, is not yet evident. A combination of factors may have caused such behavior. One was that he was too insecure to know how to lead; in the final analysis he had no clear notion of what his Weimar should look like; the smatterings of knowledge that he had were no guide, and he lent his ear to too many people for advice. Another was that he always held out the promise of money to finance great men and their projects, without, in the end, dispensing any, or not dispensing enough. Whatever his sweet talk may have been, the funds remained in abeyance. Connected to this particular fault was his belief, sanctimonious ruler that he was, that visitors should consider it an honor to be invited by him, without having to ask for additional, material, emoluments. He himself may not have had an overview of Weimar's finances: what was his personal fortune, what that of the court, how large were the state's revenues, what belonged to his wife? He must have inherited wealth from his mother Maria Pavlovna when she died in 1859, for she had come to Weimar rich and remained so, even after having spent a lot on social causes and the arts of her choice. His wife Sophie of Orange was even richer, but, until late in life, she had no cultural agenda. Earning money in mercantilist fashion for the state was a futile exercise for Carl Alexander, for he was not economically minded – during his reign the grand duchy remained an agricultural and industrial backwater.

Several case histories illustrate his deficient interpersonal skills. The prince attracted younger men in whom he recognized potential, as well as mature minds, and all stayed for some time, without becoming Weimar citizens. Some would have done so, had they had something to live on. A number of invited worthies mulled Carl Alexander's offer over, without eventually accepting it.

At the beginning Hans Christian Andersen frequented the Ettersburg soirées. The small and physically awkward Dane struck a vivid contrast to the willowy prince, who took an immediate liking to this visitor. The poet had been roaming Europe collecting accolades, was stopping over in Weimar and liked the way he was appreciated in the town of Goethe. He stayed longer. Carl Alexander suggested themes for his fairy tales. When Andersen was absent, they corresponded on intimate terms, the prince wanting to tie the poet to his duchy permanently. But then in 1849 the Deutsche Bund declared war on Denmark; General Carl Alexander of Saxe-Weimar-Eisenach had to lead a brigade in the struggle, serving the Prussians. Andersen firmly represented the Danish view of things, and so that friendship was over, although Andersen would return to Weimar in later years.[25]

In the pre-1848 revolutionary period, August Hermann Hoffmann von Fallersleben had been on the run as a liberal professor of German literature at the University of Breslau, because of some irreverent verses he had published. One of these political verses had been "The Song of the Germans," *Deutschland, Deutschland über Alles*, which was meant "as a liberal work appealing for a German national state with free institutions."[26] Under the sway of the authoritarian Prince Metternich, Prussia would have imprisoned the exile (until his pardon in 1848), who found refuge elsewhere in Germany, ending up in Weimar in the early 1850s. Carl Alexander's mandate for him was, originally, the publication of three volumes of critical texts toward the creation of a Goethe Foundation, and when this floundered, the editing of a "Weimar Yearbook for German Language, Literature, and Art." The latter Hoffmann was able to produce in six volumes from 1854 to 1857, whereupon the grand duke decided on a whim to cut off supporting grants. The Goethe Foundation never having been realized and Carl Alexander having lost interest in the, by now impecunious, scholar, Hoffmann left Weimar again in 1860, for greener pastures.[27]

By 1857 Carl Alexander wished to tie the poet Victor von Scheffel to his circle by inviting him to be librarian of Wartburg Castle, still in a stage of renovation and with no library within its walls. Scheffel was expected to write a novel for the greater glory of the grand duke and his castle, covering the complicated romantic history of that structure, "a new national epos," with special attention to the legendary singers' contest of the High Middle Ages. After much hesitation, Scheffel accepted and spent several lonely months on that isolated precipice near Eisenach (the ascent to it at that time was certainly much more cumbersome than it is even today). Alas, a novel he did not produce, merely thousands of pages of draft.[28]

The grand duke attempted to invite yet another famous poet toward the end of the 1850s, Friedrich Hebbel, with his wife Christine Enghaus, an equally famous Viennese actress, in tow. Again, Carl Alexander bestowed on him the title of "Librarian," this time not of the Wartburg but in Weimar, yet it was not clear what Hebbel was to do in that capacity, nor what his annual salary would be. A frequent staging of his well-known plays – *Agnes Bernauer, Genoveva*, and the *Nibelungen* trilogy – on the Weimar stage would have been assured, but Hebbel found Weimar "unbelievably tight and small." Hence a contract was never signed.[29] Later Carl Alexander made similar advances to Richard Voss, a minor playwright (once more to be installed as Wartburg Librarian), the poet Paul Heyse from Munich, already quite well known, Ferruccio Busoni, then on the cusp of fame as pianist and composer, and the Italian painter Aristide Sartorio, recommended by Richard Voss. Voss had been urged to recommend still others, "so that they could be discovered from Weimar for the glory of the prince." None of these men came, and when they did, put in fleeting appearances. What was worse was that Sartorio disappeared from the Weimar art academy without ever taking his formal leave.[30]

Carl Alexander's political disposition had two components, a liberal and a conservative one. It was the liberal in him who allowed Hoffmann von Fallersleben into his country. Later he would tolerate other politically undesirable professors, such as the philologist Kuno Fischer from Heidelberg, at Jena.[31] Not surprisingly, the prince had inherited his more progressive leanings from his father Carl Friedrich, who in turn had them from his father, Karl August. Indeed, although Grand Duke Carl Friedrich was said to be slow-witted and uninterested in the arts – his pastime was collecting porcelain figurines – he had an agreeable personality and was sympathetic to his subjects. There was unease during the months of revolution in 1830, when censorship increased, as ordered by Metternich from Vienna throughout the Deutsche Bund territories, hence also in the Weimar duchy. One problem was the university in Jena, where unruly students took to the streets in 1832–33 and Weimar troops tried to hold them down. Maria Pavlovna's confidant, First Minister Carl Christian Schweitzer, was the unbending conservative responsible for such action – the grand duchess remained influenced by the aura of autocracy generated by her reactionary brothers, tsars Alexander and then Nicholas, especially the latter.[32] When in 1837 the liberal Göttingen professors Friedrich Christoph Dahlmann and Jacob and Wilhelm Grimm could have been called to the University of Jena after being set upon by the reactionary King of Hanover, the Weimar rulers backed down for fear of insulting that king.[33]

During the 1848 upheaval the comparatively liberal minded Christian Bernhard von Watzdorf became the leading minister in Weimar, where the revolution itself was relatively benign, with hardly any casualties. Instead of storming the ducal castle, the commoners, many from the surrounding countryside, aimed to protect the duke and duchess; politically, they knew not what to complain about.[34] In the wake of these mildly disquieting events, Saxe-Weimar crown lands were converted into state holdings, representing an immediate personal loss to the princely family, and more freedom of the press – contra Metternich – was secured. All this was in conformity with the democratic constitution passed by the Paulskirche assembly in Frankfurt, even if some of the newly won privileges were taken away again under the Deutscher Bund, now ruled by Metternich's successor Prince Schwarzenberg by 1850.[35] Yet even then another progressive step was important: the total civic emancipation of the Jews, of which the Weimar duchy still had very few as its citizens.[36]

Carl Alexander was a member of the ducal party during the revolution of 1848, in sympathy with the demonstrators in the streets below, and was in favor of mild reforms, lest radicals take the upper hand.[37] His moderate views did not betray his fundamentally conservative belief in monarchy, however, which for him owed its legitimacy to God, still making the monarch responsible, if not accountable, for the welfare of his subjects.[38] Besides this strong belief in the union of altar and throne, he was conscious of being a *German* prince, as he appreciated everything German, in the present as in the past – hence also his predilection for German cultural achievements, such as post-Renaissance Albrecht Dürer's paintings. He read the ultra-nationalist historian Heinrich von Treitschke and abhorred Social Democrats.[39] At the same time he thought himself above other German princes, even the few remaining ruling ones (after the constant territorial revisions since the Congress of Vienna), because his Saxon duchy had not been mediatized to become part of an adjoining state, but also because he was a close relative of the ruling Romanovs in Russia.[40] Thus Russia remained his favorite in dealings of larger policy, in which he personally had little say (except that his sister Augusta eventually was to be the wife of the first German Kaiser, who as Prussian prince in 1848 was a leader of the counter-revolution and whom in his capacity as King of Prussia he tried to influence in the direction of a democratic opening). This also determined his growing dislike of Britain, although his liberal side should have predisposed him positively toward his cousin Queen Victoria.[41] His disparaging views of Britain could have been the trigger for his enthusiasm for German colonial expansion after 1880, which militated against the British domination of the seas. Carl Alexander played frequent host to Gerhard Rohlfs, one of the pioneers in German East Africa, and he sponsored festivities for and donated money to Carl Peters, who had been behind the German acquisitions in eastern Africa, and who, in Hans-Ulrich Wehler's words, was an "adventure-loving psychopath." Carl Alexander wanted, above all, to Christianize the natives, and his naïveté in matters of colonial expansion is shown by his keeping a court moor, Hussan, at his side – a romantic if anachronistic reference to a less enlightened past.[42]

Weimar and Surroundings

From the time of Goethe's death in 1832 to the beginning of the twentieth century, Weimar changed at a snail's pace, in physical appearance as well as socio-demographically.[43] Some of the retardation seems to have been the result of deliberate planning by the rulers both of the town and the ducal realm in order to preserve Weimar's museumish, cultic character. To the extent that this happened, it did so without heed to the potential for economic progress or positive social change, in that matters of cultural import always remained paramount and the proven political equilibrium was not disturbed. Here the tradition of conservative rule tempered by liberal notions, the latter encouraged by periodic revolutions or the fear thereof, maintained for town and country a status quo of comfort, security, and tranquility acceptable to most. As a personal attitude and a state philosophy, no one typified this more ideally than Grand Duke Carl Alexander himself.

Most visitors in the nineteenth century found Weimar small and forlorn, its town center with most celebrities' houses self-contained and somehow isolated from its surroundings, including, in the late 1840s, the new railway station to the north. It was described as a very quiet place, with clean but boring crooked little streets, where the last open sewer streams had been covered up only in the 1830s. The inns, including the traditional Elephant and Erbprinz in the market square, were modest, with no accoutrements of extravagance, their staff dour and taciturn, as were most ordinary burghers. Things were orderly and nary a drunk was seen, all the street lanterns were working, and everything was quite unexciting, remembered Hoffmann von Fallersleben.[44] But some observers were impressed by the verdant beauty in and surrounding Weimar: the large park to the south of the main castle, which Karl August and Goethe had designed and Prince Pückler had been enhancing. Through it ran the tiny Ilm river, continuing past the town center – a most charming romantic rivulet, with peacocks on its shores. And all over town there were fountains.[45] Yet Weimar had an aura redolent of the sarcophagus – every avenue led to the tombs of great men.[46]

Weimar's population figures give an indication of the town's languid growth. It was home to 10,638 inhabitants two years after Goethe's death; that figure had not quite doubled by 1880, and not even tripled in 1900, when other German towns were bursting due to migration from the countryside. The earlier, similarly disadvantaged Rhenish town of Worms, for instance, in 1900 had 35,000 citizens. After German unification, Berlin in 1871 was home to 865,000 persons and six years later passed the 1 million mark. In 1853, when the grand duchy contained *c.* 260,000 people, Weimar's share was about 13,000. Population growth was not helped by the outbreak of cholera in 1866 (in the wake of the war against Austria), when the town lost 58 people; typhus had already taken its toll in 1806. Equally slow was the construction of new housing, especially to the north, as the town could expand only modestly beyond its medieval walls: whereas it had 1,011 dwellings in 1843, sixteen years later there were just 44 more.[47]

Significant in this context is the proportion of the Jews: it continued to be very low, in keeping with Weimar's character as a small town, but progressive legislation in favor of Jewish immigration could have attracted more, certainly after 1848. The Jewish theme is important in view of Weimar's subsequent development, with the advent of political anti-Semitism in Germany during the 1880s and later, under National Socialism. Weimar was home to only thirty-six Jews in 1818, thirty in 1858, forty-six in 1867, sixty in 1880, and seventy in 1895. These numbers were very considerably lower than the national average. So few of the Jews practiced Judaism that the town never had a synagogue – significant for what would happen in November 1938 during Kristallnacht. One could interpret this to mean that Weimar attracted few Jews because of an anti-Semitic ducal or municipal policy, but of course the opposite was the case. In mid-century, Weimar's music director Eduard Lassen was Jewish, and Franz Liszt had many Jewish piano students visiting as well.[48] The low Jewish figures at that time must instead be related to Weimar's static character as a non-industrial and non-commercial place; had Jena's university been moved to Weimar, which would have been sensible from several points of view, a higher number of Jewish scholars and students could have been added to its head count.

Industry and agriculture in Weimar and the duchy as a whole remained behind the norm in other German states despite some impetus caused by the Industrial Revolution, especially in the second half of the nineteenth century.[49] Apart from the court administration and some retail businesses, in Weimar the main enterprises continued to be handicraft shops, tightly controlled by ancient guild codes, until more entrepreneurial freedom was decreed by law in mid-century.[50] The business of Friedrich Justin Bertuch, Weimar's richest man, continued on in the hands of his heirs under the name of Landes-Industrie-Comptoir, an early holding company, and smaller factories sprang up – a water-hose plant, gaming cards, glove and gun factories. There were two fine-quality breweries, the traditional onion market went on in October as usual, and after 1825 a wool market attracted customers. This and a concentration of wool-processing handlooms and leather works complemented the textile cottage industry still active in the satellite hamlets, as in Apolda. Cottage-industrial entrepreneurship, typically involving single families for generations, continued to determine the economy in other areas, such as hand-painting small porcelain pieces used for tobacco-pipe heads. Toward the end of the century, tourism strengthened as a viable economic alternative.[51]

Yet ambitious entrepreneurs who wished to start something on a larger scale were discouraged, as was one Carl Friedrich Zeiss, born in 1816 as the son of a Weimar master turner who, having learned the trade of a mechanic, wanted to set up shop in 1845. He was barred by the town's administration for fear that he would cause undue competition with two existing establishments. Consequently he moved to Jena to found a mechanics shop. This was the beginning of the world-famous Zeiss optical works – Weimar had missed the entrepreneurial chance of a century. A company manufacturing railway cars was not established in Weimar until 1898.[52]

None of this brought in much revenue, especially since external commerce was still impeded, certainly until a railway line was opened up in 1846–47. But it connected Weimar only to the Weissenfels-Erfurt line running north to south, a connection to southeastern Gera falling into place only thirty years later, and later still merely to other Thuringian towns.[53] During Goethe's final years the Ilm was already in use as a commercial artery, but only primitively, for floats shipping in lumber from the Thuringian Woods.[54] (For decades it remained polluted and a danger to the locals.)[55] Overall income for the duchy therefore was diminutive, for example merely 800,000 taler in 1844, with an annual deficit of 3.8 million taler.[56] No wonder if for culture the rulers had to shell out money of their own, and entire occupational groups such as orchestra musicians and choir members almost starved.[57]

Weimar's preexisting social divisions, the contrast between very rich and very poor, had not been alleviated; if anything, they had deepened. As in olden times, a major rift separated the lower and lowest classes, anyone from shopkeeper to unskilled laborer and peasant (or poorly paid musician), on the one side, from the upper, educated, bourgeoisie and the aristocracy on the other. Bourgeoisie and aristocracy were less sharply divided from one another, but distinctions were visible where it counted, as in the theater auditorium and admittance protocol at court.[58] Here grand dukes were at liberty to invite a bourgeois only if he was an artist or a scholar, but without his wife – apart from the titled, who had constitutional access. The number of courtiers and ladies-in-waiting had grown, as had the court administration and its pomp and circumstance since 1800, with the attendant costs.[59] Within these divisions there were other, more hidden ones. Men of letters who had the confidence of the grand duke, especially the unreliable Carl Alexander, snubbed those who did not, rich members of the aristocracy disdained the poorer ones, those who spoke French and English despised those who knew only German, always against the fixed background of a time-honored hierarchy of titles. Certain social clubs were forming to challenge existing clubs.[60] When Ludwig Schorn married Henriette von Stein, a relative of Goethe's friend Charlotte, he, being of value as an educated expert, had to be ennobled, if only to allow him access to the right side of the theater balcony.[61] Gossip enveloped the unwanted or the strange, such as the Princess Carolyne zu Sayn-Wittgenstein, Liszt's mistress, because, as a married woman, she was living in sin with a bourgeois musician and, for the court, because she had been officially banished by Tsar Nicholas I, Carl Alexander's uncle, and because she smoked cigars. A final line sharply separated the precious glitterati who appreciated culture, the very essence of Old Weimar, from the much larger mass (of burghers) who did not. (Before Liszt premiered Wagner's opera *Lohengrin* in Weimar in 1850, Maria Pavlovna had to buy up many of the unsold tickets for general distribution because not enough townspeople were interested in attending.)[62] But there were other, more sharply drawn, lines pitting against each other devotees of different subcultures, for example followers of Liszt versus his enemies, or the old school of painting versus the new.[63] Albert Brendel, who was an accomplished painter of animals influenced by the French Barbizon School, was ridiculed by Weimar society as the "sheep painter."[64]

An additional comment is warranted about gender and age. Weimar was turning ever more into a town of very young and very noticeably old people, with no healthy middle section.[65] By about mid-century, as industrialization spread elsewhere in Germany, in the generation of late teenagers to those in their early twenties, women were in the majority in Weimar society, and they tended to be unmarried. This demographic phenomenon may be directly explained in terms of the town's economic infrastructure: because it lacked industry and commerce, it could not attract and retain young, employable men, who were horizontally mobile enough to leave town. The army, for instance, consisted of the same old smallish number of fifty hussars, and they were paid a farthing – never enough to raise a family.[66] Men beyond their mid-twenties were leaving Weimar for employment in other parts of Germany (or, in fact, eventually for overseas), including those who had studied at Jena, for opportunities through the court were limited as well. The result was that many young women of respectable social standing went unmarried and late in the century Weimar was to possess a comparatively large number of upper-class spinsters.[67] At the same time it became a town of pensioners, many from other regions, as has caustically been observed.[68]

Franz Liszt Comes to Weimar

If the classical period of the historic founders has often been called Weimar's Golden Age, most decades of Weimar's nineteenth century have customarily been termed the Silver Age. This primarily refers to the stay of Franz Liszt in Weimar, first from 1848 to 1861, and then from 1869 to 1886. A legion of historians have traced a renaissance of culture, in line with Grand Duke Carl Alexander's oft-stated overall aims, to that musician's presence.[69] At the same time they would have had to admit that a "silver age" is logically inferior to a "golden age," and therefore that the identification of Weimar in the nineteenth century with silver would amount to concession of a decline. Insofar as the grand duke presided over bursts of culture as personified by Liszt's presence which sometimes resembled the accomplishments of Goethe's time, any highlights were insufficient to substitute for or even cover up Weimar's gross cultural loss over the entire century.

The circumstances under which Franz Liszt settled in Weimar in 1848 are complicated and cannot be considered in isolation from the events characterizing his virtuoso life in his late twenties and thirties. Born to Austro-German parents in western Hungary in October 1811, he was a teenage prodigy in Paris, French becoming his language of use, his mother tongue German a never perfect idiom, with Hungarian quite absent. Tall, lean, and handsome, with a finely chiseled face and shoulder-length hair he was attracted to women as they were to him, even as a teenager. He always possessed a charismatic, demonic quality, and both his charm and rages were the stuff of legend. Soon he was frequenting the salons of the rich and aristocratic, dazzling everyone with his prodigious piano technique. He became the first public virtuoso pianist and in his ability to fascinate audiences was second only to Niccolò Paganini before him. In the modern judgment of pianist Charles Rosen, he was "the greatest pianist who ever lived." Rosen continues: "He was the first composer who turned a musical performance into something like an athletic feat." Not surprisingly, Liszt was constantly lionized, and as he perfected his recital routine he became addicted to social intercourse almost exclusively with the European *haut monde*, in particular its women, and to lavish living. In 1833 he took up with the married Countess Marie d'Agoult, whose mother was from Frankfurt, and eventually accompanied her to Switzerland and Italy. He had three children with this mistress, of whom the oldest, Cosima, born in 1837, would in time make music history of her own.[70]

Liszt separated from Marie in 1839, because of quarrels and in order to be free to perform in concerts, but for all it was worth, they considered themselves a couple until 1844. During this period and beyond, Liszt accomplished astounding feats of travel and performance, everywhere collecting fame, money, and the, invariably sexual, favors of women. He became what the eminent British music critic Ernest Newman has described as "a pushing young careerist and social climber," who sought decorations and titles of nobility. He also became addicted to tobacco and alcohol – small wonder for a man thus taxed. A months-long affair with the Irish dancer Eliza Rozanna Gilbert, also known as Lola Montez – who in 1846 flitted to Munich and two years later would cause her lover King Ludwig I of Bavaria to lose his throne – appears to have changed Liszt's fate decisively: Marie and Franz broke off their relationship, she turning violently against him. Liszt shouldered the financial responsibility of supporting their children in Paris, where they would be educated by his mother and personal governesses, while he continued his concerts. By this time it had become clear to him that life, as he had been leading it, could not go on or he would be physically ruined.[71]

Liszt first visited Weimar in April 1840, when he took great interest in Goethe's house.[72] He played in Weimar in 1841, at which time he so enthralled the audience that Grand Duchess Maria Pavlovna and her son Carl Alexander invited him to return for the celebration of the prince's Dutch wedding in November 1842. It was then that the grand duchess enticed him to consider Weimar as his future abode, offering him the title of extraordinary Kapellmeister and a salary at her discretion. The only fixed condition was that he be in Weimar for three months each year.[73] Liszt accepted Weimar because, as Newman has plausibly explained, he wished to be in a place where, now quite secure financially, he could compose music quietly, away from limelight, rather than having to impress the world with his piano pyrotechnics. As well, he could polish his, at that time modest, skills as a conductor. Far-off Weimar would be the perfect place for this. That Goethe and the classics were the major attraction for him at this time, as supporters of a Weimar myth have liked to maintain, may be discounted, even though he was very much aware of Goethe and of Schiller, as he had already been of Dante and Shakespeare. He was, after all, steeped in French culture and too much of a cosmopolitan to be exclusively interested in the German classics, and already a product of the post-classic Romantic school (which, musically, he had been reared in and of which he was subsequently a leader, notwithstanding his reverence for Bach and Beethoven).[74]

As Liszt continued to appear on stages around Europe, rubbing shoulders with all types of nobles, giving luxurious parties, and with women flinging themselves at him, he was also maintaining a correspondence with Prince Carl Alexander from January 1844, in which ideas of Goethe and a New Weimar resounded.[75] Two years later Gaetano Donizetti, the gifted Kapellmeister of the Vienna court opera who had also been its official composer, was committed to a Paris asylum, ill with syphilis. Since 1842, Donizetti had enjoyed a loose arrangement with the Viennese court, of the kind Liszt had secured at Weimar, but with more money attached. Liszt was hoping to become Donizetti's successor, yet he was never invited. The question now became: when would Franz Liszt exchange his touring business for a more or less permanent stay in Weimar?[76]

The answer seems to have materialized in 1847, when he met Carolyne zu Sayn-Wittgenstein after a benefit concert in Kiev. Because she had had a role in the concert, Liszt fell into conversation with her. Eight years younger, Carolyne was a princess, and Liszt "collected princesses and countesses as other men collect rare butterflies." Whether he fell in love with this fabulously rich woman at that time, or ever, who owned an estate with 30,000 serfs in eastern Poland, has not yet been convincingly proved. But what is beyond doubt is that she fell in love with him, and that she wanted to get away from the husband she detested, Prinz Nicholaus zu Sayn-Wittgenstein, who was much older and a tsarist general. It was decided at that time that she and Liszt would move to Weimar, along with her young daughter Marie, where Maria Pavlovna, the sister of Tsar Nicholas, could be useful in securing her brother's consent to a divorce.[77] That Liszt did not love her, and possibly may have been interested only in her wealth is suggested less by the fact that he continued to have other casual affairs once in Weimar than, more cogently, by his serious relationship with Agnes Street-Klindworth. The young daughter of a professional master spy, she was as beautiful as she was gifted, and had come to Weimar in 1853 to sleuth around the ducal court, probably for the tsarist government, using the musician, for camouflage, as her piano teacher. Liszt continued his correspondence with Street-Klindworth even after she had left Weimar in April 1855, and visited this paramour clandestinely for trysts. One son she eventually bore was, however, not the offspring of Liszt, contrary to stubborn rumors.[78]

Eventually, the princess found out about Street-Klindworth, as d'Agoult had learned about Montez. Even if she remained adamant in her quest to get rid of her Russian husband and marry Liszt, did the musician continue to be interested in a marital union with her – if indeed he ever was, especially since soon the tsar would confiscate the bulk of her Polish fortune? This question is important not only in a continuing study of Franz Liszt's personality, but also in our search for answers to questions regarding Liszt's residence in Weimar. What did Weimar have to offer him, and why did he stay, then leave, come back and all but die there? What did he do for Weimar, and what did he neglect to do, and why? How was his fate intertwined with Weimar's for thirty years, for better or for worse?

Liszt and his princess moved into town during 1848, taking residence in the Altenburg, a multi-storey mansion the sympathetic Maria Pavlovna had put at their disposal. It stood in the outskirts of the city on the road to Jena and was large enough not only for many of Carolyne's precious belongings, but also for Liszt's assorted music and pianos. There were guest rooms for visitors, some of whom would stay for months at a time.[79]

Liszt used the Altenburg not only as a base where he could look after his official duties in the theater – when he was in town – but also to give music lessons and to entertain himself and his mistress.[80] Carolyne zu Sayn-Wittgenstein was attractive more for vivid temperament, erudition, and quick wit than physical beauty; she would converse in French non-stop, offering judgmental opinions, while chain-smoking planter cigars. Very intelligent, she had read much of world literature but knew little about music, which nonetheless was often included in the debates she favored. Her somewhat prickly personality was balanced by that of her eleven-year-old daughter Marie, a sweet, innocent beauty, whom the couple lovingly cared for. Marie was important, for eventually Carolyne was able to transfer a large portion of her wealth to her legally, so that Russian courts could not touch it: it was known that Prince Nicholas, while not opposed to a dissolution of their marriage on principle, wanted his wife's money.[81]

Frequent visitors to the Altenburg found Carolyne eccentric but mostly charming, Liszt brilliant though given to mood swings, and Marie enchanting. For more than a decade, they arrived in two discrete groupings – young musicians whom Liszt mentored, always free of charge, and accomplished artists and literati, who would move on more quickly. Among the latter were the Czech composer Bedřich Smetana, the English writers

William Thackeray and George Eliot, the Frenchman Hector Berlioz, the alluring Hungarian actress Lilla von Bulyovsky and, after the termination of his German exile, the Swiss resident Richard Wagner. Hoffmann von Fallersleben stayed for months at the Altenburg.[82]

The student musicians were mostly pianists, such as the Berlin Baron Hans von Bülow, Hans Bronsart von Schellendorf, the attractive Swede Ingeborg Starck, and the Jewish teenage prodigy from Poland, Karl Tausig. Many of these, like Bülow and Bronsart, would later also be conductors and composers, as Liszt himself now aspired to be. Violinists of future renown included Leopold Damrosch, who would decisively influence the musical life of New York, and Joseph Joachim, the close friend of Johannes Brahms who ended his career in the early twentieth century as director of Berlin's Royal Conservatory. The young Brahms himself briefly showed up at the Altenburg but, not impressed by anything he saw or heard, departed forthwith.[83]

Since Liszt was paid less than 2,000 taler annually by the Weimar court and irregularly at that, it was probably his mistress who financed sumptuous evenings of revelry and entertainment, which she always attended, unless as a woman prone to illnesses she had to visit a spa.[84] Poems were recited and music was played, sometimes with Weimar artists or notables as special guests. But by and large, Altenburg was a phenomenon unto itself; there was hardly any interaction with Weimar society and little with the ducal court. For example, when von Bulyovsky, who later starred in Dresden and Munich, visited Liszt from Pest, she did not at the same time assume a guest role in the theater, and Smetana did not conduct an orchestra. This disconnection was owing, on the one hand, to the unconventional makeup of the Altenburg's denizens, their appearance, behavior, and activities, which Weimarers of any class had difficulty comprehending. On the other hand, Liszt's relationship with the princess gave rise to scorn and gossip in Weimar streets and caused her official banishment from court. After the grand duchess had failed to secure Tsar Nicholas's permission for a divorce, Carolyne had been ordered by St. Petersburg to return to her native Poland. When she refused, she lost her entire fortune (save for what she had been able to pass on to her daughter), and the Weimar court had been impelled to ostracize her. Carolyne subsequently tried, through high-placed relatives in Rome, to have her marriage annulled by the pope, so that, as a Catholic, she could wed the devout Catholic Franz Liszt, but the Vatican's ruling kept being delayed and, as far as Weimar was concerned, she continued living in an illegitimate relationship with the musician. While courtiers and ladies-in-waiting could understand that but could not speak with her (in any case her idiosyncrasies were profoundly disliked by most), the man in the street – as in Goethe's time – resented the unofficial tolerance of adultery which, for ordinary burghers, was punishable by jail.[85]

Perhaps not least to mitigate these tensions, but certainly to reassert themselves as a viable force in Weimar's artistic and civic life, Liszt and his closest supporters in 1853 founded a club, calling it the *Neu-Weimar-Verein*, or New Weimar Association, whose members, from Liszt's innermost circle, were to meet regularly in a local inn and even at the Altenburg. Unfortunately, this club was modelled on conventional, bourgeois, patterns, hardly inspired by an artistic animus. It had an elaborate constitution with a president (Liszt), vice-president, and treasurer, and even a gazette. Its members congregated with enthusiasm for a number of months, very much like any German beer-swilling regulars, until the more critical began to stay away and the entire structure collapsed in the late 1850s, when Liszt had already decided to leave town. Apart from the bourgeois trappings, one serious fault of the venture was that although initially all progressive protagonists of culture were welcomed, music and musicians, all Lisztians, predominated from the start, due to Liszt's overbearing presence. This got worse as more non-musicians dropped out. The organization, conceived as a general platform for bold and novel ideas, was ever more turning into a Franz Liszt fan club.[86] Within Weimar's walls, the club lost its exclusivity; throughout the 1850s, there thrived three rival clubs; the opposition was often palpable. All three were populated by established worthies, some of them the descendants of iconic figures like Bertuch, Wieland, and Herder. One club even enjoyed the official patronage of Duke Carl Alexander.[87]

"Liszt-centricity" was a constant not only at the *Neu-Weimar-Verein*, where the same men fawned over him whom he knew from the Altenburg, but also, naturally, at the frequent soirées in the Altenburg itself. Here the princess for all appearances held Liszt well in check and always knew how to present herself to best effect. Liszt himself understood the mechanisms of crowd control. In his intimate circle he accomplished it by dint of his personal charisma, usually displaying joviality and sometimes displeasure, but he always knew how to dazzle in recitals. It was here that he employed the tried and proven tricks of the juggler and poseur, as when earlier, on the concert stage, he had allowed his gloves to drop ever so slowly from his hands before they touched the keys, or when he shook his fair-haired mane. Now he would play six complicated octave trills *all' unisono* with both hands when a simple trill would do. Granted, he was no Mozart, famous for elegant simplicity. Sometimes his mistress helped in the act. A visitor from Leipzig recalls, not without sarcasm, how, when Liszt had presented parts of his *Faust* symphony, all the listeners had become totally exalted, as the princess rose from her cushions, "seized Liszt and kissed him so consummately that everybody was deeply moved. (The Havana had just gone stale.)"[88]

The impression that Liszt was performing much of his music for show even in those post-golden years, in order to feed his ego, some even of his acolytes found reminiscent of his wilder concert days. Although they acknowledged his many endearing qualities, not least his tremendous generosity when he gave of his time and money, they were repelled. A showman's flair was one thing, but there were other, more significant, characteristics of the man which they came to resent. Those were musical, for as Liszt had begun to compose in Weimar, he had been inventing new harmonies as part of the *Neue Musik*, New Music, or Music of the Future, which was his creed and which he wanted musicians to play and audiences to hear. To a few of his early devotees, notably Joseph Joachim, these new sounds became anathema; they heard in them Liszt's "self-centered flamboyance," and increasingly wrote the whole man off.[89]

As Liszt was in the process of deeply disappointing musicians like Joachim, his assistant Joachim Raff, and eventually even Bülow and his closest admirer Peter Cornelius, he forwent the opportunity to create a new music school that could be lastingly identified with Weimar (as in Mannheim, for instance, in the previous century).[90] Liszt did become recognized as a pioneer in music, a catalyst for new compositions by contemporaries and successors, notably Berlioz, Wagner, and Richard Strauss. But this new trend was divorced from Weimar proper and was to remain so, and for some, including Brahms and Robert and Clara Schumann, it marginalized Liszt as an egocentric tunesmith with demonic traits.[91]

Liszt's Achievements as Music Director

In contrast to what was happening at the Altenburg, on opera and concert stages Liszt was contributing to the culture of Weimar directly and significantly, once given a chance. What hindered him most was the quantity and quality of performers at his disposal, and the intransigence of both Maria Pavlovna and Carl Alexander, whom he asked in vain to correct this by providing proper funds.[92] As early as January 1852 he warned the grand duchess that, as had been the practice under Chelard, one could not pull in as much money as possible by staging inexpensive, commercially viable productions, often by little-known composers, and that, as far as he was concerned, many props for the opera sets were shoddy. Fabrics, for instance, resembled the sofa covers in cheap hotels. Liszt desired subventions for high-quality operas to be performed, with high-quality artists, and if the taste of the Weimarers was close to zero, as he appeared to think, one should attract foreign visitors until this business model was self-financing.[93] A year later, when no change had been wrought, he threatened Carl Alexander with his resignation, but the prince, who was not yet a grand duke and was in no position to act on this, in typical fashion calmed him with soothing words.[94]

Liszt was eventually aided by the fact that Chelard was officially dismissed, in April 1851, and that thereafter, especially when he himself was absent, he could rely on two supportive Kapellmeister, Carl Stör and, soon, Eduard Lassen. Both were competent and, perhaps more important, avid Liszt followers, though not regulars at the Altenburg.[95] Until Liszt could exercise some quality control, culminating in the introduction of Wagner's creations – even within the limited means at his disposal – Weimar's opera repertory remained largely pedestrian. It included *La Fille du Régiment* by Donizetti, *König Alfred* by Raff, and *Robert le Diable* by Jacob Meyerbeer.[96] Raff was Liszt's friend, of course, and Liszt felt compelled to stage lesser works, such as Anton Rubinstein's *Die sibirischen Jäger* (1854), Lassen's *Le Roi Edgard* (1857), and Cornelius's *Der Barbier von Bagdad* (1858).[97]

Yet one of the first things Liszt accomplished was to hire new expert musicians, even if some did not stay long – another loss for Weimar. First, in 1850, was the violinist Joseph Joachim, a Jewish wunderkind who came from Bratislava via Vienna and Leipzig. Joachim was appointed concertmaster, until he accepted a better-paid position in Hanover, after only two years. In this case, the musical and personal disappointment with Liszt was surely a greater motivation for leaving than any financial one. Other new stellar instrumentalists were the cellist Bernhard Cossmann, the harp virtuoso Jeanne Eyth and the trombonist Moritz Nabich, who would even star in London. An excellent baritone who was newly employed was Feodor von Milde; he later married the superb Weimar soprano Rosa Agthe, and the two became mainstays of Weimar's public music scene. The outstanding trumpeter Ernst Sachse was another paragon of Weimar's home-grown talent.[98]

Supported by these players, but still starved of expert personnel, Liszt proceeded to conduct operas of renown, those of Gluck, Mozart, and Beethoven's *Fidelio*. He also favored contemporary works, as well as Wagner's and Berlioz's, although they had not yet passed the test of time.

Those included Albert Lortzing's *Zar und Zimmermann* and Otto Nicolai's *The Merry Wives of Windsor*.[99]

In addition, Liszt conducted concert pieces, including some of his own. Prominent in this instrumental program were Beethoven's piano works and symphonies. Liszt presented overtures by Carl Maria von Weber and premiered Schumann's dramatic tone poem *Manfred* in 1852. Of his own compositions, Liszt premiered the *Ideale* and the *Faust-Symphonie* in Weimar, on festive occasions in 1857. By that time the "newly arrived piano player, who cannot even beat time correctly," as unfriendly musicians once taunted, had become a master at wielding the baton.[100]

Amid his official duties and tending so solicitously to his private affairs, it is remarkable how Liszt became productive as an original composer, when in pre-Weimar days he had not been able to amass a wealth of experience. It is true that Liszt always complained to friends that he lacked time for composing, yet in the face of great adversity his accomplishments are impressive. Today some of the best-remembered works are his two piano concertos, the Dante symphony, and the Hungarian rhapsodies. But he also wrote fantasias and paraphrases on the favorite airs of Meyerbeer's operas, because these brought in some necessary funds.[101] Yet Liszt even ventured beyond convention. Allan Kozinn informs readers of the *New York Times* that skillful pianists like Pierre-Laurent Aimard are capable of revealing Liszt as a "futurist whose harmonic and structural ideas were so demonstrably ahead of his time that when you place his works beside those of Bartók, Ravel, Messiaen, Scriabin, Berg and a few others, the scope of his influence is undeniable."[102]

Alan Walker has detailed the musically most interesting pieces of Liszt's *œuvre*, many of which contributed to his historic fame as the creator of the, alas so controversial, *Neue Musik*. Within his orchestral work, Liszt's symphonic poems must be counted first. Before Weimar, Liszt had written very little for orchestra. He himself introduced the term "symphonic poem," in order to describe, as Walker explains, "a growing body of one-movement orchestral compositions, programmatically conceived." This implied shifts in structural emphasis involving the shape and role of recapitulations, codas, and main themes. Some of these poems dealt with unique heroes – Hamlet, Orpheo, Tasso – figures Liszt was able to identify with easily because they confronted overwhelming odds and faced seemingly insurmountable dilemmas, as he himself did so frequently. Because he was short of time, Liszt composed his *Faust-Symphonie* in only two months, in the mid-1850s; it resonated with the spirit of Goethe, whose house he was familiar with since 1840, as did the symphonic poem *Tasso* and other of

Liszt's works. Clearly, the affinity with Goethe was a cause, as well as a main consequence of the composer's stay in Weimar. The *Faust-Symphonie* was also musically original not least because it featured an early form of the twelve-tone note roll that Arnold Schoenberg would develop later. Its first performance took place on September 5, 1857, on the occasion of the unveiling of the Goethe–Schiller monument in front of Weimar's theater – another important allusion to the classical era. Liszt's Sonata in B minor was completed four years earlier; it represented "a sonata across a sonata," as its four movements were "rolled into one" and composed "against a background of full-scale sonata scheme – exposition, development and recapitulation." Before Liszt, only Beethoven had attempted anything resembling this. Once again, the structure was so novel that it foreshadowed Schoenberg's inventions, namely his First Chamber Symphony, half a century hence. Liszt's work for organ also was significant, particularly since he was the first composer to move that king of instruments out of the church and into the concert hall. Liszt's Fantasy and Fugue B-A-C-H, paying homage to one of his idols, was among the most important works for organ he created in the mid-1850s. And finally, Liszt became a mature songwriter. Having composed his very first songs in Italy, he now used verses by Fallersleben, Schiller, and of course Goethe, and eventually had eighty songs and collections to his credit. They too were musically daring, as they were characterized by "an unparalleled freedom of the vocal line, which often unfolds across an advanced harmonic texture." Moreover, explains Walker, "Liszt's penchant for plunging back and forth from one extreme key to another often means that his melodies are fraught with enharmonic subtleties."[103]

Insofar as Liszt's productivity as conductor and composer could be relied upon to progress well and found the approval of the ruling family, it was destined to go a long way in fulfilling Weimar's quest for new greatness. But three factors combined to interfere with Liszt's creative residency, compelling him to leave the town after just over a decade's stay. These were his view of the theater as primarily an operatic venue, his relationship with Richard Wagner, and his identification with Johann Wolfgang Goethe's legacy. In all of this, Carl Alexander, who wanted culture without having to invest in it, assumed a decidedly negative stance.

For Liszt, the stage became dramatic in more ways than one. As a musician, he was involved in the affairs of the theater as one of its principals. Although he kept himself formally independent because of his initial contract with the court that guaranteed him freedom in return for low wages, in an everyday relationship, even when conducting opera, he was reliant on the theater's Intendant, for better or for worse. Although in this regard he got along reasonably well with Baron von Ziegesar and his successor Baron Karl von Beaulieu-Marconnay, who nominally were his superiors, he had to see to it that the presentations of drama and of comedy on stage did not take precedence over those of opera – for budgetary considerations. After his permanent tenure commenced in 1848 that balance was not perfect, but somehow workable: in future programming, stage plays did take a back seat to opera. Liszt had to suffer contentious relations with the capable but impetuous dramaturge Wilhelm Marr, who in interpersonal dealings was so rancorous that he was pensioned off in 1855. But just in time Marr had helped in staging Liszt's own opera productions, and staged them well.[104] The fact that the theater program remained of mixed quality – far from the uniform high standard Goethe had once striven for – ranging from *Berthold Schwarz* by the Weimar-raised and usually inebriated bard Alexander Rost, to dramas by Hebbel, Goethe, and Schiller, was hardly Liszt's fault.[105] Some of the visiting actors were of the first rank: Bogumil Dawison, Marie Seebach, and Emil Devrient; others were of the parochial Weimar type who simply refused to release their long-held grip on the ducal stage, especially the locally reputed ones.[106]

One of the more substantial works performed in the early 1850s was *Das Haus des Barneveldt*, a tragedy in five acts by one Franz Dingelstedt.[107] Dingelstedt had been a Gymnasium teacher, librarian, and Intendant at the Munich theater; politically liberal, he was also a friend of Liszt's and Liszt had invited him to Weimar several times. When Beaulieu-Marconnay had to be replaced, Liszt prevailed upon the grand duke to have Dingelstedt appointed, as he had unexpectedly been dismissed from his Munich post.[108] In the following months, while Dingelstedt once again turned to mostly quality stage productions in memory of Goethe, he did so at the expense of opera, which Liszt, now Dingelstedt's formal subordinate, resented. The vacillating Carl Alexander found it impossible to escape from Dingelstedt's considerable charm and powers of persuasion, even though his wife Sophie detested the man.[109]

Matters came to a head in December 1858, when the first major work of Peter Cornelius, one of the last young men to have kept his Weimar friendship with Liszt intact, was premiered. It was *Der Barbier von Bagdad*, a comic opera with New Music harmonic elements, "not brilliant enough" for a discriminating audience, but also "not bad enough" to be a flop, as Cornelius himself divined.[110] In order to embarrass Liszt, and as he could not care less about Cornelius, Dingelstedt had delegated a claque to boo the opera at its premiere; sadly, a lonely grand duke rose and ostentatiously applauded.[111] In February 1859, Liszt handed in his resignation; his former supporter Maria Pavlovna died in June. Receiving no equivalent professional offer, he stayed on in Weimar for two more years, but he also wished to await the outcome of his lady friend's divorce proceedings, which now were in the hands of the Vatican.[112] During this period Carl Alexander tried to persuade him, once again against his better judgment, to stay, holding out great promises for Liszt in Weimar and mentioning, in particular, a future with Richard Wagner, the University of Jena, and the – just founded – ducal art academy.[113] With regard to the latter two a disillusioned Liszt replied to him in February of 1861 that "neither Jena's university nor, much less, the new painters' academy is thus far pace-setting. There are, without a doubt, in Jena very worthy men of recognized knowledge and talent; but twenty German universities possess them also, and even more. And as far as the painters' academy is concerned, it yet has to prove itself through its *œuvre*."[114] Liszt left Weimar for Rome in August, whence Princess zu Sayn-Wittgenstein had already preceded him the year before.[115]

Victorious, Dingelstedt continued his sterling productions in the theater, once more at the expense of opera, which practically withered, as did the rest of Weimar's public musical life, in a regimen of unremarkable conductors, until the advent of Richard Strauss in 1889.[116] With the classics being neglected, the Intendant's specialty now was William Shakespeare.[117] But the new achievements were not Weimar's to keep. In 1867, just after the grand duke had effected Dingelstedt's ennoblement (something he chronically and incomprehensibly failed to achieve for Liszt), Dingelstedt moved to Vienna's Burgtheater to perpetuate his fame in the service of the Habsburg monarchy.[118]

In what he called his testament, Liszt wrote in September 1860 that ten years earlier he had been dreaming of a new artistic era in Weimar, similar to that in Karl August's time, "where Wagner and I would have been the leaders, just like Goethe and Schiller then."[119] Indeed, by 1850 Wagner's compositions had started to become an integral part of Liszt's novel concept of *Neue Musik*, more important even than the music of Berlioz, whom he also admired and liked to welcome in town.[120] Liszt came to have great plans for himself and Wagner in Weimar, and Wagner was one of the important reasons why he remained there for as long as he did.

Already by early 1849 Liszt was so impressed with the work of Wagner, a composer he had met only a few times before, that he decided to stage his *Tannhäuser* for Maria Pavlovna's birthday on February 16, 1849. Thereafter it was accorded pride of place in Liszt's operatic repertory.[121] Wagner himself arrived in Weimar in mid-May, a refugee from justice in Saxony, because he had participated in the Dresden rebellion against the king. Liszt would have kept him in Weimar even then, but for the opposition of Minister von Watzdorf, since a Saxon extradition order against Wagner would surely have to be honored. Hence after a few days Wagner, with help from Liszt and Sayn-Wittgenstein, escaped from Germany via Switzerland and Paris, temporarily to settle in Zurich. The Saxon warrant was duly issued, and it remained for Liszt to perform Wagner's music without enjoying the inspiration and friendship of his artistic collaborator in person.[122]

Liszt understood Wagner's unique notion of a symbiosis of text and music, the essence of his *Gesamtkunstwerk*, and put much stock in the revolutionary musical constructions of a composer who was two years younger. Thus he next prepared a Weimar premiere of *Lohengrin* for August 28, 1850, the occasion of Goethe's birthday.[123] Liszt wished to secure his own position at court and in town with this offering as much as improve Wagner's chances for a permanent return to Weimar, the political mood at the ducal court permitting. Notwithstanding the underwhelming impression the first staging of this work made on the local public, apart from the enthusiasm of visiting international guests, *Lohengrin* too became a mainstay of the operatic repertoire for Weimar, as did Wagner's *Fliegender Holländer*, first performed there in February 1853.[124]

The entire decade of the 1850s is characterized by Liszt's manifold efforts to secure Wagner's permanent presence in Weimar, ideally with a ducal sinecure. These included not only as frequent performances of his works as possible, but also financial help from his own or Carolyne's private purse, visits to Zurich, and obtaining a pardon from the King of Saxony – where Carl Alexander joined him.[125] However, the grand duke, though seemingly an admirer of Wagner's music and also inclined to visit him abroad, was less than enthusiastic in having the composer reside in Weimar. Watzdorf warned him that this would be political folly, and hence Carl Alexander even refused to award the composer medals.[126] A plan thought out by both Wagner and Liszt to have what later became *Der Ring des Nibelungen* cycle composed and exclusively performed in Weimar, after the construction of a special theater, was also thwarted by the ducal government.[127] If that had been allowed to happen, Weimar would be today's Bayreuth. Officially, Carl Alexander claimed not to have the money. But his personal reason lay deeper, for his sense of self-importance would not allow him to be overshadowed by the illuminating presence of such an exceptional artist. Related to this, the grand duke did not want a singular domineering *Gesamtkunstwerk* for his town; he favored several smaller projects which he thought he could control. Here the amateurish nature of the, after a fashion, cultured yet insufficiently enlightened grand duke placed another insurmountable obstacle in the way of Weimar's quest for renewed greatness.[128]

Liszt's initial and long-sustained interest in Goethe and other classicists, in particular Schiller, was an additional reason for his being attracted to Weimar for as long as he was. "Liszt very consciously connected to Weimar's cultural tradition," Dieter Borchmeyer has observed.[129] There is no denying Liszt's early interest in Goethe and in Schiller, apart from Dante and Shakespeare; apparently Marie d'Agoult had read from their works to him during their post-Parisian years. In 1839, one year before he set foot on Weimar's soil, Liszt had announced that he would attempt "a symphonic work based on Dante, then another on Faust, say in three years."[130] Then, as he increasingly associated himself with Weimar, he made it his business to think more about Goethe, taking in the celebrations around Schiller, Wieland, and Herder as well. By 1848, as he was settling in Weimar with his mistress Carolyne, such an attitude for him must have become de rigueur. He must have realized that there was no better way to ingratiate himself with Maria Pavlovna and particularly with the ambitious heir Carl Alexander than to ostentatiously honor the memory of Goethe and the classics. The opportunities were many. Goethe's birthday was celebrated every August 28, and there was a Herder festival in 1850, and the visit of the noted French *Faust* translator Gérard de Nerval to the court and the Altenburg in the same year.[131] In 1857 the Goethe-and-Schiller statue by Ernst Rietschel was unveiled, and yet another one for Wieland, with Liszt participating actively. Liszt's contemporary compositions abounded with classically oriented texts.[132] In 1859 a Schiller centenary took place, at which Liszt delivered an official toast.[133]

It was in 1851, after Liszt had already realized the potential importance of Richard Wagner for a rejuvenated Weimar culture, that he conceived a master plan for a Goethe Foundation, to support German artists through regularly scheduled competitions, awarding money prizes. He had been inspired by preliminary thoughts of celebrated Goethe acolytes in Berlin, such as Alexander von Humboldt.[134] The venture, every three years, should be financed by the grand dukes, and the reigning grand duke, leading a specially selected committee of experts, should be the foundation's president. Literature, painting, sculpture, and music should benefit.[135] It was Wagner who criticized details of this scheme by telling Liszt it would not work, for such festivities would be commercially exploited by the artists, there would be rivalry among the arts, and those artists who had proved their mettle did not need them anyway. The one exception he made was for the visual arts and architecture, which were not infinitely reproducible, as were works of music and fiction.[136]

Throughout the 1850s Liszt and Carl Alexander continued to communicate about this plan, with the grand duke displaying fervor but in the end never committing himself. As usual, he kept the door ajar, employing complimentary verbiage. His failure on this front closely paralleled his inability to fund the "Weimar Yearbook," dedicated to Goethe and the classics.[137] As for Liszt, his friend and master pupil Hans von Bülow wrote to his mother as early as 1852 that Liszt had enemies in Weimar comparable to excrement at the seaside. "After all, Liszt sticks his nose in things other than playing the piano – the Goethe Foundation etc. – which rubs people the wrong way. When you come right down to it, they only allow him to entertain them in his capacity as pianist."[138] This was as sad a comment on Liszt's professionalism as it was on his ostensive interest in the classics. Insofar as such sentiment had not changed by 1861, it gave Liszt sufficient reason to assume that his art and the town of Weimar had never bonded and that, on all accounts, his impending departure for Rome now was a timely one.

To sum up the four Weimar decades after Goethe's death: they were marked by the establishment of a tradition of missed opportunities. For a few years there was hope that Maria Pavlovna and later even Goethe's two grandsons would regenerate the town's culture, which in the 1830s and into the '40s was made up of inferior productions, home-grown or imported. This hope was not fulfilled, but received new nourishment under Karl August's grandson Carl Alexander, especially after his enthronement in 1853. But despite obvious gifts and a proclivity for enlightened culture, he was hampered by an immobile court apparatus superimposed on a culture-neutral citizenry. In the end, the new grand duke's intellectual horizons proved limited, albeit pretentiously far-stretched, hence his political liberalism gradually turned into reaction, dampening for creative processes. Efforts to attract, in the manner of Anna Amalia, prolific spirits remained futile, as spirits like Andersen and Fallersleben were second-rate and the attraction chronically temporary.

With the arrival of Franz Liszt in Weimar in 1848 hopes of a cultural revival received new impetus, not least in the Goethe memorial department, for Liszt, eventually joined in this by the grand duke, became Goethe's most fervent advocate since 1832. Liszt had other qualities that augured well for Weimar: an attractive personality, international flair, and of course his virtuoso musicality, where he excelled both as a composer and creator of New Music, and as champion of the futuristic music of Wagner. For a few years, Liszt improved not only Weimar's comparatively pedestrian musical scene, but its cultural aura generally. Nevertheless, Liszt's negative side prevented ongoing success. His narcissism insulted friends who might otherwise have stayed in Weimar and, whatever the ultimate reason, he could never mobilize Carl Alexander effectively to grant financial and institutional backup for large-scale and lasting cultural projects. Those would have included the institutionalization of Wagner and his music as a Weimar hallmark. Goethe's memory, too, was revived only slowly. By the end of the 1860s, Weimar may have begun the attempt to reach a Silver Age, after the highlights set by the neoclassicists seventy years earlier, but with a dull collective mentality it got stuck in ordinary business.

CHAPTER 3

◆

Failing the Silver Age
1861 to 1901

In the 1850s Liszt had provided Weimar with some lustre, and there had been cultural highlights, such as the staging of Wagner's operas. But even before his departure, drabness returned to the town, in culture and society, and this was reinforced when Liszt's foe, the theater-obsessed Franz Dingelstedt, left for Vienna in 1867. Even though Wagner performances became something of a tradition in Weimar and Goethe and Schiller's dramas were featured (lasting changes after Liszt and Dingelstedt), mediocrity once again ruled the stage and literary circles.[1] Politically the grand duchy appeared carefully conservative without having lost its fundamentally liberal tinge; the effects of the war with France in 1870–71 did shake things up a little, with some families losing their breadwinners.[2] Polite society became stultified in efforts to while away the time; the diaries of the barons Lothar von Thüna and Carl von Schlicht display a shocking emptiness.[3]

It is therefore somewhat of a surprise that Liszt, at the end of the 1860s, resolved to return to Weimar. In part, he was following Carl Alexander's call: he had never got over what for him had been a personal loss, all questions of responsibility aside. Liszt saw the grand duke in 1864 and inspected the Altenburg, which he found enveloped in spiderwebs and dust. He had been appointed a grand-ducal court chamberlain in 1861, and in 1867 his *Heilige Elisabeth* oratorio was performed at Wartburg Castle under his direction. But there evidently was no viable position for him at that time, as his follower Kapellmeister Eduard Lassen, workmanlike if no genius, had had the musical productions well in hand since 1858. Liszt was unhappy, moving between his modest quarters in Rome and Pest. His affair with Princess Carolyne was becoming increasingly sour, for although her husband had died in 1864, the pope withdrew his final consent to their marriage shortly before the ceremony because of Carolyne's relatives' intercession. Thereafter, she became uninterested, with Liszt himself losing his fervor, doubtless also because he never lacked for female attention. Moreover, there was trouble in his immediate family. In 1857 his favorite student Hans von Bülow had married Liszt's daughter Cosima, who after 1863 was Wagner's on-and-off lover until, after divorcing Bülow and with three illegitimate children, she married Wagner in 1870. This was one of the bedrocks on which the budding animosity between the two composers was founded, Liszt gallantly taking Bülow's side.[4]

Upon arriving in Weimar on January 12, 1869, Liszt moved into the flat of a villa between the Goethe Park on the Ilm and the center of town, courtesy of the grand duke. It had three medium-size rooms and a small kitchen and could not welcome any guests to stay the night, but Liszt did employ a housekeeper and manservant. From now on he would spend almost every spring there, dividing the rest of his time between Rome and Pest.[5] He gave very few public performances, save for some in the early days and at court, to show deference to Carl Alexander. One meritorious project he became involved in was the founding of the public music school which today bears his name.[6] As a composer, in this late mature period the deeply pious Liszt had been fond of creating Catholic-inspired works, with choir and organ, such as the oratorios *Heilige Elisabeth* (1862) and *Christus* (1867). His marriage plans shattered, he had taken the lower orders in Rome and arrived in Weimar as an abbé, dressed in a long black frock. In 1870 Liszt composed a Beethoven Cantata as a paean to the older composer, but also courageously quoting a chord from Wagner's *Tristan und Isolde*, as a compliment to *Neue Musik*. According to Alan Walker, his last pieces were marked by "darkness and depression," even though harmonically they were as bold as ever, as would be his *Bagatelle sans tonalité* (1885).[7]

Liszt's main purpose in Weimar was to set himself up as mentor for advanced piano students, but he also became a magnet for visiting established musicians such as the Russian composer Alexander Borodin or the Hungarian violinist Ede Remenyi.[8] Again, he accepted no fees, instead inviting his students to dinner and always offering them wine, cognac, and cigars. Some received amounts of money from him, loans that invariably turned into gifts. Liszt just did not wish to lose the role of benefactor he had cultivated earlier – out of altruism as much as vanity.[9] Now he obviously had less to spend than before, since an absent princess could not finance him. After 1871 he received an annual salary as Royal Hungarian councillor and still worked on commissioned music for a fee, and he must have had funds saved up. It is certain that Carl Alexander gave him next to nothing.[10]

Liszt, already the creator of the modern star virtuoso type, now became the founder of the modern masterclass.[11] Most of his advanced students were above their teens, had had expert instruction in their home countries and were in control of their technique. Some, in fact, were already very accomplished, even internationally famous. His most important disciples then were the Russian Vera Timanova, the American Amy Fay, the English-German Eugen d'Albert, and the German Pauline Fichtner.[12] Hence Liszt taught them interpretation. Using himself as an example, he showed them how to generate charisma and build on it. If they had none, Liszt was not shy about getting rid of them quickly, as he did uninvited onlookers. Students would appear at regular intervals at his salon, and Liszt would choose them at random for recital, sometimes playing from orchestral scores on an upright piano alongside. With great aplomb and mimicry, he would then point out their strengths and weaknesses. Liszt himself could never be coaxed into playing, but frequently did so of his own accord, if only to uphold his famous magic and keep the alchemy going by dazzling everyone with his technique. Students, usually mortified when asked to play, had to bear his whims and froze in the vortex of his furors, but they were magnetically attracted to the man, knowing that to be with him in Weimar was an extraordinary honor which later they could flaunt, and they adored him for it.[13] On certain days there were matinees and recitals and a few Weimar regulars came to visit, with the grand duke sometimes among them.[14]

Liszt's second stay in Weimar, like the first one, had its unsavory aspects, but this time they were so strong that they contributed to his downfall. More often than not, his coaching sessions assumed the characteristics of a court with himself at the center and student sycophants servicing his narcissism. If anything, Liszt's sense of self-importance had increased and struck all but his most slavish followers as sheer vanity. The visiting Bülow once entered the salon in Liszt's absence to clean up the stable of fawning hangers-on, especially some musically incompetent young women, but next day Liszt had invited them all back, presumably because he felt adrift without his entourage.[15] Amy Fay and others noted how obsessed Liszt was in the presence of nobility, that he changed his entire demeanor when around them, and that his constant companion, who was decades younger, was the Baroness Olga von Meyendorff.[16] Indeed, as much as ever, Liszt was hankering after orders, medals, titles, and decorations. He still craved recognition and applause.[17] Once a young female violinist, for her own commercial advantage, dragged him to the photographer to have her picture taken with him, which Liszt then adorned with words of praise.[18]

Liszt was as capable of crowd control as ever. "He always fixes his eyes on some one of us when he plays, and I believe he tries to wring our hearts. When he plays a passage, and goes *pearling* down the key-board, he often looks over at me and smiles, to see whether I am appreciating it," writes Fay.[19] It appears that in that final decade and a half, Liszt could not attempt anything for the sake of a good cause, if it was not also for himself. Walter Damrosch, son of Liszt's old student Leopold Damrosch, tells how in 1882 he came visiting Liszt from New York, not least to convey greetings from his father. Meeting him at his flat, Damrosch sensed "a certain frigidity in the air" and politely took an early leave. That evening Kapellmeister Lassen told him that he had found the master in tears. Liszt had thought that Damrosch would stay and study with him (and, like his father, fall at the master's feet). "The young generation have forgotten me completely," moaned Liszt. "They think nothing of me and they have no respect for us older men of bygone days."[20] Liszt found it difficult to accept what he took to be rejection, when in fact some young people were simply in awe or very scared of him.

Liszt may have been an old man by then but his interest in young women had not abated. On the contrary, he could take his pick from the many that he attracted and who came to visit him, and Weimar's air was filled with rumors about strange goings-on at his house.[21] It is moot to speculate whether he had sexual relations with Meyendorff, who was born a Russian princess, but she did live across from his house and he spent many hours in her company.[22] The same can be said about a certain Lina Schmalhausen, a well-nigh incompetent piano player who was constantly around him in his later years and actually tried to steal his money. Apart from being dependent on her, Liszt knew this and kept her on, because she had been recommended by Augusta, the grand duke's sister and now the Kaiser's wife.[23] Liszt did have a serious affair, in Rome and already a priest (although not bound by the vows of celibacy), with a young Russian countess who, lovesick, tried to kill him with a dagger and then followed him to Weimar in 1870, starting all tongues wagging.[24]

If sex or its ramifications did not kill Liszt, tobacco and alcohol nearly did – especially alcohol. Liszt always had difficulty surviving a day without spirits in his earlier years, but on his second stay in Weimar, indulging in expensive French cognac and Hungarian Palugay wine became a way of life.[25] He took those stimulants while smoking heavy Virginia cigars, and what was worse, he was in the habit of urging them all on his male students, at least two of whom later became alcoholics: one, Arthur Friedheim, causing a brawl in a New York theater and almost being tried for murder, and the other, Alfred Reisenauer, dying of alcoholism in Riga while on tour.[26] Toward the end of his life Liszt began to mix cognac with wine and also took to drinking absinthe, that lethal concoction then wreaking havoc throughout France.[27]

Liszt showed signs of clinical depression in 1875, at the latest. At that time he experienced a breakdown because he deemed himself a failure in life.[28] This may explain his increasing substance abuse, which further contributed to a decline in health. In his last years, he was suffering from asthma, insomnia, cataract, and dropsy (edema) conditions which were compounded after he had taken a fall in summer 1881. The plumpness due to water in his feet and legs, plus prominent warts on his face, made him into a caricature of his former handsome self.[29] He died of pneumonia at Wahnfried, his daughter Cosima's manse in Bayreuth, in July of 1886.[30]

Cosima was busy with that year's Wagner festival at the time of her father's death, so he could not die in her arms. But the two had been estranged for years.[31] In fact, it was a tragedy that Liszt had by now lost virtually all of his old friends, including Berlioz and Bülow, who, like Joachim much earlier, was then firmly established in the Brahms camp. The *Neue Musik*, it seems, had not taken hold, with the exception of course of Wagner's own but he, dead since 1883, was not especially identified with Liszt. Surely unfairly, Hermann Levi, Wagner's long-time favorite conductor, had in the 1870s called Liszt "a talented humbug."[32] All music aside, Liszt's mannerisms and antics had in no small degree contributed to this.

What did such a reputation do to Weimar? Just as Liszt had not been appreciated by the town's native population during his first sojourn there, so did the burghers dislike him during the second.[33] He remained a bizarre figure whose strange activities in that villa near the park ordinary people could only regard with suspicion, especially with his ever-present aura of sexual innuendo. Although the grand duke and some notables appeared at Liszt's matinees, as he, when at all possible, appeared at court, the monarch had not officially lent legitimacy to the composer's stay in town.[34] Liszt's ducal commission being in name only, he was a private citizen surrounded by others of his kind, like the Baroness Meyendorff – a widow habitually dressed in black and with four adolescent sons – and ever-changing visitors who were just as outlandish as he was.[35] He could be seen in the park or walking about town with his white head of hair and dark clerical cassock, usually surrounded by a clutch of young, often wildly attired, people.[36] Weimar's unchanged provincialism could not bear such sights. Liszt himself, it was known, called Weimar "the little nest," and his contempt of local Weimarers who now had just as little taste as during 1850, when they had refused to purchase tickets for the premiere of *Lohengrin*, knew no bounds.[37] This was apart from the fact that, ironically, Weimar now benefited somewhat commercially, as Liszt students rented flats, rooms, and pianos, and filled taverns, inns, and shops. In fact, as in Goethe's last years, a certain Liszt-oriented tourism developed, as more established visitors like Borodin and Turgenev, but also total strangers who took a chance on seeing and meeting with Liszt, appeared.[38] Liszt as a tourist attraction became a milestone on Weimar's path to national prominence – Weimar, that provincial heart in the sylvan middle of a geographically and spiritually united Germany, as the century drew to a close. Today, of course, in the great theme park that is Weimar, Liszt's house on the park is just another monument, as if he had always been a creator of its legacy.

The Painters' Academy

As has been aptly observed, Grand Duke Carl Alexander was acutely aware that Liszt's impending departure – seriously imminent since 1858 – was going to result in a vast lacuna in the cultural landscape of Weimar, which even Dingelstedt's accomplishments could not fill. It is therefore no coincidence that he thought of art and an art academy to repair this damage.[39] The grand duke, who would pay for all the upcoming artistic activities himself, allowed himself to be guided by his aesthetic, religious, and dynastic-patriotic principles. Aesthetically, art was to represent the truly good and beautiful; physically ugly images were anathema. Art had to be divinely inspired, or reflect the presence of God in the image of nature or of history – Germany's or that of antiquity. In the late 1850s and even before the founding of any academy, one of the projects he was keen to finance was the depiction of historic themes, including excerpts from the life of Luther, in his ongoing restoration of Wartburg Castle. He engaged the Romantic painter Moritz von Schwind, who declined, however, to work on anything beyond the legendary medieval singers' contest, and the saintly duchess, Elizabeth of Hungary. Carl Alexander was imbued with the ideals of classicism, as he thought Goethe had understood it – Goethe, who had taught him and who along with his Swiss friend Heinrich Meyer had himself founded a Zeichenschule, a drawing school based on classical tenets. By 1858 the grand duke desired for his realm the foundations of an art academy dominated by genre and historical painting. He and the landscape painter Count Stanislaus von Kalckreuth went to Munich to receive additional inspiration and attempt to hire the first art instructors. After Schwind himself had shown no interest years before, the prominent

Munich art professor Karl Piloty was approached, who also declined Carl Alexander's offer. Once again the grand duke had tried to attract internationally known luminaries but had failed, so that in 1860 he settled for Kalckreuth.[40]

The monarch could have turned to Friedrich Preller, born in 1804 as the son of a Weimar pastry maker, who had been a pupil in Goethe's Zeichenschule and then, because of obvious talent, had been sent to the art academy in Antwerp. After several years in Rome he joined the Zeichenschule's faculty in 1832. He was in the center of what would become the Weimar Old Guard, traditional artists opposed to more modern concepts to be followed in a new ducal art academy. His main compatriots were another Weimarer, Carl Hummel, son of the composer, and Bonaventura Genelli, born in Berlin of Italian lineage. They all painted landscapes or genres reflecting antiquity, the Bible, and a glorious historical past; their paragons were giants of the Renaissance like Michelangelo.[41] This was not a "Weimar Painter School," but their interrelated styles may have been unique to Weimar as landscape painting was unique to the Dresden School, historical painting to the Munich School, both these modes to the Düsseldorf School, and portraiture to Berlin. Germany had not evolved and was not then evolving a unified art style, as had been happening in centralized France with its Parisian academy; what gradually developed in France as a uniform standard turned out to be a boon to that country's art scene in the nineteenth century, attracting all manner of admirers, including, of course, Germans, and soon also Germans from Weimar.[42]

Although Carl Alexander had high regard for Preller, in particular, since both shared a reverence for Goethe and the classics, he was aware that Preller was of a bygone era and, seeing himself as modern, that nowadays he should embrace more progressive trends. This did not mean that the duke wanted to lose sight of his cherished principles as he had discussed them with Kalckreuth; on the contrary, Kalckreuth should try to do justice to them with a younger team and better resources. The count hailed from the German East; after service in the Prussian army he, like all members of the aristocracy, had only had three or four options for a livelihood. He could inherit the homestead if there was one and he met the laws of primogeniture, he could become either a career officer or diplomat, or he could attach himself to one of Germany's many ruling houses as a courtier or in government. Instead, Kalckreuth's artistic talent impelled him to become a painter; his specialty became the landscape of the Alps or, more precisely, the Pyrenees, where he traveled to make sketches for the paintings he would do in his studio.[43]

After the official founding of the Weimar academy in December 1860, and to the disbelief of the Old Guard, Kalckreuth assembled around him several younger artists, all of whom Carl Alexander believed to be so independently wealthy that he did not have to pay them. (Only one of them, Count Ferdinand Harrach, actually was rich.) Kalckreuth himself, who was in need of money, received merely 1,500 taler a year. The defining specialties of these artists were traditional enough not to offend the grand duke, but most had artistic ambitions reaching beyond his own vision. In the main, Romantic images were now replacing the classicist motifs; this new Naturalism was opposed to the Old Guard's heroic style. Baron Arthur von Ramberg was assigned the professorship of historical content; he was closest in style to the Old Guard and likely to please the grand duke. Baron Carl von Schlicht would teach landscape, Harrach the painting of figures. There were also two counts from Sweden, acquaintances of Kalckreuth but of no renown.[44] By far the most important teachers, who were commoners, were Franz Lenbach (b. 1836), a student of Piloty, who demonstrated basic painting techniques, and the Swiss Arnold Böcklin (b. 1827), with years in Italy and Munich behind him, who did landscapes.[45]

Although Carl Alexander watched Lenbach and Böcklin's work with guarded approval, the two men were not happy in Weimar. They found the town altogether too provincial, resented the stodginess of its burghers and were offended by the arrogance of the court, where they had to appear on command by virtue of their office, but always without their spouses. Böcklin, who was paid 500 taler, especially chafed under what he considered to be the undue control, driven by ignorance, of the grand duke. As reported in the reminiscences of his Italian wife, he resented "having to put on breeches, buckle shoes and the gold-braided tuxedo with golden buttons and collar, to say nothing of the dagger," when ordered to appear in court. Both Lenbach and Böcklin left in 1862.[46]

In fact, several others left (as was becoming the historic curse of Weimar) in the first few years, because of manifold difficulties, not the least of which was the grand duke's reluctance to pay the faculty members properly, but there was also friction with Director Kalckreuth, over these and other issues. The count had disagreements with the ruling family as well. He did not share the grand duke's penchant for socializing with his personal, mostly aristocratic, painter colony, for example in the hunt and games; he wanted a new building for the academy which Carl Alexander did not grant; and he resented the duke's tendency to appoint faculty over his head. Kalckreuth, who could himself be irascible in communications with his colleagues and fought many little wars that damaged the school's reputation abroad, also felt personally slighted because his wife, born a commoner, was prohibited at court. Like Franz Liszt threatening repeatedly to take his leave, he was persuaded by the monarch to stay on till 1876, when he retired to South Germany and Theodor Hagen succeeded him as director.[47]

Despite these disruptions and although the personnel turnover in the academy during the 1860s was almost crippling, one achievement of that decade stands out: the fundamental grooming of Max Liebermann, later an Impressionist and one of the most significant German painters of the early twentieth century. He was trained by the Flemish painter of historical themes Ferdinand Pauwels, an academy staff member since 1862. Liebermann arrived from Berlin in 1868 and could barely suffer Pauwels's authoritarian teaching style, but he learned from the Belgian techniques of coloration that cleverly employed contrasts between light and dark. In 1873, now back in Berlin, he unveiled a late work from Weimar, of peasant women plucking goose feathers. The stark visual effect was as remarkable as the social comment implied by the genre – both a first for Weimar.[48] Were these the portents of what certain German critics later called the "Weimar Painter School"?[49]

There were several developments in the 1870s which together rendered the Weimar style of painting more mature, without making it excel in Germany. The academy brought forth teachers and students who concentrated more and more on landscape – to the dismay of Carl Alexander, whose principal preference was historical motifs. In so doing, artists like Hagen, Karl Buchholz, Paul Baum, and Christian Rohlfs might at first keep their paintings in a grayish tone (some insiders were beginning to talk of a "Weimar gray"), but they tended more and more toward lighter patterns as was already the custom in France.[50] They also paid heed to indigenous Weimar scenes and practiced *plein-airisme*, or free-air style, which meant taking the easel outside into nature and painting the entire work there, rather than finishing it after sketches, in the studio.[51]

Of particular significance were the ties Weimar artists kept with Paris, and, even more so, the School of Barbizon, in the forest of Paris-Fontainebleau, which upheld Naturalism and contributed to Realism in French landscape painting. Barbizon's specialty was to paint landscape realistically and for its own sake, thereby following seventeenth-century French and Dutch artists. Its champions were Théodore Rousseau, Charles François Daubigny, Jules Dupré, and Camille Corot. The school was becoming more popular after mid-century, its members winning recognition from the Paris standard-setting Académie des Beaux-Arts. In Weimar

Hagen and the painter of animals, Albert Brendel, were heavily influenced by Barbizon, as was – further removed – Karl Buchholz.[52]

A painter who first was a protagonist of the gray tones but then drew closer to the Barbizon style (although he had been to Paris, if not to that small village nearby) was Baron Ludwig von Gleichen-Russwurm, a grandson of Friedrich Schiller. Having lost his wife rather early in life, he left his ancestral castle in Franconia in 1869 to become a pupil of Hagen. At first enthused by being able to welcome the famous poet's descendant in his realm, Carl Alexander soon became suspicious of Gleichen-Russwurm, as he could not understand the baron's free-air mode and identified the new Realism in art with commercialism. The grand duke was still divided between his love of traditionalism and his interest in new directions, which despite the best of intentions he was incapable of comprehending.[53]

In spite of these daring and promising turns, the Weimar academy also produced works of mediocrity. There were many products of genre painting that were popular with all but the avant-gardists; they showed harmless scenes of everyday life and work bordering on bathos. In the late 1870s Carl Alexander's brother-in-law Kaiser Wilhelm I purchased a painting by one Otto Piltz, depicting some children having lunch. Weimar painters such as Piltz, Alexander Struys, and Wilhelm Hasemann often worked on motifs with the sentimentalism that produces kitsch. One telling example of this is a picture by Otto Günther of a little girl holding a wake at the bier of a recently deceased playmate.[54]

In the 1880s, the move of Weimar painters from the *plein-air* landscape style to Impressionism represented the climax in the development of the ducal art academy. In 1880, a Permanente Kunstausstellung, a permanent art exhibition, was established at what today is the Goetheplatz, in whose halls several of the pioneering Impressionists were later exhibited. Its main purpose, however, was to serve as a public platform for Weimar artists, whose work should be seen there perhaps on a lasting basis, until they were bought by an admiring public. But although members of the ducal family made it their business to patronize this exhibition regularly, including the purchase of some artifacts, many Weimar citizens, even affluent ones, ignored the permanent display – another way for them to express their disdain for high culture, as they had done with Liszt and in Goethe's time.[55]

Nonetheless, four artists who increased Weimar's reputation in this period were Buchholz, Gleichen-Russwurm, Rohlfs, and Count Leopold von Kalckreuth, the son of the academy's founder. The reclusive Buchholz suffered incrementally from depression in the 1880s, perhaps because outside of Weimar he was receiving less critical notice than in the previous

decade. Yet the quality of his work remained consistently high and innovative. When the young art student Lovis Corinth visited Weimar from East
Prussia with his teacher Otto Günther, formerly of the academy, he considered meeting Buchholz first of all, whom he thought a legend. Buchholz
committed suicide in 1889.[56]

Gleichen-Russwurm remained open to French influences, especially by
members of the Barbizon School, such as Daubigny and Corot. Yet if
anything, color and movement were more toned down in his *œuvre* than in
that of the Frenchmen, and he suggested harmony. This was evident in his
painting *An der fränkischen Saale*, completed in 1885, depicting two fish-
ermen in a boat, stolidly going about their business in the calmly flowing
Saale river, some distance from Weimar. For its model Gleichen-Russwurm
had adopted a work by Dupré.[57]

When in 1885 the thirty-year-old Leopold von Kalckreuth arrived in
Weimar, the academy acquired a progressive portrait and genre-painting
specialist. Unlike his father, who had once been his teacher, he was a down-
and-out Realist, painting, as a convinced *plein-airiste*, in a Naturalist vein. A
friend of Lenbach and Liebermann, he liked to make social comments in
his paintings of the real world and in this way resembled Gleichen-
Russwurm, but he was more poignant. It was just this aspect of his work that
evoked criticism, especially from the grand duke with his rose-colored
glasses. After Carl Alexander had appointed Count Emil Goertz zu Schlitz
as new, conservative, director of the academy, the two men were unanimous
in their opposition to both Social Realism and the *plein-air* mode. Kalckreuth
preempted his threatened dismissal by tendering his resignation in 1890.[58]

Several of Kalckreuth's paintings anticipated French Impressionism,
which was to take hold of Weimar painters by the late 1880s. Yet another
artist who came under its influence was Christian Rohlfs. Born in 1849
and a former student of the academy as well, he settled in Weimar in the
second half of the 1880s, where he turned from the painting of historical
motifs to local landscapes, especially those with bridges.[59] He and a few
others fell under the spell of Impressionism after the art critic Emil Heilbut
had given a public lecture introducing three small pictures by Claude
Monet. Rohlfs realized that he had been using Impressionist color application techniques for some time, but that the Impressionists' use of light was
something novel.[60]

As is well known, Monet, born in 1840, had received early impulses
from the Barbizon painters Daubigny and Constant Troyon; he was
beholden to the color scheme of the earlier, Romantic, painter Eugène
Delacroix. He then pioneered the brushstrokes the Impressionist group

was to become famous for, fragmenting them into broken touches. By 1870 a school was established, in the village of Chailly-en-Bière, not far from Barbizon, in the woods of Fontainebleau. In 1874 Monet was instrumental in setting up an exhibition of Impressionist works, by himself and like-minded artists such as Pierre-Auguste Renoir and Édouard Manet. It was then that the movement received its name; but in 1881 the original group was starting to dissipate.

Next to Rohlfs, Gleichen-Russwurm and then Hagen incorporated Impressionistic techniques into their works. The directorship of the Permanente Kunstausstellung was progressive enough to exhibit, in 1890–91, paintings by Monet, Camille Pissarro, Troyon, and Alfred Sisley. (It was only in 1891 that French Impressionists were shown elsewhere in Germany – at the Third International Annual Exhibition in Munich.) Meanwhile, Rohlfs proceeded to create his Impressionist picture *Strasse in Weimar* as early as 1889. It excelled in its vibrating colors, of trees and of houses, reflecting the glare of a summer heat. Gleichen-Russwurm was beginning to paint similar canvases using as his backdrop rural scenes at his Franconian estate. In Weimar, the Permanente in 1892 was showing the works of Corot, Daubigny, Troyon, and Dupré. It was the year of the grand duke's Golden Wedding anniversary, but Carl Alexander himself was not happy.[61]

As if he had wished for this, Impressionism in Weimar died out again at the turn of the century. Rohlfs left Weimar in 1901, the year that Gleichen-Russwurm died. Other adepts, such as Paul Baum, had moved away much earlier. The grand duke himself expired in January 1901, after having enforced restrictions on the art academy using the reactionary Count Goertz, and leaving it to the devices of unremarkable genre painters such as the Norwegian Fritjof Smith.[62] In modern interpretations of art in this period, a "Weimar Painter School" does not appear; the *Oxford Companion to Art*, for instance, does not mention it.[63] Once again, Weimar had thrown away the opportunity for renewed greatness.

The Young Richard Strauss

The grand duke was handed yet another chance to revive Weimar when the twenty-five-year-old Richard Strauss was hired to infuse new vigor into the music scene. Long before Liszt's death in 1886 musical events had barely sustained the cultural life of the town, and Dingelstedt's creative activities at the theater were a distant memory. Since 1887 Liszt's former master student, the pianist Hans Bronsart von Schellendorf, was Generalintendant of opera and stage and, under him, the Lisztian Eduard

Lassen, promoted to Hofkapellmeister, or court conductor, was in charge of the musical repertoire, but rather listlessly so. Weimar insiders were aware that redress was called for, not least because of the embarrassing complications with the painters' academy. Indeed, at the end of the young conductor's seasons it was stated that he had been welcomed by all those "who had hoped Strauss would usher in a new artistic era for Weimar."[64]

As he was positioned in 1889, Strauss was more driven away from Munich by the circumstances in which he had had to work in the last few years, rather than attracted by the opportunity to sharpen his skills as a conductor in what he did not know was a culturally neglected provincial backwater. As far as Weimar itself was concerned, he was intrigued by the myth that had been created by the accomplishments, real or believed, of its mavens over the decades, and he wished to be a historical part of what he believed to be the dynamic Weimar aura. Weimar was, after all, just at the zenith of a recently begun Goethe-culture revival.[65] In Munich, Strauss had been third Kapellmeister under Hofkapellmeister Hermann Levi, who had kept him from rising to greater heights, and he had been comparatively ill paid. Coterminously with his decision to leave his hometown of Munich for Athens on the Ilm, Richard's anger at Levi had been kindled by that conductor's arbitrary and entirely unexpected decision to prematurely pension off his father Franz, the principal French horn player of the Munich court orchestra, whom Wagner himself had so treasured.[66] However, as soon as Strauss had arrived in the classical heritage town in September 1889, he was shocked to discover in what a sad state the orchestra had been kept, how many musicians and singers were missing, how badly the remaining ones were performing and how ill-paid they were.[67] Lassen's humdrum repertory and professional negligence appalled him. But like Lassen, Strauss now considered himself a disciple of the New Music School of Liszt's creation, and he firmly intended to conduct Liszt, Wagner, Berlioz – and Strauss.[68] With regard to his own musical ambition, Strauss wanted to complete a few compositions he had already begun – not unlike Liszt when he had first arrived in town – thus honing his dexterity both as conductor and composer. In the operatic genre Strauss was mostly interested in Wagner's work, just as Liszt had been; he was yet to present an opera of his own. But there were operas of friends of his that he wished to stage and even to world-premier. Not all of these men were stellar; chief among them was his much older mentor Alexander Ritter, once a violinist under Liszt in Weimar and now with Levi, who was married to one of Wagner's nieces, thus making the succession from Liszt to Strauss via Wagner even more creditable.[69]

Although Strauss's Weimar salary would be as dismal as his Munich one, since the grand duke notoriously spent no money on the institutions he wished to sponsor, he was touched by Weimar's quaintness and green surroundings. He received a warm welcome from everyone, including Carl Alexander, and appreciated the goodwill extended by Lassen and Bronsart, that long-time friend of Richard's other important mentor, the – originally – Lisztian Hans von Bülow. The orchestra, also, came around to acceding to his stringent demands for improvement.[70]

Strauss commenced his Weimar work with aplomb: a performance of *Lohengrin* in October 1889, followed in quick succession by Carl Maria von Weber's *Der Freischütz*, then *Tannhäuser* and works by Beethoven, Liszt, Berlioz, and his own, brand-new tone poem *Don Juan*. Out of deference to Bülow, Ritter and Lassen he also conducted mediocre works of theirs. As singers he could particularly rely on the tenor Heinrich Zeller and the soprano Pauline de Ahna, both of whom he, as their singing coach, had caused to move from Munich to Weimar.[71] The response, into 1890 and beyond, was immediate and overwhelmingly positive. "We enjoy this youthful enthusiasm, this fiery and overwhelming power, which already appear to us as portents of the beautiful and lofty things that hopefully will come our way," enthused the *Weimarische Zeitung*. Through Strauss, Weimar's art scene had experienced "a new lift," judged concertmaster Artur Rösl in 1894, and Marie Schoder, the local soprano Strauss discovered and encouraged as a teenager until she became world-famous later at the court opera in Vienna, thirty years hence remembered Strauss as a "radiant spirit" who conducted "for the enthrallment" of all art-loving Weimarers.[72]

But there was evidence of friction early on – an indication that conditions for Strauss in Weimar, seemingly perfect in the beginning, were destined for deterioration. Although his self-definition as a Wagnerite was tolerated, his obvious predilection for Liszt and Berlioz was viewed with suspicion. Not only by the elite members of the audience who harbored negative memories of Liszt and his wily cohorts, but also by onetime dyed-in the-wool Lisztians such as Bülow, who as a current Brahms follower hated harmonic dissonances of the kind Strauss himself was favoring in his compositions. Yet even Bronsart, who wanted to steer an even course, became alarmed. The Generalintendant also took the self-confident Strauss to task several times on account of what he regarded as cocky behavior. Moreover, it could not have sat well with Strauss that on the occasion of his Weimar premiere of the ultra-modern *Don Juan* the grand duke chose to be in Italy. And Strauss's budding friendship with

Bayreuth's Cosima Wagner displeased her former husband Bülow, who often visited her, as well as the more even-tempered Bronsart. On top of that, Pauline de Ahna, a Bavarian general's daughter, expressed set views with a prickly tongue (decades later she would tell the stout opera singer Lotte Lehmann that she had "piano feet"). Hence she was beginning to annoy many, especially her chief rival, the soprano Agnes Denis who soon married the court pianist Bernhard Stavenhagen. It did not augur well for Richard in Weimar that he soon fell in love with Pauline.[73]

Perhaps inspired by his love, however, Strauss worked hard for Weimar, so hard in fact that he had little time for his own compositions. To be sure, he further developed his *Guntram* opera score, wrote a few songs and orchestrated his tone poem *Death and Transfiguration*, so that it could be premiered at Eisenach in 1890. But in the main, he taught and coached and played a leading role in Weimar's Wagner Association, which he had founded in the same year. There were daily rehearsals at the theater, for concerts and at the opera, and he regularly played the piano in local chamber groups. All this was in addition to opportunities for guest appearances elsewhere he always took advantage of, whenever given leave by Bronsart.[74] Strauss was a musical genius comparable only to his predecessor Liszt or to Wagner, whose heir he considered himself, and extremely ambitious to boot. He aimed to please Weimar notables as much as possible, and this called for social integration, as when he took his lunch each day together with Lassen at the Hotel Erbprinz and joined artists like Stavenhagen and Leopold von Kalckreuth for a beer or a card game. Although, unlike Liszt, he did not care about relationships at court, the grand duke continued to be fond of him, enthusing over a performance of *Tristan und Isolde*, even though he still found *Don Juan* too strangely avant-garde.[75]

Yet Strauss's mounting discontent was nourished, as before, by the lack of formal recognition accorded him, as shown by Bronsart's immutable reluctance to improve his status and increase his modest salary of 3,000 marks. Evidently, the grand duke himself strengthened Bronsart's position on this.[76] Trouble was now also brewing in Bayreuth, as Cosima Wagner disliked his audacious *Don Juan* and objected to Strauss's preparation of a performance of *Rienzi* in Weimar without the cuts she happened to prefer. His protégés Zeller and de Ahna stopped being invited to sing at Bayreuth as they used to, undoubtedly because Wagner saw herself thwarted in her quest to win Strauss in marriage to her daughter Eva. And as far as Bronsart was concerned, he still wanted to tone down Strauss's New Music enthusiasm, in opposition to which he was now beginning to criticize Strauss's eccentric Beethoven interpretations.[77] Strauss, on the other hand, apart from his growing trouble with Frau Wagner, found Weimar increasingly narrow and impervious to change. "I have been here for 3 years now and still play second fiddle to the old and scheming buffoon Lassen," he complained in June 1892, "and I am getting rather sick of the unhealthy circumstances here."[78] Indeed, he was beginning to cast about for a new situation, when in the summer of that year he was struck down by pneumonia. Magnanimously, Grand Duke Carl Alexander granted him recuperative leave, with pay, for a full two seasons. It seemed that for once the Weimar authorities were paying attention and making ready to step into the breach to prevent yet another let-down.[79]

During his months-long trip to the Mediterranean Strauss became even more aware of how constricted Weimar was and that he, who was already a famous maestro, was relatively neglected there. He had to leave Weimar as soon as possible.[80] Thus the search for a new platform as a conductor became his sole private preoccupation after he returned in spring 1893, apart from his love interest Pauline and the finalization of *Guntram*. At issue was where he could go, for this was also tied to the question of his first opera's premiere. Strauss preferred Munich, especially since Levi was seriously indisposed and ready to surrender his court conductor's post, because Richard's family lived there (as well as Pauline's parents), and for the signal effect a first performance of *Guntram* would have there. But although Levi went through the motions of clearing the path for him, it was obvious that he would rather have two other young conductors in Strauss's place, one from Karlsruhe and the other from Berlin. Hence vacancies to be created in those two cities would actually have suited Strauss, as second choices next to Munich. Strauss also thought of Hamburg, whose theater director expressed an interest in him, but its resident conductor Gustav Mahler would sign a new contract there in 1894. The process of getting all this sorted out took many months; certainly enough time to have enabled both Carl Alexander and Bronsart to make Strauss an offer he would have found impossible to refuse, notwithstanding Lassen's staying power. By March 1894 the Munich court theater finally came around and Strauss signed a contract as principal Kapellmeister. He and de Ahna, now officially engaged to be married, left Weimar in June.[81] In Weimar, Strauss later said ruefully, "I lost much sympathy through youthful daredevilry and exaggerations," to the extent that some people did not mind at all seeing him leave.[82]

Strauss's original plan to have *Guntram* premiered in Munich, preferably with himself as conductor, could not be realized, as events had dragged on far too long. Therefore Weimar had to serve one final time. *Guntram* became the last opera Strauss conducted there, in May 1894.[83] The premiere has been described as anything between a "a highly successful first performance" (Leonhard Schrickel) and "a flop" (Alex Ross), but in reality it was a *succès d'estime*. Although the orchestra had drowned out the singers and de Ahna's impersonation of the heroine Freihild was merely competent, the Weimar audience gave Strauss a standing ovation, with Carl Alexander and Bronsart still hoping that their young genius would stay. Strauss himself knew well that he could do better than an opera like *Guntram*, which, with scenes evoking *Tannhäuser* and *Lohengrin*, was epigonal Wagner rather than a Strauss original.[84] In retrospect, the performance was a symbolic ending to Strauss's professional stay in Weimar, as it had launched the career of, arguably, the most important composer of the twentieth century. In return, Strauss had helped Weimar to stage a comeback as a cultural center of gravity, even though this comeback would not be a lasting one.

Development of a Goethe Cult

After Strauss's departure cultural Weimar sank into grayness, as far as its music and theater, but also its literature, were concerned. For the former two, several sets of circumstances were responsible, one having to do with a conundrum regarding the long-awaited departure of Eduard Lassen as Hofkapellmeister. At one time after 1894, because Carl Alexander failed to keep matters under control and members of his camarilla, among them his daughter Princess Marie Alexandrine zu Reuss, intrigued against one another, there were no fewer than five music directors in the town simultaneously, which Strauss's friend Baron Emil von Reznicek, himself a short-term appointee, later characterized as "a comfortable swamp where you lived well."[85] Therefore, what transpired on stage under Hippolyt von Vignau, Bronsart's unremarkable successor, was predictably pedestrian. The vaunted Weimar came to have fewer performances per season than German towns of comparable size.[86] Mediocre artists performed the work of mediocre composers and acted in mediocre plays; members of the court improvised lay theater for themselves, with the grand duke cringingly applauding. Or else they kept to themselves for rigid afternoon teas and monotonous evening galas.[87] An educated bourgeoisie did not seem to care; unquestionably it had no input. No visitor of note would pass through Weimar in the 1890s until Carl Alexander's death in January 1901; no famous person sought residence. Except for the beginnings of a Goethe cult, it was impossible to tell that Weimar had once been home to the classics. One promising man who stayed briefly in the town was the young

German-Italian composer Ferruccio Busoni, later a pianist of Lisztian proportions, who collected around him foreign students as Liszt had done and, like Liszt's, they mocked the town's provincialism. "Their costumes and *coiffures* were eccentric and startling; they hailed each other with shrill musical cries, danced along the streets like a *corps de ballet* and fell into each other's arms with extravagant embraces, offering the most shocking examples of deportment to all the well-bred young ladies who walked out two and two in the sacred city of Goethe."[88]

But what had happened to the memory of Goethe, Schiller, or Herder? Although his powerful legacy simply could not be suppressed, since his death in 1832 Goethe had not been foremost in people's minds. His lack of visibility was relative, for he tended to be compared with Schiller, who was held in the greatest popular esteem.[89] One reason for that was Schiller's widespread reputation as a champion of freedom; it was in this spirit that his plays, such as *Wilhelm Tell*, were constantly being performed throughout Germany. The goal of freedom was, in time, conjoined to the aim of unity, and those twin ideals influenced Germans in states which, as members of the Deutscher Bund, were ultimately under the thumb of Austria. Already in 1847, a small Schiller museum was created in Weimar, whereas Goethe still had none. In 1859 Schiller's centenary was celebrated, in Weimar as in many other German towns. Although Schiller was not viewed in an expressly political context, he was treated as the symbol of a national German culture, on which it was now paramount to concentrate – a collective mental prelude to the wars of political unification that would commence under Bismarck in the 1860s.[90]

By contrast, even before his death it was known of Goethe that politically he had tended to side with the mighty rather than the common folk, Napoleon rather than any leader of the French Revolution having been his hero. As far as the German cause of liberty or unification was concerned, he tended to be an aloof cosmopolitan rather than an engaged democrat or nationalist. The German Romantics who had succeeded the champions of the classics at the end of Napoleon's rule, now riding the literary wave, and in keeping with the zeitgeist, looking for freedom from foreign oppression if not for national unity, condemned Goethe for his stance. Devout Christians, often in line with the Romantics, rejected him for his alleged atheism, which they claimed to have detected particularly in the second part of *Faust*.[91]

Even though Goethe had achieved the status of a polymath icon by the time he died in March 1832, a Goethe movement or Goethe cult was therefore slow in coming. Still in May of that year, the Weimar court theater organized a Goethe memorial celebration featuring creations after

Goethe's works: some poems about Goethe's Egmont or unremarkable music composed for scenes from *Faust*.[92] In the same year Goethe's old friend Karl August Böttiger proposed the foundation of a Goethe National Museum to attract admirers from abroad, on the model of Stratford-upon-Avon honoring Shakespeare.[93] Böttiger failed. Two years later an attempt in Berlin to found a Goethe Society was also unsuccessful.[94]

Schemes in 1842, this time initiated by the Deutscher Bund, to purchase Goethe's house from his heirs, in order finally to realize the older plan of a national museum, foundered on the resistance of Goethe's grandsons Wolfgang and Walther, who refused to part either with the real estate or with the poet's papers. Three years later even Carl Alexander, who was on intimate terms with both brothers, failed to persuade them to sell.[95] Hence Franz Liszt's proposal of a Goethe Foundation, published in 1851, deserves posterity's admiration, even if it was so naïve as to be unworkable, and even if it had been preceded by a futile Berlin declaration signed by Alexander von Humboldt and others.[96]

The Weimar festivities for the Goethe centennial in August 1849, which more or less coincided with the arrival of Liszt in town and in which he partook vigorously, to all true friends of the poet should have proved humiliating. Much of the pathos had nothing to do with Goethe's birth, and everything with months of failed political revolution, for which the Goethe who hated revolution, was the wrong symbol.[97] One did not really know what to say about Goethe at a time like this; embarrassed people were producing embarrassing results. Nonentities declaimed Goethe's stanzas, nameless musicians composed and conducted forgettable sound. Altogether, a carnivalesque flavor characterized the town, and the patrician would have winced had he been present.[98]

When a year later a Herder statue was unveiled in front of the Town Church, this must have restored some dignity to Weimar. Herder had been much closer to the idea of revolution than his more fortunate friend, and so, not least politically, this was more fitting. Still, as Thomas Nipperdey has noted, it was culture rather than politics that was to be emphasized.[99] Goethe received his own statue – in the same spirit – in 1857, but only in union with the popularly beloved Schiller, fittingly in front of the town's theater. For this monument Dresden's sculptor Ernst Rietschel had reduced the physically taller Schiller to match Goethe's medium height, in order to do some justice to the patronizing superiority Goethe had always exercised over his younger friend.[100]

A cultural revaluation of the poet occurred in 1861 in Berlin during a Goethe colloquium led by Herman Grimm, a noted art historian and son of fairy-tale collector Wilhelm Grimm. Again, there was a paper about Goethe *and* Schiller, but the pathologist Rudolf Virchow gave Goethe much credit when reassessing him as a natural scientist. This train of thought was continued in 1866, after Charles Darwin's publication *On the Origin of Species* (1859) when the Jena zoologist Ernst Haeckel, an avid Darwinist, pointed to a direct connection between Goethe and Darwin in his epochal *Morphologie der Organismen*.[101]

But the cultural revaluation was turned into a political process after the creation of the Second Empire by Bismarck in 1871, for the sake of legitimization. Politicized, Goethe was inserted into a national legend, because the new political construct needed a proper legacy. This need had not existed before, when the lands of Germany, "a nation of provincials," to borrow Celia Applegate's phrase, had been disparate and often at war with one another, under the First Reich – the Holy Roman Empire.[102] True enough, even before this conscious utilization of Goethe a different kind of transfiguration of the new national unity had been attempted, through concentration on old Germanic myths, polemical finger-pointing at the traditional hereditary enemy which was France, or a calculated preoccupation with Richard Wagner's music and lore. In analogy to Frederick II of Prussia, called the Great, some also hailed the new Kaiser as Wilhelm the Great. However, this particular moniker did not stick. Stressing the connection between the Iron Chancellor Bismarck and the Olympian Goethe would be more convincing as cornerstone for a new national legacy, for they could be easily identified as the most outstanding personalities in Germany of the past hundred years. What Bismarck had done through his diplomacy and the use of arms, Goethe had prefigured in the dramatization of that supreme man of action, Dr. Heinrich Faust, apart from the shadows cast by his own dynamic personality.[103] Drawing a direct line from Bismarck to Goethe, from Goethe to Frederick, and Frederick to Luther, ultimately even to Charlemagne, would create the new national legacy. In this context, the previously touted Schiller was not submerged; rather, Schiller's culture was conflated with Goethe's to round off this new tradition of German greatness, which was made to appear to culminate in Bismarck and to project even greater historic climaxes in future.[104]

What occurred here was the inventing of a new tradition, in this case to serve nationalistic purposes, as Eric J. Hobsbawm has described it for England and several other European countries, and in differing social and political settings. Poignantly, Hobsbawm speaks of "invented tradition," by which is understood "a set of practices, normally governed by overtly or tacitly accepted rules and of a ritual or symbolic nature, which seek to inculcate certain values and norms of behaviour by repetition, which automatically implies continuity with the past. In fact, where possible, they normally attempt to establish continuity with a suitable historic past." According to Hobsbawm, the posited continuity between past and present is as fictitious as is the need to constantly insist on it.[105] After 1871, this implied a repeated necessity to invoke Goethe, to conjure up Faust and interpret them both as closely interlinked with significant phenomena of the day. This was done ad nauseam.[106] A master of this practice was Herman Grimm, who in 1874–75 spoke to his Berlin university students in extended lectures in this vein, setting a much-observed precedent. Grimm broached chauvinism when he maintained that because the Germans possessed the epos *Faust*, they came first as poets, "in the art of poetry of all times and among all the nations."[107] In 1896 Professor Emil Walther maintained that Goethe, always an admirer of Frederick the Great, had laid the intellectual foundations for Bismarck's actions, and that Bismarck himself was a great admirer of Goethe, recognizing in him an archetypal statesman.[108] It is true that Bismarck knew Goethe's works well, but he himself did not make such a connection.[109]

The apogee of Goethe reverence occurred in the decade following 1885. Within the framework of a "new" tradition, it was also, appropriately, politically colored. In April 1885 Walther von Goethe, the poet's last surviving grandson, died, leaving Goethe's papers to the Grand Duchess Sophie. The Goethe mansion on the Frauenplan was left to the duchy.[110] Sophie now decided to offer the use of the papers and manuscripts to the public as her contribution to the attempt to integrate Goethe into the national mainstream. The mansion was to be converted to a Goethe Museum, the papers were to be edited and, gradually, published, in a special series as well as a Goethe Yearbook. Moreover, a Goethe-Gesellschaft (Society) was to be created, with prominent, nationally based members, to hold annual meetings in Weimar. Sophie also planned an authoritative multi-volume biography. Her constructive ideas were suited to a cultural and physical remake of the town, especially since she pledged what appeared to be private, unlimited, resources, to finance the new institutions.

In 1885 the grand duchess commissioned experts to examine the precious handwritten papers with a view to constructing a proper archive, for they had to be removed from Goethe's house, which was to be converted into a museum. But while they were temporarily kept at one of the ducal castles, she took advantage of her privileged position to rifle through them. She looked for passages compromising both Goethe and Weimar's princely house, blackening text, deleting or altering passages or causing entire documents to disappear. Much of the erotica Goethe had produced fell victim to this practice, without her realizing that some had already been published.[111] It is certain that early publicized depictions of the "Muses' Court" of Anna Amalia, as they construed their idealized scenarios, were based on this censored evidence. From the beginning, the eminent editors appointed by the grand duchess were at her beck and call, strictly beholden to her taste.[112]

The Goethe-Gesellschaft was founded in July 1885 to oversee the massive commemorative work that lay ahead, and to demonstrate the affinity of Goethe Town Weimar with the new Reich. Immediately, the new union of Weimar and Berlin was effusively conjured up: "The new German Reich was born in a time of great national and political contemplation, untouched by the prejudices and partialities, which in the case of many have hindered the proper comprehension and appreciation of Goethe in past decades. A great national empire knows how to value the greatest of its poets to the full. The foundation and preservation of the political astuteness of our people goes hand in hand with the care and support of its spiritual treasures." Among the 250 people who became founding members of the Gesellschaft that year were the high and mighty in the land, in politics as well as from academia and the arts: Empress Augusta, her daughter-in-law Crown Princess Victoria, the scientists Ernst Haeckel and Hermann von Helmholtz, the violinist Joseph Joachim, the historian Theodor Mommsen, the actress Marie Seebach, Herman Grimm and, not least, Franz Liszt. At the first regular membership meeting in Weimar a year later Grimm commenced to employ Goethe further in the design of national politics, with his keynote speech, "Goethe in the Service of Our Time." From then on, the Goethe-Gesellschaft became an ever more important ideological factor in the desired synthesis of Berlin and Weimar. "Nationality and humanity" in the new German Reich were inseparably fused, declared the philologist Gustav von Loeper in his 1890 festive address, "Berlin and Weimar," in which he equated the great Frederick and Goethe.[113]

Over time, Weimar acquired many experts to work on its vast Goethe collection, which, after 1896, was housed in a newly constructed archive of neoclassical architecture on the banks of the River Ilm. The Sophienausgabe had to be developed, volumes filled with editions of Goethe's manifold writings, many more of which were being donated in the original from around Europe. The published series was to comprise 143 volumes by 1919 and would serve for decades as the standard tool of Goethe studies. The poet's papers were soon complemented by many others contributed by the descendants of Schiller, Herder, Hebbel, and Wieland, to make the *Goethe-und Schiller-Archiv* on the Ilm an indispensable resource for research in the German classics.[114]

Weimar Moves to the Right

By the 1890s Weimar had become an arch-conservative town. Several factors contributed to this. One was the growing reactionary stance of Grand Duke Carl Alexander, who politically had exchanged the liberalism of the pre-1848 and revolutionary era for nationalism, which fed on pride in German unification and its resulting colonial achievements. This occurred in an era when, as Jürgen Kocka has written, support was given to "a kind of nationalism that increasingly moved to the right, with imperialist aggression and chauvinistic radicalization," despite "some liberal concessions and democratic elements."[115] In the 1880s and '90s Carl Alexander, the admirer of tsarist, despotic Russia, shared the popular suspicions of democratic Britain and tended to regard the French as weak, flighty, and degenerate. This expressed itself not least in his view on culture, as he disparaged the influence of French Impressionism on his painters' academy. In music, too, his narrowness scarcely tolerated foreign works, and neither could he abide the bold harmonic experiments of a Richard Strauss. The grand duke's stance was mirrored in that of his wife Sophie, with whom he shared punctiliousness in court etiquette and bigoted religious beliefs.[116] Virtually the entire aristocratic entourage reflected these attitudes. Typical representatives were the baron Hermann von Egloffstein, who habitually exulted in trivial pursuits at court, as long as they had style, and Adelheid von Schorn. She was the daughter of the art expert Ludwig Schorn, who had been ennobled so that he could sit on the right side of the theater auditorium. Along with her mother, Schorn became Liszt's and, even more so, Princess Wittgenstein's chatty confidante, even while Wittgenstein was in Rome. Like Egloffstein, this descendant of Charlotte von Stein was a faithful chronicler of Weimar's placid life. Her reports of events at court and Weimar burghers, as well as her enthusiastic documentation of the German victories over Denmark and France, were glowingly chauvinistic. Her hatred of France was palpable. The accounts of both Egloffstein and Schorn make clear how ossified Weimar had become over time, how self-servingly smug, and how dominated by an incrusted establishment increasingly governed by old age. Verily, Weimar was turning into a wealthy but mindless pensioners' refuge.[117]

Most of the pillars of the newly constituted Goethe-Gesellschaft, including their professorial presidents, and certainly all the Weimar members, believed in the trinity of throne, altar, and Goethe.[118] Anti-liberal hangers-on at court, but also persons of real influence and power in Weimar at that time were too numerous to mention. Among the latter was Richard Voss, that little playwright, who joined Carl Alexander in his rejection of progressive art.[119] Generalintendant Bronsart von Schellendorf was a prominent conservative, as was Hans von Bülow, who brought his influence to bear on visits. But so was the young Richard Strauss, whose sense of revolution pertained only to the world of music. Strauss had worked in subservient positions within court settings – in Meiningen, Munich, and now Weimar – and knew only obeisance to divinely ordained rulers, to a father, or to professional superiors. One new element which fortified this reactionary attitude in the last two decades of the nineteenth century was anti-Semitism, as it had sprung up in Germany for economic, political, and recently what were considered scientific reasons, since the late 1870s. Characteristically, Bülow, Bronsart, and Strauss all were sworn anti-Semites, Strauss having been guided by his father, Bülow, Alexander Ritter and now, subversively, by Cosima Wagner, notwithstanding the continued paucity of Jews in Weimar.[120]

Three personalities who stood out as right-wingers and helped to lead Weimar from the very last years of the century into a new epoch of political conservatism were Ernst von Wildenbruch, Adolf Bartels, and Elisabeth Förster-Nietzsche. Wildenbruch was a founding member of the Goethe-Gesellschaft.[121] His father was the illegitimate son of Prince Louis Ferdinand von Preussen who had been killed in battle against Napoleon in 1806 while only thirty-four. This nephew of Frederick the Great had fancied himself a patron of the arts, a pianist and composer, and was a skirt-chaser. The son this prince had sired with a commoner was ennobled and went on to a diplomatic career in the Prussian service. His son Ernst had been born in Beirut in 1845. He studied law and participated in Prussia's campaign against Austria in 1866 and then again in the Franco-Prussian War of 1870–71. These experiences as well as his lineage made him a rabid nationalist. His aspirations as a dramatist drew him to Weimar, where in the early 1880s Carl Alexander was already seeking to attract him permanently.[122] Both men had Frederick the Great as a great-uncle, though somewhat removed. While still based in Berlin and married to the granddaughter of Carl Maria von Weber, Wildenbruch embarked on what was in retrospect a pathetic artistic career, but as a Prussian nationalist. Although many soon saw in him the "poet of the Hohenzollerns," Ludwig Raschdau, the Prussian legate at the court of Weimar, observed drily in 1897 that after all, he was "not a genuine poet." It was clear by that time that Wildenbruch had failed in his quest to become the rightful successor of Goethe in Weimar.[123]

Already in the 1870s Wildenbruch had written a number of patriotic dramas, some of which failed to be accepted at German stages, including Weimar's own, in 1875. In all of them German or Germanic royalty were the heroes, as Wildenbruch engaged in transference via his biological grandfather; heroes who invariably fought tragic battles against duplicitous enemies.[124] In 1889 he penned a stage piece, *Der Generalfeldoberst*, which his distant nephew, Kaiser Wilhelm II, banned from all Prussian theaters, because Wildenbruch had drawn an unflattering portrait of the monarch's mother Victoria, the widow of Kaiser Friedrich.[125] Devastated, Wildenbruch turned his back on Berlin and looked again to Weimar, where he knew Carl Alexander would welcome him.[126] Testing the waters, Wildenbruch gave patriotic speeches to students at Jena University and made himself conspicuous at official functions, such as when he opened the Weimar Theater Centenary in May of 1891.[127] Bronsart von Schellendorf – who now performed Wildenbruch's pieces – and Adelheid von Schorn became close friends, and Wildenbruch made much noise about Weimar being the heart of Germany and the greenest of the German lands.[128] In that year he was commissioned to write a drama, *Bernhard von Weimar* (a theme long close to Carl Alexander's heart), in which, most certainly, the prince wished to recognize himself. But just as the Kaiser had censored Wildenbruch's Berlin work ever since 1889, Carl Alexander now sought to interfere in his Weimar work, infuriating the poet. After the premiere on the occasion of the grand duke's Golden Wedding anniversary in October 1892 Carl Alexander publicly criticized the author.[129] Wildenbruch got into more trouble when in 1896 he was awarded the newly funded Schiller Prize, not once, but twice, in an act that ignored the mercurial young Naturalist Gerhart Hauptmann, whom pundits had predicted to be the deserving winner. From now on the anti-Naturalist Wildenbruch had the increasingly influential Hauptmann clique against him, which stigmatized him further.[130] No doubt all of this had something to do with the fact that his chance at that time to become the new state secretary of culture in Weimar was scotched.[131] Nonetheless, Wildenbruch persisted in his "Teutonization of the Goethe period," as he had practiced it throughout the 1880s and '90s, trying to bring the artistic Weimar of the classics and the militaristic Berlin-Potsdam of the Hohenzollerns into a new symbiosis. He discovered Germany's enemies everywhere and made the official motto of the ruling dynasty – that the new empire was being encircled – his own.[132]

Having first spent the summer months in Weimar, Wildenbruch moved to Weimar in 1900, having built a villa there, near the new Goethe- und Schiller-Archiv, which he pompously named Ithaka, after Homer's *Odyssey*. Another writer joined Wildenbruch in Weimar in the 1890s, a young journalist originally from Wesselburen/Dithmarschen in North German Holstein, actually the same small town where Hebbel had been born. Henceforth Adolf Bartels would constantly conjure up his spiritual kinship with Hebbel, that almost-resident of Weimar, whom he now obviously wanted to succeed, just as Wildenbruch saw himself as Goethe's successor. That Bartels too, discovered a kinship between himself and Goethe is suggested by his future attitude and writings.

Bartels's credo was inspired by a melange of German nationalism, Goethe and Hebbel adoration, and anti-Semitism.[133] Born in 1862, he said that in Wesselburen he met his first Jew, who had come over from nearby Friedrichstadt to sell fabrics. His father purchased some products from this peddler which turned out to be shoddy. Bartels then observed the Jews of Hamburg, and physically they impressed him as "very strange." Later in Frankfurt, Jews in the streets and café society alienated him.[134] As Bartels began to write for newspapers and journals, he got caught up in the stream of cultural pessimism which since Schopenhauer, Wagner, and Nietzsche had gripped a large part of the conservative German bourgeoisie, regarding as its main enemy modernism in the arts.[135] Modernism, Bartels claimed, was fanned by Jews and, allied with them, international forces like the French with their inbred decadence. Having lived in Weimar since 1896, he published his first notorious book, *Die deutsche Dichtung der Gegenwart*, in which he paid some tribute to Wildenbruch and fulsome homage to Hebbel, and began to rant against the Jewish Heinrich Heine, an obsession that would characterize all his future work.[136] Conveniently for Bartels, Heine had been critical of Goethe, whom Bartels had eulogized as "the greatest of the Germans" in a poem authored as early as 1887.[137] By contrast, Heine, who had spent the last eight years of his life as a paralytic in Paris, was described by Bartels as "the father of decadence in the nineteenth century."[138] As in the case of Wildenbruch, one of the earliest supporters Bartels found in Weimar among the local establishment was Adelheid von Schorn.[139]

In 1900 Bartels composed a poem, "Friedrich Nietzsche's Grave at Röcken," in which he equated the philosopher with "Superman" and "Antichrist."[140] Nietzsche had just been buried at Röcken near Leipzig, where he was born in 1844, and Bartels had calculatingly alluded to two of the key concepts Nietzsche had created as part of his overall critical philosophy, boldly ascribing them to Nietzsche himself.[141] Although this suited Bartels's own purposes at the time, in reality Nietzsche had been wary of post-mortem idolization and had certainly never identified himself with any of the allegorical heroes he used to critique Western civilization.

In his treatment of Nietzsche's personality and *œuvre* Bartels had adopted the style of Nietzsche's sister, Elisabeth Förster-Nietzsche, who since 1897 had cared for the philosopher, by then a hopelessly debilitated man, in a villa situated on a hill in the outskirts of Weimar which she had obtained ostensibly for that purpose. Förster-Nietzsche saw, and in future would continue to see, in her brother precisely what she wanted to see, insofar as it could be of immediate use to her. By the time of Nietzsche's death in August 1900, how had this come to pass?

After having studied theology and classical languages in Bonn and Leipzig, Friedrich Nietzsche had been appointed full professor of classical philology at the University of Basel at the age of twenty-four, without even having obtained a doctorate. At Basel, his interest lay less in philology than history and philosophy, and he began to write the first of what would be more than ten monographs he produced in his lifetime, several of them in an aphoristic format. Highly musical himself, he took an interest in Richard Wagner's operas, paying tribute to him in his first book, *The Birth of Tragedy* (1872), a collection of four essays, in which he also praised Arthur Schopenhauer, the son of Johanna from the late Goethe period. His main concern here was a criticism of Western culture, as it had been dominated by rigid, rational, Apollonian forces rather than pre-Socratic creative Dionysian energy of the kind Schopenhauer had espoused and Wagner was given to. From Basel Nietzsche often came to visit Wagner and Cosima in Tribschen near Lucerne, and later in Bayreuth, after Wagner had relocated there in 1872.

In 1870 Nietzsche participated as an orderly in the siege of Metz during the Franco-Prussian War, because as a youth he had been disabled by a riding accident. It is possible that while serving there behind the lines he contracted syphilis, if he had not already done so as a student. He suffered from other ailments, such as an eye disease, all of which caused him to ask for early retirement from the University of Basel in 1879. From then on he lived on his pension in various places in Switzerland, southern France, Italy, and Germany, seeking out the best climate, as his health deteriorated further. But he wrote prolifically; among his books were *Human, All-Too-Human* (1878) and *Thus Spoke Zarathustra* (1883–85), until in 1889, in Turin, he lost his senses. Legend has it that he saw, from his window on the Piazza Carlo Alberto, a driver beat his horse so viciously that he ran out, embraced the beast and fell to the ground, weeping. One of his Basel colleagues came to fetch him, taking him to a psychiatric clinic in Basel. From there he was sent to a psychiatric ward at Jena University, close to Naumburg, which was some twenty miles north-east of Weimar, where his mother and sister were now living. He stayed at their house until 1897, when his mother died. His sister Elisabeth thereafter began to take care of him in the Weimar villa Silberblick, which she had been loaned by one of Friedrich's rich Swiss devotees, from whom it was later acquired.[142] Nietzsche remained there immobile, unable to speak or read and having to be fed, occasionally making roaring animal sounds and sometimes exhibited like a circus attraction, shrouded in a white sheet like a Brahmin, to visitors carefully selected by his sister.[143] By 1900, Elisabeth was well on her way to creating a cult around her brother. Medical indication points to paralytic syphilis as the long-term cause of death on August 25, 1900, although the trigger was pneumonia complicated by the last of several strokes.[144]

Elisabeth Nietzsche was two years younger than Friedrich and a charmingly attractive and intelligent woman when in 1885 she married Dr. Bernhard Förster, a Gymnasium teacher and one of Germany's most vociferous anti-Semites. Seeking to found a pure "Aryan" settlement, in 1887 he went with his wife to Paraguay, taking fourteen German families with him, to create the colony Nueva Germania. It soon failed, Förster having defrauded his co-settlers and being left with a pile of debt. He poisoned himself in 1889 and so, after wrapping up her Paraguayan affairs, which took years, Elisabeth Förster returned to Naumburg in 1893, to assist her mother in the care of Friedrich.[145] This is when she decided to create an enterprise based on her famous brother, eventually changing her name, legally, to Elisabeth Förster-Nietzsche. It entailed taking care of a library – Friedrich's library, collecting and editing his papers and correspondence, gradually wresting control of him from their mother, who originally possessed all the rights, and developing effective public relations.[146] Apart from the sheer technical complexity of what was going to turn out to be a lucrative business, the control of which was difficult enough (not the least of it being the constant procurement of funds), Elisabeth Förster had some psychological problems to solve. She would have to create an official persona for herself and a matching one for her brother, to present themselves to the world as a team. When all composites were fit together, which took years to accomplish, they would be parts of a big lie – the capstones of the Nietzsche Cult.[147] This was a confidence trick on a large scale. As far as she herself was concerned, Elisabeth had to convince everybody that she was the most valued person Friedrich had ever known and that in fact she had played a much larger part in his conscious life than was actually the case. In truth, Friedrich had always entertained a love–hate relationship with his sister, more hate than love, as she had jealously interfered in his personal relations, for instance when he had courted the beautiful, brilliant, Russian general's daughter Lou Andrea von Salomé, whom Elisabeth cursed.[148] In order to establish authenticity of authorship later, Elisabeth early on had to insinuate that she had collaborated with her brother on certain of his works. Moreover, she had to eliminate any extreme manifestations of political conservatism because her brother had been an outspoken critic of Prussian and German nationalism and always eschewed anti-Semitism – one of several issues over which he had broken with Wagner in 1878.[149] This was difficult for her, because enough people knew of her association with right-wing German nationalists and, through the work with Bernhard Förster, of her contempt for Jews. Conversely, Frau Förster had to mold Friedrich into a German nationalist and a fanatical believer in a Prussian-led German empire. She also had to produce proof from Friedrich that he thought her his favorite sibling, nay woman (a brother Ludwig had died when two years old) and hence someone he had loved even more dearly than his own mother. Elisabeth went to great lengths to achieve this, even if she had to forge or obliterate Friedrich's handwriting.[150]

Hence Förster-Nietzsche was construing an arch-conservative image for her brother to match her own true convictions, superimposed on the conjured image of an adoring brother, all for the sake of future manipulative schemes. Especially as she became ever more a fan of Wilhelm II's empire and wished to curry favor with the high and mighty, she proceeded to present her brother as a right-wing patriot. She did so by sifting through his fragmentary records in an effort to find material for a new book, which purportedly he had been in the early stages of conceiving, to be entitled *The Will to Power: An Attempted Transvaluation of All Values*. This would reemphasize elements Nietzsche the critic of Western culture had stressed before – his suspicion of institutionalized Christianity ("God is Dead"), his belief in the might and right of the stronger, his contempt for the weak.[151] Even in Naumburg, but especially in Weimar, Elisabeth began to employ groups of young men as editors whom she ruled with an iron hand, among them, for a while, the future founder of the anthroposophic movement, Rudolf Steiner.[152] They would assist her in selecting fragments matching her own *Weltanschauung* and readying them for publication, in the anticipation of fame and wealth. In the final years of the century, as she had acquired the copyrights of Nietzsche's already published books, she collected rich royalties, while Nietzsche's name as a philosopher was becoming ever more famous. Living in the posh Villa Silberblick with its panoramic view of Old Weimar, she adopted the trappings and the mannerisms of a rich woman, hiring staff and keeping a carriage with a liveried page.[153] She sought and found acceptance by the home-grown, conservative circles of Weimar, including the aristocratic establishment and members of the court, as well as distinguished visitors from elsewhere, the grand duke being her guest on numerous occasions.[154] In all, she made a mockery of everything her brother, that great critic of conventional society, had stood for. Thus she became living proof that within the span of a hundred years, from 1800 to 1900, Weimar had transmogrified from a place of high-mindedness and original ideas to a repository of routines and platitudes; from a meritocracy to a mediocracy.

Recapitulating, in the second half of the nineteenth century the failure of Weimar's denizens to lift their town into a Silver Age became manifest, despite some obvious highlights. These included the creation of the first master classes for piano ever by Franz Liszt, the mercurial ascent of Richard Strauss, and the anticipation of German Impressionism, on the French model, by members of the newly founded painters' academy. But these highlights were more than offset by Liszt's own transience, continued streaks of his personal venality and lack of self-control, as well as the merely respectable plateaus he reached in musical achievements. (According to Alfred Brendel, Liszt's best compositions were always those for piano, which occurred rather more before his second sojourn in Weimar.)[155] Transience and good, not great, creations also characterized the visual artists. Despite the Weimar critics' self-made, long-lasting propaganda and obviously promising beginnings, for example those of Christian Rohlfs and Leopold Kalckreuth, there never was a "Weimar School" of painting. As for Strauss, he despised much of the Weimar musical industry, came to question town and court life, had uneasy moments during *Guntram* episodes and experienced a questionable relationship with Bayreuth's imperious Cosima Wagner. One of the creeds she tried to influence him in was anti-Semitism, inherited from her late husband, and that was also the leading article of faith for new Weimar residents, pseudo-intellectuals and pseudo-literati Ernst von Wildenbruch, Adolf Bartels, and Elisabeth Förster-Nietzsche, who all pretended to act, partially, in the name of Goethe. A concerted effort to revive the memory of Goethe for twentieth-century inheritors of classical Weimar culture must remain suspect, because of its being tied into Bismarckian-era chauvinism, one egregious embodiment of which would become the Goethe-Gesellschaft. Social divisions from earlier decades were not smoothed over but, if anything, deepened with the advent of Marxism, in spite of the relative absence of industrial workers in the ducal residential town. Here, any inequities, lack of dynamics and downright inertia, creative or otherwise, continued to be presided over by Grand Duke Carl Alexander, whose aversion to modernist impulses in the arts and letters deepened to the extent that his political conservatism strengthened. In his case, both attitudes were tempered by religious bigotry. Worse, Carl Alexander furthered the progress of the politically right-wing views paired with intolerance which were captivating a substantial part of the ordinary population.

CHAPTER 4

The Quest for a "New Weimar"
1901 to 1918

IT HAS NEVER BEEN ASCERTAINED WHY ELISABETH FÖRSTER-NIETZSCHE moved from Naumburg to Weimar with her sick brother in 1897. This may have been due to a combination of circumstances. The least of these was that the Nietzsche siblings had had distant relatives living there and that Friedrich, while still sane, had casually uttered the wish to retire in Goethe's town. Ever since his early writings he was known to be fond of Goethe, if not of Schiller and especially not Liszt, whom, not unlike Wagner later, he found the embodiment of artistic vanity.[1] In the decade when the new Goethe and Schiller Archive was being developed, Elisabeth entertained visions of a Nietzsche archive to be erected as a suitable complement, with herself playing the primary role. Indeed, there were archivists working in the Goethe archive who also were admirers of Nietzsche, such as Rudolf Steiner, who was allowed to visit Elisabeth and her ailing brother in Naumburg. The members of that small Weimar circle of Nietzsche acolytes came and went, but by 1897 it was large enough to provide potential backing for a separate Nietzsche shrine.[2] Elisabeth was inspired here by the Wagner cult that Cosima Wagner was in the process of setting up in Bayreuth, not even a day's journey to the south-west. Elisabeth and Cosima had known each other in earlier years, and now each followed the other's moves suspiciously. If there was to be cult rivalry, Elisabeth would be the last to back down; she could hold court as well as Cosima.[3] To have her incipient cult elevated to court level was much easier in Weimar than in Naumburg, for there she could interlock with the grand-ducal court and take advantage of the many highborn, rich, and influential people already living in the Goethe town, or visitors from outside.[4] One of these she had in mind was Count Harry Kessler, an independently wealthy, cosmopolitan aesthete from Berlin who was drawn in equal measure to Goethe and to

Nietzsche. Like Steiner, he had been granted the privilege of seeing the great man in Naumburg, where he was overcome with emotion; he visited him again in Weimar in 1897. This was just after Förster-Nietzsche had ensconced herself in the Villa Silberblick on Luisenstrasse.[5] It was during a breakfast at Kessler's in Berlin that the count introduced Frau Förster-Nietzsche to the Belgian artist Henry van de Velde in March 1901. The peripatetic Kessler had sought him out near Brussels much earlier and, overwhelmed by his output, had persuaded him to pursue his design work commercially in Berlin. One of the first things the Belgian had done was to remodel Kessler's Berlin Köthener Strasse apartment in the *Jugendstil*, at that time on the cusp of fashionableness – the German variant of *art nouveau* that van de Velde himself had helped to pioneer.[6]

Henry van de Velde was born in 1863 and first became a painter, much influenced by members of the *plein-air* Barbizon School such as Jean-François Millet; the Impressionists Pissarro and Maurice Denis became his friends. He was close to Belgian modernists, but soon decided to move away from painting and into the arts and crafts, as well as architecture, although he had no formal training in that field. He was influenced by William Morris and the Arts and Crafts Movement in England – the idea that there had to be a connection between the arts and society, and especially the belief that artistic products should be useful. Politically, he was on the left.[7] In the late 1890s he was often in Berlin for commercial ventures there, he had earned some good money, and in 1897 his designs were featured at a Dresden exhibition to much acclaim. He was already well known as a modernist when Förster-Nietzsche met him.[8]

Count Harry Kessler was the son of an unimaginably rich Hamburg banker based in Paris and a mother hailing from Irish landed gentry; she was a renowned beauty. In 1881, when Harry was thirteen, his father had become a count. Kaiser Wilhelm I had caused that ennoblement because he much admired Alice Kessler, whose company he delighted in whenever the two families consorted with one another at a fashionable spa. According to never-ending malicious gossip Harry was the illegitimate son of Wilhelm (a vital factor in the ennoblement), but a careful arithmetic reckoning even then could have dismissed that. The over-sensitive Harry, however, smarted under this rumor all his life and, being artistically and homo-erotically inclined, tried to make up for it all by a mannered masculinity and overt displays of loyalty to the staid value system of his caste, including political conservatism. This was also the reason why originally, after university courses in jurisprudence and membership in a dueling corps, he planned to enter the Reich's diplomatic service, which stood in some contrast to his stupendous interest in the arts. In many ways, he was a torn man who would eventually suffer through the vagaries of the First World War, the growing pains of the republic (which he came to embrace, as Max Weber and Thomas Mann finally did) and the beginnings of the Third Reich, which had contempt for the likes of him and would cause him to die in exile in Lyons in 1937. Completely trilingual and equally at ease in London, Paris, and Berlin, his patriotic allegiance was to Germany, and even though in 1900 he made his home in Berlin, he was drawn to a town like Weimar magically. He owned paintings by Cézanne, van Gogh, Renoir, and Denis. At the time he was entertaining Förster-Nietzsche and van de Velde at that genteel breakfast, he was still collaborating with the editors of the avant-garde journal *Pan*, which, however, was in the process of folding. The esteemed Nietzsche, he thought, should still be given a voice there, before the printing presses stopped.[9]

At that time, Kessler and Förster-Nietzsche agreed that van de Velde ought to be relocated to Weimar, where the philosopher's sister could use the professing Nietzsche admirer to aid her in building the Nietzsche cult, and Kessler himself might spend some useful time while waiting for a diplomatic posting to come through.[10] Förster-Nietzsche already boasted of connections with the Weimar court and administration, and Kessler knew Aimé von Palézieux, who was, like Kessler, an officer in the Prussian army and, as chamberlain in Weimar, had inaugurated the Permanente Ausstellung there in 1880.[11] Indeed, in 1901 the new twenty-five-year-old grand duke Wilhelm Ernst was persuaded to appoint van de Velde as artistic adviser to craftsmen in the grand duchy, and the Belgian contractually began his work in Weimar in April 1902.[12] Wilhelm Ernst, who by temperament was rough and boisterous, did not arrive naturally at this decision, for his interests were travel and the hunt, but the canny Palézieux's influence on him was strong, he had the legacy of grandfather Carl Alexander to preserve, and he was spurred on by both his mother Pauline and his young and delicately tempered wife Caroline.[13]

By October 1902 van de Velde had set himself up as artistic adviser for small industry and handicraft; at the same time he founded a seminar for arts and crafts, where he could develop modern concepts and confer with local tradesmen.[14] Both enterprises flourished; van de Velde had been accompanied by a few of his Berlin students who assisted him and for whom he remained iconic. The aesthetics he now adhered to had moved beyond original *Jugendstil*, in that they were less floridly ornamental and more functional – van de Velde believed in the power of the sinuous line – although there were always critics who disparaged decorative

excrescences.[15] Contrary to the Belgian artist's expectations, the grand
duke financed nothing, van de Velde having to be content with the title of
Thuringian professor. He was therefore dependent on a personal income,
especially since his family was growing, and so he resorted to design and
consulting work. In this he did well, especially financially, and had the security that lay in the realization of his very own artistic ideals. In his modified
Jugendstil, he remodeled the Silberblick villa of Förster-Nietzsche (its
imposing portal can still be admired today), constructed one or two private
villas in Weimar, as well as a new building for the art academy near the
Liszt House by the Belvederer Allee. He also strove to shape the interior of
an apartment for Count Kessler at Cranachstrasse, just below Silberblick;
Kessler joined him in a separate artistic mission in 1903. Van de Velde also
accepted commissions from outside of Weimar, but could not help but
wonder why the state almost never offered him a contract.[16]

In all of this, van de Velde employed local tradesmen, who profited from
the collaboration both materially and by way of an artistic education. A
basket weaver's shop in nearby Tannroda, where Goethe's judicial victim, the
child murderer Johanna Catharina Höhn, had been born, was able to expand,
the tobacco-pipe turners of Ruhla prospered, Master Müller's goldsmithy in
Weimar flourished. The Weimar firm of Scheidemantel now exported
furniture based on van de Velde designs, and its revenues multiplied.

In October 1907 Grand Duke Wilhelm Ernst finally allowed van
de Velde to found a regular arts and crafts school (Grossherzogliche
Kunstgewerbeschule) that would attract students, including women –
although it was properly licenced only in 1908.[17] Now the Belgian artist
was able to employ several of his former students as instructors in various
design fields, whereby the cooperation with the trade shops was continued,
to everyone's benefit.[18] The school served sixteen students in 1907 and
seventy-six in 1913–14. It existed parallel to the art academy, with both of
them sharing parts of the same building. In that Saxon dynasty's sad tradition, the grand duke withheld the funds necessary for a smooth operation
of the venture, so that van de Velde himself had to subsidize the school's
budget from his own purse.[19] This situation could continue only for so
long, however. "Weimar offers few material advantages" in any effort to
attract really world-class people, van de Velde drily informed the grand
duke in October 1907.[20] On July 15, 1914, with his friend Kessler having
absconded from Weimar's confines by that time, plagued by financial losses
and with war chants in the air, van de Velde, legally a potential alien in the
German Reich, asked for the termination of his employment, which
the ruler granted only too willingly.[21] After the outbreak of World War I

the Belgian and his family were prohibited from leaving town; instead, for several weeks, he was required to report to the central Weimar police station three times daily, his walks totaling nearly ten miles. In 1917, after intervention from Berlin, he was finally allowed to leave for Switzerland, with his family having to stay in their house far out on Belvederer Allee till hostilities had ceased.[22]

For van de Velde's gradual demise, the main blame certainly lay with the unsympathetic grand duke. But the Belgian artist himself was not without his faults. He had been well known if not famous before he settled in Weimar, and he expected Weimar burghers and the court to pay him respect. There was a certain arrogance about the man, which is reflected in his posthumously published memoirs. He got himself into tactless situations in Weimar society, as when he openly declared at a dinner party that he harbored "no piety," an attitude he threatened to translate into practice by proposing to replace the high wall surrounding the garden of Goethe's house near the Frauenplan with an iron fence. Such a thing was unheard-of in the sanctum of the classicists.[23]

This arrogance was fed by a sense of nonconformity which van de Velde unquestionably possessed and which should have been a catalyst for a Weimar bent on reviving, in fact on modernizing itself. As an artist, he gave himself a precious air, showed off a French accent and displayed mannerisms, even garments, which were strange to Weimarers. It could not remain hidden that he dressed his family members, including his wife, in self-designed clothes and jewelry, which had to harmonize with the furniture and eating utensils he had also designed. He gave dinner parties that were formally ritualistic, with black suits for the gentlemen de rigueur. He communed with esoteric company, mostly transient artistic elites who themselves did not connect to the core of Weimar but were transfigured by its simple beauty and who condescended to conjure images from the bygone classics. Among those who passed through were Helene von Nostitz née Hindenburg, the granddaughter of a princess, with her diplomat husband, Rainer Maria Rilke, Gerhart Hauptmann, Hugo von Hofmannsthal, Ernst Hardt – an esoteric and temporarily much-celebrated minor playwright – and, one is tempted to say, Weimar resident Count Harry Kessler himself, who spent a total of eight weeks in Weimar in 1904 and a mere ten in 1905.[24] Van de Velde made a personal eccentric statement with the house he built for himself up on Belvederer Allee: asymmetrical, curvy and with prosceniums, a purist architect's nightmare.[25]

This villa may have been structurally sound, but van de Velde, of course, was not an architect proper, as he had never studied this specialty. He was a polymath who as an aesthete tried his hand at everything; this was very Goethean, but now would have to pass the test of time. Although he always desired an architectural division in his school, as an architectural draftsman he made egregious mistakes, such as when he placed the balcony for a restaurant right above the toilet vents. As an interior architect he had a grand piano built for Förster-Nietzsche's Silberblick salon, which looked beautiful but alas, did not give off a sound. For recitals, another piano had to be wheeled in. He wished to design and build a special theater for the celebrated German actress Louise Dumont, but the authorities would not listen to him, so this idea was quashed, and when the old theater building had to be replaced, van de Velde's expertise was ignored.[26] To be sure, an architectural division would have helped him in his rivalry with the art academy, for the academicians had been suspicious of him from the start. The academy having surpassed its modernist peak in the 1890s, its denizens now were Old School painters, and they resented an Arts-and-Crafts practician sharing quarters with them. After the academy's director Hans Olde, who had been friendly, had been replaced by the *Heimat* painter Fritz Mackensen in 1910, the directorate sought to remove van de Velde by engaging in intrigues behind his back. Or so van de Velde liked to claim in his bitter résumé of October 1915 for the grand duke.[27]

It was *völkisch* chauvinism that worked increasingly against the Belgian, who found no entry to the court and was never in working contact with the grand duke. The two royals who had helped get him appointed in 1902, duchesses Pauline and Caroline, died in 1904 and 1905, respectively. Members of the court and established Weimar citizens, such as influential descendants of the philosopher kings of Anna Amalia's time or their illustrious contemporaries such as Bertuch, routinely shunned him. To them all he was crazy, tainted with French decadence, and politically unreliable. As those difficulties were compounded over time, van de Velde's health began to deteriorate and he had to commit himself to psychiatric care outside Weimar. The one person who might have propped his spirit up effectively was Harry Kessler, yet he, who had his beautifully appointed apartment and later even a house on Cranachstrasse, was hardly ever there.[28]

Count Harry Kessler and the Weimar Art Scene

When he was in Weimar, Kessler held some social gatherings of his own, no less eclectic than van de Velde's soirées. In retrospect, the Belgian described him as ruled by a "quick intelligence, of all-encompassing *Bildung*, but also with a noble attitude." Physically, van de Velde, who himself looked somewhat like a character out of a Cervantes novel, thought him possessed of a natural elegance and, although smaller in height than average, well proportioned. His beautiful face was dominated by sharp and luminous eyes, entirely without hardness, even though his mien could sometimes be authoritarian. This description comes close to matching the full-length portrait Edvard Munch painted of Kessler when in Weimar in 1906.[29] Van de Velde joined Kessler in his desire to turn the fate of Weimar around, once more to revitalize it and mold it into the center of culture in Germany – altogether a "New Weimar." Letters Kessler sent to his friend Baron Eberhard von Bodenhausen early in the new century leave no doubt as to the enthusiasm nourishing that claim.[30]

No sooner had van de Velde been officially appointed in early April 1902, than Kessler himself put in an appearance in Weimar to talk with leading figures about reformation of the local art and museum scene. With the grand duke still in a progressive mode, and backed by Förster-Nietzsche, the new director of the art academy Hans Olde and van de Velde, Kessler conferred with Minister of State Karl Rothe and Chamberlain von Palézieux. Kessler's own vision for culture in the duchy was, typically of his grandiose concepts, as "a sort of ultimate supervision that would coordinate everything toward the general goal." A natural elitist himself, he viewed culture as a product by and for elites and, as his chief biographer Laird Easton has aptly expressed it, with himself as its priest, as of a new religion. This went against the folkish art forms coming into vogue in those years, not least in Weimar, for the peasants or the broad bourgeoisie, much of which would acquire a racialist taint anathema to Kessler.[31]

But while he arrogated the supervision of art solely to himself, the count was also still holding out for a position in the imperial foreign service. Only when these prospects had faltered by April 20 was Kessler ready for an appointment in Weimar. The realistic Rothe preferred a more modest, delimited, function and Palézieux, who must have feared for his long-maintained autonomy, wished Kessler merely to undertake the very special-ized job of modernizing the Permanente Ausstellung he himself had created some twenty years ago. Hence in March of 1903 the count was made chair of a presidium controlling the Permanente, which had now been renamed Museum für Kunst und Kunstgewerbe, for art and the arts and crafts, removed from the private ducal realm and to be financed entirely by the state.[32]

In the next two years or so Kessler proceeded energetically to organize exhibitions mostly of works by the French painters he knew, among them van de Velde's former collaborators Denis and the Belgian Théo van

Rysselberghe. But he also showed Delacroix, Signac, Bonnard, and Vuillard, as well as core Impressionists such as Monet, Renoir, and Degas. Although his predilection for modern French painters was becoming obvious as the – altogether forty – expositions unfolded, he was not averse to displaying works by German artists, such as Liebermann, the old Weimar academy mainstays Rohlfs and Hagen, the newcomer Olde (who was a neo-Impressionist pointillist) and, new on the German scene, Wassily Kandinsky and Emil Nolde. In particular, Kessler favored two sculptors: Max Klinger of Leipzig, early on influenced by Arnold Böcklin, who had been a corresponding member of the Viennese Secession and became famous as the creator of monuments to Beethoven and Nietzsche, and the Parisian Auguste Rodin. He also showed van de Velde's designs. As museum director, Kessler received no salary; the events were financed by the sale of German items the Permanente had been collecting over the years.[33]

To a very large extent, Kessler managed his modern-art administration deliberately against the background of reactionary policies enacted by Kaiser Wilhelm II and certain of his officials in Berlin. In contradistinction to Kessler or van de Velde, Wilhelm II had a simplistic understanding of art, and he believed in censorship from above. About art in general he said publicly in 1901: "Art which transcends the laws and limits set by me ceases to be art."[34] Concerning theater, he castigated the stage innovations of the young Austrian Max Reinhardt. In regard to music, it meant that daring harmonies or risqué opera librettos were taboo. Significantly Richard Strauss, in his time avant-garde, when he was appointed Erster Hofkapellmeister in Berlin in 1898, had attained that position despite the protests of the emperor. In 1905, when Strauss's opera *Salome* was to be premiered, he had to take it to Dresden because the prurient Empress Auguste Viktoria objected to its lascivious theme, apart from the bold harmonic structure.[35] With respect to the visual arts, Wilhelm wanted uplifting aesthetics to be shown, not depressing discordance. As Peter Paret has noted, for him "art should elevate, either by depicting ideal beauty or by arousing patriotic or other noble sentiments." Paret continues: "His liking for uncomplicated renderings of realistically detailed landscapes, idealized nudes, and evocative historical scenes reflected the taste of large groups of the middle and upper classes in German society."[36]

In Berlin, perhaps Germany's second most important art center after Munich, artists had to hew to these precepts or be excluded from sponsorship or exhibitions organized by official, state-supported agencies, such as the Prussian Royal Academy of Arts or the Berlin chapter of the Allgemeine Deutsche Kunstgenossenschaft. Both were beholden to the Kaiser's court painter, Anton von Werner, who had produced famous portraits of Bismarck and two representations of Wilhelm I being crowned German Emperor at the Hall of Mirrors in Versailles in January 1871. Von Werner's style was super-naturalistic; he painted details with a sense of realism only the newly invented photographic camera was capable of.[37]

In places such as Vienna and Dresden secessions from this main line had already taken place in the early 1890s, by artists who refused to adhere to the official, traditional, style in order to be recognized by the establishment. The Berlin Secession occurred in May 1898. Sixty-five artists withdrew from the Verein Berliner Künstler, close to the academy and frequently headed by Anton von Werner. They receded under the leadership of the former Weimar student Max Liebermann, who was now one of the foremost German Impressionists. His comrades-in-arms were Lovis Corinth, Walter Leistikow, Max Slevogt, and Ludwig von Hofmann, who would soon move to Weimar. Associated with them were the publishers of the journal *Pan*, which had been co-founded by Harry Kessler. The Berlin Secession commenced to organize its own shows, featuring German and especially French Impressionists, just the category of artists Kessler himself would champion. Tensions between the traditional, academic, painters led by von Werner and the Berlin Secessionists came to a head in 1903–4, when the official group, thus authorized by Kaiser Wilhelm, got ready for German art exhibits at the upcoming International Exposition in St. Louis, to open on April 30, 1904. During these preparations, works by the Secessionists were excluded. As it happened, related secessionist groupings in Munich, Dresden, Karlsruhe, Stuttgart, and Vienna would also have no presence in St. Louis.[38]

These events led to Count Kessler's second major activity in the politics of art while in Weimar: the foundation of the Deutscher Künstlerbund, conceived as a counterweight to the officious Kunstgenossenschaft. It was meant to function as an umbrella organization for all German secessionist groups and its goal was to guarantee freedom from moral constraint in art by a boycot of the official salons. Moreover, it would organize its own exhibitions as well as studios and a museum. Members should be admitted on an individual basis.[39] As Kessler himself put it, the Künstlerbund was supposed to become "an arm and, if necessary, a fist to aid German culture, protecting individuality in art and ensuring its rightful representation."[40] Kessler traveled far and wide to talk his artist friends into membership.

Grand Duke Wilhelm Ernst consented to serve as the association's protector. Why he did this in late 1903 can only have been the result of the same set of circumstances that had induced him to employ van de Velde and Kessler in the first place, primarily the influence of his mother and his wife. Moreover, in 1903 Kessler, with his considerable charm, would certainly still have been able to manipulate him.[41] But that Wilhelm Ernst would have wanted to outdo in momentum the achievements of his grand-father by exhibiting a more avant-garde attitude, as has recently been suggested, is not believable. Carl Alexander's taste in art in the last decades of his life had been approximately that of Wilhelm II at the beginning of the century (with more religious and no erotic content) and, if anything, Wilhelm Ernst's personal understanding of art must have been minimal, certainly below the level of his grandfather and even of the Kaiser. Cousins Wilhelm and Wilhelm Ernst got along well, as the Kaiser's visit to Weimar and the Wartburg in April 1901 proved, and any suggestion that the grand duke wanted to demonstrate his independence as a regional ruler in the united Second Reich by acting against the Kaiser's monopolistic art policy is far-fetched.[42] Wilhelm Ernst was a coarse man who soon after hiring the count and the Belgian master artist displayed next to no interest in any culture, for which the two men came to hate him. No sooner had the Künstlerbund been officially patronized than the grand duke leered at Kessler only a few months later, expressing his hope that this organization would soon fall apart.[43] By that time, both duchesses had died.

In mid-December 1903, the president of the new Künstlerbund was Count Leopold Kalckreuth, Kessler being elected secretary. Its first exhibition was held in Munich in 1904, with a second in Berlin a year later.[44] The paintings exhibited were all close to Impressionism and neo-Impressionism, from Germany and beyond, and when the first exponents of Expressionism showed up, their works were also included: Kandinsky's, Nolde's, Franz Marc's and Max Beckmann's.[45] Kessler himself bought *Young Men by the Sea*, a 1905 Beckmann canvas, for his museum, and not because Beckmann had been a student at the Weimar art academy in 1900–3, which was a coincidence. In this regard the Künstlerbund went beyond the Berlin Secession, whose rejection of the Expressionists spelled its own demise by 1910.[46]

The Deutscher Künstlerbund won a political victory when in February 1904 sympathetic representatives of all major parties in the Berlin Reichstag were lobbied to argue for its formal recognition by the imperial government led by Chancellor Count Bernhard von Bülow. The successful parliamentary debate could not alter the earlier St. Louis decision. It did, however, amount to a humiliation for Anton von Werner and Kaiser Wilhelm II, whose contempt for Kessler henceforth became bottomless. In this case, persistent rumors of a common ancestor for the latter two added to the rancor.[47]

Still, in November of 1905 Count Harry Kessler seemed at the pinnacle of his success. He noted in his diary: "Consider what means of influence I have in Germany: the German Künstlerbund, my position in Weimar, including the prestige despite the grand duke's stupidity, the connection with Reinhardt's stage, my intimate relations with the Nietzsche Archive, with Hofmannsthal, with van de Velde . . ."[48] When he penned these words, Kessler was already on his way down. His Weimar denouement began when, in late 1905, he was searching for a local venue for the third annual exhibition of the Künstlerbund in 1906. A promised Museum of Modern Art not yet having been realized, he approached Carl Ruland, the venerable director of the ducal art museum which, unlike the original Permanente Ausstellung, had not been entrusted to Kessler's care in 1903. Alleging that he had the grand duke's permission to set up his art displays there, he forced Ruland to move hundreds of artifacts from the entire building in a potentially damaging transport. Kessler himself recorded details of a conversation with Ruland, who was also the director of the new Goethe Museum, an architecturally extended Goethe House, and a scholar of note. Kessler's arrogant tone totally unsettled the old gentleman, so that after the chores demanded of him he chose to resign from his post. In the process, Kessler had also antagonized State Minister Rothe, who had earlier been his ally.[49]

Ruland was, in fact, not a man Kessler wanted to see as head of that rival museum. Already in November 1901 he had planned to make the job available to his close friend Baron Eberhard von Bodenhausen, who was of impeccable lineage and a connoisseur of art exactly to Kessler's liking. Besides, Bodenhausen was looking for a position in order to feed his young family. But first he had to complete a doctorate in art history at Heidelberg with Professor Harry Thode, Cosima Wagner's son-in-law. Bodenhausen's position did not materialize because Ruland would have been difficult to remove. An alternative was to install the baron as private secretary to Wilhelm Ernst, for Bodenhausen, like Kessler, was a fraternity brother of the duke from the same exclusive student corps, but Bodenhausen eschewed such service.[50] Kessler's personnel machinations displeased certain of the higher echelons in Weimar, chief among them von Palézieux, who also must have been chagrined when Kessler maneuvered a possible transfer of his Viennese friend, Hugo von Hofmannsthal, to the post of Weimar theater Intendant. Unfortunately for Kessler, the poet could not be swayed.[51]

The count was more successful in attracting yet another famous contemporary to Weimar, if, again, only periodically and at some risk. It was Edvard Munch. This early Norwegian pioneer of Expressionism after some years in Paris had been invited in the autumn of 1892 to exhibit with the Verein Berliner Künstler. Yet he was told to close after one week by the reactionaries backed by von Werner, because of his Impressionist-like style and human-emotional subject matter, much of it with sexual overtones. From that time on he consorted with Bodenhausen, Kessler, and denizens of the journal *Pan*. At the Berlin Secession of 1902, he exhibited a cycle of paintings entitled *Love*, resonant with sexuality, life, and death.[52]

Munch came to Weimar early in March 1904 mainly to paint Kessler. As he was drawn into court company, like Böcklin before him, he was constantly constricted by tuxedos or stiff overcoats, "exclusively surrounded by counts and barons." Moreover, suffering from a persecution complex and as an alcoholic, he could not stand the presence of the formal academicians of the painters' school. But he was drawn into Nietzsche's aura at the Villa Silberblick, enjoying the engaging attentiveness of Nietzsche's sister and trying his hand at portraits of the deceased genius. More often than not, however, he kept to himself, sitting with a glass of wine in the Erbprinz or Russischer Hof. He painted Kessler sitting at his desk, at the end of March. On another sojourn in Weimar in 1905, just as awkward, he could have accepted an academy professorship but again felt out of place. Once, at a grand duke's party, his borrowed formal trousers split down the middle, to everyone's embarrassment. Munch was always near that mental illness which had fatally engulfed his sister Laura. A second portrait, the famous full-length one of Kessler standing, was completed in 1906.[53]

Two days after Munch had finished his work in July, Kessler noted in his diary: "My leave granted." This was not the result of the count having summoned the Norwegian to Weimar, though Munch's presence was a contributing factor. In the case of Kessler's parting, the straw that broke the camel's back was the so-called Rodin scandal.[54]

Kessler had exhibited works by his friend Auguste Rodin as early as 1904, with mixed reviews from the Weimar Old School art lovers. In 1905, after receiving an honorary doctorate from Jena, Rodin decided to show gratitude by gifting fourteen watercolors to Grand Duke Wilhelm Ernst, mistakenly assuming that he had been behind the honor. In January 1906 these were exhibited in Kessler's gallery. Some portraits showed semi-nudes. Of these, one was particularly offensive, to the public and potentially to the duke, because it bore Rodin's inscription of thanks to him personally. As one acerbic critic commented, the woman was painted "from behind and presented to the viewer in a position that can be interpreted in no other way than that she wished to relieve herself." Kessler and the duke could not comment at the time, because the former was in London and the latter on a tiger hunt in India. After Kessler had returned and was challenged by von Palézieux about this indiscretion, he referred to a letter of thanks that had been sent to him on behalf of Wilhelm Ernst, by Cabinet Secretary Baron Hermann von Egloffstein. Often leaving his personal things at four different places and in disarray, Kessler had problems producing this letter to prove his point. Meanwhile Palézieux was gloating, almost certain he now had the reason he needed to finally rid himself of the eccentric count. An added factor in all this was that, like Kessler, Palézieux was rumored to be an illegitimate son of Wilhelm I. The matter took an ugly turn in early summer after the letter had been found and Kessler, caught in the rituals of both the aristocratic and the Prussian officer caste, challenged Palézieux and Egloffstein to a duel. This greatly displeased the grand duke for, at the least, it would lead to tension between himself and the Kaiser, as whose Prussian army general Palézieux served. Wilhelm II's dislike of Kessler was well known. Before the matter could be definitely settled, it was reported that the chamberlain had, suddenly, died of pneumonia. However, some maintained that he had poisoned himself, for they had heard his "screams and groans" all evening. An additional element in the feud was that Kessler knew of pecuniary improprieties Palézieux had committed since his founding of the Permanente and that he, Kessler, had always been at liberty to expose these. In any event, Kessler handed in his resignation early in July and from then on returned to Weimar only to visit van de Velde or Förster-Nietzsche.[55]

Despite his idiosyncrasies, what Harry Kessler achieved in matters of art for Weimar in the span of a mere three years could have formed the impetus for a return to greatness, as Strauss and Liszt had envisioned it. But like those two musicians, Kessler suffered under Weimar's double curse: a combination of inharmonious relations with the temporal ruler in a protracted period of royal patronage, and a personal sense of restlessness. The cultural deficit that Kessler, and to a lesser extent van de Velde, eventually caused through inertia, poor judgment, and physical absence, could hardly be compensated for by a creative productivity emanating from the painters' school, for ever since the 1890s, it continued on its middling course. That there was minimal coordination between its activities and the sweeping endeavors of both Kessler and van de Velde was to the academy's and, in the final analysis, Weimar's own detriment.

It is not that Weimar academy painters were not progressive after 1901 – on the whole they were. But they were not outstanding in the manner of artists in Munich, Berlin, Vienna and, of course, Paris. In October 1910, the critic Philipp Franck thought that works by Weimar painters put on public display in town made "scarcely an exciting impression." In the conservative Berlin daily *Der Tag*, he wrote that they "did not show a life beyond the present one and did not point the way ahead."[56] And this although most of the artists had been members of secessions, some of them founding ones. Kessler got along best with his old friend from Berlin Ludwig von Hofmann and the pointillist Hans Olde, until he realized in mid-decade that try as they might, their works could never attain the level of originality in which the French paintings excelled.[57] In any case, Olde would be replaced as director by Fritz Mackensen, who pandered to the new *Heimatkunst* style, which was super-patriotic to the point of racism and xenophobia.[58] It was the forerunner of National Socialist-inspired Blood and Soil art. With the exception of Beckmann and Hans Arp, the later Dadaist, no Weimar student in this period before the end of World War I reached the stature even of these mediocre teachers.[59]

Finally, it was damaging to the academy that too many instructors were seen to be leaving, a few in unsavory circumstances. The departure of the Impressionist Christian Rohlfs in 1901 for Kassel had been a great loss to the school, and in 1908 Sascha Schneider (whose traditionalism had been opposed by Kessler) took his leave, not for objective reasons but because he was persuaded to after homosexual scandals.[60] The sculptor Adolf Brütt waxed enthusiastic about the good life in Weimar, the hunt he indulged and, through that, the proximity to the grand duke, as well as the vacations he was able to enjoy with his wonderful family. But he was a womanizer and in 1910 a serious affair with his master student Franziska von Seeger forced him, too, to flee.[61] By that time it looked as if little artistic impulse had remained in Weimar.

The Cult of Elisabeth Förster-Nietzsche

In this period, and into the time of the Great War, Elisabeth Förster-Nietzsche, who had been instrumental in bringing van de Velde and Kessler to Weimar, was busy expanding her own dominion. Her tasks were gigantic. Foremost, she had to secure financial backing to guarantee the future of her institution. Part of that money would continue to come from publications of Nietzsche's surviving manuscripts and letters, so she had to keep her editing and publishing activities going. For this she had to hire suitable staff and hone her relations with publishers. In order to be a convincing match for Cosima Wagner's Wahnfried, she needed to cultivate the reputation of her Silberblick shrine, make it part salon, part mausoleum, and attract influential men and women from society, Weimar's and from abroad.

This entailed being politically shrewd and manipulating people. Here she had to balance her own political views, which were starkly conservative, with those of the *haut monde* she wanted to invite, several of whom were artists or writers and liberal to left-wing, like van de Velde. A particular problem she had to contend with here was her formerly open political anti-Semitism, which she needed to conceal in the new circles she now wanted to move in, for many educated connoisseurs were Jewish and several were rich enough to potentially lend her support. Moreover, many of Nietzsche's core followers were Jewish; Nietzsche himself had been anything but an anti-Semite.

Förster-Nietzsche had published the first edition of *The Will to Power* in 1901, which had included 483 of her brother's aphorisms. The aim had been, and continued to be, to establish him as a consistent thinker who had created a systematic philosophy, rather than someone who had just strewn aphorisms about. It mattered nothing to her that creating a systematic body of thought had always been far from Nietzsche's mind.[62] Audaciously, Förster-Nietzsche overcame the huge problem of being unable to decipher much of her brother's handwriting by hiring Peter Gast, a failed composer and old acquaintance of his, to explicate documents for her when she needed them. With Gast's help, and after further falsifications as she saw fit, a second, amplified edition of *The Will to Power* appeared in 1906. This one contained 1,067 aphorisms, with others, from the first edition, having been omitted. It was yet another hodgepodge. Critic Albert Lamm remarked in the *Süddeutsche Monatshefte* in 1906 that the entire attraction of the work had been artificially created by Förster-Nietzsche's arbitrary choice of the sensationalist title and the headings in the book; once one took those away, there was nothing in the assorted aphorisms that one did not already know from Nietzsche's earlier *œuvre*. It was especially precarious in those cases, warned Lamm, where "older passages are pasted together, which he himself had dismissed, and become works of fraud." In defense of her editing, Förster-Nietzsche published a pamphlet in 1907, in which she claimed to have been guided by her brother's lists and captions – none of which, as was discovered much later, were genuine. She alone was responsible for the emendations, deletions, and distortions, once the handwriting had been made clear to her; her helpers did not engage in forgery, but neither did they stop her.[63]

By 1904 Förster-Nietzsche had published a multi-volume biography of her brother, in the preparation of which she had taken care to include only the qualities she wanted him to have possessed and to make their sibling relationship look perfect. In her interpretation he was a strong German nationalist, against democracy and socialism, who had created the ideal of the *Übermensch* in the service of the German Reich of Bismarck's and the Kaiser's making. His relationship with her had been most loving, to the extent that he had designated her as his natural heir, record-keeper and biographer.[64] Of particular concern to her was his sexual integrity. In 1902 a Dr. Paul Julius Möbius had confirmed in a meticulous study the earlier findings that Nietzsche had died of syphilis-induced paralysis, and Förster-Nietzsche did not wish this verdict to stand. Instead, she said that her brother had taken a medication called chloral and had ingested a brown substance brought to him from Java, to help him sleep. Too strong doses of these had made Nietzsche, who always worked beyond capacity, terminally ill.[65] To substantiate her claims, Förster-Nietzsche published Nietzsche's letters, again after tampering with the evidence, sometimes using a razor blade in cases where outsiders could examine the originals.[66] She claimed a monopoly on Nietzsche's correspondence, especially an exchange of letters with Professor Franz Overbeck, a former close colleague from Basel, and when she could not get it, she sued. Some lawsuits she lost, but she also was victorious, applying a ban on the publication efforts of others. These suits cost her much money, apart from the trouble with her publishers, adding pressure on her in the continued quest for funds from stalwart friends like Kessler.[67]

Assisted by her local Weimar friends such as van de Velde, Helene von Nostitz and, when he was present, Kessler, Frau Förster converted the Villa Silberblick into a salon, as the occasions arose, not least, to draw attention away from Bayreuth. The social circles of the above three people over-lapped, and invariably, whoever visited with them also visited the villa on the hill. One of these was Erika von Watzdorf-Bachoff, a frequent guest at the Nietzsche Archive. She described Förster-Nietzsche as "tiny, round in figure, wearing children's shoes and gloves, with blue, very weak eyes, a blond wig, rosy cheeks and a small nose that was hardly capable of supporting her glasses."[68]

There was virtually no German artist or intellectual of note in those two decades till the end of World War I who did not make the pilgrimage to the new Weimar shrine. Thomas Mann, Detlev von Liliencron, Richard Dehmel, Hofmannsthal, Stefan George, Max Reinhardt, Gerhart Hauptmann, and Oswald Spengler all paid homage. Since Nietzsche's views, although controversial with many, were becoming more fashionable internationally by the day, guests from abroad also arrived, for instance André Gide. There were afternoon teas, dinners, lectures, musical recitals, and readings. And Nietzsche's sister corresponded with Maxim Gorky no less than with Gabriele d'Annunzio.[69] Yet, as in Franz Liszt's time, members of the ducal court were largely absent.

What seemed logical, the institutionalization of a Nietzsche Society, failed in 1907, but one year later a Nietzsche Foundation was created, with financial funds separate from those for the archive. Owing to Förster-Nietzsche's increasing skills in attracting and using money, however, she always had her hands in both tills. No matter who was on the supervisory boards, in the end it was she who controlled the finances as much as all other activities at Silberblick.[70]

What supported her economically? Apart from continuing the publication of edited Nietzsche works and some books of her own, which brought in a lot of revenue, she received irregular donations from Count Kessler and, ironically, a Swedish Jew of German background. Ernst Thiel, a Stockholm banker, was one of those unshakable Nietzsche stalwarts she now saw more and more of. He had translated some of the philosopher's writings into Swedish, and over a period of several years donated tens, even hundreds of thousands of marks to the wily widow. Whenever she found herself near a financial crunch, she appealed to him with heart-wrenching letters, or with tears in her eyes when she met him, and he always delivered. Politically, he was a conservative, and so in that area too they saw eye to eye. In conversation or correspondence, Jews or the thorny question of anti-Semitism, Förster-Nietzsche's Achilles' heel, were not mentioned. To Förster-Nietzsche, Thiel was important not just as a source of funds, but also because in 1908 and again in 1914 she craved the Nobel Prize and wanted him to use his influence with the Swedish Nobel Committee.[71]

In late summer 1914 Count Harry Kessler, sincere patriot that he was, but also motivated, in Ian Buruma's poignant phrase, by Nietzsche's "idea of renewal through struggle," left for the Western Front.[72] Yet before he did, he, van de Velde, and Elisabeth Förster-Nietzsche got together one more time for a most bizarre venture, in honor of the matron's brother. It concerned plans for a grandiose monument. These plans were preceded by an understanding between Kessler and Förster-Nietzsche that on recently acquired grounds surrounding the Villa Silberblick, a small temple should be built in honor of the philosopher. But the ambitious Kessler wanted more. In the spring of 1911 he conceived the idea of two statues, a temple, and a large stadium elsewhere on the outskirts of Weimar, without a direct route to the villa. In the stadium athletic games should be held, perhaps with naked youths, and ballets should take place – Diaghilev and Nijinsky had both shown interest. Inspired by Nietzsche's *Birth of Tragedy*, he and van de Velde had secured the cooperation of the French sculptor Aristide Maillol, a friend of both men, who would create the statue of a naked young Apollonian man, and, complementarily, a Dionysian man. Van de Velde was to construct a temple, and Max Klinger to sculpt suitable reliefs. A steering committee was then struck, on which were men like the wealthy Berlin industrialist Walther Rathenau and Anton Kippenberg, director of the Leipzig Insel publishing firm, with Kessler as president. Patronage and funds were sought (and duly promised) from figures such as Richard Strauss, Gustav Mahler, and d'Annunzio; two wealthy Jewish businessmen from Berlin donated 60,000 marks for purchasing the site. In this, Kessler was driven by his veneration of Nietzsche, who, he maintained against critics, had taught man to love his own body, and an ideology of anti-urbanism which, since the beginning of the new century, had become fashionable, finding its expression, not least, in the new German youth movement. Further, the idea borrowed heavily from the revival of the classical Olympic Games, since 1896 in Athens, Paris and St. Louis, with the Stockholm ones scheduled for 1912. When the costing of the entire project reached one million marks, Kessler was assured by wealthy sympathizers that such a large amount would pose no problem, and so he planned for the foundations to be laid in October 1914, the philosopher's seventieth birthday.

But complications soon arose. For one, van de Velde's three blueprints for a temple could not satisfy Kessler, who was beginning to think the Belgian had lost his touch, remarking at one time that his design had "an oppressively heavy and empty effect." In June 1912 a fourth draft was finally accepted by the committee, with Kessler's acquiescence. As for Maillol and Klinger, there is no evidence that they ever submitted anything. The greatest difficulty, however, came from the direction of Förster-Nietzsche. She was suspicious of the money from the Berlin Jews whom, unlike Ernst Thiel in Sweden, she did not know and could not steer. More importantly, this larger project was out of her hands and to be situated in an area remote from her archive, so that she formally extricated herself from those proceedings early on. What she wanted was influence for her archive and funds, and when the million marks came into play, she thought that some of this money was due to her. She pleaded with Kessler repeatedly to either shelve or delay his plans, knowing full well that without her express consent the project could never be realized. As it happened, despite the committees struck and the monies budgeted, it remained in total limbo throughout 1913 and most of 1914, when in August of that year the Great War started and it was irretrievably doomed. By this time, the count had already donned his lieutenant's uniform and van de Velde had been forced to resign his Weimar position.[73]

At the beginning of the great conflict Kessler and Förster-Nietzsche were agreed that the war enthusiasm of the German people was a wonderful thing. "If my brother were still alive today, he would have gone to war, in spite of his seventy years," Förster-Nietzsche wrote to the Thiels. Publicly she declared that *The Will to Power* was bearing fruit in the minds of German youths; how else could one explain the lightning victory over Belgium? Besides, special, inexpensive, editions of *Thus Spoke Zarathustra* had been published en masse and distributed to the army (she herself was earning a fortune). Förster-Nietzsche did not tire of writing martial articles and launching press releases. When the going at the fronts got heavier, she was dead-set against peace talks with the Allies. Those would only encourage the Social Democrats, who were endangering the monarchy in any case. At the end, in 1918, when an armistice had been signed, she, who by now had joined all manner of right-wing political organizations, declared that Germany had not really lost the war, but been stabbed in the back by her internal enemies. She was clearly in the rightist camp, where other citizens of Weimar, who were not as cultured or cosmopolitan as Kessler and van de Velde, had also been for years. Because Förster-Nietzsche was known to keep such elevated company, only few of those others would have dared to join her on the hill.[74]

Pioneers of *Heimatkunst*

Elisabeth Förster-Nietzsche's cerebral anti-Semitism, if not her highly developed sense of aesthetics, connected her to the Weimar group led by Adolf Bartels. To it belonged, loosely, lesser-known Weimar semi-intellectuals such as Ernst Wachler, Friedrich Lienhard, and the Weimar newspaper art critic and painter Mathilde von Freytag-Loringhoven.[75] They were beholden to the *völkisch* ideas that had been developing in Germany since the 1880s under the influence of Julius Langbehn's hugely successful book *Rembrandt als Erzieher*. The focus of these ideas was *das Volk*, the German people as increasingly defined from a racist perspective. This perspective was determined, on the one hand, by the people's blood. On the other, it was determined by its home (*Heimat*) – the soil on which the people lived. The "soil" was specified as rural or provincial, in stark antithesis to the city, especially Berlin. Such anti-urbanism occurred in a phase of cumulative industrialization after the founding of the Second Reich and the resultant rise of large cities. "Blood and Soil" were to become fundamentals of Nazi ideology. Much of Nazi aesthetics was based on folk culture as it arose from *Heimatkunst*, homeland art, which Adolf Bartels and his companions helped to generate and foster.[76]

Since 1901 the anti-Semite and major *Heimatkunst* protagonist Bartels had engaged in various activities in the service of this cause, at a torrid rate. Perversely, judged by quantity he was the most prolific writer in Weimar since Goethe. Much of his output appeared in the form of articles for the right-wing *Kunstwart*, the chief organ of believers in *Heimatkunst*, which, after its inception toward the end of the nineteenth century, was not averse to pointing out salient distinctions between "Germans" and "Jews."[77] In those, as in other media, he vented his ultra-nationalist and anti-Jewish spleen. Not least, nationalism meant that tribute was due to Weimar as the home of Goethe and Schiller, the green heartland of forests and hills and, as Bartels enthused, the center of gravity of the most Germanic Germany, for the most German of Germans. Bartels's anti-Semitism soon became so vicious that more moderate and respectable friends of his, his former mentor Adolf Stern, a professor of German in Dresden, and Eduard Avenarius, the publisher of *Kunstwart*, found themselves embarrassed by him. In 1905 Bartels's triumph peaked when his *Geschichte der deutschen Literatur* had reached its fourth edition, as a putative memorial in a German literary landscape free of Jews. Consequently, Grand Duke Wilhelm Ernst made Bartels an honorary professor, bestowing on him a title which this half-educated scribe now could put to good use in a world of German burghers defined by *Bildung* and attendant respectability but also, and significantly, with a growing sense of chauvinism.[78] From there Bartels never looked back. In 1907 he became a member of the *völkisch* Deutschbund, which considered itself "the core of all true Germans," in 1909 he began editing the journal *Deutsches Schrifttum*, in 1912 he drafted the statutes of the German-Völkisch Authors' Union, whose members had to swear to be free of a single drop of Jewish blood, and in 1913 he co-convened the "German Day" in Eisenach, where several *völkisch* organizations united in a Deutschvölkische Vereinigung.[79] He had cordial relations with Theodor Fritsch in Leipzig, whose Hammer firm published a "Handbook of the Jewish Question" as early as 1907, which was reprinted with striking regularity to the end of the Nazi Reich.[80] Bartels was proud to own the Goethe biography authored by Cosima Wagner's fiercely Jew-hating son-in-law Houston Stewart Chamberlain, who autographed it for him.[81]

This pernicious ideologue systematically ranted against everything that was taboo for the *Heimatkunst* movement, phenomena which he linked, in multifarious ways, to the Jews. At the center of this was a belief in the country's soil, the countryside, and, conversely, a hatred of the city, where most Jews were known to reside. By Bartels's catechism, Jews were responsible for industrialization, rationalization, and modernization, in particular the new chain stores such as Wertheim, which were proliferating in urban centers like Berlin. Examples of decadent art could be found in Impressionism no less than in operetta or on the Berlin stage, in the paintings of Liebermann, the scores of Jacques Offenbach, or the plays staged by Max Reinhardt. All three were Jewish. In literature, Thomas and Heinrich Mann as modern novelists were condemned as Jewish, albeit falsely, not to mention Jews like Arthur Schnitzler and Stefan Zweig. Hugo von Hofmannsthal was targeted, even though he was not fully Jewish. The large newspaper and book-publishing chains of the Mosses and Ullsteins and Jewish critics such as Alfred Kerr were anathema. Social democracy as a political movement went against the grain of the monarchic order, strivings for democracy were evil and the early women's rights movement led by Jews such as Hedwig Dohm were of the devil.[82] When Germany was defeated in 1918, Bartels publicly subscribed to the same stab-in-the-back legend, blaming the Jews, as did his good friend Förster-Nietzsche.[83]

What distinguished Bartels's anti-Semitism as a typical by-product of the new *Heimatkunst* ideology and placed it in a league with that of chauvinistic pseudo-scientists at that time was its racist tinge. Seemingly, it was grounded in natural science. It was the essence of Bartels's increasing radicalism that he viewed the Jews not merely as undesirable religious, economic, and cultural elements, as had been the practice until the late 1870s, but, in addition, as biologically inferior to true-blooded Germans; here he foreshadowed the National Socialists. This was a corrupted offshoot of Darwin and Haeckel's evolutionary theories and applied to the German situation what the vulgarizing Comte Arthur de Gobineau had preached in France.[84] Hence Bartels championed "purity of the blood" as the physical criterion of a superior race, and deplored miscegenation – said to be the interbreeding of Jews with non-Jews, as increasingly witnessed in recent times within the German aristocracy. (In Weimar, too, after 1912 Count Friedrich von Dürckheim-Montmartin lived in the Cranachstrasse, in one of the few houses van de Velde had built there, with a non-"Aryan" wife.)[85] In his eugenic fanaticism Bartels even went so far as to demand the resettlement of the European Slavic East with racially pure Germans who would maintain themselves there militarily – anticipating Himmler and Hitler's *Drang nach Osten* – Drive to the East.[86]

As part of his larger crusade Bartels fought two separate campaigns. One was against the German poet Heinrich Heine, who lived from 1797 to 1856 and against whom Bartels had polemicized already in the 1890s. Heine was controversial even in his lifetime, owing, to a large part, to his animosity against Goethe, whose lyricism he sought to emulate. Indeed, there was a wide belief that Heine was a lyricist second only to Goethe. But as a writer, often in a journalistically sloppy and satirical mold, he was accused by others of vapidity, even plagiarism, and he was ambivalent about his Jewishness, having converted to Lutheranism in 1825. He was living in Paris after 1831, became a friend of Karl Marx and eventually accepted a modest French pension, none of which endeared him to German nationalists. When in the 1890s a monument was to be erected in Germany in his honor, opposition from certain German quarters was so strong that a statue that was sculpted, of Heine's legendary poetic figure Loreley, eventually had to be shipped to New York.[87]

In 1906 a new call for a Heine monument was issued by the Berlin critic Alfred Kerr, one of Bartels's favorite Jewish targets. Kerr was joined by such cultural luminaries as Hauptmann, Dehmel, Haeckel, Liliencron, Klinger, and Liebermann. Bartels immediately shifted into gear and within a few months had published another book, *Heinrich Heine: Auch ein Denkmal*, in which he tried, as one of Bartels's modern biographers has put it, to kill the dead Heine's spirit.[88] Bartels held that not Heine, but Eduard Mörike was Germany's greatest poet after Goethe, and he also mentioned his longtime idol Friedrich Hebbel as an overall superior writer. Altogether, Heine had lived a second-hand life, charged Bartels, as a Jew who could never deny his true heritage, using the German language as only a virtual poet could, as mere form with no content flowing from his pen. Bartels alluded to Heine's anti-Jewish self-image as contrasting with his typically Jewish qualities: his overflowing, tasteless eroticism and bathos, the constant dissimulation, the sugary content of his scripts and, not least, the Paris mattress-bed that was his inescapable dungeon for the last eight years of his disease-ridden life. Altogether these symbolized a deplorable, decrepit, disgusting existence. Such a man deserved no monument, maintained Bartels, and after much controversy, with input from Bartels's sensationally successful screeds, Kerr's original plan was shelved.[89]

Bartels's second venture combined his desire for German theater reform with what he considered proper youth indoctrination. By 1906 the Deutscher Schillerbund had been founded in Weimar, which acted as his vehicle. Its patron was none other than Grand Duke Wilhelm Ernst, with Bartels as its secretary. Its caucus attracted twenty-eight members, half of them from outside of Weimar. One of its first keynote speakers was Baron Alexander von Gleichen-Russwurm, son of the painter Ludwig and Schiller's great-grandson. Although the first group of member names was not stellar (included were many middling German pedagogues and a few wealthy merchants), some well-known figures eventually joined, thus aiding the national collection of membership fees. Among them were the philosopher Rudolf Eucken and historian Karl Lamprecht, as well as the writers Wilhelm Raabe, Peter Rosegger, and Baron Liliencron, all staunchly nationalist. After Ernst von Wildenbruch had launched a propaganda article in the *Berliner Tageblatt*, membership markedly increased. By 1908 it was possible to design the first program for the following July: selected high-school students from all over Germany should visit the hallowed grounds of Weimar for three weeks and, in between visits to historic sights, attend plays in Weimar's theater, by Goethe, Schiller, Lessing, and Kleist. And under the new, sternly patriotic, theater Intendant Carl Norris von Schirach, this is exactly what happened. Goethe's *Egmont* was staged, along with Schiller's *Wilhelm Tell*, Lessing's *Minna von Barnhelm*, and Kleist's *Prinz von Homburg*. These idolatrous works were from the canon of Germanocentric literature; it is significant though hardly surprising that Lessing's *Nathan der Weise*, based on Moses Mendelssohn, was *not* among them. By this time finances had been enhanced by contributions from the ducal government and the town of Weimar, by the large private donation of a generous philanthropist, and by fund-raising performances in the theaters of Weimar and Hamburg.[90]

During that first summer in 1909, when the Schiller League had close to 4,000 members in more than 300 German localities, 1,800 pupils of both genders attended these new Nationalfestspiele, or national festivals, as Bartels self-importantly had styled them. They came in groups for one week each. The year 1911 saw a second event, and the third and last one before the war was held in 1913. The repertory hardly changed, with Wildenbruch's *œuvre* (he had died in 1909) included in the final productions. After World War I, events continued on an almost annual basis well into the early part of the Third Reich.[91]

Already in the first year of 1909, students and their teachers visiting from provincial towns were in the majority, but a few urban centers such as Berlin, Hamburg, Dresden, and Frankfurt were also represented.[92] All students were duly impressed; the mood of the accompanying teachers was nationalist, pro-monarchist and pregnant with awe for the classics. Invariably, Bartels himself received an ovation. The students were overfed with sightseeing, theater, and lectures; all the Weimar clichés since 1800 were rehearsed. The entire event was in the spirit of the newly invented German national tradition that reached from the Middle Ages via Luther, Frederick the Great and Goethe to Bismarck, and now also to Wilhelm II. Chauvinist admonitions were the cement holding these spectacles together. A German had to fulfill his "national duty without compensation," a feeling of "tight community, of belonging together, the national consciousness" was conjured, "national sentiment penetrated deeply" – phrases uttered to the tunes of military bands, with *Deutschland, Deutschland über Alles* constantly in the air. If there were phenomena of pre-fascism before World War I, they certainly found their expression here in Weimar at the end of the new century's first decade.[93]

Thus Bartels wished to set an example of how to shut out of German theaters German Jews and decadents like Schnitzler and Frank Wedekind, and foreigners, equally decadent and often Jewish, such as George Bernard Shaw, Oscar Wilde, and Maxim Gorky. According to Bartels, they had converted the German stage to a mere commercial business. This was his unique contribution to the badly needed reform of Weimar's local theater, until in 1915 he was ejected from the Schillerbund on account of his embarrassingly rabid anti-Semitism.[94]

Most certainly, Elisabeth Förster-Nietzsche did not socialize with Bartels at her villa, where his crude tone was sure to offend her more sophisticated visitors. Instead, she met him at a Weimar establishment called *Jungbrunnen*, or "Fount of Youth," which an anti-Semitic journalist named Ernst Wachler had founded and where she – often accompanied by her brother's former assistant Peter Gast – could give unbridled expression to hyper-nationalist and anti-Jewish sentiments.[95] As George L. Mosse has written, Wachler, whose mother was Jewish, chose to interpret Nietzsche as "the great Germanic seer, the prophet of the reborn race of heroes; not the scathing skeptic and sometime prophet of a dying religion and civilization." Not surprisingly, Wachler's son Ingolf would eventually marry Ursula Sigismund, Nietzsche's niece. He maintained ties with a variety of *völkisch*, anti-Semitic groups such as the Deutschbund, and Fritsch's radical-racist Hammer-Verlag in Leipzig. Furthermore, he was in touch with the Viennese Ostara-Verlag of Jörg Lanz Liebenfels and contributed articles to Dietrich Eckart's journal *Auf Gut Deutsch* in Munich. Both Liebenfels and Eckart influenced Adolf Hitler at different stages during this time, in his own ideological evolution.[96]

Wachler had come to Weimar from Berlin in 1902, in order to assume the chief editorship of the *Weimarische Zeitung*, where the reactionary Freytag-Loringhoven worked. He was a great believer in the Old Germans and in resurrecting what he thought was their ancient culture, which at first sight was somewhat at odds with the spirit of Greek neoclassicism that was said to dominate the Goethe town.[97] Like Bartels, however, Wachler was interested in theater reform (as Goethe had also been), and he sought to accomplish this by adopting the Greek open-air stage, filling it with

Germanic drama, drawn from the lives of heroes like Arminius the Cheruscan, who had defeated the Roman armies in the Teutoburg Forest in AD 9, close to the Externsteine pagan reliquary which was later to become Heinrich Himmler's playground.[98] Establishing such theaters for Wachler was a "Nordic Renaissance."[99]

Wachler's *Heimatkunst* contribution consisted of producing open-air plays at Thale in the Harz mountains, some sixty miles northwest of Weimar, after he had taken a leave of absence from his newspaper post. In these, he wanted to protest against all the modern theater tendencies, the decadence of French plays, the social criticism and psychological analysis of the Ibsens, Shaws, and Strindbergs. His vision was as anti-urban – especially anti-Berlin – as it was xenophobic, pointedly in contempt of Jewish agents, who, he said, profited from expensive tickets. Wachler preferred German motifs enacted by German actors: Wagner's *Meistersinger*, depictions of patricians from Nuremberg or Lübeck, wholesale merchants and sailors from Hamburg, Thuringian peasants, Jena students, and the skirmishes between Germans and Poles on the eastern border. With such figures and in such genres, he felt at one with Bartels.[100]

The shows got under way in the summer of 1903 and continued for several years. Wachler paid homage to Goethe and Schiller by upholding *Faust* and adopting Schiller's use of the choir – so redolent of organic community. He resorted to new creations by like-minded playwrights and compatriots in *Heimatkunst* such as Friedrich Lienhard, whose *Wieland der Schmied* was performed. *Münchhausens Liebeswunder* by Ernst Böttger, and *Walpurgis*, by Wachler himself, with music by Peter Gast, were staged. Wachler also offered *Widukind* and *Mittsommer*, and featured *Herzog Heinrich am Finkenherd* by Franz Herwig, *Frithjof und Ingeborg* by Paul Schmidt, as well as *Lafontaine* by Bartels. Older works included some by Goethe (*Die erste Walpurgisnacht* after *Faust*), Hebbel (*Moloch* and *Gyges*), and Kleist (*Hermannschlacht*). All his actors hailed from Weimar's stage, on loan from sympathetic, national-minded, directors.[101]

Wieland der Schmied was put on many times by Wachler, for its author Friedrich Lienhard was a close friend.[102] Born in 1865 in Alsace, Lienhard had studied Protestant theology, literature, and history in Berlin, but had failed in all subjects. By 1900 he was starting to move in and out of Weimar, in 1903 settling nearby in the Thuringian Woods and collaborating with Bartels on journals. In 1916 he chose the town of Weimar as his permanent home. The series *Wege nach Weimar*, or "A Path to Weimar," became Lienhard's very own mouthpiece in 1905, and its consecutive volumes were dedicated to individual themes: race theories à la Gobineau mixed up with themes from the classics connected to Schiller, Herder, or Goethe. Put off modernism, the specter of democracy, and the big city by his experiences in Berlin, Lienhard became yet another blood-and-soil apostle and contributor to *Heimatkunst* ideology. *Heimatkunst* was a weapon in his fight against "the dominance of Berlin," by which he meant its culture, its agents, its premieres. In the fashion of what we earlier referred to as an "invention of tradition," his specialty was twisting classical ideas to fit them to his notions of Nordic superiority, even though he meant this less in the biological-racist sense of Bartels, and more in an idealistic sense.[103] This did not mean he loved Jews. On the contrary, he deplored the course they had taken after their "complete emancipation" in the nineteenth century and in particular ranted against the Jews of Berlin. In his drama *Ahasver am Rhein*, the protagonist, Professor Hasse, is a despicable Jew.[104] During the Third Reich Lienhard would be commended for having identified, in this play, "an essentially Jewish-directed science," but his description of Hasse on the whole was seen as flat.[105] Lienhard became yet another thinker who forged a path for National Socialist ideology without later being acknowledged by Hitler and his lieutenants for the pioneering service he had rendered, to the extent that was his due.

The Conservative Style

The adherents to *Heimatkunst* were hard-core nationalists and racists who had peculiarly neo-Germanic views of culture and resented all foreign influences, particularly French ones, and in their xenophobia especially hated Jews. About 1910, they were the most radical of several circles of conservative persuasion in Weimar, including, with significant exceptions such as van de Velde, Förster-Nietzsche's own. Another set of thinkers kept more to themselves, but they all loosely overlapped and coalesced around theater directors Hippolyt von Vignau and, after 1908, Carl Norris von Schirach, a former, half-American, career officer who did not have a clue about theater direction but happened to like music. They were also imbued with the spirit of cultural pessimism that had been cultivated in the writings of Julius Langbehn and Paul de Lagarde and, of course, Nietzsche and, farther-fetched, Schopenhauer. The pessimistic view implied that Germany would be doomed without the national resurgence that many now saw evolving, and a complementary cultural renaissance. Most fancied themselves as agents of this renaissance, and they had deliberately chosen Weimar as its locus (and symbolically arranged their own domicile therein), as superficial connections could be forged to a tradition that harked back to a Goethe, Herder, or Schiller. To the extent that the classical seers had been part of a genuine spiritual enlightenment entailing values anathema to early twentieth-century conservatism, those aspects were simply ignored by these chauvinistic minds that so easily connected Goethe with Bismarck.

A thinker in this mold was Johannes Schlaf, who today is less well remembered than Bartels or Förster-Nietzsche. He was born in 1862 in nearby Querfurt, then betook himself to the University of Halle, where, like Lienhard, he broke off his studies to continue life in Berlin. Mentally unstable and sometimes in asylums (which would later cause him to compose abstruse astronomical treatises), he moved in bohemian circles. Together with Arno Holz he developed Naturalism in literature, in which area Gerhart Hauptmann, who was five months younger, soon overtook him. This may have contributed to Schlaf's rejection of that literary style in 1895. Besides prose he wrote poetry; at least one of his poems was set to music by Schoenberg.[106]

Initially under the influence of Nietzsche and later Haeckel, Schlaf adopted a scheme of biological inequalities, within which human generations could redeem themselves only through eugenic self-selection. As with Wachler and Bartels, the Nordic man was for him the ideal genotype, whose masculine manifestation he depicted as tall, blond, broad-shouldered, and square-jawed, instilled with superior intelligence and an iron will. The Nordic's seed would be superior to all others, and he would somnambulantly choose the right female partner to propagate his race. Schlaf's fictional women, too, were sexually attractive and seductive; they had the freedom to choose their mating partners. If necessary, this should be against all social conventions such as marriage. The women's ultimate instinct was to become mothers of the present-day, quasi-Nordic heroes. Woman could show true love and respect only to the man who was able to impose his indomitable will upon her, especially sexually – nothing could ring more Nietzschean! Such eugenic notions which, not least, were directed against modern female emancipationists such as Helene Lange, Schlaf shared with Bartels. But he did not necessarily place the Jews at the bottom of his racial hierarchy, although there are demeaning sketches of them in his novels, as in *Der Kleine*.[107] It is clear that Schlaf obtained his stereotypical views of Jews in Berlin, but whence his often intriguing depictions of the female body and psyche derived remains unclear, as no sexual liaisons of his are known and he remained unmarried, living with his sister in Weimar, after he had moved there in 1904. From 1910, he resided on Lassenstrasse, with the Nietzsche villa, where he sometimes visited, almost in his view.[108]

Schlaf was a staunch conservative, whose adoration of Wilhelm II and the Hohenzollerns was unflappable. In the same way as for Bartels and company, provincial Weimar, apart from the classical tradition, was for him the healing antidote to the intellectual urbanity and attendant perversions of the capital, which destroyed natural organisms. Social democracy was prone to grant inferior phenotypes undeserved privileges, and must be vehemently fought.[109] He welcomed World War I as a potential cleansing agent which would eventually ensure that German culture and German customs would colonize the rest of Europe, including the decadent French and skinflint English.[110]

One of Schlaf's writer acqaintances was Wilhelm von Scholz, who was born in 1874 in Berlin, to a father who served as Bismarck's last minister of finance. Scholz, with a doctorate in literature from Munich, had been a career officer in the 1890s and became an arch-conservative. In the early 1900s, he lived for several years in Weimar, befriending yet another conservative thinker there, Paul Ernst, who was also a friend of Schlaf's. Scholz, like Ernst, called himself a "neoclassicist." Of nobility and with impeccable manners, he was often at Förster-Nietzsche's place; whether he frequented the *Jungbrunnen* that she was known to patronize and there was in touch with Bartels, Wachler, and possibly Schlaf can only be surmised, but the possibility exists. In any event, like Schlaf, Bartels and the rest of this motley group von Scholz was sufficiently right-wing to allow himself to drift into the Nazi camp.[111]

During that time in the 1930s and '40s, Scholz wrote homilies for the Third Reich, composed verses in praise of Hitler, and published anti-Semitic commentaries. It is tempting to trace those commentaries to his time in Weimar, when a drama of his was premiered in Dresden in 1905 entitled *The Jew of Constance*. At least one scholar has held that today one cannot view von Scholz through the lens of Auschwitz, and indeed, the drama comes across as just short of philosemitic. It is about a Jew from Constance named Nasson who, after conversion to Christianity, is caught up in a pogrom during the fourteenth century, and although he could have saved himself by confirming his newfound Christianity, he decides to stand by his former compatriots and his original Judaic faith and, as a result, is burnt at the stake. As author, Scholz ostensibly commiserates with this man whose medical skills are formidable and generously offered. Nonetheless, the coda of the piece means to confirm that no matter how many times a Jew may be baptized, he will always remain a Jew. This judgment foretold to an almost exact degree how the National Socialists began to solve their "Jewish Question": by the Nuremberg Laws of September

1935 Jews were defined by bloodline (as Bartels would have had it) and not by faith. It was the racial element that was still missing from Scholz's narrative for it to qualify as a product of modern anti-Semitism.[112]

In contrast to Schlaf, who periodically was dependent on a foundation's charity, von Scholz was a wealthy citizen of Weimar, for his family owned a castle on Lake Constance.[113] Yet a third member of this conservative clique, Ernst von Wildenbruch, also had money – enough, at least, to live alternately in Berlin and Weimar, where he had his prominent villa in the fashionable Am Horn district, pretentiously named Ithaka. By now he was spending more and more time in the Goethe town, more than he had before the turn of the century. His chauvinism was expanding; in the late style of his distant cousin Grand Duke Carl Alexander, he became an inveterate foe of England, whereas he seems to have tolerated France, as whose adversary his grandfather had fallen in the field. The ultimate reason for such sentiments is difficult to determine, for, apart from Prince Louis Ferdinand, it was France that was generally alleged to be the root of the evils of modernity Wildenbruch now fought against: republican parliamentarism, societal egalitarianism, press freedom and, especially, those devious tendencies in the arts. Wildenbruch's admiration for Bismarck knew no bounds; in the manner of the formulaic "invention of tradition" he easily identified Goethe, as well as Schiller, with that statesman, and he died on January 15, 1909, in Berlin, with the words "Germany . . . Germany . . . Germany" on his lips.[114]

Wildenbruch stood for his convictions regarding Goethe and the fatherland, and he demonstrated this early in Wilhelm Ernst's regime in spring 1902, when he proposed a toast as a constituent member of the Goethe-Gesellschaft during its annual meeting: to an absent grand duke. Wilhelm Ernst happened to be on his honeymoon, and apart from Wildenbruch nobody found anything wrong with that at the time, but when a year later Wilhelm Ernst still did not turn up as patron of the Goethe Society, this sparked Wildenbruch's ire. Undoubtedly conscious of his relationship by blood to the monarch, however distant, and thus entitled to tell him a thing or two, Wildenbruch took the audacious step of publishing a polemical brochure. Wildenbruch's remonstrances against Wilhelm Ernst culminated in the bombastic sentence: "It has to be said to him, and if no one else does it, I shall, that it is the duty of a grand duke of Weimar to make sure that an institution such as the Goethe Day will not wither, will not die, and will not suffocate beneath the indifference of the indifferent masses!" After reading this, the grand duke assured him in a telegram of his concern, promising lasting redress, but soon after he gave

Wildenbruch a humiliating dressing-down in his palace. In the end the poet's action remained a vainglorious and empty posture, even from a patriotic point of view.[115]

On the whole, those last years in Weimar did not turn out very happy ones for Wildenbruch; his mediocre works were not considered at meetings of the Goethe Society as he had implied they should, and although Bartels, Wachler, Lienhard, and Intendant von Vignau embraced them and some were performed on stage, few other Germans took notice.[116]

Wilhelm von Scholz and Ernst von Wildenbruch's plays in the early 1900s featured as ingredients of an essentially mediocre repertoire on the Weimar stage; Lienhard's kept them appropriate company.[117] By the turn of the nineteenth century Weimar's main stage was no longer the pace-setting theater it had once been, under a Goethe or a Dingelstedt. Altogether, there were now some thousand theaters in the various principalities of the Reich, among which the stages attached to a court were by far the most conservative. Even in this group, Weimar came last as far as the premieres of new plays were concerned, whereas the court theater of Mannheim – where Schiller had once made his debut – was in the forefront.[118] Safest for Weimar were classical plays, and naturally those by Goethe and Schiller; also performed were Henrik Ibsen's *Wild Duck* and some works by Hauptmann, even though that socially engaged playwright was disdained as a socialist. Frank Wedekind and August Strindberg were virtually excluded as much too avant-garde.[119] Even Scholz, who made the verdant Weimar his domicile of choice for several years, admitted later that when *Faust* was given, its quality did not exceed "a provincial average," and that none of Weimar's stagings amounted to more than "common mediocrity."[120] The crux was of course that Bartels's influence was substantial: it showed not only in the relative popularity of his hero Hebbel's works, but also in the interconnection, ideological and stage-technical, with directors Vignau and Schirach. Bartels's predilections had an influence on Weimar's stage, and that stage delivered the platform as well as the human resources for Bartels's Nationalfestspiele.[121] Thus the works of playwrights regarded as "Jewish" such as Arthur Schnitzler and Hugo von Hofmannsthal in Weimar hardly had a chance. Hofmannsthal, whom Count Kessler only a few years before had tried to lure to Weimar as Intendant!

In opera and concert, matters were only slightly better. Weimar had a Liszt and Wagner tradition to preserve, and although few musicians and singers excelled – among them Richard Strauss's discoveries Marie Schoder and Heinrich Zeller – conventional repertories were executed reliably. Since Strauss, too, now belonged to the Weimar pantheon, his most modern creations *Salome, Elektra,* and *Der Rosenkavalier* could be experienced on stage, but given the reactionary local clientele, reportedly to few audiences' delight.[122] For the undiscerning there was Waldemar von Baussnern's opera *Dürer in Venedig,* with a libretto by Bartels.[123] Once again, as in the past, Weimar possessed capable, but not outstanding musical directors, the most notable of whom, after 1907, was Peter Raabe, a Liszt acolyte, who was friendly with von Schirach and the anti-Semitic Hans Pfitzner, whose opera *Rose vom Liebesgarten* Raabe introduced.[124] Significantly, like so many other Weimar culture brokers, after he had left the town in 1920 Raabe turned pro-Nazi and in 1935, kowtowing to Hitler and Joseph Goebbels, was rewarded with the presidency of the Reich Music Chamber, from which post Strauss had just been dismissed. In this capacity, Raabe discriminated against many Jewish musicians.[125]

Among the more unremarkable compositions Raabe performed in the Goethe town were the operas of Richard Wagner's son Siegfried. Neither did he forget the work of the conservatory director von Baussnern, who delighted in entertaining his friends and colleagues at home at his piano, hammering out and singing his own compositions until his voice was hoarse.[126] During the opening ceremonies for the newly built theater on January 11, 1908, Raabe conducted a "Spring Fairytale Play," with lyrics by Carl Alexander's old Wartburg librarian and current Hohenzollern disciple Richard Voss, set to music by the ambitious but unexceptional Felix von Weingartner. It received a sound thrashing by educated critics, among them Kessler's old friend Ludwig von Hofmann, who complained to Gerhart Hauptmann about it.[127]

From 1901 to 1918, the nationalist-to-radical-racist attitudes of a Kessler, Förster-Nietzsche, Bartels, or Wildenbruch were not isolated phenomena. This spectrum, applying specifically to Weimar, was but a reflection of broad-based sentiments in German society, as expressed in politics and the arts, popular culture (military bands in public parks and sentimental glee clubs in the pubs) and, not least, in scholarship.[128] What causes surprise is that it predominated in a town acknowledged universally as the cradle of the Enlightenment in Germany, one which remained progressive by degrees, into the last decades under Grand Duke Carl Alexander.

Well before 1900 Weimarers, like most other Germans, shared the imperial regime's fear of being denied a place in the sun, of being encircled, by England on the high seas which had to be navigated to protect commerce and colonies, and on land by France, which was – rightly – suspected of harboring plans for revenge for the 1871 loss of Alsace and Lorraine, and by Russia. Just before and during the early phases of World War I members of the German artistic and scholarly elite joined jingoists in declarations supporting the invasion of Belgium and the Kaiser's army, soon fighting on two fronts, with the argument that it was *Deutsche Kultur* that had to be defended. They rejected the enemies' attempt at differentiating between culture, representing positive German forces, and militarization, representing negative ones, maintaining that a strong military was needed to uphold German culture, which could one day permeate all polities and save the world. In this view a monarchic, autocratic order was vastly preferable to a democratic one. Among those artists were former Secessionists like Liebermann and Corinth, among the scholars were historians such as Erich Marcks and Friedrich Meinecke, as well as Germanist Gustav Roethe, a prominent member of the Goethe-Gesellschaft. From Weimar's University of Jena, the biologist Ernst Haeckel and the philosopher Rudolf Eucken joined in.[129] Writers and men of the stage included Gerhart Hauptmann, Thomas Mann, and Max Reinhardt.[130] Every so often, in these people's arguments, Goethe was appealed to as a patron saint. The artificially constructed legacy linking Goethe to Frederick the Great on the one hand and Bismarck (or marshals Hindenburg and Ludendorff) on the other, was invoked, time and again.[131] It was highly symbolic that, come August 1914, a miniature edition of *Faust*, that book of the archetypal, struggling, German hero, was tucked into every German soldier's backpack.[132]

Weimar's Duchy and Closure

Between 1900 and 1918 the population of both the Saxon-Weimar grand duchy and the town of Weimar as its capital grew, as it did everywhere else in the German Reich. The reasons for this are known. Industrialization created, among other improvements, better hygienic and nutritional conditions under which people lived longer. There were attendant advances in medicine; rationalization in factories, shops, and commerce; in addition, social and health insurance and pensions initiated by Bismarck in the previous century gradually broadened and improved. Moreover, emigration had stopped, with Germany now drawing in new laborers from abroad, for instance from Poland to the industrialized Ruhr Valley.[133] The grand duchy's own population grew from 120,435 in 1880 to 214,053 in 1910, Weimar's from 28,489 in 1900 to 31,848 in 1907 and 34,582 in 1910. As industrialization took hold and attracted what Karl Marx had defined as a worker proletariat, neighboring Jena with its Zeiss factories became somewhat larger than the capital. More closely tied to Weimar were the textile-producing outlier Apolda with 22,610 and the hinterland mining village of Ilmenau with 12,202 people (1910). To place that in perspective, Ilmenau had multiplied by a factor of six and now had twice as many inhabitants as Weimar had had by the turn of the previous century, when Goethe had tried to salvage its mining operations.[134]

Weimar society itself remained as divided as ever. Lines of fragmentation created several patterns, partially overlaid and interlocked. There was a social division between a tiny segment of aristocrats and courtiers, a small section of an educated upper bourgeoisie (including various artists), a larger group of lower-middle-class merchants and craftsmen (a few now aided by van de Velde's initiatives), joined slowly by what in the future republic would be a large army of clerical, white-collar, workers usually raising themselves up from the lower class. At the bottom was a larger, ever-growing mass of manual laborers, servants, and small plot holders on the edges of town. A second set of divisions existed across an employment-status matrix: a larger-than-average group of pensioners, including widows, more properly referred to as rentiers if they were wealthy, stood out from similar groupings in the rest of the Reich, even if their absolute numbers in Weimar in 1907 amounted only to 1,700 (out of 31,848).[135] This, thirdly, helped skew Weimar's population in terms of age: inhabitants tended to be either very old or very young, relatively speaking, with a middle-aged core somewhat attenuated. That suggests a fourth layer, determined by gender: just as before, young men tended to leave a town where industry, the professions, and commerce were not strongly developed and opportunities for occupational advancement, even at the ducal court, were limited. The most derogatory thing one could say about Weimar at that time was that it was a place filled with pensioners and old maids.[136] Finally, there was a fifth pattern, one defined by education, mentality, and taste. The tiny group of artists, writers, and ideologues, among whom there was no distinction to be made as to left and right wing, simply did not fit in either with the majority of the ordinary burghers or with the lofty members of the court. This suggested a virtually tripartite society of, so to speak, typical Weimar geniuses (example: Henry van de Velde), of blasé, conventionally groomed courtiers (example: Baron Hermann von Egloffstein), and of ordinary folk (example: the unnamed carriage drivers who were hit in the face by Duke Wilhelm Ernst's whip because they would not move out of the way fast enough to avoid his landau). Were those carriage drivers the people who damaged modern paintings Count Kessler had exhibited during his Künstlerbund showing of July 1906, or was it an Egloffstein?[137]

The poorest of the poor in Weimar were certainly poorer than the rest of low-wage earners in Germany, as the examples of female public-school teachers but also of unskilled Ilmenau miners show. By about 1910 Weimar-area miners were earning approximately three-quarters of the wage then offered elsewhere in that line of work.[138] Still, the evident growth of a lower class does not necessarily suggest a strong Social Democratic presence in Weimar in the years before World War I. Although signs can be found for it especially among its youth, it is not clear to what extent this growth was due merely to accidental factors, such as occasional or even targeted visits of workers to Weimar from the neighboring, decidedly more proletarian towns of Jena or Gera.[139] But it is interesting to note that in 1911–12 the left-wing socialists Rosa Luxemburg and Clara Zetkin spoke publicly in Weimar, and so did Luxemburg's partner Karl Liebknecht. Significantly Zetkin, more radical perhaps than her two compatriots, did not fare well.[140]

Having no reason to be scared by occasional forced extreme left-wing influences in Weimar's population, the grand duke of Saxe-Weimar surrendered his sovereignty under pressure not before November 1918, along with the other German ruling princes. Before that, there had been issues, some of which had been caused by the stirrups of the war, during which the duchy was to lose 4,694 lives.[141] From Weimar alone, which surrendered 4,000 men to the military, 1,341 persons died at the front, among them three women.[142] Since 1914, as in other towns and cities of central Europe, for example Berlin and Vienna, there had been shortages of foodstuffs and vital resources for the population, causing malnutrition and diseases, which administrative measures could do little to rectify.[143] In Weimar, rationing of food and fuel began in March 1915. Schools were converted to infirmaries and four church bells from St. Peter and Paul's were melted down. Some stores had to close.[144] Hence dissatisfaction within the population grew. It fed on long-standing unhappiness over the political regime, which suffered from an antiquated electoral system favoring conservative parties supported by the high, mighty, and rich. In 1907–9 the electoral district of Weimar-Apolda was represented in the Berlin Reichstag by an anti-Semite, although earlier and toward the end of the war August Baudert, a master weaver and Majority Socialist (not of Zetkin's extreme-leftist persuasion) sat in the Reichstag as well as the duchy's own Landtag. Apart from the inequitable constitution, administrative and tax reform was called for.[145] In these respects, the grand duchy of Weimar merely mirrored conditions – and demands – in other member principalities of the Second Reich.

What may have made the duchy stand out was the decidedly unenlightened disposition of its monarch, who after 1901 became incrementally unpopular with his subjects, especially after his first wife Caroline died at age twenty of pneumonia in January 1905: rumor had it that the sweet-tempered, unhappily married grand duchess had deliberately contracted the disease in a rainstorm.[146] Wilhelm Ernst, son of a well-intentioned but sickly father Carl August, and grandson of the well-remembered legendary Carl Alexander, was narrow in his interests, basic in his needs, and prone to surrender too often to wild rages. He quite obviously despised his subjects, whom he liked to call "rabble" and "bastards," and would have been sued in court for hitting a seven-year-old boy with his whip in the street but for a last-minute, financial, out-of-court settlement.[147] By early November 1918 there was unrest in the military contingents stationed in the Weimar barracks. Apparently much of this was caused by genuine leftist elements, especially after envoys of rebelling sailors had been sent down from Kiel, where the revolution started. The commanding colonel tried to keep order, and Baudert as well as Minister of State Rothe between them attempted to contain the political situation, balancing a potential brewing rebellion in the army against monarchic recalcitrance. On November 8 commotion occurred because of the presence of Jena Zeiss workers inducted into the army, now stationed locally in Weimar. Although the populace was still calm, one feared it was incitable. This all of the leaders except for the extremists, not least the grand duke himself, wanted to prevent. Later that day a soldiers' council had been formally constituted, and Wilhelm Ernst, with his family, fled the palace to seek refuge in the house of his lawyer. As the republic had already been proclaimed in Berlin, masses of people were streaming through the streets of Weimar in the expectancy of, perhaps radical, change. Baudert spoke publicly the following day, hailing the republic. But what to do with the grand duke, given the potentially explosive radicalized military which was being backed by comrades in Berlin and Kiel?[148]

On November 9 the Kaiser abdicated in Berlin and Majority Social Democrats proclaimed the republic. Baudert on that day stood at the helm of a group of moderate Majority Socialists who were trying to keep in check the more radical soldiers' council whom their once commanding colonel could no longer control. Minister Rothe and Wilhelm Ernst constitutionally still represented the old regime. Later that day Baudert went to see the grand duke and secured his agreement to abdicate. Henceforth he would live, with his family, on his estates in Silesia.[149] A new government for the Saxon-Weimar dukedom had not yet been found, its place in the new political German order not yet defined. Little did anyone know that while the era of the Weimar duchy had ended, the era of the Weimar republic was about to begin. It would last for less than fourteen years. Yet its aura would last much longer.

As one looked back in November 1918, at the end of monarchic rule throughout Germany, one could make out several themes for the duchy. Carl Alexander had passed on his political conservatism to his grandson, Wilhelm Ernst, who did not, however, share his fundamental interest in the arts over the long term. At the same time, the young grand duke's inertia in economic matters completely matched the official attitudes of the preceding regime. It was bad for Weimar that Wilhelm Ernst began his regime in the worst tradition, in which his grandfather had left it early in the twentieth century. A notorious neglect of the arts and letters in practical terms was one of its most negative aspects. The results were dull, homegrown, cultural products, on stage, in the concert halls and museums, despite the heroic efforts of Count Kessler and van de Velde to redress all deficiencies by creating a "New Weimar," profiling the visual arts. After Liszt and others, this was yet another attempt to rejuvenate a Weimar of Goethean proportions destined to fail, not least because – as in the case of Liszt – personal vanities, but also unfortunate cultural-political choices, prevailed. Moreover, since the ground had already been prepared, dark, chauvinistic conspiracies gained further strength, many in the abused name of Goethe. This meant defeat of the very same modernist trends the count and van de Velde had wanted to encourage. As Weimar became a hunting-ground for anti-urbanists, eugenicists, befuddled German-history memorialists all buttressed by anti-Semitism of various shades, and with Kessler and his friend well-nigh disabled, it lost the last vestiges of intellectual and artistic progressivism which had once developed in Goethe's orbit. Particularly viral now was anti-Semitism. In an age of Positivism, as it acquired a scientific tinge through misinterpretation of Darwin and Haeckel, a platform was created for the National Socialists, whose German chauvinism was cemented with anti-Jewish beliefs, scientifically said to be unshakable. In that sense, the likes of Wachler, Schlaf, and Wildenbruch served as pre-fascist pioneers. This group was not so secretly spearheaded by Elisabeth Förster-Nietzsche who, ironically, turned out to be the nemesis of her deceased brother, in that she came to personify some of the worst prophecies he had uttered during his lifetime. Along with Bartels, because she was highly visible, she was, locally, the most dangerous facilitator of German fascism, tarnishing Weimar's name to an extent that seemed to preclude any resurrection.

CHAPTER 5

The Weimar Bauhaus Experiment
1919 to 1925

ONE DAY, IN THE EARLY 1920S, GUSTAV MAHLER'S WIDOW ALMA traveled from Vienna to Weimar, to visit her former husband Walter Gropius, who was then heading the newly founded Bauhaus. Alma Mahler was usually helpful while in Weimar, assisting her second husband as best she could, even though she was already living with the poet Franz Werfel in Vienna, and divorce from Gropius had occurred. She also mingled with Bauhaus students, not all of whom liked her assertive manner, and spent time with some of Gropius's colleagues. One of those was Lothar Schreyer, who was boarding at a modest *Pension* in a house on the edge of the Goethe Park, in the old Marstall princely stables, once the home of Goethe's friend, Charlotte von Stein. One of Schreyer's fellow-boarders was a nineteen-year-old girl, demure but affable and a bit pudgy, who was studying the violin. Her moderately well off family had sent her there from Berlin; by her own admission the young girl just adored Goethe. When she heard, at the communal dinner table, that Alma Mahler was about to visit, she asked Frau Schreyer for an introduction to that legendary woman. The next day, Frau Mahler arrived, regal, commanding, spell-binding. She was at the height of her womanly beauty, and no one could escape her charm. As she was leaving the Baroness Stein's historic house, she encountered the young girl in the hall, violin in hand. When Frau Schreyer introduced her, the young woman curtsied, her large eyes fixed on the lady. She was clutching her violin, as if to make a statement as a musician; her dress was simple but of an artfully suggestive cut. The girl kissed the lady's hand, but did not say a word. As the girl blushed, Alma Mahler said to Lothar Schreyer: "What eyes this child has! What eyes!"[1]

The girl was Marlene Dietrich. She was studying at the conservatory, but her private violin teacher was the thirty-six-year-old Professor Robert Reitz of the state orchestra, the father of two small children. He was Swiss and very handsome, and Marlene was carrying on an affair with him. It was a hopeless situation, for Reitz would not divorce his wife. He was "still young," Marlene entrusted to her diary, and yet: "I wish somebody would come and cover much grief with all his love and lift that torture from my heart." Soon Marlene returned to Berlin to begin a new career, in cabarets and acting. She did not play much violin any more, but always had a singing saw nearby, one with which she consoled Kurt Weill in New York in 1942–43, after she had rejected his offer of the lead role in his new Broadway play *One Touch of Venus*, because she wanted film rights for it that he was unwilling to cede. At that time, Alma Mahler-Gropius-Werfel was leading the precarious existence of a refugee from Nazism on the California coast.[2]

Marlene Dietrich's presence in Weimar in the early 1920s is emblematic of the unmitigated attractiveness of the classics town, even in the turbulent aftermath of the Great War. Since early 1921, the thirty-five-year-old painter and theater enthusiast Lothar Schreyer had been in Weimar as one of the Masters at the Staatliches Bauhaus Weimar, which the architect Walter Gropius had founded in April 1919. Gropius, born in 1883, hailed from a well-respected Berlin family of architects and stage technicians and had already made a name for himself before the outbreak of war in 1914, which he had joined, not without enthusiasm, as a lieutenant.

Much of Gropius's early thinking as an architect contained the seeds of what would later blossom in the Bauhaus. Intellectual forefathers had influenced him: William Morris, who upheld the ideal of medieval handicrafts over industrial production by machines; Charles Robert Ashbee, who favored craft collectives. Both were socialists and had impressed Peter Behrens, first an arts-and-crafts teacher in Düsseldorf and later an architectural and design consultant who worked for the huge AEG concern founded by Emil Rathenau. Between 1907 and 1910 Gropius was employed in Behrens's Berlin office, learning from Behrens, occupying himself with architectural building construction and conceiving ideas for industrial mass production. Turbine factories and worker settlements for AEG were routine items on the order books. In 1911 Gropius completed the first significant project of his own: the Fagus shoe-last factory in Alfeld, a steel cage for a building without supporting walls, the empty spaces covered by glass panes. Meanwhile, the Deutscher Werkbund had been founded in 1907 by Behrens's teacher Hermann Muthesius, and both Behrens and Gropius were members. It advocated the harmonious combination of artistic design, craft production, and machine duplication.

In 1915, while Gropius was at the front, the arts-and-crafts school in Weimar found itself leaderless because Henry van de Velde had been let go, and the art academy had personnel and directional problems. Gropius was well enough known at that time for van de Velde to recommend him as his successor, and Fritz Mackensen and his staff eventually came around to the possibility of choosing Gropius as their new director. Gropius himself pursued these matters with letters to the ducal government and in person, and in early 1919 he stood a fair chance of being appointed head of the two Weimar institutions combined. The appointment materialized in April, when the schools merged, and Gropius insisted that the new institute officially be called State Bauhaus: Staatliches Bauhaus Weimar.

After the war Gropius had returned to Berlin, only to find his former employment ended, Behrens's office having had to busy itself with designs for war production. The originally rather more conservative scion of a well-established family now openly sympathized with leftist ideas, was a member of the postwar Novembergruppe founded by left-wing artists in Berlin and played a leading part in its offspring, the Soviet-council style Arbeitsrat für Kunst. Stylistically, Expressionism was very much in vogue although about to reach its peak; it had replaced Impressionism around 1910, with a few artists managing the transition smoothly; one who did was Christian Rohlfs, formerly of Weimar. The center of Expressionism in Berlin was the Sturm-Kreis headed by Herwarth Walden; it amalgamated currents from the leading art movements in Europe at the time: Italian Futurism, French Cubism, and Russian Constructivism. Walden published a magazine, *Der Sturm*, and organized exhibitions. Gropius was associated with this circle, as were leading architects, sculptors, and painters of his day, such as Otto Bartning, Rohlfs, Paul Klee, Oskar Kokoschka, Lyonel Feininger, and Lothar Schreyer, who was the journal's editor.[3]

What were Gropius's objectives? As he put it in 1919 in a famous manifesto, artists and craftsmen were to come together to construct *Der Bau*, the building of the future. This was exactly the purpose of organizing an arts-and-crafts school and an art academy under one roof.[4] In this, Gropius was motivated by a social animus: he wanted to tear down the walls that traditionally kept artisans and visual artists apart. *Der Bau* was as much a metaphor, signifying the harmonious marriage of creative ideas, as it was a physical construct, a model for rational, livable, everyday buildings of the future. Lyonel Feininger, the first Master teacher Gropius hired in May 1919, depicted it as the "Cathedral of the Future" in an Expressionist woodcut that became the symbol of the new Bauhaus.[5] Gropius wanted students, young men and women, to be taught the ideals of harmony, which they would then carry into society, by Masters of Form and Masters of Craft, the former being artists and architects and the latter craftsmen, with both categories at the same level of accomplishment, recognition, and remuneration.[6] In all this, Peter Gay has written, Gropius was "a good modernist," who wished to join "the social critics who for a century and more had been dismayed by the 'fragmentation' of German culture" (as in Wilhelmian versus New Weimar artists).[7] Gropius's concentration on crafts was in deference to the craftsmen of Weimar who would immediately benefit, and of course to van de Velde who had long championed them. In reality, as he admitted in an interview in 1969, he wanted to go there and much further, by resorting to the techniques of industry, as he had already done in Behrens's Berlin office and with the erection of the Fagus structure.[8]

To the extent that Gropius harked back to the medieval guild system, adopting the traditional title of "Master" for his professors, he was a Romantic. But at the same time, he had already demonstrated his penchant for modernism by favoring industrial mass production, the machine, and rational design. Until 1923, the Romantic side of his character predominated, putting its stamp on the Bauhaus, and this was in keeping with the Expressionist background of the *Sturm* movement and its followers, several of whom soon would join the Bauhaus. Yet another sign of this was Gropius's interest in secret societies, Masonic lodges, and astrology.[9] As far as Weimar and the classics were concerned, Gropius harbored a genuine interest in connecting with, or reviving, where necessary, the hallowed convention of that town, and thus he stood in lineage with Count Kessler and Franz Liszt. In fact, after Goethe, Gropius joined Kessler, Liszt, and Richard Strauss as a member of that very small elitist group of post-Goethean Weimar residents. Goethe himself Gropius admired, but he was suspicious of the commodification that had already set in around the poet's persona, and he mistrusted the invention of that false tradition which placed Goethe in the same pantheon as Wilhelm II, Bismarck, and Frederick the Great, to whom he showed more diffidence.[10]

By April 1, 1923, when the Bauhaus was formally anchored and budgeted for in the newly constituted state of Thuringia, Gropius had appointed most of his teachers.[11] Those included, at first, three of the traditionalist art academy professors who had chosen to be taken over: the painters Max Thedy and Walther Klemm, and the sculptor Richard Engelmann. Later the academic painter Otto Fröhlich joined them. Although Gropius himself was interested mostly in architecture, as teachers for the Bauhaus he preferred painters, because they were the ones who had "worked most systematically, had thought through specific systems, and I wanted to use the influence of these painters on architecture."[12] The first hired, Lyonel Feininger, was born in 1871 in New York of German parentage. He had worked in Weimar and its outskirts for some time, loved the territory, and by 1919 was one of the most famous Expressionist painters in Germany. Gropius knew him from the Berlin Arbeitsrat. He was not actually required to teach formal courses, but had to be available for students when they needed inspiration.[13] Gerhard Marcks and Johannes Itten arrived in October 1919. The thirty-year-old sculptor Marcks was an acquaintance of Gropius from before the war. As a *Sturm* artist, he was also a potter, draftsman, and printmaker. Gropius wanted him to lead a ceramics workshop in Dornburg, some twenty miles east (because no suitable venue could be found in Weimar itself).[14] Itten was born near Berne in 1888. He first trained to be a teacher but then studied painting under Eugène Gilliard in Geneva and Adolf Hölzel in Stuttgart, from whom he learned abstraction. After a one-man show at the *Sturm* gallery in Berlin in 1916 he decamped for Vienna, established a private art school, and frequented the salon of Alma Mahler. It was she who recommended him to Gropius, who immediately recognized Itten's extraordinary pedagogical talent. At the Bauhaus Itten came to teach the *Vorkurs* (Basic Course), a six-month (later twelve-month) preparatory program, in which students were to be readied, not least psychologically, for the form shops and workshops taught by the other Masters. The charismatic Itten brought more than a dozen of his Vienna students with him.[15] In April 1920 the twenty-four-year-old Georg Muche arrived, who had been Walden's assistant at the *Sturm* gallery. As a painter, he became influenced by Cubism and the work of Marc Chagall, also a *Sturm* gallery regular. Muche's output was exhibited alongside that of Expressionists Max Ernst and Paul Klee. Once in Weimar, he was closely associated with Itten.[16]

Five more accomplished artists would join Gropius as colleagues until the summer of 1923. In January 1921 the Bernese Paul Klee accepted a post as Bauhaus Form Master; he was largely an autodidact. Then virtually unknown to the public, insiders knew him as one of the most powerful Expressionists of the period. In 1921 alone, three monographs would be published about him simultaneously, and he had just turned forty.[17] Oskar Schlemmer also moved in around that time. Born near Stuttgart in 1888, he too had studied with Hölzel and, while living in Berlin earlier, befriended fellow artists from *Der Sturm*. In his Expressionist paintings, traces of Cubism and Hölzel's abstractionism are often visible, but Schlemmer was also a sculptor, choreographer, and stage designer. He would first direct the sculpting classes as Form Master, but in 1923 he assumed, in addition, the stage workshop, where theater arts and crafts were taught. This was after its previous director Lothar Schreyer had left. Gropius was full of praise for Schlemmer, as late as the 1960s.[18] Schreyer was as multi-talented as all the Bauhaus teachers. With proven painting, writing, and editing skills, he had arrived in Weimar in early 1921 to build up the theater department. He designed and staged a play, *Mondspiel*, which demonstrated his personal belief system in a cloyingly obtrusive way. Nobody liked it – not even Gropius – which resulted in Schreyer's departure in 1923.[19] Wassily Kandinsky came into the Bauhaus's employ in early 1923. Born in 1866, he had spent years in the Munich area as a co-founder of the *Blaue Reiter* movement and with the *Sturm* artists in Berlin, until World War I broke out. As a Russian national, he had been forced to return to the Tsarist Empire. Having worked briefly for the Bolsheviks after 1917, he left again for Berlin, with his second wife Nina accompanying him. In Berlin, however, he found that all of his paintings stored there had disappeared and what money they had fetched after sales had been devalued in the inflation. In early 1922 Gropius met him there, penniless, and hired him on the spot for Weimar. Kandinsky became a Form Master instructing in the theory of painting.[20] About a year later the Hungarian László Moholy-Nagy was engaged to take over the *Vorkurs* taught by Itten, who had left for Switzerland. Moholy-Nagy, born in 1895, was influenced by Constructivism, after having absorbed Futurist and Cubist influences. His interest lay in photo reproduction and montage, and painting, as well as the stage.[21]

Bauhaus students were free to become artists, but their formal schooling at the institution's studios and shops was in the artisanal crafts. They were expected to take art instruction after choosing teachers of their liking, which could be rather theoretical, in the artists' studios and, complementing this, hands-on training in a craft shop. The former were headed by the artists in their capacity as Form Masters, the latter by traditional master craftsmen who bore the title of Craft Master. "It was necessary to work under two different teachers," explained Gropius later, "since there were neither craftsmen with sufficient imagination to solve artistic problems nor artists with sufficient technical skills to take charge of workshop operations."[22]

After a minimum of three and a half years, including the *Vorkurs* stretch, the students could pass the regular state examinations as masters of a craft. This was conditional on having taken a journeyman exam earlier. Certified masters could go out into the industrial and commercial world; the most gifted ones, however, might be invited to join the Bauhaus faculty. This happened to the Jewish-Hungarian carpenter Marcel Breuer, who even as a journeyman, as he was helping other Masters teach, designed a prototype of what later became world famous as the clean-lined Breuer Chair – a pain to sit in but a joy to look at. By the time the Bauhaus left Weimar for the town of Dessau in the spring of 1925, there were pottery, metal, furniture, weaving, gold- and silver-smith workshops, to name only a few.[23]

More than 90 percent of the 172 students registered during the summer semester of 1919 hailed from the art academy, since word about the Bauhaus had not yet spread through all of Germany, despite Gropius's best publicity efforts.[24] During the summer, they only met Feininger and the Old School academy holdovers. Gropius himself was too busy to teach. When more students arrived from outside of Weimar, one could discern how socially dislocated they were because of the war and its consequences, most of the young men just having returned from the front. They wore field-gray uniforms which female students were eager enough to die a neutral color, as they toiled in the weaving shops and with fabrics. This being the republic, the percentage of girl students was larger than it had been in the art academy and under van de Velde, as the trend was toward the opening of higher education to women, and the Bauhaus was preceded by a reputation of progressiveness. Several students were Jewish, and several came from other countries, especially Hungary and Austria, where Itten had already left his mark. Most of them were eager, talented, and full of confidence for the future. "I think they are after something new, a new way of expressing themselves in art," remarked Feininger early on.[25] Slackers were quickly expelled, for Gropius had a sharp eye for them and it was difficult to make it through Itten's Basic Course. A few were war wounded; most were materially in dire straits, hungry, cold in winter, and ill housed, so that Gropius tried to lighten their tuition and arranged for them to sell shop products to help them subsist on the proceeds.[26]

The students, mostly an enthusiastic and gregarious lot, participated in extracurricular events, such as poetry readings – for example by visiting-writers like Else Lasker-Schüler – and regularly scheduled Bauhaus parties. At the Christmas party Gropius himself served the food. Bauhaus dances were important, and there was an idiosyncratic Bauhaus dance style resembling a hop. "Hirschfeld played his 'squeak box,' with Andor at the piano, and Schmittchen played the only piece he knew on his violin. And we improvised our Bauhaus dance," reminisced Paul Klee's son Felix. Preparing for these festivities was an essential part of the training, and the communal celebrations served one of Gropius's original aims: tearing down class barriers. For everyone connected with the Bauhaus, regardless of its inherent hierarchy, participated. Hence as a didactic function, these activities were key. On the dance floor as in studios and shops, the Bauhaus provided "a secure place for its masters and students, where the realization of their fantasies was nurtured and inspired by interdisciplinary exchanges," the psychoanalyst and historian Peter Loewenberg put it in Freudian terms. "The institution of the *Bauhaus* protected creative fantasy from immediate repression through inner inhibition and suppression by outer criticism. The intense group process of creative interaction in the *Bauhaus* was one of personal and functional interpenetration. Boundaries between individuals, between masters and students, were partially dissolved in significant ways, in an ongoing group process of regressive fusion and creativity."[27]

Today one wonders how work and play could have occurred against the backdrop of severe economic trauma throughout the republic. Even though a fixed budget was granted to the Bauhaus by dint of legislation in the Thuringian Landtag, it was barely a minimum and the postwar inflation, setting in around 1920 and reaching its peak by late fall 1923, made running the institution increasingly difficult. Training students in shops cost money, not least for materials, and the Masters had to be paid. Although Gropius wanted his students to sell products for their upkeep, he needed a share of those proceeds for the Bauhaus. He would have preferred compensation for them of gifts in kind. As the proceeds from Bauhaus products lagged, he tried to secure as much clothing, bedding, and free meal tickets for the students as possible. Bauhaus localities lacked coal for the winter and, unsurprisingly, visiting artists like Lasker-Schüler did not prove to be great magnets to the Weimar burghers who were supposed to pay admission in order to hear her talk. Consequently, faculty suffered along with the student body. In December 1921 Gerhard Marcks was afflicted with kidney inflammation because his Dornburg shop was freezing over. And on April 10, 1922, all Masters complained to Thuringian Finance Minister Emil Hartmann that their salaries were so low as to force them into debt. They demanded redress, backdated to the period from October 1, 1921.[28]

From its beginnings, the Bauhaus was never institutionally secure because of its uneasy dependence on a benevolent majority in the Thuringian parliament, which controlled its charter and budget. Founded in 1919, the interim period between revolution in 1918 and the establishment of a regular Thuringian government after elections in summer 1920, the school got its start under the aegis of transitory, left-leaning politicians, who appreciated Gropius's own socialist bent. Gropius was fortunate to have been appointed state commissar after the summer elections, which had produced a more stable and more permanent majority of left-of-center politicians, so that he was able to defend his program and his budget, whenever necessary, in the state assembly. Even then, the parties of the right, backed by the great majority of Weimar's citizenry, were notoriously against him. This situation did not change significantly when in September 1921 a new government was elected, supported by Social Democrats (SPD) and the liberal German Democrats (DDP), and tolerated by the Communists (USPD and KPD), the USPD having been an integral part of the ruling 1920 coalition. As before, the right-wing parties, led by the German Nationalists (DNVP), continued their anti-Bauhaus tirades relentlessly, their parliamentary leader being Dr. Emil Herfurth, a Weimar Gymnasium teacher. He was, without a doubt, Gropius's greatest Weimar foe during the entire Bauhaus years. Herfurth's fanatical supporter was Mathilde Baroness von Freytag-Loringhoven, the local newspaper critic and, as a student of Max Thedy, a painter of flowers and landscapes, who now served on Weimar's municipal council.[29]

For all his administrative and political duties, Gropius had less time than he should have expended to help shape the new type of artist-craftsman of his original Bauhaus vision. To be sure, his relative inactivity as a teacher was understood by his colleagues and sympathizers. Despite differences of opinion and temperament, his charisma and potential for genius captivated all of them. "Where would we be without the dynamic energy of the man?" asked Feininger of his wife at the beginning of August, 1923. "He is working through the nights until early morning, hardly ever getting enough sleep, yet he never complains or becomes embittered. If he looks at you kindly, his eyes shine as no one else's ever do." Whereas an architecture department at the Weimar Bauhaus never materialized, as proprietor of his own architectural bureau Gropius did build a house in Berlin, for which he employed Bauhaus students. And he took over the furniture shop after disagreements with Johannes Itten in 1922, as the new Master of Form.[30]

Two momentous but interrelated events occurred in 1923, which constituted a caesura in the development of the Weimar Bauhaus. The first was Itten's replacement by Moholy-Nagy as head teacher of the Basic Course. The second was a six-week exhibition of Bauhaus creations, bolstered by similarly inspired foreign imports, the core of an intermittent audit, in August and September. From an aesthetic and moral vantage point, the audit turned into a triumph, whereas the changeover of the *Vorkurs* Masters a couple of months earlier had left a few people with misgivings.

The Romantic Itten had stood for Expressionist art, as *l'art pour l'art*, paying little heed to functionality. The union between art and the crafts, which had been mandated by Gropius and which he had already, in his mind, extended to one between art and industry, was not Itten's concern. Itten's purist view increasingly met with criticism by several of his colleagues, chief among them Gropius himself, and some artistic and government voices outside. Government was keen on the commercial utilization of Bauhaus designs because that would bring in much-needed funds and extend the Bauhaus's *raison d'être*, especially in the face of unabated right-wing opposition. As far as Gropius was concerned, he finally wanted his rational *Bau* ideal fully realized. No sooner had Itten moved back to Switzerland in April 1923 than Gropius chose Moholy-Nagy as his successor, who arrived from Berlin, speaking only broken German.[31] Next to Gropius, he now became the most important faculty member of the Bauhaus.

Moholy-Nagy's Constructivist background suited Gropius because he could use it to give rise to a new, sharply defined, goal for the Bauhaus: (mass) industrial production inspired by the aesthetics of art, logic, and sobriety of style.[32] This was not really a paradigm change, for he was merely emphasizing the rational side of his artist's persona, at the expense of the Romantic. To be sure, it had been the latter that had drawn him to Itten initially. Now he was reinforced in his attitude by the new generation of Bauhaus-trained journeymen like Breuer and Josef Albers, rather than the older Masters such as Schlemmer, Kandinsky, and Feininger, who nominally might acquiesce in his new approach but, true to their original artistic selves, continued to adhere to well-worn painterly practices, without a hint of commerce.[33]

Starting in 1922, Masters and students toiled to get the Bauhaus exhibition ready, which was to last from August 15 to the final day of September, 1923. What transpired during those six weeks in retrospect must be judged the most important cultural event in Weimar since the death of Goethe and never equaled again in the twentieth or twenty-first century. Seldom had the town seen such a collection of geniuses all at once! It seemed like its decades-old quest fulfilled. If only those moments had lasted! There were lectures, concerts, theater and film presentations, and the exhibition of artifacts and a model single-family house. In an opening lecture on August 15 Gropius announced the new program of a union between art and technology under an eponymous heading: *Kunst und Technik – eine neue Einheit.* Kandinsky, author of a few books, followed this up with a talk on "synthetic art." Employing the Stuttgart dancers Albert Burger and Elsa Hötsel, Schlemmer introduced his Cubist-influenced *Triadic Ballet*, at the Weimar theater. There was much music: the young composer Hans Heinz

Stuckenschmidt, later to become the preeminent music critic of the republic, participated in a "Mechanical Cabaret," for which he had composed an avant-garde music score inspired by the Dada movement.[34] Gropius succeeded in inviting the elite of modernist composers in Europe, Ernst Krenek, Igor Stravinsky, Ferruccio Busoni, and Paul Hindemith, to perform their latest compositions; pioneer Hermann Scherchen conducted. Hindemith premiered his *Marienlieder*, Stravinsky had his *L'Histoire d'un soldat* performed and was very surprised that the previously skeptical Busoni liked it; the two men parted as friends.[35] Works of every Bauhaus Master as well as of students were exhibited in the Weimar Landesmuseum. Thirty architects congregated in Weimar in August, from Germany, the United States, France, and smaller countries, among them Erich Mendelsohn, Frank Lloyd Wright, and Le Corbusier. Altogether 1,500 visitors made the trip, many from abroad. By and large, the happenings met with a positive German press; predictably, nationalist papers condemned them.[36] The exhibition was a portent of the *Neue Sachlichkeit*, the New Objectivity, which spelled doom for Romanticism and Expressionism, and which was then beginning to show itself in the music of Hindemith and Stuckenschmidt and in other German art forms as well, such as cinema, where Fritz Lang's 1927 masterpiece *Metropolis* symbolized the triumph of a new technology.[37] By that time, the Bauhaus was a central part of this.

By way of an excursus, one should emphasize the 1923 exhibition as an international catalyst. The exhibition helped to develop international contours for the Bauhaus, which came to be pronounced decades later, when the German Gropius would be mentioned in the same breath as his world-famous colleagues, the American Frank Lloyd Wright and the Swiss Frenchman Le Corbusier. The cosmopolitanism represented by the founding faculty – the Swiss Itten and Klee, the Russian Kandinsky, the American Feininger, the Germans Marcks and Gropius and later also the Hungarian Moholy-Nagy – early on was reinforced by the presence of foreign students, especially from Austria, Poland, and Hungary, not to mention polyglot Jews from all over Central Europe. Non-German artistic styles also made inroads in the Bauhaus, such as the Dutch *De Stijl*, Cubism from France, and Constructivism from Russia. Signally, the Bauhaus's international flair became institutionalized around the middle of the twentieth century, through Gropius's directorship of the architecture department at Harvard and Moholy-Nagy's founding role in the Chicago School of Design, later part of the Illinois Institute of Technology. In Germany, as a monument to the anti-Nazi martyrs Hans and Sophie Scholl *and* in the spirit of a new beginning, the Hochschule für Gestaltung was founded in

Ulm, with Gropius's help and Max Bill, an ex-Bauhaus student, as rector. It was a legend in the late 1960s when it had to be closed for lack of funds.

Back in the 1920s, although most Thuringian politicians for the time being were mollified and willing to support the Bauhaus further, the right-wingers among them continued their campaign against what they regarded as excrescences of the modern age. They could point to the fact that, financially, the displays and performances had not been successful; just 4,500 inflation-resistant gold marks had been earned by a sale of artifacts.[38] It is true that after autumn 1923 the Bauhaus concentrated on the design of products that were beautiful to look at and actually useful in daily life, such as Wilhelm Wagenfeld's table lamps, Gunta Stölzl's hand-woven carpets and Marcel Breuer's chairs. The Bauhaus developed a typographical series, in which the practical-minded Moholy-Nagy was instrumental, and which from an aesthetic point of view was sublime. But the portfolios entitled "New European Prints" needed a mass publisher, and the German competition in prints was severe. Where were the outlets for other designs and products that lent themselves to industrial production of one sort or another, as in mural painting, stone sculpture, or wood-carving, to which the workshops now dedicated themselves?[39] The Bauhaus had given up some of its esoteric principles for the sake of applicability and everyday utility, and with a view to future industrial manufacture. But although much here was impressive, it was all too little too late. Come 1924, the Bauhaus would fall on extremely hard times.

The Bauhaus Masters

Although the Bauhaus performed brilliantly with its pedagogy, showpieces, and exhibitions from its inception in 1919, it did not go untouched by crises. But on the positive side, its development had as much to do with the visionary Gropius's leadership qualities as with the enthusiasm of its students, yet the main reason for its success must have been the quality and extraordinary harmony, barring a few significant exceptions, which ruled the faculty, today reminding us of the Muses' assembly in Goethe's time at its very best. Several factors contributed to this harmony. On the one hand, the members of the faculty, right down to Moholy-Nagy, all drew their inspiration from Expressionism and had been close, in one way or another, to Herwarth Walden's *Sturm* circle in Berlin.[40] On the other, Gropius himself had been an anchor of this circle, which he now used as a convenient reservoir for talent-spotting artists. And if he himself did not travel to Berlin to go after his quarry, as in the case of Feininger and Moholy-Nagy, *Sturm* affiliates had friends they could recommend, as Itten did in the cases of Muche, Schlemmer, and Klee. A second quality, apart from Expressionism, was the artistic versatility these men all shared and which made them understanding and tolerant in the comprehension of their colleagues' individual qualities. Shared values were a key factor. Itten, Klee, and Feininger were highly musical to the extent that music had been an alternative choice for a profession. All three were accomplished musicians even during their Bauhaus years, Feininger also composing fugues. Kandinsky partook in this love of music, even though he did not play an instrument. He had an especial talent for writing, as did Schreyer, Muche, and Moholy-Nagy. The Hungarian was keenly interested in the stage, as were Schreyer and Schlemmer. Not least, artistically there was agreement among most regarding the proper use of primary colors and form: triangles had to be yellow, circles blue, and squares red, even if the psychological properties attached to these constructs were always up for discussion.

Gropius's first appointee Feininger started drawing and painting from architecture and in that way alone deeply sympathized with the Bauhaus director, at least at the start. His earlier works from the Weimar hinterland since 1906 featured bridges and churches, towers and streets, inspired after 1911 by Cubism gleaned from the canvases of Robert Delaunay in Paris. Inside or facing these structures he painted human figures, often grotesquely exaggerated, but also symbols of technology, such as locomotives and ships. At the beginning of the twenty-first century, the American critic Sanford Schwartz brilliantly referred to Feininger's "stylishly designed images of angular and elongated buildings seen in hushed moments and of stilled seacoasts," as they were peopled or surrounded by persons with "out-of-date hats," painted in "lollipop colors."[41] These works lead straight to the cathedral Gropius commissioned from Feininger as the symbol of the Bauhaus, and they revealed this artist as the caricaturist and cartoonist at heart that he had been professionally in his Berlin years. His approach also lent itself to woodcuts, of which he would masterfully produce many. Even in 1924 the contemporary critic Willi Wolfradt credited him admiringly with being the first since Vincent van Gogh to have conveyed "dynamism" in the depiction of reality.[42]

Feininger showed Gerhard Marcks the art of wood carving, and whereas Marcks arrived in October 1919 as the sculptor that he was, he began teaching pottery for the Bauhaus at nearby Dornburg. He practiced no ceramics himself, but left this to his able master craftsman Krehan and a couple of very talented journeymen, yet did try his hand at designs. Here he combined "geometry with a local pottery tradition", according to Martina

Rudloff. By 1923, when the industrial ideal took over, he again turned to sculpting. Marcks had always preferred the purely educational impetus of the Bauhaus, liked working with genuine craftsmen (as Gropius initially said he did, too) and, like Feininger, resented the arrival of Moholy-Nagy. This was after he had already disregarded Gropius's plea for greater duplication, if not mass production, of the clay pots and vessels Marcks and his handful of students hand-crafted and which the director was so enthusiastic about. Marcks remained difficult, reserved, and conservative, as he had already been as a member of the left-leaning Berlin Arbeitsrat, and occasionally anti-Semitic, although he treasured his Jewish students. He was a Romantic and medievalist, preferring Christian motifs. When he was with his pupils and the Krehan brothers in the evening, his home-grown vegetables were consumed, schnapps made the rounds, and the dismal living and working conditions were forgotten during communal readings of Strindberg and Goethe. His journeyman-student Otto Lindig eventually made a name for himself with a series of large-format crocks and pails, which lent themselves to Gropius's vaunted industrial manufacture.[43]

Similarly to Feininger, Paul Klee, who started teaching in winter 1921, early on was subjected to several stylistic stimuli and was interested in more than one artistic or spiritual form of expression. He too came under the spell of Delaunay and Cubism in Paris and in 1914 traveled through Tunisia, which inspired pristine watercolors. At the Bauhaus, he took on the bookbinding and later the stained-glass workshop and after Itten even gave lectures in the *Vorkurs*. Interested in pictorial theories, he looked upon art as a parable of the Creation; a dialogue with nature was always essential. His color theory drew much from Goethe, and like some of his colleagues he was attracted to the esoteric, having earlier been influenced by Rudolf Steiner, theosophy, and anthroposophy. In his artistic world-view the child mattered much, but so did numbers and astrology. In Master council meetings he welcomed diversity, even strife, thinking differences of opinion would make for creative dialectics. Marvelously productive – as an artist, teacher, writer, musician, and amateur chef – he turned out a book of sketches for Moholy-Nagy's typographical series in 1925. Still during his Weimar Bauhaus years he would have an effect on French Surrealists like Paul Éluard and painters such as André Masson and Joan Miró. He often taught his Form Master classes using his own works as examples; in fact he painted canvases especially for them. When students visited him at his home to view his paintings he directed them to his aquarium and told them to watch the multi-hued fishes and their movements, to make them aware of color and of form.[44]

As a visual artist, Oskar Schlemmer came to oversee the Bauhaus's carpentry and stonemasonry shops, as well as metalworking, by 1922. At the end of that year, he also began to paint again, always concerned with the relationship of his protagonists, who tended to be abstract geometrical body shapes, to space. Moreover, as a parallel art, he was ever interested in the stage – the stage as space – and its figures, actors or dancers, mutating to a new existence: a "moving architecture," as Gropius saw it. That is to say that Schlemmer visualized the stage actor and stage dancer in space within the laws of geometry and mechanics, here following Émile Jaques-Dalcroze. This Swiss composer and music, rhythm, and theatrical-performance educator was then very much *en vogue*. In his quest for the *Gesamtkunstwerk* Schlemmer wanted to see realized within the Bauhaus, he held dance to be the archetypal, elementary form of human movement in space. Out of this were born his ideas for the *Triadic Ballet*, on which he had worked for many years before its 1922 premiere in Stuttgart and presentation under Bauhaus auspices a year later.[45]

Where Schlemmer was to triumph, Lothar Schreyer had already failed with his *Mondspiel*, notably the dance scenes in the dress rehearsal in March 1923. They struck protesting students, who, toeing Gropius's new line, currently wanted "American" things and Constructivism, as pseudo-religious. The wrath of these students, his colleagues, and particularly Gropius's, was brought down on him. The Grand Master Gropius, who once had encouraged all manner of artistic expressions in his search for the *Gesamtkunstwerk*, which he called *Der Bau*, now could be so unforgiving! Schreyer, this multi-gifted Heidelberg doctor of jurisprudence, left Weimar at the end of 1923, in recognition of the fact that at this juncture of the Bauhaus, cultic Expessionism was on the way out. But not before he impressed fellow artists with his paintings and artifacts, among which brightly colored sarcophaguses stood out – prominently displayed at his home. One was designated for his wife, the other for himself: he was so mystically touched as to convert to Catholicism later. In keeping with this arcane, archaic, symbolism, there also were South Sea sculptures, African masks, and a leopard throne, as well as the figure of the Virgin Mary, all of two meters high. Much of this was reminiscent of the theater, and not just because of the props at the *Sturm* stage, of which Schreyer had been a part in Berlin and in Hamburg as a dramaturg. In Berlin, his dramatic texts had been the Romantic Hölderlin's, Herwarth Walden's, and his own.[46]

Early in the twentieth century, sketches were made for what would become the first abstract painting in modern art. The author of these sketches was the Swedish painter Hilma af Klint, who subsequently created many abstract canvases which, buried in crates, were discovered in the early twenty-first century. Wassily Kandinsky, the man who, ever since 1910, thought that he was the first abstract painter, had no inkling that this woman existed, for she remained virtually unknown throughout her life. Born in 1862, she died in 1944, the same year as Kandinsky, having painted her first small abstract in 1906. About the Russian, art historians may now safely say that he painted his first abstract four years later, but it was not the first abstract ever. Kandinsky's was a watercolor, done in Munich in 1910, and he created others thereafter. For these, he had developed "a distinctive style of painting in which motifs were still recognizable, but the work gradually became more abstract, emphasizing the synthesis of color, line and form over straightforward representation."[47]

Kandinsky came to be obsessed with color and with form, individually and in their mutual relationship, as in more than one dimension. For instance, he would experiment with the spatial effect of black on gray, perhaps contained in a square. Taking cues from Goethe's color theory, he lectured on these subjects in a Bauhaus theory class, besides being the Master of a mural-painting workshop. Not a natural draftsman like his friend Klee, he painstakingly assigned qualities to colors, and then contemplated their relationship to forms like the triangle, circle, and square. Moreover, he related them to sound. Already in 1909 in his abstract drama *The Yellow Sound* an orchestra produced "individual colors," and a "light-yellow giant with a white blurry face" expanded his body, as the stage darkened, with "the music expressive, simulating the actions onstage."[48] In 1912 he had written about "the warmth and coldness of the colored tone," and "the lightness and darkness of same." Hence his musicality connected colors to sound frequencies; he insisted on "listening to the colors." For Kandinsky, each color possessed its intrinsic sound.[49] These associations may have had an esoteric source, but he was also intrigued by his composer friend Arnold Schoenberg, an artist deeply superstitious, who doubled as an extraordinarily good Expressionist painter. Kandinsky's versatility is not surprising and of course typically Bauhaus: like Schreyer he had a doctorate in jurisprudence and in art he advocated multiple interests and approaches. "One art has to learn from another how it puts to use its resources," he insisted, "it has to learn this in order to be able to treat its own resources in principally an equal manner."[50] Like fellow esoterics Klee and Gropius he put much stock in psychic powers, he too being aware of Steiner's thoughts and of the theosophic teachings of Steiner's precursor, the Russian mystic Helena Blavatsky, whose ideas informed many European thinkers until her death in 1891. From this it follows that to Kandinsky astrology and astronomy were significant, and he regularly had horoscopes cast for himself and his wife Nina. In his teaching and personal style, he was probably the most formal artist next to Gropius himself, albeit more respected than loved by his students and most colleagues. And he was the most famous, with the younger Paul Klee approaching him but still only second.[51]

Kandinsky's paintings had already been admired in 1913 in Munich, at the Goltz Gallery, by Georg Muche, before he had moved to join the *Sturm* circle in Berlin. In 1920 Muche became head of the Bauhaus weavers' shop and allowed himself to be influenced by Kandinsky, soon to be his colleague there, but also by Klee, by his close friend Itten, and later by his eventual successor, Moholy-Nagy. As a painter Muche liked experimenting, with photograms and mirrors, attempting to differentiate photography from painting. In the course of this, he moved back from abstract to representational art. He also distinguished himself as director of the 1923 Bauhaus exhibition and, though not an architect, designed the model house in the exclusive Weimar Am Horn district where Ernst von Wildenbruch had resided.

In Muche's cosmic world astrology figured much (he was known to explain some of this to Klee), but also the doctrine of *Mazdaznan*, where Itten shared his interests. *Mazdaznan* was a post-Zoroastrian cult containing Christian elements, founded by the American Otto Hanisch at the turn of the nineteenth century. It concerned itself with breathing exercises, a vegetarian diet, meditation, fasting, and a physical culture. *Mazdaznan* followers wore a simple, specially designed Bauhaus costume and the men would shave their heads. Strict sexual discipline obtained, and a type of flagellation was practiced where pustules were precipitated on the skin with a needle contraption, which took weeks to inflame and then to heal – the whole ritual was to aid purgation. Because a *Mazdaznan* diet was simple and less costly, in times of stringency the entire Bauhaus kitchen served *Mazdaznan* dishes, much beloved by its young disciples, but less so by more mature Bauhaus staff. If there were any visible esoteric marks of character on the Bauhaus during its lifespan, this was the most pronounced, in its Romantic phase between 1919 and 1923. However, with Itten's exit in April of that year the cult died down and Muche, who stayed on, aligned himself more closely with the anti-sectarian Moholy-Nagy and the, by then *Neue Sachlichkeit* Master Gropius.[52]

Johannes Itten became the most important Master in the Bauhaus's early, seminal phase, not just because he was the only true pedagogue to teach there, but also because through his strong charismatic personality he was able to put his stamp on the institution, in the beginning almost certainly with Gropius's approval. As he had taken formal teachers' training, he always remained interested in the child and its development, as did Klee. Itten was yet another artist who, as a budding painter, had learned from Kandinsky's art, at least by 1912, and had carefully studied his book about the spiritual roots in art, as well as the journal Kandinsky coedited, *Der Blaue Reiter*. Hence, like Kandinsky, Itten became fascinated with color and form and their interdependent relationships, in consideration of which he also looked to Goethe's color theory. But next to Kandinsky and his own teacher Hölzel, he admired van Gogh, Gauguin, Cézanne, and Munch.[53]

Yet another Renaissance man, Itten taught the Basic Course regularly after October 1919, but he also directed carpentry, carving, metal, stained-glass, and mural-painting workshops. His didactics were informed by a blend of conventional Christian religion and mystical teachings, which derived from the established sources: Steiner, Blavatsky, and even Alma Mahler's idiosyncratic brand of theosophy; she had introduced him to Gropius, but later blamed him for the smell of *Mazdaznan* garlic wafting through the place. Viewing body, soul, and spirit holistically as one unit, Itten aimed to trigger the basic creative powers he knew to be inherent in every one of his students. This amounted to teaching through a combination of "intuition and method," according to Magdalena Droste. As he adopted *Mazdaznan*, in theory and practice, initially because he himself was plagued by gastrointestinal disorders, he compelled his students to engage in rhythmic, relaxation and breathing exercises, as well as the fasting, dietary and other rites that were de rigueur. The simple-cloth monkish garb, in which he with his shaven head resembled a white Dalai Lama, was a uniform most students welcomed in times of the high cost of fashion, when they themselves were impoverished, and his following was substantial, even though he also had his share of enemies.[54]

The students in his *Vorkurs* learned from him in three unconventional albeit austerely structured stages: random artifact assemblage dictated by the intuition of the moment and available materials (mostly scrap), all manner of life drawings (not excluding that of nude models), and the analysis of Old Masters. Putting together those fantastic montages for the students could be as adventurous as it was frustrating, but invariably had liberating results, even though Itten himself might not have approved the end products. In Freudian terms, Itten was teaching them to free-associate using manual skills. This is how the Polish freshman Mirkin was observed having put together a horse: "It was a wooden board, part smooth and part rough, which had a paraffin-lamp cylinder on top with a rusty saw through it, ending in a spiral."[55] In teaching form and color as theory, Itten, like

Kandinsky, subscribed to a belief that both were determined by sound and, influenced by his Viennese composer friend Josef Matthias Hauer, attempted a synchronization of a color spectrum with a chromatic scale, positing the existence of twelve tones in each.[56] Itten's artistic aura, which enveloped the entire Bauhaus, was inward-directed, his paintings products of Expressionism as art for art's sake, the consequence of working as a humble craftsman, just as Gropius had initially advocated.[57] When that mood began to change in 1922, Itten had to be replaced by the cool and practical Moholy-Nagy. Without much ado, Itten relocated with his philosophy of art and life to Herrliberg, in the Swiss canton of Zurich, the European headquarters of *Mazdaznan*.

Gropius welcomed Moholy-Nagy as the youngest Master of the Bauhaus in the summer of 1923 for two specific reasons: to neutralize the sectarian excesses and to ready his institution for the realization of his amplified ideal, the union of art and technology. Through this, Gropius wished to further the Bauhaus's industrial potential and ensure its longevity, in the eyes of both an increasingly malevolent public and a suspicious government. Moholy-Nagy set to work exactly as Gropius envisaged. Still influenced by the Russian Constructivist Alexander Rodchenko, he eschewed intuition of the kind Itten had cherished, preferring rational science and experimentation. Although a painter, he wanted to replicate art mechanically, in a pronouncedly non-painterly fashion. So he began to teach Itten's *Vorkurs* as well as his former metalworking shop, all in the spirit of the utility-inspired exhibition of late summer 1923. In the metal workshop alone he moved to "industrial mass production by changing the priority from elaborate, precious metalwork to simple, practical, geometric designs for electrical household appliances, including light fittings." Soon the Berlin firm of Schwintzer & Gröff would manufacture fifty-three Bauhaus lamp designs. Moholy-Nagy, this painter, typographer, sculptor, photographer, filmmaker, and stage expert, who loved only the most avant-garde music, such as Stuckenschmidt's, in the last few months of the Bauhaus's Weimar existence became Gropius's right-hand man, at the expense of the director's friendship with artists such as Marcks and Feininger.[58]

The Bauhaus Crises and its Exit

A number of crises and near-scandals did much damage to the Bauhaus and eventually helped bring the institution down, to the detriment of the town of Weimar, which had forgone yet another chance to reconstitute itself as a haven of enlightenment and culture. One such crisis derived from the 1919 incorporation of the old art academy into the Bauhaus, with several of its Old Guard staff, among whom Max Thedy was the weightiest. Although he had initially agreed with Gropius's ideas for a new foundation, Thedy had considered only minor conceptual reforms for the two preexisting institutions, in particular his own. He and his colleagues then realized of what cloth the newly arriving Expressionist artists were cut, principally the first-comer Feininger, whom they disdained as a "Cubist." Neither did the introduction of the title "Master" instead of "Professor" go down well. The situation was compounded by the fact that although the new and old wing of the Bauhaus shared van de Velde's original building, Thedy and his cronies also had to camp out in the main Weimar castle for lack of space. When Itten and Gropius, not least to earn some money, concentrated on manufacturing children's toys, which were then sold by Bauhaus students in the famous market square at the 1919 Christmas fair, Thedy was shocked. He came to ally himself with the reactionary forces in Weimar itself, as well as those in the Thuringian Landtag like Herfurth and some in Berlin, so that already by 1920 he was able to secede, with the aim of reviving the traditional academy. That was accomplished de facto by April 1921, with the erection of a legally novel creation, the Staatliche Hochschule für bildende Kunst, a state academy for graphic arts, although everybody held it to be the old academy. It offered the services of Thedy, Engelmann, Klemm, and like-minded teachers, and a number of more conservatively minded Bauhaus students even moved over. Under the Old Guard they trotted along those well-worn paths, painting, in oil, conventional themes and Weimar landmarks such as "Ilm Park, nudes, castle bridge, herds of sheep, and Belvederer Avenue." But friction continued, because the new academy was still housed in Bauhaus quarters and it rivaled the Bauhaus for its budget.[59]

Gropius himself held insufficient finances. This added to the controversies with the academic Old Guard, but so did his own lack of an architecture department. After all, he had predicated his entire idea of the Bauhaus on the notion of *Der Bau*, The Building, which apart from any metaphorical significance was an architectural concept. His justified criticism of a stingy government notwithstanding, Gropius's more acerbic in-house critics such as Schlemmer wanted to take him to task for that absence, being fully aware that students had come to Weimar precisely because Gropius had advertised architecture as a specialty and in its abeyance, in some cases, were leaving town. Gropius made other excuses: for example that it would take three years of more general schooling before a specialized architectural course of study could be started. After a while he offered replacement instruction, such as classes in geometry he himself taught. But he also claimed that he was simply too busy as administrator and central figure at the Bauhaus to burden himself with the chores of teaching.[60]

As a step in the right direction, Gropius had Adolf Meyer, a journeyman and one of his assistants, teach some basic architecture skills, but not as a full-fledged Master. Meyer's main job was to help Gropius run his private architecture firm outside the Bauhaus, for which he had the so-called Sommerfeld House built in Berlin. However, this activity raised questions of ethics which were broached but never openly discussed in the Masters' council: even if Gropius employed his favorite Bauhaus students to help him in Berlin and granted them academic credit, who pocketed the earnings? If the Sommerfeld House was built in Bauhaus time, did the Bauhaus receive all the proceeds, and what share did Gropius himself receive, and on what contractual basis? Where was a full accounting? Another such project raising eyebrows was the renovation of the municipal theater in Jena. This lack of transparency provided oil for the fires many Bauhaus enemies were fanning. Similar accusations could not be leveled in the case of the Haus am Horn designed for the 1923 exhibition by Muche, but critics were asking why Gropius himself had not designed it and why, in the end, it turned out to be so grossly non-functional.[61]

Those students who left the Bauhaus for the revived academy in 1920–21 were only part of a permanently dissatisfied contingent which changed its character over time, and for varying reasons. As early as 1919 some Bauhaus students rejected Gropius's elitist approach, while those who had come with Itten from Vienna demanded preferential treatment. They wanted guaranteed lodgings in a town already filled to capacity with outsiders because of the relocated central government. Besides, they objected to all interference with their *Mazdaznan* practices. Not least because several of those students were Jewish, a protesting student faction under the young Expressionist Hans Gross sought an alliance with the prevailing nationalist forces in town backed by the likes of Herfurth and Freytag-Loringhoven. Publicly, they ranted against Jews and proclaimed the idea of a Bauhaus based on "German principles." When Gross and his group of thirteen left the institution, it was noted that several of them bore aristocratic names – holdovers from the monarchic era. Gropius thereupon decreed political neutrality for the student body. But this demand rang hollow, as he himself remained firmly allied to the political left. Nor was there peace thereafter. As late as 1923 Schlemmer remarked that a significant number of students objected to the idiosyncratic Master title; they thought that there was a surfeit of Masters and wanted to get rid of them to free up funds for student aid.[62]

The manner in which Johannes Itten conditioned those students who were fanatically loyal to him exacerbated the tension between him and Gropius, which was palpable by early 1920. It occurred notwithstanding the "creative impulses" that Georg Muche, Itten's stalwart friend, thought he could discern from productive dialectics, soon after Itten's hiring.[63] Itten exaggerated his *Mazdaznan* cult to a level where not just Gropius became concerned and, guided by its principles, he set to work an admissions committee staffed by students, in parallel to, but opposing, official procedures sanctioned by council.[64] Itten did this in full awareness of his unique position as prime educator and the only person then qualified to teach the Basic Course. By the spring of 1920 Gropius felt his fear was justified that Itten was aiming for a takeover of the Bauhaus by means of his totalist philosophy. Gropius saw Itten at work, trying to shape students' character according to holistic principles, whereas he wanted to shape artist-craftsmen (and later engineers). By December 1921 faculty members had become alarmed. Against the background of the the Itten–Gropius controversy, Schlemmer commented that for Itten's pupils in the craft shops "meditation and rites" were more important than an honest day's work. Schreyer warned Gropius that the council could be split in two and a continuing fight with Itten would destroy the Bauhaus.[65] A few months later Gropius was openly championing the Bauhaus's new utilitarian approach, with Itten clearly in opposition. Clinging to his ideal of improving a person's inner self rather than fashioning machinists, Itten began to surrender responsibility for his workshops, while still controlling the *Vorkurs*. But this, too, he relinquished by autumn 1922, after giving final notice to Gropius effective April 1923.[66]

Gropius's relationship with Itten was not helped by the appearance of Theo van Doesburg on the Weimar scene. Born 1883 in Utrecht, he began painting in a Naturalistic style, before turning to Impressionist-inspired motifs. By 1915, Kandinsky's abstractionism had clearly influenced him. Cubist, Dadaist, and Futurist currents were also leaving their mark on his work. Until 1920, after having met up with collaborators such as painter Piet Mondrian and architect J. J. P. Oud, he had founded the movement *De Stijl* – an artistic style exemplified in a journal series of the same name.[67]

Van Doesburg came to Weimar first in 1920, because he was aware that there was new and fascinating work there. Gropius's awakening trend toward a union of art and technology was not lost on him; the two had several meetings. Both men, in fact, argued in favor of an integration of the machine in artistic-industrial processes – for the sake of the common good. Weimar artistic endeavors greatly excited Doesburg, who in his own paintings indulged in "the right angle and the three primary colours, supplemented by black, white and grey." The primacy of red, blue, and yellow was of course something that Bauhaus painters like Kandinsky and Klee had long upheld, but not necessarily Itten, who allowed freedom of expression for everyone in accordance with individual choice. All in all, Doesburg was a Constructivist, who militated against Itten's Romantic Expressionism, with the aim of a more radical change for the entire Bauhaus.[68]

In late 1921 an intrepid van Doesburg returned to Weimar, expecting with certainty to be appointed Bauhaus Master; this, however, did not happen, no doubt because Gropius still dreaded offending Itten. Besides, Gropius may have been jealous. Thereupon the Dutchman set up his own studio where he himself gave courses, mostly to Bauhaus students and charging very low fees. He could afford to do so, for from the Netherlands he possessed American dollars, for which Gropius's worthless marks during a period of exorbitant inflation in Germany were no match. Personally, he cut a striking figure, with his elegantly tailored suits, black shirt, white tie, monocle, and American cap. Not to mention, in stuffy Weimar, the flair of his attractive wife.[69]

Gropius must have had serious reason to fear van Doesburg's strategic syphoning-off of students from the Bauhaus, coupled with that intractable animosity to Itten. Tension heightened when in September 1922 the Dutch artist organized an international congress of Constructivists and Dadaists in Weimar – squarely against the Bauhaus. Some fashionable not to say notorious artists of the time showed up: Kurt Schwitters, Hans Arp, El Lissitzky, Hans Richter, and László Moholy-Nagy, who then had his first look at the Bauhaus. There is no doubt that young Weimar artists were mesmerized by van Doesburg's Constructivist approach, among them Werner Graeff and Karl Peter Röhl, but also Marcel Breuer, who worked with van Doesburg's friend Gerrit Rietveld. Today it is obvious that Breuer's archetypal slatted chair (the precursor of the classic steel-pipe Breuer Chair) took more than a cue from Rietveld's famous Red and Blue Chair. By 1923, after Itten had been replaced by Moholy-Nagy, van Doesburg moved to Paris, having realized the futility of his Weimar quest, but he had managed to stir things up for Gropius and his collegium, some of whom, like Feininger, found it all unsettling. That van Doesburg had also acted as a catalyst was, at that point in time, not Gropius's main concern.[70]

Van Doesburg's shaking of the Bauhaus walls did nothing to further the integration of that institution in Weimar society, because his excoriation was further proof for the town's citizens that something with the Bauhaus was awry. Chief among those burghers were the very craftsmen whom Gropius had promised to woo, in the manner of his predecessor van de Velde. Instead, he sounded off too early and too vocally about the value of machines which, serving industry, could replace the craftsmen. This was quite contrary to the theoretical pronouncements regarding collaboration with craft shops Gropius had made in his original 1919 manifesto. In normal Bauhaus routines of teaching and of work it turned out that the Work Masters, Weimar craftsmen who were organized in guilds, were underused and also were paid less than the artist Form Masters – a condition Gropius himself thought unjust and sought to correct in the Landtag. The guilds themselves were suspicious of the Bauhaus's attempts to make money on its own by trying to sell products. Matters had come to a head by 1922, a time when Gropius was already determined to merge with industry, when the Work Masters complained they had never been given a permanent seat in the Masters' council and that in everyday practice they had been referred to, by the precious Bauhaus artists, as "auxiliary masters." Council minutes demonstrate that Form Masters actually had no interest in inviting the craftsmen to their meetings, because they believed that an artisan's deficient comprehension of things artistic precluded participation in decision-making.[71]

The craftsmen were an integral part of Weimar society which, on the whole, rejected Gropius and his Bauhaus, as it had rejected Liszt and Goethe. Its spokesmen were firmly behind Thedy and Fröhlich, when they decided to part with Gropius. Having barely tolerated van de Velde, Weimar's citizens were convinced that Gropius and his staff, let alone the students, politically were Communists and artistically, perverts. When Gropius's first employee Feininger arrived in spring 1919, they were certain he was a "revolutionary out to corrupt their youngsters." The Bauhaus's own students, those boys with long hair and girls with short skirts, were suspected by this xenophobic citizenry of being mostly foreigners, in particular Jews. As early as September 1919, when the students were to paint a ceiling in the town hall, the municipal council reneged by withdrawing its commission. Bauhaus members were regarded as weird, and as such were socially boycotted. Upstanding Weimar parents would scare their small children by threatening to send them to the Bauhaus if they did not behave. Suspicion struck even when there were no grounds: once a policeman wanted to issue a summons because someone had seen a Bauhaus teacher molest a nude model sexually, from a certain window. But from where the plaintiff claimed to have watched, one could not even see the studio.[72]

These local enemies of the Bauhaus allied themselves with the rebellious student Gross, and their opposition was fed with information from Old School painters Thedy and Fröhlich. Publicity support came from town councillor Mathilde von Freytag-Loringhoven, the art critic of Weimar's reactionary daily, the *Weimarische Landeszeitung "Deutschland"*, and Landtag deputy Herfurth. In 1920, he published a pamphlet in which he questioned the very existence of the Bauhaus in Weimar, with its classicist tradition, maintaining that he was united with the burghers by "a common love of Weimar and its art." He objected to what he identified as Bauhaus Expressionism as a one-sided form of art, dominating the traditional culture Weimar was famous for. In addition, he protested against the visible eccentricities of Bauhaus members, particularly its students who, it must be conceded, often acted provocatively in the market square, what with their garlic breath, their odd hairdos, and their monkish garb. Freytag-Loringhoven in particular resented the 1923 exhibition and polemicized against it in her *Landeszeitung*.[73]

The example of the failed integration of the master craftsmen into the Bauhaus shows that there were limits to Gropius's and his colleagues' progressiveness. This can best be appreciated in terms of their relationship to female colleagues and students. In this realm the Masters' patriarchal attitude, and Gropius's in particular, clashed with the republic's proclamation of new freedoms. In being beholden to the idea of an artisanal tradition, which had no place for women, the Bauhaus teachers implicitly had to reject educational processes for women as future Masters, which would have been in line with the new, republican, precepts of female emancipation.

Therefore, although Gropius had called for equality of opportunity for both sexes in his Bauhaus announcements of 1919, he was baffled when more women than men applied for admission by the fall. They were promptly dispatched to the weaving workshop, for, as Schlemmer was known to intone, "where there's wool you'll women find, weaving just to pass the time." Henceforth women were also allowed into the pottery and bookbinding workshops, which were considered suitably feminine. By 1920, when Gropius had admonished his teachers to let in fewer girls and not a single one into architecture (not yet extant in any case), male students were dismissing the girl students' weaving as "arty-crafty." This occurred notwithstanding the fact that the weaving shop was virtually the only craft shop making substantial product sales. On the other hand, the male Masters registered with glee that girl students had volunteered for services in the kitchen, at the expense of their creative time. Among these Masters, only Itten and Muche considered women as true equals. Almost everyone based his prejudices on clichés, Gropius applying the regnant color fetishism to the sexes, as he assigned red to masculinity and blue to femininity. Klee was convinced that genius was masculine, and Schlemmer as well as Kandinsky associated creativity with masculinity. Marcks was on principle opposed to women students and had a huge row with the androgynous lesbian Grete Heymann, as she left his workshop after having been told that she was talented yet not suitable. Marianne Brandt hardly made it into the metal workshop and flourished only under the protection of Moholy-Nagy, who regarded his own partner Lucia as his equal. But Johanna Hummel was expelled from that workshop. It is telling that no Bauhaus woman student could ever obtain an apprenticeship certificate from Weimar's chamber of commerce, which precluded follow-up careers as journeymen or master craftsmen. There is no record of Gropius ever trying to change that. One of his own students, however, Dörte Helm, did very well as a mural painter, for instance for the Berlin Sommerfeld House, but then again, she is probably the favorite he was rumored to have had a sexual liaison with.[74]

Only three prolific women today can be identified as Weimar Bauhaus teachers. In essence, Gropius and his colleagues extended the same patriarchal attitude to them as they did to female students. One was Gertrud Grunow, born 1870, who, as a pianist, had studied with Hans von Bülow in Berlin and came with her grand piano. She adhered to the exalted, esoteric, philosophy of an Itten or a Muche and taught their students "harmonization" in the *Vorkurs*, accepted by many but also silently laughed at behind her back. Grunow, like Itten, believed in the fundamental relationship between color and sound and exercised her students in dance and trance. Since 1920, she did this nominally as a Form Master, but was treated and paid like a lecturer. In 1923, when a full Master's post became open for her to fill, the Masters' council decided to fire her, effective 1924. The connection between her sudden dismissal and Itten's prior exit even then was palpable. Helene Börner taught as a Work Master; she was an old-style seamstress, weaver, and knitter. For that she was fought by Gunta Stölzl, who was developing and teaching new methods of weaving and saw in Börner the more experienced practitioner, who could squeeze her out. The women's cause at the Bauhaus was certainly not served in cases where two members of the same gender carried on crusades against each other. As it turned out, Stölzl became one of the more formidable teachers after 1925 in Dessau, at a time when the number of women Masters in the Bauhaus remained extremely limited.[75]

Still in Weimar, the Bauhaus did not collect accolades from its citizens for its sexual politics. While they could not have cared whether a female associate should be elevated to Master status or not, those citizens gossiped about alleged sexual relationships, even orgies, among its students as in Liszt's time. Yet, as Schreyer assures us, there was nothing especially wild going on in this regard, nothing beyond the usual: boys falling in love with girls and couples forming. Some actually got married. Among the teachers, Itten with his uncanny sensitivity attracted female students more than other Masters, and at least one bittersweet episode featuring a heartbroken young woman has been documented.[76]

Things were somewhat different with Gropius, for he was always the focus of attention, in the Bauhaus, in the streets of Weimar or in the political arena. A lean and darkly handsome man – and not only according to the flattering description of his onetime spouse Alma – his comportment was very masculine and his means of expression decisive, to the point where many in the final Weimar years deemed him headstrong and autocratic.[77] But these very same qualities also made him a prize for young women, many of whom had lost husbands or sweethearts in the Great War. They included inhabitants of Weimar, after it had become publicly obvious that Gropius's tortuous union with the sometime present Alma was on the verge of collapse. Walter and Alma finally divorced in October 1920, which event may or may not have been grist to the Weimar gossip mill (and further hurt the Bauhaus's local reputation).[78] But his extended affair since 1919 with Lily Hildebrandt – the wife of a Stuttgart art historian who was an accessory to the adultery and frequently came visiting – would not have gone unnoticed.[79] While Gropius was seeing Frau Hildebrandt, he also, from March 1920, carried on an affair with the aspiring writer Maria Benemann, née Dobler, an attractive Weimar widow in her early thirties, which he tried carefully to shield from the public's view as well as from Bauhaus constituents.[80] Finally, in May 1923, he began courting Ilse (Ise) Frank, his future second wife, originally from Hanover.[81]

The evidence suggests that Gropius was a habitual skirt-chaser who eventually aroused the prurience even of the politicians he depended on. In the fall of 1922 Carl Schlemmer, Oskar's younger brother and, as Craft Master, an especially invited council member without a vote, tried to get him censured by the Masters for carrying on with Bauhaus female students as well as employees. As for the latter, one of Gropius's secretaries remarked years later that whenever she was alone in the office with him, she had the feeling someone was peeping through the keyhole to catch him in "something sexual."[82] And a cleaning woman reported at the time that she had found "a discreet object" lying about in the office when tidying up.[83] In any event, Carl Schlemmer's censure motion never passed for lack of watertight proof, and a second, external investigation by Thuringian government administrators also found no fault. Schlemmer later maintained the reason for this was obvious, for Gropius had a firm grip on the Masters' council and, it might be added, had the left-wing deputies of the Landtag in the palm of his hand.[84]

Beyond such common human failings, the chronicle of the Bauhaus in Weimar must close on a sad note because of the deteriorating relationship between Wassily Kandinsky and Arnold Schoenberg. What this meant was the rupture between two epochal modernists and, writ small, was emblematic of the break between artistic modernism, symbolized by the Bauhaus, having made such a brave try at it, and the political modernism represented by the republic of Weimar, itself on the verge of decline, only months after its inception.

Schoenberg, who was a regular at Alma Mahler's Vienna soirées, by early 1919 was on an unofficial short list as new director of the Weimar conservatory, and three of his *Fünf Orchesterstücke* had their informal German premiere in Weimar on November 7. The full five pieces were performed in Weimar in December of 1920.[85] Kandinsky had collaborated with Schoenberg on the *Blaue Reiter* series; in 1912 Schoenberg had published a chapter about the relationship between music and text in a volume Kandinsky edited with his and Paul Klee's friend Franz Marc.[86] Besides, writing of color and of sound, Kandinsky had lauded Schoenberg for the use of what he called "counter-sound" in his latest quartets in his monograph on art and the spiritual of the same year.[87]

In early 1923, as the question of a new music academy director became acute, Kandinsky wrote, at the behest of Gropius, to Schoenberg in Vienna, trying to get him interested in the post. However, Schoenberg wrote back saying that for him as a Jew this was not possible. "I have heard that even a Kandinsky sees only evil in the actions of Jews and in their evil actions only the Jewishness, and at this point I give up hope of reaching any understanding. It was a dream. We are two kinds of people."[88] When Kandinsky showed this letter to Gropius, he immediately thought that Alma was behind it. For an explanation Kandinsky's widow Nina has subsequently maintained that Frau Mahler had passed on to Schoenberg the false rumor that Kandinsky was an anti-Semite, because he had resisted her sexual advances.[89] Whatever the validity of this claim, Kandinsky had not been particularly known as an anti-Semite, and he obviously treasured Arnold Schoenberg. All the same, he made the fatal mistake of writing to the composer on April 24 that if he had met Schoenberg in Berlin after his flight from Bolshevik Russia he would have discussed with him the "Jewish problem." And then he penned the fateful sentence: "I reject you as a Jew, but nevertheless I write you a good letter and assure you that I would be so glad to have *you* here in order to work *together!*"[90] The two men's friendship ended forthwith, and so did Weimar's chance, once more, of elevating its musical cachet.

Aesthetically, personally, and morally compromising circumstances within the Bauhaus contributed to external developments that cut short its existence in Weimar. After elections in Thuringia, the left-leaning majority in the Landtag was replaced by a new government in March 1924. Now the Socialist parties of the SPD and KPD together had 30 seats, as opposed to 35 held by five right-leaning parties, among which Herfurth's DNVP was the most influential. For the first time, there were seven Nazis in parliament, acting under a camouflage label, as they had been legally proscribed since Hitler's abortive November 1923 Munich putsch. To them, of course, the Bauhaus was anathema. In order to force the Bauhaus to close, the right-wing parties, calling themselves the Thüringer Ordnungsbund (TOB) or Order League, cut the Bauhaus's annual budget in half – from 100,000 to 50,000 marks, when even 100,000 had not been sufficient. They were supported by Weimar's craft associations, long disappointed in Gropius. Sloppy bookkeeping since July 1923, as it was discovered by the new political rulers, weakened the Bauhaus's case further. Gropius tried to counter such adversity by announcing the formation of an industrially viable company, since in this last Constructivist phase the Bauhaus's artistic products were selling ever better. But among other difficulties, this met with the objection of colleagues such as Marcks and Schlemmer, who wanted to see the purely educational character of their school preserved. Then a Circle of Friends of the Bauhaus was formed, which included luminaries like Albert Einstein, Gerhart Hauptmann, and even Schoenberg. It was all to no avail. In September 1924 the Thuringian ministry of education gave notice to all teachers and staff, effective April 1, 1925. Bauhaus Masters preempted being sacked by themselves declaring the dissolution of the Bauhaus, on December 26 – a step which they were legally not entitled to take. Meanwhile the nearby town of Dessau, in the new state of Sachsen-Anhalt, which, unlike Weimar, had a respectable industrial tradition, had already made the best of several offers for the Bauhaus to relocate, as a municipal institution. Gropius and his staff took the mayor up on this and by the end of April 1925 they all had gone to Dessau, with the exception of Marcks and Muche, who found new positions elsewhere. Now this last living legend of Weimar thus far had come to its end, as the Bauhaus moved on to further impressive feats in its new home, at least for a few more years.[91] The successor institution, which Gropius's former Berlin colleague Otto Bartning carried on in the Goethe town, mostly as an architecture school, was as functional as it was unimaginative, destined to be all but forgotten in the annals of cultural history.[92]

As if on cue to save Weimar, Walter Gropius and his collaborators had appeared in early 1919. It would be the last chance for the town in decades. It is interesting to imagine the Bauhaus as the culmination of prior progressive developments in Weimar since Goethe – the youthful Carl Alexander, Liszt, Dingelstedt, and Strauss – and as a platform for launching a future series of achievements. However, the previous progress line was porous and after 1923, instead of achievements there was more gloom and doom. Still, the exhibition of 1923 represented the pinnacle of original creativity for Weimar since 1832 and incidentally showed off a certain cosmopolitanism by attracting international luminaries in the arts and letters, with whom Gropius and his friends could well stand in line. In the best sense, then, Gropius was a direct extension of Kessler and van de Velde, and his left-wing ideology stood in positive contrast to the jingoism and small-mindedness of Weimar's burghers and all of Thuringia's right-wing politicians. Some of these clearly were heralds of Adolf Hitler. Unfortunately, in trying to bring the Bauhaus down, they were able to exploit Gropius's and his associates' weaknesses, such as the lack of cooperation with local artisans, fiduciary infidelities, the early leadership rift between Gropius and Itten, the lack of institutionalized architecture, Gropius's inability to harmonize with the traditional painters' school, and, potentially, even Bauhaus misogyny. Bartels and company were known to be fierce enemies of the Bauhaus and increasingly used it to justify first solid support for *völkisch*-conservative parties and later also the NSDAP. The uniqueness of the Bauhaus and its faculty lay in their ability to interest themselves in, foster, and accommodate a variety of artistic expressions, even aesthetic opposites (such as Romanticism versus Constructivism) and still obtain creative consensus. This was wholly contrary to what the succeeding Hitlerites believed in, as they adhered to, next to excessive nationalism, a creed of biologistic organicism, racist exclusivism, and overall censorship – all anathema to the pluralism and freedom, in behavior and expression, which the Bauhaus had been wont to cultivate.

CHAPTER 6

Weimar in the Weimar Republic
1918 to 1933

On Saturday, October 9, 1920, the unemployed painter Karl Büchner, armed with an open razor and a pistol, slipped into the basement of a villa at Weimar's Berkaer Strasse 11 in order to commit robbery. The house belonged to retired imperial admiral Reinhard Scheer, who was just having lunch with his family. When the maid went to check on the noise, Büchner shot her in the head. A few minutes later Scheer's wife Emilie was killed, as she was looking for the maid. Then Büchner committed suicide. He was a war veteran who, unlike Scheer, had not found peace with himself, traumatized after escaping from a collapsed dugout at the front, being out of touch with society, and with his sanity on edge.[1] By contrast, Scheer was a war hero; in summer of 1916 he had commanded the strategically unde-cided Battle of Jutland on the German side, then becoming the chief advo-cate of unrestricted submarine warfare, which had helped to bring the United States into the war.[2] A fanatical monarchist, his retirement in Weimar in late 1918 was in character with the attitude and actions of many well-to-do conservatives who, before and after the Great War, chose the sylvan German middle of Germany on the Ilm river as the basis for a comfortable, economically secure life. Scheer believed the imperial army had been stabbed in the back by traitors inside Germany, rather than defeated at the front; in 1919 he considered running as a candidate for the conservative DNVP in the new Reichstag but then desisted, because he was on the "War Criminals" list of Germans to be extradited to the Allies.[3] People the like of Scheer were anti-modernist and hated the Bauhaus.

Admiral Scheer was known as a pillar of the Lutheran Church in town, and there he congregated with notables of similar ideological persuasion, many of whom were also guests at Frau Förster-Nietzsche's cultish mansion, as Scheer almost certainly was. His villa was only a stone's throw from hers.[4]

Whereas Elisabeth Förster-Nietzsche knew Gropius and purported to sympathize with the Bauhaus, she did so not as a protagonist of the avant-garde but because she expected to gain certain advantages from the Bauhaus's own multifarious connections – in the same way that she continued her old friendship with Harry Kessler. In 1919, she exerted pressure on Gropius, because she wanted him to bring back to Weimar her old friend van de Velde, whom she knew how to manipulate. But Gropius resented the return of his predecessor; besides, his understanding of Nietzsche was limited and he was unable to share Frau Elisabeth's distorted view of her brother. Therefore in future, although Oskar Schlemmer and Lyonel Feininger were in tune with Nietzschean ideas, no significant relationship developed. Never was there a lecture by a Bauhaus Master in the Villa Silberblick, never an exhibition of its art, and its members were not invited to soirées.[5]

In the main, Nietzsche's sister continued well-tried lines of pursuit: to maintain and increase material support for her Archive and herself, to augment propaganda and continue the publication of Friedrich's manuscripts and, opportunistic as always, to steer the most accommodative political course. Publication consisted of a combination of her esoteric editing practices and the creation of works about Nietzsche, by herself, closely controlled staff and, increasingly, sympathetic Archive outsiders. From 1920 to 1929 twenty-three volumes of Nietzsche's collected *œuvre* were published, including a new edition of *The Will to Power*, under Förster-Nietzsche's tight supervision. She herself and others published separate articles and books on Nietzsche. In these, the likelihood of falsifications, elisions, and misrepresentations was high. By 1930, Förster-Nietzsche's exclusive publishing rights had nearly run out, and now Leipzig's Kröner-Verlag became the Archive's chief publisher (printing the apocryphal *Will to Power* well into the 1970s). By 1929–30 the Jena philosopher Hans Leisegang was considering an institutional association between his university and the Nietzsche Archive, but he wanted to reserve final critical judgment for himself, which Frau Elisabeth rejected. After that plan had come to naught, yet another Jena philosophy professor, the National Socialist Karl August Emge, was tied into the Archive's editing and publishing operations, with the university itself still staying out of things.[6]

By this time, at the dawn of the Third Reich, Förster-Nietzsche had found a true Nazi champion of her brother in the person of Alfred Baeumler, who since 1929 had occupied a chair in philosophy at the Technical University of Dresden.[7] Baeumler had joined the Combat League for German Culture (Kampfbund für deutsche Kultur – KfdK), created in 1928 by Alfred Rosenberg, who in Munich was not only the chief editor of the National Socialist broadsheet *Völkischer Beobachter* but also the self-styled chief ideologue of the Nazi Party.[8] Although Nietzsche's ideas were slow to penetrate the brain cells of Nazis, because much of what he had said was diametrically opposed to Nazi tenets, Rosenberg did include a reference to the philosopher in his *Myth of the Twentieth Century* of 1930, as he lauded him, rightly or wrongly, for having striven for "high racial breeding."[9] Baeumler himself remained an editor and apologist for what he thought Nietzsche represented until after World War II, writing in 1931 that a "Germanic yearning for freedom, Germanic warrior's pride and warrior's spite are alive in Nietzsche." The philosopher must have turned in his grave.[10] For his sloppy work in the early 1930s Baeumler along with Nietzsche's sister was savaged by the critics, including Walter Benjamin. Nietzsche expert Erich F. Podach accused him of falsification (for example calling Nietzsche's onetime flame, a descendant of the Russian-Huguenots, Lou Andrea Salomé, a Finnish Jew), of tactical omission, and of uncritically using Frau Elisabeth's earlier, questionable, editions.[11]

In the wake of Germany's defeat in World War I, Elisabeth Förster-Nietzsche persisted in her political conservatism, staunchly holding to the "stab-in-the-back" legend, which insisted that the defeat was due to the machinations of internal enemies, above all Germany's socialists and Jews. As an ideological establishment, the Nietzsche Archive was supported by an infrastructure of conservatives – anti-democratic because to them the new Weimar Republic brought disadvantages rather than benefits. In her leadership role at Villa Silberblick Förster-Nietzsche at the beginning of the 1920s was aided by a trio of cousins: Richard Oehler, a strongly monarchist archivist, Adalbert Oehler, who had been displaced as Lord Mayor of Düsseldorf by a Communist mob, and Max Oehler, who as an active major had lost his job with the disintegrating imperial army. Apart from editing and publishing responsibilities, these three men helped Förster-Nietzsche with the organization of various events, which were to be in memory of Friedrich Nietzsche as much as they were designed to augment Frau Elisabeth's already formidable aura.[12]

As countervailing statements to many celebrations initiated by the new republic, the Archive put on a series of events and sponsored associations, which mostly benefited Förster-Nietzsche. It may seem beside the point but is fully in keeping with the Weimar myth construction that she may have believed that all of these would honor this town of geniuses. In 1919, a Nietzsche Society was founded in Munich, made up mostly of conservative yet cosmopolitan intellectuals and artists, such as Hugo von Hofmannsthal and Thomas Mann. In 1921 the seventy-fifth birthday of Frau Elisabeth was celebrated in Weimar, and on that occasion she received a Festschrift and an honorary doctorate from Jena.[13] In 1926 the Society of Friends of the Nietzsche Archive was constituted, formed to a large extent of conservatives and Germanocentrists (many of whom later turned to Nazism), such as the Cologne Germanist and former Stefan George disciple Ernst Bertram, a friend of Mann's.[14] Both Bertram and Mann had contributed to the 1921 Festschrift. Moreover, in 1926 Elisabeth's eightieth birthday was celebrated, with requisite pomp and circumstance. The two newly founded Nietzsche organizations, together with the Nietzsche Foundation of 1908 hosted a well-publicized convention between October 5 and 17, 1927, in honor of Nietzsche's birth eighty-three years earlier; this was attended by many luminaries, including the philosopher Max Scheler. The Archive also secured enough money to finance a Lassen Prize (named not after the nineteenth-century conductor, but a wealthy Hamburg donor), awarded for the first time in 1919: to Thomas Mann for his nationalist-colored tract *Betrachtungen eines Unpolitischen* (1918), and later to the cultural-pessimist writer Oswald Spengler. Both were attuned to Nietzsche.[15]

In the structure of ideas, a problem was developing for the Archive in the 1920s, because representatives both of conservatism and of democratic liberalism came to play prominent roles there and were on a collision course, though the former eventually prevailed. The most prominent conservative to align himself with the Archive and openly profess his fealty to Förster-Nietzsche was Spengler. If not uncritically, he had dealt with Nietzschean ideas in his increasingly popular *Decline of the West* (1918 and 1923), and apart from the Lassen Prize was influential in the various Nietzsche support groups. Probably no one gave as many talks at the Archive as he did, among them one entitled "Blood and Money" in February 1923, and another at the conference of 1927 – an address which revolted Kessler.[16] As the count was becoming more left-wing – a member of the German Democratic Party (DDP) which had been instrumental in forging the new republican constitution, and a firm supporter of a universal League of Nations concept – he came to abhor Spengler, who ideologically and by physical appearance, with his beefy build and shaven head, was the count's very opposite.

Why the mentally and physically refined Kessler, who maintained his house on Cranachstrasse just below the Nietzsche shrine even after he had lost his Weimar offices, remained so loyal to the Archive is something of an enigma. But one must remember that he believed deeply in the ideas of Nietzsche, still trusted the various publications now appearing and, above all, was personally loyal to Elisabeth Förster-Nietzsche in an Old School, chivalrous sort of way. Nonetheless, as he became more and more ostracized in German society because of his post-1918 liberal-cosmopolitan views and sympathy for the republic, he had difficulty comprehending her political attitudes, since she was moving even more to the right than she had ever been.[17] Thomas Mann, too, had become a supporter of the Weimar Republic, after the assassination of Foreign Minister Walther Rathenau, the son of Emil, in June 1922, and while this did not dent his relationship with Weimar and Frau Elisabeth's Nietzsche cult, his relationship with Bertram was beginning to cool, to the extent that Bertram was openly professing National Socialism. Yet it is likely that both Bertram and Mann were among the group of German intellectuals supporting a third bid by Förster-Nietzsche in 1922 for the Nobel Prize in Literature, because she thought, as she wrote to Ernst Thiel in Sweden, that her literary production was "of great cultural significance."[18]

The prize money would have been welcome, because after the Great War Elisabeth Förster-Nietzsche was in greater need of funds than before. Imperial war bonds which she had signed for had defaulted, and the inflation of the early 1920s took its toll, even if publications brought in steady money. In December 1919 Ernst Thiel was able to give her another 100,000 marks as a Christmas present, but then he too fell victim to business failure and hence one of the matron's reliable sources of income vanished. In 1926 she was able to snatch a Hindenburg grant of 450 marks monthly from a new government she despised; the loyal Kessler had been instrumental there. The Society of Friends raised money for her, and the Hamburg cigarette manufacturer Philipp Reemtsma, who favored nationalist causes, granted her an annual 20,000 marks after 1928. Another small, regular, income came from the new Nazi Thuringian education ministry headed by Wilhelm Frick in spring 1931, so as the Third Reich was ushered in early in 1933, Förster-Nietzsche was not exactly rich, but the financial affairs of her institution were in order and she could enjoy a comfortable living.[19] It helped that she won a lawsuit against Kröner Publishing in 1930 that ceded her sole author's rights for *The Will to Power* – an irony of Nietzschean proportions because now it was official that her brother had never written the book, as she had claimed for decades.[20]

By this time, Förster-Nietzsche could have properly been called a bona fide National Socialist. It had not always been so. Having started out in Wilhelmian times as an anti-Semitic conservative, she remained a convinced monarchist throughout the war, until at the beginning of the republic which she came to hate she joined the DNVP, the German National People's Party of Emil Herfurth, who wanted to destroy the Bauhaus. The DNVP was known to harbor as its main goal the unseating of the republic and its parliamentary system by voting against its measures in parliament, to effect a return of the monarchic system. That would have suited Förster-Nietzsche just perfectly, as she would have preferred to be called "Your Excellency" rather than receiving an honorary doctorate from Jena in 1921.[21]

As it happened, she arrived in the National Socialist camp by detour, via the Italian Fascist minister-president Benito Mussolini, who was a declared admirer of Friedrich Nietzsche. After the Italian dictator had made positive statements about the philosopher publicly in 1924, Förster-Nietzsche gratefully reciprocated by declaring her admiration for Mussolini a year later. The first public lecture on Mussolini in the Nietzsche Archive was given in 1928, and the dictator sent her a congratulatory telegram on her eighty-fifth birthday in 1931. In January 1932 the play *Campo di Maggio* was staged in Weimar. The venal Duce had co-authored it with the opera librettist Giovacchino Forzano but had it performed all over Europe under his own name (It dealt with Napoleon's allegedly heroic hundred days on Elba.) Because Mussolini was supposed to be there, on the invitation of Förster-Nietzsche herself, Adolf Hitler decided to come over from Berlin to attend. In between acts, one of Weimar's more prominent National Socialists decided to introduce the leader of the Nazi party to Förster-Nietzsche, who was at the theater. Hitler, who liked spending time in Weimar between his stays in Munich and Berlin, paid the first of several visits to the Archive after that performance. This was nine years after Förster-Nietzsche had observed the November Munich putsch with sympathy, certainly for the audacious young Hitler, but more pointedly for the seasoned World War I general Erich Ludendorff, Hitler's partner in high treason, who was the idol of every DNVP member. After January 1930, when a regional Nazi-led government was in place in Thuringia, its most prominent minister Frick carefully cultivated friendship with Weimar's guardian of the Nietzsche sanctum. Her vanity having been flattered, Förster-Nietzsche then transferred her political loyalty to the Nazis, not least because she was receiving funds from them. Her entire staff, foremost her acting chief archivist Max Oehler, had long ago taken that step.[22]

Weimar's Right-Wing Culture

In the greater Weimar circle of conservative intellectuals and pseudo-intellectuals, artists and pseudo-artists, Elisabeth Förster-Nietzsche's recently acquired new relative Ernst Wachler continued to stand out, more so than did his friend Friedrich Lienhard. Wachler's visits to the Nietzsche Archive were now becoming more frequent.[23] In 1926, he published a brochure in the service of a Nordic Germany. Ranting against the national capitulation of 1918, which like Förster-Nietzsche he attributed to inside traitors, he once again urged mental concentration on the values of *Heimat*, the homeland, as the panacea for all ills befalling the country. At the center of evil threatening *Heimat* he placed current foreign influences, such as the French and "Americanization," and incoming eastern Jews who only sought commerce by deceit. For Wachler, those Jews were instrumental in an ongoing "Semitization of the Occident." In education, he wanted all Jewish content purged, for example in biblical instruction any stories from "far-away Jerusalem." Like Nietzsche, he disdained the Christian Church and Christian thought. He wished eugenics to be used for racial improvement, the same thing which Alfred Rosenberg later said Nietzsche had wanted. He also wanted Nordic values, Germanness, and images of *Heimat* to continue to be presented on stage, as he had earlier tried to do with his open-air theater, but such implementation seemed less conceivable now.[24] In contrast to Wachler, his companion in battle Lienhard had become more muted after the defeat of 1918; the national humiliation did not buoy every conservative's spirit. But even as he had to resign himself to the republic, he, too, saw Germany's enemies personified in the Jews.[25] His name, like Wildenbruch's, would gain renewed currency in the Third Reich.[26]

Although Johannes Schlaf shared many of these sentiments, his personality was somewhat more complex. After he had guarded prisoners of war near Weimar for ten months toward the end of the world conflagration, he came to see that Germany had suffered an unjust, humiliating, defeat. In 1918 Schlaf, along with luminaries like Thomas Mann and Arno Holz, his erstwhile partner in the founding of Naturalism in literature, had signed a declaration against the Western Allies, warning them against reprisal and vindictiveness. Although he initially sympathized with the DDP, because he detected elements of populism in it, he soon discovered that the new German parliament, which in the first half of 1919 congregated in Weimar, was a place of idle chatter. Therefore he moved in a *völkisch* direction, to the DNVP and, like Wachler and Lienhard, deepened his belief in all things Germanic. In this, as he admitted, he was following the racial theories of Count Gobineau and H. S. Chamberlain. By 1925, he was visualizing a Führer figure without yet endorsing the newly arising NSDAP and Hitler, but he agreed with their antipathy to what he regarded as aberrations of modernity: movies, mass sports, and venues of public yet debauched entertainment such as liquor bars. In May 1932 he attended a *völkisch* writers' conference at Wartburg Castle, where he bonded with Will Vesper, soon to be one of the official Nazi bards. Schlaf's anti-Semitism at this time was verbal but reserved for Jews from Europe's East. Since he had a Christ complex, irrevocably setting him apart from his former idol Nietzsche, he ceded credit to the Jews as a people for having produced such a savior of mankind and hence advocated that assimilated, baptized, German Jews more emphatically embrace their Germanness. He was shocked by the assassination of the Jewish Walther Rathenau in 1922, not only because he rejected violence, but also because he had seen in him a strong leadership figure who might help pull Germany out of its present doldrums.

Schlaf's protracted poverty was due to his notorious lack of literary output and stood in inverse relationship to his huge self-esteem. This essentially gifted writer came to neglect prose and poetry for the sake of his astronomical experiments, culminating in the geocentric conviction that the sun revolved around the earth. In some occult way known only to himself, he tied this to the apparent superiority of the Nordics; he expected a new Nordic tribe at the North Pole to take over the governance of mankind. To the extent that his constant appeals to university scholars regarding his cosmogenic theories received no response, he suspected a conspiracy against him and drew parallels with Goethe, who, as Schlaf was not slow to point out, had also turned against what had become entrenched as the Scientific Revolution. At the same time Schlaf, who along with his sister was living solely on handouts of one kind or another, like Förster-Nietzsche expected to receive the Nobel Prize – he thought his imminent in 1922 – and ingenuously delighted in the creation of Schlaf festivals, Schlaf museums, Schlaf associations, and Schlaf linden trees, usually in his birthplace of Querfurt, just north-east of Weimar.[27]

There is ample evidence that Schlaf considered himself as a genius, and therefore thought that Weimar was worthy of him. Interestingly, with his sense of the esoteric he was one of the few conservatives in Weimar who appreciated the Bauhaus. That is to say, he enjoyed the company of certain Bauhaus students, whom he invited to his home for cigar-smoking, song, and discussions. Still, when the Bauhaus's fate was decided in 1924, he sat on a local committee which ruled that its financing by the Thuringian government should cease, to be assumed by the Berlin government, knowing full well that such a solution was impossible. Later, in the Third Reich, he passed disparaging comments about Expressionist art and Walter Gropius.[28]

Meanwhile Adolf Bartels, the patron saint of all Weimar right-wingers, continued on his mission of baiting the Jews. In his approach, he vacillated between the downright vulgar and the pseudo-scholarly. In this connection, eugenic concepts which he had uttered before 1918 were now more strongly emphasized, as he believed all Jews were related through incest, and must be kept strictly apart from Germans. He strove to document the power of Jews in the political, economic and especially cultural life of the new republic, singling out (next to Heinrich Heine, the figure of the past he loved to hate), Walther Rathenau. Old canards were repeated, such as that Christ had been an Aryan and that Jews were innately promiscuous, and credence was given to anti-Jewish conspiracy theories, like the tsarist police invention that the Elders of Zion were secretly ruling the world. New was the accusation that German-born Jews had shirked war service, whereas statistics proved the exact opposite. Bartels often overreached himself in identifying Jews, as when he called the composer Max Bruch and the politician Karl Liebknecht Jewish. When Georg Kaiser, the reigning Expressionist playwright in the early 1920s, was placed on Adolf Bartels's index he protested (which did not reflect well on Kaiser), but Bartels only continued to jeer at him. Bartels meant to be charitable as well as humorous to Jews when he declared: "We do not want to beat them to death," which of course was exactly what the National Socialists proceeded to do later, even not far from Weimar, in Buchenwald. Bartels was to become a member of the National Socialists' party in the mid-1920s.[29]

Bartels also fought Ernst Hardt's appointment as the new theater Intendant following Carl Norris von Schirach; evidently he was considered for the post himself, but despite his theatrical experience had no interest in it.[30] He did not need it, because his books and brochures were flying off bookstore shelves now – a reflection of the right-wing conservatism that was spreading within large parts of the German population at the time. He was especially successful with the publishing firms of Reclam and Westermann, both with new editions of old writings and ever newer publications which, alas, repeated much of the older propaganda. Hence he became successful in two ways. For the first time, he could make a comfortable living as an author. And as a consequence of his growing popularity, a fan club, the Bartelsbund, was founded in 1920 near Leipzig, with a Thuringian chapter in Kölleda, just outside Weimar. Even as respectable a man as Dietrich Schäfer, an arch-conservative historian from the University of Berlin, joined up. The Bartelsbund existed until 1929, when it was merged with a larger *völkisch* conglomerate.[31]

After World War I, Bartels's political reactionism first manifested itself, as in many other Weimar cases, through membership in the DNVP. Bartels, like the others, was a loyal monarchist who principally compaigned for the return of Kaiser Wilhelm II. Logically tied to that goal was a desire to destroy the newfangled republic, whose parliamentary democracy Bartels detested. But through Ernst Graf zu Reventlow Bartels eventually found his way to the Nazis. Count Reventlow hailed from Husum, in the vicinity of Bartels's birthplace Wesselburen. As in the case of Hebbel, this immediately distinguished Reventlow in the eyes of Bartels, steeped in his Blood and Soil ideology as he was. The half-Danish, and hence, for Bartels, Nordic Reventlow had taken on a kind of caretaker role on behalf of illegal Nazis in the North, after Hitler's Munich putsch in November 1923; although his was a caretaker role among several. Within the Bartelsbund, Bartels had lectured on Hitler as early as May 1923, and as he drew closer to Reventlow during Hitler's absence in captivity he came to appreciate the unbridled anti-Semitism of the Nazis. In 1924, when members of the DNVP proceeded to support the Dawes Plan that was to help the republic get on its feet again economically, Bartels claimed those conservatives had done so in the interest of Jews. He also claimed, not without a basis in fact, that several Jews represented the DNVP in German parliaments. Bartels made his views public in yet another new brochure, published in 1924, in which he now fully endorsed the National Socialists, but with little mention of Hitler. Still, the two men met in March of 1925, when Hitler was staying in Weimar, and then again in July of 1926. By 1927, after Hitler had published the second volume of *Mein Kampf*, Bartels was fully won over. He acted as a co-founder of the Weimar KfdK and was on good terms with the Nazi-supported Thuringian government. By July 1932 a new fan club had been founded, the Adolf-Bartels-Bund, in far-off Wesselburen.[32]

One of Adolf Bartels's close acquaintances in and around Weimar was Paul Schultze-Naumburg, the uncommonly gifted son of a painter and an architect, who had been born in Almerich near Naumburg in 1869, some twenty miles from Weimar. Both men published often in *Der Kunstwart*. Schultze-Naumburg resembled van de Velde in that he had begun his professional life as a painter, then, after a minimum of formal study as an architect, switched to the design and construction of buildings. Like van de Velde, he was also interested in interior design, down to furniture and decorations, and took an interest in garments for women, whom he wanted to liberate from physical restraints such as corsets. Moreover, there were early signs of sympathy with modernism, as Schultze-Naumburg partook in the Secessions of Munich and Berlin, in 1893 and 1897 respectively. But

while van de Velde turned to *Jugendstil*, Schultze-Naumburg's development was arrested, moored, as he was, in the German *Biedermeier* style that
had been popular from Goethe's time until mid-century. He advocated
simplicity for houses to be lived in, also finding this quality in the English
country-house style of the late nineteenth century. The dwellings he began
to build in Germany after 1900 were upscale, of simple but expensive materials such as brick and wood and glass, and they conveyed feelings of
comfort and day-to-day livability. Schultze-Naumburg became much
sought after as an architect all over the country, even fashionable, and he
was also asked to build schools, sanatoriums, and factories. Between 1901
and 1917, he set out his ideas in a series of nine published volumes which
he entitled *Kulturarbeiten*, as by 1901 he was living in a house he had
constructed for himself and his growing family in Saaleck, just south of
Naumburg – a picturesque mansion in a picturesque landscape, overlooking
the Saale River, a model of organic integration. He conceived this as the
center of an artists' colony, as he invited colleagues and students there to
workshops, where furniture-making and house-building could be studied.
Although like Schlaf and Lienhard he was ideologically opposed to the
city, Schultze-Naumburg was open to all manner of technical novelties
such as the bicycle, the automobile and, especially, the camera, which he
came to use prolifically in his own work. He also accepted commissions in
big cities, including Berlin, although there he preferred the leafy suburbs
such as Zehlendorf, where he built solid mansions for wealthy burghers,
most of them Jews. Grand Duke Wilhelm Ernst appointed him professor
in 1903, and he received honorary doctorates from Tübingen in 1923, and
Stuttgart in 1929.[33]

With his early progressive history and respectable professional achievements, Schultze-Naumburg became one of the most reactionary architects
of the 1920s and an inveterate foe of the Bauhaus. Idealizing Goethe's
vaunted garden house in the park on the Ilm, where the poet had first
trysted with Christiane Vulpius, he constructed a myth around the gabled
roof (as on the garden house), declaring it "Nordic" and comparing it positively with the flat roofs favored by Bauhaus modernists, especially once
they practiced architecture in Dessau after 1925. Not only did Schultze-
Naumburg attempt to make a sounder economic argument on behalf of the
gabled roof vis-à-vis the flat roof in a copiously illustrated brochure he
published in 1927, but he also resorted to ideological reasoning when he
declared that most Germans had a deep craving for "the way the roof fits
on a Nordic house."[34] His widely accessible theses actually held up better
than the technical explanations Bauhaus apologists printed in obscure

journals for narrow specialists.[35] A few years later, Schultze-Naumburg had become one of the most active speakers throughout Germany, in the service of Rosenberg's Kampfbund für deutsche Kultur.[36]

How had this former Secessionist got to such extremes? Schultze-Naumburg's fundamentally conservative disposition as an artist had prompted him to support the monarchy and Germany's effort in World War I; he had built the imposing Cäcilienhof castle for Crown Prince Wilhelm in Potsdam from 1912 to 1917. After the defeat, like Bartels and Förster-Nietzsche, he joined the German National People's Party (DNVP). But in 1924 he met the newly resurrected leader of the NSDAP at one of Elsa Bruckmann's soirées in Munich. Her husband Hugo was the leading racist publisher in Germany, along with Julius Lehmann, whose Munich salon Schultze-Naumburg also frequented. Gobineau, Chamberlain, the Bayreuth Circle led by Cosima Wagner's daughter-in-law Winifred, and the *völkisch* eugenicists Alfred Ploetz and Fritz Lenz were further influences.[37] Although Schultze-Naumburg was not overly anti-Semitic (what with the many Jewish customers he had), it was the racist-eugenic aspects of National Socialism that he tied to his views on superior Nordic architecture which most motivated him. In 1926, he made succinct race-hygienic observations at an international art exhibition in Dresden, which on account of its modern exhibits he labeled "pornographic," and in 1928 he published another widely available booklet entitled "Art and Race" that compared the works of current Expressionist painters with physical images of the insane. Handy with his camera, he had included many graphic pictures. Although Joseph Goebbels never conceded it (because Schultze-Naumburg was then somewhat *non grata* in the Third Reich's hierarchy), he most certainly used this as a model for his own notorious Exhibition of Degenerate Art in 1937. About the Expressionists Schultze-Naumburg said that the ugliness they presented in their creations reflected nothing but the ugliness residing within themselves. Axiomatically citing as his proof the converse, he pointed to Leonardo da Vinci.[38] By 1930, this architect had joined the Nazi Party and was getting ready to enter the service of Thuringia's new Nazi government.[39]

One of Schultze-Naumburg's protégés toward the end of the 1920s was Hans F. K. Günther, born in 1891 in Freiburg, who had a doctorate in linguistics and German literature. Günther moved quickly from German nationalism – he had volunteered for war service in 1914 – to Nordic racism, as a man of letters, as was Bartels, coupled with a sense of aesthetics, as was the case with Schultze-Naumburg. It is possible that as a student in Paris in 1911 Günther had been repelled by what he conceived as the frivolous French way of life, as many Germans liked to claim, and that subsequent trench experiences bolstered his faith in the Fatherland. What might have been decisive were stays in Norway and Sweden between 1923 and 1929; his second wife was Norwegian. He was able to make ends meet in Scandinavia without really laying the foundations for a career; when he returned to Germany he was caught up in the beginnings of a long-lasting stretch of unemployment and cutbacks for civil servants, including Gymnasium teachers: teaching was the profession he was qualified for, and was poised to enter.[40]

An early decisive influence on Schultze-Naumburg was Professor Eugen Fischer, the medically trained anthropologist whose lectures Günther absorbed while a student in Freiburg.[41] In 1908 Fischer had been in the German colony of South-West Africa (today's Namibia), where he had studied the native population as well as the Rehoboths, persons of mixed race, about whom he had published a famous book in 1913. It advocated, among other things, that the Rehoboths' treatment by the white men be "good, just, stern and not pampering." For they resembled their Hottentot ancestors more than their Boer ones, especially with regards to energy. "The constancy of will, to pursue a certain issue, the energy that the European has – this is missing." After a close reading of the book there can be no question that Fischer believed in the superiority of the white over the black race and that in retrospect he endorsed what had been Germany's first genocide, the protracted war against the Herero and Nama tribes of South-West Africa, between 1904 and 1907. Eventually the war was won by the Germans, after 80 percent of those peoples had been eliminated. The Germans had executed the native men or placed them in concentration camps, and forced their women and children into the Kalahari Desert, where they died of thirst. It is unknown whether Fischer as a scientist had had a hand in sending containers filled with Negro skulls to Germany, but many were found as late as summer 2011 in Freiburg and Berlin's university hospital Charité. Fischer served as that university's rector during the Third Reich, after special appointment by Hitler, and was a section chief at the Kaiser-Wilhelm-Institut (Anthropology), where he had full knowledge of the ongoing genocide of the Jews and was in working contact with Dr. Josef Mengele of Auschwitz.[42]

Under the influence of Fischer, but also because he became interested in the origin of human tribes through his language studies and, like so many of his generation, having read Chamberlain and Gobineau, Günther published his first book in 1920. It was entitled *Knight, Death and Devil* and praised, in the cultural-pessimistic vein of intellectual forebears such as

Schopenhauer, Langbehn, and Lagarde, the ideals of the hero and of Nordic Man. In a nutshell, Günther maintained that after earlier heroes such as Luther, Frederick the Great, Goethe and Bismarck, in present times real heroes were few and that those who did exist were of Nordic stock. The anti-heroes were the modernists, liberals, republicans, and (female) proponents of women's emancipation, and they were, he implied, anything but Nordic. It is significant that Günther reached these conclusions as a linguist, not as a natural scientist or medical scholar, as Fischer had been, who could more properly trace his scholarly genesis to scientists like Haeckel, Rudolf Virchow, and Darwin.[43] From the beginning of his work as a student of race until the end, therefore, Günther's work was organized within, at best, linguistically determined categories and largely according to criteria of his own invention. These had had scant if any precedence in scholarship and must be regarded, as Elvira Weisenburger has put it, as the fruits of Günther's "very own race psychology."[44] Somehow Günther was able to get his knight-and-devil book published by the eugenically minded Julius Lehmann in Munich, who at that time was also beginning to meet with Hitler socially and who then personally encouraged Günther to write a second book, on the racial makeup of the German people. Günther managed to publish this with Lehmann in 1922, a year before he set out for Scandinavia.[45]

The book turned out to be a subjective admixture of syncretic observations and apodictic claims. Syncretic, because Günther had, after much reading and study in museums, chosen to repeat, randomly or in any fashion that suited his preconceived opinions, material already published by others, whether genuine scientists from the *Anthropological Review* or racist pamphleteers like the Frenchman Georges Vacher de Lapouge (1854–1936). Apodictic, because frequently Günther would posit certain conditions without backup of any sort, not even one of his many photographs.[46] As an example of this reasoning, he maintained, without documentation, that Nordics had the greatest propensity for cleanliness and had indeed invented soap and hairbrush, or that only Nordics could properly breed and tend to horses, in this totally ignoring Arabs, the English, or North American native peoples.[47]

Among the four current German "races" Günther placed the Nordics expressly at the top, and the *Ostisch* – a term he had invented – at the bottom. Two others in between were the *Dinarisch* and the *Westisch* – those types, like the Nordics, he had previously encountered in the literature. He admitted that all types were now commingled and that scarcely 8 percent of pure-blooded Nordics still existed, at least in Germany. He allowed for the presence of all four tribes (plus Negroids and Jews) in other European countries as well, notably France, England, and Italy, but those did not concern him and added nothing to his main argument.[48]

According to Günther, the Nordics were of high physical stature, blond, blue-eyed, and long-headed. The long head indicated the highest level of intelligence possible. Their chief distinctions were "capacity for judgment, honesty, and courage." Of all tribes around the globe, they possessed the highest proclivity toward great statesmanship, toward sports, and the smallest chance of becoming criminals. On the minus side – not real minuses for Günther – they tended to be careless and casual, hard and cold in temperament, and given to gambling and betting.[49]

Günther liked the *Dinarisch* less, not least because, like the two remaining tribes, originally they did not hail from Europe's highest North. According to Günther, the *Dinarisch* had some redeeming qualities such as greater emotional capacity and talents for the arts such as music; hence he counted Mozart, Liszt, and Wagner among them. The *Westisch* had even fewer positive qualities, and Günther irredeemably detested the *Ostisch*, because he found them square, squat, and of uncontrolled sexuality, quite unlike the Nordics.[50]

It was not just by implication that Günther placed the Jews, as a foreign "tribe" living among the Germans, at the very bottom of his racial hierarchy although, unlike Bartels, he did so in a studied and restrained fashion. On the Jews, he published an appendix at the end of his volume, soliciting the readers' interest by painstakingly quoting Jewish sources in order to conjure an impression of objectivity. Photographs once again illustrated his theses.[51]

Since all of that material was repeated, with complementary asides and illustrations, in yet another book he had printed in 1930, again by Lehmann, it can serve as the basis for a more sustained analysis. Günther published it and others like it after the phenomenal success he had been having with his first treatise on the German people's race, which would sell 400,000 copies by the end of World War II, in various editions.[52] In 1930, in a tome entitled *A Racial Analysis of the Jewish People*, Günther repeated well-known clichés and imparted new information about the Jews, differentiating little between those living inside and outside of Germany. In the great majority of cases, his allegedly new information was as malicious as were the clichés, clearly identifying Günther as an enemy of Jews. He would dwell on physical characteristics, such as thick lips, protruding eyes, flat feet, and heavy eyelids, and he drew the number "6" to impart authenticity to "the Jewish nose."[53] By Günther's catechism, Jews tended to have strong hair, kinky-haired beards, and "pallid, yellow-matte" skin.[54] Tautologically, he talked of

"Jewish gestures," without explaining what these gestures were and why "Jewish," and added that red-haired Jews might "give off the smell of goats."[55] As was in keeping with a growing body of Nazi ideology by the turn of the 1920s, he placed more weight on inherited traits than on acquired ones and drew conclusions about character. In stating that "the Jewish walk can be silent or slithery," he alluded to deceit and swindle, and he pointed to male Jews as potential sexual predators who preferred impregnating blond and blue-eyed German girls.[56] Günther capped his diatribe with an account of Jewish influence in current German state and society: after having increased the wealth of international Jewry through their role in World War I (echoes of the 'Stab in the Back' Legend), German Jews were now controlling financial institutions, the press, the universities, theater, and art. It did not bother Günther that he was committing errors in the manner of Bartels, whose favorite organ *Kunstwart* Günther cited as a source when claiming that Jews were taking over German literature: he identified the painters Picasso, Feininger, Kandinsky, and Max Pechstein as Jewish and, like Bartels, maintained that Heine's real name had been Chaim Bückeburg. By way of conclusion, Günther called for a strict separation of Germans and Jews, stopping short of hinting that one could beat them all to death, as Bartels had done earlier.[57]

Contrary to what some scholars have maintained, Günther did not become "one of the principal racial experts under the Nazi regime," because he lacked the modicum of formal scientific training that would render himself credible even in a polity wont to utilize pseudo-science.[58] He was a popularizer of truths, half-truths, and falsehoods, his argumentation was impressionistic, what scant evidence he had was anecdotal. As a popularizer, National Socialist politicians and more rigorously trained race scientists like Eugen Fischer and Fritz Lenz welcomed him. By propounding the superiority of the Nordic-German type and the miserableness of the Jews, Günther aided German public opinion in its growing rejection of the Jews and, ultimately, in acceptance of their total disappearance.[59]

A few years before Hitler's assumption of power the racist Blood and Soil work Adolf Bartels had started with the early *Kunstwart* came full circle through the efforts of Hans F. K. Günther and both these men's ideological fellow travelers. In fact, it had ramifications beyond 1933 that came to full fruition only at the height of World War II.

Immediately after World War I a cross-fertilization of ideas set in which revolved around the concepts of Nordic superiority especially vis-à-vis Jews and Slavs, the priorities of (German) blood and soil and, after the loss of German territories in the East, the right to conquer eastern European territory. This implied the necessity of new Germanic-German settlements and the attendant subjugation of indigenous eastern peoples. In 1919 Bartels publicly advocated the creation of "colonies of military men-in-training" as far as western Russia; the area would have to be "Germanized," with painstaking attention to racial eugenics; swamps had to be cultivated; Jews would be put on ships in Odessa and sent across the Black Sea: "We need land."[60] These goals resonated with Günther one year later when he stated in his knight-and-devil volume that a heroic race had an obligation to hate, that its heroes were given the courage to break new ground and drain swamps, and that as Nordics they were legitimized to do so by invading foreign soil: "The hero may ransack whatever he finds." In his 1922 race analysis Günther enlarged on this and mentioned "a special lust for conquest, and strength for conquest, possessed by Nordic tribes."[61]

It was in the same year of 1922 that Bartels received credit from the *völkisch* writer Bruno Tanzmann near Dresden whom he had been mentoring for some twenty years, going back to the early times of the *Kunstwart*. Tanzmann (b. 1878) was interested in the future of the German farmers, Germanic history, and new settlement; not without means, he had once promulgated his ideas through his own "Swastika" publishing firm which, however, went bankrupt. Now he lauded Bartels, as "herald of race and home-bred art", and his positive influence on agrarian community and culture. Ever anti-urban, one would have to encourage more settlement, urged Tanzmann, ideally in the East and, if necessary, by fighting Poles and Russians.[62] A couple of years later Tanzmann teamed up with Willibald Hentschel, also of Dresden and born in 1858, who had once been an assistant to Haeckel at Jena. He was an even more pronounced anti-Semite, interested in Aryan breeding colonies (ideally of 100 men mating with 1,000 women), for the propagation of the Germanic race. With variations, both sets of ideas conformed to schemes of Bartels and Günther; Hentschel saw in Albrecht Dürer's knight, the centerpiece of the engraving *Knight, Death and the Devil*, the prototype of the Germanic hero.[63] By 1924 Tanzmann and Hentschel had formed one of the republic's innumerable youth groups, with 100 members at first and 2,000 in 1929, about 10 percent of them being girls.[64] They called themselves the Artam League and next to the Hitler Youth later went down in history as Germany's most right-wing youth organization.

Tanzmann's Artam motto of summer 1924 had been "Against the East Now Let Us Ride," but in lieu of a Slavic conquest in eastern Europe the *Artamanen* had to resign themselves to less spectacular activities. So they hired themselves out for simple room and board to replace Polish migrant workers on East German estates. It was hard labor, and in their free time, they honed tenets of Nordic racist ideology under a set hierarchy of leaders. A department for race science was established by the fall of 1927, inspired by Günther's racial analysis of the German people. What were believed to be Germanic rites were performed and Germanic plays staged, such as those by Friedrich Lienhard at a summer convention in Pretzsch on the Elbe river, in 1926. Hans Severus Ziegler, a young Weimar protégé of Bartels and of Schultze-Naumburg, talked to the Artam Thuringian chapter in September 1928.

Günther became a member of an Artam support organization, and often from Scandinavia, yet always when in Germany, he was available for guidance and advice. One of the section leaders was the Bavarian university-educated agronomist Heinrich Himmler, born in 1900, who as a twenty-four-year-old had enthused over Günther's knight-and-devil tome, as he noted in his diary: "A book which in wisely conceived words and sentences expresses what I feel and think, ever since I have begun to think." Himmler became the Artam League's regional leader for Bavaria.[65]

Yet another supporter of the league was Richard Walther Darré, Swedish-German-born in 1895 in Argentina, who had gone to school in Heidelberg and Wimbledon and then fought for the Kaiser on the Western Front. Like Tanzmann, he became concerned with the fate of the German farmer and studied to become an agronomist, specializing in colonization. Sharing the anti-urbanism and xenophobia of the Artam League and its backers, he too joined the support group, encouraging the young men and women to incorporate biological criteria for training, after 1927.[66]

Darré, Günther, and Himmler all met through the Artam League, at various times, most likely in the villa of Schultze-Naumburg, who sympathized with their ideals. Haus Saaleck, perched on a cliff over the Saale, ironically was situated beneath the decaying Saaleck Castle, where the two murderers of the Jewish Walther Rathenau had hidden in July 1922 until one of them killed himself, as police shot his companion to pieces.[67] From the mid-twenties to the early 1930s the so-called Saaleck Circle gathered there, with some Nazi grandees such as Rosenberg, Goebbels, Göring, and Frick also passing through. In due time, Schultze-Naumburg invited Hitler, who was in direct communication with Artam head Hans Holfelder, after he had met him at Hugo Bruckmann's in Munich, and Hitler came to Haus Saaleck at least twice. It is reasonable to assume that Bartels, Hentschel, and Tanzmann, all of them living close to Saaleck, were also guests of the circle.[68]

Darré had already published one book on Blood and Soil and farmers, when in 1930 Schultze-Naumburg invited him to stay at his mansion to finish writing a follow-up volume. Darré began this book with a quotation by Schultze-Naumburg from the *Kunstwart*; he defined his new work as a "requirement for the creation of a new aristocracy," wishing to merge the "trinity of peasant, *Volk* and nobility" into one. His point of departure was the principle of congenital inequality; like Günther and other ideological friends he placed the old Germans at the pinnacle of a racial hierarchy, following their history through the centuries, only to conclude that many of the qualities that determined their former ranking had been lost. To recover these, land was necessary, farms were needed, and Poles had to be replaced in the German East by select Germans willing to settle. Darré singled out the *Artamanen*'s current efforts as exemplary. But as yet, there was no mention of conquering Slavs beyond German borders, and on the question of breeding, too, Darré proved conservative. Instead of Hentschel's breeding farms he preferred monogamy, if among superior species, although he did not rule out sterilization among the lower ones. He ranted against manifestations of modernity such as "Hawaiian Jazz Bands" and the Dessau Bauhaus, where the Jews undoubtedly had wrought mischief. Regarding Jews in general, he respectfully deferred to Günther, whom he cited affirmatively a number of times, as he cited Nietzsche and Schultze-Naumburg.[69] Whereas after 1930 the *Artamanen* came to suffer from attrition, only to be absorbed into the larger Nazi youth movement later, their seminal, pioneering imperialist-eugenicist ideology was carried further by Himmler and Darré, and several *Artamanen* proceeded to join the Nazi Party's SS, which was led by Himmler after 1929. Himmler appointed Darré as his first chief of the SS Race Office in 1931 (later known as SS-RuSHA), which selected SS candidates biologically and even appraised their brides, according to Günther's criteria. During World War II, prominent SS officers with an Artam record occupied themselves with desettlement and resettlement issues in important ways. These imperialistic visions entered the realm of reality when after autumn 1941 the Germans were coming to enjoy ultimate military success in the East, the murderous *Generalplan Ost* took shape, and Himmler's second in command Reinhard Heydrich was setting himself up as the uncompromising ruler of the Czech Protectorate. In 1942, when mechanical mass killing of ethnic enemies began in earnest, ex-Artaman Rudolf Höss was already installed as commandant of Auschwitz; his wife, Hedwig, too was a former Artam girl. By then *Artaman* alumnus Wolfram Sievers was executive secretary of Himmler's research organization Ahnenerbe, whose research interest was in the German ancestral heritage and from where, as an organizational platform, he supervised the planned evacuation from Italy of South Tyroleans of German stock, with an initial view to resettle them, after its conquest, in the Crimea. Sievers also directed cultural looting expeditions in Poland and the western Soviet Union. (After 1945, both Höss and Sievers were hanged.) Himmler's entire concept of resettling the western part of the Slavic East with Germans owed much to his early experiences as an *Artamane*. His earlier projections included plans for militarily fortified borderland farms, occupied by elite SS warriors, who would till the soil during daytime while watching out for rebellious Slavs at night, poised to attack from the East, where they had been pushed by force.[70] These Artam-inspired plans were never realized.

Goethe Is Nationalized

In Franz Liszt's old haunts, the Altenburg mansion on the road to Jena, on February 9, 1911, a wintry day, Professor Bernhard Suphan, the director of the Goethe and Schiller Archive, piled up several volumes of the Herder edition he was working on. Then he climbed on top with a rope and hanged himself. He had been unable to continue with his work, and with his life. As a widower, he could not raise his children by himself. Worse for him, in the nearby archive, he was completely overcome by a chronic lack of staff and financial resources.

Suphan, born in 1845, the son of a Nordhausen barber, had been a Gymnasium teacher in Berlin, where Wilhelm von Scholz, one of his pupils, remembered him as eccentric but brilliant as a German literature scholar. He received the title of Prussian professor in 1886 and call to Weimar as director one year later. His work there was first-rate.[71]

Suphan barely finished the so-called Sophian edition of Goethe's writings, with the last index volume appearing posthumously in 1919. Altogether there were four parts, comprising 143 volumes. Letters between Goethe and Karl August were also published. Otherwise, there was little progress in the Goethe and Schiller Archive. The stasis between the two world wars was marked by slow overall indexing beyond the earliest stages, and few additions to the holdings. There was one important new acquisition in the form of the playwright Georg Büchner's papers, donated by the Leipzig Insel publisher Anton Kippenberg in 1924. After that year, the Archive was co-sponsored by the new state of Thuringia, a remaining grand-ducal escrow fund, and the Goethe-Gesellschaft. Its vice-president in 1932 was the archivist and Goethe specialist Hans Wahl, who had become director of the Goethe National Museum (essentially Goethe's historic mansion on the Frauenplan) in 1917 and of the Archive in 1928. If

Suphan had been an avid nationalist, yet capable idealist who could not cope with the vicissitudes of life, Wahl was capable but a political opportunist. He was one of the underwriters of the Weimar chapter of Rosenberg's KfdK in 1928 and in 1945 offered his services to the invading Soviet army. When their leaders asked him whether Hitler had ever had anything to do with the iconic museum Wahl denied it, as he denied it to the US *Stars and Stripes* reporter Klaus Mann, Thomas's oldest son. Yet it had been he himself who had led the Führer on a grand tour of Goethe's house in March of 1925.[72]

Already by the turn of the century Goethe was being appropriated ever more by the chauvinists and xenophobes of the Second Empire, after the initial founding of the Goethe-Gesellschaft in 1885. Of this, albeit in an extreme form, Adolf Bartels had been a striking example. During the Great War this process continued, and after its shameful end for Germany it intensified. In this, conservative culture brokers were spurred by the negative example of what they called the dissolute gutter culture, perpetuated by leftists on the Bauhaus model, by Dadaists and anarchists flourishing in the cabarets, dance halls, theaters, and cinemas of Berlin, Frankfurt, and Hamburg. Those were the pollutant champions of modernity, the backers of the new democratic republic, whom the established pillars of the Goethe-Gesellschaft had to withstand, had to defeat. Whatever was usable of Schiller was, incidentally, part of this effort. Not much else from the Weimar classics served their purpose.[73]

The aura spread by the reactionary Goethe-Gesellschaft weighed heavily on all official or public creations of intellectual products involving Goethe's name or Goethe's ideas. Right-wing publicists and scholars engaged Goethe in the service of their ideology, on the model of Chamberlain, who had written just before the war that Goethe had been an exemplary German patriot and an exemplary anti-Semite.[74] After World War I, these two values became the bedrock of the new conservatism; almost the entire academic discipline of German literary studies was based on them.[75] Goethe's cosmopolitanism was contrasted with the observed plebeian comportment of the new republican politicians – Philipp Scheidemann, Friedrich Ebert, and their Jewish colleagues Otto Landsberg and Eduard David. If Goethe was said to be an idealist, they were materialists.[76] In this, the invented tradition that had placed Goethe between Luther and Frederick the Great on the one side and Bismarck on the other was frequently referenced. Armand Crommelin related the "artist Goethe" to the "artist Bismarck" in 1919, and three years later Thomas Mann, in the last stretch of his nationalist phase, likened him, next to Bismarck, to Luther, when he wrote: "He is the most

German poet for the reason that he is Germany's greatest."[77] The racists Wachler and Günther used Goethe as their witness and increasingly, as Hitler became known as the "Führer" of his National Socialist party, Goethe too was described as a "Führer," not of a mere political formation, but of the entire German nation.[78]

In the Goethe-Gesellschaft, the succession of presidents symbolized political reaction from the beginning, a reaction which itself harked back to Goethe's own time. If something rang false with the Gesellschaft in the 1920s, this quality can immediately be traced to Grand Duchess Sophie, who founded it in 1885, only to begin manipulating the Goethe papers in the interest of the ducal house. However, one may go further back, to the Goethe era, and be reminded that in the early nineteenth century the multi-talented but precocious young writer Bettina von Arnim had engaged in futile attempts to ingratiate herself with, perhaps to seduce, the poet, while, at the same time, insulting his partner Christiane by calling her in public a "blood pudding gone crazy". Thereafter Goethe had forbidden the von Arnims entry to his house. Bettina von Arnim's son-in-law happened to be Herman Grimm, the son of Wilhelm Grimm, who after Bismarck's unification wars was one who set the tone for the nationalistic Goethe interpretation to follow, as professor of art history in Berlin.[79] The first advisers for the newly founded Goethe Archive appointed in 1885 had been the Germanists Wilhelm Scherer and shortly thereafter his pupil Erich Schmidt, both teaching in Berlin and falling into that tradition. Schmidt became president of the Goethe-Gesellschaft in 1906, until his death in 1913. Just before that, he dismissed Ludwig Geiger, who had been the Jewish editor of the *Goethe-Jahrbuch* since 1880, because he did not like Jews.[80] Schmidt's colleague in Berlin was the pro-monarchy Germanist Gustav Roethe; he headed the Society from 1921 until his death in 1926. A year after that Roethe and Schmidt's student Julius Petersen took over as president; he was a Berlin University chairholder since 1921. In so many ways, Petersen eventually catered to the Nazis.[81]

Gustav Roethe passionately hated Jews, the republic and all the manifestations of modernism.[82] From Berlin he carried on a lengthy correspondence with Society presidium member Friedrich Lienhard in Weimar about the possible creation of a "German Academy," to be coupled with the Goethe-Gesellschaft, through which unwanted influences could be curbed.[83] In August 1924, on the occasion of his patron's birthday 175 years earlier, Roethe gave a festive speech in Weimar in which he strongly polemicized against the French (who had recaptured Lienhard's birthplace of Alsace) and equated Goethean thought with Germanic thought and, by extension, German thought. In a crafty parallel to current democratic developments, he lauded Goethe for having controlled the rabble by siding with the aristocratic Napoleon, praising the Olympian's opposition to "equality." For Roethe, as for others before him, Goethe was firmly ensconced in the elysium of Luther, Frederick the Great, and Bismarck. Here, the invention of a false tradition worked once more. Clairvoyantly, Roethe concluded with the salutation: "The way that Goethe shows us is the German way. Goethe, we greet you, we thank you, you, our friend, our hero, our Führer!"[84]

In his capacity as Berlin professor and president of the Goethe-Gesellschaft, Petersen showed no particular aversion to Jews, but in his public demeanor as a right-wing patriot he was scarcely less vocal than Roethe had been. As the Berlin scholar Eberhard Lämmert has explained, the aim was, after the catastrophe of 1918, "to safeguard the German spirit against similar defeat."[85] Such *Weltanschauung* had ramifications for the Society in 1929, when new presidium members were to be elected. Significantly, the personality of Thomas Mann once more came into play. Mann had managed his ideological changeover from conservative monarchist to republican-by-necessity (*Vernunftrepublikaner*) during 1922, and because of this had not been elected to the Goethe-Gesellschaft in that year. He had been backed by the Berlin chapter of the Gesellschaft, which was more liberal than Weimar's mother organization, as it stubbornly rejected the new political order. In 1929 Mann again became a candidate, but now was opposed by his erstwhile friend, the increasingly fascistic Ernst Bertram, who had been proposed by the Hamburg chapter – just as reactionary as Weimar's. In keeping with his public conservative utterings on the state of the nation, Goethe's place and that of the Goethe-Gesellschaft in it, Petersen as president made sure that Bertram won the day.[86]

Thomas Mann never became a presidial member of the Goethe-Gesellschaft, but he attained a dubious prominence as he was moved to deliver a key address during the Goethe Festival of 1932. The event had been painstakingly planned by Petersen and his staff. The centenary of Goethe's death had been conceived, in Weimar, as a demonstration against the German republic, which in March 1932 was on the brink of failure.[87] The formal call to participate in the festivities of Weimar's "Goethe Year" had an imperialistic ring; principally, it was addressed to all Germans in the world. It was signed by President Paul von Hindenburg, Chancellor Heinrich Brüning, and other German notables, virtually all from the right of the political spectrum. Although National Socialists (and Communists) refrained for tactical reasons from participation in these events, two known

Nazi men of letters had signed the declaration, Rudolf Georg Binding and Erwin Guido Kolbenheyer. Moreover, the key concept *Volksgemeinschaft* (biologically defined people's community) was prominently mentioned, which had a racist connotation and was an integral part of the propaganda arsenal of the NSDAP. Wilhelm von Scholz had signed as president of the poetry section in the Prussian Academy of Arts, and so, on behalf of Weimar and the Goethe-Gesellschaft, had Hans Wahl and Julius Petersen.[88]

The ceremonies beginning on March 21 included an elaborate procession to Goethe's burial site, in which Feodora, the widow of the last grand duke, took part; this in itself was an affront to the republic.[89] Speeches included one by Kolbenheyer and one by Hans Eibl, a *völkisch* literature scholar from Vienna.[90] Petersen's address turned out to be an exercise in nationalist and pseudo-religious phraseology, as he compared Goethe to Jesus Christ.[91]

Thomas Mann had been among the original signatories of the official invitation, along with Gerhart Hauptmann (who subsequently withdrew). Whereas Hauptmann then as later was known to be a political opportunist, Mann's name should not even have appeared on the paper. By conviction, he opposed any attempt to demonstrate against the republic at that time, and Petersen and his Goethe-Gesellschaft colleagues, knowing this, had tried to avoid him, as before.[92] However, along with Hauptmann and Petersen himself, as well as a few others, Mann had been singled out as a recipient of a new Goethe Medal to be bestowed by President von Hindenburg; hence Mann, unaware of the kind of company that would surround him there, may have felt impelled to participate.[93] As it turned out, once in Weimar and awkwardly received by the organizers, he felt distinctly uncomfortable, eerily touched by the many signs of Nazism already visible.[94] For all of Thuringia had already experienced the first regional Nazi government in Germany's history, from January 1930 to April 1931, and the political constellation was such that Thuringia would enter upon a second such government in August. Significantly, Mann excused himself from the graveyard procession on the grounds that he had no top hat.[95] Nonetheless, as Hans Rudolf Vaget has emphasized, Mann was "a formidable expert in all matters relating to Goethe." Hence his talk, opening official events on March 21, not surprisingly turned out to be well crafted and marked by profound insight into a personality whom he himself, only a few years later, would brilliantly portray in a new novel.[96] At the end of his speech, Mann issued a warning regarding the impending destruction of German democracy. Perhaps against his better knowledge, he urged his listeners to keep believing that this democracy, while it lived, had the power to lead into a new and worthwhile future. And he cited Goethe as having said that it was imperative to love not what was dead, but what was alive.[97]

Few of those who listened to the Nobel laureate agreed with him, and reactions in the German media were largely negative.[98] The great majority of visitors to these Goethe festivities were either looking back to the monarchic era as was ex-Grand Duchess Feodora, or into a future under National Socialist auspices. The Nazis themselves hurled slurs at Mann, insulting him as a "so-called European (with Portuguese blood)," who had been tasteless enough to lower himself from the world of Goethe to the nether regions of cheap political criticism.[99] The writing was on the wall. Weimar was already well primed and poised, in 1932, to enter the Third Reich.

The Weimar Republic in Weimar

The German Republic had been proclaimed in Berlin by Philipp Scheidemann, parliamentary spokesman of the moderate Majority Socialists (SPD) in the Reichstag, on November 9, 1918, two days before Germany's armistice with the Western Allies. Scheidemann, a former journalist, and Friedrich Ebert, a saddler from Heidelberg and the leader of the SPD, did not want radical changes from the monarchy, whose Kaiser had just abdicated, instead they strove for a democratic, parliamentarian republic, in line with the strong recommendations of US President Woodrow Wilson. Wilson had made peace contingent on such a transformation. First on the agenda of Scheidemann and Ebert therefore was to elect a constituent assembly from among the legitimate political parties, appoint a chancellor and elect a president, as well as propagate a republican constitution. Under the intermittent chancellorship of Ebert a provisional republican government found it impossible to pursue this business from the capital of Berlin, because it was beset by a riotous naval brigade and breakaway extreme SPD leftists led by Karl Liebknecht and Rosa Luxemburg. All of them wished to complete the revolution of the proletariat started by the mutinous sailors in North German ports in the fall of 1918, and which was spreading to other German cities. To keep these left-radical elements in check the right-wing socialist Gustav Noske was called upon, whom Ebert had appointed as commissioner for war. Noske now summoned some of the Freikorps, bands of demobilized imperial soldiers loyal to the old order, who followed, willy-nilly, whatever former imperial commander would command them. In Berlin the clashes between left and right were fierce; on January 15, 1919, the Freikorps caught Liebknecht and Luxemburg and murdered them. Difficulties were compounded by an extremely harsh winter and the effects of an Allied blockade, which kept essential goods from reaching the city. Moreover, an influenza epidemic was killing thousands of already malnourished Berliners.[100]

In the Reichstag building, the interior had been demolished.[101] This symbolized the chaos, within which constructive governance of Germany from its capital of Berlin was presently impossible. But there were deeper reasons why the politicians, for a while at least, wanted to move away from Berlin to begin their work. South Germans were tired of the dominance of Berlin and Prussian militarism since the Bismarck era. Hence a compromise might be found by situating the new central government somewhere in the middle of Germany. Others resented the big-city culture that Berlin represented and preferred a town of medium size, untouched by the urban modernism of which Berlin was the avatar. In line with that was the desire of many to connect a new democratic government with vestiges of the past that bespoke traditional culture.

During the second half of January, these points were seriously considered by politicians and administrators, until a shortlist of venues was drawn up, consisting of Frankfurt am Main, Nuremberg, Würzburg, and Weimar. It is not certain who had actually made the choice of Weimar – apparently several people thought of it – but it quickly emerged in the lead. Although currently it lay in a sea of leftist would-be revolutionaries, with Thuringia and especially neighbouring Saxony inhabited by a dissatisfied proletariat, it had a very conservative reputation, what with its classics tradition, steadfast artisanal middle class, and well-to-do rentiers. Against its surroundings it was easily shielded by a military cordon. It lay virtually in the center of Germany yet was not too far from Berlin, where some administrative branches would remain, and its celebrated cultural reputation might curry favor with the Allies, with whom a peace treaty had to be signed and who would be suitably impressed by the irenic Goethe and Schiller tradition. It had never been a physical or spiritual locus of militarism as had the storied small town of Potsdam near Berlin. Logistically, it appeared suitable because of its practical experience of tourism, which had created a sufficient number of hotels, restaurants, and watering holes. Hence on January 20 the decision was made to move the provisional national assembly to Weimar, where it would hold meetings in the theater for as long as necessary. On February 6 the designated president Ebert opened the first parliamentary session in Weimar's rearranged theater auditorium. Scheidemann had been appointed chancellor.[102]

Weimar itself was deeply affected by the change from provincial capital to seat of the national parliament. As over 400 deputies, a press corps of

1,000, scores of blue-frocked Berlin policemen, and a Freikorps of at least 4,000 Freiwillige Landesjäger (volunteer soldiers conscripted locally) were moving to the small town, revolutionary worker bands from industrial outposts like Gera and Jena did their best to create havoc. They were ripping out the railway tracks around Weimar well into the summer, until after February the only reliable route was that between Weimar and Jena. Since communication with and transportation to the capital had to be secured, new telephone facilities were installed and the sidewalks torn up, and a twice-daily airplane shuttle had to be established. As new people moved in, inns were crowded and private dwellings requisitioned, which made renting – for instance for Bauhaus personnel and students – very expensive. The soldiers squatted in villages and everywhere food was becoming scarce and expensive, as Weimar was not exempt from the Allied blockade and ration cards proved inadequate. It was difficult to get into the city, because special passes had to be displayed to guards, and inside Weimar too there were many controls. General Georg Maercker's Landesjäger were everywhere, on rooftops, in windows and doorways, even hiding in the bushes with machine guns. Indeed, a putsch by the outlying radicals was feared. Some workers, like those on the railways, attempted strikes, but these were always suppressed.[103]

The good burghers of Weimar liked none of this; their theater and opera productions had been relocated to inferior venues, their public places taken away from them, and their shops overrun. Since they did not really know or care about what was going on, although most were glad to be rid of their intemperate grand duke, they protested by displaying the old black-and-white imperial flags that were now illegal. As the parliamentary sittings dragged on into summer, the citizens became restless and started cursing the authorities. The deputies, too, and the many visiting correspondents soon found Weimar unspeakably boring, having exhausted the restaurants, the Liszt House, the Goethe Museum, the Ilm park and what few diversions there were in off-site recital halls and cinemas. Most had come without their wives, because it would have been too expensive to bring them.[104]

After its move from Berlin to Weimar, the national assembly would face three important tasks: the passage of a constitution befitting a democratic republic, the proper installation of a republican president, and the signing of a peace treaty with the Western Allies. All were accomplished before the assembly's permanent return to Berlin in August 1919, but each had its own attendant problems, the consequences of which would weigh on the republic in the future and crimp its day-to-day efficacy.

A constitutional proposal calling for a republic of confederated states and with due recourse to the revolution of 1848–49 had been presented by State Secretary Professor Hugo Preuss in Berlin at the end of January, and finally passed in Weimar on July 31. It took heed of many of President Wilson's prior admonitions (Wilson had been professor of political science at Princeton), in particular, on the American pattern, his call for a strong president. Doubtless the Germans thought that in heeding this advice they would please Wilson and his peace offerings would be commensurately mild. But there were a number of things wrong with the constitution from the start.

Anachronistically, the republic remained a *Reich* – an empire, which signified expansionist aspirations. The strong presidency was to contribute to the downfall of the republic later because Article 48 allowed the head of state too much power through the invocation of emergency legislation: this could be done at the behest of a strong chancellor, who in this manner could mutate into a quasi-dictator and ignore parliament. This occurred during Heinrich Brüning's so-called presidential dictatorship in the early 1930s, weakening the republic's fibre and ushering in Hitler's rule. Furthermore, the constitution was backed by the parties of the so-called Weimar Coalition, an alliance between the liberal German Democrats (DDP), Ebert's Majority Socialists who had supported the Kaiser's war effort (SPD), and Catholic Center party (Zentrum). In the Berlin elections for the constituent assembly on January 19 they had received 75, 163 and 71 votes respectively, and hence possessed a majority over the opposition (112). Principally in opposition were the Independent Socialists (Communists – USPD) and the reactionary German National People's Party (DNVP), who were bent on preventing or unseating the republic and astringently opposed the constitution, if from opposite sides. As the political right became stronger in Germany after 1920, it was the DNVP and, later allied with it, Hitler's NSDAP which claimed that the constitution was the work of left-wingers and Jews as, indeed, the DDP and SPD harbored many Jewish members. As if to validate this argument, it was frequently emphasized that Preuss himself was Jewish. Moreover, it did not augur well that while the constitution was passed in Weimar on the last day of July, 1919, it was signed (by a Socialist president) only on August 11 in Schwarzburg, a Thuringian spa, because Ebert had chosen to vacation there at such an inopportune time. In the final analysis, as Fritz Stern has observed, even a perfect constitution in 1919 – and this was regarded as such in its time – could not help solve Germany's problems as a divided country, "with elements at both ends of the political spectrum irreconcilably opposed to liberal democracy."[105]

Ebert took his formal oath as president of the republic on August 21, the last day of the assembly's Weimar sitting, significantly in the absence of all DNVP members. In several respects, his choice as president did not help the republic on its way. His determination, in alliance with Scheidemann and Noske, in keeping down a series of leftist uprisings, especially in Berlin, did not endear him to the radical wing of his party, the Independent Socialists, who under Liebknecht had not supported the war effort and who now liked to portray Ebert as a puppet of the bourgeoisie. While some of these Independent Socialists remained within the new parliamentary system as USPD, others had already formed the Communist Party of Germany (KPD) in Berlin, on January 1, which stayed, as yet, outside of government and then would work hard to unseat it. None of this contributed to Ebert's political fortunes. On the right, however, Ebert was viewed not as a member of the respectable classes but a petit-bourgeois parvenu, who on arrival dared to ride, literally, on a sleigh to his new residence in Weimar's main castle. In public addresses he took great pains in conjuring up the "Weimar Spirit," referencing the classics, such as when he pointed to *Faust*, and *Wilhelm Meisters Wanderjahre*, Goethe's mature novel, on February 6, for which he was derided by the philistine establishment.[106]

Finally, Weimar came to be unhappily associated with the shameful end of the war and precarious new beginnings through the signing by its National Assembly members of the Paris Peace Treaty. Ultimately, that treaty was determined by the Council of the Big Three in Paris, staffed by the leaders of France, Britain, and the United States. Germany had to assume full responsibility for having caused the war and substantially diminish its armed forces. France wanted material and financial reparations from Germany to compensate for its huge losses and as punishment, as well as territorial revisions to Germany's disadvantage, not least for security reasons. Included in this was the goal of the Rhine as a binational border or, at the very least, the indefinite occupation of the left bank of the Rhine. Britain coveted some reparations to help pay its war debt (mostly to the United States) and for the reconstitution and safeguarding of its superiority on the high seas, but sought to keep Germany's economic infrastructure intact, so that continued commerce with the country was possible. The United States originally had upheld the benign and fair-sounding principles of Wilson's Fourteen Points, which had served as a basis for the November 1918 armistice and which, the Germans unstintingly believed, would serve as premise for the final peace. Under constant pressure from France's Georges Clemenceau and Britain's David Lloyd George, however, Wilson had been attenuating those principles, mostly to salvage for himself the plan for an international League of Nations, to preserve peace and establish democracy wherever possible, especially in Germany. One large plank in this platform had been national self-determination, meaning that a people, or a minority thereof, would not be ruled by foreigners. The Germans banked on this in particular, because they thought it would prevent the separation of German-inhabited borderlands, Alsace-Lorraine in the west on behalf of France, and parts of Silesia in the East, coveted by Poles.

The formulation of the peace terms to be offered by the Allies took place in Paris during 1919, with much bickering between Clemenceau and Lloyd George, which invariably had to be resolved by Wilson. When the German delegation under Foreign Minister Ulrich Count Brockdorff-Rantzau were summoned to appear in the French capital on May 7, they were still under the impression that they could negotiate on the basis of the Fourteen Points. But for starters, the 180 members were surprised when they were deposited by the French in "the cold and gloomy Hôtel des Réservoirs" in Versailles. They worked feverishly on their dossiers, the count preparing two possible replies to the Allied peace offer, one mild and curtly accepting, the other long and defiant. Meanwhile, someone was playing Liszt's Hungarian Rhapsodies on a hotel piano in order to obstruct the enemy's eavesdropping. Brockdorf-Rantzau was then summoned to the Hall of Mirrors in Versailles to be told of the peace terms. It was here, after the defeat of France, that Bismarck had ushered in the Second Reich in 1871. No negotiations were allowed. In shock, the count presented his longer speech and returned to the Réservoirs hotel in a daze.

Back in Weimar, the National Assembly considered what they thought were dictated, crushing, peace terms. Long deliberations among the deputies ensued, on whether to sign or not. The more on the political left one stood, the more one was inclined to sign, because it was known that otherwise the Allies would march onto German soil, something that during the entire world war had not happened. The right, at least, feigned resistance. So on June 20 the government resigned over the peace dispute, with president-designate Ebert forming a new cabinet on June 22. The next day marked the Allied deadline for treaty acceptance. The Social Democrats Otto Bauer and Hermann Müller replaced Scheidemann and Brockdorff-Rantzau as chancellor and foreign minister. Outside Weimar's theater, some of General Maercker's patriotic troops were threatening revolt, should this peace be signed, and could be restrained by Ebert and their commander only with difficulty. At the eleventh hour Weimar's assembly accepted the terms. On June 28 Müller, together with his colleague Johannes Bell, traveled to Paris to sign the peace documents. Bell was the new minister for traffic, but also for the colonies. Germany had just been surrendering its colonies.[107]

With the national government returning from Weimar to Berlin in August, the day-to-day business continued in a capital that had become much safer. But the name "Weimar Republic" stuck to this new German polity, for better or for worse, in all cases associating the town of Weimar with a history it was not responsible for, whether it be further social and political disquiet or the modernist culture, hitherto known as "Weimar Culture," emanating from Berlin. As for the disquiet, events even in 1919 could have derailed the new democracy. Soviet republics sprang up in Bremen and Bavaria, a miners' strike in the Ruhr, left-radical terror in Leipzig, and revolutionary leftists taking over in nearby Gotha, in January and February alone. The following months saw a Soviet republic in Brunswick, a left-radical putsch in Hamburg, general strikes in Berlin, the Ruhr Valley and Württemberg, and corresponding reactionary backlashes. Poles revolted in Upper Silesia and Freikorps moved to the Baltic lands to try to claim them for Germany. There were a trial and extremely light sentences for the murderers of Liebknecht and Luxemburg in Berlin; one killer escaped and fled to Holland. Under Cologne's Lord Mayor Konrad Adenauer, parts of the Rhineland, encouraged by France, considered separa-ration. War wounded and children were starting to populate the city streets as beggars, with Germans still dying from disease and hunger, as the Allied blockade wore on till mid-July and its effects much later. Otto Dix from Gera would soon paint demobilized soldiers, beggars, and street urchins in grotesquely Expressionist fashion.

Anti-Semitism was rife. The black market thrived, thought to be driven by Jews. In Berlin the French sergeant Paul Manheim, a Jew, was mobbed and stabbed to death. Russian-Jewish Marxists of the likes of Karl Radek and Pavel Axelrod were milling about, undermining the new democracy, and the Communist Reichstag deputy Hugo Haase, another Jew, was shot with lethal consequences in broad daylight. As for the democ-racy itself, already in the general elections of June 6, 1920, the three parties of the Weimar Coalition lost their majority, ushering in a gradual move to the right for the republic.[108]

The first stress test for the town of Weimar, as an integral part of the Weimar Republic, came in March 1920, in the form of the Kapp Putsch. As the great majority of enlisted sailors and soldiers as well as their officers were to be permanently dismissed from the former imperial armed forces throughout Germany, true to the terms of Versailles, two upper-echelon commanders protested. Walther Baron von Lüttwitz, the commander of troops in central and eastern Germany, and Captain Hermann Erhardt, commander of the marine division Erhardt Brigade, conspired with the lower-level monarchist bureaucrat Wolfgang Kapp to overthrow the Berlin government. Having got wind of this beforehand and, to avoid being incapacitated, the government on March 13 first repaired to Dresden and then to Stuttgart, while Kapp proclaimed himself chancellor, with the aim of restoring the monarchy. In Weimar General Gustav von Hagenberg commanded regular army troops, taking commands from Lüttwitz. Although not all of his soldiers were loyal to him and he had to call in Landjäger Freikorps from Naumburg, there were skirmishes between his soldiers and armed workers, many of whom had entered town from surrounding industrial strongholds. In Weimar, as in Berlin, several workers were killed. The two leading politicians of the legitimate provisional Thuringian government at the time, Majority Socialist August Baudert and liberal democrat Arnold Paulssen, were briefly detained. But for once the Social Democrats and Communists (USPD) stood together, and it was Baudert who convinced the local putschists of the foolhardiness of their venture. What made them hesitate was the fact that, four days later in Berlin, Kapp had already given up, in the face of a general strike set in motion by the self-exiled Ebert government. This strike, helped along by hundreds of thousands of dissatisfied workers throughout Germany, affected Weimar less than the industrialized Ruhr, for instance, where it created absolute chaos, but it, too, was a foretaste of the social and political unrest that would afflict the Goethe town in future. In 1920 the Bauhaus, shaken at its periphery by all these events, was working hard to establish itself in Weimar, and in spring 1921 Walter Gropius, in league with left-wing, republican politicians, constructed a monument for the Kapp Putsch Fallen (*Die Märzgefallenen*) of cement, still visible in the Weimar cemetery today.[109]

Adolf Hitler and the Nazi Party in Weimar

One day in early spring of 1932, as Emmy Sonnemann, a well-respected actress at what was now the German National Theater (Deutsches Nationaltheater – DNT) in Weimar, had her usual coffee and cake in the Café Kaiser in the Parkstrasse, a commotion set in. A group of men entered the establishment, visiting politicians, so it seemed, and Sonnemann along with her Jewish bosom friend, the actress Herma Clement, wanted to leave in order to make room. But the leader of the group prevented this, charmingly approaching her and bidding her to speak to him about her theater work in Weimar, which now reached back six years. He was extremely knowledgeable and told Sonnemann about Weimar perform-ances he himself had seen in the past. His judgment was sound, thought the actress, and his erudition amazing. The man was Adolf Hitler. He was there to meet with local Nazis and discuss political strategy.[110] Hitler had first come to Weimar on an official visit in March 1925, a few weeks before Walter Gropius and his team left town for Dessau. Their art would not have appealed to Hitler's sense of aesthetics, although both men liked the Goethe Park, where Hitler would always make sure to spend time relaxing, between political meetings and speeches.[111]

When Hitler arrived in March 1925, Weimar had been the capital first of a newly constituted state of Thuringia for five years, replacing the old grand duchy, and now as a part of the federated republic, which anachron-istically continued calling itself the German Reich. Constitutionally, it had been in limbo from the time that August Baudert had advised Grand Duke Wilhelm Ernst to abdicate in November 1918 and spring–summer 1920, when the new Thuringian state had legally been formed. Baudert, a moderate member of the revolutionary workers' and soldiers' council active in Weimar and authorized by it, had served as state commissar. Elections in Saxe-Weimar-Eisenach on March 9, 1919 produced a provisional leftist-liberal coalition under Baudert. It was this government that instituted the Bauhaus. On May 1, 1920, a federal law by the Reich government in Berlin decreed the creation of the new state of Thuringia, which eventually would consist of seven former principalities in Thuringia, Saxe-Coburg in the South having decided to join the new state of Bavaria and Weimar's larger neighboring city of Erfurt staying with Prussia. Each of the principalities had ratified this law on its own by the end of June 1920. Hence by the time the former geographic entity of Thuringia had evolved into a federal state of the German Reich with its capital in Weimar, the onetime grand duchy had been much enlarged in terms of territory and population.[112]

Regular Thuringian elections were held in the summer of 1920, producing a coalition of SPD, USPD, and DDP. This government, too, remained favorable to the Bauhaus. But it fell in the autumn of 1921, and after new elections a Socialist majority was in power, tacitly supported by the recently constituted, extreme left-wing Communist Party (KPD). Again, for the Bauhaus this was a positive political backdrop. It ended after elections in February, 1924, when the right-wing-dominated Thüringer Ordnungsbund (TOB) government was formed that lasted, in various combinations, until fall 1929. Hitler's National Socialist German Workers'

Party (NSDAP) was officially not a part of this, but supported the government from the sidelines, as it had supported earlier right-wing oppositions,
sometimes under a camouflage label, during phases when it was outlawed.[113]
The strong representation of left-wing parties in the new Thuringian
Landtag after 1919 at first sight is surprising, given the old grand duchy's
predominantly conservative social makeup. But it has to be remembered
that the new federal state was now more than three times as large as the old
one and that the newly added territories were inhabited by more people of
proletarian or impoverished agrarian background.[114] They were inclined to
vote Socialist or Communist but, disappointed by the scant economic
improvement, they were beginning to turn to radical parties on the right
toward the middle of the 1920s. After 1918, there were more industrial
workers in the enlarged state, hailing from Gotha (railway wagons,
airplanes), Zella-Mehlis (weapons), Maxhütte-Unterwellenborn (mining),
Gera, Greiz, and Mühlhausen (textiles). There were an oil refinery in Rositz
and concrete works in Göschwitz. Added to these were the old grand-ducal
Zeiss-Jena factories, textile mills in Apolda, and railway wagon manufacture (dating from 1898) in Weimar itself. Much of the economic infrastructure continued to consist of agriculture, but always of the middling
and smallest-farming type, with hardly a large estate dotting the verdant
landscape.

Characteristic of Thuringia was the widespread, traditional, cottage
industry, particularly in the Thuringian Woods to the southwest, where
porcelain ware and toys were made by hand and poverty was chronic. While
small farmers might shun left-wing parties, agricultural and cottage workers
were likely to be drawn to them. What industry there was in Thuringia
tended toward the manufacture of finished products that were dependent
on export (such as weapons and the optical equipment of Zeiss), but such
export lagged in times of economic distress, as during the Allied blockade
and the exponential inflation. Just as the old grand duchy had never been
an economic powerhouse, with hardly noticeable improvements since the
turn of the century, so too the new Thuringian state belonged among the
have-not provinces of the Weimar Republic. In 1929, Thuringian wages
were "at the very bottom of the scale" in the entire Reich.[115]

In the town of Weimar itself, its population almost 46,000 strong in
1925, the old socio-economic pattern persisted by and large, with wealthy
rentiers and aristocrats, the highest government and civil servants forming
the upper crust, and a slowly growing middle class of merchants, upwardly
mobile artisans, lower-level administrators and professionals such as physicians and lawyers below it.[116] At the bottom was a, now broader, working

class, a mix of skilled workers, preindustrial laborers, indigent tradesmen, and transmigrating country folk.[117]

Hitler made his way into Thuringia generally and Weimar in particular through individual appearances there, on which occasions he demonstrated a combination of political skill and personal charisma, and through organizations he had been able to rebuild after proxy and rival parties had spread during his Landsberg incarceration. By 1922–23, there were local Nazi party chapters in Jena, Gotha, Gera, and Ilmenau. The Ilmenau group had been founded by Fritz Sauckel, born in 1894 in Franconia, a merchant-marine sailor who had been detained in France during World War I. Thereafter, he attended the technical college in Ilmenau but never finished his course, and so extreme right-wing activism became his main occupation. From Coburg across the border from Thuringia, he along with a small loyal troop tried to get through to Munich to assist Hitler in his November 1923 putsch, but was stopped by police. In Landsberg prison during 1924 he was in contact with Hitler, who recognized Sauckel early on as one of his truest followers. In 1925, Sauckel became executive secretary of the newly formed Nazi *Gau* of Thuringia – *Gaue* were Nazi-defined areas of party jurisdiction led by *Gauleiter* – under Dr. Artur Dinter, a chemist and racist author. Dinter, a follower of Chamberlain's race theories, was as vicious an anti-Semite as Adolf Bartels, with whom he became good friends, the salient difference being that Dinter, even more stringently than Bartels, defined the Jew biologically. In his most notorious novel, *The Sin against the Blood* (1918), sold tens of thousands of copies, Dinter had maintained that once persons were contaminated with Jewish sperm, all their descendants were to be counted as Jews. The archetypal victim of a Jew's sexual penetration for Dinter was, inevitably, a blond Aryan woman. These stereotypes matched, sometimes more and sometimes less, those presented by other racist writers of Dinter's time, Günther and Darré included. Dinter who, like some in this group, also believed that Christ was an Aryan (as did Johannes Schlaf), was appointed by Hitler, from within the prison gates, as the leader of all camouflage Nazi cells in Thuringia, in July 1924.[118]

In addition to Hitler's incarceration in Landsberg on April 1, 1924, the NSDAP had been proscribed throughout the Reich, so that camouflage organisations took its place, some for the South of Germany, and different, rival ones for the North. In any event, they often touched on or merged with the rightist fringes of the DNVP, following racialist goals and upholding as their paragon General Erich Ludendorff, the other failed putsch leader, as much as Hitler himself. Since Ludendorff had enjoyed the good fortune of being acquitted at the Munich Putsch trial, he was free to travel the country and beat the *völkisch* drum. During the regional Thuringian elections of February 10, 1924, which fell short of providing a working majority for what came to be called the Order League parties (TOB), seven members of the Vereinigte Völkische Liste (United *Völkisch* List) were also elected: these consisted of Ludendorff and Hitler followers. Dinter, that fervent Hitler disciple, was leading them. He argued that he could not join the TOB in a ruling coalition, because one of its constituent parties, the DDP, included Professor Eduard Rosenthal of Jena, who had drafted the new Thuringian constitution (on the model of the federal Weimar one) and was a Jew. Nevertheless, Dinter pledged to support the TOB on key issues from outside the government caucus, on condition that for Thuringia, the Nazi ban be lifted. The TOB granted this on March 3 and hence presented Hitler with his first legal platform in Germany after the putsch of November 1923, including the invaluable right to speak publicly. This he was still unable to do when the Weimar *völkisch* groups convened a rally in his absence on August 18, 1924, at which leading Munich Nazis such as Gottfried Feder, Alfred Rosenberg, and Wilhelm Frick were present and made speeches. The main speaker, however, was Ludendorff, who, like the others, openly commiserated with the captive Hitler. That was without a doubt another chief accomplishment of Dinter. Yet another consisted of his official rant in parliament against the Jews; he actually anticipated Hitler's early Third Reich persecution of German Jews when he demanded that Thuringian Jews be dismissed from their professions, and managed to force the resignation of the Jewish head of the Thuringian state bank, Walter Loeb, as well as that of a Jewish, Socialist, judge.

Dinter was assisted by Weimar's Hans Severus Ziegler, the acquaintance of Schultze-Naumburg, who had put himself in charge of a small weekly newspaper called *Der Nationalsozialist*. Ziegler produced and distributed it regionally with the help of a young, thickset, local lad by the name of Martin Bormann, whose ascent in the Nazi hierarchy Ziegler would henceforth champion. Whereas Bormann was of humble background, Ziegler – like Dinter – was an example of the conservative educated German elite which slowly but surely was now placing itself at the service of the Nazis. Ziegler's father was a banker and his mother hailed from the Schirmer family in New York, perhaps the most important American serious-music publisher of its day, which later issued Schoenberg's works. Ziegler, born in 1893 and educated in elite German schools as well as at Cambridge, came under the spell of Bartels as a young boy and possibly met Dinter through him. In affairs of culture, he had unquestioningly adopted Bartels's standard. Hence what annoyed him about the Bauhaus was that in the winter of 1919–20 at its first Christmas party "unwashed and uncombed young men and women jazzed up all German Christmas songs, on the piano in the auditorium of Jena's municipal theater." He eventually studied German literature in Greifswald and obtained his doctorate with a thesis on Hebbel, Bartels's literary hero. On March 1, 1925, as the NSDAP was being re-founded, Hitler appointed Dinter Gauleiter for Thuringia, with Ziegler as his deputy.[119]

On March 22, 1925 – coincidentally the day of Goethe's death ninety-three years before – Hitler made his first official visit to Weimar. It was followed by three more that year. The first was undoubtedly motivated by thoughts about the possibility of moving the NSDAP headquarters from Bavaria to Saxony or Thuringia. When in March of 1924 the Thuringian Landtag had rescinded the prohibition of his party, Hitler considered Weimar to be a good organizational platform from which to operate. As he had had to travel from Munich to Berlin and back in the past, he had found Bayreuth, and now Weimar, a good resting place in between. Although Hitler was not a classics fan and Goethe or Schiller – unlike Richard Wagner – had not figured in his political thinking or current personal tastes, he, like so many before him, liked Weimar's intimate small-town atmosphere, the parks, the castles, and the aura of the cults, including that of Nietzsche. Everything was close together – hotels, cafés for relaxation, and an abundance of meeting halls. The theater, as he later told Emmy Sonnemann, was of repute and appeared to offer enough Wagner; Bayreuth was nearby in any case. He also was impressed by the progress his organizations had made there, and by the capable people behind them, chiefly Dinter and Sauckel. If his party moved its seat to Weimar, Hitler was one step closer to Berlin and a national government, something that the Munich putsch had failed to attain.[120]

Hitler arrived in Weimar in March to deliver four public speeches. He was well if not enthusiastically received. It was the Deputy Gauleiter Ziegler who met him at the train station and acted as his guide. Ziegler was accompanied by a star-crossed seventeen-year-old Gymnasium student by the name of Baldur von Schirach, the son of Carl Norris von Schirach, the former theater Intendant who had assisted Bartels with his Schiller festivals, from a long-established noble family. The older Schirach had been dismissed by Baudert in 1918 and been replaced by the Socialist Ernst Hardt, now the aristocrat's lethal enemy. Schirach had been a staunch monarchist and sued the authorities, who for a while had to continue to grant him his annual salary. He was a pronounced anti-Semite; as a leading member both of the ultra-nationalist Goethe and Shakespeare Societies he belonged to the pillars of the citizenry. Since Carl Norris Schirach was half American and had married a patrician American from Philadelphia, his son Baldur was three-quarters American, which created a bond with Ziegler, who was familiar with English-speakers, and was yet another sign of the potential for cosmopolitanism that Weimar, at a different level, could have profited from. But the opposite was the case, for Baldur had attended a private school in nearby Bad Berka, whose director Hermann Lietz was a narrow, anti-Semitic chauvinist. Both Baldur and his father had been followers of Ludendorff and naturally approved of *völkisch* goals.[121]

Apart from the speeches, Hitler tried to sort out the controversy embroiling Artur Dinter, who had been rejected by some of his earlier followers, in part because he dedicated more energy to the question of an Aryan Christianity than to party business. For the time being, Hitler made no changes, but he must have been aware that both Sauckel and Ziegler were at odds with Dinter. Hitler spent some time in discussions with Ziegler in his comfortable house at Luisenstrasse 10, just down the hill from the Nietzsche Archive and around the corner from Count Harry Kessler's villa on Cranachstrasse. During those discussions, a proud Baldur was standing guard outside. Hitler then was introduced by Ziegler to Bartels in his modest, book-lined, flat on nearby Lisztstrasse 13. The two men agreed on much but diverged when it came to the ideal form of government. While the monarchist Bartels was in favor of an elective emperorship, Hitler thought a young and energetic man, schooled in private and political virtues by a circle of elders, should be put in charge of a nation. Then thirty-five years old, Hitler was obviously thinking of himself as dictator.[122]

After the formal founding of a Weimar Nazi chapter by Ziegler on April 6, Hitler returned on July 12. This time he was convening the leaders of twenty Gaue and eighty local chapter leaders from all over the Reich, in order to help heal the rift in the right-radical movement between North and South. In that sense, Weimar was proving its worth, geographically and psychologically, by being situated in the center of Germany. Yet another two-day visit took place around October 28, when Hitler addressed an audience of 800 in Weimar's large meeting hall at the Erholung club, where Goethe, Schiller, and Liszt had been known to spend time. He attended the opera and there was invited to visit the Schirachs at their stately villa at Gartenstrasse 37 next day, not far from the historic cemetery. Baldur's regal mother thought Hitler a real patriot. The older Schirach now warmed to Hitler, not least because at the opera he had observed him properly attired in tails. Baldur himself, on turning eighteen, had joined the Nazi Party. Again, he could hardly contain his admiration for the Nazi Führer. Hitler was impressed with the young man, who had a penchant for writing poetry, and invited him permanently to Munich. After botched university studies in German literature, Baldur became Hitler's leader of the Nazi Student League in 1928. In 1933 Hitler would appoint him Reich Leader of the Hitler Youth (HJ) and, in 1940, Gauleiter of Vienna. Von Schirach would spend twenty years in Spandau Prison after 1945, as one of the major war criminals.

By the time Hitler came to Weimar a fourth time in 1925 on December 13, he had given up his idea of moving his offices there. Munich was, after all, too important – too many Nazi organizations had taken root there by now, and the ban on the party in Bavaria would eventually be lifted. In December, Hitler addressed 120 guests in the modest Hotel Hohenzollern near the railway station, trying to collect funds. Matters for Hitler and his NSDAP were looking up. Internal leadership difficulties were in the process of being smoothed out and, albeit slowly, the Nazi Party was attracting more people every day. In Thuringia by the end of the year, the party had 600 members organized in almost 100 chapters.[123]

Encouraged by his successes in Thuringia throughout 1925, Hitler decided to push on in 1926, strengthening his movement. He had to repair the existing fragmentation, so in February he held a leadership meeting in Bamberg, during which he got the left-leaning renegades led by Gregor Strasser on his side. By April, he had the support of the former journalist and friend of Strasser Joseph Goebbels. To consolidate things further and tie his lieutenants irrevocably to him, Hitler planned a show of strength, again in Weimar and building on recent accomplishments there. It was to be a huge party rally with himself visibly at the center. By now Hitler knew that everything he needed for that was at his disposal in Weimar, not least the goodwill of the regional and municipal governments. Once again, it helped that Weimar was central enough to attract all and offend no one: every German could get there in less than a day's journey. He could shame the republic by holding events in the DNT, which for months had been the home of the national parliament; official permission to speak publicly and an effective local party apparatus would aid him. As Hitler put it shortly before the mass meeting in the party paper *Völkischer Beobachter*, he wanted to give the German people "visible proof of the recovered inner health of the movement."

From the point of view of Nazi Party history the rally of July 3 and 4, 1926, Hitler's first since the reconstitution of the party and the first outside of Munich, was a great achievement. There were nearly 8,000 participants, including many from out of town, with, at its core, 3,600 storm troopers (SA) and 116 black-shirted elite guards (SS). They staged marches through the main market and the narrow streets, with thousands of onlookers cheering. This time Hitler stayed at the famous Hotel Elephant, from which he acknowledged the mass ovation, outstretched arms offering the Roman salute, now obligatory in the movement. Speeches were delivered, some in the theater, by Ziegler, Rosenberg, Frick, Goebbels, and of course Hitler himself, and important organizational decisions were made. For example, the Hitler Youth was newly founded, albeit not under Baldur von Schirach, as Ziegler later claimed and so many authors have mindlessly copied from his memoirs.[124] Also in 1926, increasing votes in Thuringian communal elections as well as in towns such as Gera and Schleiz attested to Hitler's overall success. In the judgment of Sir Ian Kershaw, Hitler had demonstrated that his NSDAP "was turning into a new type of political organization – a Leader Party. Hitler had established the basis of his mastery over the movement."

Nonetheless, from the perspective of civil law and order the rally was a disaster. Perhaps few Weimar burghers would have realized this, but the physical excesses it generated provided a foretaste of what would happen under Nazi rule in future years. All over Weimar, frequently drunken Nazis provoked both the Weimar police and ordinary citizens. There was arson; two workers were thrown into the Ilm. Girls with bobbed hair – the big-city fashion of the modern twenties – were molested. Weimar's Jews, when identified, were harassed. One murder occurred, that of Paul Schmidt, a policeman. On duty near the station, he was shot and died a few days later. Hitler was embarrassed, but he may not have known that Schmitt had been a card-carrying Nazi Party member.[125]

Nazi Government in Weimar

After Hitler had been released from Landsberg in December 1924, he had resolved never to seek national political power through a *coup d'etat* again, but to travel the parliamentary route, utilizing every legal trick in the book to cut corners. Alas, in this regard, in the years after 1926 that saw a climax in Weimar, the Nazi Party in Germany made fair rather than spectacular progress. Its membership increased from approximately 55,000 for the original party in October 1923 to double that for the newly constituted one five years later, and 150,000 in October 1929. In both local and state elections its vote began to rise – 5 percent of total votes for the Saxon Landtag,

4 percent in Mecklenburg, and 7 percent in Baden. In Thuringia in 1927, Landtag elections produced results still under 5 percent. In June 1929 the party conquered its first municipality in Germany as a whole when it assumed the reins in northern Bavaria, in the Franconian town of Coburg, critically close to the Thuringian border. Hence, as Sir Richard J. Evans has aptly remarked, "in the autumn of 1929, the Nazi Party was still very much on the fringes of politics."[126]

In Thuringia generally and in Weimar in particular, few successes could match Coburg, as the party could not tactically avail itself of any political opportunities that offered themselves because of the TOB's frequent administrative and financial difficulties. This restriction obtained, notwithstanding the fact that Hitler replaced the sectarian Dinter with the much more dynamic Sauckel as Gauleiter in September 1927. Two months later Weimar, that quaint green-belt convention center for all German patriots, hosted a Nazi Reich Leader meeting at which Hitler railed against what to him were cultural contortions of the modern twenties, specifically "nigger- and jazz music." Seemingly following up on this, Rosenberg founded his Munich Combat League for German Culture (KfdK) in 1928, with a Weimar chapter established by Ziegler. He was actively joined in this by Bartels, the older Schirach, Schultze-Naumburg, Hans Wahl, and Wilhelm Deetjen, who led the Weimar-based and chauvinistically tainted Shakespeare Society. On that occasion, Ziegler delivered his leading address on the topic "Bolshevization Threatens German Culture." Under the roof of the KfdK, it was easy to condemn what were regarded as manifestations of the gutter culture of the Weimar Republic, as Carl Norris von Schirach did in January 1929, when he protested against the Max-Reinhardt-style staging of Shakespeare's *Romeo and Juliet*, from the platform of the Shakespeare Society.[127]

Thuringian elections in December 1929 finally afforded the National Socialists the first chance to install a Nazi-controlled government in Germany at the regional level. This was a greater coup than Coburg! After the wobbly TOB coalition had fallen, the Nazis campaigned rigorously, especially in small towns, of which there were many, and in rural areas. In Thuringia, the lumpenproletarian lower middle class had long been disappointed with the left and with the four bourgeois parties. The DNVP in particular chalked up strong losses. Eventually, Socialists and Communists together ended up with 24 seats in the assembly, against 23 for the original TOB parties. But the National Socialists, now as a fully united faction, garnered 11.3 percent of the votes, which gave them 6 seats out of 53. Therefore, because neither the bourgeois right nor the proletarian left was able to form a government and new elections were unthinkable, the Nazis became kingmakers, and more. They decided to enter the government on condition that two key ministries were ceded to them and they be allowed to furnish two cabinet members. While the head of the government was Erwin Baum, from the Landbund agrarian party, Hitler personally insisted that his confidant Wilhelm Frick enter the cabinet, assuming the interior and education portfolios, and that Willy Marschler, a sales clerk from Ilmenau, be appointed junior minister without portfolio (*Staatsrat*). Even before the government was formed, Sauckel declared publicly in December, true to the new strategy of his party: "With our mandate we do not wish to serve the current state – on the contrary, we want to destroy it."[128]

Hitler's choice of Frick was clever and yet another sign of high political astuteness in the Nazi Party's rise to power. Hitler regarded him as an "energetic, audacious and ever responsible bureaucrat of exceptionally high capabilities and a fanatical National Socialist." Frick had been born in 1877 in the Palatinate, obtained a doctorate in law and become a civil servant in the government of Bavaria, where he had directed the political police between 1919 and 1921. Having involved himself in Hitler's putsch he received a 15-month jail sentence, which, however, was suspended. Since May 1924 he had been representing one of the Nazi camouflage parties in the Reichstag, and in 1927 he was the leader of the seven-member Nazi Party caucus there. He was intelligent, possessed of good manners and a personality so charming that soon he lured Schultze-Naumburg's second wife away from the architect's Saaleck mansion and into marriage.[129] It has been said that the governance which now unfolded in Thuringia for the Nazis was a "dress rehearsal" for the anticipated assumption of national power in the future. That might be too strong an interpretation, for a dress rehearsal has a finite quality, and one always knows the date of the premiere. Since in Thuringia a premiere was not in sight yet, one could speak, more realistically, of an experiment in manipulative democracy.[130]

The measures enacted bear this out, and they were justified, in this deflationary era of an incremental depression, by the need to save money. Frick's rule since January 26, 1930, claims the Thuringian Social Democrat Hermann Brill in retrospect, "consisted in a series of legal infractions." One of the first decisive acts passed was an emergency law covering the period January to September 1930 to enable all manner of authoritarian changes. Democratic laws could now be abrogated and undesirable personnel dismissed, chiefly from the SPD and KPD camps, and notably in bureaucracy and education. This was negatively balanced by an increase in Thuringia's police presence. A new law of March 14 removed police forces from municipal control, placing them directly under Frick's interior ministry. Since Sauckel, the Landtag's Nazi speaker, was officially endorsed by the government as Thuringia's Gauleiter, he was also given power over the police, reducing it more to the status of an arbitrary party SA or SS. Moreover, the right of free assembly was curtailed and press freedom diminished – again mainly to hurt the Marxists. Scores of Communist teachers and state officials were dismissed, which was all the easier since parliamentary opposition was rendered ineffective because in the Landtag the SDP and KPD were at loggerheads.[131]

Advocating stricture and censorship along those lines, three interrelated actions followed – milestones on the Nazi Party's road to full political power. The most spectacular was the appointment of the then unemployed schoolteacher Hans F. K. Günther to a professorship in social anthropology at Jena, on October 1, 1930; effectively this meant a chair in race science. Frick, as minister of education, was responsible for the appointment, probably on Hitler's personal orders, after he had met Günther personally at Schultze-Naumburg's. Frick's initial proposal was rejected by most of the faculty, whose executive committee could not be convinced that Günther's "publications demonstrated original scientific achievements." However, it was enthusiastically received by a strongly entrenched right-wing student body. (Baldur von Schirach was now leader of the Nazi Student League, which had an influential chapter at Jena's university.) Not only was this the first such appointment in Germany's history, but Günther was not even an anthropologist by training and, beyond his doctorate, lacked certification as a university teacher (*Habilitation*). Hermann Göring and Hitler himself attended Günther's inaugural lecture. Surrounding this promotion of a mere secondary-school teacher were the appointment of Schultze-Naumburg as head of Weimar's art and architecture schools, making him successor to Gropius and to Bartning, who had resigned. Moreover, Bartels became an adjunct professor at what used to be the Bauhaus; he announced lectures on German literature and was also to lecture at Jena.[132] A second educational innovation was the planned introduction in Thuringian schools of special prayers which were barely concealed diatribes against Germany's former enemies and the Jews, and propounded the "Stab in the Back" Legend. This conformed with Hitler's goal "to put the entire school system to the service of educating Germans into becoming fanatical nationalists." Whereas three of these prayers were eventually disallowed by the republican supreme court in Leipzig, two of them were left standing and came into daily use in all the schools.[133]

A third ordinance had been drafted by the Nazis' culture expert Hans Severus Ziegler; it was an edict against "Negro culture" and, just as Hitler had demanded in Weimar earlier, forbade the staging of modern plays, the performance of atonal music or jazz, and visiting cabarets or risqué circus acts. Those were the typical expressions of what was already internationally known as the progressive art of the new republic, mainly generated in Berlin. As a token of this policy, Oskar Schlemmer's frescoes from the Bauhaus period were destroyed in the van de Velde building near the Liszt House, and seventy Expressionist paintings, including works by Klee, Kandinsky, Feininger, and Emil Nolde, were removed from exhibits in the ducal museum.[134] There were telling ramifications of such novel authoritarian rule – in the defense of Weimar's classical tradition, as Sauckel claimed. Films were censored, especially if they had a semblance of sexual content. (Some such films were arguing for sexual hygiene and against paragraph 218, prohibiting abortion; others were, admittedly, just smut.) Erich Maria Remarque's pacifist book *All Quiet on the Western Front* was banned as reading matter in schools. The theater was cleansed. Hence the avant-garde theater director Erwin Piscator was hampered in his attempt to tour Weimar with his Berlin ensemble, but in this case too the Supreme Court exerted some control over Nazi capriciousness.[135]

On the other side of these destructive measures, the Nazis tried to achieve something positive for themselves. In the cultural arena, the KfdK organized its first national convention, at which it was reiterated that theater, architecture, literature, music, and the visual arts must be shielded from what were described as pernicious influences. Schultze-Naumburg, who grandly set the tone here, supported by the new adviser on art and Thuringian KfdK leader Ziegler, was vigorously applauded by Frick, Rosenberg, and Darré. Günther, Schirach, Goebbels, and Göring put in appearances, and Artam section leader Friedrich Schmidt called for a "campaign of German youth into eastern lands." Beyond these cultural-political efforts, two attempts were undertaken, albeit rather clumsily, to obtain German citizenship for Hitler by making him a Thuringian official. One was a short-lived attempt to get him appointed as head of the art and architecture school – Hitler, as Nazi director of the Bauhaus! The other was to install him as commissar of gendarmes in the small township of Hildburghausen in the South, yet lest he open himself to ridicule, Hitler wisely declined.[136]

The government fell in early April 1931 after a non-confidence vote from the majority of parties.[137] The next Nazi cabinet would not arrive in Thuringia until summer 1932. But in the interim, the Nazis had put their stamp on Weimar, and on the rest of Thuringia as well. In 1930, they had won the important Reichstag elections of September 14 for all of Germany,

1. The eighteenth-century Weimar Muses' Court as imagined by painter Theobald Freiherr von Oer, 1860. Friedrich Schiller is seen reading to a select group of savants and court nobles in Tiefurt, near Weimar. Johann Wolfgang Goethe, with his hand in his vest, is standing to the right. Christoph Martin Wieland is seen communing with a young woman in front of Schiller.

2. The statue of Weimar Duke Karl August, a passionate huntsman, at the Platz der Demokratie. In his time at the turn of the seventeenth century this was the Fürstenplatz. On the left is the famous Anna Amalia Library, the former Grünes Schloss, behind the duke a princely residence, the Fürstenhaus, today the Franz Liszt Conservatory.

3. The Goethe-and-Schiller statue in front of what is now (2013) the Deutsches Nationaltheater Weimar. The statue was created by the Dresden sculptor Ernst Rietschel for festivities in 1857. The physically taller Schiller has been reduced in size to make Goethe appear equal in height, at the dawn of a Goethe renaissance in the second half of the nineteenth century.

4. Goethe's garden house in the Ilm park as viewed in modern times. It was at this retreat that Goethe, who had designed the park, first met with Christiane Vulpius, and later repeatedly for trysts.

5. The statue of Johann Gottfried Herder, created in 1850 by Ludwig Schaller, in front of St. Peter and Paul's, which colloquially was known as the Town Church or, later, the Herder Church. This is where Herder, as the chief theologian of the duchy, held his sermons.

6. Grand Duke Carl Alexander and his, originally Dutch, wife Sophie, on the occasion of their Golden Wedding Anniversary, October 8, 1892. The pious but enlightened couple had commenced their reign in 1853. During his lifetime Carl Alexander was proud that as a child he had sat on Goethe's knees.

7. Franz Liszt in the 1880s, toward the end of his life, in front of his Weimar residence. He is dressed in the clerical garb of a Catholic abbé. Surrounding him are his favorite students at the time. In the front row, Arthur Friedheim sits to his right, and Alfred Reisenauer is the second to his left.

8. Liszt's future son-in-law Richard Wagner, 1861 in Paris. By this time, Liszt's efforts had failed to draw Wagner to Weimar permanently, one of several reasons why he himself left Weimar for Budapest and Rome in 1861. Nonetheless, Liszt had succeeded in premiering Wagner's opera *Lohengrin* at the court theater in 1850.

9. Weimar court theater director Franz Dingelstedt, a brilliant artist, whom Grand Duke Carl Alexander called to Weimar in 1857, on Liszt's urgings, after Dingelstedt had lost his position in Munich. But because Dingelstedt preferred theater over opera, he ungratefully intrigued against Liszt, thus contributing to the musician's departure in 1861. This portrait is from the 1840s.

10. Richard Strauss in his early twenties, before his Weimar court appointment in 1889. Once there, he took little interest in town life or the court, concentrating, instead, on music and winning the heart of his lead soprano, Pauline de Ahna. He married her after his stay in Weimar, and after Cosima Wagner in Bayreuth had dismally failed to interest him in her daughter, Eva.

11. The poet Ernst von Wildenbruch, a distant relative of Grand Duke Carl Alexander, who moved from Berlin to Weimar in 1900. As a rabid German nationalist, he was the author of pathetic dramas, not all of which were performed at the Weimar court theater. His influence in Weimar in the early twentieth century signifies a precipitous cultural decline coupled with a rise in chauvinism.

12. Grand Duke Wilhelm Ernst, the grandson of Carl Alexander, and his first wife Caroline. She was only twenty when she contracted pneumonia and died in 1905; many said she had sought her death in a rainstorm. The cause was her husband, whose insensitivity made her suffer. The duke's vicious temper matched his penchant for authoritarian rule.

13. Portal of the Nietzsche Villa Silberblick, early twentieth century, designed by Belgian artist Henry van de Velde in *Jugendstil* fashion. Together with Count Harry Kessler, he sought to create a "New Weimar," after Goethe's and Liszt's. Here the arts would again flourish. But van de Velde and Kessler were opposed by Wilhelm Ernst and his entourage. Their efforts floundered long before World War I.

Friedrich Ebert
Reichspräsident

14. Friedrich Ebert, a Social Democratic saddler from Heidelberg, the first president of the new German republic in 1919. His parliament was temporarily installed in Weimar's former court theater seen at the top of the picture. Although a sincere democrat bent on good government, Ebert became the butt of ridicule, especially from the political right. While cabinet and parliament moved back to Berlin in August, the new German polity henceforth was known as the "Weimar Republic," a historic misnomer persisting to this day.

15. Under the auspices of the new democratic republic, architect Walter Gropius influenced and encouraged by van de Velde, founded the Weimar Bauhaus, in early 1919. After only a few years, its sober, innovative style became legendary, but its modernism was anathema to the growing front of German ultra-nationalists. Gropius and his school were pressured by regional politicians to leave Weimar around April 1925.

16. Leading Bauhaus faculty in Paul Klee's Bauhaus studio, Weimar, April 1, 1925. From the left: Masters Lionel Feininger, Wassily Kandinsky, Oskar Schlemmer, Georg Muche, and Klee. The group is about to repair to its new domicile, the town of Dessau in neighboring, and more tolerant, Sachsen-Anhalt.

17. Marlene Dietrich, born 1901, starring as Lola-Lola in *The Blue Angel*, produced 1930 in Berlin. It established her international fame and brought her to Hollywood. In the early 1920s she had been studying the violin in Weimar, befriended Bauhaus members like Lother Schreyer and carried on a steamy affair with her violin teacher, Robert Reitz.

18. A poster for the summer 1923 Bauhaus exhibition, designed by Kandinsky. It is typical of Kandinsky's Bauhaus painting style. The exhibition attracted internationally famous artists such as Igor Stravinsky and Frank Lloyd Wright and represents not only the highlight in Bauhaus history, but also the apex of Weimar's cultural development since Goethe's death in 1832.

19. Elisabeth Förster-Nietzsche at the entrance of Villa Silberblick, probably in the early 1920s. The villa was now not only her residence but also the official Nietzsche archive, attracting many famous visitors. The Förster widow, while endowed with intelligence and great charm, championed right-wing causes and eventually lent official support to the Nazi movement, which iconized her.

20. The *völkisch* author Friedrich Lienhard, in the 1920s. Anti-urban and increasingly anti-Semitic, Lienhard was a pre-National Socialist culture broker based in Weimar, who smoothed the path for Nazi men of letters, art and music, before Hitler's political takeover.

21. Funeral parade for Admiral Reinhard Scheer, with Reichswehr troops marching past the Herder Church, November 1928. Once Kaiser Wilhelm II's architect of unrestricted submarine warfare during World War I, Scheer had retired in Weimar – as did so many affluent, right-leaning pensioners at that time.

22. Hans Wahl, director of the Goethe house and museum, probably in the late 1920s. Wahl served as director in the late imperial era, the republic, under the Nazis, and during the beginning phase of Weimar's Soviet occupation. In the late 1920s, he was a local founding member of Alfred Rosenberg's anti-Semitic Combat League for German Culture.

23. Adolf Hitler leaving the Hotel Elephant in Weimar's market square in October 1934, with Gauleiter Fritz Sauckel on the left. The hotel, dating to the Middle Ages, was one of Weimar's most famous hallmarks and had been a temporary home for all of Weimar's greats. Not to be outdone, Hitler had a special suite there built for himself, as would the head of the GDR, Walter Ulbricht, during the Communist regime after October 1949.

24. Reich Propaganda Minister Joseph Goebbels with Weimar's own, Hans Severus Ziegler, on the occasion of German "Book Week" in Weimar, 1938. Thuringian Theater Commissar Ziegler, always in search of higher office, wears the uniform of an SS officer, although he is gay, knowing full well that the SS dispatched homosexuals to concentrations camps.

25. Adolf Hitler during one of several official Nazi Party gatherings in Weimar, early in the Third Reich. To his left marches Gauleiter Fritz Sauckel, behind him are black-uniformed SS, and he is hailed on his far left by storm troopers. Hitler enjoyed Weimar, because a sojourn there usually afforded him more peace and quiet than in other towns.

26. Buchenwald concentration camp after liberation by U.S. troops, April 1945. Near the gate stand two inmate survivors, while a well-fed American soldier is walking toward them. The JEDEM DAS SEINE entrance sign, built by a former Communist Bauhaus student, was removed when the occupying Soviets adapted the camp to imprison German captives of their own.

27. Lawyer Bernd Kauffmann, director of the 1999 Weimar Culture Year and, coterminously, annual Kunstfest manager from 1992 to 2001. Although talented, he was a controversial culture broker, backed by right-wing government interests, who failed – once again – to restore Weimar to even a semblance of its early greatness.

28. Nike Wagner at a Weimar press conference in 2003, one year before she became Kunstfest director for ten years. As a direct descendant of Liszt, Richard and Cosima Wagner, much faith was placed in her to complete convincingly what her predecessor Kauffmann had attempted to begin. Up to and including 2013, her record is, on the whole, a more convincing one.

29. A condemned house in the Gerberstrasse near the Ilm river, which was claimed and repeatedly occupied by left-wing-anarcho youths, after German reunification in 1990. It was a symbol not only of the persistent poverty in postwar, run-down, Weimar, but also of the social and political protest Weimar left-leaning citizens voiced against skinheads and other neo-Nazi groups. Their members often laid siege to this house, which borders the section of Weimar (Jakobsviertel) that Hitler partially razed, to make room for bombastic party structures.

which made them the second-largest party in the national parliament.[138] What worked in favor of the Nazis after April 1931 was the continuing high rate of unemployment in Thuringia, higher in fact than the Reich's average. While the government continued to be led by Erwin Baum with the tacit support of the SPD, the Nazis under the direction of Gauleiter Sauckel were doing everything to destabilize it. Hitler himself was in Weimar as often as he could manage, eight times in 1932 alone, and he spoke locally six times during this interlude. Meanwhile, the Nazi Party was growing throughout the Reich, winning, in the summer of 1932, the governments of Sachsen-Anhalt, Oldenburg, and Mecklenburg.[139]

Thuringia's cabinet fell, characteristically, at the end of July 1932, over the feeble economy, when the SPD opposed an increase of taxes to bolster the state budget. In the ensuing elections of July 31, the Nazis became the largest party, with 42.5 percent of the vote, with the SPD and KPD together reaching only 40.4 percent. This would give the Nazis 16 seats as opposed to 25 for the Socialist parties, so that, when they teamed up with Baum's agrarian (Landbund) members, Sauckel's Nazis ended up with 32 deputies in the Landtag. This now was a clear majority, as the remaining bourgeois parties had shrunk into oblivion.[140]

Under Sauckel as new head of the cabinet, the government extended many of the rulings from 1930–31, but it now had a compounded problem with growing unemployment and mass poverty on its hands. Although the Nazis had campaigned strongly on the back of economic issues, many of their promises turned out to be hollow. No emergency crisis program was instituted, as the Reich, still ruled by a succession of right-wing but not yet Nazi governments, was blamed. There were none of the work creation schemes that had been pledged, and the advertised reduction in ministerial salaries proved merely cosmetic. The withdrawal of financial support from the Israelite community in Weimar was explained as economically necessary, but clearly was a seriously intended anti-Semitic blow. The anti-Jewish as well as anti-Marxist bias was exercised in schools and in the cultural institutions, when more teachers were dismissed, and the theater program was censored. Ziegler, who had been restored to cultural power (as had Schultze-Naumburg for the academies), preferred Nazi content fabricated by scribes such as Johst and Kolbenheyer.

After innocent tête-à-têtes with Hitler, actress Emmy Sonnemann fell in love with Hermann Göring, who had recently lost his Swedish wife Karin. Sonnemann became Göring's mistress, and they were married in April 1935. (Sonnemann's Jewish friend Herma Clement had already come under Göring's special protection in 1933 and was acting in Berlin's

Staatstheater.) At Jena University, the National Socialist professor Emge, Förster-Nietzsche's confidant, became the official curator, supporting, among others, Günther and Bartels. All the while, the number of unemployed rose until it reached 11.5 percent by 1932–33 – a new record – and exports, on which Thuringia depended, declined further. The primitive Sauckel, who was not averse to beating up fellow parliamentarians outside government buildings, promised new anti-Semitic measures in the area of ritual slaughter (*shechita*) and boycotts of Jewish shops, delayed only in the interests of the Thuringian retail trade. In all, confident Nazis were setting the stage in Thuringia, as they were doing in other German states, for Hitler's national takeover to occur smoothly early in 1933.[141]

Looking back on 1933, this was the apex of a complex development that had begun in 1918. Their intellectual and political pioneers having cleared the path by the second half of the 1920s, the National Socialists under Hitler had proceeded to entrench themselves in Weimar, and all of Thuringia. Characteristically, what happened was that the arch-conservative and *völkisch*-attuned had made the decisive move to fascism, thereby enabling themselves to be of full service to the Nazis. In this, an admixture of radicalized nationalism and anti-Semitism had served as the leitmotif. For Bartels and Wachler, Jew-hatred may have been the strongest component; for Förster-Nietzsche and Schlaf it was probably chauvinism. Members of the new Saaleck Circle had added impetus for these tendencies, while at the same time drawing into their midst actors from outside: Günther, Darré, Himmler and other *Artamans*. The convergence of those two streams – the traditional conservative one and the Saaleck pro-eastern-settlement one – had produced a new type of Weimar-born, fanatical functionary, who would serve in an activist liaison between the old, more passive, reactionary elites and the active, ruthlessly forward-looking fascists. These men were Hans Severus Ziegler and Baldur von Schirach. Their activism had assured Hitler and his party a positive, and lasting, reception in the town of Goethe. In addition, Hitler had imported his own adjutants, Dinter and Sauckel, to entrench his movement in Weimar. The town was ideally suited to guarantee the survival of his party through clever machination, which would exploit intricate political constellations in the Thuringian parliament. Hence Hitler had been able to gain political clout. Unsurprisingly, given the fertile fascist climate, the first German regional Nazi government had been established in Thuringia by January 1930, with Weimar as the hub; this experience had been repeated in August of 1932. By this time, resident conservative associations such as the Goethe Society had been playing the game not necessarily of Hitler, but certainly not against him. What they had been against, supported in this by the Nazis and their local adjuncts, was the new German republic, which had had the bad fortune to have been established in Weimar. It was accused of having instituted what looked like weak democratic government and of having signed a shameful peace with the Western Allies. By 1933, the ground for a National Socialist Third Reich had been prepared in many ways in Weimar – through intellectual exercises, political maneuvers, and physical exertions like mass rallies. In this, when suitable, the tradition of the classics had been abused by right-wingers, with the obvious objective of hampering new democratic beginnings.

CHAPTER 7

Weimar in the Third Reich
1933 to 1945

"THE ADMIXTURE OF HITLERISM AND GOETHE AFFECTS ONE RATHER strangely," commented Thomas Mann in his distinctive manner after his Weimar visit of March 1932. "Of course, Weimar is a center of Hitlerdom. Everywhere you could see Hitler's picture etc. in National Socialist newspapers on exhibit. The town was dominated by the type of young person who walks through the streets vaguely determined, offering the Roman salute, one to the other."[1]

The stamp of Hitlerism Thomas Mann observed during the tortuous death of the republic may have been more visible on Weimar than on other mid-size German towns, a mere four months before the National Socialists took over Thuringia for good. After Hitler's national victory in January 1933 Weimar remained the capital of Thuringia, and here Hitler could count on a vast majority of Nazis. NSDAP membership figures demonstrated this two years after Hitler's assumption of the chancellorship. By 1935, among all the German states in the Reich federation, Thuringia, with its Nazi population, was in the upper quartile. Whereas in the Reich the percentage of Nazi Party members at that time was 3.78, in Thuringia it was 4.[2] For Weimar alone, these values were disproportionately higher. According to a conservative estimate for the period from 1933 to 1945, the Nazis' percentage in the Reich population was 11.7, versus Weimar's percentage of 14.3.[3] Nazi Party membership in individual professions, such as physicians in Thuringia, was also higher than their counterparts in the Reich.[4] This lends credence to the postwar observation of the Jewish Weimar accountant Rudolf Cohn, who was losing his clients after 1933 and charged that "90% of Weimar business people were members of the party."[5] All this is not surprising, given the steady move of Weimar to the ideological and political right even before the turn of the nineteenth century, under the intellectual leadership of Adolf Bartels, and the path-breaking role the town had played in the public comeback of Hitler after December 1924. The bureaucratically wily Wilhelm Frick, the dynamic if non-charismatic Fritz Sauckel, and the intellectually pretentious Hans Severus Ziegler had been the leading drivers here and, with Frick working in Berlin, Sauckel and Ziegler could continue their Nazi politics until Thuringia was one of the most National Socialist provinces in Germany and the town of Goethe and Schiller near the top of Nazified cities.

Gauleiter Sauckel took advantage of the strong pro-Hitler mood in Weimar to eliminate or coordinate democratic institutions quickly. Parallel to other German states, or *Länder*, but more brutally than in most, he began by dispatching his enemies of long standing – foremost the members of the KPD, but also the SPD. (This occurred well into wartime. The Weimar Social Democrat Kurt Nehrling, a forty-four-year-old locksmith, was arrested in 1943, accused by an SS court of high treason, and executed in Dachau in September of that year.)[6] Against the backdrop of special emergency ordinances promulgated centrally in Berlin, for instance on February 28 after the Reichstag fire of the day before, Communists were declared enemies of the state and clapped into prison and the first concentration camp in the nation, at the small airport site of Nohra near Weimar. If they had not already been dismissed by previous Nazi-controlled governments, Communist and Socialist public servants, teachers, and officials were fired and often arrested. Sauckel's executive organs carrying out these actions were the brown-shirted SA and the black-shirted SS, who, as in other parts of Germany, were temporarily charged with assisting the regular police. Other republican parties either merged with the NSDAP or dissolved themselves. The Thuringian parliament was at first suspended and, after a special law of January 1934 which coordinated all *Länder* with the Reich government, formally abolished. Weimar's municipal council became an organ of the Thuringian state, where Sauckel in May 1933 assumed the office of Reichsstatthalter, a powerful, newly instituted, governmental post that complemented his party position as Gauleiter. It enabled him to be in total control of the government as he saw fit, without actually having to carry out its tedious day-to-day business. He could appoint and dismiss ministers and was responsible only to Hitler. Sauckel's powers were amplified when in March 1942 Hitler named him plenipotentiary for transporting foreign, pressganged, workers to Germany and keeping them alive just barely, as slaves for the war economy. Thuringia and Weimar in particular were affected by this as, increasingly, armament production plants were situated there. For the suffering and death Sauckel inflicted on those captives he was later hanged at Nuremberg.[7]

The important state ministries, such as the ones for education and for justice, soon became extensions of their central counterparts in Berlin. Judicial procedures were tightened and sharpened, to the disadvantage of all defendants, especially political ones. More arbitrary categories of "political crime" were created. These actions sprang from the philosophy of totalitarianism that was Hitler and Sauckel's creed. Individuals had to submerge themselves in the racially defined *Volksgemeinschaft*: "The misplaced reverence for a singular person," wrote one Nazi commentator in 1935, "had to give way to the, hitherto neglected, reverence for the community."[8]

On the economic front, Weimar continued to suffer from the ramifications of the Great Depression that had started in Germany after 1929 and had struck this small town and its hinterland uncommonly hard. Unemployment rose until the beginning of 1935 but then began to subside, because of the introduction of military conscription and as the armaments industry was cranked up. Along with industrial expansion, Weimar's population rose from 46,003 in early 1933 to 51,285 in 1936, then to 59,637 in 1939, and reached 65,361 in 1941. Clearly, surrounding rural dwellers were drawn to burgeoning city factories, and in wartime there was also an inflow of civilians from air-raid-endangered centers such as Berlin and the highly industrialized Rhineland. Even in the years of peace, major projects helped Thuringia's and in particular Weimar's infrastructure: work began on Thuringian *Autobahnen* in July 1934 and the stretch between Weimar and Jena was opened to traffic in August 1939. By February of 1936, Weimar's inefficient, low-volume wagon factory had become part of the much larger Berlin-Suhler-Waffen complex and now was making guns and airplane parts. The influx of people encouraged the construction of housing, and military barracks (and, even before 1939, air-raid shelters). After November 1934, tourism was actively supported, for a post-Depression German population that felt sufficiently prosperous to afford high discretionary spending.[9] In the concentric rural green belts around Weimar smaller industry was boosted, such as button-making, the manufacture of glassware like test tubes, and low-voltage lamps. Agriculture itself benefited from increased veterinary aid to livestock farmers, especially to combat tuberculosis in cattle, as well as aid to beekeepers, in the form of technical schooling, and seed-distribution and monitoring for all active farmers. In addition, international exports were to be facilitated in cooperation with experts from the port cities of Hamburg and Bremen.[10]

The industrial activities were intensified after the outbreak of war in September 1939. Already in May of that year Sauckel had established the "Sauckel Works" in Weimar, as part of the huge, multi-faceted, Wilhelm-Gustloff-Werke, whose ultimate goal was the fabrication of weapons and armament-related products. Until 1945, this firm branched out into the wider region, including the nearby concentration camp of Buchenwald. In the underground warrens of Nordhausen-Dora, V2 rockets were eventually assembled, and in similar shafts near Kahla Messerschmitt 262 jets were being built – all by prisoners. The fact that Germany, including Weimar, by 1938 was suffering from an acute shortage of skilled workers was one of the chief motives for Sauckel's machinations to import captured foreign workers. The demographic picture of Weimar, which, small-townish in the early 1930s, had still been characterized by an over-representation of white-collar employees and public servants (more than 50 percent of the employed), noticeably changed until early 1945. In the sprawling Sauckel Works in Weimar alone, 25.8 percent of the working population were foreign laborers, 1.4 percent prisoners of war, and 42 percent inmates of Buchenwald concentration camp. The rest were regular German workers, who, if male, drifted continually in and out of military service.[11]

Enforcing Nazi Culture

As in the case of the economy, the Thuringian Nazi authorities were able to build on pre-1933 foundations to extend their control over culture. In this, they were aided by personnel and institutional circumstances. Apart from Sauckel himself, the person who lent continuity to new regime ventures was Hans Severus Ziegler, who assumed several roles within both the state and the party to exert his ideological influence. At one point he became so powerful that Sauckel wanted to have him removed to Dresden. Hitler, however, would have none of that, although he knew that as a homosexual Ziegler was really not acceptable in the Third Reich, for usually gay men were shunted off to prisons and concentration camps. Yet Ziegler survived prosecution in a court of law as well as temporary suspension from his posts and simply carried on.[12]

He had been instrumental in founding the Combat League for German Culture (KfdK) under Rosenberg and continued in its leadership as Thuringia's most prominent functionary. The KfdK still organized specifically Nazi cultural events in Weimar, especially those of a mass character, but its main role was the ideological guidance of theater audiences and, where possible, the program of the stage itself. Ironically, when in 1934

Hitler had appointed Rosenberg official deputy for the ideological indoctrination of the German people, his KfdK had already lost much clout in
the face of other Nazi agencies. They were supervised by more powerful
men, in particular Goebbels, who was now minister of propaganda and
people's enlightenment, and later even Himmler. By June 1934 the KfdK
had reinvented itself as the NS-Kulturgemeinde (NSKG), or National
Socialist Cultural Community. It held sway over theater patrons and also
directed book clubs, but sank into insignificance as Goebbels's own Reich
Culture Chamber, founded in November 1933 (with Richard Strauss as
president), was spreading its tentacles regionally and locally. Ziegler,
however, remained active by virtue of his office as deputy Gauleiter and
plenipotentiary of the party for cultural matters in Thuringia. In September
1935 the NSKG still had 3,000 members.[13]

With or without party organizations such as the KfdK or NSKG Ziegler
retained his power in Weimar's theater, first in a general role as state commissar
for the stage, and then in a hands-on function as Generalintendant, after
September 1935. Not least because of his special relationship with Hitler, the
theater received subventions from the Führer's private purse as well as
generous state subsidies and was able to embark on structural renovation. As
its content was tightly controlled, its repertoire was either shallow and non-
political, or spiced with political content, and of the lowest quality in both
categories. Into the first fell a fairy tale in 1933–34 authored by the local
NSKG chief Hans Joachim Malberg, for which Ziegler himself had composed
the incidental music. Into the second category fell Christopher Marlowe's
play *The Jew of Malta* (c.1589), cunningly adapted to the regime's anti-Semitic
campaign by the dramaturg Otto zur Nedden in 1938. Other stock-in-trade
playwrights were the Nazis Johst and Kolbenheyer. Weimar's theater became
a caricature of its classical archetype until in October 1944 it was closed, as
Goebbels was shutting down all cultural activities in the Reich. Thereafter it
was used for the production of ordnance by the Siemens & Halske concern.[14]

Weimar's musical events after 1933 belied the former existence of a
Hummel, Liszt, or Strauss; they were traditional and executed without flair.
Weimar became a fulcrum of Nazi musical activities organized by
unbending Nazis. For instance, along with Berlin and later Graz, Weimar
became one of the leading places for the musical education of the Hitler
Youth. Although the conservatory's director Bruno Hinze-Reinhold had
been a member of the KfdK, he resigned in 1933, yet not because of a
fundamental conflict with National Socialism, but because of friction with
younger and politically more agile faculty members. He was followed by
Felix Oberborbeck, a Nazi who later repaired to Graz, where as rector of its

conservatory he lamented that faculty and course offerings were "still below the National Socialist standard of education." Oberborbeck's Weimar successor in 1939 was Paul Sixt, a Ziegler protégé, who also conducted symphony and opera and in 1938 had been instrumental in organizing the Düsseldorf exhibition of "degenerate music."[15]

Sixt and Ziegler were able to move this exhibition to Weimar in the spring of 1939, where it constituted the highlight of musical life from 1933 to 1945, albeit a sadly negative one. In Düsseldorf as in Weimar, individual audio-booths enabled visitors to listen to samples of music composed by moderns such as Kurt Weill, Schoenberg, Stravinsky, and Hindemith. In the official exhibition guide, Ziegler referred to his mentor Adolf Bartels when he emphasized that "degeneracy" in the arts was due to the harmful influence of Jews, and he reminded his readers that Richard Wagner, generations ago, had tried his best to demonstrate to all Germans the influence of Jews particularly in music. The show drew 50,000 visitors from all over Thuringia; some came in special trains.[16]

This Weimar exhibit was conjoined to one with "degenerate art" as its subject; it constituted Goebbels's original, villainous, concoction of avant-garde visual art from Munich in 1937, now, as an itinerant show, visiting Weimar as its seventh stop. From March 23 to April 24, 1939, the same 50,000 Thuringians could look at works from the condemned Bauhaus period and its modernist aftermath. Originally these had included paintings by Klee, Kandinsky, and Schlemmer, but now the collection was already diluted in content, as items were being sold off, to fill the Nazi state's coffers. At that time paintings by avant-garde artists originally from Weimar museums were being burned in Berlin, having been transported there two years previously, after others had been dispatched for commercial gain, including lithographs, watercolors, and drawings by Bauhaus icons Feininger and Klee.[17]

In addition to these policing activities, Nazi cultural censure touched film and book distribution. In Niedergrunstedt just south-west of Weimar, on June 21, 1933, the works of Erich Maria Remarque, Franz Werfel, Stefan Zweig, and Kurt Tucholsky were burned, among others, mirroring the more spectacular autos-da-fé in university towns. Libraries were searched for suspicious titles, and in February 1934 their directors received lists of recommended German books for acquisition that bore "the spirit of the Third Reich."[18] If Harry Kessler, who left Germany as an exile for the south of France in 1935, had visited van de Velde's famous old pre-Bauhaus building before his death in 1937, he would have been aghast at the mediocrity of the art and architectural work being done there. After 1930, under Schultze-Naumburg, whom the regime steadily marginalized, the school had deteriorated even further from the time of Otto Bartning, and until his retirement in 1940 sank to the bottom of the German ranking – below similar institutions in Stuttgart, Düsseldorf, and Berlin. Weimar's students were not able to obtain a degree equivalent to that of a university-certified engineer, but then they also did not need Gymnasium credentials to enter. Throughout the Third Reich the Staatliche Hochschulen für Baukunst, bildende Künste und Handwerk struggled in vain to attain academic equality with the traditional technical universities such as Darmstadt's or Dresden's. The school, comprising architecture, visual arts, and the arts-and-crafts now was the very opposite of what Gropius and his colleagues had once visualized for it.[19] If Weimar itself had only a second-rate architectural school, it could enhance its academic reputation by strengthening its ties with Jena's university. This had been done successfully as far back as the time of Schiller, when Goethe was in charge of it. After 1933, universities comprised one area in which, as far as culture, art, and higher learning were concerned, Sauckel in his capacity as Reichsstatthalter, mandated by the state rather than the party, was able to exercise authority over his jealous rival, State Councillor Ziegler.

Then appeared Karl Astel. Born in 1898, he had been active in World I, the Kapp putsch of 1920, and Hitler's Munich Beer Hall putsch of 1923. A fanatical Nazi, he joined the NSDAP in 1930, around which time he also obtained his medical doctorate from Würzburg University. Thereafter he practiced sports medicine at the University of Munich and became a personal friend of Sauckel. Early on under extremist influences such as that of Hans F. K. Günther, and of more established experts like Ernst Rüdin in Munich and Eugen Fischer in Freiburg, Astel came to believe in the improvement of the German race through radical eugenic engineering. Here Sauckel saw eye to eye with him. Thus in April of 1933, the Reichsstatthalter commissioned Astel to establish a Landesamt für Rassewesen in Thuringia, a State Office for Race Studies, to be located in the capital of Weimar. After this had begun to function in July, Astel was appointed full professor of eugenics and hereditary race science at Jena in 1934.[20]

Astel practiced a "crude combination of technocratic initiatives and racist utopism." From his base in Weimar, he proceeded to look into the racial lineage of thousands of Thuringian families, divided into occupational categories. For example, he collected statistical data on 20,000 farmers, as he did on craftsmen. Soon, every third Thuringian citizen was on record. (In a similarly Orwellian project, Dutch demographers were then registering their citizens, so when the occupying Germans were swooping down on Dutch Jews, they could swiftly be caught and deported.)[21] At the same time, Astel established training centers to qualify assessors in nearby Bad Berka and in Egendorf, further to the south. Already by 1935, Astel had schooled 10,848 officials, among whom, at 2,653, Nazi political leaders furnished the largest, and physicians, at 583, the second-smallest contingent (the smallest being from the Nazi Women's League). His ultimate goal was, as he said in 1937, to ensure that the German race be given whatever was necessary for survival, against "the craziness of racial aliens and the racially perverted, Jews and degenerates," who would have to be kept in check. He networked with like-minded colleagues in the Reich, and in February of 1935 Professor Rüdin visited, to speak on "Predictions of Hereditarily Diseased and Normal Children" – the strongest signal yet that "euthanasia"-killing of the feeble was on its way. Eventually, more than 650 Thuringians became its victims, one of the highest regional levels for the Reich. Astel himself carried out sterilization in his Jena clinics, operating on 1,593 men, women, and children from January 1934 to January 1937 alone.[22]

Astel coordinated his Weimar work as a public servant with that at his academic chair in the University of Jena. He did so in accordance with his superior Sauckel, who announced to students in the winter of 1936–37 that they represented "the best selection of the nation, according to their racial aptitude, industry, and strong will." Even before he became rector in 1939, Astel wielded sweeping influence within the university, which showed itself in the methodical cultivation of key disciplines such as law, medicine, and the natural sciences, as well as the hiring of new faculty. Until 1935, when Günther moved to Berlin, he and Astel, together with the zoologist Victor Franz and the anthropologist Gerhard Heberer, constituted the highest concentration of racist scholars in any German institute of higher learning. Anti-Semitism pervaded all programs, especially when Bartels, who had never completed university studies himself, was engaged to hold lectures. After Günther's departure, Astel wished it to remain that way. This was not altogether easy because he frequently had to force the hand of the man in charge of final decisions, Berlin's Reich Education Minister Bernhard Rust. With the support of his friend Sauckel and because of his closeness to Himmler and the SS, however, Astel was able to employ, over time, Günther Franz, who in 1938 proceeded with a lecture series ideologically justifying the pogroms of Kristallnacht, and Lothar Stengel von Rutkowski, who combined race biology with law. Johannes von Leers was hired, really in his hobby field of race history (like Bartels or Günther, the man had no university teaching qualifications) but, nominally, as a marine historian. Bernhard Kummer, similarly under-qualified, became a lecturer in Old Nordic languages in 1936 and a full professor in 1942. Falk Ruttke, already an official commentator on forced sterilization, like Rutkowski was given a chair in race and law, in 1940. Like Günther Franz, Heberer, Leers, and Astel himself as well as many others in that university, Ruttke was personally close to Himmler and ostentatiously wore his black uniform. Berthold Kihn, a pediatrician, assumed a chair in psychiatry and during the war euthanized children. Through his Weimar office Astel himself was in charge of all such actions, and his fanaticism as a National Socialist eugenicist never wavered. In 1943, he lectured to hundreds of Norwegian students, resistance fighters imprisoned in Buchenwald, trying to convince them that as "Nordics" they should willingly embrace the neo-Germanic creed. By this time Jena had acquired one of Germany's strongest reputations as a Nazi university; it was one of only four allowed to remain open during the final war years. From a post-Third Reich perspective, this was a dubious honor for neighboring Weimar. When the war was lost in early 1945, Astel gave up and put a bullet through his head.[23]

A Nazi Sanctuary and the Nietzsche Tradition

How important was Weimar in Hitler's overall scheme of things after he had assumed power in the Reich on January 30, 1933? How did the degree of Weimar's importance affect the town's development from 1933 to 1945? To assess these factors, one might begin with a statement from the generally unreliable memoirs of Hans Severus Ziegler. He maintains that in 1928 Hitler said to him that he "just loved" Weimar, that he needed Weimar and had great plans for it.[24] Other memoirists have established that Hitler had been genuinely fond of Weimar, ever since he had got into the habit of visiting it in 1925. This accords with the recollections of the actress Emmy Sonnemann in her enthusiastic accounts of her meetings with Hitler, in the Goethe Park or the cafés in town. Friedrich Christian Prinz von Schaumburg-Lippe, an early member of the Nazi entourage, recalls that Hitler liked Weimar because he could preserve his privacy there, as he walked undisturbed from the Hotel Elephant to cafés or shops.[25]

It is easy to see why Hitler would have felt comfortable in the cozy atmosphere of the Goethe town, although he was minimally concerned with the classic aura that had made its name and had no affinity with Goethe or Schiller. Traveling often between Munich and Berlin and back, Hitler paid several visits to Weimar and frequently spoke there publicly, notwithstanding his many visits to neighboring Bayreuth.

But the fact that after January 1933 the Weimar visits were becoming rarer, whereas Hitler's interest in Bayreuth and the Wagner family never waned, gives one pause to think.[26] If Hitler's admission to Ziegler of 1928 was true, then one must note that Hitler had also included Bayreuth in his praise, by mentioning the two towns in one breath. So had Elisabeth Förster-Nietzsche's decades-long design to make Weimar superior to Bayreuth not come to fruition, after all? For the period of the Third Reich it is known that Hitler's preferred cities, quite apart from Bayreuth, were first Munich and then Linz, where he had lived during his youth and might one day retire. Over time, he devised plans to beautify those towns, endow them culturally, and significantly monumentalize their architecture. New, grandiose structures he also planned for Berlin and Nuremberg, in cooperation with his personal architect Albert Speer. Hitler had to govern from Berlin, as the capital of the Reich, which he wanted to elevate to the status of "capital of the world," hence it had to be overwhelming. And Nuremberg had become the site of the party rallies – *after* Weimar, significantly, for Nuremberg was the home of Wagner's *Meistersinger*, and Weimar was simply too small to accommodate the frenetically adoring masses that Hitler was now becoming used to. Hamburg with its stunning waterfront villas was also to be further beautified, to become the greatest port. Hamburg, Munich, Nuremberg, Berlin, and Linz were to be singled out as *Führerstädte*.[27]

Therefore, on balance it is probably safe to say that in past accounts, the importance of Weimar for Hitler has been much exaggerated, especially by those who spent time with him there before 1933. On the other hand, Hitler was indebted to Weimar's citizens and municipal and regional governments for having afforded him the opportunity to restart his career there in 1925, and to hold his first large party rally in 1926. (Characteristically, however, Hitler did not acknowledge Weimar's hospitality in his rally address of July 4, 1926, even in a single sentence.)[28] Weimar's right-wing burghers recognized and serviced his political needs, and the town as such made him comfortable physically and mentally. Weimar was neither too large nor too small for him to stay there, more for relaxation than official business, whenever the spirit moved him and time allowed, after 1933. About this, there must have been agreement between him and Fritz Sauckel, one of his most obsequious Gauleiter, and it was Sauckel (along with the similarly slavish Ziegler) who entertained great Nazi plans for Weimar, more often encouraged or simply tolerated by Hitler than contradicted – Hitler was not a micro-manager. Was Weimar going to be made into a Nazi sanctuary?

The assumption that Sauckel, not Hitler, was the main driving force behind a renewed quest for Weimar's greatness is supported by the grandiose architectural visions Sauckel entertained for the classics town. As early as May 1933 he proposed to Hitler that a huge new complex of buildings be constructed, for party institutions, the government, and himself as Reichsstatthalter. Originally Sauckel wished to use the Goethe Park next to the Ilm river, a scheme rejected by Hitler. Eventually, vast tracts of land near the Landesmuseum were chosen, in the northern district of town, between the historic market and the railway station.

Of the ten architects, among them Schultze-Naumburg, who had handed in blueprints for the remodeling, Hitler, advised by Albert Speer, ultimately selected Hermann Giesler. Next to Speer and, until his death in 1934, Paul Ludwig Troost, who had built the Munich Haus der Deutschen Kunst, Giesler was Hitler's favorite architect. Construction began, carefully timed, in July 1936, exactly ten years after the symbolic Weimar party rally. The Asbachtal park, a charming green belt that had marked the border between south and north Weimar, was erased, along with proletarian living quarters in the historic Jakobsvorstadt. Altogether, 445 dwellings for 1,650 people, including around 150 houses and over 79 businesses, were marked for demolition, and most were indeed razed. A new imposing square, the Adolf-Hitler-Platz, incorporating the old Karl-August-Platz, was created, leading to a Halle der Volksgemeinschaft for 15,000 visitors. The largest building, a Zentralministerium, was planned to the northeast of this complex near the Ilm, to house, among others, Astel's race office. War priorities after 1939 slowed the construction process, so that the last important discussion regarding future work was held in February 1942. Then all activity ceased in July of 1944, as armament production and key decisions at the fronts took center stage. Meanwhile, by a law of 1937 many private owners had been forced to accept compensation below market value, others had been forcibly resettled, and the town had been forced to surrender valuable real estate gratuitously. A total of 27.5 million marks had been expended by mid-1944, including 3 million of Hitler's own money. Of all the buildings planned, however, only two or three had been partially finished, in Brutalist style.[29]

Hitler had planned such a Gauforum for every Gau capital in the Reich; hence Weimar could lay no claim to having been singled out. But what did make this special was that once more Weimar was used as a testing ground, in that the Nazi government had begun its Reich reconstruction activities early here, and nowhere else. This was unquestionably due to Sauckel's perseverance, yet might have been doomed to failure, but for Hitler's overall compliance. Sauckel, on his own, constructed new living quarters for the military (Weimar's tradition as a garrison town was now revived), for workers in the Gustloff-Werke, and for some of the people displaced by the Gauforum upheavals. Hitler, on the other hand, proved his relative fondness for Weimar once again when he had Giesler rebuild the medieval Hotel Elephant in 1937, with architectural input by himself personally, such as sketches for a multi-vehicle underground garage, a stylish hotel bar, and a special flat for the Führer's future visits. The newly enlarged hotel was opened, with much fanfare, in 1938.[30]

But apart from the monstrous urban restructuring, which took years to develop and held little promise of being completed within a realistic time span, how could the Nazi rulers capitalize on Weimar's tradition as a cultural icon? How could Weimar itself accommodate National Socialist rule within its walls, given the sympathetic presence there of long-time right-wing extremists? The key problem, of course, was that by its very nature the Nazi movement had never been concerned with high art or intellectual pursuits, let alone caring for the classical era of a Goethe or a Schiller. Because conceptually, the German Enlightenment of the late eighteenth century and National Socialist ideology were anathema, continuing any kind of classics worship by Nazis would have to assume some form of compromise.

The Nazis first tried to instrumentalize idolatry they themselves had helped to foster before their national takeover, and it involved not the princes of Weimar's classical era but a sometime critic of it: Friedrich Nietzsche. Participating in the Nietzsche cult, such as it was in 1933, and even making it one's own was not an easy matter, because not all Nazis could accept what Nietzsche stood for. Hitler himself, who had never mentioned Nietzsche in *Mein Kampf* and did not give much thought to the philosopher's ideological uses, conveniently continued his personal friendship with Elisabeth Förster-Nietzsche and hence lent an official air to the connections between his party and government on the one side, and the Nietzsche Archive on the other.

After meeting her personally for the first time in 1932, Hitler saw the Förster widow again on February 2, 1933, during the celebration of Richard Wagner's passing, when Weimar's theater performed *Tristan und Isolde*. At that point, Förster-Nietzsche issued a permanent invitation to Hitler, specifying later that it was her dearest wish to serve him a vegetarian breakfast at her house. To the Jewish benefactor Ernst Thiel in Stockholm she sang the praises of the "wonderful Führer," doing her best to explain to him why Germany now had no choice but to enact anti-Semitic measures. Yet she allowed that the severity and suddenness of those measures was disturbing: "surely one could have waited with that." Nonetheless, Thiel was warned not to listen to foreign anti-German propaganda in these matters and was assured that milder laws would come to pass, permitting the regime "to preserve the best of the foreign race as Germans."[31] That in reality she now had chosen to demonstrate her anti-Semitic feelings more openly became clear in early November, when during another visit from the Führer the old lady presented Hitler with a copy of an anti-Semitic petition her husband had delivered to Bismarck in 1880. Her accompanying comment was that ever after, opponents of the petition, meaning Jews, had pursued the couple as far as Paraguay, because her husband had been a pioneer of the anti-Semitic movement in Germany. As calculated by Förster-Nietzsche, Hitler's subsequent support proved unstinting. In May 1934 he granted her a monthly stipend of 300 marks, in July he returned once more to Weimar to relate to her details of his visit with Mussolini in Italy the previous month. Still another visit to Villa Silberblick took place in October.[32]

Then, on November 10, 1935, Förster-Nietzsche died at the age of ninety. On the next day Hitler, accompanied by Sauckel and Baldur von Schirach, was at the Archive, attending a special ceremony. Apart from the homage paid to the dead woman and her philosopher brother, the event provided another welcome platform for anti-Semitism, when the deceased's cousin Adalbert Oehler pronounced Bernhard Förster "a genuine German man," one of the few in his time "who had had an open eye for the egregious dominance of Jewry." As Hitler placed a wreath on Elisabeth Förster-Nietzsche's grave in Röcken the next day, he must have done so knowing that thus far, the Villa Silberblick and its Archive had served his movement well.[33]

For the future, the directors of the Archive wished things to remain this way, for they themselves would benefit. But apart from Förster-Nietzsche's personal relationship with Hitler, which was all the smoother because her rivalry with Bayreuth of the mid-1920s had finally been laid to rest, institutional developments in the Archive after January 1933 were turbulent. Several forces were working at cross-purposes, threatening to tear the entire structure apart. A scholarly group under Jena professor Karl August Emge strove to bring about the *Historisch-Kritische Gesamtausgabe* (*HKG*), a definitive critical edition of Nietzsche's *œuvre*. It is surprising that despite great difficulties altogether nine volumes were actually published by 1942, at which time editors became incapable or unwilling, money dried up and paper for the printing presses was unavailable. The editorial board made do without Alfred Baeumler, who had assumed high functions in Rosenberg's new ideological party office. But Emge, who threatened to take control over the entire Archive, was opposed by Max Oehler, the leading archivist, in league with Adalbert and Richard Oehler. Max Oehler's aim was to hire out the Archive as "a fount of ideas for the Nazi state." Already in May

1934 a conference was organized on the topic of Germanic Law, to which Rosenberg, Hans Frank (later the governor-general of Occupied Poland) and the professors Hans Freyer and Martin Heidegger were invited. In October another event celebrated Nietzsche's ninetieth birthday, when he was stylized as an "innovator for a time of great leadership and heroic comportment." Förster-Nietzsche herself was then too old to involve herself in the minutiae of these squabbles; she had been trying hard to finish her book about Nietzsche and the women in his life, which she managed just before she died. After her funeral Max Oehler, freed from her tethers, got the upper hand, so that Emge decided to resign. Spengler had already left the advisory board a few weeks earlier, declaring that "either one concerns oneself with the philosophy of Nietzsche, or with that of the Nietzsche Archive."[34]

As a replacement for Spengler, Heidegger now joined the board. Rector of the University of Freiburg and officially still known as a National Socialist, Heidegger's main concern was to create a new, unadulterated version of Nietzsche's *Will to Power*. The problem was that for this work as for other projects substantial funding was necessary, the securing of which lay in the hands of Emge's foe Max Oehler. In the following years, several agencies of party and of government were approached, mostly with negative results, for they were clamoring for control of one sort or another. At various times after 1935, Himmler's research organization Ahnenerbe, Goebbels's propaganda ministry, and Bernhard Rust's education ministry could have taken the reins and ousted the Oehler clan. Hitler became too busy with foreign policy and the war to concern himself with lesser matters in those years. So the person who prevailed in the end was Rosenberg. Heidegger, already, by conviction, somewhat removed from Nazism, resigned his responsibilities in 1942, because he had witnessed too much incompetence in the Archive (not least the discovery of new forged letters thus far hidden by Förster-Nietzsche). Now the Archive was Rosenberg's to take over. That he did not do so had to do with his new duties as minister for the occupied eastern territories (since 1941), decreasing resources and, within the Nazi hierarchy at home, his declining prestige. The Nietzsche Archive did serve secondary functions as an ideological training camp for schoolchildren and contingents of soldiers on furlough, and the like, but it had lost its former mark as a Nietzsche edifice, to say nothing of a salon for Weimar's sophisticated *haut monde*. Rosenberg officiated during a final event, on the centenary of Nietzsche's birth in October 1944. On that occasion he spoke about "the National Socialist movement" as a bastion against the non-Nazi world, in the same way as Nietzsche had once stood against "the powers of his day." In mentioning German defeats on the battlefield, he was, ironically, endorsing Nietzsche's dictum that weaklings should be pushed, in order to accelerate their fall.[35]

Rosenberg's participation in celebrations staged by the Nietzsche Archive so late in the war illustrates his rising interest in the philosopher over time, for which, in no small measure, the persuasive Baeumler was responsible.[36] This as much as Hitler's enduring friendship with Elisabeth Förster-Nietzsche opens up the larger question of how important Nietzsche's philosophy actually was for the Nazis. This issue has been raised before, and it is of interest whether the philosopher was a genuine precursor of Nazism or whether certain National Socialists simply twisted his ideas and abused him. The Israeli historian Steven E. Aschheim has reconceptualized the issues in order to explain to what extent Nietzschean ideas actually did pervade the theory and practice of National Socialism and the Third Reich. At the core of this was the Nietzschean formula of "transvaluation of all values": it was anti-values that informed Nazi dogma, such as illiberalism, anti-humanism, anti-rationalism, and anti-democracy. All of those were historic antipodes to the Enlightenment which Nietzsche himself abhorred. Seemingly in line with Nietzsche, the Nazis were against the "tyranny of objectivity," as for them "there was no absolute truth, only the need to create one's own culture."

In a fundamental way, writes Aschheim, Nietzschean precepts permeated all areas of life in Nazi-controlled society: education, science, scholarship, jurisprudence, and ceremonials. An important element was Christianity, its origins and its consequences. Although Nietzsche was no anti-Semite of the beer-garden variety, he blamed the Jews for having generated the Christian religion and its wider value system. After the Jewish Mary, Jesus, Peter and Paul, Christianity aimed to neutralize hierarchies whose essentially defining characteristic was inequality. In particular, Nietzsche's stance suited Rosenberg, whose two main belief systems were anti-Judaism, and the rejection of Christianity and its institutions. Nietzsche's thought aided the Nazi regime in its application of the inequality principle during bio-political actions such as sterilization and euthanasia of the physically and mentally weak, and in the denial and ultimate removal of Jews. It was not universal humanity that was the goal to be striven for but, as Aschheim interprets Nietzsche in Nazi terms, a racial-hierarchically defined polity in which the *Übermensch* – Nietzsche's archetypal "Blond Beast" – would rule. The *Übermensch* and his progeny must be encouraged to "live dangerously," as practiced by the SS (and, even earlier, by Hentschel and Himmler's *Artamanen*). *Übermenschen* would be prepared to embrace Nietzsche's call "to love your destiny," as Rosenberg did when he addressed the Weimar congregation in the face of military adversity. In the larger geopolitical picture, Hitler's grand plans for the remaking of Europe, his vision of a Grossgermanisches Reich, were another exemplification of Nietzschean transvaluation, for the remaking of Europe under neo-Germanic hegemony had not been conventional German policy in recent times. The National Socialists rationalized the limitations of Nietzsche's personal anti-Semitism, says Aschheim, by claiming that during his lifetime the theoretical and practical skill-sets necessary for the execution of radical anti-Semitism (and which, said leading Nazis, Nietzsche too held to be indispensable), were not yet available. But they were in place after 1933; hence Nietzsche would have been a model National Socialist.[37]

Such casuistry, as Aschheim has delineated it, was demonstrably supported by declarations and actions other than those Rosenberg, the chief ideologue of the Nazi movement, was responsible for *ex officio*. National Socialist proponents of Social Darwinism Alfred Ploetz and Fritz Lenz, who influenced the course of "mercy-killing" in the Third Reich, believed early in Nietzsche's judgment that weaklings should perish.[38] Already in his novel *Michael* of 1929 Goebbels had his hero place into his desk drawer a copy each of the Bible, Goethe's *Faust*, and Nietzsche's *Thus Spoke Zarathustra*.[39] Governor-General Hans Frank delivered a very similar embrace-your-fate (English for the Nietzschean formula *amor fati*) address at Cracow, his Polish seat of governance, as Rosenberg, on the same occasion in fall 1944.[40] SS elite troops were indoctrinated with the hardness principle, as articles in Himmler's publications *Das Schwarze Korps* and *SS-Leithefte* show. In an essay entitled "Our Hardness," one SS journalist wrote in the January, 1943, edition of *SS-Leithefte*, at the beginning of the fiercest year of extermination of Jews in the Third Reich: "This now is the toughness which the people of poets and thinkers has struggled to arrive at. Only the resolute man, the man who knows what he wants, will win in this decisive contest of peoples and ideologies."[41] Nietzsche could not have said it better. Moreover, an article from November 1943 by SS War Correspondent Zimmermann was entitled: "We Must Become Ever Harder."[42] And in "War without Mercy" in the December issue SS readers and their clans were informed, in reference to recent successes of the Red Army, that "we have entered into the arena of a battle that is without mercy."[43] In these war years, Nietzsche's thought did not just touch the SS. Wehrmacht troops were furnished with special editions of *Zarathustra* and *Der Wille zur Macht* as a matter of routine, to steel them in war against the enemy.[44]

Yet it will be remembered that similar volumes were handed out to German soldiers before they were rushed to the trenches in World War I. So what was truly special about Nietzsche in the Third Reich? Leading National Socialists other than Rosenberg ignored him as inconsequential, while others still went further, claiming that his belief system was contrary to Nazi *Weltanschauung*. Dietrich Eckart, Hitler's Munich mentor from the early Nazi movement days, had always claimed Nietzsche was simply mentally ill. After 1933, at the universities of Frankfurt and then Heidelberg, the influential pedagogue Ernst Krieck railed against Nietzsche, as did the historian Christoph Steding, in one of Nazi Germany's official research institutes. Invariably, such Nietzsche critics took umbrage at the philosopher's stand on race, he who prided himself on his (certainly imaginary) aristocratic Polish roots. Heinrich Härtle, who actually worked under Baeumler in the Amt Rosenberg, even though admiring of Nietzsche, developed a trenchant line of arguments against him. Although Nietzsche despised Jews because they had spawned Christianity, maintained Härtle, he was known for having attacked anti-Semites in his day and had many Jewish friends. His disagreements with Richard Wagner had been mainly because of the Jewish Question and he had been an enemy of Bayreuth. Nietzsche held the Lamarckian view that Jews could develop and be assimilated by the German people over time, as he thought that so-called pure races could not exist in any case, only mixed ones. Moreover, Nietzsche had scoffed at proactive attempts to ameliorate a race through breeding experiments. "Thus Nietzsche has removed himself completely from a realistic racial policy. His racial insights do not lead him to an organic conception of the *Volk*, and it is not the *Volk* that becomes the building block for his political model, but the European blending of races." In the end Härtle deplored the fact that for Nietzsche, "Master Race" really did not have racial but corporativist or social-class connotations. Corollaries of these central views, argued Härtle, were Nietzsche's notorious opposition to Bismarck's Second Reich, no less than his negation of *Volk* and nationalism. In all, Nietzsche had an inorganic view of Europe.[45]

Beyond these speculations for or against the philosopher, Hitler had a few reasons of his own why Nietzsche idolatry should not go too far. He had to be careful not to be seen merely as an executor of Nietzschean thoughts; his own cult must not be overshadowed by a Nietzsche cult. Hitler had, after all, developed individual ideas about nation, state, and race and wished to be taken seriously as an independent thinker. In *Mein Kampf* alone, references to Schopenhauer, Wagner, Bismarck, and Chamberlain would not call into question his own originality. If he was seen as a direct extension of Nietzsche, Germany's most famous philosopher after Kant and Hegel, however, Hitler's uniqueness would be impugned. And this is why Hitler's book ignored him.

Altogether, these considerations formed a major reason why Hitler's visits to Weimar, and in particular the Villa Silberblick, became even more sporadic after Förster-Nietzsche's death in October 1935. They could also have affected the sluggish progress in the construction of a final monument to honor Nietzsche, next to the Silberblick estate.[46] The venture was eerily reminiscent of Kessler's, van de Velde's and Förster-Nietzsche's pre-World War I plan to memorialize Nietzsche with a stadium, and it was to fail just as spectacularly. During his visit to Weimar in October of 1934 Hitler, Sauckel, and Nietzsche's sister had discussed the idea of a Nietzsche memorial hall to be erected alongside Villa Silberblick. Disagreements occurred early when Hitler and Sauckel opted for a ceremonial character, whereas Förster-Nietzsche preferred practical functions such as a congregation hall and a library. Nonetheless, 50,000 marks of government money were committed by October 1935, and Schultze-Naumburg was charged with the execution of the project. After Elisabeth Förster-Nietzsche's death the Nazis supplied further funds and a neighboring lot was purchased. By August 1938 a rudimentary structure was completed, and steps were now taken to work on replicas of typically Nietzschean symbols to adorn the interior: eagle, snake, and lion, but also a bust of Hitler. The heads of Dionysos and Apollo were to be among the ornaments, along with those of famous poets, musicians, and thinkers. Schultze-Naumburg traveled to Italy to search for a suitable Dionysos statue – it was to be his last commission in the service of the Nazi movement. Mussolini, enthusiastic about Nietzsche as always, could help. A marble figure of Dionysos, copied from a Greek original, was found near the Via Appia. Although it had an arm missing and the head and beard were damaged beyond recognition, the statue could be restored by an Italian artist. Finally, on January 29, 1944, after Mussolini had been deposed, and under the personal care of Wehrmacht Mediterranean Supreme Commander Field Marshal Albert Kesselring, the sculpture arrived at the Weimar railway station. Braving a British air raid, Archive director Max Oehler transported it himself to the half-finished edifice at the top of Luisenstrasse, only to discover later that it was too tall to fit into the designated hall. Further renovation to the large building was called for, but the vagaries of war prevented this. Until 1942, the project had cost 560,000 marks, and 150,000 were still needed.[47]

Sports Meets, Mass Rallies, and Congresses

In the face of Hitler's decreasing interest in Weimar after 1933, Thuringian and Weimar Nazi grandees were doing their best to reevaluate the town for their own purposes. They knew well that in the Third Reich, aesthetics and totalitarianism had entered a workable alliance. "The aestheticization of politics was one of the foremost purposes of National Socialist propaganda," maintains the Münster historian Hans-Ulrich Thamer. "Images and signs, demonstrations and open spectacles were primarily used to secure broad approval and an identification by the public with the Nazi movement and its rulers."[48]

In this effort Weimar, which stood for aesthetics, was seized upon as a traditionally famous place. Fame might be determined by the classics, but to some they were not a prerequisite. What mattered was that Weimar and its arts and letters showed the potential for being attached to a vibrant, neo-Germanic, National Socialist tradition. In Hitler's Germany, such a tradition was in a continuous process of being invented in the same manner in which the earlier one had been, to use Hobsbawm's paradigm, for the late nineteenth century, connecting Goethe to Bismarck.

Goethe aside, it behoved a town with a cultural reputation such as Weimar's to be tied into new textures of culture and learning. And so in June 1934 a tradition of annual "Book Weeks" was inaugurated, and in June 1936 the Deutsche Tonkünstlerfest (German Composers' Festival) was held. The latter was in fact a venerable institution sponsored by the Allgemeiner Deutscher Musikverein harking back to Liszt, but now judged out of character with Nazi tenets and therefore on the verge of dissolution. In June 1938 Weimar University Student Days were organized, featuring cultural and competitive-sports programs for Nazified students.[49] Hitler put in one of his rare appearances in Weimar in 1936, in an official capacity, which had nothing to do with culture but with the town's earlier function as a Nazi stepping-stone to power. It was in commemoration of his first party rally outside Munich, ten years ago to the day, in 1926. From July 3 to 5, 1936, Hitler took part in preliminary ceremonies for his massive Gauforum project and politely acknowledged that Weimar had hosted him in July 1926, at a crucial point in his political career. Over three festive days, between party rallies and marches, Hitler, Sauckel, Reich Interior Minister Frick, and other Nazi bosses made public speeches, but there were only two cultural offerings – very untypical of Weimar. On Friday, the 3rd, the first movement of Beethoven's Fifth Symphony was performed, before an evening of Wagner's *Tannhäuser*. In this context Weimar's Wagner tradition was incidental, for almost all events were Nazi-specific and could not even remotely be tied to the town's storied reputation. On July 4 the Weimar State Orchestra played "Storm, Storm, Storm," a text by Hitler's deceased friend Dietrich Eckart, set to music by the obscure composer Hans Gansser.

(Gansser had ingratiated himself with the Nazis earlier by writing a song entitled "For the Führer.") The national anthem and the Nazi signature "Horst-Wessel-Lied," which conjured up doom for all Communists and enemies of the Nazi revolution, were intoned by the goose-stepping jack-boots, while Hitler Youths formed their own choruses and choirs. In the cinema, a propaganda film showed *The Way to Freedom: A Nazi Village Assembly from 1925*. To round things off, well-known marches such as the *Badenweiler* and *Preussens Gloria* were played by the band of Hitler's special bodyguards, the SS-Leibstandarte – German Nationalist, but easily utilized by Nazi propagandists.[50]

Already by the mid-1930s party leaders other than Hitler, Sauckel, or Ziegler had designs on Weimar as a place with potential to enhance the standing of the Nazi regime, with a focus on the cultural, where applicable. Chief among them were Reich Youth Leader Baldur von Schirach and Minister Joseph Goebbels, who had both been reared against a background of culture. Schirach, the native Weimarer, had a theater Intendant for a father, an opera singer for a sister, and always fancied himself a poet. He respected the classics, especially Goethe. Goebbels, although from a lower middle-class family, held a doctorate in German literature from Heidelberg and was the author of a novel; his Berlin ministry was officially in charge of culture. In 1923, Goebbels had written his dissertation on the early nineteenth-century Romantics, some of them contemporaries of Goethe; the topic had been suggested to him by Professor Friedrich Gundolf, one of the foremost Goethe experts of his time.[51]

In 1937 Schirach extended full Hitler Youth dominance over the Schiller Festival, proceeding to adapt it to Third Reich needs. After having stopped its performances under the aegis of the Schillerbund during World War I, the festival, serving German youth since its inception, had been revived in 1921 as a republican venture and from then on took place regularly, beginning every June after the end of the normal repertoire.[52] Schirach's aim in 1937 was to completely repoliticize the event. When spawned in 1906 by the Schillerbund under Schirach's father Carl Norris and Adolf Bartels, it had been an ultra-nationalist affair, but its political agenda had been attenuated during the republic. Hans Severus Ziegler, as supervisor of the Weimar stages, after 1933 did his part to bring the festival ideologically in line again; he also led the overarching Schillerbund. By 1937 the celebrations functioned under the official label "Weimar Festival of German Youth."[53]

Paying its deep respect to co-founder Bartels, the festival now became primarily a political platform for the Hitler Youth. Not least, it turned into a tool of Nazi social engineering in that Hitler Youth auditors comprised not just high-school students but also young workers and shop apprentices, who would all rub shoulders in Weimar. This was the constantly restated aim not only of Ziegler but of Schirach and his cultural aide Karl Cerff. The program featured ideologically useful plays by Schiller, but also Goethe and Heinrich von Kleist, and operas by Wagner.[54] Conveniently, other cultural events could be included with the aim of ideological training, as was done in 1938. On average, the youths camped out in Weimar for four weeks. It was in summer 1938 that Schirach started quoting Hitler from *Mein Kampf* and reminding his listeners that the Germans, the people of poets and thinkers, had now metamorphosed into a "nation of poets and soldiers."[55] The boys and girls needed no reminder that Austria had just been incorporated into the Reich and the regime was coveting Czechoslovakia, with French and British politicians becoming concerned. Cerff, a high SS leader, spoke of the moral right of every German to defend his sense of entitlement in the world on the basis of his "valuable German blood."[56] For good measure, a commissioned lecturer, Professor Ewald Geissler, denigrated the literary style of the Jewish Heinrich Heine and Franz Werfel. "We have found that the same German word can have a totally different sound, a noticeably flatter quality, if spoken by a Jewish mouth."[57] Important policy directives were also issued. Dr. Jutta Rüdiger, under Schirach the chief of all girls in the Hitler Youth, made her underlings aware of the *Glaube und Schönheit* (Faith and Beauty) program, whose aim it was to select well-shaped blond females and prepare them, through special routines such as calisthenics, to become breeding mates for the most desirable elite of young men, destined to be leaders.[58]

In the summer of 1939, the German Reich was a mere two months removed from a new world war. Hence the underlying tone of the Schiller Festival turned more militant. Youths were reminded of Goethe's opinion that wearing a uniform was a good thing, or Schiller's that life had to be put at risk in order to be won for good. Sauckel and Hitler's long-term plans for Weimar as a newly constructed Gau, meaning party administrative center, were explained in some detail. The pledge to serve the socially disadvantaged was renewed.[59] The next festival began on June 12, 1941. By that time, the bellicose German Reich had been victorious in the West, and when the festivities were concluded, the Soviet Union had been invaded. The language of the speakers thus was appropriately martial, with strong imperialistic undertones. Future recruits had to be properly, and quickly, indoctrinated. Hence HJ-Oberbannführer Otto Zander, now the director of culture for the Hitler Youth, in his opening address alluded to the fact that apart from Weimar's, additional cultural meetings were currently being planned for Danzig and West Prussia, Strasbourg, and Upper Silesia – all recently reconquered. Culture in Germany clearly had become political: "Whoever among Germany's youth is active in cultural matters and a leader, must have, to say the least, an eye for large spaces and the greatness of the Reich, such as our soldiers have acquired after several thousand kilometers of marches in war."[60] There was a further Schiller Festival in 1942, but thereafter the war's exigencies forced an end to the venture.[61]

Whereas Goethe and Schiller played nominal but still official roles in the festivities of Baldur von Schirach, their appearance was more incidental in the festivities of Goebbels. The culture minister had delegated two of his experts, Wilhelm Haegert and Rudolf Erckmann, to organize annual gatherings of poets, formally as an introduction to the 1938 "Book Week," starting in the fall, at which he himself would officiate at the end.[62] As Frank Trommler has observed, Goebbels wanted to use these Weimar poets' meetings "as instruments for integrating important writers into his propaganda machine; in return they received increased recognition as the embodiment of German culture."[63] That was the plan, but whether the writers really were important was a question, and what recognition they received remained open. In any event, the thirty-five-year-old Erckmann got to work in Weimar. He was the more studious of the two functionaries; a philologist with a doctorate, he had been employed by Goebbels's ministry since 1934.[64] His boss Haegert back in Berlin, although four years younger, was a veteran of the early Nazi movement and, more practical, had studied law and had served as a deputy Gauleiter. He had been chief of staff and head of propaganda in Goebbels's ministry and in 1938 was one year short of being appointed chief of its literature department.[65]

And so in late October 1938 Ziegler and Bartels on behalf of Weimar welcomed 250 authors to the town, of whom only six were invited to speak, however, apart from Erckmann, who led the proceedings.[66] None of those seven speakers was prolific. Erckmann set the tone of mediocrity by condemning the "madness of so-called Expressionist poetry" as a manifestation of the spiritual decline of the bygone liberal period, which was synonymous with "the work of the Jewish world enemy."[67] This fit the Nazi mood, a few days before Kristallnacht, the horrors of which Goebbels was about to unleash. Erckmann did not fail to mention the political background for the event: Weimar, the "town of great German poetry," had been chosen to summon German authors, in recognition of Austrian literary achievements and what had been inherited from Sudeten German poets – those Germans with Czechoslovak citizenship who were just being annexed to the Reich.[68]

Another speaker was Robert Hohlbaum, an Austrian originally from the Sudetenland, who after serving in World War I had become a rabid nationalist and moved to Nazi Germany in 1933. Hohlbaum paid tribute to Goethe and Schiller, as well as to the currently leading National Socialist writers – Edwin Erich Dwinger, Hans Zöberlein, Werner Beumelburg, and Rudolf G. Binding, most of whom could not be relied on to appear in Weimar. In large part, Hohlbaum's speech was a paean to Hitler.[69] In keeping with the Austrian–Sudeten theme, other speakers in 1938 were Heinrich Zillich, originally from Austro-Hungarian Siebenbürgen, and Josef Weinheber, who lived in Vienna. Zillich, whose anti-Semitism was particularly fierce, had recently been received by Hitler. Weinheber, after severe bouts of alcoholism, was to take his own life during the Red Army advance on Vienna. Pouring scorn on Remarque's *All Quiet on the Western Front* and lauding Hitler's *Mein Kampf*, Weinheber credited National Socialism with social progress: his own elevation from simple postal worker to published author.[70]

By the time of the second meeting in the fall of 1940 the war was on and the martial tones were shriller. That Germany had recently subdued France spurred the organizers on. In his speech of welcome, Erckmann reminded his guests that German writers had already been invited to visit Wehrmacht soldiers on the Western Front.[71] This time Hanns Johst stood out, the former Expressionist dramatist, president of Goebbels's Writers' Chamber, and a general in the SS. It was he who had written: "Whenever I hear the word culture, I reach for my revolver," a phrase notoriously attributed to Göring. To National Socialist events in Weimar in the past, Johst had been no stranger. This time his talk was all military; there was nothing relating specifically to Weimar or the classics. "Under the sign of war it goes without saying that the fighter's spirit, the soldier's input, the hard edge of the word moves to the foreground." And he reminded his listeners that the idea of the future was tantamount to German *Lebensraum*: the National Socialism of Adolf Hitler."[72] The speakers following Johst were as insignificant as those from previous meetings, even in Nazi terms: Kurt Hesse, Ludwig Tügel, Hermann Burte, and Carl Rothe. In their speeches, bristling with warlike aggression, Hitler was mentioned as often as Goethe and Schiller combined.[73]

The 1941 Convention gave the Nazis an opportunity to impress foreign collaborators who had been invited to join their German colleagues. Such a notion was about as far removed from Schiller and Goethe's thinking as could be. Not that these collaborators had any active role to play or were allowed to speak. On the contrary, the German press had been instructed by Goebbels's ministry that "the names of the foreign authors may be mentioned, but their works not especially singled out."[74] The Nazi sympathizers and practicing fascists either came from Axis member countries like Italy, or neighboring nations like Holland, which Hitler planned to integrate into his Great-Germanic Reich in one capacity or another.

In October 1941 these foreigners in Weimar were a motley group. They arrived from as far north as Sweden and as far south as the Balkans. Professor Alfredo Acito represented the Italian Ministry of Popular Culture. Professor Veikko Antero Koskenniemi came from the Finnish Academy. He had translated Goethe into Finnish, himself wrote prose in a chauvinistic vein and saw in Hitler the long-awaited savior from Bolshevism. After a trip to Nazi Germany in 1935 his anti-Semitism had hardened. Then there was the Romanian Ion Sân-Giorgiu, who had studied in Germany. Close to the fascist Iron Guard and an inveterate Jew-hater, he was known for the swastikas he liked to pin to his clothing. Josef Nyirö was a fascist journalist and Catholic priest from Hungary, and Filip de Pillecyn came from the right-wing Flemish movement.[75] Perhaps the most important were the French "collabos," as Frederic Spotts has described them, both from Vichy France and the Nazi-occupied northern French half.[76] Abel Bonnard, a former follower of Charles Maurras, the anti-Semitic founder of the *Action Française* who was himself a Germanophobe had been an advocate of fascism since the 1930s. A future education minister in the Vichy regime after 1941, he would be expelled from the Académie Française after the war and condemned to death *in absentia*, having sought refuge in Franco's Spain. Pierre Drieu La Rochelle was ruled by a fear of Bolshevism, believing, like Koskenniemi, in Hitler's pan-Germanic vision as a cure. After the liberation of Paris he finally succeeded in committing suicide in March of 1945. Robert Brasillach too had been close to Maurras. He was destined to sign a declaration demanding that members of the French Resistance be executed.[77] In 1945 he himself was shot after trial, having been denied a pardon by General de Gaulle. Marcel Jouhandeau was yet another fascist writer. First he was not sure if he should go on the Nazi journey, but after all, these Frenchmen had been promised a three-week tour of the Reich prior to Weimar, with all expenses paid.[78] When he had finally decided to join his compatriots, Jouhandeau noted in his diary: "For whom or for what am I here? Because from the time I knew how to read, understand and feel, I have loved Germany, her philosophers, her musicians and I think that nothing could serve humanity better than our understanding with her. In 1940 I observed very closely what happened and it is undeniable, unless one is less than honest, that the Germans could have treated us worse after their victory." Upon his return,

Jouhandeau wrote in the *Nouvelle Revue Française*, "I was finally able to live for a few days close to people who were yesterday our enemy but whose tact towards us amazes me."[79]

For this 1941 conference, Wilhelm Haegert, Erckmann's superior, had come down from Berlin. Harping on the theme of anti-Bolshevism that was shared by all participants, in his opening remarks he warned of "hordes of Huns and Mongols" that could potentially invade Western Europe. Conveniently, he conjured up the "European spirit," which had been passed down from Charlemagne – here was a concession to the French – and said that today it was the cement holding together "the Germanic Race, the creator of our European culture, the most highly developed flower of mankind."[80] No less than Goebbels spoke next, inspired by the power of the "battle front."[81]

After those orators, only minor German writers held forth, including Bruno Brehm, who was born in Bohemia, and Moritz Jahn from the hinterland of Bremen, a former public-school teacher who wrote in North German dialect. While Brehm warned mostly of the Jews, in particular the Jewish political commissars of the Red Army, Jahn, apart from his own anti-Semitic diatribe, got in a few references to Goethe, Schiller, and Herder.[82]

The fall of 1942 saw another meeting at Weimar, now that Hitler had enjoyed some victories on the Eastern Front. But the overall success of this conference was dubious, for invitations were honored by only a few foreign fascists. Jouhandeau, for example, had now excused himself.[83] That October the prominent Edwin Erich Dwinger was the keynote speaker, his address competing with a speech by Johst. Keeping to the previous theme of anti-Bolshevism, Dwinger had been well chosen, for he was a former prisoner of war in Russia and then had fought the Red revolutionaries on the White Russian side.[84] Now Dwinger seized the occasion to remind his audience that Europe was in the shadow not just of Bolshevism, but also Americanism, for the United States had been in the war for almost twelve months. As for the Soviet phenotype, said Nazi expert Dwinger, in its crude outlines alone it embodied Marxist ideology, the result of a collaboration between "primitive Russians and Jews."[85]

One of the concluding features of the 1942 writers' meeting was a speech by Haegert paying homage to Weimar's own Adolf Bartels. Haegert praised Bartels for having metaphorically attached "the yellow star," decades ago, to the perfidious "Jew literati," who were just as disgraced by it then symbolically, as Jews were in the present day by wearing stars of cloth. That, for Haegert, was the legacy of Weimar, not Goethe, Schiller, or Herder.[86]

Altogether, the relevance of the poets' meetings had proved a questionable one. A Europäische Schriftsteller-Vereinigung, a European writers' union, established at the 1941 Weimar congress was already failing. It had been placed under the presidency of Hans Carossa. This prominent German novelist, who later said he had never been a Nazi, publicly confessed to admiring both Goethe and Hitler, but was claimed by the Nazis as one of their own and during the war was a favorite cited in SS publications not seen by the general public. Now he graciously made his services available.[87] Despite the reasonably well known Carossa, designed as a counterweight to the London-based PEN Club, the Vereinigung never had a chance.[88] Somehow, for the propaganda ministry, a repeated foray into Weimar had not borne fruit. Thus for the future, any further events were cancelled.

Weimar Icons

Somehow, the Third Reich found it difficult to establish organic ties with Weimar, either through a personal predilection of Adolf Hitler for the town, or through some significant institutional link. Still, Weimar was too important in the recent history of Germany not to be inserted into a legacy the Nazis were construing for themselves, to be remembered after a thousand years. With Nietzsche's persona not suitable and his philosophy only partially useful, could not a prominent resident of Weimar be built up as a symbol, an incarnation of National Socialist values, someone who already had a convincing stature? Among contemporaries, hardly anyone qualified as such a figure. Both Hans Severus Ziegler and Baldur von Schirach were too young and did not have the gravitas commensurate with Weimar's reputation. Johannes Schlaf, while becoming ever more convinced of Nazism and soon embracing its vicious Jew hatred, was not a sufficiently public figure and was increasingly controversial because of his abstruse astronomical theses. Although he had become a member of the Prussian Academy of Arts, he had not served Nazi publicity in any constructive way as a writer, as had Kolbenheyer, Johst, or Dwinger. Besides, in 1937, he moved back to his birthplace of Querfurt. Still, when he died of a stroke in February 1941, after praising Hitler for having awakened the spirits of the German "*Volk* and race soul," he was given a bombastic funeral with all the Nazi trappings.[89]

So somehow it looked as if Adolf Bartels, whose fealty to Hitler after 1933 was as little in doubt as Schlaf's, could be the movement's elder statesman in Weimar, in the manner of Hitler's mentor Dietrich Eckart in Munich before the Beer Hall putsch. However, too close an association by

the Nazi regime with Bartels would also have its dangers, especially internationally, for he was primarily known as a garrulous anti-Semite. Whereas
Schlaf had found his place in literary history as one of the co-founders of
Naturalism and his name was mentioned by some in the same breath as
that of Arno Holz and Nobel laureate Gerhart Hauptmann, Bartels was a
second-rate journalist who had earned neither the doctoral nor the professorial title he bore. If he had thought, like Ernst von Wildenbruch before
him, that he could be Weimar's Goethe of the post-classical century, this
promise had not been fulfilled. All the same, ever since Hitler's private
meeting with him in 1925 the Nazis had courted Bartels, and in the persons
of Ziegler, the younger Schirach, and Weimar's own Rainer Schlösser, who
became Reichsdramaturg under Goebbels in Berlin, he had three powerful
supporters.

Throughout the Third Reich Bartels received many honors, usually on
the occasion of his birthday, ritually celebrated in Weimar. In 1933, for his
seventy-first, he was granted an honorary pension from the state of
Thuringia. Ziegler as director of the Weimar theater then had his 1902
play performed, *The Reichstag of Worms*, and a Weimar street was named
after him. On his seventy-fifth birthday in 1937 Bartels became an
honorary citizen of Weimar, while Hitler endowed him with the Order of
the Eagle Shield, for civilians the highest order in the Reich. A year later
Bartels, a newly created honorary doctor of the University of Leipzig,
assisted Haegert at the poets' meeting. A Bartels Foundation was established in 1941 for the purpose of awarding a "Dietrich Eckart Prize" –
20,000 marks for the best work in literary criticism. The year 1942 was a
halcyon one for Bartels, for he reached eighty and was much feted. By the
NSDAP he was honored with the Golden Party Badge, and Professor
Heinz Kindermann, a noted Germanist from Münster, published a more
or less definitive verdict: "At this time, as racist principles, thanks to
National Socialism, are the common point of departure for our thoughts
and judgments, Bartels can witness with a sense of satisfaction how the
axioms he enunciated long ago are gradually becoming self-evident, as part
of our national-historical consciousness." Bartels died in March of 1945,
before any of the victors could indict him for his intellectual crimes.[90]

However, for the purpose of gaining a spiritual foothold in Weimar,
Bartels too was proving unsuitable; he was a *quantité négligeable*. Therefore,
in the final analysis, the Nazis as a new-German movement could not
afford to pass by the two main pillars of Weimar's classical era: Goethe and
Schiller. Opposite an elusive, ahistorical Hitler, Goebbels, who organized
the poets' meetings, and Rosenberg, who was being won over to Nietzsche,

inspired a bevy of writers – academics and propagandists alike – to return to Weimar's roots, with von Schirach and Ziegler lending a hand. In his autobiographical novel *Michael* (1929) Goebbels had made many references to Goethe and his works, even if Goebbels, the cynical intellectual, had found the second part of *Faust* too intellectualized for comprehension. Rosenberg, despite caveats, had extolled the wisdom of Goethe the polymath in his *Myth of the Twentieth Century* in 1930.[91] But as both authors' qualifying treatments show, adapting Goethe, no less than Schiller, for Nazi *Weltanschauung* and totalitarian rule was problematic, for what some Nazis had to say in the poets' favor could be neutralized by the counterarguments of others.[92] In this sense then, the two poets resembled Nietzsche.

As far as Goethe was concerned, caution was expressed from on high. In a Goebbels propaganda ministry directive to writers dated August 28, 1939, on the occasion of Goethe's 210th birthday, it said that he should be portrayed as a fighter and someone who abhorred the French Revolution. By no means should he be characterized as a cosmopolitan European, and his relations with Napoleon ought to be treated gingerly. Under the caption "Racial" hints were given as to how to deal with Goethe's attitude to Jews. The organic and emotional aspects of his character should be stressed, as well as his "fight against theoretical and intellectual over-education." The latter instruction seemed fully in line with the earlier skepticism expressed in Goebbels's novel.[93] Whereas Goethe had been pushed into the right-wing corner by the nationalistic Old Guard in the Weimar Republic, headed by the Goethe Society, many National Socialists after January 1933 wanted to make him one of their own. As part of this process they seized on the two volumes of *Faust*, the poet's magnum opus. There was much about Doctor Heinrich Faustus, the *Tatmensch*, man of action – that could easily be equated with Goethe himself: he reminded them of Hitler. Faust–Goethe was interpreted as a Nordic Superman who at the end of the second volume led a Master Race.[94] According to Goethe's tale, Faust had forcefully taken land for settlement, foreshadowing Hitler's Blood and Soil philosophy and territorial *Drang nach Osten*.[95] That had been a veritable *Artamanen* goal. But the parallels did not end there. As a token of his wisdom and power, Faust went blind at the end of his life, as Hitler had been blinded in World War I, toward the end of his conventional life.[96] A Germanic Faust loved the Germanic Gretchen, blond, and beautiful as the archetypal German woman.[97] Yet in his sagacity and as a great leader, Faust forsook marriage with her, as did Hitler with any woman during his career. One writer spoke, numerologically, of the interregnum the German people had suffered from Goethe's death in 1832 to Hitler's ascent in 1933 – an entire century without leadership![98]

Other authors latched onto episodes from Goethe's biography or the utterances he left to posterity, as they saw fit. To the prurient, Goethe's whole life was a paragon of clean living and the opposite of the lifestyle – excrescences of the asphalt culture and alleged to be Jewish – observed in the cities, at the end of the republic.[99] Jewish overemphasis on reason and rationality was contradicted by Goethe's stress of the organic, for instance in the way he observed nature and as it informed his views in science.[100] Goethe was interpreted as a precursor of racial hygiene, said Ziegler and others, because he had pointed to blood as "a very special fluid" – thus converting a mere allegory to a physiological fact.[101] Much quoted, most notably by Schirach, was Goethe's paradigm about young men who should be in uniform and, complementarily, about girls preparing for motherhood.[102]

Politically, Goethe had done as much right as he could have been expected to, given the limiting circumstances of his time. He hated catering to the masses, hence hated democracy, liberalism, and the French Revolution.[103] As a minister of the duchy, he had, like Hitler, been interested in the proper education of the young.[104] While the historian Heinrich Ritter von Srbik asserted that Goethe had been the model of a German patriot anticipating national unity, the jurist Ernst Rudolf Huber went a step further by maintaining that Goethe had upheld the ideal of organicism that eventually became the chief building block of Hitler's totalitarian dictatorship.[105] Historian Erich Marcks amplified the formerly invented German national tradition (Hobsbawm) by adding Hitler to the end of the genealogical chain: from Luther to Bismarck, including Goethe.[106]

Other Nazis' opinion *against* Goethe was usually fixated on his cosmopolitanism, his tendency to flee narrow spaces and roam afar, both physically and figuratively. This was said to be responsible for preventing him from being a genuine German nationalist. Many critics connected this to Goethe's positive personal relationship with Napoleon, who kept Germany down on the pattern of the current Western Powers, even though some Nazis could well see that the French emperor, as a type, had been the greatest of great men, similar to Hitler. Goethe's worldliness caused him to become a member of Weimar's Masonic lodge Amalia, an embarrassing detail for regime leaders who were in the process of persecuting German Freemasons as "internationalists." Goethe's humanism, an offshoot of the classical era he was a product of, was tied in certain ways to his Catholic Christianity and kept him, as Professor Walther Linden charged, from being a "heroic activist," Nazi-style.[107]

A point of particular contention was Goethe's treatment of Jews. In principle, National Socialists appreciated that Goethe had rejected Jews as a collective; however, he had been fond of individual Jews such as the young Felix Mendelssohn and youthful adoring women like Rachel Levin-Varnhagen. It was obvious to these Nazis that Goethe had not liked the Jews, had colored them negatively in his comedy *Jahrmarktsfest zu Plundersweilern* (second version 1778) and had protested against the 1823 liberal ducal provision allowing Jews to marry Christians. They further approved of the characterization of Mephistopheles in *Faust* as Jewish, or so they thought. But they were suspicious of Goethe's objective, dispassionate view of the Jews; hence when the Berlin University linguist Franz Koch stated that Goethe "does not hate the Jews," this was meant as a reproach. In that sense Goethe, the reluctant leadership figure, was not even close to Hitler. As August Raabe put it: "Hitler professes openly that he has learned to hate the Jews, whereas Goethe sees in Mephistopheles a mere phenomenon of nature, which cannot be judged on moral grounds."[108]

Within such conflicted interpretations, could not the Goethe-Gesellschaft create an equilibrium? This was impossible, for like Goethe's legacy, the Society never became fully integrated into the Third Reich. For this already sufficiently right-wing body, that was certainly not for lack of trying. During its June 1933 annual meeting in Weimar, when President Julius Petersen was in the United States, his friend, the Leipzig publisher Anton Kippenberg, led proceedings as vice-president. He allowed the presidial member Ernst Bertram, a long-time Nazi, to speak of current times as "a significant turning-point in the German people's history." Kippenberg himself, although leaning more to the political center, greeted the new Hitler movement "with the warmest wishes," hailing the (military) spirit of Potsdam in the interest of a possible rejuvenation of the nation. Weimar's local poet Heinrich Lilienfein also spoke; formerly he had been a leading member of Rosenberg's Combat League for German Culture. But significantly, Reichsstatthalter Sauckel, who had been officially invited, excused himself, saying he was ill.[109]

For the June meeting of 1935 Petersen was back as president and ingratiated the Society with the regime, as he held one of the most compromising speeches of his career. Even though Jewish members, some from abroad, were still attending, Petersen extended his blessings to the "black fellows and the brown comrades" of the SS and the SA and hailed the Führer on account of his foreign policy. Similar plaudits went to Rosenberg. Ziegler spoke at least twice, and so did Werner Deetjen, president of the German Shakespeare Society and an early supporter of the KfdK. This time, Reich Education Minister Bernhard Rust excused himself and, what was worse, even Adolf Hitler abstained, an ominous symbol of the Society's unpopularity with the Nazi leadership.[110]

In fact, Petersen was pleading with his members to court more newcomers, for the current membership was in danger of fading. But such weakness could be redressed only with difficulty, especially because some Jews had been leaving and the remaining ones were forced out by Kristallnacht 1938. After the 1938 meeting, at which Petersen once again paid homage to the Führer, Kippenberg took over as president for 1939, after which year the organization abolished its presidency and held no more annual meetings in Weimar.[111]

Despite being out of grace with the Reich leadership, it is hard to see how the Goethe-Gesellschaft could have been a place of "inner emigration" for real or potential regime opponents, as has variously been claimed. Before 1933 and through the early regime years the Society had been far too reactionary and on the verge of Nazism to serve as a platform for resistance. Too many genuine Nazis were leading members of it in any case, such as Ziegler and, after 1938, Bartels. Before cessation in 1943 its journal was mostly edited by Nazis. Judged by his utterings, long-time president Julius Petersen must also be counted among the Nazis, although in his case one never quite knew when opportunism was being substituted by faith.[112]

Petersen was symptomatic of the worst that was happening to Goethe scholarship in particular and German literature studies generally in the Third Reich. A facile Nazification of the entire field was under way. Emblematic of this was an essay Petersen published in 1934, in a formerly scholarly journal onto which after January 1933 he himself had helped to slap a *völkisch* title. He applauded Giuseppe Mazzini as a precursor of Italian Fascism, used references by the Nazi poet Kolbenheyer to Faust, and polemicized against the Jewish writers Gustav Landauer and Erich Mühsam. Landauer had been murdered by Freikorps in Munich in 1919; Mühsam perished in Oranienburg concentration camp in 1934. Petersen thought that Germany was currently being saved by National Socialism and described Goethe as a quasi-forerunner of the Third Reich. Nietzsche's Superman was acclaimed, and so was Gobineau as founder of modern race theory. As the converse to this list of achievements, Expressionism was condemned and the Geneva-based League of Nations reviled as "monkey theater." Hitler, once again, received kudos.[113]

Petersen continued on this course from the time he left the headship of the Goethe Society to his death in August 1941. All the while he served as the most important scholar and teacher of the "Berlin School" of German literature, which was rooted in the chauvinism of Roethe, Schmidt,

Scherer and Herman Grimm, influencing scores of future German chair-holders – including Benno von Wiese, who, at Münster and Bonn, was Petersen's successor in eminence during the early Federal Republic even as a former card-carrying Nazi Party member. On the other hand, Petersen helped some Jewish colleagues to emigrate and assisted others while still in Germany, and was maligned for this by the envious Franz Koch, his less prolific colleague in Berlin and one of the most fanatical National Socialists in the university.[114]

Apart from any difficulties the Goethe Society experienced in the Third Reich, many Nazis thought they could make better use of Schiller than of Goethe. This was in keeping with Schiller's easier accessibility in the nineteenth century, but not for all the same reasons. One common one was that Schiller, who, unlike Goethe, had supported the French Revolution for a time, could be depicted as more popular with the masses, so that Nazi leaders like Goebbels early on painted him as a potential Nazi revolutionary. After January 1933, it became fashionable in Germany to label Schiller a "revolutionary" for or against several institutions or causes: through his dramatic character Wallenstein he had been revolutionary in wanting to chase foreigners out of Germany, against the Catholic Church, or, through Joan of Arc, against the French. Wilhelm Tell had been revolutionary in wanting to kill the Austrian-Habsburg deputy Albrecht Gessler, who enslaved the Swiss in the fourteenth century. Karl Moor in *The Robbers* was revolutionary in his capacity as a socialist (as in "National Socialist") leader. It saved Schiller's Nazi image that he had eventually condemned the French Revolution, which turned the regime's focus back on his nationalism (another myth emanating from the historic Schiller). Hitler himself had a problem with this interpretation of "revolutionary," because he himself had put down brown-shirted SA followers of Ernst Röhm during the Night of the Long Knives on June 30, 1934, hence signaling the end of all (Nazi) revolutions. Therefore, when Hitler appeared during pompous Schiller festivities in Weimar on November 10, 1934, for the celebration of the poet's 175th birthday, he arrived in tails rather than a brown party uniform and pointedly left the keynote speech to Goebbels. But this gesture also, once again, displayed Hitler's personal aversion to figures of the classics, although he seems to have preferred Schiller marginally to Goethe, for what that was worth.[115]

As for Schiller the nationalist, this image had also been projected by German patriots during the nineteenth century. After the Anschluss of Austria in March 1938, *Wilhelm Tell* was performed in Vienna with the actors wearing Tyrolean costumes (the Austrian Tyrol bordered on Swiss

Graubünden), and similar scenes were enacted later after the annexation of parts of Czechoslovakia and newly Polish, formerly Prussian, Posen (Poznan) – actors wearing the respective ethnic German costumes. Early on during World War II Professor Petersen hailed Schiller for inspiring Wehrmacht soldiers in their foreign campaigns.[116]

There was much to be gotten out of Schiller in racial terms, and here the similarity with the nineteenth century ended. Schiller himself could be shown to have been very tall, blond, and blue-eyed – the picture of a model "Aryan". His characters were often said to be Nordic (or Gothic), such as Tell, and Tell's wife Hedwig. When a film of *Tell* was made in 1934, with a script by Hanns Johst, none other than tall, Valkyrian, Emmy Sonnemann, soon to be Göring's wife, played Hedwig. Also Nordic was the Miller family from *Kabale und Liebe,* and of course Swedish King Gustav Adolf, who commanded the Swedish people's army as an organic, Germanic, unit, in *Wallenstein.* The Poles, from whom Demetrius (the hero of Schiller's last, fragmentary, drama) stemmed, were in disarray because, it was argued, of racial inferiority. Schiller's treatment of the Jews fell within this racist matrix. Moritz Spiegelberg of *The Robbers* was portrayed unsympathetically with what were said to be typically Mosaic traits: cunning, deceptive, greedy, and ugly to look at. For Nazis, he suffered a deservedly violent, shameful, death.[117]

Great emphasis was placed on Schiller's own fighter and heroic leadership qualities. Such could be seen in the paradigm of his personal fight against disease: he died prematurely, having completed more than three lifetimes of work. In Fiesco, Wallenstein, Karl Moor, and Tell Schiller had, albeit tragically at times, created images of great Führer personalities. Indeed, the homo-erotically inclined Ernst Bertram saw in Schiller the very essence of heroic man. In *The Bride of Messina*, it was asserted, the princes of Messina were rulers over racial inferiors, in accordance with the principle of natural selection; this would appeal to Nietzscheans. In the words of literature professor Herbert Cysarz, Schiller as a tragedian had established an influential "school of heroism."[118]

However, as in the case of Goethe there were detractors who pointed out faults and inconsistencies, rendering Schiller questionable in any scheme of Weimar symbolism. For one, he had not been as interested in Germanic lore as in plots from the classics, which now raised suspicion. His somewhat comical treatment of the Jew Spiegelberg gave rise to the question of how seriously he had taken racial issues and whether his teachings suited current times. Spiegelberg was simply not convincingly evil enough. Professor Linden found Schiller too rational (influenced, after all, by Kant), unlike Goethe, whom Linden felt to be more emotional and organic, and therefore closer to the people. For others there was too much international content in some of Schiller's dramas, such as *Wallenstein* and *Joan of Arc*. What should have been purely German causes were often not transferable; they remained Swiss or French or Bohemian.[119] Nonetheless, as in previous decades, Schiller's plays proved highly successful on the German stage. In 1934–35 Schiller was the most popular dramatist in the theaters, *Wilhelm Tell* being performed 472 times. At 1,764, there was an explosive rise in the number of his plays being produced up to the 1941–42 season, after he had long topped Shakespeare, Goethe, Kleist, and Hebbel.[120]

To be sure, this ascendance had not been without hitches. On June 3, 1941, Hitler had issued an order forbidding all performances of *Wilhelm Tell* and removing the play from school texts. Too many Nazi complaints had reached Berlin over the years; the parallel between Gessler and Hitler had been just too obvious; tyrannicide on stage would invite assassination of the Führer. (A similar motif was observed in *Fiesco*, but that play was never touched.) Second, the Swiss's quest for independence from the Habsburgs was suspicious at a time when Hitler himself was beginning to eye Switzerland for possible annexation. Furthermore, the Swiss would-be murderer of Hitler, Maurice Bavaud, whose assassination attempt dated to 1938, had been executed just two weeks before, which, naturally, left the Führer resentful. *Tell* was not the only Schiller drama causing consternation. For years in *Don Carlo*, the Marquis of Posa's plea to King Philip II of Spain to grant freedom of thought had met with stormy applause in German theaters, first in 1933 in Bremen, thereafter in Hamburg, Munich, Berlin, and Dresden. With Hitler himself abstaining, the matter was brought before Goebbels, who decided to leave that play alone. This may have been one convenient way for the regime leaders to demonstrate self-confidence, but the repeated critical occurrences in Nazi eyes did nothing to heighten Schiller's popularity. In the end, Schiller remained as useless to the regime as Goethe, certainly not suitable as a Weimar Nazi icon.[121]

After January 1933, no princes of poetry or masters of painting moved to Weimar in order to raise its sunken profile. Either there were none in Nazi Germany or those that remained had been muffled. But even years before the Nazi takeover, Weimar had been left alone by creative elites. Instead, based on their machinations during the republican years, National Socialists high and low when in power tried to avail themselves of Weimar's cultural capital by aligning and coordinating what to them seemed useful, with questionable success. Starting early in the regime and implicitly backed by a large Nazi majority in town, Hitler's lieutenants founded racial-policy agencies in Weimar and utilized Jena University for the implementation of criminal demographic schemes: sterilization and euthanasia facilities. With conventional cultural institutions like theater, music, and the academies having been shrouded in mediocrity even before 1933, it seemed that matters could hardly deteriorate, but they did. Hitler himself got accustomed to Weimar mostly as a place of personal relaxation, apart from its occasional use as party showcase. Personally, he put no stock in Nietzsche, Goethe, or Schiller, as indeed he had never displayed true interest in philosophy or the German classics. It was the men of his entourage who saw potential in Weimar to be selectively exploited: Sauckel with an extended Gauforum, Baldur von Schirach with youth rallies, Rosenberg with Nietzsche, and Goebbels with Book Weeks and writers' conventions. For earlier vehicles of Weimar culture, such as they were, this meant being pushed into the background, if not total liquidation. After the death of Elisabeth Förster-Nietzsche in 1935, her dream that the Archive would become a major Nazi think-tank was not fulfilled, and the Goethe Society, despite its notorious pro-Nazi obsequiousness, was shoved into oblivion. What is remarkable about the overall structure of Weimar, however, is that its industry gained currency, due to the progress of rearmament, and that as a consequence of that, Weimar's population, always slow to grow, appreciably gained in size. Apart from increased war demands, the municipal population also grew because of new services Weimar was to render, with its infrastructure having been enlarged after the founding of Buchenwald concentration camp in 1937.

CHAPTER 8

Buchenwald
1937 to 1945

AT THE BEGINNING OF 1938 THE FORMER BAUHAUS STUDENT FRANZ Ehrlich was busy with an important project. He was designing a slogan in large letters later to be worked into a meters-high iron arch. The inscription was to read: JEDEM DAS SEINE, or To Each His Due. Later in 1938, after finishing in a metal shop, this cynical motto was fixed in iron latticework high above the main entrance of the concentration camp of Buchenwald.

Most certainly, this was a belated Bauhaus product the school's founder Walter Gropius would never have been able to imagine. No greater contrast could have been construed for the Germany of the 1920s and '30s: individualistic design by the artistic avant-garde on the one side, and brutal fascistic oppression on the other. So how did Ehrlich manage to move between two such extremes? He was born in 1907 in a Leipzig suburb as the son of a mechanic. After training as a cast-and-die maker he became a machinist and eventually a mechanical engineer. Having visited the famous Bauhaus exhibition in nearby Weimar in 1923, he decided, four years later, to enroll. From 1927 to 1930, he attended the Dessau Bauhaus, studying chiefly under Klee, Kandinsky, Moholy-Nagy, and Schlemmer. He learned Bauhaus-style design work, which would later characterize his Buchenwald lettering, under graphic design teacher Joost Schmidt. In 1930, he received his Bauhaus diploma.

Politically sensitized from the days of his youth, he became the student representative in the Bauhaus Masters' council. Since 1927, he had been a member of the German Communist youth movement, joining the KPD in 1930. Hitler's assumption of power in 1933 drove him into the Communist resistance, and in 1935 he was arrested, tried for conspiracy to commit high treason and sentenced to three years in penitentiary. He had spent two years in the prisons of Waldheim and Zwickau when the SS came for him in 1937 and carted him off to the Buchenwald camp, which was in the process of construction. There he toiled in the quarry, as a carpenter, and in the building unit. He was forced to draw up what was to become Buchenwald's signature sign. Until his release in 1939 Ehrlich was active in the Communist camp resistance. Thereafter, during the war, he was assigned to the infamous punitive battalion 999 but miraculously survived the front. After 1945, still a loyal Communist, he involved himself in the development of the German Democratic Republic (GDR).

Ehrlich was designing the entrance sign because the SS had forced the first inmates of Buchenwald to construct the camp virtually on their own. He was working alongside fellow inmates, but not necessarily those from Germany's very first concentration camp, Nohra, less than four miles from Weimar, although possibly some prisoners from Nohra, which was already closed, were his cell mates. Opened on March 3, 1933, Nohra had reached its maximum number of 220 prisoners, all Communists, around March 12, after transfer from Thuringian police and SA holding stations. How many inmates Nohra had received from Weimar's Gestapo prison is not known, although certainly there were Weimarers in Nohra.

As far as Jews were concerned, until Kristallnacht in November 1938, they were not generally sent to concentration camps because of their ethnicity or religion, but for real or contrived crimes, and as regards Weimar itself, the Nazis had never considered it as afflicted with the "Jewish Question." One reason for this surely is the fact that Weimar had always had disproportionately few Jewish inhabitants.[1]

It is salutary at this time to remember that the town of classic idealism and of humanism had a tradition of indifference if not hostility to Jews that stretched back even before the arrival there of Goethe – not an unqualified friend of the Jews himself. Inspired by the religiously anti-Semitic Martin Luther, the rulers of Weimar and Jena had forbidden Jews to settle there, and this changed only under Dowager Duchess Anna Amalia in 1770, when Jacob Elkan became Court Jew. A few Jewish families followed him, engaging in trade and commerce. But thereafter, the openings for Jews remained tight, and despite occasional progressive legislation (such as that of 1823), Jews were not encouraged to move to Weimar until the end of the nineteenth century.[2] By then, anti-Semitism was brewing in all the newly unified German lands, including Weimar. Here especially, Adolf Bartels wielded his evil influence even before 1900, and in the 1920s, with the entrenchment of political conservatism, the rise of the Nazis, and Hitler's repeated appearances in Weimar, things got worse for the Jews. In 1925,

100 Jews lived in Weimar, some of whom were openly molested during the Nazi Party rally of July 1926, with no defense offered to them by fellow citizens or the municipal bureaucracy and police.[3] In the months of Nazi rule before 1933 Weimar Jews had a foreboding of what might be in store for them after a national regime change.

In early 1933, proportionally speaking, Weimar had approximately four times fewer Jews among its citizens than the Reich, whose Jewish population was already very low, at approximately 1 percent.[4] Such singularity made the forty-three Jewish families, comprising 105 persons, eminently visible in Goethe's small town.[5] It also made them easy targets for bad treatment. Jews who were later hiding from Nazi capture in large, anonymous cities like Berlin, could not have existed in Weimar. Hence from the beginnings of the Third Reich Weimar's Jews suffered the full force of gradually accelerating anti-Semitic measures.

The first of those was a boycott of Jewish stores organized by the SA that began in March–April 1933 and was periodically renewed until Kristallnacht in November 1938. Signs were posted near the stores warning non-Jews to stay away, and photographs were taken of those who still dared to shop. Notably affected by this were Heka, a small department store in the center of town, two large textile businesses, Hermann Tietz and Sachs & Berlowitz, as well as the Leopold shoe store.[6] Smaller vendors, who had movable stalls, could still try to get by from strategic positions in the main market, near the Hotel Elephant.[7] As early as 1934, systematic "Aryanization" began, meaning the wrongful acquisition of Jewish businesses by "Aryan" rivals, who were expeditiously aided by the authorities. As in other German towns and cities, Weimar's Jewish stores typically were efficiently run and offered good merchandise for a decent price – often during times of special sale. A case in point is Sachs & Berlowitz. Early in January 1933, three weeks before Hitler came to power, this firm not far from Friedrich Schiller's historic house in the Schillerstrasse offered ladies' stockings for 50 pfennig on a special sale rather than the normal RM (Reichsmark) 1.90, because they were slightly discolored. Regularly, a child's coat could be bought for less than a mark. (For comparison: in 1933 in the larger city of Magdeburg, a 1 kilogram rye-bread cost 27 pfennig, in cosmopolitan Dresden 32 pfennig. On average, a male skilled worker in the Reich received 79.2 pfennig per hour.) Israel and Lucie Berlowitz, the owners of the store, who had employed close to eighty clerks at an annual turnover of 1 million marks in a business worth 781,000 marks, in October 1938 were forced to sell it for 715,000 marks. Of this amount the couple never saw more than 6,000, after being held in concentration camps and finally having emigrated to Britain. In a parallel case, the Leopold shoe store was "Aryanized," after allegations of "race defilement," meaning the sexual exploitation of dependent female employees, had been leveled against the owner.[8]

The Nuremberg Race Laws of September 1935 brought additional hardships, signally affecting Jewish children in the schools. Unrelentingly, pressure was applied to them or their parents to make them withdraw from classes. By November 9–10, 1938, when Kristallnacht, the pogrom of broken glass, occurred, there were no more Jewish children in Weimar schools.[9] The pogrom itself was not as spectacular in Weimar as in other German towns and cities because Weimar's Jewish community had never been large enough to sustain a synagogue – it had been served by Erfurt's. Nonetheless, one last Jewish business was still operating in the town, the doll store at Teichgasse 6 of Hedwig Hetemann, who was popular with all small children. Its display window was smashed and the toys thrown into the street. Old Widow Hetemann herself was manhandled, as were other Jews, shops or no shops. Altogether, twelve arrests were made, most of them of boys and men, and only temporarily. Hetemann herself was later put on a transport to a Polish liquidation camp, where she was murdered.[10]

The next station in the martyrdom of Weimar's Jews was their concentration in so-called Jew Houses, beginning in 1940. There were three of those, where the remaining Jews of Weimar (many had already left or died) were held. By fall 1941, these Jews had to wear the yellow cloth Star of David on their garments when in public, could keep no pets nor ride public transport and were on strict food rations, with their physical mobility severely curtailed.[11] They were held in those cramped dwellings until the Nazi leaders had decided, after the Berlin Wannsee Conference of January 20, 1942, to transport all German Jews to the conquered East for extermination, through hard labor, shooting, or gas. Weimar saw three principal deportations from the Jew Houses, instigated by the SS, starting on April 14, 1942, at which time a train took the victims to the Majdanek annihilation camp near Lublin in Occupied Poland. Included in this transport were Jews from all over Thuringia, who had been collected and held at the Gestapo prison. This was located in the Marstall, the princely stables, once the domicile of Charlotte von Stein under Duke Karl August, and Marlene Dietrich in the early 1920s. Another transport on May 2, 1942, took more Jews from all over the province to Majdanek, followed by yet a third, on September 20, when a train brought elderly Jews to Theresienstadt (Terezín) in the Czech Protectorate. Although it was theoretically possible to survive Theresienstadt, because no extermination facilities were installed there, nutrition, sanitary, and general living conditions were so bad that most of the old people fell ill – if they did not die immediately. Once weak and sick, they were shoved onto a freight train headed for nearby Auschwitz's gas chambers.[12]

During the extreme phase of anti-Semitic oppression, the cruelty of leading Weimar National Socialists affected the fates of its resident Jews as shown in the cases of Rosa Schmidt, Emil Fischer, Ludwig Leopold, Eduard Rosé, Jenny Fleischer-Alt, and Otto Eisenbruch, all of whom were destined to die unnatural deaths.

When Hitler spoke in the down-market Hotel Hohenzollern in December 1925 and used it as his organizational headquarters during the party rally of 1926, he could not have known that Rosa Schmidt, the wife of proprietor Arthur Schmidt, was Jewish. Arthur Schmidt had assumed the hotel's management in 1922; no one in Weimar knew of the Jewish origins of his wife Rosa, née Grill-Freimann, originally from East Prussia. But during a closer examination of the hotel's personnel by the Gestapo in 1943–44 her ethnic identity was discovered and she was arrested in late 1944. Theoretically protected in a so-called mixed marriage with a non-Jewish husband, this was now said to be voided by what was labeled deceit. Consequently, Rosa Schmidt was deported to Auschwitz and died there on November 28.[13]

The buffo bass Emil Fischer had suffered from anti-Semitism in Weimar already in the 1920s. Doubtless this had to do with his engagement for the SPD and his active role in the Erfurt synagogue. In July 1926 Hitler's party rally rowdies accosted him. Early in 1933 he was dismissed from the opera, even before the Law for the Reconstitution of the Civil Service, which mandated such measures nationwide after April. Fischer's work for the synagogue continued, and in 1938 he was driven out of the house at Weimar's Hellerweg 26, a dwelling in whose reconstruction he had invested over 20,000 marks. Now all his property rights were annulled. With some members of his family, Fischer moved back to his birthplace, Amsterdam. But pension funds the Weimar Opera remitted to him monthly were minuscule. Fischer would have emigrated to South America, where his stepsons lived, but for his patriotism as a German. Alas, at the beginning of 1943 the occupying Nazi forces arrested him, sent him to the Dutch concentration camp of Westerbork and eventually to Sobibor in Poland, where he suffocated in a gas chamber on May 28, 1943.[14]

After having been accused of sexual misdemeanors, Ludwig Leopold, the shoe-store owner, was sentenced by a Weimar court to two and a half years of penitentiary, on fabricated evidence. Leopold appealed the verdict, but meanwhile Nuremberg Gauleiter Julius Streicher was spreading contrived accusations against him throughout Germany in his semi-pornographic rag *Der Stürmer*. In late 1935, the higher court in Leipzig ruled against Leopold. As he was stuck behind bars, his wife Elfriede was being leaned upon by Nazi authorities to sell their business far below its true value. By August 1942 she was on one of the transports to Majdanek, on the way to her death. Ludwig was taken straight from the penitentiary to Theresienstadt and then to Auschwitz, where he died.[15]

Eduard Rosé had married Gustav Mahler's sister Emma and, as principal cellist, had been concertmaster of the Weimar State Orchestra. He was the uncle of Alma Maria Rosé, who would die 1944 in Auschwitz and, posthumously, become the heroine of the controversial film *Playing for Time* in 1980, co-authored by Arthur Miller. In autumn 1941, at eighty-two years old, Eduard Rosé petitioned the Gestapo to release him from wearing the yellow Star of David, using as justification his status as a Protestant Christian. To the Gestapo, this amounted to impudence and so, two weeks later, Rosé found himself in the Marstall behind bars. The secret policemen now searched for and found several irregularities in his papers, all on technicalities. Besides, Rosé had not been buying his groceries in shops specially designated for Jews. He was formally charged with fraud in a court of law, carted off to one of the Jew Houses and on September 20, 1942, was transported to Theresienstadt, where he died four months later.[16]

Rosé had been sent to a Jew House at Belvederer Allee 6, once a stately villa that had belonged to Professor Friedrich Fleischer, a painter, and his wife Jenny Fleischer-Alt, a soprano – like the cellist, originally from Vienna. Jenny Fleischer turned seventy-six in August 1939. In her early Weimar days at the opera, she had been a favorite of Grand Duchess Sophie, who acknowledged her as a sterling musician during a time of relative artistic dearth. Originally from Bratislava (Pressburg), she too had become a Christian. Having stopped her singing career in 1891 because of her marriage, she had been teaching at the Weimar Conservatory since 1920. Comfortably off, the childless couple had lived in the Belvederer Allee villa, steps from the original Bauhaus, since 1900. But when Friedrich died early in 1938 Jenny Fleischer lost the "Aryan" protection afforded her by a mixed marriage and became prone to persecution as a Jew. This jeopardized her position and that of cohabiting relatives and her devoted household help, seven in all. Using legal trickery, the Weimar Nazi authorities limited Fleischer's access to her well-filled bank accounts, which made caring for a household of seven increasingly difficult. By 1940 the Gestapo was beginning to turn the Belvederer Allee villa into a Jew House by moving other Weimar Jews there, including Rosé. All newcomers were devoid of funds.

By 1942 the inhabitants of the Jew House had hardly any money to survive on, as the authorities curtailed Fleischer's provisions further. Jenny Fleischer-Alt, having heard of the impending deportations and seeing no way out, took poison on April 7, 1942.[17]

Finally, there is the tragic story of the fishmonger Otto Eisenbruch, whose father Emanuel was originally from Prague. In 1924 Otto married an "Aryan," Gertrud Klein, a local Weimar girl. Like Fischer, he was a Social Democrat, and even a member of its paramilitary wing. In 1934, the authorities rescinded the German citizenship of Otto and his parents; they returned to Prague, and Gertrud filed for divorce. Otto Eisenbruch's parents and his daughter Ruth – only half Jewish – were murdered by the Nazis in their eastern camps. Otto himself was sent to Dachau concentration camp and from there, in 1941, to Buchenwald. He was killed in Buchenwald on July 18, 1942.[18]

Buchenwald in the Concentration Camp System

In August 1939 there were approximately 21,000 prisoners in the German Reich's six concentration camps. One of these was Buchenwald, erected after June 1937 on the Ettersberg, five miles north of Weimar. It was to become the second-worst of the camps, after Mauthausen, near Linz. Based on the Reichstag Fire emergency legislation of February 28, 1933, camps had sprung up by the dozen and were run in an uncoordinated way by police, Gestapo, SA, SS, and the paramilitary veterans' organization Stahlhelm. By late spring of 1933 as many as 45,000 inmates had been held as internal enemies of the state, at that time mostly Communist, Social Democratic and trade-union men, but after relatively quick releases that number had dropped to 27,000 by the end of July. About two years later, there were only 4,000 inmates. By this time, the commandant of the Dachau camp, SS-Gruppenführer Theodor Eicke, socially unstable and once the inmate of a psychiatric hospital, had been in office for a year as inspector of the concentration camp system, specially appointed by Heinrich Himmler in his capacity as chief of the political police. After Himmler had become chief of all German police forces as well as of the preeminent paramilitary party formation, the SS, on June 17, 1936, he was in a position to reorganize the entire concentration camp system. This he did by dissolving the smaller camps, consolidating the larger ones and founding new ones, now centrally under his and Eicke's personal command. By early summer of 1937 Sachsenhausen had evolved from the Oranienburg camp north of Berlin, and in July the foundations for Buchenwald had been laid. Mauthausen was added in August 1938, after the

Anschluss. That year saw a significant increase in the overall number of concentration camp prisoners: Austrians in spring and summer, and victims of Kristallnacht in November and December. By the end of June there were 24,000 prisoners, with the pogrom adding another 30,000 Jewish ones, mostly males, for a total camp population of 54,000. Because the great majority of pogrom Jews were released, by August of 1939 the camps held approximately 21,000 prisoners. Then the war began, and non-citizens of the Reich became captives at an alarming rate. In the spring of 1942 there were around 80,000; between July and November of that year their number had sprung to 180,000. Half of those inmates died. In January 1945, the concentration camp system held c. 715,000 prisoners, over one quarter of whom were women and 200,000 Jewish. They were guarded by some 40,000 SS men.[19]

In concentration camp practice, the SS men were at liberty to treat their charges in any way they pleased, because they were not constrained by conventional legality. By June of 1934 Eicke, backed by Himmler, had introduced the Dachau model, which meant isolation of the camps from the civic justice system. Inmates were in the concentration camps not by any rule of law but within the extraterritorial jurisdiction of the SS (and, after June 1936, SS *and* police), which saw itself as an extension of the traditional legal norms. Inmates were never sentenced to a concentration camp term, not by a legal court and certainly not by Himmler's personnel in the camps themselves. This led to the notorious practice by SS or Gestapo of fetching inmates, who had served a legal term in a civic institution, at the prison gates and carrying them off to a camp, where they would stay for indefinite terms, legal prison time served notwithstanding. However, SS and Gestapo always could arrest victims directly, without recourse to the legal system or having to check prisons and penitentiaries.

In line with this self-arrogation of authority, the Dachau model also came to mean the execution of a camp-specific disciplinary and penal code, at least in theory; in practice its arbitrariness soon resulted in chaos and uncontrolled brutality. Yet another aim of the model was complete isolation of the camps from the public, although hiding prisoners or guards became ever more difficult, for as the war dragged on, the camps grew in size and there was interaction with outside industry. Furthermore, the inmates were to be systematically intimidated, certainly to the point where escape from the camps would be impossible and fewer draconian punishments necessary.[20]

In accordance with Eicke's original scheme, Buchenwald belonged to category II, designed for prisoners who could be reformed by National

Socialist criteria only with difficulty. Mauthausen was the only camp in category I, where such reform was thought impossible; hence the higher degree of severity. Dachau, theoretically a reformist institution, was in category III, with supposedly easier conditions.[21]

This system, if it ever was one, did not end until early 1945 with the death marches – inmates being driven by SS guards on foot to other camps, or simply into nowhere. Many times movement also took place by cattle train. Death marches were concentration camps in motion. Since each camp's SS was trying to hide from the invading Allies, using another camp as a potential target, total chaos resulted. "The death marches were completely pointless, except as a means of inflicting still further enormous suffering on those designated as the regime's internal enemies."[22]

Buchenwald concentration camp was founded after Eicke, in the course of his expansion, had expressed the desire to extend his imprisonment powers to Thuringia, which he called "the heart of Germany," in 1936. At the same time, the region's Gauleiter Sauckel, always bent on increasing his prestige, was advocating the addition of SS battalions to his realm, where he was an SS-Gruppenführer, or general, himself. As far as Himmler was concerned, he had already agreed with Hitler that Germany needed more concentration camps, to contain what was called the internal enemy.[23]

The first 149 inmates arrived at the Ettersberg location on July 16, 1937, from Sachsenburg camp – now defunct – furiously driven by the SS to start building the new camp. In the first few years, conditions for Buchenwald inmates, terrible as they were in all the camps, were worse because of the slavery involved in the construction phase, as all of Buchenwald had to be built by relatively few prisoners. By spring 1938 there were just 2,500 men to finish that job. The first Jews, five hundred in number, arrived in June. In September 2,300 political prisoners were shipped in from Dachau, including many Jews – former servants of Kurt von Schuschnigg's Austro-Fascist regime. After Kristallnacht, Buchenwald received 10,000 more Jews during November and December, most of whom were released again upon promising to emigrate. Thus until the outbreak of war Buchenwald held three main categories of prisoners: political and criminal ones, and Jews.[24]

From the beginning the criminals (called Greens because of their green triangles) were powerful, eventually contributing significantly to some sort of camp self-administration, which was tolerated and later even encouraged by the SS, including police functions. So the SS were free to perform less work and instead could devote themselves to corrupt activities, such as extorting money from Kristallnacht victims. (Many of those were rich and had brought cash to the camp, to be used to their advantage.) Already in those early years the criminals were challenged by the politicals for administrative control, a contest the politicals won decisively only in 1943. While the politicals, mostly German Communists, were ascending, they had to pay heed to new groups of inmates dumped into the camp by the German overlords, as World War II ran its course: French and Belgian Resistance fighters, captured Poles, non-submissive Dutch, Czechs, and Danes and, eventually, numerically the largest group, Soviet POWs. Although the French constituted an imposing presence, no one could, especially after 1943, rival the Marxist politicals, who enjoyed the protection of the SS.[25]

The SS camp's highest leadership was comprised of Karl Koch, a mid-level SS officer, who had headed a number of other camps before arriving in Buchenwald. Cruel and given to corruption like his underlings, Koch's personality was overshadowed by his promiscuous and spoiled wife Ilse. Their illegal activities in the camp, including sexual affairs, became legend. Following his removal by suspicious superiors in December 1941 Koch was replaced by Hermann Pister, a less colorful and erratic but, for prisoners, more forgiving commandant. After trial Koch was shot by the SS, whereas Pister was hanged by the Allies after the German capitulation.[26]

As in the case of other concentration camps, Buchenwald's prisoner numbers escalated after September 1939. At the end of August 1943 there were just under 20,000 inmates, but by the end of that year there were 37,000. At the end of August 1944 approximately 82,000 inmates were crammed into the camp; that number had climbed to around 110,000 in January 1945. At the last roll call on April 5, 1945, 80,900 prisoners were registered; thereafter, because of deaths and evacuations by the SS, the population had declined drastically to 21,400 by the time of the American troop arrival. Evacuations and death marches known to have taken place before then were to Theresienstadt (1,500 souls) and, probably, to Flossenbürg and Dachau (over 22,000 souls). Until April 1945, many thousands of prisoners had been taken by the SS to Buchenwald's satellite slave camps, eighty-seven in all and usually situated next to an armaments production site, as close as Eisenach's BMW works or as far as Essen's Krupp steel mill. In 1943 the most important of these was Mittelbau-Dora near Nordhausen, Thuringia, where 30,000 Buchenwalders toiled under inhuman conditions to assemble V2 rockets. Because of its size alone, it became an independent camp in the fall of 1944. Another large complex was the nearby Deutsche Ausrüstungswerke (DAW), which made carbines. Since spring 1943, Buchenwald had its own armaments concern in the shape of Gustloff II, right next to the barracks. This became the target of a fierce air raid on August 24, 1944, which also hit the camp, killing some 320 inmates and 80 SS.[27]

The Americans arrived in the afternoon of April 11, 1945. Officers Egon W. Fleck and Edward A. Tenenbaum of Eisenhower's Third US Army, led by General George Patton, were the first to reach the camp by jeep. They were surprised to find just under 900 Jewish children there, the youngest three years old; among the older ones was the Romanian Elie Wiesel, who was sixteen. The SS had fled, and inmates of the camp demonstrated a workable form of self-administration, to which many owed their survival, sustained by the leaders of about 800 core Communists. Later reliable estimates ascertained that altogether 277,000 inmates had passed through the Buchenwald camp, of whom 56,000 had died.[28]

Themes of Buchenwald

In Buchenwald, inmates spent their lives under unimaginably horrible conditions, which were, however, generally in line with those of other German camps. And so was the SS staff, by and large. Eugen Kogon, student of the corporativist and Fascist-leaning Othmar Spann, who spent years in the camp after being caught in Vienna as an extreme right-wing Catholic publicist supporting Austro-Fascism, after having been disabused of earlier radical convictions, used Buchenwald as a model in analyzing the concentration camp system. His comprehensive study was published as early as 1946 in German and subsequently became a standard work of Nazi historiography, currently in its thirty-first, unchanged, edition.[29]

It is difficult to begin listing details of the inhuman treatment prisoners were subjected to in all the Nazi concentration camps. Because the justice system, with its norms observed to a large extent even in Nazi Germany, played no supervisory role in the camps, not only the prisoners' length of stay was arbitrary, but so were the circumstances of their punishment. Almost all activities could be life-threatening, and breaking the rules was inviting certain death. Visibly resisting the SS's orders was as foolhardy as trying to escape. To find a survival mode was difficult, because once the SS or kapos (inmate functionaries) had singled out an inmate, for whatever reason, they could do with him as they pleased. The other pitfall was that often inmates committed infractions thinking they had not broken any rules. Sometimes a prisoner was caught by the cunning SS in a conflicting set of rulings, for instance when his cap was thrown in the direction of barbed wire and he was ordered to fetch it. If he refused, he would be shot for disobeying a command. If he ran toward the fence in order to retrieve it, he would be shot for trying to escape.[30]

In Buchenwald – as in other camps – sanitary conditions were indescribably bad. Toilets consisted of open latrines into which one could fall or be pushed, headfirst. There were SS canine patrols with dogs trained to maim and kill prisoners. From the beginning, inmates had to wear wooden shoes that caused foot injuries and sometimes had to be abandoned for the sake of work efficiency. Prisoners were drilled to make up their bunks in Prussian military style, with not a crease in the bedclothes showing. They could be beaten on their bare buttocks, but also on the kidneys, usually twenty-five strokes from a lead-enforced leather whip; many did not survive this ordeal. In a detail composed mainly of Jews, heavy stones had to be carried to one place, often up a steep incline, only to be moved to another place the next day, and to yet another the day after. The chore of Sisyphus! Food was extremely bad, and scarce to boot: prisoners caught stealing it would often lose their lives. If the theft was from comrades, prisoners themselves could do the killing. Indeed, one of the truly frightening aspects of camp life was prisoners turning on each other: "Prisoners who abused their comrades or even beat them to death were typically never punished by the SS and so had to be hunted down under the prisoners' own form of justice." Roll calls in snow, rain or extreme cold would go on for hours; often the prisoners were not allowed to stir. Laziness on the job would be defined as broadly as possible and could be interpreted as sabotage, with the most dire consequences. There were medical experiments on humans to cure typhus, yellow fever, and diphtheria, or to treat men's homosexuality. After the pain, many gay inmates died.[31]

Like all concentration camps, Buchenwald was characterized by a few particularly notorious phenomena. The cruelty of Karl and Ilse Koch and SS-Hauptscharführer (Sergeant) Martin Sommer possibly was without parallel. The torture they meted out in the quarry and the confinement bunkers appeared to have been devised in Dante's Hell.

But not quite. In the hellhole that was Mauthausen the quarry was the defining mark of evil, where inmates were killed by heavy boulders and scores of them joined hands to jump from above, to what they hoped would be a liberating death below. Still, Buchenwald's quarry was operational even one year earlier and its nefarious properties could have served as a model. In Buchenwald's quarry – as no doubt in Mauthausen – inmates would be pushed over the precipice by sadistic SS. This happened especially to members of so-called punishment companies or to Jews. Ordinarily, the boulders had to be transported, with or without lorries, from the quarry, a few kilometers away from the main camp, back to the camp gate for repairs inside, or, as the war demanded, to construction sites further out where the armament factories were being built. Inmates could be crushed by the stones, by lorries out of control, or could be shot by the sentries for slacking. In the first few years, every Buchenwald guard received three days off in Weimar, for having shot a prisoner.[32]

Another torture method characteristic of Buchenwald was suspending prisoners from trees in the thickly wooded surroundings. With their feet a few inches from the ground, their arms were slung around a tree trunk and their wrists tied to nails in the tree. They hung there from a half-hour to as much as three hours or even longer, with the SS guards often tearing at their sides or striking them with whips. Soon screams turned to whimpers. Some inmates died during this procedure; most came down with permanent damage to their joints and tendons.[33]

Of lethal consequence could be a series of bunkers or arrest cells, some for solitary confinement, overseen by Martin Sommer. In one larger bunker where there was no light, furniture, or heating, several inmates could be confined for weeks on end with a minimum of food. Sometimes the SS sent kapos in there, after they had been aiding regular guards. They were regularly killed once inside by their former victims, being handed from one inmate to the next for individual treatment. In this way, the SS could rid itself of unwelcome witnesses of its own crimes, once those kapos had fallen out of favor. In other, smaller bunkers, prisoners had to stand motionless from morning till night. Once they were observed to stir, they were brutally beaten. Sommer himself also liked to enter in order to strangle his victims, or to administer fatal injections of air or milk.[34]

During the war years, Buchenwald possessed facilities for the mass murder of Soviet prisoners. According to Timothy Snyder's research, these "strikingly resembled Soviet methods in the Great Terror." In a large room made up like a clinical examination facility, there were SS men in white coats, pretending to be physicians. The prisoners would be stood against the wall in such a manner that the nape of their necks would be against a hole. From an adjoining room, SS men then shot through the necks with a pistol. "Batches of thirty-five to forty corpses would be taken by truck to a crematorium: a technical advance over Soviet practices."[35]

Of course Buchenwald had real camp doctors who, besides administering wholly inadequate care to the prison population, were interested in conducting medical experiments. In a typhus laboratory Dr. Waldemar Hoven burned hundreds of captives with phosphor; they suffered extremely painful deaths. Hoven had been hoping to develop a typhus antidote. The physician Karl Erich Wagner, not yet a medical doctor, wanted to write a medical dissertation on tattoos. Hence he had newcomer inmates searched for tattoos anywhere on their bodies and killed them for his research if any were discovered. An inmate called Paul Grünewald wrote the dissertation, passing it off as Wagner's. As part of the medical experimentation program, human heads were shrunk to the size of a fist. Several samples were sent to the chief of concentration camp doctors, Dr. Enno Lolling in Berlin. Other heads were kept in the camp for the pleasure of the SS, in particular Karl and Ilse Koch.[36] Altogether, Buchenwald's medical science fit the Nazi pattern of charlatanism, bordering on criminality.

Within Buchenwald's violent and criminal SS, the first commandant Karl Koch stands out, for the length of time he was tolerated by Himmler and because he was, in spite of this, one of very few officers to be tried by an SS court and then shot. Like many SS leaders, such as Theodor Eicke or Reinhard Heydrich, he had been ill-adjusted to postwar society and fallen short of success. Born in 1897, he lost his job as a bank clerk after committing fraud during the Depression. As such failures often did, he joined the SS in 1931, and in 1935 became captain of the guards at Esterwegen concentration camp. As Buchenwald commandant, he grossly enriched himself while philandering at night in Weimar. He presided over "comradeship evenings" with his SS staff, when alcohol was limitless, as was the food, much of which was taken from inmates' provisions. He also acquired a riding stable. In November 1941 Koch was arrested and removed from Buchenwald; thereafter he served, for a time, as commandant of Majdanek liquidation camp. In September 1943 he was again arrested, tried in Weimar, chiefly on charges of sabotaging the war effort, and condemned to death late in 1944. He was executed in early May of 1945. Koch's excesses were not necessarily graver than those committed by other SS officers, but he suffered the additional misfortune of having the regional SS leader against him, Josias Erbprinz zu Pyrmont, a fomer adjutant of Himmler's, who insisted on having him removed.[37]

Ilse Koch was unique in the history of Nazi concentration camps because she wielded power without playing an official role. In her position as the wife of a commandant no one forced her to get involved in the goings-on of the camp, as no one forced Commandant Rudolf Höss's wife, the former Artam girl Hedwig, in Auschwitz. Yet, unlike Höss's wife and those of other commandants, Ilse Koch chose to be part of the camp's regimen and for this became known, and feared, as *Die Kommandeuse*.

This woman, born 1906, a former secretary in a cigarette business, was an attractive reddish blonde with an excellent figure, which she sought to accentuate by wearing short skirts and tight sweaters. Karl's second wife since 1937, she was a nymphomaniac who carried on affairs with Dr. Hoven and the deputy commandant. She would also pick out good-looking inmates for the night, only to have them shot in the morning. Her appetite for luxury being at least as large as her husband's, she took baths in Madeira wine and was keen on collecting tattooed skin, from which she had lampshades made. She took pleasure in sexually exciting the inmates with provocative walks through the camp; anyone who looked at her too obviously could be marked for punishment. She also rode through the camp on horses from the stable, which Karl had made available to her. She remained in Buchenwald after her husband's removal in November 1941, but along with him was charged in the Weimar trial almost two years later. Set free for lack of evidence, she was tried by the Americans in 1947 for having had prisoners murdered for their tattoos, and condemned to life in prison. Like so many other German war criminals in those years, she was released early, in October 1949, but the Germans arrested her again and sentenced her to a life term in January 1951. She committed suicide in her cell fifteen years later.[38]

More so than Karl Koch, Martin Sommer, who kept an electrically lit skull in his office, embodied pathological sadism in Buchenwald. The many forms of torture he invented earned him the description "a beast in human shape." A handsome man, this monster was born on a farm just twenty-five miles from Weimar. Focussed on a military career, he joined the SS in 1933. He was twenty-two when he began his tenure of terror in Buchenwald, in 1937, after having served as a guard in other camps. He stayed until fall 1943, when he too was scrutinized in the course of the Koch trial. Avoiding proceedings against him, he came to serve in an ill-fated military unit near Eisenach, from which he returned badly wounded.

It takes effort to list all of Sommer's devilish practices not only because they were so deplorable but also because there were so many of them. His fiendish imagination came up with ever new ones. They included sticking an inmate's head into the latrine while administering a beating to his buttocks. Sommer was one of the most active SS men in hanging prisoners from trees. He devised a system of water torture, with drops battering the victim's head monotonously. He enjoyed killing inmates with iron tools and once crushed a prisoner's skull with a vise that he turned on the head slowly. He withdrew food from inmates till they died and was adept at giving lethal injections. His beatings of inmates shackled to radiators were as notorious as his strangulations, of which he is alleged to have committed at least 150.[39]

After the Kochs and Sommer were removed from Buchenwald in fall 1943, self-administration of the camp under the control of the SS led by

Pister came into full force. Indeed, the relationship between SS and prisoner elite is one of the more interesting elements to study in the sociology of Buchenwald, as is the intra-prisoner group dynamic. Both were, of course, related. Once a captive understood how prisoner elders were dependent on the SS but could in turn influence it, and once he understood how these elders ranked the rest of the prison population, his chances of survival improved.

Members of the prisoner elite, which, to a greater or lesser extent after the fall of 1941 was dominated by German Communists (the Reds), were extremely circumspect. They sized up inmate categories collectively, as well as captives individually, who were to be fought, ignored, or somehow utilized, even wooed, in the Communist cause of survival. For the Reds, ideological conviction and nationality of a prisoner were of paramount significance. When 349 Norwegian students arrived in January 1944 who as "Nordics" were to be indoctrinated by the Nazis, including Karl Astel and his staff from Jena, the elite left them alone as inconsequential and not dangerous. When Soviet POWs were driven in in large numbers, the Communist elite should have welcomed them as brothers-in-Marxism, but instead decided they were primitive, illiterate, and most of all dangerous. They had to be carefully watched and possibly dispatched. Two thousand Danish policemen were not an issue either way. Members of the French *Résistance* might be useful, as long as they did not possess an ultramontane, nationalist, or aristocratic background. In this respect Spanish Civil War veterans from the Republican side could mostly be relied on. When toward the end of the war British and Canadian officers arrived who had functioned as agents with the *Résistance*, the camp elite was sympathetic, even though it could not prevent the hanging of these men as spies. Neither could, or would, it do anything about Jews, of German or foreign nationality, who, in great numbers, were regularly tortured to death or shipped off to eastern liquidation centers.

The inmates' regime began in summer 1937 with the Greens, who were gradually allowed to control certain offices in the camp, providing opportunities for the SS to enrich themselves illegally. Those offices were the records office (*Schreibstube*), which kept a prisoner card file, settled the inmates' block assignments or work-detail arrangements, and looked after the allocation of food. Another important office was the infirmary (*Krankenbau*), which the SS tended to avoid because of fear of contagion and which therefore was ideally suited for prisoners' clandestine meetings. The labor records office (*Arbeitsstatistik*) became more important as the war progressed, because it would consign inmates to outside commandos such as work in Dora-Mittelbau, which usually amounted to a death sentence. There were also a firefighter department and a camp police, both run by prisoners.

From the beginning, the criminal Greens were in the habit of putting down the politicals, mainly Communists, who were rivaling the criminals for control. After May 1938, when the Bavarian Flossenbürg concentration camp had been built, more and more Greens were transferred there, so that politicals could put themselves in charge by 1940–41. It helped that Dr. Hoven, seeking the Reds' favor, aided them by administering as many killer injections to the Greens as possible. There were other, brutal, methods of killing on both sides, depending on the physical strength of the individual adversaries. By this time, the SS was letting the Reds have their way because the Greens had been participating in their graft and had to be removed as unwelcome witnesses. The politicals, by contrast, appeared to be squeaky-clean – as in fact they mostly were, being interested only in total administrative and therefore survival control. But by the beginning of the war, when many Buchenwald Greens were languishing in punishment companies at the military fronts, other Greens were shipped in from outside, and the battles started anew. These were not settled with a definitive victory on the Reds' side until fall 1943. From this time it held true that as corruption by the SS grew, even after Koch's departure, so grew the power of the Red camp elite. Their representative Ernst Busse was to reign in the infirmary, and Walter Bartel ruled over the labor records office. For the sake of an orderly administration, these Communists tried to be just and govern without excesses, but physical cruelties were known to be perpetrated, though nothing on the scale of the SS. By and large the judgment is warranted that as terrible as the first two years of the camp had been, the last two years were much more bearable. Communist sub-rule of the camp undoubtedly rendered its liberation by the Americans much easier.[40]

Konzentrationslager Weimar-Buchenwald

Imagine a concentration camp in Thuringia, Germany, at the end of the 1930s. The camp's postal address is "Konzentrationslager Weimar-Buchenwald."[41] Imagine a professor of German literature at Cologne University ten years later, making a momentous statement: "Between us and Weimar lies Buchenwald. There's no way we can get around that."[42] Imagine an oak tree on the grounds of Buchenwald concentration camp, revered as the Goethe Oak by the SS, whose top echelons are beside themselves when it is destroyed by an air raid on August 24, 1944.[43]

Three different images from different time zones! Are they meaningfully connected?

The existence of an oak tree in the camp, which Goethe was fond of visiting and into which he carved inscriptions with a knife, may have been the stuff of legend, but if it was, the SS proudly believed in it.[44] It suggests the SS respected the Goethe tradition and Weimar, even if it interpreted the great poet in a typically National Socialist vein. Significantly, the SS leadership had listened when the Weimar chapter of the NSKG, the Rosenberg-controlled culture organization, had protested in summer 1937, as the new concentration camp near Weimar was to be named the Ettersberg Camp. Thereafter it was SS-Gruppenführer Eicke who told Himmler that the name Ettersberg could not be used, because it was connected with "the life of the poet Goethe." Eicke instead proposed the name "Hochwald," and Himmler finally decided on "Buchenwald," meaning Beech Woods.[45]

So did this mean that the Rosenberg devotees, Eicke, and Himmler recognized the incompatibility of SS enforcement practices and classical ideals? Would they have wanted to keep the names of Buchenwald and Weimar separate, because each meant different things? Their official naming of the camp Weimar *and* Buchenwald, separated by a hyphen, would suggest otherwise, as they appear to have seen Buchenwald as a part of Weimar, the way Manhattan is a part of Greater New York. A Greater Weimar? There were five miles of forest between the camp and the railway station of northern Weimar, where the inmates usually arrived. There are forests there today, and the buses that go out there from the center of town still indicate as their final destination "Weimar-Buchenwald." And Buchenwald's postal address still is D-99427 Weimar-Buchenwald, as there is a Weimar-Tiefurt (D-99425), and a Weimar-Mitte (D-99423).[46]

The Cologne professor of German was Richard Alewyn. His statement regarding Weimar and Buchenwald was predicated on caution. It set up a situation of "us," the postwar generation in West Germany, and Weimar, then of course in Communist East Germany, but separated from West Germany's new beginnings in democratic politics and culture by an evil Buchenwald. The lesson of his image was that although West Germans were trying to be moral without fail, as was the classical Weimar with which they wanted to identify, they would have trouble doing so because the fiendish Buchenwald would interfere. Hence Alewyn suggested a separation between Buchenwald and Weimar, but at the same time warned that West Germany was tainted by Buchenwald's past and hence would experience difficulty likening itself to a model Weimar. The Goethe expert Alewyn had the authority to speak on such cautious note because he was a bona-fide victim of the Third Reich. A student of Friedrich Gundolf (who had been Goebbels's teacher) and Karl Jaspers at Heidelberg, he had done postdoctoral work with Julius Petersen in Berlin and then assumed an associate professorship in Heidelberg in 1932. Because one of his grandmothers was Jewish, he had been forced to relinquish his post in August 1933. Petersen hated to see him go, but did nothing to help. Alewyn spent his subsequent professional life in Paris and London, Austria and Switzerland, until in 1939 he was able to teach at a college in Flushing, New York. In 1948 he returned to Germany, when he took over Ernst Bertram's chair in Cologne.[47]

In the final analysis Alewyn's remark implied responsibility by Germans after 1945 for Buchenwald – all Germans, including Weimar's citizens. But Weimarers did not see it that way when, on April 16, 1945, more than a thousand of them were obliged to march the five miles from the town's railway station to Buchenwald camp, to take a closer look. The American officers who forced them were incredulous in the face of their reaction. For while the citizens, some of them finely attired, admitted shock at what they saw – emaciated inmates, piles of corpses, lampshades made from human skin – they loudly professed their innocence. A few days later the Goethe Museum's director Hans Wahl, the same one who had co-founded the Weimar KfdK and shown Hitler the Goethe treasures, joined other town dignitaries in writing a letter to the US authorities, denying that "the inhabitants of Weimar and its surroundings had known about the atrocities of Buchenwald and remained silent, for which they were now regarded as sharing in the guilt." It would be unjust to attach to "the population of the old culture town of Weimar" a stigma that it did not deserve. And the Lutheran superintendent of the Weimar diocese issued a directive to all pastors to include, in the coming Sunday sermon, a statement saying that in Buchenwald "events have come to light which, to this day, have been totally unknown to us." The directive continued: "Hence we may confess before God that in no way do we share in the responsibility for these barbarities."[48]

The Weimar citizens, in particular the museum director, mayor, and divines, all were lying, and if they did not see what was going on at Buchenwald, they did not want to see. In reality, there existed many everyday connections between Weimar and the camp, from the beginning to the end. Many of these were parts of a tight administrative, commercial, and human-relations network. There was no escape from this.

Buchenwald was not administratively isolated from, but became an incorporated constituency of the Town of Weimar on April 1, 1938.

Application for this had been filed by Weimar's town council in September 1937 because of expected gains in municipal revenue. An early consequence of this was postal and telegraphic integration; the camp could be reached under a Weimar telephone number and had its own Weimar suburban post office in October 1938. Buchenwald as a legal suburb of central Weimar also meant that Weimar's citizen registry became Buchenwald's. From 1937 to March 1945, 33,791 Buchenwald deaths were entered into that registry, a number much too large to be overlooked. The registry's keepers alone were authorized to inform next-of-kin of an inmate's death, and could have spread details in town. When Buchenwald received a branch registry on April 1, 1938, it was named "Weimar II." Moreover, Weimar's civic responsibility for Buchenwald's prisoners extended to the burial system. Until the camp had its own crematoria in 1940, all deceased inmates had to be cremated in central Weimar and their ashes interred in the main cemetery, not far from the sarcophaguses of Goethe and Schiller. The town received 20 marks per cremation. The smell of burnt flesh regularly reached the poets' tombs, the Nietzsche Archive and the former Kessler domicile at nearby Luisenstrasse and Cranachstrasse, and it wafted to countless private dwellings. Inmates' cadavers were transported down the road from Buchenwald in wooden boxes, on trucks turning right at the main station and continuing past the Goethe and Schiller statue on Theaterplatz, to Wielandplatz, whence they turned right again to the cemetery and crematorium. Once, on the Wielandplatz, some boxes fell from a truck and split their covers. Corpses lay on the pavement for everybody to see; the bodies looked "mutilated," remembered one undertaker's helper.[49]

Certain matters of Buchenwald health and hygiene also fell within the jurisdiction of the town. Weimar hospitals treated inmates and SS alike, until the camp received its own infirmary in summer 1938. Some Buchenwald inmates were forcibly sterilized in Weimar. When the danger of a typhus epidemic arose in 1939 because of deteriorating hygienic conditions in the camp, the Weimar officer of public health looked upon this emergency as a communal health issue and became active in October. After the beginning of the war and with the introduction of food rations, the nutrition office of Weimar extended its purview to Buchenwald, as foodstuffs for inmates had to be apportioned. It was during this collaboration between SS and the nutrition office that SS corruption reached its apex.[50]

Furthermore, Buchenwald being incorporated within Weimar had certain juridical and zoning implications. When an SS guard had been murdered by two Buchenwald fugitives in 1938, the inmates, once recaptured, were tried by a Weimar Nazi Special Court and executed on the

Ettersberg in the presence of a mass of prisoners, as well as a public pros-
ecutor and his staff, who also read out the formal indictment. Several
Weimarers were onlookers as the men were hanged. Undoubtedly most
had traveled to Buchenwald by car, on the single road from the train station
in Weimar's north. A year later there was also a municipal bus service in
place, with the Buchenwald line serving Weimar commuters six times a
day, on rides lasting thirty minutes each and costing 40 pfennig.[51]

Weimar's firefighters were responsible for the camp until spring of
1939. Until 1942, Buchenwald received its water supply from the town.
And lest the SS commandants forget that Weimar had been Goethe and
Schiller's town, Wahl and Weimar's mayor Otto Koch commissioned
Weimar carpenters to take furniture measurements from the inventory of
both the Goethe and Schiller museums to be handed to Buchenwald
carpenters for the manufacture of wooden boxes for the safekeeping of
chairs and tables.[52]

Apart from administrative ties, from the early days of Buchenwald
there was a remarkable interchange of people. The reinforced presence of
the SS in the region was announced in the local Weimar press, for example
in an interview with Himmler in January 1937. In October one could read
in Weimar broadsheets that "the VIIth SS-Sturmbann of the third SS
Death Head's Unit Thuringia" was moving into concentration camp
Buchenwald. Buchenwald was mentioned often in the papers from then
on. In December the papers noted that the music corps of the third Death
Head's Unit would give a free public recital on Weimar's Theaterplatz, near
the famous Rietschel statue. German shepherds owned by Buchenwald SS
competed in Weimar dog shows, it was written, one being Commandant
Koch's own. There were press notices about an SS-Sportgemeinschaft
Buchenwald – SS men playing soccer against neighboring clubs such as
Luftwaffen-Sportverein Weimar.[53]

Press notices aside, the burghers of Weimar entered or came very close
to the camp on various occasions over the years. Nobody conducted more
business with Buchenwald than Thilo Bornschein, an anti-Semite and
Nazi of the first order, who in 1933 became party chapter leader
(Ortsgruppenleiter) for Weimar. He was also an SS officer, and by 1935 a
Weimar councillor. Bornschein delivered virtually all the foodstuffs to
Buchenwald by 1940 and became indecently rich enough to purchase the
modernist, exclusive, Bauhaus-Muche's Haus am Horn. For 1941 alone his
firm registered a turnover of half a million Reichsmark (RM). Bornschein,
charging usurious prices with Commandant Koch's connivance, eventually
became involved in the outright graft of the Buchenwald SS leadership and

was tried and sentenced to a prison term, but because of his SS incorporation he seems to have gone free. After 1945, he resurfaced in West Germany,
apparently continuing with his life as if nothing had ever happened.[54]

Altogether, there were forty Weimar firms in business with the concentration camp from 1937 to 1945. Hans Kröger enjoyed a near-monopoly as
supplier to Buchenwald after he had acquired, for a farthing, the "Aryanized"
Herman Tietz mixed-goods department store. The historic Court
Apothecary on the main square supplied SS physicians Hoven, Ding-
Schuler, and Eisele with drugs. The town brewery Deinhardt shipped
excellent beer to all SS men. Butcher Karl Daniel sold sausage for the SS's
and inmates' consumption alike; during the war he was cutting corners and
his sausage, now dubbed "rubber sausage," became so bad that even inmates
would not touch it. Weimar's banks kept accounts for the SS and inmates
– at least those who were expecting money from their relatives (which the
SS could then swindle them out of).[55]

Other Weimar contacts with Buchenwald were non-commercial.
Acquaintances of the SS staff often visited and stayed in the camp overnight, to the extent that Koch began to issue warnings. Professor Gerhard
Offenberg, the director of the architecture school once called the Bauhaus,
early on was invited to inspect the ongoing construction on the Ettersberg,
was given a tour of the camp as it then existed and, as he recalled in 1973,
found "everything perfectly in order." The venerable town theater put on
performances for SS leaders in their casino. Buchenwald itself had a small
zoo that invited Weimar citizens and their children to pay a visit. Entry
cost 50 pfennig for grown-ups and 20 for children. Uniformed SS men
showed visitors around and answered questions, but the camp itself was
taboo. Moreover, in August of 1939 the SS corps organized a summer
festival for Weimar citizens, old and young, on a large site next to the camp.
The SS impressed with sausage stands, colored balloons, variety skits, and
music and dancing. One enthusiastic observer reported: "There were three
giant podiums for dancing and one for the band. Also many game booths,
shooting and sausage kiosks around the large festival site. Everywhere
something was frying and steaming. Two huge oxen were grilled on spits."[56]

The SS men themselves were often in Weimar; several actually lived
there, their children attending school alongside Weimar's children. After all,
the Weimar-Buchenwald SS detachment was 4,000 strong, and growing.
Those who lived in special settlements in a large radius around Buchenwald
and Weimar were frequently in town for their daily business. They and their
families sought to integrate themselves with Weimar's population, many
forming functional relationships and personal friendships in town. Their

presence in Weimar was so large that the theater embarked on a dedicated SS subscription series. One of the many unsavory aspects of the SS in Weimar was their fondness of disreputable establishments and predilection for brothels. Beyond brothels, SS men took pleasure in chasing the local girls and stealing them away from younger Weimar men. Commandant Koch had several liaisons in town; one was said to be with a dancer.[57]

If Buchenwald's SS roamed about Weimar, their charges were even more conspicuous. From 1939, camp inmates were employed on construction sites by the firm of Majewski & Thiele or in the municipal slaughterhouse. Hotel Elephant employed ten inmates. Prisoners also toiled on Sauckel's unfinished Gauforum or for the produce wholesaler Mennong. These ventures were lucrative ones for the SS; it received 5 RM for a skilled worker's eight-hour day, and 3 RM for an unskilled one. During the war the moving firm of W. Staupendahl paid just 2 marks for the services of Russian POWs. By this time Gustloff Works I and II, the latter right next to Buchenwald, forced a total of 5,000 inmates onto assembly lines, shoulder to shoulder with 2,000 conscripted foreign workers and 1,000 regularly employed Weimar civilians. It is inconceivable that those civilians would not have noticed details that identified workers from a concentration camp. Those contacts were intensified when during air raids toward the end of the war inmates were forced into communal shelters, such as the one near the town cemetery that today serves as a giant underground garage. Between 1942 and 1945, Buchenwald prisoners slaved in at least sixty Weimar firms and administrative offices, totally without payment.[58]

Conversely, several Weimar citizens served time in Buchenwald, although their number is not certain. As is possible in a totalitarian police state, some were arrested and carted to the camp on a whim. This happened to two older civil servants and the surgeon Maximilian Schreiner, who had witnessed a brawl in a restaurant, between three high-placed Nazis and another guest, in May 1938. After they had challenged the Nazis to compensate the guest for damages, they were trucked to Buchenwald for several weeks, just to intimidate them. Yet this could not have been for political reasons, as the three had been going on hunting and social drinking bouts with the Nazis. A similar case is that of the Weimar pastor Alexander Wessel, who spent some time in Buchenwald in 1941, after he had bickered about the government. But Wessel was a "German Christian," a member of a movement following Schlaf and Dinter in believing Jesus to be "Aryan" and principally collaborating with the regime. More critical today and deserving of more serious analysis is the case of twelve Jews from Weimar who were arrested in the aftermath of Kristallnacht, among them Israel

Berlowitz, mentioned earlier. Although most survived that particular ordeal, the chemist Dr. Hans Salomon, who owned a medical laboratory near the Sophienhaus, did not. He was taken to Buchenwald on November 10, 1938, only to die after his release from the camp in December. Along with Salomon, the Weimar Jews Ernst Bendix and Albert Ortweiler, a merchant, died before being released from Buchenwald.[59]

Weimar citizens must have seen the surviving Jews as they returned to town from the camp, since they often observed future inmates arriving at the train station. Countless times they were witnesses to the inhuman treatment those received, as they boarded the SS trucks or were driven on by foot. In early 1945, they witnessed death marches of inmates through Weimar as Buchenwald was in the process of dissolution. Many were afraid at that time and shortly after, when some inmates were free, that they would be physically attacked. But the prisoners were attacking no one, they were weak, tired, and in near-disbelief at having escaped with their lives.[60]

In reconsidering Richard Alewyn's warning about the proximity of Weimar to Buchenwald and what the town's citizens knew, two factors seem important. One relates to the geographic and logistic ties between Weimar and the camp. The evidence at hand leaves no doubt about the deep involvement by Weimarers in the nearby concentration camp's affairs. Here individual judgments would have to decide the degree of guilt with which each citizen became afflicted. The second factor involves mental awareness, the realization that Weimar, as a bastion of Classicism and Idealism, would change its fundamental character after association with the wellspring of evil. How would Weimar burghers view their hometown after 1937, and were they concerned about how outsiders would view it? How large was the comprehension in town that Buchenwald represented something abjectly malevolent, even according to the value system of a nationalist dictatorship? The strongest indication we have that Weimarers knew before summer 1937 that the construction of a camp on their municipal outskirts could constitute a moral issue and affect Weimar's historic reputation, is the protest that was launched by Nazis, attempting to salvage the uniqueness of the Ettersberg. Yet even if the name was spared, what it stood for was still drenched in blood.

The End of National Socialist Weimar and Buchenwald

Since the beginning of the war the Town of Weimar had an arrangement with Buchenwald's SS leadership that in case of need occasioned by an Allied air raid, Weimar citizens could use the camp's infirmary. However, it would never come to that; instead on August 24, 1944, Buchenwald itself was hit by a British air strike. The armaments works Gustloff II had been targeted and indeed, it was almost totally destroyed. The outskirts of the camp were also hit and altogether approximately 320 inmates died. Among them was Princess Mafalda, the daughter of King Vittorio Emanuele III of Italy, who was married to Prince Philipp of Hesse, a great-grandson of Queen Victoria and a powerful Nazi who had had a falling-out with Hitler. Also killed was Rudolf Breitscheid, a prominent Social Democrat and, like Mafalda, kept in a special barracks for VIPs. In addition, eighty members of the SS guard squad were killed, and a total of 1,500 people injured. Certain of their own impending death, fighters of the *Résistance*, among them the British and Canadian spies, watched this infernal spectacle with sarcastic glee, while Ukrainian SS guards were chasing prisoners trying to escape. If Dante's visions had invented Buchenwald, they had not invented these scenes.[61]

The Buchenwald bombing occurred against a background of worsening conditions in the Third Reich, which affected the concentration camp and Weimar alike. The decisive turning point in the war came for Hitler with the disastrous defeat of the Sixth Army at Stalingrad on February 2, 1943. Later that year, Allied bombings of German strategic objects started in earnest, with armament resources in the Ruhr Valley of the west particularly badly hit. Himmler replaced Wilhelm Frick as interior minister in the fall, but with no visible effect.

Things went further downhill in 1944. The Western Allies invaded the French mainland on D-Day, June 6, and began to fight their way eastward. On July 20 Hitler barely escaped an assassination attempt. With personnel resources depleted and armed forces weakening, a people's militia (Volkssturm) was established in the fall, comprising all men from ages sixteen to sixty, and charged with defending the home turf. In December Hitler started his Ardennes Offensive in the West, but it imploded for lack of fuel. By this time, more political power had shifted from government to party agencies, the Gauleiter having received all responsibility for holding the Home Front. This meant mounting arbitrary powers and further cuts in personal freedoms, as the party collaborated more closely with police, Gestapo, and SS.

It enraged German citizens to observe how, by the end of 1944, party functionaries were getting ready to desert their posts and flee to safer areas. This trend increased in 1945 while, at the same time, the party's terror multiplied. Summary courts martial combed German lands for deserters or defeatists; people were shot on suspicion on the spot and soon they were hanging from lampposts. Indeed, in the entire Reich 600,000 German soldiers were avoiding frontline service, maintained Weimar's native son Martin Bormann, now head of the all-important party chancellery. By the end of January 1945 Soviet troops had crossed into German territory and were advancing on Berlin. Meanwhile, most Germans kept hoping for the advent of miracle weapons, fulsomely promised by the leaders and sweated over by many Buchenwald inmates in Dora-Mittelbau, who were building them. Every day, essential materials such as oil, cement, steel, and coal were becoming scarcer. By the end of March the enemy had crossed the Oder in the East and the Rhine in the West. Patton's Third US Army was on the march to central and southern Germany, reaching Thuringia on April 1. Ten days later, he was in Buchenwald, and on the following day had occupied Weimar. This was after Himmler had warned that all resident males of any German house with a white surrender flag would be shot. Moreover, Himmler, Bormann, and head of military staff Wilhelm Keitel had commanded that all towns be defended to the last man. Hitler committed suicide on April 30, and Germany capitulated on May 8–9.[62]

The Allies' progressive victory on land was helped along significantly by British and American advances in the air. British Air Marshal Arthur Harris had decided already in 1942 to bring the Third Reich to its knees by bombing not only industrial sites, mostly in the Ruhr, but also cities. In January, February, and March of 1943 Berlin was, for the first time, seriously hit; after the raid on March 1, there were 700 deaths and over 60,000 people lost their homes. July 1943 saw the terrible fire-bombing of Hamburg, with a loss of 40,000 lives. By 1944, moreover, the Allies had found ways to bomb oil sites, southeast of Germany, in Romania. In 1943, 206,000 tons of Allied payload were dropped on Germany. This had increased to 1,188,577 tons by the end of 1944.

During that year, German air defenses had noticeably slackened. Also, the Allies had found ever better methods of making their planes fly longer routes, and for more hours. So it was decided to attack cities in more eastern parts of Germany, one being Nuremberg of Nazi lore, which was struck on January 2, 1945. Altogether 1,800 people died. Dresden was targeted on February 13–14. Although it did not have any war industry of note, it was a strategic railway junction. A total of 25,000 people perished in that fire-bombing, which was carried out in several stages, trapping unsuspecting residents.[63]

Air-raid-related events in Weimar mirrored these larger developments. On May 27, 1943, there occurred the first air attack on Weimar, which caused little damage or loss of life. With the exception of the Buchenwald attack, there was little thereafter, and Weimarers thought they were untouchable, just like the citizens of Dresden. But on February 9, 1945, one week before Dresden, there came a massive assault, lasting more than twelve minutes. After 481 tons of ordnance had been dropped by Allied planes, 462 people were dead. The Goethe Museum, the Schiller House, the theater, and Herder's Church of St. Peter and Paul as well as the northern part of the historic central square were all hit. In a nursery school at Richard-Strauss-Strasse 4, near the theater, eighty of ninety children were killed, in addition to all the staff. Margot Köhler, a teenager who sometimes helped out, came to take a look. What she saw shocked her: "Everywhere sat or lay children and grown-ups, their lungs having burst. Soulless, they stared at us." Friedel Winter lost her daughters there: Christa, who was four years old, and the seven-year-old Monika. Winter's family was destroyed when her husband Herbert, a clockmaker, did not return from the front. There were perhaps ten subsequent bombings. Intermittently, low-flying aircraft aimed and shot on sight. One attack came on February 23, killing thirty-two in the Am Horn area of the town. On the 27th, 118 POWs, Americans, British, and French, were killed on the open road; it is questionable if the low-flying attackers had not seen them. The last raid on Weimar, on April 10, left five civilians dead. Two days later American troops occupied the town.

During those air attacks on Weimar, 535 houses were destroyed, 1,254 civilians were killed, as well as 600 inmates, on town assignments and at Gustloff II. The Frauenplan quarter, in front of the Goethe Museum, had been erased, although both Goethe and Schiller's tombs had been brought for safekeeping to Jena. This destruction of tangible symbols of classic Old Weimar does raise the concern that the Allies wanted to get rid of what they knew to be tokens of former German greatness, as if to demolish the country's hubris. The idea brings back images of Buchenwald as a structure next to Weimar, more precisely: of Buchenwald *in* Weimar. Visions of this last scenario were not far-fetched, for concentration camp inmates were clearing away Weimar's after-attack rubble on a regular basis.[64]

Bombing raids were only one factor contributing to the final aura of dissolution and destruction in National Socialist Weimar. The town was being turned upside-down by dictatorship and war even before the terror of the bombs began. In the theater, a munitions factory had been installed. The party, together with the Gestapo, was trying to take full control, even as Gauleiter Sauckel was seen fleeing the city center twice, and returning once. In the old Marstall, the Gestapo executed all surviving prisoners. Courts-martial justice ran rampant, as looters were killed on the spot, and hundreds of army deserters held up in Weimar were led to the Webicht, a small adjoining forest, to be shot. A hastily assembled Volkssturm of boys and pensioners pretended to defend the town, but on hearing the rumble of American tanks threw away their guns and ran.[65] Weimar, as Hitler had known it, had ceased to exist.

Within the Nazi concentration camp system, it is problematic to single out one camp as the most terrible site. But by all accounts, as of 1937 Buchenwald had assumed that dubious reputation, certainly for Germany itself; it may also have been a model for Mauthausen, which was set up in annexed Austria only a year later. It is indeed difficult to imagine SS personnel more fiendish than Karl and Ilse Koch, and Martin Sommer, to imagine torture and killing practices more vicious than tree-hanging and the quarry killings. So why are such comparisons even worth a mention? Because they are juxtaposed with a consideration of the historic Goethe, his confrères, and their classical environment, which was Weimar. Even contemporaries could not get Goethe out of their mind, whether they worked on blueprints for the camp or had to live with the certainty that Buchenwald would henceforth be an integral part of their topography. Weimar's communal denial of mid-April 1945, its claim of ignorance, was, as Richard Alewyn had clearly seen, a morally questionable method of whitewashing oneself, in total disregard of the hard facts. But it was to parallel official German attitudes toward the Nazi regime for decades to come.

To Weimar citizens with open eyes, Buchenwald served as a reality check, making them aware that their small town's fate had, after January 1933, been tied more closely to Germany's national fate than before, indeed to the entire world after September 1939, when war industries were established and, eventually, Allied air raids began. As in the case of Heidelberg (on account of its unique beauty and university tradition), there had been a belief among Weimarers that the enemy would not destroy their town with bombs, because of its classical legacy. In reality, the Western Allies' sparing of Weimar for many months had been for purely strategic reasons. Goethe, in fact, meant more to educated Russians than to the British or Americans, and it was the latter who were doing the bombing. When those bombs hit, especially in February of 1945, the Weimar burghers' disingenuousness anticipated their disbelief of a few months later, that Buchenwald horrors should be associated with them in any way.

CHAPTER 9

Weimar in East and West Germany
1945 to 1990

FRITZ GOES WAS TALL AND ATHLETIC. ON THE BRINK OF A CAREER IN the Wehrmacht he had given up a place on the 1936 Olympic running team to join an elite regiment. During the war his unit was sent to the Eastern Front; on the Crimea around Easter 1944 Goes experienced defeat and retreated with his troops to Romania. On vacation with his in-laws in early summer, the thirty-one-year-old major met Marianne Simson, a film starlet reputed to be one of Goebbels's mistresses. She had just played Die Mondfrau in the color film *Baron Münchhausen*. Dejected, Goes told her of his defeat but Simson, a Nazi Party candidate seven years younger, romanticized the disaster. In July Goes got involved in the Stauffenberg plot against Hitler, and when he again met Simson he deplored its recent failure. Shortly after, Simson received Goes in a Berlin hotel room, draped in a negligee, but Goes later said he resisted her. Nonetheless, she denounced him to the Gestapo, and Goes was almost hanged. After Germany's capitulation on May 8, 1945, Goes, released from British captivity, settled in western Germany. Simson, on the other hand, was arrested by the Soviet NKVD in Berlin, charged with being an accomplice of the Gestapo and eventually sent to Buchenwald, which the NKVD had converted into Sonderlager 2, or Special Camp 2. From there, she was transported to the Waldheim penitentiary in Saxony. Upon release in 1952, Simson assumed smaller roles on southwest German stages, keeping a low profile until her death in 1992.[1]

East-German-run Waldheim was a common destination for inmates kept for years in Sonderlager 2. And while Simson may have been guilty, driven by political fanaticism and because she had taken revenge on a war hero who had spurned her, her detention for seven years most certainly outweighed her sins. Had she moved to the western part of Germany right after the war, she would have been spared this. By May 8, 1945, it was clear that Germany was to be split into an eastern, Soviet-ruled, part and a larger western part, administered by the Americans, British, and French. The town of Weimar was in the East and hence, for decades, it was to lose much significance for Germans in the West. A lot of this had to do with western Germany's special path after the catastrophe, which separated it ever more from the eastern part, politically, socially, and economically, and, not least, mentally.

Weimar between West and East

The history of Weimar after 1945 unfolded against the backdrop of East–West relations, and those were, to a large extent, determined by indigenous developments in eastern Germany and, often in stark contrast, those in western Germany. At first, West Germany was divided into three zones. But these American-, British- and French-controlled units became a sovereign state, the Federal Republic of Germany (FRG), in May 1949, after having introduced a stable Deutsche Mark under Chancellor Konrad Adenauer. A free market economy under Economics Minister Ludwig Erhard guaranteed prosperity, which hugely accelerated after 1952. The American Marshall Plan having helped economically, the FRG became a solid member of the Western Alliance, led by the United States, which culminated in rearmament and inclusion in the NATO defense pact after 1955.

In these circumstances, for West Germans relations with the disadvantaged eastern neighbor were secondary and, to all intents and purposes, Weimar became a distant memory. After the formation of the German Democratic Republic (GDR) in October 1949, the FRG refused to recognize it as a sovereign state and regarded recognition by any other nation as a hostile act. As late as 1969, the Bonn ministry for all-German affairs published a lexicon, as a handbook for "the other part of Germany." In keeping with this view of things, the FRG proclaimed the need for reunification of the two halves after general and free elections in both polities. With the GDR claiming reunification itself, but under Communist rule and within the Soviet-controlled bloc until the late 1960s, there were scant points of contact. Cold War events and the erection of the Berlin Wall in August 1961 reinforced the hiatus. The disconnection extended as far as the political parties: East Germany's newly formed Socialist Unity Party SED did not correspond effectively with West Germany's KPD, which by 1949 was merely marginal and by 1956 was prohibited. The situation improved somewhat in 1971, after the less doctrinaire Erich Honecker had succeeded the Stalinist Walter Ulbricht as head of government in East Berlin. For his state, Honecker gave up the goal of reunification under Communism; this trend had been slowly under way since the late 1960s. The Bonn government under chancellors Willy Brandt and Helmut Schmidt came to recognize the GDR as a sovereign state, and likewise suspended reunification. In 1973, a Basic Treaty was ratified by the Bonn parliament establishing formal relations with the GDR, and both sovereign states joined the United Nations. What followed were economic aid programs extended by Bonn to East Berlin; the more largesse and the more frequently supplied, the more morose East Germany's command economy became over time. The apex of a series of improved bilateral communications was reached when Chancellor Helmut Kohl formally received Honecker in Bonn, in September 1987. This was two years away from the fall of the Berlin Wall, a torch event signifying the collapse of the Communist East German system, politically, economically, and socially. A year after that, in October 1990, the two parts of Germany reunited.[2]

If West Germans thought little about Weimar, they tried to think nothing about Buchenwald. This was in keeping with the West Germans' tendency during the first two postwar decades to dissociate themselves from the negatives suggested by the Third Reich, by claiming that they themselves had been either victims or not involved. Whenever obvious perpetrators such as Adolf Eichmann were found out, West Germans would identify them as *the only* guilty agents. That was the attitude Weimarers had adopted when they were forced by the US Army to confront the Buchenwald camp in April 1945, and it manifested itself again when Buchenwald guard Martin Sommer was tried in Bayreuth at the end of the 1950s. In the German press, Sommer was demonized as "The Beast from the Buchenwald Camp," and his wife Barbara, a nurse he had recently met while in hospital and who had been a child in 1945, was dismissed from her job. Only a few readers cautioned in letters to the editor that moral blame was being unjustly shifted or ignored, that Sommer possessed all-too-human qualities and that, regarding his bad characteristics, there was a Sommer in every German.[3]

Press reports about the monstrous Sommer and his devious wife were designed for the man on the street. Certain intellectual circles practiced a similar type of apologia using not Buchenwald – it was excoriated – but Weimar itself, or the idea of Weimar. This amounted to a collective "denazification" of the entire nation. If, for one part of West Germany's populace, Buchenwald was said to stand for the evils of National Socialism worth condemning, for another part Weimar and Goethe stood for the humanity encapsulating the true Germany.[4] Germany's national legacy as a salient one, emblematized by Goethe, was molded into that invented tradition from the late nineteenth century and conveniently extended, according to the needs of the day, as far back as 1914, or 1918. Because Weimar was situated in East Germany and therefore inaccessible, a virtual Weimar was created, inhabited by a poet Goethe and his prodigious cohorts. On Goethe one could reliably lean. It was a simple matter of collective identification with the great man. This phantasm was perfected in the Germanist seminars of the universities. Here the Gundolf school of conservative Goethe studies now ruled, under Friedrich Gundolf's student Professor Benno von Wiese, in Münster and later in Bonn. From 1936 von Wiese had enjoyed a professorship in Erlangen, while his two closest friends, Hannah Arendt and Richard Alewyn, had had to flee Germany. Apart from having been a member of the NSDAP, Wiese had held at least four other Nazi offices, something he now was eager to suppress, as he presided over the emerging apostles of literary criticism.[5] In 1963 their representative, the editor of a Festschrift for von Wiese, thanked him for his "liberal spirituality and personal charisma."[6] In a less obtrusive manner, von Wiese's Berlin colleague Friedrich Meinecke, the doyen of German historians, professed a belief in Goethe's healing powers. Meinecke was a liberal conservative, but with early anti-Semitic leanings, who, although skeptical of the Nazi phenomenon, had hailed Hitler's early martial victories as an expression of "the revolutionary dynamics of the Third Reich." Now, in 1946, for German society's moral cleansing, he advocated the creation of a network of local "Goethe Congregations" throughout the land.[7] Such a redemptive interpretation of Goethe and the classics was practiced by students and scholars-in-the-making until they began to rebel against traditionalist society in general and ossified university structures in particular after 1965, one consequence of which would be the rise of the Baader-Meinhof terrorist gang, but with a more sober professorial generation having evolved by the 1970s as well. This generation, led by scholars such as Eberhard Lämmert and Karl Otto Conrady, proceeded to initiate critically enlightened Goethe discourse.[8]

In so doing, it was able to refer to an important public debate from as early as the 1940s. In 1947 the German philosopher Karl Jaspers had been chastised by his conservative – in the Meinecke mold – colleague, the Bonn Romance scholar and cultural critic Karl Robert Curtius. Jaspers, with a Jewish wife, had lost his Heidelberg chair under the Nazis in 1937 and since 1943 had suffered from a writers ban. Having retired after the war to

Basel he traveled to Frankfurt to receive the Goethe Medal, and for a lecture, on August 28, 1947. The gist of his talk was that Germans should not hide behind Goethe in an effort to escape from the memory of Nazism, or even to whitewash themselves. Jaspers humanized Goethe by emphasizing some of his weaknesses, thereby advancing the argument that Goethe was ill suited to serve as a pretext for a fundamentally spotless German legacy that would allow one to ignore Nazism. There could be no recourse to Goethe to obtain "liberation from the burden which has been placed upon us." Jaspers was taken to task by Curtius, who accused him of having belittled the Olympian and of misunderstanding German history.[9] But the philosopher was echoed two years later by his student, the Germanist Alewyn, as he warned that Weimar's golden past could never absolve the German people of the guilt projected by Buchenwald.[10]

Few West Germans traveled to Weimar after May 1945. But of the ones who did, disproportionately more went during the Honecker era after 1971 than during the Ulbricht era. At the beginning of the East–West divide, visitors usually came in groups attracted to official functions being staged in Weimar, by virtue of its classics reputation. Typical were the West German delegates to conventions organized by the revived Goethe-Gesellschaft, which was officially ideology-neutral and for many years led by an astute Gymnasium principal from West Berlin. As an example, 200 members of the West German chapter of this society were in Weimar for the annual meeting of May 1958. Throughout the 1950s, a West German delegation of scholars under von Wiese's direction regularly met with East German counterparts in Weimar to prepare a *Schiller-Nationalausgabe*, an all-German comprehensive edition of Schiller's works. When the groups of editors met in West Germany, it was in Marbach near Stuttgart, Schiller's birthplace, which housed a growing stock of literary materials, rivaling the Goethe- und Schiller-Archiv of Weimar. In November 1959 Hans-Dieter Roos from the *Süddeutsche Zeitung* in Munich was able to inspect the Schiller-Museum, and two years later Karl Korn from the *Frankfurter Allgemeine Zeitung*, equally sympathetic, followed suit with a visit to the Goethe-Museum. In November 1964 a "Weimar Academy" invited East German as well as West German writers for discussions in the Hotel Elephant. Here it was Günter Grass and Hans-Magnus Enzensberger who showed themselves least willing to take in East German propaganda.[11]

After 1971, West German tourists increasingly visited the local Weimar shrines, such as the Goethe and Schiller Houses, and their tombs.[12] So many thousands of West Germans traveled to Weimar over the years that the FRG press came to dub the town first the "Muses' Court of the SED," and later the "Disneyland of Classical Literature."[13] Of some significance was the partnership between Marx's birthplace Trier and Weimar in the 1980s, which sent delegations from one town to the other – Weimar's having been carefully handpicked. For the West Germans, this was a mixed blessing. To the last, Trier citizens bussed to Weimar were coolly received and strictly prohibited from mingling with ordinary Weimarers. This changed only in 1989, when the end for the Communist republic was near.[14] After the fall of the Berlin Wall in November of that year West Germans came more frequently and in greater numbers. Pending reunification with the FRG, Trier construction experts visited Weimar in early 1990 with the aim of buildings restoration.[15] But other West Germans expected too much, too soon. Horst Krause from Hanover found mostly "dirt, drab house façades, hardly air to breathe and little culture."[16] Krause was correct regarding the buildings. But as far as tokens of culture were concerned, he could have looked somewhat harder.

Buchenwald Legends and Monuments

In April 1945 a small group of men emerged from Buchenwald concentration camp to begin assuming responsible positions in regional government and administration, briefly under the American, thereafter the Soviet occupation of Thuringia. Most of them were the leaders of the Communist underground of a few hundred men that had closely collaborated with the SS and eventually taken the upper hand in the running of the camp. They had been instrumental in handing Buchenwald over to the Americans in April, after camp commandant Pister, scared by ever closer US tank rumblings, had expressly asked them to do so. Among the most important were Willi Seifert, born in 1915, who had learned masonry and been a captive at Buchenwald during its entire history. Here he had been put in charge of its dreaded labor records office. After 1945, he would rise from municipal comptroller in his native Plauen to lieutenant general of the People's Police (Vopo). The mason-turned-general supervised the construction of the Berlin Wall in 1961. Erich Reschke, a locksmith born in 1902 who had participated in the ferocious revolt of Hamburg Communist workers in 1923, in 1945 was made chief of the Thuringian regional police. Walter Bartel was a forty-one-year-old former sales clerk from Brandenburg, who, in exile, had enrolled in the Moscow Lenin Party School and hid a few years in the Czechoslovak Republic, before the Nazis caught up with him. After liberation, Bartel became personal advisor to Communist Central Committee Chairman Wilhelm Pieck – just returned from

Moscow – in East Berlin. In Buchenwald, Bartel had shared leadership of the Communist-led International Camp Committee with forty-eight-year-old former grinder Ernst Busse. On his release, Busse was set to assume the interior ministry of Thuringia.[17]

The alleged actions of Busse, Bartel, and their friends especially in the final few months of Buchenwald contributed to the legend of what current Buchenwald Memorial Warden Volkhard Knigge has called "the birth of the GDR from a more or less idealized and heroicized Communist resistance."[18] The legend became official copy in all East German publications and was repeated countless times even by serious authors such as the onetime Leipzig Germanist Hans Mayer, who wrote, after having fled to West Germany in 1963, that Bartel and his men "by virtue of their own power prevented a final massacre before the arrival of the liberators."[19] In formulating this legend, Bartel had, against the truth, allowed the American troops two extra days before liberating the camp, to invent more time during which his resistance group would have disarmed the SS.[20] This GDR foundation legend was institutionalized through the erection of a Buchenwald memorial on the Ettersberg by September 1958. Created by the East German sculptor Fritz Cremer, it had a 50-meter-high bell tower and a large, imposing group monument depicting eleven inmates.[21] Until 1990, the lead theme of commemorations and exhibitions on the Ettersberg was not the suffering of the Jews and other prisoners, persecuted on religious or political grounds, but solely that of the steadfast Communists, with an emphasis on former party leader Ernst Thälmann, who had been brought there to be killed by the SS in August 1944.[22]

The Buchenwald founding legend, although it persisted and came to serve its purpose for one faction of GDR leaders, was already deflated in 1945, on the initiative of another faction – the Ulbricht Group. This core of twelve German Communists had arrived from Moscow exile in East Berlin on April 30, 1945, led by the former Leipzig carpenter Walter Ulbricht, who had been chosen personally by Stalin to rebuild the German Communist Party and spearhead a Communist administration in the Soviet-occupied zone. Stalin mistrusted any non-Soviet Communists who had been incarcerated by the Nazis or were in exile in the western hemisphere, such as Spanish Civil War veterans who had fled to Mexico. The orthodox Stalinist Ulbricht made certain that one of his own representatives was sent to Weimar under the fledgling Soviet administration of Thuringia in July 1945, as chief of the KPD, to countermand the growing influence of men like Busse and Reschke. To apply further pressure, in October 1946 the SED, under Ulbricht's control, appointed a committee to probe the past of these annoyingly ambitious Buchenwald ex-inmates. It developed a set of criteria by which the men in question were to be scrutinized, with the ultimate aim of their removal. In time, Busse, Bartel, Reschke, and others were questioned in Berlin on issues such as their general behavior in Buchenwald with special attention paid to their SS relations, their attitude toward captured Soviet soldiers, and their morals, with a view to the camp brothel – which on higher orders had been off-limits for Communist cadres. It was important for the East Berlin leadership to deal with these points in a timely fashion, for the Americans were about to stage a Buchenwald trial near the former concentration camp of Dachau, at which compromising details about the former Communist kapos could be revealed. The sooner the Buchenwald functionaries disappeared or were neutralized, the better it would be for the overall credibility of the SED and the power schemes of the Ulbricht clique. This clique succeeded in the review proceedings without being able to extinguish the founding legacy as such, because it had already entrenched itself and was proving its worth in helping to justify Communism in eastern Germany. Nonetheless, Ernst Busse was found to have frequented the Buchenwald brothel and to have had a hand in the death of at least one Soviet officer, who had tried to escape but then been caught by the SS and killed. Busse was clearly suspect as one of the chief kapos in the camp infirmary who had been in a position to administer lethal injections to rival prisoners, including other German Communists and Soviet POWs. After interrogation by Ulbricht's cronies, Busse was dispatched to the Soviet Union, where he died in the Vorkuta Gulag in 1952. Reschke also was sent to the Gulag, on similar charges, but permitted to return, finally to rise to the position of a police lieutenant colonel in the penal system. Bartel too came under examination, was dismissed from his Berlin party position and afforded a chance to retrain. Somehow he managed a Leipzig doctorate in German history, ending his career as a chair-holder at the Humboldt University in East Berlin.[23] Ideology in East Germany often trumped expertise.

In March of 1990, a few months before the GDR's extinction, the Humboldt University historian Kurt Pätzold, a former junior colleague of Bartel and leading Communist expert on the Third Reich, spoke in Weimar about the Hitler–Stalin non-aggression pact of August 1939. Thereafter he was asked about "inhuman conditions" that were known to have existed in the Buchenwald camp, when the Soviets were keeping Germans there between 1945 and 1950. Pätzold deflected all queries, pointing instead to American maltreatment of Wehrmacht POWs in the Upper Rhineland meadow camps shortly after the war, and to Nazi "euthanasia." The

Russians, insisted Pätzold, had actually been rather liberal in their zone of occupation. Pätzold lost his Berlin chair in 1992, two years after the reunification of the two Germanys, for having impeded students on political grounds.[24]

The historian may have been caught unawares by those questions, for whatever had happened in Buchenwald after the Soviets had taken it over for their own purposes had been officially taboo and certainly never a part of the memory work directed onsite by the authorities. Over the decades, this neglect had grated on former inmates and their relatives, especially since many of the prisoners had been innocent. On the eve of the old regime, they demanded justice and an opening of the records.[25] But it would take years until the entire truth could come to light.

Stalin's Buchenwald

As the Red Army advanced westward across Poland and eastern Germany in early 1945, it not only captured Wehrmacht soldiers but was also making arrests of German civilians. Stalin needed them to work in the Soviet Gulag, but as his secret-service chief Lavrentiy Beria informed him in April, of the 138,660 Germans thus far caught less than half were physically fit to work. Stalin agreed to Beria's proposal to send fewer Germans to the Soviet Union and intern more of them in Germany itself. The idea of Soviet internment on German soil was based on Beria's directive of April 18, and it meant resorting to facilities already in existence. The Soviets began with altogether twenty-eight camps east and west of the Oder river and later in the year had around ten in eastern Germany, of which the former Nazi concentration camp Sachsenhausen near Berlin was the largest, and Buchenwald, now called Sonderlager 2, the second-largest. From 1945 to their dissolution in 1950, 122,671 inmates would pass through those ten camps, of whom 15 percent would be transported to the Soviet Union. Of the total, 42,889 would die. Through Sonderlager 2, 28,500 prisoners would move and 7,113 would perish. On camp termination, 7,073 Buchenwald inmates were released, 2,415 were handed over to the GDR judicial system for trial and execution or incarceration, mostly in Waldheim penitentiary, and 264, including the members of the burial commando who knew altogether too much, were transferred to the Soviet Union.

The Soviet camps, including Sonderlager 2, were closed because in September 1949 Pieck had asked Stalin to do this, after inmates freed in 1948 had settled in western Germany and spread adverse propaganda. It was argued that after the establishment of the GDR as a sovereign state its government would be capable on its own of policing political enemies. Besides, formal denazification had been declared at an end. Stalin having agreed, Sonderlager 2 was dissolved beginning in January 1950 and formally handed over to the East Germans on December 21, 1951, whereupon they began to fashion their GDR-specific Buchenwald Memorial.

The mode of suspect capture and the manner of their captivity in Germany – they were generally not required to work – begs the question of motivation on the part of the Soviets. In the end, only a two-part rationale holds up: first, Germans had to be punished collectively, nominally for National Socialism but regardless of their crimes, and second, Lenin's early maxim, that terror was an effective tool of governance, was still valid. As the Sonderlager 2 survivor Ernst Klotz has noted: "Terror is the means by which one can effect a maximum of governance through a minimum of exertion."

Like the other camps, Sonderlager 2 was run by the NKVD, which had special troops on the payroll of the Soviet interior ministry. This secret-service staff was augmented by Red Army soldiers. The initial consignment of prisoners arrived in Sonderlager 2, as forty-six prisoners from Erfurt entered the infamous main gate on August 21, 1945. Prisoners were always delivered on the instigation of the Soviet authorities, who usually held them in local NKVD basements first and interrogated them under torture, throughout Thuringia. Most prisoners came from Weimar, Jena, Erfurt, and Arnstadt and their environs. Terror spread because the inmates were often arrested on the spot, wherever they happened to be, in the clothes they were wearing that day, and without their kin being notified. Sonderlager 2, like the other prisons, was tightly sealed off, since officially it did not exist, and news neither entered nor exited. Family inquiries were never answered. When inmates were let go, no advance notice was given outside, and when inmates died, no one beyond the camp was told. This conformed with Soviet practice, especially that during Stalin's Great Purge from 1934 to 1938. After an inmate's release, he or she had to maintain strict silence and was disadvantaged in civilian life for years – in searching for work or in health care. Soviet or German police maintained tight supervision.[26]

The demographics of Sonderlager 2 differed from those of the formerly Nazi Ettersberg camp in significant respects. The Russians sent entire batches of people to Sonderlager 2, or had them released or transferred in large groups, without German Communist administrators interfering. Hence inflow and outflow were more erratic after 1945 than they had been under the Nazis. But these movements also illustrated the huge power of the Soviet occupying power in the Eastern Zone during the first few postwar years. In January 1946 over 5,000 inmates arrived from Landsberg on the Warthe, dispatched by the Soviets; others came later from camps to the east of Weimar – Torgau, Ketschendorf, or Mühlberg. About Ketschendorf, especially ghastly stories circulated. In early February 1947 over a thousand inmates left Buchenwald for camps in Kazakh Karaganda, where Stalin had already resettled Soviet Volga Germans, and in summer 1948 the first large group of almost 10,000 inmates was freed.[27]

By far in the majority were males in the age bracket of early twenties to the sixties. Most of them were from the small or medium Nazi hierarchy – mere Nazi Party members were typical, local block or cell wardens frequent. Many had been rounded up in everyday situations, often as a result of denunciations. Thuringia being largely agrarian, farmers predominated who had not fought at the front but tilled the land for the sake of the national economy, while also taking on Nazi offices. Moreover, craftsmen and small factory owners were brought in. There were many railroad employees, who might have serviced cattle trains to Auschwitz, Majdanek, or Sobibor, but certainly not all did. Anyone with a Slavic name had been suspect to the conquerors, hence men from Silesia or Posen or East Prussia were now entering Buchenwald who had earlier trekked west and had had no Nazi connections. Older men had been in the Volkssturm and were caught. Several hundred SS men were prisoners, but they were segregated and eventually shipped to Russia. Formerly high-placed functionaries were rare, such as the physician Gerhard Wischer, who had wrought evil in the euthanasia actions and in 1948 came from Mühlberg. He was a prisoner physician until in February 1950 he was taken to Waldheim, charged with murder by the Germans and condemned to death. He was hanged on November 4.[28]

Next to the men, there were boys in the camp, ranging from age fifteen to just over twenty. Altogether, they comprised approximately 4 percent of the prisoner population. Most had been arrested, like Joachim Heyne in Jena, on suspicion of having belonged to the Werwolf, that SS-directed suicide squad of Hitler Youths the Nazi regime had set up at the end of the war to sabotage and kill the advancing victors. Other Thuringian youths never made it to the camp. Fifteen adolescents from Eisenach were shot on transport to Buchenwald after they had been denounced as Werwolves. Actual Werwolves, however, had been minuscule in number and had succeeded only once, in March 1945 in Aachen, in killing anybody of importance. Hitler Youths like Horst Kranich of Lübben fared particularly badly during initial arrests, because they were invariably tortured to force confessions about Werwolf membership, whereas in fact few had ever heard that name. Among those young prisoners in Sonderlager 2, who lived intermingled with the older inmates and were remembered as rather cheerful, were three boys from Berlin, all seventeen years old. Their entire school class had escaped Berlin's bombing through flight, with three teachers, to Poland, whence they moved to Thuringia to escape the Red Army. They found refuge with farmers near Camburg, but the Soviets caught up with them, tortured them on the Werwolf charge and threw them into Buchenwald. The three teachers, who had accompanied them to the last, perished in the camp; two of the boys eventually were released, stricken with tuberculosis.[29]

The third prisoner contingent were women who, much like the boys, were more resilient than the men in sustaining hardship. Segregated from the males, their numbers always were around 1,000. They tended to be from their early twenties, up to middle age and had been members of the female Hitler Youth, the BDM, where they had held senior leadership positions (and were suspected of being in the Werwolf), or other ancillary formations of the Nazi Party, such as the NS-Frauenschaft. A few had been SS guards or worked as secretaries for the Gestapo; Elfriede Böttcher, one of Bormann's secretaries, was typical of them. On the whole, they were less ideological or political than their male counterparts and their sense of camaraderie was much stronger. Several had been raped in the NKVD dungeons, although in the camp itself such barbarity abated. As in the case of the male cohorts, many did not know why they had been arrested, as they just happened to have been somewhere suspicious at the wrong time. However, the Soviet definition of "suspicious" was an elastic one. For example, anyone who lived near or crossed the inter-Allied zones, to the Red Army was suspect.[30]

Sonderlager 2 was staffed by a Soviet outer commando and a German inner commando, comprised of inmates (kapos), which took over the more immediate guard duties. Whereas the Soviets seldom showed themselves to the inmates, the German camp administration looked after day-to-day camp business. These Germans therefore were comparable to the Communist semi-autonomous administrators of Buchenwald under Nazi rule. This was all the more true as the German officials under Soviet auspices invariably were ex-Nazis who carried themselves proudly and loudly and were generally despised and hated by the mass of prisoners. Yet it has to be said that although this German kapo elite was brutal and often arbitrary in its actions, it was not set on a potential destruction course for the prisoners, as the SS guards and sometimes their Communist sub-chieftains had been under Hitler. Neither were the Soviets bent on systematic annihilation of their charges. Although their penal philosophy is still unclear, it is certain that the East German camp system was intended neither for labor nor reeducation, but instead was an extension of Stalin's personal sense of hatred for and unremitting punishment of former Nazis, possibly innocent victims notwithstanding.[31]

If an endless chain of cruelties had dominated Nazi Buchenwald from 1937 to 1945, interminable hunger controlled Sonderlager 2 after 1945. Because it was a hunger that never went away, it affected the inmates to the point where they could do nothing else but wait for food, consume it – often in a pathologically ritualistic fashion – and indulge in grotesque cookbook fantasies while waiting for the next feeding. The chronic food shortage led to gruesome scenes. One day ex-Hitler-Youth Günter Ochs observed a huge soup container being spilled on the pathway. At once the surrounding inmates were lying flat on their stomachs, slurping the liquid. "It was a humiliating sight. Human beings who threw themselves down like animals. Just to pick up the grub that one threw at them. Like hungry pigs before the trough, where one pounced on the other."[32] From the Soviet side, the scarce food supply was the result of a combination of two factors. One consisted of true shortages in eastern Germany, particularly until 1947, which tormented civilian Germans as much as Russian occupiers. The other factor was a genuine desire for revenge, in Joseph Stalin's mold. Altogether, an inmate received as little as 1,600 calories per day, far below the minimum for survival, generally held to be above 2,500 for an adult. The main staples were a heavily water-saturated bread, and soup of barley and later potato scrapings, which turned disgustingly gelatinous. To this were added 15 grams of sugar and something masquerading as malt coffee. An occasional herring was passed around, pieces from which as many as six inmates would devour. Tubercular beef was in the supply chain. Vegetables constituted the smallest part of a daily diet that was so insufficient as to weaken the immune system. If the males had the gravest problem with this as they habitually ingested more, women inmates complained less because they received rations equal to the men's and boys'. But it was women who were bothered by the lack of hygiene more than men; for instance, worms and fleas in their barley. Hence women did not suffer as much hunger as did men, their immune system did not deteriorate as quickly, and they did not die of hunger-related diseases as did men. Still, overall nutrition did not improve until 1948, when the closing of the camp was near and the Soviets wanted to save face, as they released their prisoners.[33]

Malnutrition and a consequent systemic protein deficiency in Sonderlager 2 resulted in oedema or swelling of the legs and abdomen, including the scrotum. The dynamic of the tissues was upset and a redistribution of fluid was caused. "Water was always in the legs and feet during the day," remembers Hans Wagner, "and when during evenings and at night I put them up for relief to sleep, the water was in my abdomen and scrotum early in the morning." Such oedema was treated by sticking needles into the body. Pellagra, where the buttock skin falls apart, linked to vitamin-D deficiency, was another of the more visible manifestations. Yet another disease directly influenced by nutrition was tuberculosis, which appears to have been the camp's most potent killing agent. In May 1949, 30 percent of all Buchenwald inmates were said to be sick with TB. Dysentery and all manner of stomach and gastrointestinal disorders were rampant. Other ailments were furuncles (boils) and abscesses, which, untreated, could lead to overwhelming infection and sepsis. All these were compounded by the effect of lice, fleas, and other pests.

Absent corrective diets and supported by minimal medications and a merely rudimentary medical apparatus, for instance razor blades to lance those boils, the collective prognosis for inmates' health improvement was decidedly negative. Here the physicians could not help; often they were German specialists like Dr. Wischer, who had been caught in Nazi institutions of public health. This takes into account that the juveniles among the inmate population were less prone to affliction and the aetiology in women's cases on the whole also was much better. At all events, it did not help that many prisoners in winter were stuck with the summer clothing they had been caught in, and in summer with tweeds and woolens.[34]

Not being allowed to work, what was an inmate going to do, since he knew neither the reasons for his arrest nor the time he had to serve? As it turned out, boredom was a fiendish category of torture, one the Soviets had purposely devised. By and large, inmates were prohibited any diversions except for board games, and some played chess for eight hours a day. Illegally, lectures were scheduled, and any piece of paper with a text on it was craved, but there were few of those to go around. Some did, much worn, until they disintegrated. Part of a German–Latin dictionary that was found was treated like a secret treasure. Only in 1948 were single newspapers allowed, which had to be read to groups. Making music and singing too were forbidden; of course there were no instruments. Any transgressions were punishable by stretches in a bunker, often in solitary confinement. Again, women prisoners fared better in this regard, for they were allowed sewing and knitting, and they would form circles for gossip. Yet when a small percentage of the prison population was drafted into work, they found it as exacting as it had been under the Nazis (said those who had been in both regimens), especially the burial commando, whose staff would be let outside the gates to throw, sometimes frozen, corpses into pits.[35]

The one form of entertainment the Soviets scheduled was a series of stage programs called Kultura, where plays and variety shows were produced with live music, and even dances arranged with the women captives. However, the Soviets were keen on dancing with the women exclusively, and overall it became clear that Kultura was to be more for their pleasure than for that of the inmates. Here many of the more energetic younger prisoners participated, as stage hands or coiffeurs to the actors, but the scheme lasted only through the first few months. When five youths escaped in December 1946, having abused their relative freedom of movement, security was tightened and in the process Kultura was scrapped, never to be revived.[36]

Was there a connection between Soviet Buchenwald and Weimar, as there had been under Nazi rule? Not really, because the Soviets had their own resources and the camp was hermetically sealed. But obviously, there were prominent Weimar burghers there, such as Max Oehler of the Nietzsche Archive and Otto Koch, the last Nazi mayor, who both died there. Not so well known was Dr. Rudolf Scheel, former Intendant at the Berlin Theater am Nollendorfplatz, who had been at Weimar's DNT in 1928 and now became known for expert *Faust* stagings at Kultura. The Thuringian Social Democrat Bruno Threyse, who had suffered in Nazi concentration camps and then been appointed director of the Weimar criminal police under the Americans, was interned by the Soviets in early 1946. (This happened against the background of a power struggle between Communists and Social Democrats in Thuringia, which continued until the formation of the SED in April of that year.) Among those less unfortunate than others was a barber from nearby Apolda who had been caught at a wedding party and been brought to Buchenwald in tails, which he would never shed. Then there was Elli Marschall from neighboring Pössneck, born in 1922 and a former member of the BDM and NS-Frauenschaft, who as a salesgirl in a grocery store had been wrapping her wares "in old fascist magazines and newspapers, which in this fashion she distributed among the population and thereby violated the orders of the Soviet occupying powers" – thus her confession, undoubtedly extracted under torture. Hans-Georg Rudel was sixteen when the German police came for him at Weimar's Hänselweg in March 1946, holding him in a cage at the town hall in the market square until he ended up in the court of justice, the old Marstall of Gestapo infamy. Here the NKVD officers, who kept the Marstall as their headquarters until 1950, beat the ex-Hitler Youth excessively, asking the usual question about a Werwolf Hans-Georg never knew. He spent twelve months in Buchenwald and, as usual, was obligated not to talk about it when he was released, back to the Weimar Marstall that had swallowed him and many others, as if Goethe had never set foot there.[37]

The Demographics of Communism

Ever more unsightly due to progressive decay, Weimar nevertheless was one of very few presentable towns in the German Democratic Republic. The true nature of this republic has been widely debated. It has been called a "deeply bourgeois country with authoritarian gubernatorial structures, but bereft of a bourgeoisie" (Wolf Lepenies), and an "outright Communist dictatorship" (Konrad Jarausch). With obvious reference to the Soviet Union, Hans-Ulrich Wehler judges that the GDR was "the totalitarian party dictatorship of a collaborationist regime on the basis of occupational Communism." Similar is the definition of the GDR by Peter Graf Kielmansegg, as a "party dictatorship with totalitarian aspirations."[38] "Party dictatorship," because one-party rule by the SED predominated, with an additional block of four bourgeois parties doing the masters' bidding. "Totalitarian aspirations" but never fulfillment, because the dictates of its Marxist ideology never succeeded in permeating society as a whole, although the attempts were manifold and ruthless. But all the characteristics of a totalitarian state were present: official dogma informing coordinated ancillary organizations such as the FDJ and restricting individual freedoms; a command economy tied to multi-year plans; ideology-infused education; a strong military presence directed against extraneous foes, real or imagined; and a secret police with their political prisoners. This police force, dubbed the Stasi, planted more and more spies within society and was able to manipulate the lives of citizens in untold ways, down to the fabrication of pornographic entanglements for blackmail, as happened to the novelist Günter de Bruyn.[39] In Weimar, toward the end of the republic, a Stasi telephone network extended its tentacles, from headquarters on Cranachstrasse – the former Palais Dürckheim designed by van de Velde – to other strategic buildings in town, especially the Hotel Elephant, which was fully bugged. This at a time when the civic telephone directory contained scarcely more than ten pages.[40]

In accordance with agreements between Moscow and the Western Allies dating back to September 1944 Soviet troops entered Thuringia while it was still under US occupation, and by July 3, they had replaced the

American Third Army in Weimar. For a few weeks they were content with the US-appointed Hermann Brill as German governor of Thuringia, Brill being an SPD survivor of Buchenwald and democratically minded. But the Soviets, aided by Ulbricht, put in their own deputy and set up a branch of SMAD, the Berlin-centered military administration (regionally: SMATh, for governmental purposes in Weimar). Thuringia was now enlarged, after the inclusion of the formerly Prussian jurisdiction of Erfurt. One of the first tasks to be accomplished was to find replacements for former National Socialists in regional government and administration, in addition to the schools. This posed problems because of a dearth of talent, and lower-ranking Nazis were eventually retained. Several now joined one of the four nominally independent non-Socialist parties, in particular the NDPD. There were regional and municipal elections, but the SED always won a large predetermined majority, with candidates of the bourgeois parties, including East CDU and NDPD, toeing the Communist line. In fact, these parties, in their tiny minority, were never independent. Between 1950 and 1952, after the commutation of the Soviet Zone into the German Democratic Republic, the traditional state of Thuringia, even as a recently enlarged entity, was dissolved, so that Weimar became part of one of the fourteen newly created districts, in this case the Erfurt District, with Erfurt as the capital. Weimar's loss of the regional seat of government was a huge prestige blow to its citizens, from which they never recovered in the GDR era, and this remained a complaint even after the Berlin Wall had fallen in 1989.[41]

As society was gradually coordinated, private homes were taken, individual businesses were expropriated and surrounding farms partitioned and collectivized; the presence of the Stasi assured noiseless transformations. Communist uniformity entered institutes of higher learning and schools. However, the Lutheran Church could be accommodated only with difficulty, although eventually, as was the case all over the GDR, certain of its representatives collaborated closely with governmental offices, no less than with the Stasi. Nevertheless, in Weimar as elsewhere the Lutheran Church often offered shelter to the leaders of incipient resistance movements, up to 1989, with the much smaller Catholic dioceses remaining on the sidelines.[42] There had been some non-religious-inspired opposition in the 1950s, but it was effectively stifled. Hence in June 1955, the teacher of Russian Gerhard Benkowitz and statistician Hans-Dietrich Kogel, who worked for the town council, two young men who had expressed their anger in acts of sabotage, fell victim to a show trial. Benkowitz's father had been transferred to the Soviet Union in 1945. After they had rehearsed partially false confessions for public display, they were guillotined, with Ulbricht endorsing the sentences. Their wives were each condemned to twelve years in prison. In 1957, after a group surrounding student pastor Martin Giersch had damaged election posters, there were more arrests. At that time, the church jurist Gerhard Lotz, a Stasi mole, helped to convict the resisters.

After the death of Pastor Oskar Brüsewitz, who had set himself on fire because of the suppression of his church in August 1976 in nearby Zeitz, the opposition especially of young people grew in all of the GDR, including Weimar. More often than not, the Church acted as a shield. In 1978, under Pastor Erich Kranz, whom in 1945 the Soviets had dispatched for seven years to Bautzen penitentiary, a "Friday Circle" sprang up in Weimar, clamoring for peace. A "Monday Circle" had replaced it by 1982, attracting young dissidents who adhered to the punk culture, listened to rock music, drank recklessly and experimented sexually much more widely than was common in the, normally prudish, GDR. This group, with the budding writer Holm Kirsten in the middle, was tried for anti-government graffiti actions and sentenced to several months in jail in February 1984. When its members got out, several of them were allowed to leave the GDR for West Germany.

By that time, such a departure had become a realistic possibility for dissidents. However, once they had applied to the authorities for a legal transfer, they would be harassed and disadvantaged at work, as was amply demonstrated in the German feature film *Barbara* (2012). In Weimar, such would-be emigrants would occupy the Herder Church, in order to lend emphasis to their demands for exit visas. In one such instance in December 1988, protesters were set upon by the church superintendent, Pastor Hans Reder, a known collaborator of the Stasi. Reder actually went so far as to fetch the secret police and have the supplicants arrested. With emotions boiling at that time, Reder was given early retirement in March 1989.[43]

After the formation of the new Land Thüringen (State of Thuringia), just under three million people lived within approximately 10,000 square miles. The population included about one million refugees from the East, who were settled there because relatively few dwellings had been destroyed in Weimar and its surroundings, in comparison with Saxony, for example. This demographic surplus resulted in one of the highest population density rates (per square mile) in all of Europe after the war. Weimar itself had 57,396 inhabitants on August 1, 1945, including 7,498 war evacuees from the western provinces and 1,551 eastern refugees. On December 1, there were already 62,768 persons in Weimar, of whom 61 percent were female.

Because of the refugees, the total number rose further, to 66,659 by the end of October 1946, with the percentage of females now at 58. After 1950, the Erfurt District became much smaller than the former State, at about 4,500 square miles, and the population of Weimar itself shrank. The town was home to 64,452 people in 1950, and 64,151 in 1967 – due to population transfers to the west of Germany and a residential-population decline that afflicted all of the GDR. The overall decline persisted, so that the numbers were 63,910 for 1986, 63,412 for 1988, and 61,583 for 1989.[44]

The physical condition of old and new residents of Weimar at the beginning of the Soviet Zone and into the Democratic Republic was alarming. People were liable to contract diseases such as TB, with dangers exacerbated by insufficient nutrition. Especially dire conditions extended into the 1946–47 so-called hunger winter and let up only gradually, not helped by rationing. In October 1949, the farmers of nearby Heldrungen had to be persuaded to supply their produce, so that Weimar's traditional annual onion market could be reopened in October (they would rather have bartered it for richer returns on their homesteads). Yet a year later, it took merely an hour for the festival's onion stands to be stripped bare. But in the 1950s, as the GDR's populace accommodated itself to agricultural restructuring within a planned economy, entailing the expropriation of individual farmers and the organization of collective combines, the food supply became steady if never abundant. The proverbial banana that was missing everywhere in the GDR for decades was also missing in Weimar, despite East Berlin's friendship with Cuba. Other serious problems, however, notably in the 1940s, were suicides and an irregular water and fuel supply. In time, Weimar developed a capable public health-care system that was mercifully inexpensive for all citizens to use – as everywhere else in the republic – and it provided state-financed vacations for its loyal workers, as well as modest care for its elderly. By the mid-1970s, the Weimar physician–patients ratio was 1:500, and the dentist–patients ratio 1: 1,600. This was considered excellent by world standards. Such positive statistics notwithstanding and unbeknown to the average Weimar citizen, the GDR's medicinal and health system was in a worsening crisis, analogous to the economy, causing physicians and public-health staff to migrate to the West in droves by 1989.[45]

Residents of Weimar found it difficult to locate dwellings, because serviceable buildings were either bombed or getting too old for habitation. Altogether, eight camps for refugees came into being on the outskirts of town, such as on unsightly Buttelstedter Strasse near the station in the north. If by February 1947 6,000 families were looking for homes, this situation eased only gradually, so that forty-two years later 3,586 dwellings were still needed. In the last half of the 1940s, almost no houses or apartments were restored – just 49 out of 1,300 bombed-out ones by 1950. New housing was built only after 1953, but the new flats were cramped and spartan. From 1958, entire streets were being renovated in the city center, which eventually included a pedestrian zone from the Frauenplan, via the market over to Schillerstrasse, something the classics-obsessed Ulbricht himself had strongly urged.

Well into the 1980s, however, the municipal sewerage system remained primitive in stretches not unlike that of Goethe's time, and garbage disposal for the citizens was dismal, discarded mattresses sometimes damaging the garbage trucks. Building materials such as roofing tiles or plastic pipes remained shoddy and in short supply, resulting in mold, rot, and rainwater leaks en masse. Early in 1989 construction foreman Bernd Hildner referred to "the still fairly gray Weimar," when asked about the overall progress he had made.[46]

Of the spotty reconstruction the fate of Weimar's showpieces, the hotels Elephant and Erbprinz, was emblematic. After the Soviets had moved into town, the former Adolf Hitler storey at the Elephant was turned into the base for a radio station, which later moved next to the Nietzsche Villa Silberblick. Until 1954, Soviet officers used the Elephant as permanent quarters, and it was only then that it was reopened to the public. By 1966 it had been converted into Weimar's Interhotel. (Interhotels were luxuriously appointed showpieces in GDR towns and cities, to attract western tourists with western currency, while over-charging East Germans in East Marks.) Still the best hotel in town, in 1989 it demanded 112 DM for a single room. But its old charm having largely disappeared, the Elephant was not as efficient as the excellent modern Interhotels in Leipzig, East Berlin and even Gera. Still, more affluent Weimar youths could meet at the bar there to dance the twist and consume Black Sea champagne for an expensive 23 East Marks a glass. The Elephant lost its neighbor, the traditional Erbprinz, latterly renamed Parkhotel, where Liszt once stayed for months: it was demolished in 1988. The city authorities planned to tear down and rebuild the place, but after its demolition nothing was ever done and a huge gap remained on the market square well into the twenty-first century.[47]

Even within the GDR's feeble economic infrastructure Weimar was not a powerhouse. As always, in agriculture it was not spectacular, due to its patterns of small-farms and given that much of its hinterland was wooded, not arable. Its industrial production continued to be middling, attenuated by the sudden loss of armaments and the ruthless removal of key factories by the Soviets. By April 1948, 109 Weimar firms had been confiscated, previously in heavy industry or owned by Nazis, of which 36 were then returned. The confiscated factories were either dismantled and shipped to the Soviet Union (as happened to much of Zeiss in Jena, including staff), taken over and run by Soviets, or handed outright to Land Thüringen.

What remained for Weimar were a few domains of heavy industry, some railcar works having been converted to harvester and large-crane manufacture. Watch-making established itself in a larger way, with Zeiss parts and Uhrenwerk Weimar brands. There was a firm making firearms, for hunting. Weimar also specialized in the construction of hydroelectric power plants, and had Zeiss branches set up, as well as, from the 1950s, outposts of the Robotron computer works. This company had spread from Dresden to Erfurt and established several outlets in town. As Kristie Macrakis has demonstrated, the GDR became obsessed with computer technology, viewing microelectronics as a symbol of highest human achievement. It went to absurd lengths to impress its own citizens, who purchased Robotron's overpriced computers because of its monopoly. These units were never suited for export to the West, as they were always ten years out of date. West Germany, for instance, had its own, far advanced Siemens computers. In any event, the FRG remained East Germany's skeleton in the closet. East German progress reports habitually referred to increases merely in their own production numbers, avoiding a broader comparison with corresponding FRG statistics.

Whereas 91.2 percent of Weimar's industrial production had been in public hands by 1955, it was 100 percent by 1959. The nationalization of industry also applied in agriculture, when combines (LPGs) started to be created after land expropriations, by fall of 1952. Trade shops were forced into the concentration of so-called ELGs, central purchasing and supply agencies, from the late 1940s to the 1950s. In October 1948, for example, SMATh had forced the collectivization of some 100 master butchers in Weimar County, including Apolda, by prohibiting them from undertaking independent slaughter. During 1956, the remaining private retailers merged and joined the state-owned Handelsorganisation (HO), which, much maligned in jokes for its interruptions in supply, in theory marketed to consumers everything from potatoes to Trabant automobiles. By 1958 the people were able to benefit from a reduction in food and consumer-product prices, and the last vestiges of rationing disappeared. Gradually in the 1960s and '70s, some private entrepreneurs were allowed back into the economy on a modest scale, but the state became their sales agent.[48]

From the Weimarers' perspective as consumers, conditions improved progressively into the 1980s, with Zero Hour in 1945 marking the low point of departure. At that time, men and women improvised, simply to stay alive. With private enterprise still barely extant, it was common to go to a tinsmith to hand in two steel helmets in order to receive a cooking pot, which had been forged from yet another helmet. Weimarers went to dye shops to have Wehrmacht khaki dyed and re-tailored for a farthing. Because of the scarcity, the dyes were smuggled in from the Western zone. The first state-run HO outlet in Weimar was opened on November 29, 1948, and from then on the rule was the sooner one wanted a product, the more expensive it would be. This held true well into the 1980s, at the end of which people were rushing to buy a certain color TV model for 6,200 marks, of which there were five to be had immediately, while a few doors down a television outlet offered comparable models of a different brand for 4,125 marks, after some time. At the beginning all HO products were very expensive – a kilogram of butter costing 130 marks – but prices came down in time.[49] The television set, like the car and later the computer, was a token measure of prosperity and general well-being for Weimarers, as for all GDR citizens. Thus in 1965 of every 100 Weimar households, 47 had a TV, a figure that rose to 71 in 1970 and 80 in 1973 – still a long way off from FRG ratios. Here it should be remembered that the average wage in Weimar then was around 1,000 marks a month, and a pension under 500 marks. How to buy a car on that income? The most popular automobile in the GDR always was the Trabant 601 (popularly dubbed Trabbi), of which the Standard in 1985 cost 8,500 marks, and the Universal S de Luxe 9,700 marks. The waiting period for the Trabbi, which uniformly had an engine of two cylinders, generating 26 horsepower for its top speed of 67 miles per hour, was 13 to 15 years. But in Weimar newspaper want-ads, used, older Trabbis were offered for thousands of marks more and could be instantly purchased.[50]

At the end of the 1980s, one of the most acute maladies of the economy was a particularly steep scarcity of skilled labor in a society chronically short of talent, owing, not least, to the notorious GDR population decline. As documented for Weimar, this manifested itself, for the consumer, in sluggish sales and services, so that, for example, the precious Trabbis could never be adequately serviced. Other bottlenecks were in the construction industry. At the beginning of the end for the republic, social workers and local politicians were quick to identify a correlation between labor shortages and increased juvenile delinquency, as youths, aware of their indispensability, were becoming cocky. This had already been a sore point in Weimar's postwar history, when in May 1945 the old Marstall building had been wrested from the Gestapo and – save for its basement – converted into a home for youth. In the 1970s, another such home was the "Walter Ulbricht" clubhouse at the Goetheplatz – transformed from Klub Erholung of yore.[51] Then, by 1950, Weimar had the highest rate of youth criminality in the entire GDR (and the highest rate of prostitution). This persisted despite a strong FDJ presence in town and exhibited itself increasingly throughout the 1980s in acts of youth vandalism, robbery, alcoholism, and unprovoked attacks.[52]

Without a doubt, the high incidence of prostitution in town sprang from the presence of Soviet military personnel in Weimar and its surroundings. Weimar was, after all, first SMATh and later Red Army Occupation headquarters for the Thuringian region, and nearby Nohra had been converted to a Soviet base. In Weimar and Jena tanks were stationed, and Ohrdruf, to the south, housed motorized artillery.[53]

No sooner had the Red Army taken over Weimar on July 4, 1945, riding in on trucks and horse-drawn buggies, than its officers were confiscating flats in expensive villas, while most troops were shunted to drab Wehrmacht barracks in Weimar's north. Eventually, there were 10,000 men in Weimar and 5,000 in Nohra, not counting all the women, some of whom were in khaki. From their apartments and houses, German occupants were evicted practically overnight. The Soviets occupied the Hotel Elephant, devoid of the leather furniture the Americans had stolen, and started balalaika song and dance. Marching music, Russian, and trans-Caucasian melodies as well as the smell of a mixture of disinfectants, machorka tobacco, and schnapps would be everyday hallmarks of the Soviet presence in Weimar for decades to come. The Soviets also seized the only working hospital left in town, the storied Sophienhaus of Carl Alexander's reign, converting it to a barracks that would be used till 1951. They put heavily pregnant women out into the street, and military vehicles, for long-needed repairs, into the large kitchen. Operating rooms were used for the slaughter of cows and pigs. In the streets, soldiers mingled with the local population; they waded into public pools, often without swim trunks; they toasted each other at the onion market. As Weimar and some Soviet families lived next to each other, Soviet children loved playing with the German kids, often a game of "war." Many came home to puzzled Russian parents, speaking only German.[54]

Official contact between the Red Army and Weimar's population was relegated to visits by local work brigades of Soviet installations, and carefully orchestrated social events with speeches, toasts to eternal friendship, and much drinking in semi-public venues. Minor Soviet soccer stars also played for "Motor Weimar." But because officers' families were living next to burghers, private relationships developed, sometimes enhanced by commercial enterprises. The officers would attempt to sell watches or gasoline to the civilians, and near Nohra there was barter – watches for pork sides, or gasoline for lard. Officers' wives accepted jobs on farms or in shops for extra money, and though this was illegal, it was invariably tolerated. There were commercial transactions in Soviet army retail outlets, where Weimarers would shop for products they could not normally acquire, and Russians, Armenians, or Kazakhs emptied Weimar HO (supermarket) shelves, whenever there was a novelty item for sale, perhaps porcelain from Ruhla or toys from Georgenthal. Such Soviet cleanouts often were resented by the Germans. Aiding these exchanges were meetings under the banner of German–Soviet friendship that became institutionalized; becoming a faithful member of the Gesellschaft für deutsch-sowjetische Freundschaft was looked upon as toadying.[55]

Generally, in the Weimar population, the Soviets, officially called "die Freunde," were not popular. They were, after all, the victors, and what was held especially against them was their treatment of German girls and women. Resentment built up against the background of the terrible stories that were heard about the conquering Soviets and German females of all ages during the occupation of Berlin, as well as eastern territories like Silesia. According to estimates, 1.4 million women were raped by Soviet soldiers in the easternmost German territories eventually cut off from the German Reich, between 95,000 and 130,000 in Berlin, and half a million in what was to become the GDR. The severity of rape cases in Thuringia alone can be gauged by the fact that on August 29, 1945, Minister President Rudolf Paul promulgated a Law of Pregnancy Interruption.[56] How many women were raped in Weimar at that time is not known, but the number was high enough for women not to risk going out alone at night, and those who did might be attacked in the open as well as in Russian quarters. "The soldiers stood in the street at night and tossed the women from one to the other; one never knew how this ended," remembers Hildegard Delank, then nineteen. Officially, such infractions were sternly punished by the enlisted men's superiors, and officers controlled themselves more than the men. However, Gisela Hamann, in her early twenties, was unpleasantly surprised in her apartment building by a Georgian colonel. After Hamann reported him to the authorities, he was not seen again.[57] The wide availability of Weimar women who would offer themselves to the soldiers in return for material favors seems to have had no influence on rapes.

Romantic liaisons between the Soviet military and Weimar women were discouraged, and where they occurred, tragedy could result. In one instance, a Russian officer who had fallen in love with a German girl was immediately transferred elsewhere. When the two happened to run into one another in Gera, the officer rented a hotel room and shot first his girlfriend, then himself. In another case an enlisted Russian man met a waitress in the Felsenkeller restaurant, down the street from the Nietzsche Archive. The two became lovers and had two children. When the soldier wanted to get married, he was ordered back to the Soviet Union, having to leave his family behind. Only in the 1950s were the marriage restrictions relaxed; in Weimar, few unions resulted.[58]

The continuing friction between the Russian occupiers and the Weimar populace showed itself in several ways. For years, quite apart from Sonderlager 2, Weimar's Soviet Military Tribunal continued to sentence offenders of the new political order, or mere bystanders, to long incarceration or death. Culprits would often be sent to the Soviet Union, to the Gulag, or for execution. There was a high rate of criminality around town, and traffic fatalities, as a result of gross Soviet negligence, were hardly ever prosecuted. Weimar children were forced to learn Russian in school or join the German–Soviet friendship society, both of which they routinely resented. One indicator of the true nature of the relationship between Soviets and Germans was the disorderly condition of the Red Army cemetery in the Goethe Park near town. This was one where hundreds of common and mostly very young soldiers lay buried, who were not victims of the war theater, but had died as a result of ill-treatment at the hands of their officers (much of which violence the Weimarers were constantly witnessing in town), malnutrition, or disease. Weimar citizens came to hate the cemetery – an eyesore even today – and the town council balked at having to assume its upkeep.[59]

East Germany's Classical Heritage

One main motive for the westward move of the Soviet conquerors in early 1945 had been to root out fascism, in their defeat of the Third Reich. A value system dictated by humanity should replace it. Stalin, who in February 1942 had pronounced that the Hitlers come and go whereas the German people and the German state would remain, wanted a process put in place by which Germans could be disabused of fascist ways by undergoing reeducation in humanity, or democracy, or whatever Stalin understood by those terms. While still in Russian exile during the war, hardened German

Communists like Ulbricht who were to be charged with the rebuilding of Soviet-occupied Germany agreed that a return to humanity would mean recourse to the classical ideals of Goethe and Schiller and a corresponding renunciation of Nietzsche, who allegedly had done his part in spawning fascism. After Ulbricht and his entourage had returned to Germany in early summer of 1945 and the Soviet military administration, SMAD, was being set up, the ideological groundwork was prepared to revive the humanist ideals of Goethe and his circle, and bureaucratic mechanisms were devised to implement these ideals.[60] A cultural heritage for Germany with Goethe at the center, leading from the end of the eighteenth century straight to 1945 had, in the way in which it was now being proposed, not been in the annals of German history, nor did it reflect reality. Instead, as an artificial construct in the manner of earlier Goethe-centric "inventions of tradition," it was to provide legitimization for the German Communist polity that was to be created. The foremost Communist leaders Ulbricht, Pieck, Otto Grotewohl, and Anton Ackermann claimed that as early as the first half of the nineteenth century the fathers of socialism Engels and Marx had placed their faith in Goethe and the classics, that the late nineteenth-century socialist author Franz Mehring had idolized Schiller and that Lenin had also revered those enlightened thinkers as forebears of the socialist creed. This thread logically led to Ulbricht who, as a carpenter's apprentice in Leipzig, had avidly studied the classics and loved reciting them. In March 1962 Ulbricht publicly referred to Goethe's *Faust*, in particular the last stanzas of Part II, where the dying Faust exults about "standing on free ground in the company of a free people." The "free ground" for Ulbricht was the soon-to-be-perfected Communist state (as opposed to the monopoly-capitalist-dominated West), with the "free people," of course, that state's peasants and workers. Ulbricht adopted from Lenin the "Enforcer Theory," where he envisaged the socialist peasants and workers "enforcing" the humanity that the savants of the classics, as a utopia, had so championed. In line with this reasoning, Ulbricht came to see his people as currently writing the third part of *Faust*, hence as the true executors of Goethe's lifework. Ulbricht wanted his GDR, explains the Berlin sociologist Wolf Lepenies, "not just to write a socialist *Faust*, but also to live it."[61]

The classics-legacy calumny was the second of two tall tales attempting to justify the origins of the German Communist state in terms of Weimar, the first being the Buchenwald liberation legend. The classics plot hatched by Ulbricht and his cronies as far back as Moscow further explains why his group would have been eager to dislodge former camp inmate Ernst Busse and his comrades, after July 1945. And to the extent that the Busse circle's relationship with the presiding Soviet authorities was fated to turn out negative, because of the harm they were alleged to have caused to Soviet POWs in the camp, Ulbricht's relations with the SMAD were positive. Believing in the salvific mission of culture to redress Germany's past failures and prepare it for the future, the Soviets had created a special contingent of culture-controlling officers, all of whom were highly educated, admiring lovers of the German classics, and completely fluent in German. They were headed by a colonel, Professor Sergei Tulpanov, a political economist from Leningrad, who had fought his way into Nazi Germany amid the regular troops and in 1945 came to direct censorship, information, and propaganda for SMAD. In effect this meant that he could shape all culture, just as Stalin wished. He did this until September 1949, on the cusp of the Soviet zone turning into a Soviet satellite republic, when he was promoted to general and eventually recalled to Moscow. His main aides were Grigorij Weiss and Alexandr Dymshits, two equally erudite scholars of Jewish background (as were others in Tulpanov's Berlin staff), who were as much admired by their German collaborators as they were feared. Germany had a great history and a great democratic tradition, Tulpanov said, addressing the parliament of FDJ, the new Communist youth organization, in April 1946. "You have to recover the German culture for yourselves," he continued. "This is the time for German youth to return to the traditions of the best of their nation, to the ideals of Lessing and Herder, Marx and Engels, Bebel and Liebknecht, Goethe and Schiller."[62]

Under Tulpanov and beyond the time when Ulbricht was replaced by Honecker in 1971, the classics highway was followed assiduously by East Germany's culture brokers with scarcely a deviation. Two milestones on this road were central preparations for the Goethe Year in 1949, and the Bitterfeld conference ten years later, yet the conceptual bases for these events were different. Although problematic because of his complex personality, Goethe appeared to be the most rewarding and the easiest to navigate with for the GDR elite's purposes. Among all of Weimar's geniuses, he would therefore be politically applied in a fashion much stronger than had been the case under Nazism, and more officiously. Goethe, and more specifically his *Faust*, exemplified what the German Communists wished to identify with; he was meant to be the paragon for all strata of their society, foremost Marx's iconic peasants and workers. Hence on the occasion of the poet's 200th birthday Goethe's plays were staged in all the theaters, speeches and celebrations were held in his honor, and congresses were scheduled, with much of this in Weimar itself.

However, even if the union between Goethe and the GDR's worker class was loudly proclaimed, the rulers knew well that this was an empty formula, because it was obvious that in daily practice, workers and farmers could not concern themselves with an ancient poet named Goethe. Clearly, then, the GDR proletariat had not even begun to assume that Faustian role of "enforcer of humanity" which, according to Ulbricht's theory of heritage, or *Erbe*, had been prefigured for his state in Goethe's *Faust*.[63]

This shortcoming had to be addressed at the Bitterfeld conference in April 1959. Bitterfeld was a grimy industrial town between Weimar and Berlin, which Ulbricht deemed suitable for conveying his message, namely that workers and culture unite. With the classics as a model of creativity and invoking the "poetic principle" (Frank Trommler), Ulbricht sought to instil in manual workers the impulse to create, using pen, paintbrush, or musical instruments, in their spare time. Seasoned writers and artists should visit the industrial combines and mentor laborers in higher skills. The hidden agenda here was overall achievement of greater industrial productivity for the GDR, spurred by the mechanism of auto-reportage: workers were expected to put on paper their impressions of a bygone time – lower productivity or sanitary deficiencies in the capitalist age, or lockouts and unemployment, as a negative contrast to the improvements in the factory halls under the present leadership.

The East-Berlin-motivated "Bitterfeld Way" failed, because blue-collars could not be enticed to put anything in writing, let alone create paintings or compose music, especially after hours, Johann Wolfgang Goethe or not. A follow-up Bitterfeld conference in April 1964 corrected nothing. Hence, after Ulbricht's departure in 1971, a revision of the entire Bitterfeld concept was in the offing.[64]

One of the arguments the Communists used in riveting the German classics to their own history was that previously in Germany, Goethe, Schiller, and Herder had been wrongly appropriated, even falsified, by their bourgeois interpreters. Whereas there is truth in that, the revolution-bent Communists, just like the Nazis before them, twisted reality to make things fit their ideology. The most significant distortion concerned the classical thinkers' situation in society and their literary treatment of political and social inequality. The East Germans maintained that the thinkers all kept up the good fight "against feudal societal order," as Ulbricht put it in 1960. Goethe, Schiller, and Herder, from whose surnames the "von" was expunged because it connoted ennoblement, were called revolutionaries, and as such true friends of the French Revolution. Limitations in their stance, as when Goethe appeared too elitist, were said to be due not to their own personalities, but to adverse circumstances determined by the times – the "German Misery," as Friedrich Engels had called them.[65]

This might have bothered those who knew better, members of the educated elite, intellectuals, and academic professionals. But they had been mollified. In fact, after 1958 the East German regime had every reason to concentrate on workers via its, officially named, "Bitterfeld Way," because by pronouncing its classics legacy early on, it had been catering to intellectuals, artists, and other members of the upper middle class to an all-too-visible degree, no matter how askew its interpretations. Intellectual overtures involving the classics had been necessary while the borders to the West were not yet sealed (as they were after August 1961) and when a Workers' and Peasants' State-in-the-making was risking the exodus of officially designated class enemies, whose skills were coveted by the West. But the fact was that Ulbricht was in dire need of this former upper class's educated experts himself, for the building of his polity. Therefore a tribute paid to the classics was – apart from Ulbricht's and Pieck's personal beliefs about culture, Marxism, and *Erbe* – a convenient, gratuitous, device for gaining credibility among the onetime elite. As well as what upper middle-class people were sure to appreciate as concessions by East Berlin in the cultural sphere, they were, well into the 1950s, also to benefit materially, through higher compensation, awards like the richly endowed Nationalpreis, as well as education, insurance, and pension benefits.[66]

In order to channel the energies of educated collaborators, the ruling Communists created a Deutscher Kulturbund, or Culture League, as early as June 1945.[67] Its president was Johannes R. Becher, a former Expressionist poet, colorful yet personally unstable, who had been born in 1891 in Munich as the son of a high-placed jurist. With his upper-class background, Becher understood the value of a cultured elite, and for the direction of the Kulturbund surrounded himself with well-known artists, writers, and scholars. To constituent meetings in June and July 1945, in as yet undivided Berlin, the philosopher Eduard Spranger was attracted, as were the theater critic Herbert Ihering, the professor of medicine Theodor Brugsch, and the physicist Robert Havemann. Gustav Dahrendorf was there for the SPD, and Ferdinand Friedensburg for the CDU. In addition, representatives of the two churches came. Actor Paul Wegener read a public oath, avowing that "we must bring back the spirit of Goethe. This is the task of the Culture League." Gerhart Hauptmann, after his compromise with the Nazi regime, accepted the honorary presidency.[68]

Much of the very early success of the Kulturbund hinged on Becher's charismatic personality, apart from the cravings of many East Germans, and some West Germans, for cultural nourishment. Becher had suicidal tendencies; at Easter in 1910 he had formed a suicide pact with a girl-friend, shot her and then himself, but he survived. Eventually he dropped out of medicine and philosophy studies and by 1919 had joined the Spartacus League and the KPD. Then he came to the attention of Bertolt Brecht and Thomas and Heinrich Mann and was materially supported, for some time, by Count Harry Kessler. In 1921 he had an acrimonious exchange with Adolf Bartels, who had accused him publicly of being a Jew. Becher wrote – and Bartels published this – that he was finally able to excrete that piece of feces named Adolf Bartels. After some hesitation, Becher came to adore Goethe, and as a Communist sitting in the Reichstag he was able to travel to the Soviet Union several times. It is probable that during the 1920s he had become a Stalinist, a stance he never surrendered, for after he had sought exile in Moscow in the early 1930s he was person-ally not touched by the purges, unlike so many other Germans. Back in Berlin in the summer of 1945 and thereafter, his personality was domi-nated by a mixture of self-doubt and self-grandeur. Several contemporaries have commented on his tendency to compare himself with Goethe, as had Bartels.[69]

Becher was heavily influenced by Georg Lukács, from a wealthy Jewish-Hungarian family, who also spent years of exile in Moscow, during the fascist Horthy years. Apart from Marx and Engels, Lukács had been under the sway of Max Weber, as well as the philosophers Heinrich Rickert and Georg Simmel, and during the 1919 Bolshevik Béla Kun regime in Budapest became a commissar who ordered the execution of several hostages. A polymath, Lukács concentrated on German literary criticism and, quite like Becher, came to idolize Goethe and especially his *Faust*. Goethe to him was a precursor of the French Revolutionaries. He completely subscribed to the Marxist *Erbe* theory, the legacy legend for German Communism and the Communist state-in-gestation and, directly or indirectly, supplied many ideological cues to Becher and his political friends. A dour Stalinist and Soviet-beholden till his fall in 1956, Lukács was as much opposed to modernist influences in art and literature as any hardliner and, looking backward, his special hatred was reserved for Nietzsche (whom he had worshiped in his youth), as a chief culprit in the rise of fascism. He took literally Goethe's dictum that the manifestations of Romanticism showed disease and drew immediate inferences for the current avant-garde.[70]

With chapters in each East German district and in all the towns, the Kulturbund, which possessed barely one hundred members at its inception, came to have 22,000 at the end of 1945, 90,000 in May 1947, and 45,000 in July 1956, with hundreds in the western zones, where, besides Berlin, it had branches in Frankfurt and Munich. Yet only a small minority of those were from the proletariat. The 1947 peak and subsequent decline can be explained in terms of the Cold War, which was then just commencing, as the established branches in the western sectors of Berlin were shut down by the Western Allies in November (and western Germans disabused). The Allies claimed – as the Americans in particular had been emphasizing from the beginning – that the Kulturbund was a propaganda instrument of the Soviets, although SMAD spokesmen always insisted that it was politically neutral. And whereas the Kulturbund organized art exhibitions, poetry readings, musical events, film screenings, and learned lectures that were appreciated in a German world still largely bereft of cultural offerings, it was clear that behind the scenes the Soviets were pulling the strings. For instance, they frequently saw to it that Russian content was included and exercised censorship at many levels. Their influence could also be discerned in the Kulturbund's publications, the journals *Aufbau* and *Sonntag*, and the books published by its Aufbau-Verlag. After the proclamation of the GDR in fall 1949 the Soviets' influence waned and East Germans were allowed to enter into more cultural-political ventures of their own. This was certainly true after 1954, when Becher himself had assumed the newly founded ministry of culture. However, no matter what the proceedings were and regardless of its membership, Goethe and the classics always remained the centerpiece of the Kulturbund's activities.[71]

From the beginning, a Goethe legacy was tempered by Soviet controls, many of which were exerted through the Kulturbund. This was notably the case when the Stalinist campaign against Formalism was launched in East Germany in the latter half of the 1940s. Anything in the arts and letters that was abstract was labeled Formalist; later Formalism, for these critics, segued into modernism. Georg Lukács preached that the wholesome simplicity of Goethe and the classics corresponded with currently valid Socialist Realism, and that the classics' antipathy to the Romanticism of the early nineteenth century matched the Communists' opposition to non-harmonic and anti-humanist abstracts. Lukács's acolyte Becher shared these views, and Becher's friend Professor Hans Mayer spread them early from his Leipzig chair in literary criticism.[72]

The East German anti-Formalism crusade got under way in earnest after Alexandr Dymshits had published an article attacking Picasso and Chagall, as well as leading German exponents of modernist art such as Karl Schmidt-Rottluff and Karl Hofer, in November 1948. In the same year

Becher and his friend Alexander Abusch publicly turned against decadence in literature. In 1950 Becher reinforced his demand that German writers heed the principles of Socialist Realism. One year later Formalists were accused of having caused "a break with the classic cultural heritage." Around that time, Munich's Carl Orff's 1949 oratorio *Antigonae*, performed in Dresden in 1950, as well as the East German Communist composer Paul Dessau's opera *Das Verhör des Lukullus* (1951) were singled out as formalistic. After the East German revolt of June 17, 1953, Becher became the first minister of culture in 1954, and interior controls relented somewhat. But in the main, anti-Formalist, anti-modern, anti-decadence, and anti-revisionist censorship continued, blessed, as alleged, by Goethe, if only vicariously. Implied in the censorious actions during this Cold War phase was an anti-American thrust, for the United States were said to be ruled by jazz, boogie-woogie, chewing gum, and other forms of decadence, to which in the 1960s rock music and jeans were added. The Hungarian Revolution (1956), the construction of the Berlin Wall (1961), and the defeat of the Prague Spring (1968) all strengthened the hardliners, so that the threat of anti-Formalist repression hung over every artist and intellectual virtually during the entire Ulbricht era until 1971. One of the last significant state actions under Ulbricht was SED Central Committee member Abusch's condemnation of Goethe's *Faust*, staged at the Deutsches Theater Berlin, as "anti-Faust," in 1968, because, in Abusch's judgment, "it was unfortunately missing a reflection of Goethe's humanism."[73]

Few independent minds could persevere under such scrutiny. The two strongest who managed not to get completely silenced were Hanns Eisler and Bertolt Brecht. Both experienced the wrath of the party hacks, but were sufficiently prominent to survive, if with bruises. Thus Eisler admitted to mental depression and creative inertia after he had been chastised, for having violated the classics *Erbe* code after authoring a *Johannes Faustus* libretto in 1952. It was intended for an eponymous opera he then never composed. In the opera, Faust was to appear not as the habitual all-round hero who would battle Engels's pervasive German Misery, but as a man who himself became part of that Misery. This was so because, according to Eisler, Faust, first an idealistic if unsteady humanist, during the sixteenth century turned against the peasants in the historic Peasants' War and betrayed them. However, as Hans Rudolf Vaget has pointed out, "the proponents of GDR orthodoxy stubbornly clung to the illusion of a progressive Faust." Hence Abusch's vehement reaction: "As a whole, his [Eisler's] work is thematically flawed and, beyond that, a mix of contradictory elements." Eisler's main mistake was that he had "trivialized, even ignored the spiritual and poetic importance of Goethe's work for German national literature and for the history of the German people."[74]

The comrade-in-arms who tried to defend Eisler was Bertolt Brecht, who had got to know the Schoenberg student well during their common wartime exile in California. Brecht himself was threatened during 1952 and 1953 after having staged a drama of his based on the *Urfaust* first in Potsdam, and then in the Deutsches Theater. Here he, too, demythologized the hero and made him look more like a villain, whose attitude to the innocent Margarethe, for instance, was nothing short of smutty. He saw Faust as a sly opportunist, "narrow, domineering, always ready for anything." The censor Johanna Rudolph, who, as a former piano teacher, was believed to be qualified for that role, found this eminently offensive, accusing Brecht in the SED organ *Neues Deutschland* of being cosmopolitan and formalistic.[75]

After Ulbricht's retirement in 1971 those strictures were loosened, because Honecker was not so obsessed with the classics. By his time in office, the GDR had justified its existence and was not dependent any more on Goethe for a *raison d'être*. What occurred was not exactly a paradigm change, because the *Erbe* theory was as valid as before, even though the GDR's Enforcer role was seen as weakened. Rather, that theory was modified, in the sense of being broadened into a canon that allowed for more discussion of Romanticism and, by extension, modernism in the arts and letters. Honecker himself sanctified the changes in a speech of December 1971, where he famously declared that "there can be no taboo for the arts, as long as the secure point of departure is Socialism." Such a revised attitude was called for all the more now as it was realized how sadly the Bitterfeld Way had failed: workers continued in their disregard of Goethe, instead preferring lighter fare, romance novels and tabloids such as *Deutsches Sportecho*, while the, comparatively few, intellectuals and artists kept themselves isolated in the arcana of learning and taste. In the final analysis, Marxism could no longer be accepted as having logically evolved from the Enlightenment, as the *Erbe* theory had taught; instead, there was a break between the two phenomena.

The greater value placed upon the Romantics at the expense of the classics was exemplified when in 1972 Ulrich Plenzdorf (b. 1934) published a novel in the journal *Sinn und Form*, co-founded by Becher, which later became a sensational success, when dramatized on stage. Named "The New Sufferings of Young W.," it told the story of Edgar Wibeau, who, having found part of Goethe's Werther novel in a damaged paperback, retreats to a garden shack, where he dictates his impressions of the strange book into a tape recorder (the name of Goethe is missing from the book and never occurs to him). Like the historic Werther, Wibeau is a thoroughly disillusioned young man, unrequited in love, but also failing in his workers' brigade at the plant. At the end of Plenzdorf's piece Wibeau dies, not by suicide but as the result of an explosion as he is trying to construct a new paint sprayer – because he wanted to excel on the assembly line.

This amounted to a criticism of the *Erbe* theory in several ways. Plenzdorf had returned to the young Goethe of *Sturm und Drang*, closer to Romanticism than to the classics, and the Wibeau of the play did not commit suicide but died as a result of errors in technology – an area the mature GDR thought it could pride itself on internationally. Wibeau had found the novel in an incomplete condition lacking Goethe's name – as if Goethe had been incomplete. All in all, a critique of the GDR and its teleologically evolving production system was implied, besides a parody of Goethe, scarcely fit to be of further use to the *Erbe* theorists.

In 1973 Brecht's Goethe-critical attitude of the 1950s was vindicated in an article by Werner Mittenzwei, a respected Germanist. Biographies of Romantic poets were published, not by state-salaried scholars but freelance writers: of Kleist by Christa Wolf and Anna Seghers, of Jean Paul by Günter de Bruyn, and of Hölderlin by Stephan Hermlin. As the avant-garde was more readily accepted, aberrations of Formalism were ignored and former taboos tolerated: rock music, jeans, and jazz, and long hair for young men. In the 1980s the GDR took in "rather more of its history," in the phrase of Harold James. Attention was drawn to Martin Luther, earlier a reactionary villain, even to Frederick the Great and Bismarck, as important national statesmen. This concentration on the past led to newer, major biographical treatments.

But the Old Guard had remained watchful. When in 1976 the satirical singer-songwriter Wolf Biermann was barred from returning to the GDR after a Cologne concert in November, it was clear that dissension would be punished. The former Stalinist (and co-founder of the Culture League) Robert Havemann, an ever more effective GDR critic, was progressively stripped of his offices. In the judgment of Konrad Jarausch, "party hard-liners suspected that 'the principle of socialist realism' was being challenged in formal and ideological ways." Whereas the *Erbe* theory was still alive, the question became increasingly whether the classics Enforcer of Ulbricht's and Becher's imagination was still there to do his job, or had already been excoriated.[76]

Weimar the Classics Enforcer

In the mid-1970s the GDR historian Edgar Hartwig, most certainly on higher orders, wrote that "the socialist revolution offered all working people the opportunity to appropriate the valuable treasures of mankind's culture." He continued, emphasizing that "the new relationship of the ruling working class to the cultural heritage manifested itself not only in the spiritual assumption of humanist ideas, but also in real humanism within socialist society." And: "The cultural achievements of this town more and more came to be valued as an expression of the politics of the worker and peasants' state." Hartwig's convoluted sentences were meant to signify that in many ways Weimar had assumed the role of the classics heritage Enforcer for the republic. But was it really so?[77]

Supported by the Soviets, the German Communist rulers lost no time in rebuilding the sites of the classics as best they could with their limited means, such as the Schiller and Goethe Houses, the Ilm park and the Herder Church, as early as 1945. Russian diplomats and the highest commanding officers made frequent visits to Weimar during that year, sometimes accompanied by Ulbricht, to pay their respect to the town's anointed geniuses.[78]

The Thuringian branch of the Kulturbund recognized the reconstruction of the town's cultural infrastructure as crucial. Beyond that, it mobilized local intellectuals, even if they had served the Nazis – for lack of qualified staff. To this group belonged the poet Heinrich Lilienfein and Professor Hans Wahl. Lilienfein had helped to build the Combat League for German Culture, signed a special letter of devotion to Hitler in 1933, and in 1944 was declared "irreplaceable" by the regime and therefore safe from the front. Hans Wahl had also been behind the KfdK, was an ex-Nazi Party member and personal tour guide for Hitler at the Goethe House. He had commissioned the construction of wooden crates by Buchenwald inmates. Now Wahl was asked to stay on as director of the classics sites. Nonetheless, as secretary, the Kulturbund installed a reliably anti-fascist journalist, Franz Hammer, in Nietzsche's deathbed room at the Silberblick villa, which Hammer immediately converted into a kitchen. Over time, a full cultural program was developed, meetings, concerts and congresses were arranged and the Goethe Society was revived. Until 1947, Theodor Plivier, author of the bestselling novel *Stalingrad* (1945), was president of the Kulturbund chapter, but because he was lazy and more interested in show than work, he was let go, whereupon he absconded to Switzerland. Parallel to Berlin central, the Kulturbund in Weimar grew, not least because it was less obviously political and because educated people, rather than dyed-in-the-wool Communists, saw it as a kind of refuge. In July 1946 it had 3,982 members; this grew to 14,000 by the end of 1947. In the 1950s the Culture League began to lose influence. But it remained important as an organizational agency and one of several agencies of censorship. As late as spring 1989 – months before the Berlin Wall came down – its Weimar mandate included cultural municipal affairs and it possessed the right to send delegates to executive councils of government, as did the SED.[79]

When Hans Wahl died in February 1949, he received a state funeral, yet he had done little, if anything, with Weimar's classical treasures. They were too dispersed, and he was never a Communist. His successor was Gerhard Scholz. For several reasons he, too, was unsuitable for implementing the *Erbe* theory. For one, though now an SED member, Scholz had never been a Communist, but in the 1920s had belonged to the left-Socialist SAP (Sozialistische Arbeiterpartei), which Willy Brandt also belonged to, and which caused both men to be in Swedish exile during the Nazi regime. Scholz, born in 1903 and with experience as a junior Gymnasium teacher, yet without a doctorate in his chosen field of German literature, was fascinated by Goethe, but the romantic young Goethe who had written *The Sorrows of Young Werther*. Although this ran counter to the catechism of Georg Lukács, which at the time was informing the canon of East Germany's classics legacy, Scholz was called to Weimar in 1949. In a style so typical of the GDR, he was handed a professor's title and proceeded to teach in Goethe seminars for a group of young sectarian followers, in the Villa Silberblick, from which Hammer and his cohorts had been removed. Scholz's followers would, nonetheless, form core cadres of the GDR's university Germanists in the 1950s and beyond. But around 1950, besides this esoteric teaching for which he had no mandate, Scholz did little in Weimar. He neglected the museums and forgot the mounds of unsorted papers in the Goethe and Schiller Archive. And it was no secret that he disliked Lukács. Clearly, Scholz could neither curate the shrines nor help develop the means by which Weimar would transform itself into the embodiment of the classics Enforcer.[80]

Pressure was applied to Scholz, so that he left Weimar in September 1953, to assume a chair at Berlin's Humboldt University. His successor was Helmut Holtzhauer, born in 1912. Like Scholz, not only did he lack a doctorate, but, a bookseller by trade, he had not even been to university. Subsequently being made a "doctor" and "professor," he became yet another beneficiary of GDR academic-title largesse. Yet his appointment was strategically significant, for he had previously headed an art commission, attached to the SED, which had been a major censor and driver against

Formalism. Holtzhauer, a staunch Stalinist and loyal to Lukács's tropes, was put in charge of the newly constituted NFG, or National Research and Memorial Sites of Classical German Literature in Weimar, as of February 1954. As they were being restored, these would eventually comprise thirty-two different objects, including castles, museums, and parks.[81]

Well into the 1960s, the NFG acted like a demonstrator for the classics, by organizing events mainly meant for workers – there is scant mention of peasants. Events were also designed to attract foreign visitors, preferably those from the West, for the sake of official GDR recognition, but those were few and far between. Mostly it was workers' brigades that were moved in by the busload, so they could be familiarized with the famous sites as well as with key writers of the past and present, such as Lessing, Goethe, Hauptmann, and Johannes R. Becher. As for the foreigners, between October 31 and November 4, 1960, a "Goethe-Colloquium" was held, "to crystallize the materialist and dialectic strands in Goethe's thought." Seventy-three guests arrived from Socialist countries with but one from the West. Still, over the years, more visitors came from countries such as Denmark, Italy, or the United Kingdom. As for the archives, constructive beginnings were under way to put them in order; from the difficult years of the Third Reich they had been left in a parlous state, and there was never enough money, nor were there sufficient experts, to do the work. Often the projects were extraneous and politically colored, as in 1963 when, for Ulbricht's seventieth birthday on June 30, appropriate citations had to be collected.

Nonetheless, visitors to the NFG continued to arrive – from 94,000 in 1951 to over half a million annually after 1960, almost all of them on officially sponsored group tours. (After 1975, in a more relaxed atmosphere, over one million a year came.) Workers and young members of the FDJ were supposed to be impressed with shows such as "The Workers' Movement and the Classics" (in 1964), or "Art of the Classics" (in 1974). But by the early 1970s the initial *Erbe* impetus had weakened, workers and youth groups somehow could not be interested in Goethe, and Western visitors found it difficult to travel on their own, because their currency was exchanged for East German marks at par and thus rendered practically worthless. Holtzhauer, the undying classicist, was against any modernizing trends, even in architecture or landscape, so that Weimar's sites remained unattractively presented for longer than necessary. At any rate, quick decisions on renovation, and the realization of bolder, newer, ideas were difficult to obtain, because the NFG became interdependent with no fewer than three Berlin agencies: the state secretariat of universities, the ministry of people's education, and Becher's own academy of the arts.[82]

Whereas Becher's Kulturbund had little to say in matters of the NFG, it was one of the pillars on which the revived, Weimar-based, Goethe-Gesellschaft rested. This society could do nothing for the GDR's classics legacy, but was useful to East Berlin, and to Weimar, in other ways.

During the Kulturbund's denouement, the Goethe Society was essential in continuing to attract the educated to the GDR. Because, in addition, a large minority of its membership always hailed from West Germany, it served as a platform for the Communist regime to sound out the political mood and politicians' intentions in the suspect West, at least during the long-lasting Cold War. On the other side, the West German members, most of whom, by background and temperament, resembled the Society's arch-conservative membership of the Weimar and Third Reich years, had the same Trojan-horse objective. Because in the first GDR phase the East Berlin government held up the official goal of reunification, the Goethe-Gesellschaft possessed political significance for it, as the Society could serve as an initial bridge between the two populations, once such a unifying process materialized. Its other use, for the East Germans, was to hurl invective against West Germany when called for, as in August 1960 in Weimar, when Bonn was well on its way with rearmament, being solidly tied into NATO, and scores of East Germans were leaving. At that time, Culture Secretary of State Abusch was clashing with Tübingen's pedagogy professor Andreas Flitner over the social utopia expressed in Goethe's *Wilhelm Meisters Wanderjahre*. By 1967, when it looked as if the GDR was accepting permanent separation from the FRG, thus propounding an official two-state theory, the Goethe Society was in danger of being destroyed by being cut in two, with West German members about to be left in the lurch and certainly without Weimar to convene in. But at the last minute Ulbricht, the Goethe sentimentalist, prevented this. He knew full well that ideological hardliners such as the literature scholar Wilhelm Girnus and censor Johanna Rudolph were on the Society's board and that, beyond that, the Society's membership was fortified by what was internally called the SED nucleus, to say nothing of the many secret-police moles. Holtzhauer, too, who was first a board member and then president from 1971 until his death in 1973, was considered a hardliner, but he was succeeded by his deputy Karl-Heinz Hahn, a moderate well liked by the West, who had also followed Holtzhauer as general director of the NFG. In all, as a token of international prestige, if not as a classics Enforcer, the Goethe-Gesellschaft was important to Weimar. Its membership, from the two Germanys and other countries as well, fluctuated between 4,000 at war's end to approximately 1,000 in 1958, and 5,000 in 1989. For its 71st general meeting in Weimar in May 1989, the Goethe town was host to 1,600 visitors.[83]

The most notable event in Weimar during the life of the Communist republic, cultural or otherwise, must be seen in the festivities for the Goethe Year 1949, at which Thomas Mann once more officiated. Like Goethe Society rituals, in the end these ceremonies had less to do with the enforcing theory than with demonstrating to the West a sense of moral and cultural superiority, at the threshold of the Soviet zone's statehood.[84] The Goethe Year, the bicentennial commemoration of Goethe's birth, was followed in 1955 by the Schiller Year, memorializing Schiller's death – less bold and of less propagandistic value, but also in the presence of Mann, just three weeks before his death. Everyone was surprised to see the novelist again, for when he had been invited for Herder celebrations in December 1953, he had declined for health reasons.

Weimar's Goethe festival began in March 1949 with speeches to the FDJ by Honecker, Mayer, and Grotewohl, who had led the East SPD into union with the East KPD in April 1946, to form the Socialist Unity Party (SED). None of the speeches were remarkable, although they all hitched themselves to the classics Enforcer theme in the manner of the great mentor Lukács. There were additional events for blue- and white-collar workers in June. The highlight of course was to be the visit by Thomas Mann, who then spent from July 31 to August 2 in Weimar, having arrived from Frankfurt. His speech there was repeated in Weimar on August 1, under the motto "I know no zones," thereby lending official credence to the Communist republic-to-be. Along with others, including Becher, Mann received a Goethe Prize, the money for which, 20,000 marks, he gifted toward the total reconstruction of the Herder Church. (He had donated a comparable sum from his Frankfurt prize to West German indigent writers.) Becher himself spoke on August 28, on the subject of "Goethe the Liberator." In inimitable Becher style, this turned out to be a self-serving affair, one during which the renegade Expressionist, according to one observer, appeared to repeat the phrase "I and Goethe" more than was necessary.[85]

In Weimar, Thomas Mann came across to most as aristocratic, secretly laughing, and unapproachably aloof. There were a number of issues surrounding his speech which even today throw an interesting light not only on the poet's Weimar hosts but also on Mann himself. Coming to Communist East Germany shortly after a visit in Frankfurt, and offering, word for word, the same address, may have sat ill with many East Germans and the accompanying Soviet military brass, and this made Mann palpably self-conscious. So much so that at one time he condescendingly assured his audience that Weimar was not really in the East, thereby implying that the whole of Eastern Europe, and certainly East Germany, was a social and cultural backwater. To dispel the appearance of collaborating with Communists, Mann wrote to a West European friend that, lo and behold, there were also non-Communists in Weimar's municipal council (meaning East CDU representatives, among others). Mann must have known that this council was deliberating whether to confer the town's honorary citizenship on him, something that he finally accepted. According to council minutes, one reason for its hesitation was a discussion by several deputies of whether Mann should have remained in Germany during Nazi rule, in order to help avert evil. This argument played on a theme Mann himself had been annoyingly familiar with ever since he had left Switzerland for the United States. The charge returned to haunt him, before and after his carefully mapped out visit to Germany in 1949. Two lesser West German writers in particular were applying pressure to Mann, one being Walter von Molo, who had accommodated himself to the Third Reich with difficulty, in relative isolation. He felt, as did Manfred Hausmann, that Mann should now return to the country of his birth, rather than resume residence near Zurich. Hausmann, like Molo, had made concessions to the National Socialists while they were in power, in his case by glorifying Hitler's Wehrmacht and publishing in Goebbels's broadsheet *Das Reich*. Now he was accusing Mann – against all truth – of having asked Interior Minister Wilhelm Frick to allow him back into Germany from Switzerland, in 1933. Yet another matter that irked many West Germans as well as a good number of Easterners was that Mann saw fit to ignore the evil the Communist regime had spawned since 1945. He was keeping silent about people disappearing from the streets, silent on the incipient campaign against Formalism, and was ignoring Sonderlager 2, while in Weimar he was hobnobbing with Red Army Colonel Tulpanov. Regarding the camp, Eugen Kogon had published an open letter in the July 29 issue of *Neue Zeitung*, stating that it was incumbent on Mann to raise flags of protest.

But why should Mann have meddled with that kind of politics, when it must have been his understanding that there were mostly Nazis in the camp? His priority was to assuage, not to incite. That was also the tenor of his address, which, in the opinion of Karl Robert Mandelkow, was not one of the poet's better speeches on Goethe, but instead, "rather more on the modest side."

Right through three-quarters of his talk, Mann explained his stature as an emigrant, defending himself against the charge of having forsaken his fatherland. At the same time, he tried to calm the East Germans' fear of foreign occupiers, reminding them that the Nazi "occupiers" had been worse. Such advice must have rung somewhat hollow in his audience's ears, once they reminded themselves that Mann had said the same in Frankfurt, about the Western Allies' armies stationed in West Germany – hardly an apt comparison! When Mann finally launched into Goethe lore, he dwelt mainly on *Faust*, with the quintessential message that "the good works" by Faust were really "of the Devil." For his Weimar listeners, what was that symbolic of?[86]

The Herder festival of December 1953 and the Schiller Year in April–May 1955 both were slanted more heavily than the Goethe events to service the *Erbe* ideology. During the Herder celebrations comments that Herder had made against a false cosmopolitanism, at this, the height of the anti-Formalist campaign, were turned into a historic battle against modernism. In 1955, Becher argued that Schiller's concept of freedom could now be applied against looming NATO threats. Schiller had stood for the idea of German national unity – just as GDR politicians now wanted reunification, on their terms. The misappropriation thesis also was applied, in that Becher accused the FRG of having adopted and misinterpreted Schiller's exhortation. And "decadent modernism" was condemned, against the backdrop of "real modernism," of the kind Schiller was alleged always to have championed.[87]

In his address, Otto Grotewohl too paid tribute to the *Erbe*. As part of the German Miseries – including the predominance of Prussia and an exploitative class system – Engels had deplored the history of Germany as a divided fatherland, and this had meant working towards "national unification." Schiller had been a critic of the feudal order, and added as his target "capitalism-in-the-making." Grotewohl even named the FRG's chancellor Konrad Adenauer, Defense Minister Theodor Blank, and the generals Adolf Heusinger and Wolf Graf von Baudissin as putative aggressors. Warmongers had no right to call on (and falsify) classical German thinkers because they were in the process of preparing for atomic war.[88]

To all this Professor Lukács from Budapest was listening; it was his last visit to Weimar before he was toppled by the Soviets during the abortive Hungarian revolution in the following year. No speech by him has survived for posterity and according to the records, none was delivered. Thomas Mann's address was perfunctorily on Schiller; the only concession he made to the politics of the day was that he expressed his personal desire for German unification, without, however, saying on whose terms.[89]

Mann might have been invited to a Nietzsche memorial, had the GDR leaders decided to honor that philosopher on the occasion of his death in Weimar, in 1900. For that, 1950 would have been a logical year, and they might have remembered Mann's earlier commitment to the Nietzsche Archive as well as his high opinion of the onetime classics professor. Indeed, in February 1925 Mann had written that he saw Nietzsche more and more "in the forefront with Goethe, as the prophet of the new and future humanity."[90] Be this as it may, closely following Lukács, German Communists regarded Nietzsche as anathema. His papers having been moved, under Soviet auspices, from the Villa Silberblick to the Goethe- und Schiller-Archiv, his sister's former home was utilized by the NFG in various ways. Although no East German was allowed near Nietzsche's correspondence or manuscripts, in the early 1960s two Italian scholars were granted permission to reedit some of his works – presumably, to show the attractiveness of Weimar to potential foreign visitors and help bring in hard currency. Those professors managed to produce some printed volumes, but they died during the GDR's lifespan. It was only during an ideological thaw in the very late Honecker era that voices were allowed to call for a renaissance of Nietzsche studies. Nevertheless, at the end of the Communist republic, no GDR citizen was able to look back on an indigenous Nietzsche tradition. After all, Nietzsche had been the one immutable negative in the classics legacy.[91]

Other Weimar Culture

If anything, Weimar defined itself through culture, even beyond the classics, and it was culture-loving officers of SMATh who urged and assisted in the remaking of Weimar's theater, the conservatory, and the architecture school. Not least, their goal was reeducation from fascism. With their help, the University of Jena became the first university in the Soviet zone to open its doors to students, on October 15, 1945.

As before, Weimar's DNT was host to drama and comedy productions, opera and concerts. For music, the chief conductor from 1945 to 1956 was Hermann Abendroth, whose appointment to Weimar flew in the face of official policy directed against former Nazis, who were all to be dismissed from public office. Apart from the NSDAP, Abendroth had been a member of Rosenberg's KfdK and the director of music education in Goebbels's Reich Music Chamber. He had conducted under the auspices of various Nazi agencies, including the pointedly anti-Semitic Reich Music Festival 1938 in Düsseldorf, initiated by Hans Severus Ziegler. It was a blow to

Weimar's reputation as a cultural center that Abendroth had arrived from Leipzig, demoted from his post at the renowned Gewandhaus orchestra by the Soviets, on account of his Nazi entanglements. Nonetheless, for Weimar Abendroth was now good enough. Never one of Germany's illustrious conductors, during his Weimar decade he would direct opera and concerts capably, if not brilliantly. The SED awarded him its Nationalpreis in 1952 and the Vaterländischer Verdienstorden (National Order of Merit) two years later.[92]

Abendroth's repertoire came to consist of well-tried classical and romantic fare – music that he knew. Hence in good time he easily complied with the anti-Formalist directives of the late 1940s and 1950s. There was plenty of Mozart and Beethoven, Verdi, Liszt, and Wagner. Absent during those orthodox years were exponents of the Second Viennese School led by Schoenberg, and Schoenberg's own student, GDR resident Hanns Eisler, still in the crucible. Among the well-known moderns, Russians like Prokofiev and Shostakovich were represented, as were the officially approved Paul Hindemith (with his neoclassical opera *Cardillac* of 1926) and Comrade Rudolf Wagner-Régeny – he too a former Nazi conformist.

Abendroth's politically pliant successor was Gerhard Pflüger, followed by a score of competent but never outstanding conductors, who likewise toed the party line in repertoire and style. The DNT, including symphony and opera, serviced more and more state-anchored youth groups and mass organizations such as the Communist trade union FDGB, inviting busloads of workers and peasants to its hallowed grounds. In 1958, the DNT's maximum capacity mark of 1,056 visitors per season had been reached. By the 1970s, after the Formalist debate had run most of its course, the repertory was loosened somewhat, allowing for more aesthetically risqué works such as Richard Strauss's opera *Salome* and the progressive West German Hans Werner Henze's compositions. In 1983 Weimar-born and educated conductor Peter Gülke left the GDR while on a tour of the FRG; he was good enough to become a professor in Basel. He had been blamed for the flight of some musicians to the FRG and been repeatedly interrogated by the Stasi. Apart from the secret police, his departure was a sad comment on the, overall pedestrian, quality of music in Communist Weimar; his memoirs serve as a testament of disillusionment.

What held true for music also applied to the spoken word on stage. With the anti-Formalist debate well on its way in 1950, the Stalinist Karl Kayser was appointed Intendant. In the words of one obedient historian, under this former trade unionist the DNT joined other "pioneers of Socialist cultural policy." Drama and comedy were even more amenable to the necessities of Socialist Realism in Weimar. True to the classics legacy, stagings of Goethe and Schiller plays were de rigueur, and here especially *Faust*: during the 1948–49 season alone, Goethe's masterpiece was performed forty-one times. Several other playwrights coopted were contemporary Soviet ones, such as Gorky, Alexandr Korneychuk, and Konstantin Simonov. But Brecht was performed only in 1958, two years after his death, as the covenant with Socialist Realism was sacrosanct. When a refurbished building for the DNT was opened in 1975, its chief dramaturg Sigrid Busch declared, in a programmatic yet monstrous sentence so typical of the GDR bureaucracy: "We continue learning how to fulfil the 'requirements of the day,' in realizing the dialectical union in our planning and the design of our repertoire: to bear witness, with works of the present and the classical heritage, how for the first time in history Socialist society creates the preconditions for a free, sovereign development of man and his capabilities." The results of such an ongoing ideology-driven policy were obvious throughout the entire course of the GDR, so that even in the mid-1960s a visiting West German man of letters could judge anything in the cultural sector of Weimar, measured by universal standards, as characterized by "much and often very honest striving, but little palpable success."[93]

The DNT regularly performed the compositions of two of its associates, Ottmar Gerster and Johann Cilenšek, both of whom taught full-time at the conservatory. They too were former Nazis who adapted themselves well to the new regime, both winning the coveted prizes. Gerster had composed a combat chorale for the Nazified German Christians to stanzas by Baldur von Schirach and, like Lilienfein, had been handpicked for Hitler's Wartime Indispensable list. Cilenšek was an ex-Nazi Party member. To the extent that especially Gerster had already worked for one totalitarian regime, he found it easy to accept commissions from the Communists. As conservatory director from 1948 to 1955, he wrote a "Cantata for Youth" in 1950, to be performed with the school's FDJ choir in state combines. Cilenšek, who was director from 1966 to 1972, excelled with chamber-music pieces, some of which were presented to the work brigades.

In 1987 Cilenšek composed a *Rondo Pensieroso* for accordion – a logical consequence of the folk-music teaching tradition that was established at the Weimar Conservatory in 1950, after the establishment of a special *Volksmusik* division. It featured instruction in mandolin, recorder, zither, and accordion, with the purpose of bringing folk music to the common people, in accordance with most orthodox SED directives. In the serious-music area, the repertoire was much like that for the DNT, with GDR creations and staples from socialist countries, in particular the Soviet Union, predominating. Increasingly more important than the music itself, right to the late 1980s, so it appears from the records, were Communist indoctrination and training, as well as inter-Socialist congresses. FDJ cadres heavily infiltrated the student body of the conservatory, now renamed "Franz Liszt," and the faculty was ruled by the SED. Hans Pischner, who taught harpsichord, put pressure on all students to join the Society for German–Soviet Friendship in the late 1940s, and Weimar delegations of instructors as well as students regularly visited other Eastern Bloc countries to compete in state-sponsored contests. Students were sent into factories to perform, and workers shoulder to shoulder with farmers were encouraged to apply for courses of study, not just in accordion or zither. These efforts were supplemented with courses in Marxism-Leninism and classes in the Russian language. Through all this, the quality of teaching and of learning clearly came to suffer, even in the eyes of ideologues, so that as early as the 1950s a theory conference was organized, "for the improvement of the academic niveau."[94]

After the war, the conservatory was reopened on May 25, 1946, and on August 24, the school of architecture welcomed its new students. For a few, potentially pioneering years, it would represent yet another chance for Weimar at artistic revival, spurred by a Bauhaus rebirth led by Hermann Henselmann.

Henselmann had been commissioned by the authorities in late July 1945, and after months of deliberation and planning, Weimar's new Hochschule für Baukunst und Bildende Künste (College of Architecture and the Visual Arts) – historically the successor to the Bauhaus – began teaching. Henselmann, born 1905, had been a student at Berlin's progressive Kunstgewerbeschule, an arts and crafts academy, always inspired by the principles of the Bauhaus. With a Jewish father, he had been endangered under the Nazi regime and been seconded to assist in the building of aircraft plants in Prague, when in spring 1945, as a convinced Communist, he joined the restructuring efforts in the Soviet zone. An admirer of Expressionist painters such as Dix and Kokoschka, and architects like Gropius and Le Corbusier, he was a mercurial figure, with a weakness for alcohol and women, as his long-suffering wife Irene, whose sister had married the increasingly dissenting physicist Robert Havemann, attests. While in the Goethe town, Henselmann eschewed dogmatism and censorship; he kept an open house with social *jours fixes* for faculty and students, reminiscent of the Bauhaus. For Weimar's art academy, Henselmann entertained plans for open concepts, discursive teaching including a *Vorkurs*, and a production-geared curriculum – all patterned on the Bauhaus. In his inauguration address in August 1946 he referred not only to Goethe, but also to van de Velde and Gropius, using them as contrasts to the Nazi architects Paul Schultze-Naumburg and Hermann Giesler.

In his hiring policy, Henselmann dismissed nineteen out of twenty-one faculty members, holdovers from the old establishment, most for political reasons. In their stead, he proceeded to contract former Bauhaus students such as Peter Keler, Hans Hoffmann-Lederer, and the surrealists Heinz Trökes and Mac Zimmermann, both of whom commuted to Weimar on a weekly basis from Berlin. Yet he also asked the traditionalists and staunch SED members Siegfried Tschierschky, a construction expert, and Fritz Dähn, a mural painter, who then lost no time in contributing to his demise. As it turned out, Henselmann was not a Socialist Realist, but a Socialist Romantic, who was trying to square the circle in his quest for progress and personal celebrity.

It fits this contradictory portrait that Henselmann was both a close friend of the modernist teachers he was hiring, on the one side, and Ulbricht, Grotewohl, his immediate boss Paul Wandel as well as Alexandr Dymshitz, on the other. Although his superiors had been advocates of certain Bauhaus ideas early on, given its quasi-Socialist pedigree, and Henselmann himself, as an upright Stalinist, was not unsympathetic to the rigorous tenets implied by anti-Formalist screeds, he was inexorably drawn into the vortex of two incompatible ideals. As Dymshitz embarked on his anti-modernist campaign ever more vigorously, eventually exorcizing Karl Hofer who had been the teacher of Hermann Kirchberger, a mural painter employed at the Weimar school, Henselmann was becoming increasingly uneasy. He felt that his financial means were being cut, bureaucratic red tape was put across his path, and approval for faculty hirings withheld. But rather than making a stand, which his enormous authority as an architect and his personal connections even then would have permitted him to do, he chose to acquiesce in Weimar's disadvantageous situation while seeking to accommodate himself. By 1947 talks were under way to lure his rare talents to Berlin, for greater things, in the eyes of the regime leadership. Henselmann left Weimar in the summer of 1949, soon to plan sections of the Stalin-Allee in that hideous neoclassicist style. His close friend Brecht enthused over the plan to create thousands of dwellings in Berlin, for the proletariat. Post-Weimar, Henselmann rose in stature to become the GDR's most famous architect.

His move away from Weimar prompted an exodus of architects and painters Henselmann had attracted. Trökes left, as did Zimmermann and Hoffmann-Lederer, by 1950–51 – all for West Germany. The most infamous case involved Kirchberger, whose "Formalist" mural in the DNT was painted over by order of Thuringia's culture minister Marie Torhorst, after acrimonious debate, centering on the alleged uselessness of that kind of art for the people. "The majority of workers as well as many intellectuals took the position that this painting does not meet the requirements of our time" – thus Torhorst's justification. Instead, Socialist Realism was upheld as dogma for decades to come, with the traditionalists Dähn and Tschierschky assuming leadership roles in the Hochschule. Predictably, they were succeeded by kindred spirits, at a time when the school had long been converted to an architecture and engineering center, with its newly founded art department – the one that Henselmann's followers had been attracted to – already closed in July 1951. The prerogatives of the GDR called for technicians, not artists for art's sake! As a by-product of such an attitude the carriers of official ideology, such as SED and FDJ, entered the institution housed in van de Velde's original building, and its educational path closely came to resemble that of the conservatory. Both schools were reduced to ciphers signifying mediocrity – the old, new, qualifying mark of this new Weimar. In the architecture school, references to Gropius and the Bauhaus were allowed again only after Honecker had embarked on a more pragmatic course, but by that time the gesture was devoid of meaning.[95]

Deconstructing the Old Regime

When East German citizens began to dismantle Communism in the late 1980s, they did not mean to destroy their state with the aim of joining the FRG. They wanted to reduce the current shape of Communist government to a humanized, livable form of socialism by stripping it of its originally Stalinist, totalitarian, attributes. They wanted enlarged personal rights, freedom of movement – including the freedom to travel abroad by the removal of the Berlin Wall, a multiplicity of political parties independent of the monopoly SED, free and general elections at every level, the freedom to congregate and demonstrate, an enhanced economy that would produce for them a greater variety of consumer goods, better efficiency and quality in goods and services (especially in the public health system), the return of private economic initiative, and, high on their list, the removal of the detested secret police, which, using everybody, was spying on everybody. Few wished for what thinking heads still regarded as repressive Western capitalism, and those who coveted it would eventually find a way to transfer to West Germany, even if it was a long and arduous path.[96]

In Weimar, as in most other municipalities of the GDR, long-festering discontent among youth and church parishioners came to a head early in the spring of 1989 on the occasion of the annual local elections. On May 7, new town council members were to be voted into office or, put more realistically, the candidates preordained by the SED (including some from the four ancillary parties) were to be rubber-stamped by an unfree electorate. Suspicious, critical Weimar burghers attempted to monitor the election process by checking the vote counts at the polls, particularly those in the booths at the town hall. But they were dissuaded by the incumbents, and a strong presence of Stasi and People's Police threatened them. When eventually the leaders of the dissidents received access to the election numbers, it turned out that 7 percent of total votes, which had been against regime candidates or been purposely voided through destruction, had been officially discounted. Even though the election had already been seen as rigged in other ways, this was a particularly blatant case of franchise fraud, in an atmosphere of abject popular distrust, signally exposing the sham democracy of the GDR. Anger over this scam would begin to motivate the oppositional actions of the months to come, well into 1990. And none of those actions were without risk to life and limb.[97]

In the weeks after the election, there was social and political disorder of various degrees in Weimar, culminating in a sense of dissolution after November, as the events in Berlin were reflected locally. On the one hand, Weimar's administration continued as before, with the CDU Lord Mayor, Professor Gerhard Baumgärtel, officiating. An architect from the building academy, he was the first who was forced to concede shortcomings in the construction industry, which had resulted in the protracted suffering of people without proper homes. Baumgärtel presided over other economic maladies symptomatic of the self-propelled failure of the republic during those months, for example inefficient meat production and consumer distribution. In Weimar, "the queues in front of the retail outlets speak a distinct language," observed Heinz Schmigalle, head of the meat division in the ELG, who was already taking a lead in Weimar's silent revolution and later refounded its SPD. Cash registers and scales were utterly archaic, the delivery fleet truncated, and the workforce of butchers reduced in size.

On the other hand, Weimar's clerics continued to lead protest groups, meeting with parishioners in three or four churches and in communal halls, once even in the DNT, always aware of Stasi spies in their midst. One such spy was Martin Kirchner, the legal councillor to Thuringia's Lutheran bishop Werner Leich in Erfurt, who on September 10 joined three pastors, among them Weimar-born Christine Lieberknecht, in authoring the so-called Weimar Letter. It was sent to the leaders of the SED-aligned CDU, asking for the resignation of their superior Gerald Götting, as well as internal reforms – Götting resigned on November 2. Lieberknecht serviced village parishes just north of Buchenwald; other Weimar area pastors placing their safety on the line were Edelbert Richter, Erich Kranz, and Christoph Victor.

A third contingent contributing to the aura of disquiet consisted of youths of the kind Holm Kirsten had spearheaded several years earlier. He himself was now still active, as was his father, the well-respected author Wulf Kirsten. As dissidents, they were constructive, as were Wulf Kirsten's protesting friends. Of a different ilk, if equally dissatisfied, were asocial, even criminal youths of skinhead appearance and neo-Nazi persuasion, whose presence in GDR society had been troubling the state security organs for years. Weimar being a long-suffering hotbed of youth turmoil, the rowdies could always serve as a pretext for the Stasi to employ heavier policing tactics. There was a Müller Gang, for instance, which terrorized soccer games (as such gangs would do in the West) and tried to inflict harm on the Buchenwald Memorial. These posses were not the offspring of a lumpenproletariat, but of well-off parents; they were not unemployed, but apprentices and students. Yet they chose to marginalize themselves by blaming the country's insufficiencies on foreigners in Weimar – Vietnamese and North Koreans, blacks from African Socialist states, Cubans, and even Soviets. On July 11 a group of Africans was cornered by the skinheads at Platz der Demokratie near the main castle and almost lynched.

All the while, Weimarers were leaving their town for the West in droves. The more affluent or those with foreign connections had removal vans come in from West Germany and, after finally having secured permission from the state, were loading their belongings on the trucks. Others could be seen, with baskets and suitcases and surrounded by their children, waiting at the station for the West-bound trains. After Hungary had fully opened its borders with Austria on September 11, many left for that country by car. In May Weimar's daily *Thüringische Landeszeitung* had already published instructions how to prepare oneself for vacation trips. Banking on the fragility of the Trabbis, the paper wrote that spark plugs should not be forgotten, nor should spare transmission belts, extra cables, and fuses.[98]

By October the brave and pace-setting Leipzig dissidents were demonstrating for the world to take note, carrying not torches but lit candles as a sign of non-violence, for some weeks. Weimar's dissidents emulated this on October 24, when a *Demo* was organized, more or less spontaneously, by the youth group close to Holm Kirsten, starting from Platz der Demokratie. Representatives from alternative political groupings such as Neues Forum, Demokratischer Aufbruch and soon the newly constituted SPD also participated. For several months, the Tuesday *Demos* became a Weimar tradition. They would stop at Vopo headquarters and were slowly winning over the regular police as allies. With the Stasi, negotiations were tougher. There was always a threat that Stasi members would tragically interfere; later it was learned that they had a hotel in the south of Weimar prepared for mass internees. At the same time, public dialogues were held with government politicians such as Baumgärtel, who nonetheless absented himself from Weimar's peaceful revolution by accepting the central construction ministry in East Berlin, on November 17. This brought charges that he wanted to shed responsibility for mismanagement in Weimar's past administrations. In public discussions, the topics were invariably similar: freedom for new political parties, freedom to travel, a stop to the punishments of students, environmental protection in a Weimar landscape gray under layers of pollution. Wulf Kirsten and Heinz Schmigalle were the most vocal protesters arguing for change. "It was an exciting time," remembers Holm Kirsten.[99]

The big change, which Germans called *Die Wende*, came on the day the Berlin Wall was broken through, November 9. Immediately, masses of East Berliners were in West Berlin, and in the coming weeks Weimar's citizens too traveled by train to Berlin or drove their Trabbis across the western borders into Hesse or Bavaria, being paid 100 DM per head from FRG jurisdictions as "welcoming money." Now a new notion took hold, beyond that of improving but nevertheless retaining a Socialist GDR. "The opening of the Wall," noted Neues Forum member Christoph Victor, "has given rise to the idea of reunification." This idea was becoming more popular with Weimar's population as the new year of 1990 began.

During December 1989 Weimar dissidents were able to dismantle Stasi headquarters on Cranachstrasse, but when they attempted to collect the paperwork to learn who had spied on whom, they found that all records had been destroyed. This mirrored the situation throughout the GDR at the time. However, seventy-four full-time spies could be identified, as well as four hundred unofficial collaborators, such as the church official Kirchner, who had staked out Weimar and its hinterland.[100]

Soon Stasi personnel changes became emblematic of one of the dire social problems plaguing the classics town: the imbalance between employed and unemployed. Increasingly, because of the dysfunctional economy and the resulting disruption of supplies and services, capable people who were gainfully employed had to be dismissed. A hundred workers were let go on the construction site of the new Interhotel on Belvederer Allee, for instance, a few yards down from van de Velde's original home, although on the whole construction workers were sorely needed. Up to a hundred Stasi officers joined this growing army of the unemployed, their chances of finding new jobs in West Germany nonexistent. Indeed, the FRG highlighted the other side of the problem, as hundreds of well-qualified workers now moved legally across the border to relocate for better-paid work. In Weimar's polyclinic system, twenty-two nurses had left by November, as well as three anesthetists – eighty workers in all. From Weimar's symphony orchestra after a tour, three musicians had remained in West Germany. And, as in earlier months, youths qualified to start as shop trainees were nowhere to be found. These cases complicated an overall situation that clearly displayed all the symptoms of a completely bankrupt GDR.[101]

The ongoing problem with right-wing youth compounded difficulties. In Weimar, radically indoctrinated skinheads as dissatisfied with the social and political situation as anyone who was peacefully demonstrating, continued to vent their anger with the state by blaming foreigners. In late January 1990 a young African was beaten after he had entered a bus with his Weimar area girlfriend. Some time later skinhead miscreants clobbered a bus driver after molesting his passengers. Well into spring and summer there were outbursts, repeatedly against young Vietnamese who were selling trinkets at the train station and whose women, under threat of deportation, were forbidden, by state law, to become pregnant.[102] Indeed, apart from the political uncertainty, demographic complications resulting from unemployment, the dearth of skilled workers, and radical youth unrest constituted issues that Weimar would have to come to grips with in the post-Wall era.

In recapitulating this more recent history, one can say that after 1945, with regard to Weimar, West Germany and East Germany followed different paths. Whereas West German contact with Weimar was sporadic, notwithstanding the occasional evocation of Goethe in the manner of Friedrich Meinecke, a succession of Soviet and East German regimes that ruled over Weimar utilized the town and most of what it stood for. Via the classics and especially Goethe, Weimar was subjectively revalued in the service of Communist ideology and politics. Such efforts were reinforced by the Soviets, who claimed that German classicism had been sanctioned by Marx, Engels, and Lenin and thought it could be part of an arsenal of ideological weaponry to eradicate fascism. Hence Weimar served in the construction of a creation myth. At the same time, the seeming simplicity of the classics was used to defeat what were seen as the evils of Formalism, or degenerate avant-garde modernity, around 1950. In this respect, the German Communists behaved like their precursors, the National Socialists, at the other end of the ideological spectrum.

To the extent that Nazism and Communism coincided, Weimar in Soviet-controlled Germany did share characteristics of the Hitler state. Buchenwald concentration camp, instead of being closed, was continued as an instrument of oppression against real and imagined enemies of the polity. It then served as a memorial site, servicing a broader legend monopolized by Communist martyrs, some of whom were reputed to have been virtual founders of the new Soviet-sponsored state. As a clear consequence of this, dissidents in Weimar were persecuted, as they had been under the Nazis. The secret police spied on every citizen, whose social and economic progress depended on toadying to the powers that be. There were few islands of resistance; among them were parts of the Lutheran Church.

In many ways Weimar served as a fount of ideological control over all GDR citizens through the activities of the Deutscher Kulturbund, which had been created early by relentless Stalinists with firm pro-classical beliefs. Those activities were supported by the GDR's first ruler Walter Ulbricht because of his own naïve love of Goethe and the classics. Nonetheless, after Ulbricht had been dismissed from office by Erich Honecker's clique in 1971, deferring to classical edifices became a new, entrenched way of life for Weimar. The NFG, parallel to Bitterfeld-conference schooling practices, was supposed to imbue workers, farmers, and sales clerks with classical ideas, with the aim of keeping them subdued, regime-reverent, and work-efficient. The revived Goethe Society, on the other hand, was meant to act as a liaison between East and West, exploiting the West's good faith in an attempt to eavesdrop on its political leaders. Altogether, the cultural niveau of Weimar from 1945 to 1990 was as low as ever, and economically it had sunk below the National Socialist standard. When demonstrators pleaded for political change after the spring of 1989, they did not do so because they wanted to resurrect Weimar as the center of German neoclassicism. They did it because they wanted to be free and enjoy a decent standard of living, more comparable to that in the West.

CHAPTER 10

Weimar after the Fall of the Berlin Wall
1990 to 2013

SHORTLY AFTER THE POLITICAL CHANGEOVER OF OCTOBER 1990, THE *Wende* which made Weimar a part of the Federal Republic of Germany, a group of West Germans are sizing up what appears to be the Hotel Elephant in Weimar's picturesque market square. The West Germans, now dubbed *Wessis* as opposed to East Germany's *Ossis*, are attempting to purchase it on the cheap. Their conversation with the comely young concierge is condescendingly cordial, and the young woman takes the banter with good humor. Certain of an easy conquest, the leader of the group, Herr Drepper, inquires about the former Walter Ulbricht Suite; a friend waves a Sony radio in the air with which he claims to find all the hidden bugs. The concierge only smiles and answers demurely, and it is clear that Drepper wants to buy her too. Eventually he invites her out to dinner.

The scene is not real; it is part of Rolf Hochhuth's play *Wessis in Weimar*, which caricatures the impudence of West Germans as they try to get the better of the, seemingly, naïve East Germans. Hochhuth captures the mood of despondency among many former GDR citizens, after their initial joy over liberation from corrupt Communist rule. He catches their silent resentment against the arrogance of the *Wessis* with their unabashed quest for unfair advantage. He alludes to an atmosphere heavy with ramifications of a principal divide between Eastern values, experiences, tastes, and styles, and Western ones, dominating developments for years after 1989.[1] And it is true: in moments of key decision-making a West German, more often than not, would win against an East German, beginning with the Chancellor in Bonn. West Germans claimed, successfully, that they knew what was best for the country and best for Weimar, meaning mostly themselves. This was not always for the bad, but all the same, Weimarers felt pushed back, insulted, alienated. As one Weimar newspaper put it in the early 1990s, there was bitterness that Westerners were "less interested in a lively culture than in available real estate."[2]

Interactions between Weimar's *Ossi* majority and the newly influential minority of *Wessis* occurred against the backdrop of a Red Army presence. Soviet soldiers continued to cohabit in the town and its environs, in formal isolation from the Germans, but still overshadowing their lives. A humiliating symbol of defeat, Soviet troops, massively stationed in outlying Bad Berka and Nohra, were increasingly unpopular in Weimar. They had ruined parts of the Ettersberg with heavy military gear, dropped scrap metal everywhere in the landscape, and devastated rural pathways with their tanks. Thousands of acres of arable land had been polluted with toxic waste. Officers living in Weimar left their garbage outside for pickup, but without the contractually mandated Soviet payments, collection never happened and the garbage festered. Nohra-stationed Mi-24 helicopters were annoying, given their low flights and unbearable noise. When in October 1990 a Soviet "Day of the Open Door" invited German visitors to the 8th Guards Regiment stationed around Weimar, few citizens showed up. Ceremonies at the military cemeteries decreased. In September 1991 Colonel Ildar Garipov surrendered the Ettersberg terrain to German authorities. Already during 1991, 40,000 of the 80,000 Soviet troops based in Thuringia were sent home. By February 1993 the rest had followed. The question now was what to do with the dilapidated living quarters of the army.[3]

Weimar Recaptures its Culture, 1990 to 1998

Thuringia was recreated as a state and incorporated in the Federal Republic by official contracts signed on October 3, 1990, along with four other East German states – former districts of the GDR. The new *Bundesland* was composed of the onetime GDR districts Erfurt, Gera, and Suhl, and at 10,048 square miles comprised less territory than before 1945. In area and with 2.6 million inhabitants, Thuringia turned out to be the smallest of the five new FRG states. Weimarers had been hoping to recover capital status for their town but, as under Communist rule, were to be disappointed, since Erfurt eventually continued in that role. This would create new dimensions of rivalry between Weimar and Erfurt – Weimar as the cultural and Erfurt the administrative hub, but with each wanting parts of the other. A Thuringian election on October 14 confirmed the East CDU (Christian Democratic Union) as the largest party. In the former GDR, the SED had transformed itself into an electable democratic party called PDS; SED satellite parties East CDU, LDPD, and NDPD merged with Western parties, the former tending to Chancellor Helmut Kohl's CDU and the latter two to the Free Democrats (FDP). The SPD was revived. Important smaller parties – born in the last months of the GDR – which had sparked the silent revolution of 1989, united to form Die Bunten or The Colored Ones, for they included the Greens. To it belonged the 1989 key democracy movers Neues Forum and Demokratie Jetzt, but as time would show, they came to have little influence and, unlike the PDS, hardly participated in government. Josef Duchac, an East CDU functionary from Gotha, who had been active in regional politics before the *Wende* and had acted as a plenipotentiary in the Erfurt assembly for the new Land-to-be, was confirmed by Bonn as the chief candidate and emerged as minister-president after having been authenticated by the new Landtag on November 8. As the CDU had failed to gain a majority, it entered into a coalition government with the FDP.[4]

From the beginning, the Thuringian administration was fraught with turmoil, which led to questionable government. It was haunted by vestiges of a Communist past, by inefficiency, graft, and corruption, all of which were compounded by differences in qualification and mentality between the home-grown politicians and newly brought-in Western ones. The latter usually prevailed, often smugly, and this caused anger among native government colleagues no less than the native population.

The first scandal sprang up around Minister-President Duchac himself. In 1991 it came to light that the fifty-three-year-old former Sudeten German, a chemical engineer, in his CDU post at Gotha had collaborated with the Stasi. Worse, loyal to the SED, he had worked against the pro-democracy movement of 1989, whereas now he claimed he had supported it. Duchac stubbornly kept denying the need to resign until in January 1992 he was replaced by Bernhard Vogel.[5]

Vogel was a seasoned politician from Rhineland-Palatinate, successor of Helmut Kohl as minister-president there from 1976 to 1988. Six years older than Duchac, he had a doctorate in political science and was a professional center-right politician. His tenure in Thuringia was soon criticized not for flaws or inability, but for his having been parachuted into Thuringia by the federal government without electoral process. He had yet to represent a Thuringian riding, and there had been no general election.[6] As undemocratic as the opposition, mainly the SPD, found this to be, it was soon obvious that Vogel, in what was discerned as typical *Wessi* style, macro-managed affairs sovereignly, while allowing favorites of his to micro-govern through his ministries as they saw fit. As long as these favorites, most of them transferred from the West, did not threaten his supremacy, seemingly anything they did was sanctioned at arm's length. This could lead to bad administrative moves, at a time when so many reforms were necessary. Evidence of this soon surfaced. Finance Minister Klaus Zeh was accused of somehow having doubled the pay of public servants. Interior Minister Willibald Böck was found to have taken at least 20,000 marks in bribes, and Social Affairs Minister Hans-Henning Axthelm, against regulations, had procured for himself a luxury government limousine. After backing these men unconditionally at first, Vogel dismissed Böck and Axthelm in the summer, whereas Zeh stubbornly stayed on.[7]

One of Vogel's cronies, who eventually became his heir apparent, was Dieter Althaus, born 1958, from the Catholic Eichsfeld enclave north of Erfurt. To Althaus was entrusted the culture ministry, a sensitive post in a federal state that was charged with guarding Weimar's cultural tradition. This math and physics teacher, of the East CDU, by some was regarded as not beyond suspicion concerning his public behavior toward the pre-1989 government. Nonetheless, he was accepted as a native Thuringian, albeit one too much under the sway of the invasive Vogel. Still, his indigenous Thuringian status did not help him in his deliberations with the main culture managers of Weimar over the years, who would all hail from West Germany.[8]

In the fall of 1993 Interior Minister Franz Schuster was discovered to have hired a West German specialist for the establishment of a security service, analogous to the federal Bundesverfassungsschutz. But the candidate turned out to be a felon – thus initiating a long series of malfunctions in Thuringia's Verfassungsschutz over the years.[9] The felon's successor, Helmut Roewer, again from Bonn, eventually neglected to order a proper watch over a trio of young neo-Nazis originally from Jena, who after going underground at the turn of the decade proceeded to murder a policewoman and nine foreign workers throughout the FRG. (After the suicide of two male suspects, the third, Beate Zschäpe, was put on trial for homicide in Munich, in early summer 2013.)[10] Schuster himself, another Western import, was charged with claiming too high a salary. And in early 1994 it turned out that two ministers who had resigned had allotted themselves unauthorized pensions. When Vogel was forced to comment on the Schuster case, he said that he would have the regulations changed, so that the minister could keep all overpayments legally.[11]

After a state election in October 1994 had produced a great coalition of the ruling CDU and the SPD, things got scarcely better. Thuringia was chronically out of money, and mishaps, such as the theft of classified computer hardware, continued to dog the government.[12] Vogel continued to be fond of appointing Western associates; his parliamentary speaker, Wolfgang Fiedler, had to resign in October 1996 after having visited a brothel in a state of drunkenness.[13] In 1998 Schuster's economics ministry was charged with a huge mismanagement of funds, and Interior Minister Richard Dewes of the SPD still owed his cabinet an explanation for the computer thefts. Cynical, it was Dewes who in May called the Erfurt coalition "a broken-down marriage."[14]

Good government would have been mandatory in the decade after 1989, when Thuringia, and with it Weimar, was suffering serious economic stress. It came in the aftermath of reunification and immediately produced disillusioning unemployment figures. Here West Germany was also affected, because it had to assume a large burden resulting from the political and economic changes. This happened contrary to Kohl's earlier promises that East Germans would prosper and West Germans would not bear the cost; his government had "soothingly promised that it could be costless to unite the country socially and economically," in the words of Charles S. Maier. This notwithstanding, West Germany's overall productivity was consistently higher, and its unemployment statistics were always more benign than those of the new eastern states.[15] Among those, Mecklenburg-Vorpommern or Sachsen-Anhalt usually fared worst, but Thuringia was often next. Whereas there was always an employment gap between the FRG and Thuringia, Weimar consistently lay somewhere in between. Thuringian Altenburg in the East was the most seriously affected, with Weimar's neighbor Jena, still thriving on its unique Zeiss optics works, the best performer. At Zeiss, Lothar Späth was based as general manager, a close friend of Vogel's as CDU minister-president of Baden-Württemberg, a position he had had to resign in 1991 because of suspicion of corruption. Sömmerda, however, a small town just a few miles northwest of Weimar and with high-technology industries on life support, was in constant distress.

Hence the unemployment rate in Thuringia jumped from 11 percent at the end of 1991 to 18 percent in early 1992, when the effects of restructuring were becoming palpable, and then remained near there for most of the 1990s. It was lower in 1989–92 because workers were still kept on in redundant jobs, as had been the practice in the GDR. At the start of the '90s, the FRG's jobless rate was under 10 percent; in 1996 it had moved slightly higher, with Weimar's being somewhere between Thuringia's and the FRG's, in December 1997, at 19 percent. The entire former GDR had jumped from 2.7 percent unemployment to over 15 by 1992, staying there till the mid-1990s. Sömmerda, however, regularly showed values as high as 18.8 percent (in July 1995), 24.4 (February 1996), and 15.7 (November 1998).[16] Those were crisis statistics.

One immediate reason for increasing joblessness was the sudden disappearance of the formerly reliable Eastern Bloc markets, since the Soviet Union and its satellites were themselves crumbling. The Soviet Union alone, as Gerhard A. Ritter has specified, had constituted "between 36 and 39 percent of the GDR's foreign trade, and almost half a million job sites were directly or indirectly reliant on this trade."[17] Thus in the early 1990s, the Weimar watch factory put hundreds of workers on notice, and the heavy-machinery manufacturer Weimar-Werk switched employees to short term. Both inevitably folded. The giant, formerly GDR-owned, retail and restaurant chain HO was being dissolved, with viable assets acquired by financially powerful West Germans and scores of Weimar workers marked for the dole. The public service, too, such as Weimar's municipal government with a surplus of 2,500 full-time workers, was letting people go in droves, for a town of Weimar's size "could not afford them."[18]

In Weimar, as in all of Thuringia and the former GDR, women were affected more acutely by unemployment than men. In Goethe's town in December 1991, 60 percent of all persons out of work were female; there were 66.5 percent two years later. If anything, the differential between women and men increased throughout the 1990s. The reason for this was that although women had been used to working in the GDR more than their counterparts in the FRG, they were never as well trained as men and now, the less skilled one was, the earlier one was fired. Provisions for children were also not as generous as they had been under Communism, so that more of the younger women with toddlers had to stay at home.[19]

Young people also suffered. In the early 1990s training positions in shops and factories for school leavers were scarce because of the decrease in production, and potential trainees left for West Germany. When more openings became available adolescents had already gotten used to the westward drift. Later in the 1990s, during months of apprenticeship shortages, primary-school-leaver boys and girls staying in Weimar displayed a tendency not to bother with training, instead joining the army of unskilled workers or taking low-level clerical or retail jobs. Others decided to remain in school in order to prepare for university.[20]

Socio-economic hardship caused by joblessness was compounded by a dreadful housing situation. In Weimar in 1990 many buildings stood empty in the town. The irony was that the 4,500 people looking for a decent place to live in late 1990 could not move into them because of the buildings' decrepit state. The town proceeded to spend more money reconstituting its inner core, renovating historic façades and propping up shops, than investing in the construction of new social housing. House owners who were sufficiently wealthy to renovate their homes and create more apartments for renters refrained from doing so because low rents were still frozen from GDR times – hence little could be earned – and the houses sometimes were beyond repair. In some cases also, where the state or Soviets had been owners, original ownership status was in dispute. In December 1992, 26,000 housing units were in use throughout Weimar, with another 8,600 needed. The return of close to 1,000 formerly Soviet-occupied dwellings helped after 1992, but throughout the 1990s, improvements were gradual. Typical of much poor housing were the conditions at Berliner Strasse 9, in the industrial section of Weimar-West, in April 1993: "desolate plumbing, low water pressure, a broken air vent, blind windows and shredded wallpaper in the staircase." In the Landfried tenements, north of the railway tracks and near the Soviet barracks, impecunious renters fearing burglars tied tin cans together and placed them at their front doors, as a makeshift alarm system. By mid-1994, 3,252 people were still without homes, but now recently deregulated rents had soared by a factor of 5. By the end of the 1990s low renters were beginning to be kicked out of their flats, as landlords were bent on home improvement and setting new, high, rates.[21]

For ordinary people in the 1990s, Weimar was not an attractive place to live: the town had 63,412 inhabitants in 1988, but only 58,826 at the end of 1992. Population growth was negative, with young persons and qualified workers of all ages moving to the West, especially from the health sector. Hence fewer children were being born, against the backdrop of a lower fertility rate in the entire former GDR. In Goethe's town, 779 people died in 1991, but only 398 were born. And as Weimar was losing what little industry it had acquired since the 1910s, it was taking in more older people from West Germany, reemphasizing its historic character as a pensioners' town. Clearly, however, the gentility of late nineteenth-century rentiers had not yet been recovered.[22]

New building construction in Weimar affected historic restorations, closely tied to the town's classical heritage, but also the erection of hotels to draw wealthy tourists from the West. After all, Weimar still defined itself chiefly through culture. It was important how the pillars of its cultural infrastructure were dealt with, after decades of Communist abuse, beginning with the national memorial sites (NFG).

Annually funded, as of 1996, with 13.4 million marks by Bonn and Erfurt, the NFG (reconstituted as Stiftung Weimarer Klassik in 1991 and, later, Klassik-Stiftung) embarked on what appeared priority projects such as restoring Ettersburg Castle to be used as a museum and intimate stage.[23] It patronized the revitalized Goethe-Gesellschaft, which, for its 74th annual meeting, anticipated a thousand guests from the world over in June of 1995.[24] It organized a Herder Memorial Year early in 1994, featuring symposiums, an exhibition, and concerts.[25]

But the Stiftung met with problems along the way. The Goethe House, also in line for major renovations, was on the verge of becoming the victim of its own success, because too many tourists were trudging through its hallowed spaces. When in 1994 700,000 visitors came to Weimar, almost all from West Germany, 300,000 of them shouldered their way through Goethe's house on the Frauenplan. In 1996, there were two million visitors. On a hot summer day 1,000 visitors would produce 2.11 US gallons of human-generated fluids in the Juno Room alone. Moreover, the wooden floors had to be replaced every eight weeks on average. It was therefore decided to allow no more than 800 visitors a day into the Goethe treasure, however badly this would cut back on needed revenue.[26]

Furthermore, as they were preparing an edition of Goethe's diaries unsullied by ideology, directors of the Goethe and Schiller Archive were appalled by the condition of many manuscripts, which after gross negligence by GDR archivists were disintegrating. More money than was available was immediately needed for repair work. Besides, Michael Prinz von Sachsen-Weimar, the grandson of Wilhelm Ernst and Feodora, was laying claim to all manuscripts, arguing that his ancestor, Grand Duchess Sophie, while generously allowing their use by scholars in 1885, had never renounced the family's property right to them. In byzantine fashion, the rights of up to half of all the archive's contents were contested by mid-1998, and the case was entering the courts.[27]

How difficult it was to institutionalize new, meaningful, events is shown by the Nietzsche example. Nietzsche studies had been revived with the reopening of the Nietzsche Archive as a memorial site and the curation of Nietzsche's writings in the Goethe and Schiller Archive in 1991–92. In November 1993 there was a symposium. But who was being invited and what was being discussed? When in October 1994 the extreme right-wing Berlin historian Ernst Nolte was called upon to deliver a paper, other Nietzsche scholars canceled and the classics foundation was forced to call off the entire conference. In 1997 an ex-GDR politician, who had condemned the philosopher under Communism, was scheduled to speak at the convention "Nietzsche within Marxism." Thereupon the respected philosophy professor Manfred Riedel, who had planned to read from his recently published book on Nietzsche, withdrew in protest. On the other hand, a proposed "Institute for Philosophy of the Present" at the Archive never materialized.[28]

The most valuable asset of the classics foundation was the Anna Amalia Library, which housed thousands of precious volumes, many from the duchess's own collection, in a beautiful rococo building. This complex near the market square was arguably the most attractive site in all of Weimar and traditionally drew many tourists. But, after decades of inattention, it was in terrible repair, and books as well as original scripts were in danger of spoilage. Critics such as the *Frankfurter Allgemeine*'s Thomas Steinfeld by 1997 were blaming local and regional politicians as well as Weimar's cultural-event managers for this. "It is one of the grave neglects of Weimar culture politics after 1990 not to have treated the Anna Amalia Library consistently as a research library," Steinfeld complained. "Weimar is home to testimonials of a culture whose gravitas and breadth have little to do with the dalliance that manifests itself throughout town in art festivals and professorial self-importance."[29]

Steinfeld was alluding to the cultural leadership in Weimar, which in recent years had been anything but solid. In terms of the culture foundation alone, what he meant can be demonstrated. The foundation's director since February 1990 was Lothar Ehrlich, born 1943, a Germanist and professor at Erfurt's teachers' college since 1980, who by March 1992 was made to resign as president of the new Stiftung. He was later found to have had Stasi connections, but at the time it was surely because an *Ossi* could not be tolerated in Weimar's defining, showcase, cultural institution. If truth be told, Ehrlich had been no more than a mere administrator of culture, not an innovator.[30] His successor was, predictably, a *Wessi*, the forty-seven-year-old Bernd Kauffmann, a culture broker from Hanover. Kauffmann was routinely versed in matters of culture *and* politics, but although he had dabbled in stage direction, he was by training a jurist and not a humanities scholar. He had not even earned a doctorate. In appearance he was lean and handsome, with long hair down to his shoulders, just like Liszt. *Der Spiegel* once described him as a man with a dandy's mask.[31] He was perhaps more of a manipulator than a curator of culture, and wedded to modernism. With his constant creation of idiosyncratic neologisms and never without his elegant cigarette holder and Italian pointed shoes, he was seen by Weimarers as exotic, more out for himself than having the interests of the classics town at heart. But those, in the Weimar of old, had often been identified with stodginess and inertia. Kauffmann, on the other hand, preferred a Weimar "that is not just taken seriously as a depository in the manner of a mausoleum."[32] And charge ahead he did. In his inauguration address as Stiftung president on July 7, 1992, he programmatically invoked the need of the foundation to restore, within its given possibilities, "something of Weimar's avant-garde function," alluding unmistakably to the legacies of van de Velde, Count Kessler, and Gropius.[33] As his first invention Kauffmann created a fellowship program for foreign scholars to study within the classics edifices of Weimar, but it was also on his watch – until April 1998 – that the shrines continued to crumble and Nietzsche events went awry.[34]

The German National Theater (DNT) of Goethe fame, Weimar's second cultural bastion, from the GDR era could only improve, now that Communist interferences were removed. The DNT was receiving 16 million marks per annum by 1993. But as far as its State Orchestra was concerned, even Weimar critics were never quite happy with its performances, what with featuring works by local composers such as Baldur Böhme, with Hans-Peter Frank conducting, in November 1997! Böhme's Third Violin Concerto Opus 87 suffered from a state of "internal fracture," carped Weimar's Hans-Jürgen Thiers.[35] A concert of music by Mozart, Strauss, and Ulrich Schultheiss with little-known soloists Jutta Zoff and Johannes Walther, under Heinz Finger's baton, in February 1991 was of mixed quality.[36] One month later violinist Antje Weithaas played Mozart's Violin Concerto in A major KV 219 technically correctly, but "bereft of all spirited imagination."[37] Ten months hence Peter Gülke's interpretation of Mahler's Fifth Symphony exhausted every detail of the work but remained without inspiration.[38] In December 1992 Bruckner's Eighth Symphony was rendered, under Hans Wallat, merely capably.[39] And in May 1995 the critics wrote of the mezzo-soprano Christine Hansmann and the guitarist Antje Stahl's "virtuous and homely" music-making.[40] Indeed, four months previously Klaus Bennert of *Süddeutsche Zeitung* had concluded that the Staatskapelle Weimar under Frank was "really quite respectable. The musicians from Weimar form a rather solid, sound-conscious ensemble, albeit not equally staffed in all sections. Strong quality differentials between excellent results and mediocrity characterize the brass section, above all."[41] This was killing with faint praise.

In opera in April 1991, Thiers found the Leipziger Uwe Wand's design of *Turandot* opulent in the appointments, but questionable in interpretation of details, especially when the musical score was shamefully disregarded. Singers Catherine Kelly and Klaus Gerber just passed muster.[42] Even less convincing were Reiner Goldberg and Michael Junge two months later, in *Tristan und Isolde*. Still, a new beginning had been made, and Valhalla was said to be expecting "its old gods."[43] *The Bartered Bride* in

September 1992, however, was again rated negative, and *Fiddler on the Roof* more than a year later, although a hit with the audience, also missed critical acclaim.[44] On the other hand, Alban Berg's *Wozzeck* of January 1996 found favor with *Süddeutsche Zeitung*, even though much of the staging's naturalism was simply thought "unnecessary."[45] Drama and comedy on the DNT's stage engendered equally mixed reviews.[46]

The DNT almost came to grief when in 1994 its East German director, Fritz Wendrich, was replaced by a West German, Günther Beelitz from Munich, who proceeded to change its ballet arrangement, letting all the current dancers go. They had been classically trained, whereas Beelitz preferred a modern and more variable, smaller, corps. Worse, toward the end of the decade, for the sake of cost-cutting, Thuringia's government was set to merge Weimar's theater with Erfurt's. To this Beelitz, even as he acknowledged the fiscal straits, vehemently objected. But overall he was unhappy with the existing Weimar facilities, because technically the DNT stage was becoming outdated and all its facilities were much too cramped. By summer 1998 Beelitz was in a clinch with the town council, which was contemplating his pre-contract dismissal. Beelitz also suffered a collision with the music director, and himself was looking at other job opportunities. But by autumn, miraculously, he had worked out a DNT survival plan.[47]

After 1989, Weimar's Liszt-Hochschule für Musik was on an arduous quest for profile, and the quality of its graduates did little to spread its reputation as a premier school. It entered the new era under a cloud of ideological suspicion, as Professor Diethelm Müller-Nilsson, its rector for many years, was internally pressured to resign over possible political compromises in the Communist past.[48] Evidently the West Germans did not find this institution of the greatest significance, for Müller-Nilsson's elected successor was an East German colleague, Wolfgang Marggraf, like his predecessor hardly distinguished. Wolfram Huschke, a Weimar politician as much as a musical pedagogue, succeeded him in 1993.

Both under Marggraf and Huschke the main issue for the college became how to stand out in an FRG topography of already world-renowned academies – now twenty-one, to be exact. An early motto that was proclaimed for Weimar was the "connection of theory and practice," but such was scarcely unique.[49] Not even in the former GDR was this college now preeminent, as could be gleaned from its budget: whereas Dresden's school received 100,000 marks a month, Weimar got the same amount *per year*. That meant leaving chairs unfilled and hiring fewer and fewer part-time teachers – hardly conducive to quality instruction. The school's existential doubts were galvanized into a crisis when it became apparent that students as well as teachers were staying away from its traditional International Music Seminar. This seminar had been a well-known institution in GDR times, when mostly Eastern Bloc students had frequented it annually for fourteen days in the summer. They had been sponsored by their home countries and been content with spartan room and board. After 1989, this type of student could no longer register because of the prohibitive currency exchange, and West German students saw no reason to visit Weimar in place of the more renowned academies in Cologne or Detmold. Significantly, guest instructors also canceled, being offered too little and fearing for their reputations. Stifled by impotence, Rector Huschke showed himself increasingly unrealistic. In terms of music education, he announced in June of 1993, he wanted Weimar to become "the Salzburg of the North," at the same time offering no solution for rejuvenating the Music Seminar. After 1993, this seminar slowly lost significance.[50]

The former attraction of the Music Seminar aside, the quality of Liszt Academy students remained unconvincing. Time and again when young artists were performing, they earned no plaudits, save, at best, vague patronizing advice from critics. Thus in November 1990 guitarist Ulrich Leopold and percussionist Heidi Leistner-Mayer, offering contemporary works, were said to manage only "edgeless, weak-breasted splashings," feeding into "boredom."[51] In February 1993 composition students Hubert Hoche and Gunnar Dietze were thought promising but – as a sarcastic phrase had if – fell short "where notes are obedient."[52] And Vivian Hanner, singing Brahms lieder in early 1995, was found technically wanting, lacking depth and breathing badly. "No master has yet fallen from the skies," comforted the music critic; after all, "the young singer has come to Weimar to study."[53]

More and more, after 1989, young West Germans came to Weimar to study, at what used to be the Bauhaus. The GDR's Hochschule für Architektur und Bauwesen (HAB) survived the *Wende* as purely the engineering and architecture school the Communists had shaped it to be in the late 1940s. Art had been excised. During the changeover in 1990–91, West German censors combed the curriculum for quality and ideology, deciding to preserve only the faculties of architecture and construction engineering. An examination of faculty, which would take years to arrive at realistic conclusions, was initiated. The HAB could have been closed down, but Hans-Ulrich Mönnig, its young, energetic rector since spring 1989, did everything to prevent that. Yet in the fall of 1991 controversy arose on account of Mönnig's own political past before and during the months of change. Some saw in him a stooge of the SED who had been appointed by the old regime to steer a course of stability, while he himself maintained that even if he had talked to the Stasi in uncertain times, his long-term goal had been a democratic reformation of the college. Early in 1992 Mönnig, who specialized in architecture for the tropics, was dismissed by the Erfurt government – presumably in yet another attempt to replace an *Ossi* with a *Wessi*. But after Mönnig had taken the HAB to court on a technicality, he had to be reinstated. Nonetheless, he took his leave a few months later, as his regular rector's term was ending.[54]

In this case the government allowed the college to deal with the appointment of a new rector from among the ranks of its own, East German, faculty, many of whom, however, were near retirement. It was fortuitous that in October 1992 they elected Gerd Zimmermann, a forty-five-year-old historian and theorist of architecture originally from Brandenburg. Zimmermann shrewdly realized that for the sake of survival, the HAB had to newly brand itself and adopt a mission. He, who had been an assistant professor during the regime change, worked hard to accomplish both. Zimmermann's dual tactic was to adopt part of the traditional Bauhaus's identity, and develop a vision for teaching and research in a Bauhaus mode. He was careful not to go too far too fast. In conformity with Bauhaus ideals he instituted a new faculty of design, incorporating art, and later one of media technology, which utilized computers. This was along the lines of the marriage between art and technology that Gropius had advocated. Zimmermann repeatedly said that while he rejected a complete reincarnation of the Bauhaus of old, he wished to emulate it in its fundamentals. In April 1996 Zimmermann had managed, against the resistance of older colleagues beholden to the past, to have the HAB renamed Bauhaus-Universität. Moreover, later in the summer he embarked on Bauhaus-like projects in architecture, such as modern settlements patterned after, and surrounding, Muche's Haus am Horn.[55]

A new Weimar cultural icon, if with a decidedly tragic connotation, was the Buchenwald Memorial. It was opposed to a Goethe legacy, to an extent no one could have imagined in the 1920s, before the National Socialists overran the town. But now it had to be accommodated in moral, aesthetic, and touristic terms, as 136,000 visitors came in 1992, 200,000 in 1994, and 400,000 in 1996 – many inspired by the film *Schindler's List*.[56]

After East German directors had failed by 1991 (one had worked closely with the Stasi), the West Germans felt justified in installing the young Hessian historian Thomas Hofmann at the helm. A historic commission was set up headed by the Stuttgart professor of contemporary history Eberhard Jäckel, a scholar beyond suspicion. Painstakingly, no East Germans were appointed to this body by the Thuringian government, which thought them all to be tainted. Hofmann and the commission soon had to contend with various Buchenwald victim groups, among whom the International Buchenwald Committee (IBKD) was the strongest. Its main spokesman was Emil Carlebach, from a Frankfurt Jewish family, who had become a Communist in the early 1930s, spent years in Nazi jails and in 1937 was cast into Buchenwald, where the Communist shadow leadership placed him in charge of the Jewish prisoners. After his liberation in April 1945, he was one of the founders of the international survivor lobby, which henceforth was dominated by Communists anchored in the GDR. Carlebach was a dour Stalinist who rejected any claims by other survivor groups, including those representing non-Communist Jews, religious factions, or Sinti and Roma. He was most opposed to the lobby formed by onetime inmates of Soviet Sonderlager 2. Hofmann claimed not only that the IBKD's influence was unduly powerful, but also that there were too many Communists on the staff of the Memorial, since it had been passed down to him from the GDR era virtually without transformation. Increasingly frustrated in his position, Hofmann resigned in March 1994. This was an unsettling time for the Memorial; not only had Hofmann the Erfurt ministry of culture against him that had appointed him, but also the historic Buchenwald commission and soon his successor, the forty-year-old historian Volkhard Knigge, who came from Essen. To this day Hofmann's position remains puzzling. For while he complained about GDR vestiges in the former camp, he was himself accused of not having got rid of ex-Communist associates among his staff of nearly fifty, including his deputy, a woman who once collaborated closely with the SED.[57]

Be this as it may, the Memorial continued to be rocked by indignities and scandals, although the monopolistic Carlebach was effectively discredited by the Erfurt ministry in July of 1994. The question of who could legitimately represent the tens of thousands of former inmates furthermore haunted the site. And although it served the important purpose of an exhibition venue, a meeting ground for youths in need of enlightenment, for victim groups to gather, or for Israeli visitors to engage in discourse with remorseful Germans, it also invited new agents of destruction.[58] Those were right-extremist skinheads and neo-Nazis who by 1994 were taking pleasure in defiling the site. Soon one embarrassing incident followed another. Their actions were facilitated by a disproportionately large presence of right-wing youths in Weimar, by a right-leaning regional police force that looked the other way, and by the comparatively light sentences meted out to culprits after conviction, if there were any at all. Not far from Weimar's center, in a chronically dilapidated section of town close to the

Goethe and Schiller Archive, those right-wing youths would do battle against anarchist-leftist youths, who occupied desolate buildings in the Gerberstrasse.[59]

A heritage foundation, a time-honored stage, a conservatory, an architectural academy, and a sombre memorial of international significance – after 1989 influential West Germans had made sure they became stakeholders in most of Weimar's cultural *richesse*. But Weimar was the town of Goethe and Schiller, national heroes, and should be brought back to life as a symbol of national unity defined by culture in a more authoritative manner, one where the government's hand was clearly visible. A cultural symbol of reunification! Hence Walter Priesnitz, state secretary in Bonn's ministry of inner–German relations, in early 1990 came up with the idea of an art festival, or Kunstfest, to be established and financed by Bonn. Chancellor Helmut Kohl could forever demonstrate his presence in Weimar by initiating this, and West Germans could demonstrate superiority over *Ossis*. Priesnitz was stoutly CDU from his student days; he was a veteran of ex-Alfred Rosenberg associate Theodor Oberländer's refugees' ministry under Adenauer. An equally reliable CDU member was his boss the minister, Kohl's long-standing confidante Dorothee Wilms. The Kunstfest was to be a monument to Kohl's statesmanship; it was thought ideal to fit into the "blooming landscapes" the chancellor conjured up for Germany's East in July 1990.[60] Alas, in Bonn by October 1998 Kohl's cabinet would be replaced by the SPD–Green coalition under Gerhard Schröder. The new chancellor was less keen on the Kunstfest. By that time, however, West Germans had a secure foothold in Weimar, the Kunstfest was firmly based for better or for worse, and in Thuringia, the Christian Democrats were deeply entrenched.

The organizer of the festival was to be Kari Kahl-Wolfsjäger, a Norwegian-born journalist raised in England, with iron-clad ties to Bonn. A board of trustees would include her and Johannes Gross, a reactionary publicist of darkish reputation, along with conservative Joachim C. Fest, the noted Hitler biographer and co-publisher of the traditionalist establishment daily, *Frankfurter Allgemeine Zeitung*.

Kahl-Wolfsjäger's credentials were a doctorate and five years of experience in having organized a summer music festival in the Bavarian spa of Kissingen, a town much smaller than Weimar and innocent of culture. With Bonn forwarding the funds, Kahl-Wolfsjäger grandly called herself Intendantin and planned the first Weimar Kunstfest still within GDR jurisdiction, for July 1990. Since there was a sense of urgency, things had to get moving. She utilized her existing connections, mainly to musicians, to patch together four weeks of highbrow entertainment, all in a traditional mold and safely revolving around Goethe, Schiller, J. S. Bach, and Liszt. Weimar or other GDR artists were not invited.[61]

The first festival, with Minister Wilms as patron, lasted from July 16 to August 12. With the mere half-million marks that Bonn supplied and given the emergency preparation, Kahl-Wolfsjäger could not engage the cream of international artists. And hardly would she have been acquainted with them. By all accounts, next to Goethe's *Faust Part 1*, conventionally conceived and executed, the festival featured music by Schumann, Dvořák, Hugo Wolff, and Mendelssohn. The performers were as conservative as they were second-rate; the only artists of note were actor Will Quadflieg, long past his prime, and the chamber ensemble Musica Antiqua of Cologne. Pianist Alexis Weissenburg neglected to show up, as did several other soloists, and pianist Peter Buchbinder from Vienna disappointed with too robust an approach to the keyboard. The logistics, as manifested in road signs and the program notes, were askew; events were listed for more than one location; no-shows were announced at the last minute. Worst, ticket prices were too high for most Weimar burghers to afford, and local artists were ignored. "No one took out time to ask questions. A 'Kunstfest Weimar' was assigned to the Goethe town," wrote Hamburg's *Die Zeit* sympathetically.[62]

For the second Kunstfest one year later, Bonn contributed 800,000 marks and a condescending opening speech by the new patron Rita Süssmuth, the CDU president of the Bundestag. This time events were being supported by the new Lord Mayor, Klaus Büttner, a former head of the CDU lawyers' association from Fulda, who had been catapulted into Weimar by Bonn, just in time to be of service. (On arrival, Büttner imme- diately took up residence in Belvedere Castle and locked onto the highest salary notch available to him.) Again a humdrum program was pursued, this time including a piano quartet from Weimar's conservatory which, like the visiting artists, was no more than respectable. The tenor Hans Peter Blochwitz appeared for a second time (and would again in 1992); he sat on the trustees' board. For lack of better connections, Kahl-Wolfsjäger had invited other artists for a second time as well. There was a repetition of the cancelations fiasco and of general confusion, and again music preponder- ated. Even with American cellist Yo Yo Ma as the star attraction, those forty events, as in the year before, failed to thrill; the program lacked distinction.[63] In a year of rising job losses, forty Weimar musicians wrote a letter, objecting to not having been employed. But since this went to Büttner, it got nowhere. Still, this time around Weimar notables took issue with Kahl-Wolfsjäger and the phalanx of West Germans backing her, and the local press teemed with resentment. There should be more program-ming of the avant-garde and, again, Weimarers must play an active role. In fact, specific Weimar themes – perhaps involving Count Kessler – should be considered, and the emphasis on music had to go.[64]

The third Kunstfest of summer 1992 was not significantly different from the two preceding ones. Even if variety and quality had improved marginally, the chief complaint remained that Weimarers were left out of an experience "superimposed" on their town by *Wessis* and touching only few of them.[65] Consequently, Weimar's town council, in conjunction with the Erfurt government, voted for change. By the end of 1992 it was decided that Bernd Kauffmann, the director of the classics foundation, should take over from the cloying Kahl-Wolfsjäger. From now on the Federal Republic would pay half the cost, with Thuringia and the Town of Weimar sharing the rest. Even though Weimar itself now had some say in the matter, 75 percent was controlled by a CDU de facto anchored in the West, and Kauffmann was yet another West German. But since for practical purposes the Stiftung had been made into the legal carrier of the Kunstfest, the whole event would gravitate more to the East.[66]

As it turned out, Kauffmann now found himself in his true element: art of the avant-garde. He duly shifted emphasis from music to stage and the conference hall and, supported by 1.8 million marks at first, proceeded to invite mostly internationally well-known artists. Those could be German, from other European countries, or from the remaining four continents. From 1993 to 1998, it is difficult to fault Kauffmann for lack of imagina-tion or taste; if anything, he was too esoteric. He also now included Weimar, even themes from the classics and culture, in many variations. If he took up risks and performances subsequently flopped, those were the dangers any modernist impresario would have to be prepared to incur.[67]

Early, in 1993, Kauffmann placed a huge black cube into the courtyard of the main castle with a makeshift stage; it housed an audience of 450. He opened the art festival that June with a ballet by the Lausanne Ballet Company of Maurice Béjart, of twenty-three dancers presenting *Faust Variations*. As an avant-garde piece, this might have served as Kauffmann's signature event, and it was a world premiere. The dancers hailed from nine countries and moved to the music of Bach, Schubert, Stockhausen, and Weimar's own Franz Liszt.[68] The following symposium on "Nationalism and Cosmopolitanism" with public intellectuals, some from outside Germany and aided by interpreters, including, for example, Karlsruhe philosopher Peter Sloterdijk, was a failure: "a lively, combative discourse remained absent."[69] Ödön von Horváth's *Tales from the Vienna Woods* was brilliantly insouciant: the protagonists "love, screw around, exchange obscenities, and copulate."[70] American post-bebop jazz musician Eddie Daniels, the reigning champion of the modern clarinet, performed and workshopped with pianist Chris Jarrett, the younger brother of Keith.[71] It was, however, a mark of second-best that Kauffmann failed to engage Keith Jarrett, then the uncrowned king of jazz piano and long feted in Europe. At the end of the summer's six weeks there was a cost overrun of 2.5 million marks, with the surplus assumed by Erfurt. Nonetheless, German newspapers praised Kauffmann for achieving a good mixture of tradition in art with modernism.[72]

Predictably high-class happenings filled the summers to follow. The Kunstfest was notoriously too long, however, and was costing more and more money, embarrassing a town that was chronically on the breadline.[73] There were daring modernist installations such as one by the T.S.-Eliot-inspired American director Robert Wilson, to the music of Philip Glass. Goethe, Faust, and even Herder were always, somehow, present, if rarely, for some reason, Schiller. An event with the controversial filmmaker Hans-Jürgen Syberberg featuring readings of Nietzsche's last, confusing Turin "madness letters" (one of which addressed his "mistress" Cosima Wagner) turned out ludicrous; a Herder symposium was too arcane to draw visitors; Hans-Magnus Enzensberger's screwball drama Down with Goethe was based on a "flat script."[74] Redeemingly, the Brazilian pianist Nelson Freire dazzled, the Palestinian-British violinist Yfrah Neaman shone, as did twelve cellists from the Berlin Philharmonic.[75] The intriguingly original South African Handspring Puppet Company came all the way from Johannesburg. Strindberg's drama Met vuur spelen (Playing with Fire) featured the beguiling French actress Emmanuelle Béart, and Bleiche Mutter, Zarte Schwester, an outdoor installation on the Ilm meadows near the Belvedere Castle featured celebrated actors Hanna Schygulla and Bruno Ganz.[76] In those six years, visitor numbers rose from 15,000 in 1993 to 33,000 in 1998.[77] The entire series, which had begun with forty events, finished with eighty-four in 1998, at a cost exceeding 3.7 million marks.

If the slate of programs was impressive, the chief flaws had remained, for while a few excellent Weimar artists such as the DNT's veteran actor Detlef Heintze had been used in productions to good effect, others, such as Hans-Peter Frank as conductor, had not worked out well. This was a trade-off Kauffmann knowingly had chanced: resorting to local potential would nurture patriotic sentiment but risk offending artistic sensibilities: there was no compromise. On the audience side a similar Faustian bargain had been struck, for if most Weimarers took pride in the festival, they themselves found the performances too abstract and, as ever, unaffordable. Hence the symbolic affronts: the black cube was damaged with acid, and Weimar burghers never were admitted to the trustees' board.[78]

Neither were they represented on the board for Weimar as European Culture Capital, even as preparations for it were in full swing. The history of this phenomenon reads much like the history of the Kunstfest. Like it, Weimar in the role of culture capital, on the occasion of Goethe's 250th birthday in 1999, was to be a catalyst in the process of successfully riveting the new German East to the old German West, with the Christian Democratic government in Bonn demonstrably the riveter. The idea had come from Dietmar Keller, culture minister of the GDR early in 1990, when it was already clear that the West would merge with the FRG. It was enthusiastically embraced in Bonn and passed to the conference of FRG culture ministers, which approved it. Klaus Büttner, the CDU Lord Mayor of Weimar, then charged ahead in 1992 in formulating an application for the European Community, hiring in 1992 without tenders the Fulda advertising firm Cre Art as adviser. Nuremberg and Cracow also were in the running, but Weimar appeared an early favorite for this latest in a succession of culture capitals, which had, since the inception of the series by Greece's Culture Minister Melina Mercouri in 1985, included Athens, Berlin, and Glasgow. Weimar was to be the first East German town so honored and, so far, the smallest. As the grandees of Bonn, Erfurt, and Weimar were expecting carloads of money for municipal reconstruction and cultural outfitting of the event, ordinary Weimarers remained remarkably cool. If they warmed to the prospect of money being offered for the city's infrastructure (and more jobs for themselves), they could not be lured by cultural events, which, as they were just witnessing in the case of the Kunstfest, would be abstract and elitist.[79]

Weimar was chosen by the European Union administration in Brussels early in November 1993. As many Weimarers celebrated, many more remained skeptical. Weimar's council, which was overseeing a debt of 20 million marks, relied on Walter Priesnitz's promise of money from the Federal Republic; he was now secretary of state in the key interior ministry. By mid-1995, a total of 48 million marks had been budgeted, to come from Bonn, Erfurt, and eventually Weimar itself. Later it was clear that 383 million marks had to be earmarked for Weimar's infrastructure alone, and by the end of 1998 close to 2 billion had actually been invested. Predictably, Weimar had benefited from a huge financial waterfall, far beyond comparison with any other small East German city in the throes of reconstruction, and far ahead of any West German one engaged in routine infrastructural improvement.[80]

Whereas town council and state government could implement the physical improvements, including those pending for monuments and cultural buildings, the question arose as to who would take charge of programmatic content. A separate board of trustees was staffed by outsiders such as former French culture minister Jack Lang and the Spanish Buchenwald survivor Jorge Semprún (a former minister of post-Franco-Spain), in addition to Minister-President Vogel and Kunstfest Intendant Kauffmann. A competition for director was announced, and 112 candidates applied. In what now seems like a calculated move, Kauffmann withheld his candidacy. He probably knew that because strings were being pulled in what was basically a CDU establishment, he would be chosen in the end; his previous job, after all, had been as a cultural administrator in the CDU government of Lower Saxony and as such, he had become Kunstfest director. Duly appointed in November 1995, Kauffmann finalized his contract with the Erfurt government only in April 1996, to his maximum advantage, although he acted as Interimsintendant in the meantime. By mid-1996 he was president of the classics foundation, Intendant of the Kunstfest, Intendant of "Kulturstadt 1999," as well as custodian-designate for Expo in Hanover, planned for 2000. For appearances' sake, he surrendered the foundation headship in April 1998 and announced that from Expo, he would merely collect expenses (whatever their size might be). It is significant that no Weimar newspaper commented on the behind-closed-doors appointment and that, as far as is known, none of the 112 unsuccessful competitors ever sued. Only Munich's *Süddeutsche Zeitung* raised the issue. But the Social Democrats' Edelbert Richter, one of the leading 1989 movers for a *Wende*, chastised Kauffmann for his "pretentious attitude," as *Der Spiegel* joined in to savage the culture broker.[81]

Although Kauffmann had been chosen as an obviously suitable front man for the Erfurt ruling clique, he soon had a falling-out with some of its leading members. Owing to his imperious ways but also to tardiness in planning, by May 1997 he had the powerful economics minister Franz Schuster against him. Schuster accused Kauffmann of inertia, and Kauffmann charged Schuster of tailoring the tourism business for 1999 to the needs of Thuringia, at the expense of all else. Kauffmann surrounded himself with a group of Weimar businessmen and went ahead with economic schemes of his own, thus incurring the wrath of Erfurt politicians. Trying to please everybody, the avuncular head of government Vogel sat on the fence for long, doing nothing. At the dawn of the festival, which was to coincide with the 1999 Kunstfest, millions of taxpayers' money had been wasted because of this lack of coordination, and more discord between Weimar and Erfurt had been sown.[82]

Discord also ensued between Kauffmann and Weimar's citizens over what many disapproved of as his avant-garde spleen. In particular, he had invited a French installation artist, Daniel Buren, to permanently anchor colored pylons in the Rollplatz, a less famous but still treasured Weimar hallmark next to St. Jacob's Church, where Goethe had been married. It was now being used as a parking place in a town increasingly overrun with tourists. Buren's plan would have changed this historic square forever, and especially citizens living in adjoining houses were enraged. No local argument could sway Kauffmann. In the end, the issue was put to a council vote and soundly defeated. For Kauffmann, it portended worse things to come.[83]

Weimar, Culture Capital of Europe, 1999 to 2003

Although Weimar was Europe's cultural capital only in the year 1999, it remained so in the town's corporate mentality for a number of years, for better or for worse. Kulturstadt functions began on February 20 and ended on November 9 – the day of the year when Hitler had staged his Munich Beer Hall putsch in 1923, the former occupying powers allowed both the FRG and GDR to join the United Nations in 1972, and the Berlin Wall came down in 1989.[84]

The events of the Culture Year coincided with those that would have constituted that year's Kunstfest, but were drawn out for much longer. Kulturjahr-Intendant Kauffmann applied the same artistic sensibilities he had demonstrated for years in the execution of the annual Kunstfeste, as those had, indeed, doubled as rehearsals. Again it was the avant-garde that reigned, and Kauffmann scored some notable successes. He acquired for loan a large collection of modern art owned by the Cologne gallerist Paul Maenz, including works by Rob Scholte, Sylvie Fleury, and John Armleder.[85] He engaged Daniel Barenboim, who put together an ensemble of young musicians from Israel and Arab Middle Eastern countries, Barenboim regretting that it was too small to play Wagner. Yo Yo Ma also came back in. The leitmotif here was Goethe's *West-Eastern Divan*. Weimar, according to *Welt am Sonntag*, paraphrasing the Israeli Barenboim, represented the worst and best of German history.[86] A Faust piece by the Brazilian Ismael Ivo's dance theater with Mephistopheles as the principal rated a good review.[87] Maurice Béjart returned to present *Don Quichotte* and *Che Guevara* in a "Balletical" premiere which gained him an ovation.[88] The expatriate South African jazz pianist Abdullah Ibrahim, a solo guest of the 1996

Kunstfest, revisited with a trio and excelled once more; but twenty violinists of the European Youth Orchestra backing him were thought unnecessary.[89] The British singer Marianne Faithfull, once the lover of Rolling Stone artists Mick Jagger and Keith Richards, was welcomed as the "icon of enlightened groupiedom," and for the local critic put in a tenuous performance.[90] Even less appealing was the Meryl Tankard Dance Theater with *Possessed*, which reminded the *Süddeutsche Zeitung* of "Riefenstahl aesthetics." And the Austrian actor Klaus Maria Brandauer's recitations from Goethe's *Egmont* were negatively credited with the "charm of the 1960s."[91] Altogether, and perhaps mercifully, there was less from the classics here than at any of the previous art festivals.

However, Kauffmann ran into serious trouble with a number of offerings on account both of organizational and artistic weaknesses. At the opening in February it was revealed that the Goethe Museum as part of the Goethe House complex, after renovations, would not be ready for visitors until the summer. Although the fault for this lay in negligence by the Erfurt government, it was now the Thuringian minister of culture who blamed the museum's director and, by extension, Kauffmann. This added to the list of complaints Erfurt was gathering against the Intendant and that would eventually spell his demise.[92] A more prosaic problem but of the largest symbolic significance raised itself during festival time, when Kauffmann forbade the hawking of Thuringian bratwurst near key cultural events, including those on the Ilm meadows. Although the famous regional specialty had never been sold there in the past, Weimarers maintained that if they were to enjoy the Kulturjahr in the way of a folk festival, as had been projected, bratwurst stands would have to be tolerated even in the Goethe Park. The controversy garnered headlines in the entire German press, pitting elitist *Wessi* against folksy *Ossi*.[93] But a veritable scandal arose when an exhibition of paintings from three historic eras caused Weimar citizens' blood to boil, because once again they felt themselves insulted by the West. Kauffmann's art experts, among them Bauhaus University historian of architecture Achim Preiss who originally came from the West, had set up a show of Nazi paintings from Hitler's personal collection at one level of the infamous, half-finished, Gauforum structure from the Third Reich. This may have been appropriate, but paintings by GDR artists were shown at a level immediately above that, badly hung and with hardly any space between them. There was gray shelving for background, looking like garbage, the lighting was dim, inscriptions were barely legible, and catalogue entries often false. The obvious intention was to discredit all East German art and, by its location and proximity to Nazi artifacts, define it clearly as realist *and* totalitarian. At this, not only Weimarers were incensed. Hundreds of visitors from East and West who penciled opinions into a comments book were predictably divided: on the whole, the Westerners liked this exhibition, while the Easterners from all over the former GDR acridly remarked that once again, the West was out to get them. Consequently, Kauffmann could not prevent many prominent East German artists who were represented, among them the prominent Willi Sitte, from offering protests, and several wanted to withdraw their works. However, because of legal contracts only one, Elena Olsen, in the end succeeded, after having sued in Jena's court on a technicality, but there was a disruptive ending when the show closed earlier than planned.[94]

For all practical purposes, the great event was over the day after Goethe's birthday on August 28. A huge outdoor celebration with plenty of bratwurst, beer, and wine satisfied the plebeian and the sophisticated among the Weimar revelers alike. Outside tourists, who had seen much art and frequented restaurants and hotels, also had helped in the ongoing commodification of Goethe and the classics. Thousands had purchased Goethe mugs, Goethe paperweights, Goethe lenses, Goethe-shaped chocolate, and even Goethe vibrators, which were tastelessly advertised in the local press.[95] Goethe had once again been used, and the town and the state of Thuringia money-wise had, temporarily, profited. Billions had been expended. But, as Roger Cohen from the *New York Times* remarked, "friction has also stirred between the 'Wessis' from the former West Germany who have dropped anchor here to direct many of the cultural events, and the 'Ossis' who feel resentment over what they call the 'Western conquistadors'."[96] Indeed, in the final analysis at least 7 million visitors had been received in Weimar. But at the end of the year, so it was discovered, the actual budget for cultural events was overdrawn by 12.7 million marks. Bernd Kauffmann had to take the blame.[97]

As far as his future in Weimar was concerned, this put the careerist's fate as much in doubt as the art festival itself. Kauffmann was in a bind. For that significant shortfall, he was taken to account both by the state government and the town; because he had been elitist and stand-offish, most Weimarers now loathed him. Objectively speaking, of course, despite some serious blunders as with Buren and the art exhibition, his avant-garde presentations had been as appealing as the ones he had staged within the regular Kunstfest formats before 1999, and once again Weimar had attracted international attention, even though the aesthetic cost had been too tight a concentration on dance and the political cost a passing-over of Weimar talent.[98]

Knowing that his value as a prop for West Germans had expired, because by now they had firmly established themselves and *Ossis* and *Wessis* were beginning to meld, Kauffmann tried to play his cards close to his chest, as was his wont. He claimed he had no Weimar obligations beyond 1999, although he could easily have assumed the directorship of the classics foundation after the May 2001 contract expiration and, had he apologized for his budget overdraft, would in all likelihood have been retained as Kunstfest director indefinitely, especially since the Weimar notables knew no one else of his caliber. To add to this complication, the new culture minister Dagmar Schipanski (after the Landtag elections of September 1999 had returned Vogel's CDU) was against him, favoring more conventional programming, and Weimar itself was too bankrupt to make financial overtures. In any case, by a new interim contract Kauffmann was obliged to organize the Kunstfeste until 2001; for 2000, he had to do this with 1.8 million marks, an amount he promptly (and justly) denounced as insufficient. Because preparations for that year's festival had started too late, it turned out to be a more mediocre affair, drawing merely 10,000 visitors. Something similar occurred in 2001, when 12,000 people arrived. The sheen was off Weimar's culture, so it seemed, and critic Thomas Steinfeld mourned that when all was said and done, Weimar had allowed itself to be turned into a circus, "which cost a lot of money, but after the gala performance of 1999 left only devastated grounds, on which no grass will grow for years to come."[99]

On August 31, 2001, Kauffmann resigned his last position in Weimar, as Kunstfest president, preparing to depart for Berlin, where a similar but much more lucrative job – creating an arts foundation for a bank cartel – awaited him. Weimar carried on with interim celebrations for 2002 and 2003, as the future of the Kunstfest was in the balance. But having learned their lessons, in hiring a new director the culture bosses embarked on a proper competition, and in July of 2002 Nike Wagner, the leading candidate, met with the Lord Mayor. After having spelled out her conditions of 1.15 million euros' financing for the festival and 95,000 euros in salary for herself (Kauffmann had received a mere 30,000 marks per annum), Wagner signed for two trial summers in January 2003.[100]

In the person of Nike Wagner, yet another star seemed to be approaching Weimar, after a void of many decades. A descendant of Liszt and Wagner and the daughter of the controversial yet brilliant Wieland Wagner of Bayreuth, the fifty-seven-year-old theater and literature scholar was freelancing out of Vienna, while married to a Swiss musicologist based in Salzburg. She was polyglot and cosmopolitan, having studied in Vienna and Paris, and had a doctorate on Karl Kraus from Northwestern University near Chicago. She was known as the author of several articles and books, one on the Wagner clan, in which she displayed insight, wit, and refreshing self-irony. Conscious of her lineage, she showed the same intellectual passion for the abstract as had Kauffmann, but without affectations and much more down to earth. Even though in some ways she came across as arrogant, she liked to emphasize that she considered herself "merely as a small offspring" of the mighty Richard. The Weimar culture mavens liked her and could immediately sense that her own good feelings for the town were not feigned, as Kauffmann's had been, but genuinely derived from the respect she had for Liszt, whose biography was to become a leitmotif for future festivals. It also seemed that she had a feeling for the people, as indeed she had spent part of her life in nearby Franconian Bayreuth, a small town like Weimar, with deft and forthright burghers, whose dialect (not too dissimilar from Weimar's) she knew well. If there was a problem, it was that she was waiting for the directorship of the Bayreuth Festival, by the time her uncle Wolfgang died. Was this a risk the Weimar town council and Erfurt's government were willing to assume?[101]

When an interim Kunstfest director was sought for the post-2000 seasons, people in the know first thought of Stephan Märki.[102] Effective September 2000, he had become the successor to DNT intendant Günther Beelitz, who had left for Heidelberg. Märki, forty-four, was born in Berne; he was a former photographer, rally-car racer, and trained actor. He came from a theater in Potsdam whose direction he opposed, and before that had been active on the Munich scene. Märki was dedicated to the classics and wished to take the DNT away from its focus on ballet, to return it to the plays of Goethe and Schiller. Moreover, he agreed with the town leaders that Weimar's theater should remain in Weimar, a legacy of the Goethe years, rather than be fused with institutions in Erfurt. After all, the DNT had three times as many visitors per annum as Weimar had inhabitants. And yet, since the Beelitz days, the Weimar-to-Erfurt transfer option was officially still on the state government's books, and the new culture minister Schipanski was an ardent advocate. Altogether, Märki wanted to restore the DNT as Weimar's own, to a first-rate standard, since several outside experts had recently been commenting on its striking mediocrity.[103]

For a start, Märki presented an intelligently crafted *Faust* performance, which in August 2001 received a coveted Bavarian state prize. Other offerings, however, for example Wedekind's *Lulu* and Brecht's *Baal*, in 2001 and 2002 respectively, did not fare so well with critics. They had been staged in a phase of theater personnel dismissals. Meanwhile, Erfurt kept pressing for the merger, as all Thuringian theaters were to be consolidated because of a chronic financial deficit. Nonetheless, Weimar's town council kept opposing this, until a municipal vote in February 2002 settled the issue, definitively in favor of independence. Märki had helped in the struggle, as he had devised a cost-cutting model preempting DNT strike action and freezing the annual budget, at least until 2008. Employees would hold the line on wage hikes and instead, become financial stakeholders. In revamping the DNT, it was said, Märki's reformation had been less of an artistic than an organizational one. All told, by the first decade of the twenty-first century Märki had positioned himself next to the Bauhaus University's Gerd Zimmermann and, soon to come, Nike Wagner, as a manager of culture with integrity and promising plans for the future.[104]

After Kauffmann had surrendered the classics foundation headship to interim president Jürgen Seifert in 1996, it should have been clear that a rigorous pursuit of Klassik-Stiftung matters would be slow in coming. Seifert was a mid-level culture administrator from Erfurt who did not have much clout and was due to be pensioned soon anyway. Hence any of the faults that had plagued the Stiftung in the past were continuing and, with time, would make its precious objects even less presentable. With official monies being scarce and budgeted for Kunstfest or Kulturjahr priorities, the Anna Amalia Library continued to succumb to moisture and mold, and its volumes further disintegrated. The roof of the Schiller House was still in a state of bad repair, and the complete publication of Nietzsche's works in new, unabridged editions, was as ever in doubt.[105]

Kauffmann returned briefly as classics president after his Kulturjahr stint, and after his resignation the forty-four-year-old Frankfurt lawyer Hellmut Seemann was hired in June of 2001. Along with law, he had inter-mittently studied German literature and philosophy, but had no advanced degrees and was not known as a scholar. Still, besides rhetorical skills he possessed a sharp eye and immediately realized the necessity of securing all the precious collections, pressing for more financing and especially urging the overdue restoration of the duchess's library. It was early on his watch that an understanding was reached between the Stiftung and the ducal family regarding ownership of the Goethe- und Schiller-Archiv records, resulting in no changes, but with the aristocrats being paid some ample compensation.[106]

One reason why Weimar's citizens, and indeed Thuringia's, were not fully enjoying the Kunstfest events of the 1990s was that they suffered disproportionately more than their Western cousins from unemployment and lower incomes. This condition continued perceptibly into the Kulturstadt phase from 1999 to 2003. On average between 1998 and 2003, Thuringia had one and a half times more unemployed per capita than the FRG; and with respect to individual incomes it was last among all federal states. If its standing in the unemployment ranking had improved (here it was now at the helm of the five new states), this was merely due to investment of millions of dollars until 2000 into the Weimar region, on account of the culture year. The indebtedness of private individuals and businesses was also much higher than in the West, and there was a noticeable rise in bankruptcies.[107]

Particular sore spots in the economy were in the construction industry, as Thuringia remained an under-industrialized region and no new factories of note were built, but also because creating new dwellings would only produce units nobody bought. Even though rent controls had been relieved, renters were not interested in newly built flats, as it was much cheaper to live in the old cement-block module housing of the GDR era, now becoming increasingly available. Next to construction firms, the public service was making workers redundant or not offering training spots for school-leavers.[108]

Among those out of work, females continued to suffer more than males, but the differential was dwindling, because women were adapting more rapidly.[109] Youths went on to join the unemployment queues, as more traditional shops were folding and apprenticeships in a trade became scarcer. But the more intelligent they were and more training they already had, the easier it was for them to move west, so that Thuringia (like all of the GDR) gradually became depleted of its young.[110] The westward drift remained a huge problem: the younger one was and more qualified, and preferably female (young women feared to get stuck in a marriage with an *Ossi*), the stronger was the West's allure. As before, certain sectors, such as health, were especially at risk. The fact that Western municipalities were paying a moving bonus caused much resentment in Thuringia. Neighboring Bavaria and Hesse, but also North Rhine-Westphalia were the main beneficiaries of these transfers.[111]

Apart from certain gender and generational cohorts, fate had singled out a few more occupational groups for special adversity, in Weimar as in all of Thuringia. One was composed of the pensioners, whose payments would lag behind the Western standard for years. Another were the teachers, who suffered doubly. First, thousands had to be let go after 1990, following long periods of tortuous investigation for SED or Stasi activism. Second, those who were allowed to stay received less salary than their Western colleagues (as did Jena and Bauhaus University professors), but some also had to be dismissed or switch to part-time work because of a drastic drop in the birth rate shortly after the *Wende*. This made itself felt in primary, and eventually secondary schools, causing classes to dwindle in size. In the face of these crises, neither pensioners nor teachers found it easy to relocate in the West.[112]

Altogether, Thuringia received not nearly the investment from outside which it needed to reform itself, even counting the Kulturjahr funds. Promises made by Bonn were reneged on, such as building an extra track for a high-speed train from Nuremberg to Erfurt, the better for Bavarians to see Chancellor Kohl's new "blooming landscapes" and contribute to the tourism potential. Nor did Minister-President Vogel carry the load expected of him. In July 1999 Thuringian trade union leader Frank Spieth accused him of having promised 100,000 new jobs for the state in 1994. Instead, tens of thousands now were on the dole.[113]

Amid the green if not exactly blooming Thuringian landscape, and affected by most of its woes, Weimar was the only town in the former GDR that registered any net growth, but its population – 64,000 by 2002 – was becoming rapidly older. This suggests that the surplus was made up of pensioners from the West, who found it relatively cheap to reside there. Conversely, interviews recorded in Weimar's daily press over the years suggest that younger Weimar-born people had no use for the town, as it was regularly dead after 7.00 p.m. ("they're folding up the sidewalks"); that few under twenty-five were drawn to either Kunstfest or Kulturjahr events; that students of the new Bauhaus often preferred this university only because they could not get into a corresponding course, especially in architecture, in the West; and that older people moving to Weimar were intrigued by its patina of culture, even if they did not understand Goethe and had to live in one of the suburban, GDR-typical *Plattenbauten* – monotonous, prefabricated concrete high-rises without elevators. In Weimar, joblessness increased in comparison with that of Thuringia as a whole after 1999, no doubt because the Kulturjahr monies had been spent. Unemployment was at 15.5 percent in August 2001, 15.9 percent in August 2002, and 16.8 in December 2003. (The corresponding numbers for Thuringia were 14.9, 15.5, and 15.6.) Apart from its culture, Weimar had less industry than Jena and less administration than Erfurt, its more immediate, and considerably larger neighbors. A Fujitsu Siemens computer plant in nearby Sömmerda (heir to the dubious Robotron-Kombinat works) could employ a few hundred Weimarers who commuted there, with the future of that venture uncertain. The watch factory had shut down, and so had the wagon works of old, in the North, beyond the railroad tracks. Industrial branches affected by shortages in the market included construction and most trades, whose shops were poised to close, such as butchers', painters' and automobile repair. In 2000, one year after the massive culture displays, almost every fourth Weimarer, man, woman, or child was receiving emergency social aid. Weimar civic leaders kept hoping for tourism to resume after 1999, but there had been comparatively few hotels built in town for fear that they would have to be left empty after the 1999 climax. A glimmer of hope for the local economy was that in December 2002 planning got under way for a new shopping center to be drawn up at the site of the Nazis' Gauforum. A rudimentary structure was already standing; the infamous art exhibition had been held there. All that had to be done was to build it and fill it with restaurants and shops. It would be called Das Atrium.[114]

Wagner's Weimar, 2004 to 2013

Cultural developments, which once again defined Weimar after 1989, occurred in the shadow of a pronouncedly right-wing state government in Erfurt and often despite the inertia of a town council that after July 2006 had a Social Democrat as Lord Mayor. In elections of September 1999 Bernhard Vogel's CDU was returned as the ruling party, and the minister-president made his favorite, Dieter Althaus, CDU majority leader. Whereas Vogel's grand-seigneurial style of governance continued, he himself began to show less interest in Thuringia, gravitating more to Berlin, in support of Angela Merkel, who increasingly took charge of the federal CDU. Weimar's politicians had little reason to be happy with Erfurt, especially since Culture Minister Schipanski tended to be less than generous with funds, obviously comprehending little about culture. Besides, Dagmar Schipanski in those years was too interested in becoming federal president of Germany to care about her portfolio. In April 2001, six Weimar mid-level culture managers, frustrated beyond belief, were preparing to leave town.[115]

Meanwhile, the series of scandals in Erfurt had not let up. Interior Minister Christian Köckert had to resign in October 2002 because electronic data containing classified information once again went missing. Contemporaneously, Justice Minister Andreas Bickert withdrew at a point "when his affairs had been more or less forgotten." Vogel's cavalier handling of these issues prompted the Weimar press to comment on "the comfy blanket of non-transparency" in Thuringia – as always.[116]

In June 2003 Vogel decided he had had enough of provincial politics and in the interregnum after the Kulturjahr determined to resign his fief. This ushered in the era of Dieter Althaus, who was appointed head of government. At first this minister-president was very popular because he was the first native politician to head a cabinet and could turn on personal charm when necessary. But it soon became obvious that he was fond of making decisions all by himself, surrounded by his yes-men, and that he did nothing to reduce unemployment, for which he was duly blamed. Nonetheless, in the elections of June 2004 the CDU once again received an absolute majority, for which Althaus took the credit. And now it was Culture Minister Jens Goebel who continued Dagmar Schipanski's dreaded cutback policy. Althaus's first real crisis, which was typical of the far right-wing drift of Thuringia's Christian Democrats, arrived in May 2008 when Peter Krause, after Althaus's nomination, was to succeed the unpopular Goebel. It was discovered that Krause had previously worked with several right-extremist organizations and had been editor of *Junge Freiheit*, a weekly bordering on neo-Nazism. This augured badly for a state with a Buchenwald Memorial. Hence in the face of protests, Krause had to withdraw his candidacy, and this almost toppled Althaus.[117] He himself made bad headlines when the press repeated rumors of an affair he allegedly was having with a woman from his home district of Eichsfeld, and that she now was pregnant. The practicing Catholic, married with two children, denied this vehemently and quickly the gossip subsided. But in early January 2009 Althaus was involved in a ski accident in the Austrian Alps, which killed a Slovak mother in the prime of her life, with whom he had collided after violating a right of way. Not much later an Austrian court convicted him of a criminal offense. Although against all reason Althaus insisted even from his sickbed that he wished to carry on and, ostentatiously, the majority of his party, especially Vogel, backed him, the CDU lost the August 2009 Landtag elections. In September, a coalition government was formed with the SPD under Christoph Matschie, who now became culture minister. The new minister-president was Christine Lieberknecht (CDU), the same who had co-authored the courageous "Weimar Letter" of defiance against the head of the East CDU in 1989. For the past twenty years, she had served in government as minister or caucus leader, and although, according to the newspapers, she had urged Krause to stand his ground when he had been pressed to resign, she had opposed an extension of the Duchac regime of the early 1990s, and recently that of Althaus. How would Thuringia fare under Lieberknecht?[118] By September 2013 state attorneys were investigating three ministers of her government for financial and other irregularities, including the minister-president herself.

The question has been raised whether such a government was efficient enough to direct Thuringia's economy in a period of prolonged trauma, including months of instability during the financial crisis of 2007–9.

Statistics show that the notoriously negative themes continued. In unemployment, the numbers for Thuringia were 17.1 percent in December 2004 (an increase of 1.5 percentage points from a year before), 17.9 percent in January 2006, and 10.7 in January 2010. Women still suffered disproportionately to men, and youths more than older cohorts. However, since Thuringia was not as strongly tied to foreign exports as were the states of West Germany such as Bavaria, the worldwide financial crisis did not hit it quite as severely. This is why joblessness figures held steady throughout the latter part of the first decade of the new century, and even decreased. Analogously, women's employment actually improved, and young people found jobs more easily. Youths were even needed in apprenticeships because the fertility plunge of the early 1990s made itself felt around 2006. On the other hand, the overall population of the state continued to decline, and was becoming older. For April 2004 it was observed that Thuringia suffered from "growing emigration, imminent senescence, and the lowest wages in Germany." By mid-2008, the economic crisis was beginning to reveal some of the structural weaknesses of all of East Germany versus the West: 30,000 jobs had been lost since 1990; East Germans still were earning considerably less; there were many more poor people per capita; and overall, the five new federal states were consuming more than they produced. Concerning all of this, Thuringia's ranking had improved within the former GDR, but still was far below the average for the FRG.[119]

Although its unemployment numbers were consistently higher than Thuringia's on the whole, maintaining an earlier unpleasant trend, Weimar's situation improved in other ways, as an after-effect, no doubt, of the monetary infusions of the 1990s and undiminished tourism. The latter was reinforced as Nike Wagner's Kunstfest was entrenching itself. Weimar's ever greater scourge was that it was losing mid-generation workers and in particular those who would run a mid-size business right in town. Because the municipal government had forbidden automobile traffic in the inner core for the sake of pedestrian mass tourism, Weimarers went shopping in Erfurt or Jena, leaving the town's commercial infrastructure to wither. Although now there were a few more industries such as Schering pharmaceuticals, Coca-Cola, and auto-parts manufacture, and the Atrium shopping center came to employ some 450 Weimar residents, earnings remained low as in all of eastern Germany, and hundreds of citizens commuted for work to outlying western states. Weimar's positive demographics could not conceal the irony that even though by the end of the first 2000 decade Weimar was now one of three Thuringian municipalities that was growing (from 64,500 in 2004 to 64,720 in 2008), it assumed an even sharper profile as a pensioners' retreat. Indeed, West Germany was spitting out its old people into the classics town, while sucking in Weimar's young.[120]

The dire economic straits caused authorities to announce a cut in their subsidies to the Buchenwald Memorial in October 1999, from 12 million marks to 6 million. This brought about an immediate threat by Volkhard Knigge to resign his directorship.[121] This affair represented only one of several dangers to the Memorial in the period after the Kulturjahr. Since having accepted a professorship at Jena, Knigge himself was spending fewer and fewer hours at the Ettersberg, leaving the everyday business of the Memorial to a less charismatic deputy.[122] It now fell to him to guarantee that Buchenwald remain immune to the struggle of the survivor interest lobbies still claiming exclusive rights to the site, among whom unreconstructed Communists and Jews once again predominated. Moreover, Buchenwald still attracted Holocaust deniers and violent skinheads who took pleasure in inflicting damage on concentration camp property or demonstrating near the crematorium with the Nazi salute. They militated as much against (imaginary) Jews as against visible minorities – asylum seekers from Africa and Asia.[123] And whereas Buchenwald served a salutary purpose when organizing exhibitions, readings, and conventions, as well as hosting VIPs like Chancellor Gerhard Schröder in April 2005 and President Barack Obama (whose great-uncle Charles Payne had helped liberate the camp) in June 2009, it also acquired, inexorably, the cachet of a tourist attraction and hence commercialization.[124] Thus, as it drew in an excess of 600,000 visitors in 2003, mostly from Western Europe, the United States, and Israel, it seemed like just another Nietzsche Archive or Goethe-Schiller monument, a natural accessory of picturesque Weimar to be checked off in the travel guide, beyond any moral judgments.[125] This was defusing the original warning by Richard Alewyn: "Between us and Weimar lies Buchenwald." The commercial-versus-moral risk was heightened by the insufficient alignment of the Memorial with events of the annual Kunstfeste, from the early 1990s, and the 1999 Kulturjahr. From February to August 1999, when Weimar was the Cultural Capital of Europe, only twelve in the hundreds of projects dealt with Buchenwald, although some of them were long-lasting installations.[126]

In the case of the Deutsches Nationaltheater, against the backdrop of fiscal strictures, parochial intrigues came into play that almost scuttled promising opera and theater. To be sure, during his rise to prominence in Weimar Generalintendant Stephan Märki proved controversial. In drama, with his penchant for works from the classics, he was known for an avant-garde touch, always with a sense of "overarching aesthetics." In Schiller's

Maria Stuart during the 2005 season, for instance, he presented a more skeletal version than the original, with condensed dialogue, to crystallize the "political instrumentalization of a personal conflict" – between Stuart and Queen Elizabeth. In Schiller's *The Robbers* Märki conjured images of a young Berlin woman who had been kidnapped to endure abuse and torture – in a bizarre, modern, reality show. The occasionally brutal scenes on the film screen shocked the audience and, worse, unsuspecting members of the theater corps, who submitted a formal protest for not having been informed beforehand. Märki later claimed, not very convincingly, that beforehand even he had not known the full extent of the abuse. But having been dealt a better hand in opera, Märki also was responsible for an expert *Tosca* and a very good *Ring* cycle, even if his presentation of GDR Siegfried Matthus's opera *The Infinite Story* was found less convincing by *Süddeutsche Zeitung*. Altogether, critics from a metropolis such as Hamburg thought the DNT was supporting a "solid local operation."[127]

Irrespective of his artistic merit, in the years since he was hired the Swiss Intendant almost fell victim to the local rivalry between Weimar and Erfurt, compounded by the personal preferences of individual politicians. The fact that the Thuringian government, for the third time since 1990, was attempting to fuse Weimar's theater with Erfurt's by 2007 indicated a fundamental jealousy by the reigning CDU politicians of Weimar's cultural legacy, tempered – only seemingly paradoxically – by a complete lack of understanding of things cultural. It was a variant of the old power play; the patterns of the past were repeated. In fifteen years of rule, the government should have got used to the special financial needs that Weimar had for its culture, whatever its distinction, and not have deprived it of necessary funds, as Minister of Culture Jens Goebel was again trying to do in the early 2000s. It was only after several high-profile artists of the DNT, including the Texan-born music director Carl St. Clair, had given notice and Märki himself was considering offers from Berlin and Munich that Minister-President Althaus made one of his spontaneous decisions in telling Goebel to switch course. This came about after Weimar citizens had, once again, collected over a thousand signatures in favor of what they considered to be *their* DNT.[128]

If Weimar's stage was saved for the time being, Märki's directorship had not yet been. He had spoken out against right-wing, aesthetically tradition-alist, Peter Krause who wanted to be culture minister, and he had antagon-ized officials in Erfurt's ministry with his criticism of their merger plan. "Revenge" against Märki, as Munich's main newspaper labeled it, was afoot after 2007. His contract was to run out with the 2008 season, and so machinations were set in motion to prevent its renewal. Forthwith the Erfurt ministry and Krause allied themselves with Weimar's Lord Mayor Stefan Wolf, a right-wing SPD man who happened to dislike Märki's artistry. Wolf was manipulating economics by claiming that Märki's "Weimar Model" had not saved the funds it had purported to save, quite apart from the truism that after ten years, it was time for a change. (The fiscal argument was groundless, for in this regard the DNT was ahead of comparable German theaters, such as Darmstadt's and Kassel's.) In 2007 Weimar's town council, under the influence of Wolf and the new member Krause, used a legislative prerogative to block the continuation of Märki's contract. The German press was aghast, the *Berliner Zeitung* finding this "bare of any respect as well as stupid." And indeed, immediate protests from the DNT's employees and Weimar's population alike forced a reversal of that process, so that Märki was free to stay till 2015.[129]

The president of the classics foundation was facing similar opposition from politicians and culture brokers, but over different issues, some raising the question of competence, which never had concerned Märki. After having been appointed in the summer of 2001, Hellmut Seemann proceeded to administer an organization that had not borne the consequences of visionary change from 1990 to 2001, least of all under the indifferent Bernd Kauffmann. Antiquated structures from GDR times had ossified, artifacts and inventory had decayed, no new projects had been put in place. In the first few years in his new office Seemann presided over the temporary closing of seven of Weimar's eighteen museum and memorial institutions, including the Liszt House, as well as a massive evaporation of funds. Exhibition sites were suffering because there was no air conditioning (hence foreign galleries would not lend paintings), Nietzsche seminars were floundering, and there was a surplus of politically unscreened founda- tion employees with nothing meaningful to do. Gallerist Paul Maenz was threatening to withdraw his collection of modern works, because he felt it was mismanaged and complained that Seemann habitually ignored his mail. By autumn 2005 Maenz had removed his treasures. For July 2004 an external commission was appointed to look into the situation of the Klassik-Stiftung. It was headed by Klaus-Dieter Lehmann, the president of Stiftung Preussischer Kulturbesitz (Prussian Cultural Legacy) in Berlin, Germany's largest cultural foundation before Weimar's. Its findings were devastating. Against the background of a catastrophic reduction in visitor numbers after 1999 it noted individual errors such as insufficient computer usage, a lack of orientation after the foundation's fusion with Weimar's various art collections, and questionable uses of funds. In general terms, Seemann was described as being devoid of abstract conceptualization and lacking a sense of direction. After analyzing the report, *Süddeutsche Zeitung*'s Jens Bisky remarked that the Klassik-Stiftung was ruled by a "combination of provincial stubbornness, scholarly naïveté and general cluelessness."[130]

Surprisingly, Seemann accepted the verdict with equanimity, but not without reminding his critics that nominally, he was responsible for only one year of alleged mismanagement since 1990. At the same time he promised to implement whatever detailed recommendations would be forthcoming in the summer of 2005. On all fronts, Seemann had his work cut out for him. He was challenged anew in September 2004 when the precious Anna Amalia Library partially burned down, a disaster many Weimarers had been expecting for some time. This was the logical result of past neglect – as the famous rococo upper storey was destroyed along with 50,000 books and 37 oil paintings, and 62,000 volumes were damaged. Nonetheless, the fact that Seemann, supported by millions of extra euros, was able to oversee the rebuilding and reopen the library almost filled with replacement books as early as September 2007 was a credit to his administrative expertise. Other things connected with this library which Seemann managed to accomplish, after new funds had been made available (from the FRG, Thuringia, and Weimar), were the construction of a subterranean book depository and, connected to it, a modern study center with truly stupendous facilities.[131]

But after 2004 there were other problems haunting Seemann, who, ever the administrator of tradition rather than innovator with a vision, still lacked a concept, for a town like Weimar. Even though money had been made available, the construction of a new and spacious Bauhaus museum to replace the cramped one opposite the theater could not be completed before 2010, as he had promised. Exhibitions that he organized, about Friedrich Schiller and Franz Liszt, experts found unfocussed and not worthy of Weimar's cultural legacy. When a Spanish art collector was bent on purchasing the Marstall building, Charlotte von Stein's onetime home and, subsequently, the headquarters of the Gestapo and NKVD, the Klassik-Stiftung at first gave signs that it was interested but then missed a legal deadline. As the owner, the Town of Weimar, notoriously in arrears, had no choice but to sell, and everyone blamed Seemann.[132]

The president's ten-year contract came up for renewal in 2010. Most Thuringian mandarins expected the jurist to be sacked in favor of a Germanist from Berlin's Humboldt University, after a slate of twenty-seven candidates had been reviewed. But Seemann had had the temerity to reapply, and after he and the Germanist had made the shortlist, the Berliner announced preconditions that were impossible to meet, virtually withdrawing his candidacy. Although Seemann by then had the new culture minister Christoph Matschie totally against him, in addition to a goodly number of town councillors and the majority of his supervisory board, he was reelected apparently by default, for another term of four years. Only in Weimar, detractors now were harping, could such a farce transpire.[133]

Franziska Gräfin zu Castell-Castell was in the Herder Church, listening to a cantata concert conducted by the American harpsichordist Joshua Rifkin, on September 2, 2004, when the big library fire broke out. The newly hired general manager of the Kunstfest and her boss, Nike Wagner, were irritated by police sirens disturbing the heavenly performance. They ran out into the nearby market square and, confronted by a wall of flames, shed tears of sorrow. Later that evening, organizers and artists huddled together in their usual haunt, the Osteria Bertagnolli near the Stein House, trying to make sense of it all. Rifkin later donated part of his fee to the reconstruction and held a special benefit concert.[134]

The fire might have come as a bad omen for Nike Wagner's art festival. After all, she had spent months preparing it and it had had a promising opening on August 20. Dedicated to her great-great-grandfather, she had permanently named it *Pèlerinages*, after an early Liszt piano cycle. Under the composer's vicarious patronage, "Pilgrimages" connoted the path, the quest, the pilgrimage, beginning with Liszt's, then Weimar's through the decades, and its visitors', who had notoriously come and gone, and, last but not least, Nike Wagner's own, for whom Weimar was beginning to feel like a long-lost home. She had got off to a good start, had hired mostly musicians to make this primarily into a music festival, and had at her disposal approximately 2 million euros, a million coming from Thuringia, a half-million from the FRG, and almost another half-million collected from private donors by Countess Castell who, through her relations, knew many potential donors.[135] Wagner had struck a new covenant between Weimar and the Buchenwald Memorial by realizing that each Kunstfest should be opened by a special commemorative address followed by a music presentation. For 2004 this was to be Richard Wagner's *Lohengrin-Overture* and Gustav Mahler's *Lied von der Erde*, both appropriately somber. Memorial Deputy Director Rikola-Gunnar Lüttgenau thanked Wagner for remembering Buchenwald within the festival's framework. As artist in residence the Hungarian-British pianist András Schiff had been engaged, for a period of two weeks – a personal favorite of Wagner's. There were other musical offerings, such as by Rifkin, and stage pieces, such as *Johnnys Jihad* about the American Taliban sympathizer John Walker Lindh, all till September 19.

Despite a rounded program which filled Nike Wagner with satisfaction, the drama *Johnnys Jihad* by Marc Pommerening highlighted one of several problems which befell even this well-conceived arts event right from the outset: the Kunstfest was too experimental, too arcane. These qualities complemented Wagner's personality but, as much as they delighted most of the out-of-town visitors, they did not touch the locals. In that respect Wagner's curriculum had much in common with the artistic-event presentations of Bernd Kauffmann. Both their tastes were similarly refined by an abstract proclivity, albeit focussed differently, with Kauffmann's firmly on dance. The Weimarers also disliked the new French Kunstfest label and resented the high price of admission, and besides, Schiff's attitude was strange. He categorically refused to play Liszt, as he disliked him intensely, but had had three grand pianos brought into town, for playing other composers. On the organizational side, an attempt by Countess Castell to sell at the festival wine made by her relatives, the princely house of Castell-Castell in Lower Franconia, annoyed Weimarers as a self-serving intrusion. Yet another factor that would haunt Wagner's tenure for some years, from the 2004 season onwards, was the fear that she would leave little Weimar for Bayreuth. No matter how loudly she protested how fond she was of the classics town, few people in Weimar believed her.[136]

In the 2005 season Wagner's situation was complicated by unwanted interference – a sign to her that her pilgrimage to Weimar was not really taken seriously. The town had scheduled an unrelated open-air concert during the *Gedächtnis Buchenwald* (Buchenwald Memorial) without consulting her, and 300 Weimar personages were to be absent, on a previously arranged trip to Amsterdam.[137] But the program went as well as the year before, with approximately 10,000 people attending (compared to 13,000 in 2004). The financing had remained roughly the same, although there was writing on the wall that it would deteriorate in future. The culture presented was above reproach: Karl Amadeus Hartmann's First Symphony, Wolfgang Rihm's *Penthesilea Monolog* and Mahler's Fifth Symphony being among those selected. András Schiff returned for a second year as guest conductor, as he would for every year until 2007.[138]

On August 15, 2006, Wagner's contract was renewed for another three years. Now as in the following seasons, she hit her stride once more offering expert musical fare, where the traditional was combined with the experimental. The Canadian pianist Louis Lortie shone with Liszt's adaption of Wagner's *Tannhäuser-Overtüre*, and John Cage's *Mozart Mix*, a random collage of Mozart fragments on tape, was played. The eccentric pianist Igor Pogorelich, accompanied by the Young Philharmonic Orchestra of Thuringia, showcased Rachmaninoff, but to mixed reviews. There was a video installation by the Parisian Esther Shalev-Gerz that caught much interest. In subsequent seasons, Daniel Barenboim returned with his West-Eastern Divan Orchestra, and dance troupes performed. Violist Tabea Zimmermann came with the Mozarteum orchestra from Salzburg, and an exhibition, "Why Does Carl August Need a Goethe?" excited many. Schiff's student Gábor Csalog excelled, playing Liszt and Ligeti, and an African Dance Company, Correspondances, garnered bad reviews. Jazz trumpeter Till Brönner was accompanied by Hamburg's NDR Big Band, and Arnold Schoenberg's son-in-law, composer Luigi Nono, was featured; all of these in 2009. During that summer, 9,000 visitors arrived, and Wagner was reengaged until 2013, to complete her ten years. For 2011, she was contracted to celebrate Liszt's 200th birth year, with 2013 to be dedicated to great-grandfather Richard. In 2010 – an *Art Brut* exhibition was running at the time – the Federal Republic reduced its commitment from 500,000 to 300,000 euros, thereby overthrowing Nike Wagner's earlier expectations.[139]

True to a Lisztian aphorism, one of her art festivals had the motto "Unlucky Stars." Throughout the run of those ten years of annual festivals, Wagner was unable to shake off unlucky stars, whatever artistic success she demonstrably had. That Bayreuth suspicion Weimar citizens found hard to defeat until 2013, when Wagner had accepted her final contract. She actually did apply for the top Bayreuth director's job, together with the Belgian Baron Gérard Mortier, in August 2008. Although she was legally entitled to do so because her current contract had not yet been extended beyond 2009, it looked bad.[140] Another unlucky star was surely her continued disconnection from the ordinary people of Weimar, who appreciated her unassuming presence in town, as they saw her walking her large dog in the Ilm park, but had difficulty in comprehending her unconventional opinions, however brilliantly expressed they were in the local press. "A Weimar resident does not view the Kunstfest as 'his' Kunstfest, but as an elitist event of high culture and the avant-garde," complained hotel director Stefan Seiler. He wanted more of a folk-festival atmosphere, such as had existed even under Kauffmann, in his opening days, the proscription of bratwurst notwithstanding. Nike Wagner would have none of this.[141]

On Friday, August 25, 2006, something occurred that altered the character of the Kunstfest as an agent of reconciliation, as a new source of trust, between Weimar and Buchenwald. Nike Wagner's original, irenic, intention was jeopardized when the CDU politician Hermann Schäfer gave the opening address at the *Gedächtnis Buchenwald* commemoration in the Weimarhalle near Weimar's Jakob's Quarter. He spoke before the inaugural concert of Mahler's Fifth Symphony, with the Weimar State Orchestra under the baton of Michael Gielen, whose mother had been Jewish. Other Jews, survivors of Buchenwald, were in the audience, when Schäfer proceeded to lament the fate of Germans as refugees from the eastern territories, at the end of the last war. Having mentioned Elie Wiesel perfunctorily, Schäfer waxed sentimental about "twelve to 14 million fugitives and refugees," about "the victims of the SED regime," and "the terrible fate of our evacuees." In essence until the end, he had said not a word about the Jewish victims of Buchenwald, nor any of its other victims.[142]

After the embarrassing event, the search was on for the culprit. Who was responsible for this blunder? Nike Wagner immediately distanced herself, claiming that after she had invited Schäfer he had gone off topic "cruelly," by not addressing the crucial issue of Buchenwald's victims. Schäfer, on the other hand, insisted that he had been asked, first in a letter and subsequently during a telephone conversation with Franziska Castell to speak about the German refugee problem. When queried, Castell flatly maintained that he had lied.[143]

Part of the key to this debacle may be found in the public and private personalities of Schäfer and his superior, the federal minister of state for cultural affairs in Chancellor Merkel's office, CDU politician Bernd Neumann. Schäfer, born 1942, was a conservative Catholic who was adjunct professor of history in Freiburg and Karlsruhe, yet without having specialized in the Third Reich and with hardly any publications to his name. Nevertheless, he had been asked to assume the directorship of the Museum of German History which Chancellor Kohl, advised by a circle of right-wing conservatives, had opened in 1994 in Bonn.[144] The Museum had recently organized an exhibition documenting the expulsion of Germans from the East before and after 1945 which, in Germany, had found general acclaim.[145] When Wagner had first invited Schäfer in her letter of March 8, she had referred to that event, linking its success to Schäfer's qualifications as a contemporary historian and his expertise as director of the Bonn Museum. She also mentioned that she had asked Schäfer because her original choice for speaker, Schäfer's superior Neumann, had had to decline the offer.[146] Would she have known that Neumann himself was a former refugee, having been born in East Prussia in 1942 and driven from his homeland as a child? Was it Neumann who had suggested his deputy Schäfer as his replacement?

In the following months, several details surfaced that threw rather more light on the matter. After Wagner's March letter had been made public, it became clear that although Schäfer had totally erred in the choice of his subject for the Buchenwald speech, it was Nike Wagner who had placed emphasis on German refugees in her missive, without stressing the need to concentrate on Buchenwald's Third Reich victims. When confronted with these facts, Wagner denied any responsibility, maintaining that she was no schoolteacher and any invited speaker on Buchenwald should know for himself how to deal with its significance. As regards the telephone conversation between Castell and Schäfer, it was discovered that Schäfer was an old acquaintance of Castell's father-in-law and that neither he nor the countess might ever divulge who had said what.[147]

After having been widely publicized in Germany, the case was resolved badly, with Wagner continuing to protest her innocence in a situation where she clearly bore at least nominal, if not moral, responsibility, and Schäfer being retired from his museum directorship in 2007. Castell and Wagner parted a few months after the incident, officially on excellent terms, but not without witnesses having heard Wagner repeatedly utter invective against the countess.[148] Wagner went on to engage high-ranking CDU politicians as memorial speakers in future: it was Federal President Horst Köhler in 2007, a truly safe choice, and Neumann in 2008, which invitation, after what had happened, stunned observers. But Neumann, after all, was the man from whom the federal monies for the Kunstfest came! In the main, in August 2008 Neumann as festival speaker gave an account of what his office had been doing for the Buchenwald Memorial in the past, and what remained to be done. "This was commemoration as an administrative act," quipped the *Frankfurter Allgemeine Zeitung*.[149] Obviously, Neumann had not heeded calls for his own resignation, which had been strongly voiced throughout the republic, as had those for his deputy.[150] When all was said and done, it was clear by 2008 that culture in Weimar was still to be controlled by the reigning politicians, the very same ones who had entered Goethe's town after the fall of the Berlin Wall. Questions of humanity as dictated by the Buchenwald concentration camp and its anti-Nazi victims had to assume second place.

Weimar's culture as a permanent platform for West German political interests? Nike Wagner may have acquiesced in this as an inevitable condition of her tenure. Toward the end of her Weimar pilgrimage, it was business as usual for her. Yet by now, the Buchenwald scandal aside, she knew something about the town's provincial mentality. "Liszt was too great, too visionary," she pronounced in August 2011, "Weimar was too small and too normal." Still, normal or not – there was going to be a festival after Wagner. Such was the decision of the Weimar magistrates in October 2012. Starting with the 2014 season, the Kunstfest would be the responsibility of the theater Goethe had founded.[151]

The main themes of this, for the time being final, phase in the history of Weimar are, first, the attempt of West Germans to gain a dominant influence in the town and, second, efforts by the town, with the help of West Germans, after decades in a cultural coma, to regain its former cachet. If Kessler and van de Velde had sought to create a "Second Weimar," this may be looked upon as a serious attempt to repeat this quest.

Not unsurprisingly, the West Germans latched onto culture as their viable instrument of control. This control took a detour, via the Thuringian government in Erfurt, with whom Weimar stood in perennial rivalry. It was exercised by the ruling CDU party, conservatives who contemporaneously managed to launch a West German mayor in Weimar, one who would do their bidding. Cultural rejuvenation of the former idyll would fit neatly into Chancellor Kohl's overall plan for "blooming landscapes" in East Germany, with Weimar supplying the culture. Historically, Kohl would get the credit. The overall launch in 1990 was spotty, however, because questions of agency remained murky. The first Kunstfest organizer had dubious qualifications, and the co-sponsoring Thuringian government was ridden with ineffiency and corruption. Issues of improper finance dogged even those most willing to compromise. The Buchenwald Memorial was mismanaged, with the twin image of Weimar-cum-concentration-camp hardly a public concern. When Kahl-Wolfsjäger was succeeded in 1993 by Bernd Kauffmann, he turned out to be much more capable, inventive in an avant-garde fashion, but his work was marred by one-sidedness and self-love. These were parallels to Liszt, Kessler, and even to Gropius. Kauffmann's constant squabbles with either the regional government or the town and egregious event-planning mistakes during the Culture Year of 1999 caused his departure in 2001, which by then had long been overdue. Kauffmann worked alongside colleagues in charge of other cultural institutions such as the DNT or Klassik-Stiftung; they ranged in capability from bad to middling (Beelitz, Huschke), to excellent (Zimmermann, Märki), but overall, the financial uncertainty, an absence of conceptional direction, and political infighting prevented ultimate success.

During the first decade of the twenty-first century friction between *Wessis* and *Ossis*, as it had manifested itself in Weimar and interfered with growth, was subsiding. This meant renewed opportunities for the cultural regeneration of a town that continued to be economically precarious and demographically challenged. The one constant to the end of the 2000–2010 decade was continuing, firm, rule by the CDU, at least at the most important level: the regional government. In the person of Nike Wagner a new torch-bearer had arrived by 2004, welcomed by all. By this time DNT director Märki was persevering against all odds. Although the former building academy could not truly revive the spirit of the original Bauhaus, the very declaration of intent by its leaders augured well for the future. If Weimar had made a comeback since its glory days in the late eighteenth century, time would have to tell if its politicians, intellectuals, and artists could make it credible.

Epilogue

In April of 1995 a journalist working for the Dutch television program *Brandpunt* (Focus) called me from Amsterdam. He asked questions regarding the biography of a German literature scholar by the name of Hans Schwerte. Professor Schwerte was the rector emeritus of the Technical University of Aachen which, among German institutes of higher learning, enjoyed a sterling reputation. Schwerte's main claim to fame was a study of Faust and Faustian qualities, published in 1962, in which he had condemned the usurpation of the Faust theme and, by implication, of Goethe, by nationalists and right-wingers, beginning with the "Berlin School" founded by Herman Grimm and ending, via Arthur Moeller van den Bruck and Oswald Spengler, with Alfred Rosenberg. By contrast, Schwerte had described Thomas Mann's relationship with Faust as that of an enlightened author dealing with the Faust theme convincingly. Within his disquisition, Schwerte explained Albrecht Dürer's Knight, Death, and Devil motif, a "Germanic-German Horse-Rider's Myth," as a parallel to the Faustian theme. In both the motif and the theme, wrote Schwerte, analysts could see how "the German" was intricately related to "the Tragic."[1] The dualism found in Faust's persona – good residing next to evil – also characterized the Dürer copperplate engraving, depicting a heroic and morally highly motivated horseman fighting the Devil, to the death.

Schwerte knew what he was writing about, for he himself was living a dual life. As I knew from my previous work on the SS Ahnenerbe and now was verifying with the Dutch journalist, he was a former SS officer. What I learned during the telephone conversation was that he had assumed a new identity after World War II to begin a career as a university teacher. I was only familiar with his SS activities during the war. Under Wolfram Sievers, the executive secretary of Himmler's Ahnenerbe organization, he had risen to the post of SS plenipotentiary in all matters of ideological schooling in the Occupied Netherlands, Belgium, Denmark, and Norway. As such, he shared responsibility for the deportation of 349 Norwegian anti-Nazi students to Buchenwald in 1944.[2]

And so in April 1995 the pieces of this strange puzzle were starting to fit together, only to make headlines in the months to follow. Schwerte's real name was Hans Ernst Schneider. He had been born in East Prussian Königsberg in 1909 and as a student of German literature in Berlin had been exposed to the teachings of Julius Petersen. Having received his doctorate on Turgenev and German literature from the University of Königsberg in 1935, Schneider, as he admitted later, was under the influence of *Artamanen*, those pre-SS eastern-settlement fanatics who had originated close to Weimar and were especially strong in Germany's eastern provinces, which were also inhabited by Poles. Whether Schneider met the ex-*Artamane* Sievers in East Prussia is doubtful; it probably was an SS leader by the name of Rudolf Jacobsen, a former *Artamane*, who took him under his wing and with whom he later collaborated in the SS-Ahnenerbe's offices. In 1937 Schneider joined the SS and early in 1938, full-time, its Race and Settlement Main Office (RuSHA), run by the onetime Artam supporter Richard Walther Darré. RuSHA was Jacobsen's institutional home. Later that year Schneider changed over to Sievers and Himmler's Ahnenerbe. It was the *Artamanen* who had placed special emphasis on the Knight, Death, and Devil theme – now a leading motto of the SS.[3] SS Colonel Walther Wüst, the president of the *Ahnenerbe* and a confidant of Himmler's, published *ex cathedra* on this Dürer theme, and so did Schneider himself when he authored an article for Goebbels's broadsheet *Das Reich* in 1943, in which he celebrated "Nordic Man" and his Great-Germanic mission.[4] During that year, Schneider's own familiarity with death deepened. Although he himself successfully avoided being sent to the military front as a member of the Waffen-SS, he participated in the search, mostly at Dutch universities, for utensils that would help Ahnenerbe researchers conduct lethal experiments on humans. Schneider assisted in the procurement of microscopes, centrifuges, and crucibles for Professor August Hirt, who was conducting illicit mustard-gas experiments that resulted in many deaths, and assembling a collection composed of the skeletons of murdered Auschwitz inmates at the University of Strasbourg and nearby concentration camp Natzweiler. And Schneider did the same for Dr. Siegmund Rascher, who was killing Dachau concentration camp prisoners in pressure chambers.

Having changed his name to Hans Schwerte, and posing as a discharged Wehrmacht soldier, after May 1945, Schneider remarried his wife

Annemarie for appearance's sake and posed as stepfather to his little daughter. In 1948 he managed a second doctorate in his field on Rilke, at the University of Erlangen, where he soon became assistant professor. On Erlangen's faculties were at least four, formerly influential, Ahnenerbe scholars whom he knew well, and it is clear that they covered for him. (One was Professor Lothar Zotz, a leading, and personally charming, prehistorian from the Ahnenerbe, whom I interviewed and corresponded with at length in the early 1960s. Although at the time it was obvious that I wanted to know everything about the Ahnenerbe, Zotz, feigning total innocence regarding Himmler's regime, kept his mouth shut about Schneider/Schwerte. The entire affair is a devastating comment on the post-Nazi situation of German universities, well beyond the 1960s, which has yet to find its chronicler.)[5] The year 1962 saw the publication of Schwerte's *Faust* monograph, which created a favorable impression especially among younger scholars of German literature, because of his ostensibly liberal, critical, stance. His elevation to a full professorship at Aachen occurred in 1965, and his appointment to the rector's office in 1970. Schwerte served in that capacity until 1973, but even then there existed a number of Germanists in Germany who knew his real identity. Throughout, Schwerte carefully cultivated the leftist-liberal reputation for which the students of Aachen University adored him. He was often in Holland, his former main stomping ground, on official missions sanctioned by North-Rhine-Westphalian politicians, some of whom were close personal friends. The Belgians and Germans bestowed their highest medals on him. He outed himself in 1995 when the rumors surrounding him had become indefensible and Dutch journalists decided to call his bluff. After his discovery, he lost his pension and most titles and medals, dying at the age of ninety in 1999, peacefully in his bed, without ever having been tried.[6]

Inasmuch as Goethe had spoken about Faust as a man whose breast was inhabited by two souls, duality was also a theme that ruled the history of Weimar.[7] From its zenith in the early 1770s to well into the twenty-first century Weimar's history was characterized by the highest peaks and the lowest valleys. The town's initial greatness, anchored in culture and high-mindedness, lasted from approximately 1775, when Goethe arrived there, to 1805, when Schiller died and Goethe fell into momentary impotence. If this stretch represents a strong ascendancy, the period from 1937 to 1945, when the Nazis' Buchenwald predominated, marks the depths of decline, by the criteria of culture and morality. The apposition of an illustrious Weimar and a criminal Buchenwald most aptly symbolizes the duality.

Certainly after Goethe's death in 1832 the downturn continued throughout the nineteenth century, notwithstanding several noble attempts to counteract it. Highlights in what became a continuous quest were Franz Liszt's arrival in Weimar in 1848, the founding of the painters' academy in 1860, the release of the Goethe papers in 1885 and the appearance of van de Velde and Count Kessler at the turn of the century. Each of those events at first showed promise and then ended in frustration. By around 1900, according to the seismograph of genius, Weimar had settled somewhere below the 1832 mark. On the other hand, a myth had been concocted over the decades whose aim it was to prop up Weimar's reputation artificially, with the help of a crude nationalization, especially of Goethe and Schiller, in the cause of new, state-sanctioned, chauvinism. This myth was destructive and never to be quelled. In 1919, the simultaneous establishment of the new German republic, signaling progressiveness in politics, and the Bauhaus, signaling advances in aesthetics, gave rise to huge new opportunities. But these were crushed when the reactionary forces that had now anchored themselves everywhere in Germany but specifically in Weimar, aided by the Weimar Myth makers, gained the upper hand, causing the progressive democratic impulses to disappear and the avant-garde to be put to flight. The indigenous Weimar reactionaries who had held the town down for decades were helped from the outside by fascist powers which by 1930 had taken control. The nadir was reached in 1945, when one dictatorial regime of terror was exchanged for another. When it had been passed, a new climb to the top was attempted in 1990. This ascent, as encouraging as it was, became fraught with difficulties. For one, rival claims to competence by the East and West Germans precluded genuine cooperation, especially in the realm of cultural rejuvenation, where it counted. And for another, the models of the Weimar classic age appeared in many cases too distant to be realistically and effectively emulated. Was Weimar still taken seriously? Anticipating the 1999 Culture Year with skepticism, Sybille Berg commented in 1997 for *Die Zeit*: "Without Goethe the whole town would perhaps have been covered in concrete by now, levelled to the ground and super skyscrapers on top. Seventy stories. And autobahns, to drive away foul air. Weimar, not more than a small town at the end of the world, passed its climax some time ago, some time 200 years ago. But today it makes a good museum."[8] With all that was left and resurrected, by 2013 Weimar was, at best, one center of interesting cultural activity (and moral contemplation) in Germany among many.

A number of sub-themes characterize Weimar to this day, some marked by dualism. From Goethe's time, high-mindedness and the peaks of creativity were consistently countermanded by pettiness of thought and mean-spiritedness. The Weimar savants suffered from this; Goethe suffered from it when he cohabited illegally with Christiane Vulpius and their first child, August, was born out of wedlock. Liszt kept tongues wagging after the middle of the nineteenth century because of his illicit union with Carolyne zu Sayn-Wittgenstein, and in later decades when he attracted unconventional students. Thereafter, Ferruccio Busoni bore the same fate. Van de Velde and Count Kessler made themselves the butt of popular jokes because of their eccentric personalities and, in the case of the Belgian, also because of weird disciples. Regarding their youthful clientele and their personal makeup, Walter Gropius and his Bauhaus Masters were fated to endure the worst, because of how they looked, what they did, and what they said.

Here one might be tempted to associate the common people's base impulses with political conservatism, given that most Bauhaus leaders and van de Velde originally hailed from the political left. But van de Velde's friend Kessler, a prominent victim of derision, was a staunch conservative, and for the nineteenth century a correlation of vicious narrow-mindedness with political conservatism does not appear plausible, because high and low attitudes cut across all class lines, as did superior and negative creativity. After 1925 such juxtapositions were moot in any case because left-wing currents *and* a profusion of talents – in literature, the visual arts, and music – were absent from the town. When political and cultural diversity returned to Weimar by 1990, the dichotomy between populist-grounded anti-avant-garde sentiment and progressivism in the arts returned as well, but because of the long Communist interlude, this at first appeared to occur in a politically neutral zone. That was in contrast to what had been happening after 1918, when Weimar forces which opposed the left-leaning Bauhaus, supported in equal measure by an unenlightened petite bourgeoisie on the one side and scions of the *haut monde* such as Carl Norris von Schirach and Mathilde von Freytag-Loringhoven on the other, segued easily into National Socialism, pre-1933 Thuringian Nazi government and, ultimately, the Third Reich. Weimar was essentially a small town with a provincial mentality, where intrigues tended to hold sway and large-culture projects had no place, charged supporters of Stephan Märki as late as 2008. This dictum was as valid at the beginning of the twenty-first century as it had been in the middle of the twentieth, or the start of the nineteenth.[9]

Endemic political conservatism was aided and abetted by biological scientism that was to lead to racist xenophobia, particularly against Jews. Racism was in keeping with intellectual currents in other German locales

such as Chamberlain's Bayreuth – in Weimar there existed, not coincidentally, connections to the post-Darwinian thought of Jena University's Ernst
Haeckel. A distinctive Weimar anti-Semitic tradition was established with
the move to the Goethe town by Elisabeth Förster-Nietzsche and Adolf
Bartels in the late nineteenth century, causing an entire procession of anti-
urban, anti-Jewish thinkers such as Wachler, Lienhard, and Schlaf to follow.
By the early twentieth century their Germanocentric, xenophobic, thought
had been galvanized, with the more technological and anthropological ideas
of Schultze-Naumburg and Hans F. K. Günther, into a stream of Weimar-
specific racism that generated neocolonial notions regarding allegedly inferior Slavs in the East, as well as nurturing the *Artamanen* and their successor
organization, the SS. When National Socialist ideology took hold in
Weimar through the machinations of the Schirach family, Sauckel, Ziegler,
and Hitler himself, all those early influences were easily merged. In the
mid-1920s, Hitler was attracted to a quintessentially conservative, provincial, non-industrial small town, with its neoclassical tradition already
fetishized, strategically situated in the center of Germany, from which he
could ideally plan his demagogic schemes. Demographically, it was in spaces
such as Weimar's – Protestant, middle-class, and semi-rural – that Hitler's
party would be most successful during its rise to power.[10]

Yet another quality militating against a post-1832 return of Weimar to
historic greatness was the transience of culturally productive residents, of
whom the post-World War I ones could have battled right-wing extremism,
had they been of a liberal persuasion. At all events, among creative spirits
who sought refuge in Weimar the only great ones who permanently stayed
were those of the classics phase: Goethe, Schiller, Herder, and Wieland.
Liszt certainly intended to do so but was prevented from continuous residence since 1848 by a lack of institutional backing for his projects. As a
foreigner, van de Velde was never fully accepted to begin with, and Gropius
was driven away by an Old Guard's aesthetic arguments and adverse political currents. The long interregnum from 1925 to 1990 forced Weimar into
catatonic shock. When Bernd Kauffmann arrived in 1992, his potential for
ongoing work in Weimar was large, yet because of folly both on his and the
Weimar citizenry's part, this innovative impresario left town. So, eventually,
did Stephan Märki and Nike Wagner, the other two productive mavens of
the post-Berlin-Wall era, with their administrative legacies more pristine
than Kauffmann's. Might it be that a forced attempt to connect to the
classics in all those post-1832 cases hastened those protagonists' demise?
Not as a rule, for in 1862 the gifted painter Arnold Böcklin also departed
Weimar after a short while, without having linked his work to the

illuminati of the eighteenth century. "It always was the fate of Weimar to form a beginning, a platform for artists," but to attach great men like Goethe forever seemed to have become much rarer, mused Weimar aristocrat Wanda von Puttkamer early in the twentieth century.[11]

Possessed of an elusive attractiveness and marked by dissonance, Weimar always meant many things to many people at various times in its history: a town to live in, an ideal, a seat of government, a myth, a source of bratwurst, a pensioner's haven, a place to peddle neoclassical kitsch, a festival site, an onion market, an object of real-estate speculation, a center of Nazi and Soviet oppression. Its self-conception was often different from the way it was viewed in the rest of Germany, or throughout the world. Too often, and not to its advantage, its green-forest, green-meadows charm in combination with its distinguished past seduced the more sophisticated of its denizens, and even out-of-towners, into divining its fate, its future, without basis in fact. More often than not, those advocates were chasing after a utopia. Franz Liszt, for example, decided that the town should become the host of a classics foundation, with scarcely any chance of financial backing. Van de Velde and Kessler wished to turn Weimar, irreversibly, into the fulcrum of German culture, in the face of massive adversity. Neither of these attempts lacked hubris. Moreover, in early 1919 Intendant Ernst Hardt resolved without proper authorization that the municipal theater be called Deutsches Nationaltheater – a designation it has kept to this day – although it was clear even then that the basis for national government would be returned to Berlin. In fact, by 1937, there existed three other Nationaltheater in Germany: one in Munich, one in Mannheim, and one in provincial Osnabrück.[12] As for the Bauhaus University, conceived as the worthy successor to its famous archetype, in the fall of 2013 it was decided that in future it would have to shed sixty teaching positions.

In the early 1990s ex-Chancellor Helmut Schmidt declared Weimar to be the future seat of a German National Foundation, and although that organization was founded there, its center of gravity did not turn out to be Weimar.[13] By a cruel but highly significant stroke of misfortune, President Hilmar Hoffmann failed in the mid-1990s to make Weimar the administrative hub of the Munich-based Goethe Institute he headed, which was demonstrating German cultural acumen worldwide.[14] And in a more recent act of gross exaggeration Hellmut Seemann identified the 1999 Culture Year events as a historic climax, logically following on from the halcyon years of the Bauhaus.[15] In reality, the Bauhaus exhibition of 1923, the most important cultural event in Weimar since Goethe, has never been surpassed.

Notes

Chapter One: A Weimar Golden Age, 1770 to 1832

1. Hufeland, *Leibarzt*, 50, 72.
2. "About the True Conception of Classical Authority" (Walter, "Herder," 37). Also Francke, *Geschichte*, 71; Heintze, *Chronik*, 18.
3. Heintze, *Chronik*, 66.
4. Bruford, *Germany*, 250; Francke, *Geschichte*, 140.
5. Walter, "Herder," 37–39, 45; Francke, *Geschichte*, 72–74, 78–86, 90–94, 110–16.
6. Walter, "Herder," 45; Kühn, *Weimar*, 83–84.
7. Heintze, *Chronik*, 22.
8. Ibid. 18; Francke, *Geschichte*, 73–74, 78; Bode, *Musenhof*, 117.
9. De Staël, *Germany*, 141–43; Bode, *Musenhof*, 90–93.
10. Günzel, *Fürstenhaus*, 63.
11. Messner, *Nationaltheater: Anfängen*, 8; Huschke, *Musik*, 20. On salary: Zaremba, *Herder*, 162.
12. Oellers/Steeger, *Weimar*, 89; Berger, *Anna Amalia*, 93.
13. Hufeland, *Leibarzt*, 68; Oellers/Steeger, *Weimar*, 89. Also see Hinderer, "Classicism."
14. Boyle, *Goethe*, vol. 1, 240; Seemann, *Anna Amalia*.
15. This principle is aptly articulated in Berger, *Anna Amalia*, 63–64.
16. Borchmeyer, *Zeitbürger*, 26; Safranski, *Goethe*, 21.
17. Boyle, *Goethe*, vol. 1, vii, viii (quote), ix, 6.
18. De Staël, *Germany*, 157.
19. Haufe, *Humboldt*, 151.
20. Nietzsche, *Menschliches*, 118, 360.
21. Jaspers, "Menschlichkeit," 79.
22. Scholz, *Seele*, 255–59.
23. Borchmeyer, *Zeitbürger*, 114–15.
24. Böttiger, *Zustände*, 67; Koopmann, *Stein*, 28.
25. Bode, *Musenhof*, 167; Boyle, *Goethe*, vol. 1, 194–95.
26. Boyle, *Goethe*, vol. 1, 246, 251; Borchmeyer, *Klassik*, 50.
27. Boyle, *Goethe*, vol. 1, 240–45; Borchmeyer, *Zeitbürger*, 117.
28. Boyle, *Goethe*, vol. 1, 249.
29. Bode, *Musenhof*, 169, Wieland quoted ibid.; Borchmeyer, *Zeitbürger*, 116.
30. Bode, *Musenhof*, 198; Koopmann, *Stein*, 28.
31. Hufeland, *Leibarzt*, 45–46; Bode, *Musenhof*, 169; Kühn, *Weimar*, 52.
32. Vehse, *Hof*, 49.
33. Böttiger, *Zustände*, 289–90 (quote); Steiner/Kühn-Stillmark, *Bertuch*, 48–49.
34. Bode, *Musenhof*, 190–91; Zaremba, *Herder*, 111, 152–53, 161–62.
35. Hufeland, *Leibarzt*, 52–53, 77; Francke, *Geschichte*, 87–88; Richter, *Herder*, 193.
36. Irmscher, *Herder*, 26–28; Richter, *Herder*, 194; Zaremba, *Herder*, 211, 216, 219–22.

37. Francke, *Geschichte*, 135–36.
38. Kühn, *Weimar*, 38; Zaremba, *Herder*, 112, 222; Oellers/Steeger, *Weimar*, 72–73; Tobler (May 1781) and Wieland (May 1785) in Richter, *Herder*, 212–13, 238–39.
39. Vehse, *Hof*, 52; Dreise-Beckmann, "Musikleben," 68.
40. Bode, *Musenhof*, 193–95; Ventzke, "Hofökonomie," 20.
41. Bruford, *Germany*, 84–85.
42. Berger, *Anna Amalia*, 75–76; Dreise-Beckmann, "Musikleben," 63–64.
43. Messner, *Nationaltheate: Anfängen*, 6.
44. Kühn, *Weimar*, 26.
45. Berger, *Anna Amalia*, 245–49; Berger, "Rückzug," 138.
46. Bruford, *Germany*, 29–34.
47. Vehse, *Hof*, 151–52; Bode, *Musenhof*, 196.
48. See Müller-Seidel, *Geschichtlichkeit*, 37.
49. Kühn, *Weimar*, 85–86.
50. Günther et al., *Weimar*, 21, 79, 285.
51. Boyle, *Goethe*, vol. 1, 252; Wilson, *Goethe-Tabu*, 31.
52. Vehse, *Hof*, 71.
53. Ventzke, "Hofökonomie," 21–48.
54. Goethe on February 24, 1784, in Fiala, *Amtstätigkeit*, 8–10; Willy Flach ibid., 17; Borchmeyer, *Zeitbürger*, 109–10; Boyle, *Goethe*, vol. 1, 253–54.
55. For background, see Wehler, *Deutsche Gesellschaftsgeschichte: Erster Band*, 218–40, 254–67.
56. Wilson, *Goethe-Tabu*, 51–66, 94–116, 182–83, 205–35, 243–48.
57. Boyle, *Goethe*, vol. 1, 252; 199; Borchmeyer, *Zeitbürger*, 138; Vaget, *Dilettantismus*, 55–63.
58. Oellers/Steeger, *Weimar*, 80; Borchmeyer, *Zeitbürger*, 138–39.
59. Boyle, *Goethe*, vol. 1, 343; Messner, *Nationaltheater: Anfängen*, 17–21; Dreise-Beckmann, "Musikleben," 70; Conrady, *Goethe*, vol. 1, 393–401.
60. Boyle, *Goethe*, vol. 1, 94–95, vol. 2, 204–5; Böttiger, *Zustände*, 33; Sengle, *Goethe*, 28, 239.
61. Messner, *Nationaltheater: Anfängen*, 22–25; Damm, *Christiane*, 155.
62. Safranski, *Schiller*, 202, 262–63; Borchmeyer, *Klassik*, 212.
63. Schmidt-Möbus/Möbus, *Kulturgeschichte*, 152;
64. Safranski, *Schiller*, 133, 202–3; Damm, *Schiller*, 98; Borchmeyer, *Zeitbürger*, 220.
65. Günther, *Weimar*, 52; Damm, *Schiller*, 97.
66. Zaremba, *Wieland*, 196, 203.
67. Vehse, *Hof*, 96; Damm, *Schiller*, 70, 77–78; Safranski, *Goethe*, 52.
68. Zaremba, *Herder*, 212; Damm, *Schiller*, 77, 144–45.
69. Damm, *Schiller*, 142.
70. Borchmeyer, *Klassik*, 213–17; Safranski, *Schiller*, 271–73, 341–42.
71. Oellers/Steeger, *Weimar*, 103; Damm, *Schiller*, 100, 115–16; Safranski, *Goethe*, 69–70.
72. Borchmeyer, *Klassik*, 214.
73. Humboldt to Georg Forster, January 10, 1790, in Haufe, *Humboldt*, 27.
74. Unseld, *Goethe*, 245–46; Safranski, *Schiller*, 342; Damm, *Schiller*, 140–41.
75. Damm, *Schiller*, 97–99; Safranski, *Schiller*, 300–3 (Schiller quoted 303).
76. Hans-Jürgen Schings in *SZ*, October 13, 2009.
77. Safranski, *Goethe*, 100–3, Schiller's letter quoted 100.
78. Damm, *Schiller*, 145–46, 152; Safranski, *Schiller*, 314, 329, 363; Borchmeyer, *Zeitbürger*, 200–1; Vaget, "Wilson," 344.
79. Goeken, *Herder*, 93–94; Zaremba, *Herder*, 208; Berger, *Anna Amalia*, 206.
80. Damm, *Schiller*, 200; Safranski, *Schiller*, 402–3; Friedenthal, *Goethe*, 357 (quote).
81. Barner, "Goethe," 79; Oellers/Steeger, *Weimar*, 138–39; Safranski, *Schiller*, 422.
82. Oellers/Steeger, *Weimar*, 138; Safranski, *Schiller*, 422.
83. Damm, *Schiller*, 249–54; Oellers/Steeger, *Weimar*, 139.
84. Barner, "Goethe," 80; Safranski, *Schiller*, 442; Damm, *Schiller*, 256–60 (quote 258).
85. Barner, "Goethe," 77, 81–83; Boyle, *Goethe*, vol. 2, 226–28, 255; Safranski, *Schiller*, 404, 464.
86. Bamberg, *Jagemann*, vol. 1, 240; Berger, *Anna Amalia*, 189.
87. Günther, *Weimar*, 59.
88. Kühn, *Weimar*, 102–4; Messner, *Nationaltheater: Anfängen*, 26–31; Safranski, *Schiller*, 505–6, 453, 462–63, 471–73.

89. Genast, *Zeit*, 64–68, quote 83–84; Bamberg, *Jagemann*, vol. 1, 90, vol. 2, 285–86.
90. See Berger, *Anna Amalia*, 210–11.
91. Böttiger, *Zustände*, 48–59, 79; Steiner/Kühn-Stillmark, *Bertuch*, 54–56; Berger, "Rückzug," 141, 150, 164; Berger, *Anna Amalia*, 155–56, 178–79.
92. Kühn, *Weimar*, 106–7; Safranski, *Schiller*, 495. Mann's portrait was for 1816, but certainly applicable fifteen years earlier. *Lotte in Weimar*, 330–82.
93. Vehse, *Hof*, 86; Kühn, *Weimar*, 108; Boyle, *Goethe*, vol. 2, 264; Oellers/Steeger, *Weimar*, 144.
94. Kühn, *Weimar*, 46.
95. Herold, *Mistress*, 320–23.
96. Eberhardt, *Umwelt*, 9–10; Rost/Backhaus, "Weimar," 30. For 1786, Riederer indicates 6,265, for 1800 approximately 8,000 ("Grösse," 99).
97. Quoted in Kühn, *Weimar*, 21; Vehse, *Hof*, 57.
98. Vehse, *Hof*, 57; Kühn, *Weimar*, 21; Klauss, *Alltag*, 15, 45; Boyle, *Goethe*, vol. 1, 233–34.
99. Roemer, *City*, 72; Huschke, "Betrachtungen," 542.
100. Bruford, *Germany*, 211; Huschke, "Betrachtungen," 542–43; W. Wölfling (1796) in Pleticha, *Weimar*, 12; Watson, *Genius*, 521.
101. Kriesche, *Stadt*; Steinfeld, *Weimar*, 18–19.
102. Hunstock, *Weimar*, 40–44, 54.
103. Benz, *Heidelberg*; Otremba, *Würzburg*.
104. Roemer, *City*, 72.
105. Bruford, *Germany*, 31; Eberhardt, *Umwelt*, 36, 41, 45.
106. Eberhardt, *Umwelt*, 67–70; Sengle, *Goethe*, 24–26.
107. Willy Flach in Fiala et al., *Amtstätigkeit*, 20–25; Riederer/Wahl ibid., 60–61; Eberhardt, *Umwelt*, 56–65; Boyle, *Goethe*, vol. 2, 299–300.
108. Bruford, *Germany*, 97; Klauss, *Alltag*, 16; Ragwitz/Riederer, *Zwiebelmarkt*, 61.
109. Klauss, *Alltag*, 15; Boyle, *Goethe*, vol. 1, 234, 236; Hunstock, *Weimar*, 164–67.
110. Sengle, *Goethe*, 27; Ventzke, "Hofökonomie," 39–40; Hunstock, *Weimar*, 79, 338–41. By 1795, approximately 350 soldiers were stationed in Weimar (Riederer, "Grösse," 93).
111. Klauss, *Alltag*, 18; Batts, "Side," 29; Steiner/Kühn-Stillmark, *Bertuch*, 58, 69, 70 (quotes), 72, 93, 94, 99.
112. For the pre-1848–49 Revolution existence of this class in the whole of Germany, see Conze, "Voraussetzungen."
113. Eberhardt, *Umwelt*, 85; Sengle, *Goethe*, 25.
114. Eberhardt, *Umwelt*, 35, 39–40, 53, 66.
115. See Müller-Seidel, *Geschichtlichkeit*, 37–38; Sengle, *Goethe*, 27; Borchmeyer, *Zeitbürger*, 109.
116. See n. 54, above.
117. Schleif, *Diener*.
118. Eberhardt, *Umwelt*, 23, 30, 104; Hufeland, *Leibarzt*, 76–79; Francke, *Geschichte*, 87–88, 137–39; Schwabe, *Selbstbiographie*, 21.
119. Conze, "Mittelstand."
120. Kühn, *Weimar*, 24; Huschke, *Musik*, 24; Messner, *Nationaltheater: Anfängen*, 28.
121. Vehse, *Hof*, 72, 132; Zaremba, *Herder*, 230; Oellers/Steeger, *Weimar*, 173; Damm, *Schiller*, 218.
122. Scholz, *Leben*, 10–29.
123. Goethe, *Faust*, 134–222.
124. Conze, "Voraussetzungen," 124.
125. Scholz, *Leben*, 21–29; Frede, "Todesstrafe," 386–87; Wilson, *Goethe-Tabu*, 7–8; Vaget, "Wilson," 338–39.
126. Koopmann, *Stein*, 224; Eissler, *Goethe*, vol. 1, xxvi, 52, vol. 2, 1019–22.
127. Vaget, "Introduction," xviii.
128. Eissler, *Goethe*, vol. 2, 1071–72, 1287–90.
129. Ibid., vol. 2, 1070; Koopmann, *Stein*, 191, 255; Boyle, *Goethe*, vol. 1, 260–61.
130. Watson, *Genius*, 95–101; Marchand, "Becoming Greek."
131. Johann Wolfgang von Goethe in *Winkelmann*, 222.
132. E.g. (apart from Madame de Staël) historian Nikolai Karamzin, writer Wilhelm von Humboldt, and philosopher Joseph Rückert (Haufe, *Humboldt*, 63–64; Greiner-Mai, *Weimar*, 62; Pleticha, *Weimar*, 16).

133. See Hufeland, *Leibarzt*, 67; Mandelkow, *Rezeptionsgeschichte*, vol. 1, 135; Wilson, *Goethe-Tabu*, 292; Otto, "Goethe," 16; Bollenbeck, "Weimar," 214; Berger, *Anna Amalia*, 239–41.

134. Francke, *Geschichte*, 74, 112.

135. Böttiger, *Zustände*, 76; Berger, *Anna Amalia*, 240; Wieland to Gleim, May 15, 1785, in Richter, *Herder*, 238–39.

136. Müller-Seidel, *Geschichtlichkeit*, 36 (quote); Goeken, *Herder*, 90; Gillies, "Herder," 90.

137. Boyle, *Goethe*, vol. 1, 248; Borchmeyer, *Zeitbürger*, 111.

138. Kühn, *Weimar*, 104; Sengle, *Goethe*, 18; Borchmeyer, *Klassik*, 51–52; Boyle, *Goethe*, vol. 2, 264; Safranski, *Schiller*, 300.

139. Bruford, *Germany*, 324; Baeumer, "Begriff," 40; Grimm/Hermand, *Klassik-Legende*, 11–13; Barner, "Goethe," 83.

140. Kühn, *Weimar*, 20–21, 38; Bode, *Musenhof*, 218; Otto, "Goethe," 16.

141. Vehse, *Hof*, 86–87.

142. Merseburger, *Mythos*, 161–66.

143. Walter, "Herder," 59.

144. Zaremba, *Herder*, 163, 183, 199–200, 213–14, 217, 251; Goeken, *Herder*, 98; Richter, *Herder*, 269–70, 274, 289–90.

145. Richter, *Herder*, 219–21, 224.

146. Gillies, "Herder," 94; Zaremba, *Herder*, 204–5; Richter, *Herder*, 269.

147. Gillies, "Herder," 95–96; Oellers/Steeger, *Weimar*, 145–46; Zaremba, *Herder*, 196, 204, 213–14, 217–18; Richter, *Herder*, 269–70.

148. Schmidt-Möbus/Möbus, *Kulturgeschichte*, 141–42.

149. Jagemann in Bamberg, *Jagemann*, vol. 1, 97.

150. Böttiger, *Zustände*, 221; Gillies, "Herder," 94; Damm, *Christiane*, 120.

151. Bamberg, *Jagemann*, vol. 1, 97; Damm, *Christiane*, 134, 191, 195–96, 260–61, 275; Damm, *Schiller*, 221–22; Safranski, *Goethe*, 167–68.

152. Oellers/Steeger, *Weimar*, 192; Borchmeyer, *Zeitbürger*, 296; Wilson, *Goethe-Tabu*, 39.

153. Oellers/Steeger, *Weimar*, 200–1.

154. Seibt, *Goethe*, 9–11, 21–25; Pleticha, *Weimar*, 240–55; Schopenhauer in Houben, *Damals*, 10–11 and in Pleticha, 247–49; Merseburger, *Mythos*, 126–28; Zaremba, *Wieland*, 258.

155. Borchmeyer, *Zeitbürger*, 296; Berger, *Anna Amalia*, 235; Merseburger, *Mythos*, 124–25.

156. Merseburger, *Mythos*, 125–26.

157. Seibt, *Goethe*, 31–35; Houben, *Damals*, 27; Oellers/Steeger, *Weimar*, 211–12; Unseld, *Goethe*, 389–90.

158. Seibt, *Goethe*, 115–37, 150, 157 (1st quote); Haufe, *Humboldt*, 203 (2nd quote); Zaremba, *Wieland*, 264.

159. Merseburger, *Mythos*, 132–33.

160. Ibid., 140–47; Gebhardt, *Handbuch*, 85–92.

161. Merseburger, *Mythos*, 147–48; Sengle, *Goethe*, 236; Borchmeyer, *Zeitbürger*, 110; Günzel, *Fürstenhaus*, 94; Wilson, *Goethe-Tabu*, 291.

162. Merseburger, *Mythos*, 148–51 (Goethe quoted 150); Bahr, "Juden," 106–8; Schmidt, *Familien*, 8–14, 19–22, 45–47; Müller/Stein, *Familien*, 9–13. Unfriendly remarks about Jews are in Goethe, *Faust*, 152, 233.

163. Eberhardt, *Umwelt*, 18, 24; Riederer, "Grösse," 100–3.

164. Table in Eberhardt, *Umwelt*, n.p.

165. Ibid., 27–29, 50–52.

166. Günzel, *Fürstenhaus*, 124; Post/Werner, *Herrscher*, 307; Jena, *Quartett*, 181–83.

167. Vaget, *Goethe: Der Mann*, 117–20.

168. Huschke, *Musik*, 39–78; Houben, *Damals*, 275.

169. Messner, *Nationaltheater: Anfängen*, 32–43.

170. To Böttiger, December 10, 1821, in Houben, *Damals*, 246.

171. Schopenhauer ibid., 275–76, 301–2.

172. Kühn, *Weimar*, 137 (quote); Günzel, *Fürstenhaus*, 122.

173. Vehse, *Hof*, 86.

174. Berger, *Anna Amalia*, 235.

175. Safranski, *Goethe*, 304; Borchmeyer, *Zeitbürger*, 298.

176. Jena, *Quartett*, 181; Günzel, *Fürstenhaus*, 124.

177. Oellers/Steeger, *Weimar*, 263; Conrady, *Goethe*, vol. 2, 513–31.
178. Borchmeyer, *Zeitbürger*, 297 (Goethe quoted *ibid.*); Seemann, *Weimar*, 182–84.
179. Borchmeyer, *Zeitbürger*, 302–3; Oellers/Steeger, *Weimar*, 192–93.
180. Willy Flach in Fiala, *Amtstätigkeit*, 24, 26.
181. Werner Heisenberg, "Die Goethesche und die Newtonsche Farbenlehre im Lichte der modernen Physik" (1941), in Mandelkow, *Urteil*, 233. Also see Hubert Spiegel in *FAZ. NETonline*, July 20, 2010.
182. Gräbner, *Weimar*, 94; Schopenhauer in Houben, *Damals*, 36–41; Huschke, *Musik*, 41. On the beginnings of Weimar tourism during the time of Goethe, and thereafter, see Jens Riederer, "Wallfahrt nach Weimar: Die Klassikerstadt als sakraler Mythos (1780 bis 1919)" (ms., July 2013).
183. Schopenhauer in Houben, *Damals*, 56–57, 67–68, 114, 328–29; Humboldt in Haufe, *Humboldt*, 207–11; Vehse, *Hof*, 171; Unseld, *Goethe*, 508.
184. Humboldt in Haufe, *Humboldt*, 203, 217–18, 224; Safranski, *Goethe*, 305–6.
185. Steinfeld, *Weimar*, 263.
186. Humboldt in Haufe, *Humboldt*, 212–13; Damm, *Christiane*, 435–36, 458.
187. Damm, *Christiane*, 502–7.

Chapter Two: Promising the Silver Age, 1832 to 1861

1. Oellers/Steeger, *Weimar*, 322.
2. Grans, *Jahre*, 4 (first quote); Gerstenberg, *Zeit*, 3 (second quote); Bernhard von Beskow (1834) in Greiner-Mai, *Weimar*, 188.
3. Immermann, *Poesie*, 651–53; Preller, *Tagebücher*, 17; Pöthe, *Ettersburg*, 68; Günzel, *Fürstenhaus*, 125.
4. Schorn, *Weimar: Karl Friedrichs*, 237; Bollenbeck, "Weimar," 214.
5. Schorn, *Weimar: Karl Friedrichs*, 30–31.
6. Grans, *Jahre*, 3.
7. Ibid., 1–2; Schrickel, *Geschichte*, 179–82; Messner, *Nationaltheater: Anfängen*, 44.
8. Sangalli, *Weimar*, 60–66.
9. Messner, *Nationaltheater: Anfängen*, 44–45; Huschke, *Glut*, 97–99; Seibold, *Schumann*, 152.
10. Schrickel, *Geschichte*, 179–82.
11. Clarkson, *History*, 254–55; Raeff, *Russia*, 28–29; Schrickel, *Geschichte*, 211.
12. Pöthe, *Carl Alexander*, 57; Günzel, *Fürstenhaus*, 127–28; Jena, *Quartett*, 192–94.
13. Pöthe, *Ettersburg*, 14–22, 28–29, 46, 58, 83; Pöthe, *Carl Alexander*, 209.
14. Sangalli, *Weimar*, 42.
15. Mommsen, *Ordnung*, 14.
16. Egloffstein, *Weimar*, 3; Matthes, *Carl Alexander*, 4, 6.
17. Cornelius, *Briefe*, vol. 2, 50, 123; Borodin, "Erinnerungen," 41; Stradal, *Erinnerungen*, 39; Egloffstein, *Weimar*, 22, 58–59; Schorn, *Weimar: Karl Alexander*, 43; Matthes, *Carl Alexander*, 5; Pöthe, *Carl Alexander*, 256.
18. Carl Alexander, *Tagebuchblätter*, 38; Steiner, *Lebensgang*, 159.
19. Carl Alexander, *Tagebuchblätter*, 51–52; Matthes, *Carl Alexander*, 7; Reuter, *Kinde*, 407; Pöthe, *Carl Alexander*, 408; Ziegler, "Carl Alexander," 152–55.
20. Immermann, *Poesie*, 661–62; Wagner, *Leben*, vol. 2, 669; Raschdau, *Weimar*, 183.
21. Schorn, *Weimar: Karl Alexander*, 10, 14–15, 158; Kühn, *Weimar*, 160; Sangalli, *Weimar*, 38–39; Reuter, *Kinde*, 269; Jena, *Quartett*, 256–57; Raschdau, *Weimar*, 16, 36.
22. Carl Alexander, *Tagebuchblätter*, 51; Matthes, *Carl Alexander*, 13.
23. Reuter, *Kinde*, 308; Egloffstein, *Weimar*, 40–41; Raschdau, *Weimar*, 3, 15, 84, 175; Puttkamer, *Hof*, 20, 135; Ziegler, "Carl Alexander," 160–62.
24. Kalckreuth, *Wesen*, 157; Jung, *Liszt*, 292; Schorn, *Weimar: Karl Alexander*, 4; Pöthe, *Ettersburg*, 97.
25. Steinfeld, *Weimar*, 141–42.
26. Watson, *Genius*, 299.
27. Hoffmann, *Leben*, vol. 5, 232–47; vol. 6, 5, 277–78; Gerstenberg, *Zeit*, 26–27, 61.
28. Schmidt-Bergmann, "Scheffel," 222–27 (quote 224).

29. Friedrich Hebbel to Christine Hebbel, June 24, 1858, in Greiner-Mai, *Weimar*, 228 (quote); Grans, *Jahre*, 58–59; Gerstenberg, *Zeit*, 54–55.
30. Carl Alexander, *Tagebuchblätter*, 55–57; Voss, *Leben*, 173–75, 186–87, 195–97; Dent, *Busoni*, 128; Scheidig, *Malerschule*, 212–13 (quote 212).
31. Gerstenberg, *Zeit*, 29; Jonscher, "Grossherzog," 22.
32. Merseburger, *Mythos*, 189–92.
33. Günzel, *Fürstenhaus*, 128.
34. Genast, *Zeit*, 354–62; Biedermann, *Leben*, 119.
35. Merseburger, *Mythos*, 192–98; Jonscher, "Grossherzog," 20; Jena, *Quartett*, 198–200.
36. Bahr, "Juden," 109. See p. 49.
37. Pöthe, *Carl Alexander*, 87–89; Jonscher, "Grossherzog," 21.
38. Ziegler, "Carl Alexander," 159.
39. Carl Alexander, *Tagebuchblätter*, 25; Egloffstein, *Weimar*, 58–59, 88.
40. Ziegler, "Carl Alexander," 160–62; Reif, *Adel*, 2.
41. Wehler, *Deutsche Gesellschaftsgeschichte: Zweiter Band*, 720, 755; Raschdau, *Weimar*, 104, 182; Rössner, "Weimar," 86; Merseburger, *Mythos*, 229–30.
42. Wehler, *Deutsche Gesellschaftsgeschichte: Dritter Band*, 984 (quote). See also Facius, "Carl Alexander," 343–52; Pöthe, *Carl Alexander*, 102–3; Rössner, "Weimar," 54, 74–75, 85.
43. Elements of progressive change, but also of stalling, from 1850 to 1905, are described at some length in Schrul, "Umweltgeschichte," 264–419.
44. Hoffmann, *Leben*, vol. 6, 1–2; Julius Rodenberg (1856) in Pleticha, *Weimar*, 367; Raschdau, *Weimar*, 19; Klauss, *Alltag*, 18.
45. Stahr, *Weimar*, 7–9; Fay, *Music-Study*, 220; Huth, *Skizzenbuch*, 2.
46. Klauss, *Alltag*, 13.
47. Keyser, *Städtebuch*, 389; Schorn, *Weimar: Karl Alexander*, 163; Raabe, *Liszt*, 100; Jonscher, "Grossherzog," 21; Roemer, *City*, 90; Large, *Berlin*, 9.
48. Keyser, *Städtebuch*, 390; Müller/Stein, *Familien*, 24.
49. See Raschdau, *Weimar*, 19; Kuhn, *Weimar*, 129.
50. Hoffmann, *Leben*, vol. 6, 2; Greiner-Mai, *Weimar*, 181; Jonscher, "Grossherzog," 22–23.
51. Gräbner, *Weimar*, 94–96; Huth, *Skizzenbuch*, 4–5; Klauss, *Alltag*, 18; Schley, *Nachbar*, 13; Keyser, *Städtebuch*, 389.
52. Hellmuth/Mühlfriedel, *Zeiss*, esp. 15–20.
53. Keyser, *Städtebuch*, 389–90.
54. Gräbner, *Weimar*, 36.
55. Schrul, "Umweltgeschichte," 353–59.
56. Walker, *Weimar Years*, 94.
57. Raabe, *Liszt*, 103–4; Huschke, *Musik*, 114, 151–52.
58. See Hoffmann, *Leben*, vol. 6, 5; Voss, *Leben*, 38; Scheidig, *Malerschule*, 83. For all of Germany: Reif, *Adel*, 61.
59. Merseburger, *Mythos*, 188–89.
60. Hoffmann, *Leben*, vol. 6, 68; Kuhn, *Weimar*, 129; Egloffstein, *Weimar*, 100.
61. Raabe, *Liszt*, 102.
62. Schädlich, *Hochschule*, 11; Raabe, *Liszt*, 115; Walker, *Weimar Years*, 125.
63. Raschdau, *Weimar*, 19.
64. Scheidig, *Malerschule*, 110.
65. Kalckreuth, *Wesen*, 44.
66. Kühn, *Weimar*, 125.
67. Reuter, *Kinde*, 229.
68. Easton, *Count*, 100.
69. Typically, see Kühn, *Weimar*, 158; Messner, *Nationaltheater: Anfängen*, 58.
70. Charles Rosen, "The Super Power of Franz Liszt," *NYRB* (February 23, 2012): 19–21 (quotes 19); Walker, *Virtuoso Years*.
71. Newman, *Liszt*, 76–108 (quote 105); Kapp, *Liszt*, 14–15, 20, 45–47; Schorn, *Weimar: Karl Alexander*, 44; Taylor, *Schumann*, 181, 212; Sheehan, *History*, 632, 661.
72. Seemann, *Weimar*, 191.
73. Walker, *Weimar Years*, 6, 103; Messner, *Nationaltheater: Anfängen*, 45.
74. Newmann, *Liszt*, 139–41; Alan Walker et al. in *Grove Music Online*; Ehrlich, "Liszt," 37–39.

75. Huschke, *Glut*, 101; Jung, *Liszt*, 96–99.
76. Gerstenberg, *Zeit*, 9–11; Huschke, *Musik*, 104; Altenburg, "Liszt," 11; Walker, *Weimar Years*, 106; Mary Ann Smart in *Grove Music Online*.
77. Newman, *Liszt*, 157–59 (quote); Gerstenberg, *Zeit*, 11–12; Merseburger, *Mythos*, 208.
78. Newman, *Liszt*, 172; Pocknell, *Liszt*; Walker, *Weimar Years*, 210–11, 220.
79. Raabe, *Liszt*, 102.
80. On absences, see Bülow's complaint in *Briefe*, 363, 369, 372; Walker, *Weimar Years*, 86.
81. Hoffmann, *Leben*, vol. 6, 58–60; Bülow, *Briefe*, 235–36; Pöthe, *Carl Alexander*, 266.
82. Weissheimer, *Erlebnisse*, 42–43; Lachmund, *Leben*, 111; Grans, *Jahre*, 39.
83. Joachim/Moser, *Briefe*, vol. 1, 473; Lachmund, *Leben*, 111–13; Gerstenberg, *Zeit*, 20; Bülow, *Briefe*, 232, 318; Walker, *Weimar Years*, 184; H. E. Krebiel/Beatrix Borchard/Christopher Fifield/John Warrack/Bruce Carr/James Deaville in *Grove Music Online*.
84. Bülow, *Briefe*, 329–31, 372–73; Walker, *Weimar Years*, 86, 103–4.
85. Bülow, *Briefe*, 440; Walker, *Weimar Years*, 10–11, 82–86, 98.
86. Hoffmann, *Leben*, vol. 6, 32–33, 51–55, 64–68, 275; Weissheimer, *Erlebnisse*, 51–52; Grans, *Jahre*, 40; Cornelius, *Briefe*, vol. 1, 200–1; Gerstenberg, *Zeit*, 48–61; Walker, *Weimar Years*, 228, 252–55.
87. Hoffmann, *Leben*, vol. 6, 112–15; Biedermann, *Leben*, 121–25; Gerstenberg, *Zeit*, 50–51.
88. Weissheimer, *Erlebnisse*, 17–20, 40–41 (quote 40); Newman, *Liszt*, 204–6.
89. Watson, *Genius*, 460 (quote); Moser, *Brahms*, vol. 1, 38, 126, 181, 239, 278; Joachim/Moser, *Briefe*, vol. 1, 24, 32, 135, 298–99, 302, 398, 406, 456; vol. 2, 80, 86; vol. 3, 42; Moser, *Joachim*, 106–7.
90. James Deaville in *Grove Music Online*; Moser, *Joachim*, 82–83, 97–98; Greiner-Mai, *Weimar*, 221–22; Cornelius, *Briefe*, vol. 2, 207–8, Gerstenberg, *Zeit*, 21.
91. Seibold, *Schumann*, 252–53; Moser, *Brahms*, vol. 1, 18–23, 274–77, 329.
92. Bülow, *Briefe*, 348, 364, 369, 389; Raabe, *Grossherzog*, 29.
93. Raabe, *Grossherzog*, 31–37; Walker, *Weimar Years*, 135–36.
94. Huschke, *Musik*, 134–36; Jung, *Liszt*, 127–29.
95. Huschke, *Musik*, 182; Huschke, *Glut*, 138; Brian Primmer/Sarah Hibberd and Gaynor G. Jones in *Grove Music Online*.
96. Stahr, *Weimar*, 113; Huschke, *Musik*, 137.
97. Gerstenberg, *Zeit*, 19, 59; Gaynor G. Jones in *Grove Music Online*.
98. Walker, *Weimar Years*, 100–1.
99. Huschke, *Musik*, 137–39.
100. Gottschalg, *Liszt*, 4 (quote); Dömling, *Liszt*, 115; Altenburg, "Liszt," 14; Seibold, *Schumann*, 238.
101. Schorn, *Weimar: Karl Alexander*, 43–44; Moser, *Joachim*, 96.
102. April 25, 2012.
103. Alan Walker in *Grove Music Online*.
104. Grans, *Jahre*, 6; Pöthe, *Carl Alexander*, 204; Huschke, *Musik*, 140; Messner, *Nationaltheater: Anfängen*, 47.
105. Gerstenberg, *Zeit*, 44; Grans, *Jahre*, 6, 37.
106. Gerstenberg, *Zeit*, 43.
107. On March 8, 1851 (Schrickel, *Geschichte*, 201).
108. Gerstenberg, *Zeit*, 52; Messner, *Nationaltheater: Anfängen*, 47.
109. Gerstenberg, *Zeit*, 53–56; Pöthe, *Carl Alexander*, 204.
110. Cornelius quoted in Preller, *Tagebücher*, 45. The opera was musically more influenced by Wagner (and Lortzing) than Liszt, in particular *Lohengrin* (Deaville in *Grove Music Online*).
111. See the vivid description by composer Felix Draeseke in Zur Nedden, *Festschrift*, 39–42; Preller, *Tagebücher*, 45–46; Huschke, *Musik*, 142–43.
112. See Raabe, *Grossherzog*, 69–72; Messner, *Nationaltheater: Anfängen*, 48; Walker, *Weimar Years*, 497–98.
113. Raabe, *Grossherzog*, 73–75; Grans, *Jahre*, 71.
114. Liszt to Carl Alexander, February 12, 1861, in Raabe, *Grossherzog*, 77.
115. Gerstenberg, *Zeit*, 60.
116. Huschke, *Musik*, 143–44.
117. Gerstenberg, *Zeit*, 56–57; Messner, *Nationaltheater: Anfängen*, 48; Pöthe, *Carl Alexander*, 208–10.

118. Pöthe, *Carl Alexander*, 210.

119. Dated September 14, 1860, in Greiner-Mai, *Weimar*, 236.

120. Schorn, *Weimar: Karl Friedrichs*, 304; Gerstenberg, *Zeit*, 17, 19; Schrickel, *Geschichte*, 189–90; Huschke, *Musik*, 104–5, 139.

121. Schorn, *Weimar: Karl Friedrichs*, 257; Gerstenberg, *Zeit*, 15–16; Huschke, *Musik*, 121–24.

122. Wagner's flight from Weimar is detailed in Wagner, *Leben*, vol. 1, 486–91; Gottschalg, *Liszt*, 37–39. Also see Walker, *Weimar Years*, 116–18; Pöthe, *Carl Alexander*, 265–67.

123. Altenburg, "Liszt," 12.

124. Jung, *Liszt*, 116–17; Gottschalg, *Liszt*, 43; Huschke, *Musik*, 124–27; Walker, *Weimar Years*, 124–25.

125. Jung, *Liszt*, 144–45; Walker, *Weimar Years*, 118, 126, 241; Pöthe, *Carl Alexander*, 270.

126. Wagner, *Leben*, vol. 2, 775.

127. Raabe, *Grossherzog*, 45–46–74; Huschke, *Musik*, 129–30; Messner, *Nationaltheater: Anfängen*, 58.

128. Gottschalg, *Liszt*, 45; Pöthe, *Carl Alexander*, 271–73.

129. Borchmeyer, "Liszt," 69–71 (quote 69).

130. Newman, *Liszt*, 38, Liszt quoted 83.

131. Bülow, *Briefe*, 237; Huschke, *Musik*, 124.

132. Liszt, *Schriften*, vol. 5, 113–28; Altenburg, "Liszt," 15–17; Ehrlich, "Liszt," 38–39.

133. Jung, *Liszt*, 176–77.

134. Liszt, *Schriften*, vol. 5, 3–80.

135. Ibid., 81–109; Altenburg/Schilling-Wang, "Vorwort," vii–xii.

136. Gerstenberg, *Zeit*, 24–25; Walker, *Weimar Years*, 128–29; Borchmeyer, "Liszt," 71–81.

137. Raabe, *Grossherzog*, 27–29, 56–64, 76; Gerstenberg, *Zeit*, 27. Also see Borchmeyer, "Liszt," 73–76, and p. 45, above.

138. January 21, 1852, in *Bülow, Briefe*, 417.

Chapter Three: Failing the Silver Age, 1861 to 1901

1. Schrickel, *Erinnerungen*, 221–30; Huschke, *Glut*, 140–45; Messner, *Nationaltheater: Anfängen*, 58.

2. Merseburger, *Mythos*, 226–28; Günther, *Weimar*, 111.

3. Thüna, *Erinnerungen*, 42–43; Schlicht quoted in Scheidig, *Malerschule*, 15.

4. Hilmes, *Herrin*, 75–175; Raabe, *Liszt*, 214–15; Walker, *Final Years*, 193–96.

5. Ramann, *Lisztiana*, 242–45; Raabe, *Liszt*, 216; Marggraf, *Liszt*, 41; Walker, *Final Years*, 196.

6. Thüna, *Erinnerungen*, 67; Schorn, *Weimar: Karl Alexander*, 192; Hartwig et al., *Festschrift*, 24–27; Walker, *Final Years*, 207–9; Pöthe, *Weimar*, 169, 190.

7. Alan Walker in *Grove Music Online*; Borodin, "Erinnerungen," 27; Minor, *Fantasies*, 94–106; Marggraf, *Liszt*, 43; Ross, *Rest*, 39.

8. Schorn, *Weimar: Karl Alexander*, 188; Borodin, "Erinnerungen," 28–29.

9. See Newman's criticism in *Liszt*, 242–43. Also Fay, *Music-Study*, 244.

10. Lachmund, *Leben*, 235; Raabe, *Liszt*, 216; Walker, *Final Years*, 414.

11. Walker, *Final Years*, 228–29.

12. Wunderkind d'Albert, like Tausig before him, arrived as a teenager. See Raupp, *d'Albert*, 23–26; Fay, *Music-Study*, 221–22.

13. Plastic examples of instruction are in Jerger, *Klavierunterricht*, 29–43. Also see Lachmund, *Leben*, 36, 58, 63, 106–7, 216; Stradal, *Erinnerungen*, 28–29; Fay, *Music-Study*, esp. 212–14, 222.

14. Thüna, *Erinnerungen*, 66, 103; Walker, *Final Years*, 202.

15. Walker, *Final Years*, 243–45.

16. Fay, *Music-Study*, 235, 259. Fay wrongly elevates Meyendorff to countess. Also see Stradal, *Erinnerungen*, 65–66.

17. Newman, *Liszt*, 224.

18. Stradal, *Erinnerungen*, 112.

19. Fay, *Music-Study*, 227 (quote, italics *sic*), 228.

20. Damrosch, *Life*, 36–40 (quotes 37–38).

21. Schorn, *Menschenalter*, 238; Corinth, *Selbstbiographie*, 119; Reuter, *Kinde*, 377; Borodin, "Erinnerungen," 30; Stradal, *Erinnerungen*, 21, 111.
22. Stradal, *Erinnerungen*, 106; Walker, *Final Years*, 198–99.
23. Walker, *Final Years*, 414.
24. Kapp, *Liszt*, 78–79; Newman, *Liszt*, 250–79.
25. Raabe, *Liszt*, 225; Stradal, *Erinnerungen*, 57; Schorn, *Menschenalter*, 384.
26. Walker, *Final Years*, 242; Stradal, *Erinnerungen*, 141; Lachmund, *Leben*, 77, 118.
27. Walker, *Final Years*, 411–12; Ramann, *Lisztiana*, 253.
28. Ramann, *Lisztiana*, 52.
29. Schorn, *Menschenalter*, 390–91; Stradal, *Erinnerungen*, 139; Walker, *Final Years*, 403–5.
30. Raabe, *Liszt*, 226–27.
31. Walker, *Final Years*, 415.
32. Quoted in Newman, *Liszt*, 209.
33. Borodin, "Erinnerungen," 24.
34. See Meyendorff's complaint, paraphrasing Liszt, in van de Velde, *Geschichte*, 253.
35. Fay, *Music-Study*, 260.
36. Reuter, *Kinde*, 226; Stradal, *Erinnerungen*, 40; Lachmund, *Leben*, 89–90; Schlittgen, *Erinnerungen*, 63–64.
37. Stradal, *Erinnerungen*, 94–95.
38. Gottschalg, *Liszt*, 142–43; Walker, *Final Years*, 253–54.
39. See Schorn, *Weimar: Karl Alexander*, 96–97.
40. Carl Alexander, *Tagebuchblätter*, 52; Preiss, "Hochschulen," 16, 19; Pöthe, *Carl Alexander*, 351–53; Ziegler, "Carl Alexander," 152.
41. Preller, *Tagebücher*, 9, 44, 107; Kalckreuth, *Wesen*, 18; Scheidig, *Malerschule*, 10; Preiss, "Hochschulen," 17–18.
42. Champa, *Painting*, 11–12; Scheidig, *Malerschule*, 19.
43. Preiss, "Hochschulen," 18; Scheidig, *Malerschule*, 23.
44. Schorn, *Weimar: Karl Alexander*, 147–50; Kalckreuth, *Wesen*, 52–55; Winkler, "Dokumentation," 60; Scheidig, *Malerschule*, 15–21.
45. Champa, *Painting*, 29; Scheidig, *Malerschule*, 23–24, 44–45.
46. Runkel, *Böcklin*, 85–96 (Angela Böcklin's quote 91).
47. Schorn, *Weimar: Karl Alexander*, 149; Kalckreuth, *Wesen*, 18, 52–53; Scheidig, *Malerschule*, 13–15, 46, 49, 51, 77–79, 90.
48. Scheidig, *Malerschule*, 52, 92; Ziegler, *Kunst*, 133; Gronau, *Liebermann*, 44–48; Küster, *Liebermann*, 24–31; Watson, *Genius*, 506.
49. Scheidig, *Malerschule*, 210; Ziegler, *Kunst*, 164; Honigmann, "Vorwort," [n.p.].
50. Ziegler, *Kunst*, 139, 143–44; Ziegler, "Klein-Paris," 15.
51. Nissen, *Seele*, 83; Ziegler, *Kunst*, 66–67, 72.
52. Nissen, *Seele*, 84; Ziegler, *Kunst*, 140–43; Scheidig, *Malerschule*, 86, 109.
53. Pöthe, *Carl Alexander*, 366; Ziegler, *Kunst*, 100–2, 143; Scheidig, *Malerschule*, 87–88.
54. Ziegler, *Kunst*, 130–35.
55. Scheidig, *Malerschule*, 134–35; Pöthe, *Carl Alexander*, 363; Ziegler, *Kunst*, 152–54.
56. Corinth, *Selbstbiographie*, 114; Ziegler, *Kunst*, 162.
57. Ziegler, *Kunst*, 103–4.
58. Ibid., 79, 165, 202–4; Kalckreuth, *Wesen*, 170, 181; Pöthe, *Carl Alexander*, 371–72; Scheidig, *Malerschule*, 139–40, 162–63.
59. Ziegler, *Kunst*, 163–64; Scheidig, *Malerschule*, 137–38.
60. Ziegler, *Kunst*, 169, 171.
61. Ibid., 169–89, 206, 213–14; Ziegler, "Klein-Paris," 22; Scheidig, *Malerschule*, 167–68, 209–10.
62. Ziegler, *Kunst*, 68–69, 194, 198; Pöthe, *Carl Alexander*, 373; Scheidig, *Malerschule*, 164, 210–13; Ziegler, "Klein-Paris," 20–21; Preiss, "Hochschulen," 24.
63. Osborne, *Oxford Companion to Art*. Cf. Champa, *Painting*, 33; Mommsen, *Ordnung*, 30–31; Peillex, *Painting*, 49–50; Holt, *Classicists*.
64. Artur Rösl deposition (spring 1894), Richard-Strauss-Institut, Garmisch-Partenkirchen, S4.6.
65. See Strauss's quote in Olhoff, "Berufung," 163.
66. Birkin, "Concert Hall," 3–6; Schuh, *Jugend*, 36, 159.

67. Schuh/Trenner, *Bülow*, 85–86.
68. Schuh, *Jugend*, 194–95; Schrickel, *Geschichte*, 231; Messner, *Nationaltheater: Anfängen*, 59.
69. On Ritter's influence, see Schuh, *Jugend*, 137, 155–56; Ross, *Rest*, 15.
70. Schuh, *Eltern*, 113–14, 118–19, 121; Schuh/Trenner, *Bülow*, 86; Birkin, "Concert Hall," 8; Schuh, *Jugend*, 161, 181.
71. Schuh/Trenner, *Bülow*, 85, 88; Schuh, *Eltern*, 115, 117, 120–22; Birkin, "Opera House," 10–11, 18; Birkin, "Concert Hall," 10–12.
72. *Weimarische Zeitung* of November 2, 1889, quoted in Birkin, "Concert Hall," 11; Artur Rösl deposition (spring 1894), Richard-Strauss-Institut, Garmisch-Partenkirchen, S4.6; Schoder quoted in *Theater- und Musikwoche* 1, no. 29 (1919): 7.
73. Schuh, *Jugend*, 191, 195, 207–10; Birkin, "Opera House," 19; Pöthe, *Carl Alexander*, 286; Lehmann anecdote told to author by Gabriele Strauss, Garmisch, October 5, 2004.
74. Birkin, "Concert Hall," 10, 13–14, 18; Gutheil-Schoder, *Erlebtes*, 7–8; Schuh, *Eltern*, 132, 140, 152; Schuh, *Jugend*, 254–56.
75. Birkin, "Concert Hall," 22; Nissen, *Seele*, 85; Pöthe, *Carl Alexander*, 287; Schuh, *Eltern*, 146; Kalckreuth, *Wesen*, 167.
76. Schuh, *Jugend*, 161, 249; Voss, *Leben*, 196.
77. Schuh, *Jugend*, 243, 252, 256; Walter, *Strauss*, 93–95.
78. Strauss quoted in Schuh, *Jugend*, 253.
79. Walter, *Strauss*, 97.
80. Schuh, *Eltern*, 173, 180.
81. Ibid., 167–70, 175–76, 182–86, 191, 194; Schuh, *Jugend*, 270, 328, 334–41, 344–45.
82. Strauss quoted in Schuh, *Jugend*, 256.
83. Schuh, *Eltern*, 195; Schuh, *Jugend*, 329, 335, 339–41; Birkin, "Opera House," 33.
84. Ross, *Rest*, 16; Schrickel, *Geschichte*, 233; Schuh, *Jugend*, 369; Huschke, *Glut*, 154; Birkin, "Opera House," 33; Bryan Gilliam in *Grove Music Online*.
85. Raupp, *d'Albert*, 100–5 (quote 105); Schrickel, *Geschichte*, 235–40; Pöthe, *Carl Alexander*, 287–90.
86. Messner, *Nationaltheater: Anfängen*, 61.
87. Raschdau, *Weimar*, 22, 28, 88, 91, 103, 111; Egloffstein, *Weimar*, 68, 101–2; Schrickel, *Geschichte*, 240–41; Reuter, *Kinde*, 309–10.
88. Dent, *Busoni*, 125–27 (quote 127).
89. Walther, "Goethe," 373; Berghahn, "Weimar," 65; Borchmeyer, "Goethe," 191, 194; Oellers, "Sophienausgabe," 103–4.
90. Berghahn, "Weimar," 67–71; Mommsen, *Avantgarde*, 22–25; Pöthe, *Carl Alexander*, 167–68.
91. Borchmeyer, "Goethe," 189; Mandelkow, *Rezeptionsgeschichte*, vol. 1, 162.
92. Böhme, "Was," 10.
93. Böttiger proposal in Greiner-Mai, *Weimar*, 186–87.
94. Pöthe, *Carl Alexander*, 151–52.
95. Ibid., 186–87.
96. Merseburger, *Mythos*, 207–8.
97. Barner, "Goethe," 89; Borchmeyer, "Goethe," 193; Mandelkow, *Rezeptionsgeschichte*, vol. 1, 85; Greiner-Mai, *Weimar*, 181; Lepenies, *Kultur*, 383–84.
98. Details in Schorn, *Weimar: Karl Friedrichs*, 285–88.
99. Ibid., 289–90; Huschke, *Musik*, 124; Gerstenberg, *Zeit*, 46; Nipperdey, "Nationalidee," 559, 585.
100. Schmidt-Möbus/Möbus, *Kulturgeschichte*, 222–23; Merseburger, *Mythos*, 213.
101. Mandelkow, *Rezeptionsgeschichte*, vol. 1, 153–56, 187.
102. Applegate, *Nation*.
103. Grimm, "Goethe," 460–63; Walther, "Goethe," 377–79; Borchmeyer, "Goethe," 196; Vaget, "Faust," 146–47; Barner, "Goethe," 89.
104. Wildenbruch, *Werke*, 398; Nipperdey, "Nationalidee," 543, 564; Berghahn, "Weimar," 72; Wahl, *Religion*, 22–28; Mandelkow, *Rezeptionsgeschichte*, vol. 1, 135.
105. Hobsbawm in Hobsbawm/Ranger, *Invention*, 1–13, 263–78 (quote 1).
106. Berghahn, "Weimar," 72–75; Bollenbeck, "Weimar," 216–18; Borchmeyer, *Klassik*, 61; Wichert, "Bismarck," 322, 325; Ulbricht, "Goethe," 115–20; Mommsen, *Ordnung*, 76.
107. Grimm, "Goethe," 460–63 (quote 463).

108. Walther, "Goethe," 362–89.
109. Bismarck, *Gedanken*, 132, 161; Gall, *Bismarck*, 49, 460, 514.
110. Golz, "Goethe- und Schiller-Archiv," 13; Oellers, "Sophienausgabe," 107; Buchwald, *Geschichte*, 326.
111. Raschdau, *Weimar*, 37; Golz, "Goethe- und Schiller-Archiv," 15; Jena, *Quartett*, 258; Pöthe, *Carl Alexander*, 191.
112. See Vaget, *Goethe: Der Mann*, 17–18.
113. Goetz, *Jahre*, 33–41 (Kuno Fischer's words 33–34: first quote); Schorn, *Weimar: Karl Alexander*, 264–66; Mandelkow, "Goethe-Gesellschaft," 340–46 (second quote 344, third quote 346); Oellers, "Sophienausgabe," 108–9; Golz, "Goethe- und Schiller-Archiv," 17–18; Ulbricht, "Visionen," 24.
114. Egloffstein, *Weimar*, 65–66; Oellers, "Sophienausgabe," 110–11; Buchwald, *Geschichte*, 366–69; Golz, "Goethe- und Schiller-Archiv," 16–40.
115. Kocka, *Society*, 24.
116. On Sophie, see Raschdau, *Weimar*, 102–3.
117. Egloffstein, *Weimar*; Schorn, *Weimar: Karl Alexander*.
118. Merseburger, *Mythos*, 235–38.
119. Voss, *Leben*, 273.
120. For Strauss see Schuh, *Eltern*, 127–29; Schuh, *Jugend*, 205; Kater, *Composers*, 243–45.
121. Goetz, *Jahre*, 35.
122. Wildenbruch, *Grossherzog*, 13–14; Egloffstein, *Weimar*, 19; Blumenthal, *Wildenbruch*, 18–19; Wildenbruch, *Werke*, 199.
123. Elster, *Wildenbruch*, 50 (first quote); Raschdau, *Weimar*, 119 (second quote).
124. Litzmann, *Wildenbruch*, 21–22; Elster, *Wildenbruch*, 30, 50.
125. Elster, *Wildenbruch*, 51.
126. Litzmann, *Wildenbruch*, 127–28.
127. Egloffstein, *Weimar*, 17–18; Litzmann, *Wildenbruch*, 125–26; Wildenbruch, *Werke*, 397.
128. Litzmann, *Wildenbruch*, 125, 232; Elster, *Wildenbruch*, 54; 60; Wildenbruch, *Grossherzog*, 12; Wildenbruch, *Werke*, 211–22, 397.
129. Elster, *Wildenbruch*, 55; Wahl, *Religion*, 193; Merseburger, *Mythos*, 233.
130. Elster, *Wildenbruch*, 56–59; Wildenbruch, *Werke*, 211–22.
131. Raschdau, *Weimar*, 119.
132. Bollenbeck, "Weimar," 218 (quote); Wildenbruch, *Werke*, 398; Litzmann, *Wildenbruch*, 16–19; Elster, *Wildenbruch*, 49, 54.
133. Fuller, *Grandfather*, 59–61.
134. Bartels, *Weshalb* (quote 3).
135. See Stern, *Politics*; Mosse, *Crisis*.
136. Bartels, *Dichtung*, 22–31, 41, 228–30. Also Detlef Cölln in Cölln, *Bartels* (1935), 14–15.
137. "Goethelied" (August 28, 1887), in Bartels, *Gedichte*, 131.
138. Bartels, *Herkunft*, 10.
139. Walter Loose in Loose, *Festgabe* (1944), 55.
140. Bartels, *Gedichte*, 154.
141. For the burial August 28, 1900, see Hoffmann, *Geschichte*, 48; Peters, *Schwester*, 244.
142. By devious means. See Peters, *Schwester*, 225–30.
143. Testimonies and photographs in Volz, *Nietzsche*, 491–504; Schumacher, *Stufen*, 199–200.
144. Förster-Nietzsche in Volz, *Nietzsche*, 298, 305, 505; Hayman, *Nietzsche*, 349–50.
145. Hayman, *Nietzsche*, 342.
146. Ibid., 347.
147. Cancik, "Nietzsche-Kult Wilhelminischen," esp. 406–7; Aschheim, *Nietzsche*, 46–48.
148. Binion, *Frau Lou*.
149. See Heftrich, "Goethe," 17–18.
150. Diethe, *Sister*, 83–93; Hoffmann, *Geschichte*, 31–46; Naake, *Nietzsche*, 24–28.
151. Peters, *Schwester*, 236–37.
152. Steiner, *Nietzsche*, 185–90.
153. Baron Detlev von Liliencron (March 7, 1900) in Greiner-Mai, *Weimar*, 252; Hayman, *Nietzsche*, 349; Peters, *Schwester*, 236.
154. Naake, *Nietzsche*, 33–34; Günzel, *Fürstenhaus*, 171.

155. Alfred Brendel, "A Pianist's A-V," *NYRB* (July 11, 2013): 25. See Honegger/Massenkeil, *Lexikon*, 132–33.

Chapter Four: The Quest for a "New Weimar," 1901 to 1918

1. Naake, *Nietzsche*, 25–26.
2. Ibid., 24, 37–39; Hoffmann, *Geschichte*, 31; Pöthe, *Weimar*, 81–85, 90–94.
3. Aschheim, *Nietzsche*, 46; Naake, *Nietzsche*, 25; Diethe, *Sister*, 89; Easton, "Rise," 499.
4. Naake, *Nietzsche*, 24–25, 41; Peters, *Schwester*, 244.
5. Easton, "Rise," 499; Hoffmann, *Geschichte*, 34.
6. Van de Velde, *Geschichte*, 161; Föhl, "Kunstpolitik," 66; Easton, "Rise," 500–1; Michèle Lavallée/Jane Block/Paul Kruty in *Oxford Art Online*; Watson, *Genius*, 508–10.
7. Redslob, *Weimar*, 110; van de Velde, *Geschichte*, 54; Föhl, *Architekt*, 17–24.
8. Van de Velde, *Geschichte*, 139; Post/Werner, *Herrscher*, 392.
9. Easton, *Count*, 13–96; van de Velde, *Geschichte*, 161.
10. Van de Velde, *Geschichte*, 54, 188; Föhl, "Kunstpolitik," 69.
11. Peters, *Schwester*, 245; Easton, "Rise," 502–3.
12. Van de Velde, *Geschichte*, 196–98; Post/Werner, *Herrscher*, 391–93.
13. Dolgner, *Weimar*, 7, 14–15; Post/Werner, *Herrscher*, 394.
14. Van de Velde, *Geschichte*, 211; Easton, *Count*, 104–5; Dolgner, *Weimar*, 12.
15. Dolgner, *Weimar*, 8; Redslob, *Weimar*, 43; van de Velde, *Geschichte*, 309; Easton, *Count*, 105.
16. Hoffmann, *Geschichte*, 55; Peters, *Schwester*, 246–48; van de Velde, *Geschichte*, 254; Nostitz, *Europa*, 106–7.
17. Dolgner, *Weimar*, 13; Post/Werner, *Herrscher*, 395; Müller, *Women*, 8; Winkler, "Dokumentation," 96–97.
18. Van de Velde in Winkler, "Dokumentation," 97–99, 105–7.
19. Ibid. 107–8, 116; van de Velde, *Geschichte*, 291–97; Post/Werner, *Herrscher*, 396, 398; Föhl et al., *Bauhaus-Museum*, 21–26; Schädlich, *Hochschule*, 18–19.
20. Letter of October 8, 1907, printed in Winkler, "Dokumentation," 99.
21. Van de Velde in Winkler, "Dokumentation," 117; Föhl, *Architekt*, 247–63.
22. Van de Velde, *Geschichte*, 373–74, 377, 381–84; Post/Werner, *Herrscher*, 402.
23. Van de Velde quoted in Easton, *Count*, 105; van de Velde, *Geschichte*, 295; Föhl et al., *Bauhaus-Museum*, 20; Post/Werner, *Herrscher*, 399.
24. Föhl, "Kunstpolitik," 77; Scheffler, *Jahre*, 28–31; Redslob, *Weimar*, 110; Nostitz, *Europa*, 105; van de Velde, *Geschichte*, 219, 298–302.
25. Nostitz, *Europa*, 104; Steinfeld, *Weimar*, 223–24; Preiss, *Abschied*, 127.
26. Van de Velde (March 1910) in Winkler, "Dokumentation," 107; van de Velde, *Geschichte*, 294; Post/Werner, *Herrscher*, 397–98; Hecht, *Streit*, 9; Föhl, "Kunstpolitik," 77–78; Taube, *Wanderjahre*, 269.
27. Van de Velde to Grand Duke Wilhelm Ernst, October 1, 1915, in Winkler, "Dokumentation," 113; van de Velde ibid., 106; van de Velde, *Geschichte*, 297; Dolgner, *Weimar*, 15; Post/Werner, *Herrscher*, 401.
28. Van de Velde, *Geschichte*, 297, 345–46; Föhl, "Kunstpolitik," 72; Post/Werner, *Herrscher*, 400–1.
29. Van de Velde, *Geschichte*, 159–60 (quote 159); Munch's portrait on dust jacket of Easton, *Count*; original in Oslo Munch Museum.
30. See Simon, *Bodenhausen*, 64–71, 82–83.
31. Easton, "Rise," 514; Easton, *Count*, 102; van de Velde, *Geschichte*, 227; Kessler to Bodenhausen, April 6, 1902, in Simon, *Bodenhausen*, 68 (quote).
32. Preiss, "Hochschulen," 28; Föhl, "Kunstpolitik," 67–68; Post/Werner, *Herrscher*, 406–7.
33. Easton, "Rise," 510, 514; Easton, *Count*, 103, 121; Föhl, "Kunstpolitik," 74–76; Post/Werner, *Herrscher*, 408–9; Annegret Friedrich in *Oxford Art Online*.
34. Penzler, *Reden*, 61.
35. Watson, *Genius*, 525; Kater, *Never*, 9.
36. Paret, *Secession*, 27, 86.
37. Paret, *Art*, 165–80.

38. Paret, *Secession*, 113–55; Maria Makela/Beth Irwin Lewis/Cynthia Prossinger/Helmut Börsch-Supan in *Oxford Art Online*.
39. Easton, *Count*, 110.
40. Kessler, *Künstlerbund*, 15.
41. Merseburger, *Mythos*, 257, 261–64.
42. Penzler, *Reden*, 25–26. Suggestion is in Post/Werner, *Herrscher*, 379, 410–12.
43. Post/Werner, *Herrscher*, 413.
44. Van de Velde, *Geschichte*, 242–43; Kalckreuth, *Wesen*, 295–99.
45. Easton, "Rise," 515–16; Nabbe, "Zeichen," 310.
46. Beth Irwin Lewis in *Oxford Art Online*; Easton, *Count*, 114–15.
47. Easton, *Count*, 113–14.
48. Easton's translation as quoted ibid., 145.
49. Müller-Krumbach, "Kessler," 206–20; Post/Werner, *Herrscher*, 412–13.
50. Simon, *Bodenhausen*, 64, 68, 70–71; Easton, *Count*, 102; Post/Werner, *Herrscher*, 412.
51. Easton, *Count*, 128; Föhl, "Kunstpolitik," 74.
52. Paret, *Secession*, 50–51; Reinhold Heller in *Oxford Art Online*.
53. März, "Portrait," 185–91 (Munch's quote 185).
54. Kessler quoted in März, "Portrait," 191.
55. Easton, *Count*, 146–54 (first quote 151, second quote 154). Also see Watzdorf-Bachoff, *Wandel*, 142; Post/Werner, *Herrscher*, 415–27; Föhl, "Kunstpolitik," 86–87.
56. Reprinted in Winkler, "Dokumentation," 84–85. Also see Feuchter-Schawelka, "Kampf," 220.
57. Easton, "Rise," 510; Easton, *Count*, 121.
58. Feuchter-Schawelka, "Kampf," 223–24; Post/Werner, *Herrscher*, 385–86.
59. Feuchter-Schawelka, "Kampf," 221–22; Greta Stroeh in *Oxford Art Online*.
60. Post/Werner, *Herrscher*, 381; Feuchter-Schawelka, "Kampf," 219.
61. Steckner, *Brütt*, 51–54, 313; Brigitte Hüfler in *Oxford Art Online*.
62. Förster-Nietzsche quoted in Hoffmann, *Geschichte*, 50; E. Holzer ibid.; Naake, *Nietzsche*, 61.
63. Lamm quoted in Hoffmann, *Geschichte*, 68–69. See also Förster-Nietzsche, *Nietzsche-Archiv*, 42; Diethe, *Sister*, 96–98.
64. Förster-Nietzsche, *Leben* and *Nietzsche-Archiv*, 9.
65. Möbius, *Nietzsche*, esp. 50–97; Förster-Nietzsche, *Leben*, vol. 2 (*Zweite Abtheilung*), 898–932. Also see Förster-Nietzsche, *Der einsame Nietzsche*, 519–50; Peters, *Schwester*, 249–51; Volz, *Nietzsche*, 4.
66. Wollkopf, "Nietzsche-Archiv," 127–28; Naake, *Nietzsche*, 62–63; Schüssler, *Hardt*, 102.
67. Peters, *Schwester*, 251–53; Naake, *Nietzsche*, 64, 66–68.
68. Watzdorf-Bachoff, *Wandel*, 125.
69. Peters, *Schwester*, 268; Oehler, *Zukunft*, 12; van de Velde, *Geschichte*, 229; Wollkopf, "Nietzsche-Archiv," 129; Scholz, *Ilm*, 97–98, 103–4; Nostitz, *Europa*, 113–14; Pöthe, *Weimar*, 22, 95–104.
70. Peters, *Schwester*, 265; 130–33; Hoffmann, *Geschichte*, 89; Naake, *Nietzsche*, 49.
71. Naake, *Nietzsche*, 48; Hoffmann, *Geschichte*, 70, 88; Peters, *Schwester*, 262–63, 271–77.
72. Ian Buruma, "The Chatty Chronicler," *NYRB* (January 12, 2012): 18.
73. Easton, *Count*, 185–194 (Kessler quoted 193), 220–21; Nabbe, "Zeichen," 306–22; Peters, *Schwester*, 269–71; van de Velde, *Geschichte*, 250–53; Wollkopf, "Nietzsche-Archiv," 133–35.
74. Peters, *Schwester*, 273 (quote), 275–77; Naake, *Nietzsche*, 70–73; Diethe, *Sister*, 137–40; Kirsten, *Weimar*, 132–33; Wollkopf, "Nietzsche-Archiv," 135.
75. Biographical data on Freytag-Loringhoven in Günther et al., *Weimar*, 126.
76. See Adolf Bartels, "Heimatkunst," *Deutsche Heimat* 1, no. 1 (1900): 10–19, esp. 17–18. Critically: Applegate, *Nation*, 104–6; Bergmann, *Agrarromantik*, 102–21. On Langbehn, see Stern, *Politics*, 131–227.
77. Mommsen, *Ordnung*, 72–73. See "Jüdische Schauspieler," *Kunstwart* 7 (1893/94): 134–36.
78. See Bartels, *Geschichte*, e.g. 588–90; Bartels, *Lebensarbeit*, 16; Fuller, *Grandfather*, 73–74, 77–78, 87.
79. Merseburger, *Mythos*, 271.
80. Fritsch lived from 1852 to 1933. See his *Handbuch*. For deference to Bartels, see 89, 355, 570. Also Ulbricht, "Regeneration," 197, 203.

81. E. Reimers in Cölln, *Bartels* (1935), 43.
82. Bartels, *Rasse*, 46–47, 56, 194–95; Bartels, *Gedichte*, 58, 71–72, 81, 88, 161–62; Bartels, *Judentum*, 17–19, 22; Merseburger, *Mythos*, 272; Fuller, *Grandfather*, 79–80.
83. Fuller, *Grandfather*, 152.
84. Bartels, *Judentum*, 20; Bartels in Loose, *Festgabe* (1944), 31–35; Bartels, *Rasse*, 72–73, 189, 192; E. Reimers in Cölln, *Bartels* (1935), 41.
85. Bartels, *Gedichte*, 20; Hinze-Reinhold, *Lebenserinnerungen*, 47; Bartels quoted (1901) in Walter Loose, in Loose, *Festgabe* (1944), 30, and for 1908: 34; Bartels, *Rasse*, 189; Günther et al., *Weimar*, 191.
86. Bartels, *Rasse*, 196–97; Bartels (1908) in Loose, *Festgabe* (1944), 34; E. Reimers in Cölln, *Bartels* (1935), 41.
87. Bernstein, "Heine's Versatility"; Watson, *Genius*, 300–1.
88. Bartels, *Heine*; Fuller, *Grandfather*, 115.
89. Bartels, *Heine*, esp. 28, 94–96, 116–20, 288–89, 362–63; Bartels, *Heine-Genossen*, 74–90; Bartels, *Judentum*, 11–12; Fuller, *Grandfather*, 114–25.
90. Bartels, *Nationalfestspiele*, 1–6.
91. Loose, *Festgabe* (1944), 117–18; Bonn, *Jugend*, 92–97, 258–67.
92. Bartels, *Nationalfestspiele*, 122–26.
93. Ibid., 8–17, 28–29, 47, 63, 67, 71, 77, 100–1, 112, 118–19.
94. See the somewhat superficial analysis in Fuller, *Grandfather*, 89–91.
95. Günther et al., *Weimar*, 475–76; Fiedler, "Weimar", 139–40; Pöthe, *Weimar*, 157–58.
96. Mosse, *Crisis*, 82; Naake, *Nietzsche*, 88; Ulbricht, "Kulturrevolution," 44; Ulbricht, "Regeneration," 198, 204.
97. See his *Zukunft*, esp. 7, 22.
98. Steinfeld, *Weimar*, 201; Mosse, *Crisis*, 80; Kater, *"Ahnenerbe"*, 54–56, 80–81, 90.
99. Ulbricht, "Regeneration," 199.
100. See Wachler's exposition of 1893 in *Heimat*, 24–35, of 1903 in Weimar, esp. 5, and Wachler, *Freilichtbühne*, 46–53.
101. Wachler, *Freilichtbühne*, 9–32; Wachler, *Sommerspiele*, 3–24.
102. Wachler, *Freilichtbühne*, 31, 47, 51.
103. Ulbricht, "Regeneration," 199, 204; Langenbucher, *Lienhard*, esp. 19, 51, 64–65, 92–114; Merseburger, *Mythos*, 267–69; Müller-Seidel, *Geschichtlichkeit*, 5. Also see Lienhard, *Nordlandslieder*; Lienhard, *Vorherrschaft*, 18 (quote), also 44; Lienhard, *Oberflächen-Kultur*, esp. 58–61.
104. Lienhard's quote in Müller-Seidel, *Geschichtlichkeit*, 5. Also see Lienhard, *Vorherrschaft*, 29; Lienhard, *Ahasver*.
105. Barthel, *Lienhard*, 132–36, quote 133.
106. *Waldsonne*. See Schönberg, *Lieder*. Also Albrecht et al., *Lexikon*, vol. 2, 269.
107. See esp. 300–11. In Schlaf's novel *Mutter Lise*, the young Danish Jew Silvercron is sickly and, still a student, commits suicide (esp. 302, 324). See also Schlaf, *Reich*, 119, 143, 285; Schlaf, *Die Suchenden*, 277, 310–11; Kafitz, *Schlaf*, 21–161; Aschheim, *Nietzsche*, 85–92; Kurt Meyer-Rotermund in Bäte et al., *Schlaf-Buch*, 59–60.
108. Schlaf, *Leben*, 45–46, 48; Ludwig Bäte in Bäte et al., *Schlaf-Buch*, 26–27.
109. Schlaf's facsimile testimony in *Das Land Goethes*, 108; Schlaf's strongly autobiographical novel *Der Kleine*; Kurt Meyer-Rotermund in Bäte et al., *Schlaf-Buch*, 52–56.
110. Kafitz, *Schlaf*, 163–84.
111. Scholz, *Ilm*, 97–98, 103–4; Schlaf, *Leben*, 46; Albrecht et al., *Lexikon*, vol. 2, 286; Günther et al., *Weimar*, 390.
112. Scholz, *Jude*; Žmegač, *Jude*, 21–55; Albrecht et al., *Lexikon*, vol. 2, 286.
113. Bäte, *Akte*, 21–29, 34–39; Albrecht et al., *Lexikon*, vol. 2, 286.
114. Quoted in Elster, *Wildenbruch*, 67. Also see Wildenbruch's poem for Schiller, "Heros, bleib bei uns!" (1905), reprinted in Oellers, *Schiller*, 484–89; Wildenbruch, *Grossherzog*, 9; Wildenbruch, *Werke*, 264–67; Wahl, *Religion*, 265–70; Litzmann, *Wildenbruch*, 274.
115. Wildenbruch, *Wort*, 8–27 (quote 15); Litzmann, *Wildenbruch*, 263–68; Post/Werner, *Herrscher*, 85–86.
116. Wildenbruch, *Werke*, 275–76; Goetz, *Jahre*, 53. Also see Litzmann, *Wildenbruch*, 275, 284.
117. Schrickel, *Geschichte*, 246, 253–54.

118. Messner, *Nationaltheater: Anfängen*, 61.
119. Krell, *Das*, 11.
120. Scholz, *Ilm*, 107.
121. Bartels, *Nationalfestspiele*, 4–5; see pp. 120–22, above.
122. Messner, *Nationaltheater: Anfängen*, 63; Okrassa, *Raabe*, 34; Schrickel, *Geschichte*, 245–54.
123. Loose, *Festgabe* (1944), 55.
124. Okrassa, *Raabe*, 30–39; Huschke, *Glut*, 167–72.
125. Raabe, *Kulturwille*, 20, 29, 37, 60, 63, 65, 87; cases of non-"Aryans" Heinrich Unger and Wolfgang Stresemann in Wulf, *Musik*, 131–32; Kater, *Muse*, 19–20. In this regard alone, the overall benevolent characterization of Raabe by Okrassa runs contrary to the facts.
126. Hinze-Reinhold, *Lebenserinnerungen*, 45–46.
127. Post/Werner, *Herrscher*, 438; Okrassa, *Raabe*, 29. See Voss's 1914 poem, "Der Kaiser, unser Kaiser!," in *Das Land Goethes*, 123.
128. Wehler, *Kaiserreich*, 105–41; Wehler, *Gesellschaftsgeschichte: Dritter Band*, 1066–1295; *Gesellschaftsgeschichte: Vierter Band*, 69–111.
129. Post/Werner, *Herrscher*, 356.
130. Mommsen, *Ordnung*, 144–47, 185–87, 211, 222–23; Mommsen, *Avantgarde*, 140; Roethe, *Art*, esp. 9–19, 32, 42–46, 51; Wichert, "Bismarck," 332–33; Lepenies, *Kultur*, 48, 58–60; Watson, *Genius*, 531–36.
131. Roethe, *Art*, 14, 25, 31, 47; Mommsen, *Ordnung*, 182; Ulbricht, "Visionen," 25; Lepenies, *Kultur*, 49, 59, 61, 214. Also see Wichert, "Bismarck," 326–29; Golz, "Goethe-und Schillerarchiv," 46; Mandelkow, "Goethe-Gesellschaft," 346; individual contributions to *Das Land Goethes*.
132. Jasper, "Faust", 180.
133. Wehler, *Kaiserreich*, 41–59; Wehler, *Gesellschaftsgeschichte: Dritter Band*, 493–699.
134. Keyser, *Städtebuch*, 389; Eberhardt, *Umwelt*, 14; Rüss, *Dokumente*, 19.
135. Entry 81 in Rüss, *Dokumente*, 19.
136. See Scholz, *Ilm*, 89; Taube, *Wanderjahre*, 20.
137. Scholz, *Ilm*, 94–95; Mauersberger, *Hitler*, 49; Müller-Krumbach, "Kessler," 221.
138. Calculations on the basis of figures in Post/Werner, *Herrscher*, 305–6; *Statistisches Jahrbuch* (1923), 301.
139. Wiesner, *Ernst*, 36–56; Rüss, *Dokumente*, 87–88; Walter, "Thüringen," 26.
140. Rüss, *Dokumente*, 90, 94, 97.
141. Ibid., 6.
142. Günther et al., *Weimar*, 489–90; Günther, *Weimar*, 134.
143. Rüss, *Dokumente*, 6; Post/Werner, *Herrscher*, 487–90. For Berlin, see Large, *Berlin*, 127–35; Vienna, see Kater, *Never*, 47–48.
144. Günther et al., *Weimar*, 490.
145. Post/Werner, *Herrscher*, 491–94; Günther, *Weimar*, 27–28.
146. Mauersberger, *Hitler*, 48.
147. Ibid., 50; Post/Werner, *Herrscher*, 196.
148. Post/Werner, *Herrscher*, 502–10.
149. Ibid., 510–15; Baudert, *Ende*, 18–31.

Chapter Five: The Weimar Bauhaus Experiment, 1919 to 1925

1. Schreyer, *Erinnerungen*, 211–14; Dietrich never mentioned the affair and the true reason why she left Weimar: Dietrich, *Nehmt*, 42–45.
2. Weber, *Villen*, vol. 5, 176 (Dietrich's quotes ibid.); Hecker, *Weimar*, 73–74; Kater, *Composers*, 65; Hilmes, *Witwe*, 319–85.
3. Droste, *Bauhaus*, 16–17; Scheidig, *Bauhaus*, 6–16; Hüter, *Bauhaus*, 205; Winkler, "Dokumentation," 123–25; Wahl, *Meisterratsprotokolle*, 13–14.
4. Droste, *Bauhaus*, 17.
5. Reproduction of Cathedral ibid., 18.
6. Gropius in Hüter, *Bauhaus*; Droste, *Bauhaus*, 18–22.
7. Gay, *Modernism*, 314.
8. Gropius interviewed in *Der Monat* (June 21, 1969): 80–81.

9. Schüssler, *Hardt*, 175; Jaeggi, "Mysterium," 37–43.

10. Gropius in Hüter, *Bauhaus*, 204; Meyer, *Briefe*, 109; Schüssler, *Hardt*, 176; Mauersberger, *Hitler*, 137; Findeli, "Goethe," 109.

11. Wahl, "Bauhaus," 23–24.

12. Gropius interview, *Der Monat* (June 21, 1969): 81.

13. Schlemmer in Hünecke, *Schlemmer*, 69; Scheidig, *Bauhaus*, 18; Isaacs, *Gropius*, 209.

14. Droste, *Bauhaus*, 22–23; Martina Rudloff in *Oxford Art Online*.

15. Ute Ackermann in Wahl, *Meisterratsprotokolle*, 30; Anna Rowland in *Oxford Art Online*.

16. Droste, *Bauhaus*, 23–24; Anna Rowland in *Oxford Art Online*.

17. Droste, *Bauhaus*, 62; Ann Temkin in *Oxford Art Online*.

18. Gropius in Schlemmer et al., *Bühne*, 87; Scheidig, *Bauhaus*, 24; Karin von Maur in *Oxford Art Online*.

19. Droste, *Bauhaus*, 24; Hünecke, *Schlemmer*, 105.

20. Vivian Endicott Barnett in *Oxford Art Online*.

21. Terence A. Senter ibid.

22. Quoted in Droste, *Bauhaus*, 34.

23. Scheidig, *Bauhaus*, 7; Droste, *Bauhaus*, 35, 75, 86, 98; Argan, *Gropius*, 23–24; Föhl et al., *Bauhaus-Museum*, 50–52, 68–70.

24. Ute Ackermann in Wahl, *Meisterratsprotokolle*, 24.

25. Lyonel to Julia Feininger, May 21, 1919, in Ness, *Feininger*, 99.

26. Ness, *Feininger*, 104, 106; Scheidig, *Bauhaus*, 6; Hünecke, *Schlemmer*, 72; Neumann, *Bauhaus*, 124, 146–47; Wahl, *Meisterratsprotokolle*, 91, 106.

27. First quote by Felix Klee in Neumann, *Bauhaus*, 25, also 26; last quotes Loewenberg, "Bauhaus," 223–24. Also see Droste, *Bauhaus*, 37–38; Feininger, "Bauhauskapelle."

28. Hüter, *Bauhaus*, 222–23; Wahl, *Meisterratsprotokolle*, 103, 148, 370.

29. Wahl, *Meisterratsprotokolle*, 284; Ute Ackermann, ibid., 25; Droste, *Bauhaus*, 46–47; Stenzel/Winkler, *Kontroversen*, 52–65; Hüter, *Bauhaus*, 32–33; Ulbricht, "Willkomm," 22–23; Günther et al., *Weimar*, 126.

30. Scheidig, *Bauhaus*, 25; Droste, *Bauhaus*, 44–45, 82; Föhl et al., *Bauhaus-Museum*, 62–64; Lyonel to Julia Feininger, August 1, 1923, in Ness, *Feininger*, 127 (quotes).

31. Scheidig, *Bauhaus*, 31–32; Droste, *Bauhaus*, 60–61.

32. Gropius declaration, February 3, 1922, in Hüter, *Bauhaus*, 230–31; Gropius (1923) in *Staatliches Bauhaus*, 10–15; Föhl et al., *Bauhaus-Museum*, 45, 100; Stenzel/Winkler, *Kontroversen*, 65.

33. See Tagebuch Schlemmer, June 1922, in Hünecke, *Schlemmer*, 93; Lyonel to Julia Feininger, October 5, 1922, in Hüter, *Bauhaus*, 236.

34. Stuckenschmidt, *Musik*, 5–9.

35. Stravinsky, *Autobiography*, 107–8.

36. Scheidig, *Bauhaus*, 33–36; Droste, *Bauhaus*, 105–9; Föhl et al., *Bauhaus-Museum*, 84, 98–100; Stenzel/Winkler, *Kontroversen*, 78; Isaacs, *Gropius*, 296–301.

37. Brockmann, *History*, 85–86.

38. Wahl, *Meisterratsprotokolle*, 313; Hüter, *Bauhaus*, 41.

39. "Zu unseren Abeiten," *Junge Menschen* 5 (November 1924): 187; Scheidig, *Bauhaus*, 37–43; Droste, *Bauhaus*, 79–99.

40. Walden/Schreyer, *Sturm*.

41. "Oddly Brilliant Beginnings," *NYRB* (September 29, 2011): 24.

42. Wolfradt, "Feininger," 167 (quote); Coellen, "Feininger," 132–37; Muche, *Blickpunkt*, 133–34; Scheidig, *Bauhaus*, 18; Luckhardt, *Feininger*, 33–38, 172–77.

43. Martina Rudloff in *Oxford Art Online* (quote); Scheidig, *Bauhaus*, 18, 23; Droste, *Bauhaus*, 68–70; Stephan, "Bauhaus," 9–10; Hartog, "Bildhauer," 17–19; Jakobson, "Dornburg," 21–27.

44. Weber, *Bauhaus*, 130. Weber's account on the whole is unreliable; it contains many distortions and mistakes, such as that Grand Duke Wilhelm Ernst was a progressive left–wing monarch (74). Also see Paul Klee, in *Staatliches Bauhaus*, 24–25; Klee, *Moderne Kunst*, 51–53; Ann Temkin in *Oxford Art Online*; Scheidig, *Bauhaus*, 63, 65; Muche, *Blickpunkt*, 144; Wahl, *Meisterratsprotokolle*, 154; Föhl et al., *Bauhaus-Museum*, 42–43, 88–89; Baumgartner, "Itten," 108, 110, 112; Okuda, "Klee," 57–61.

45. Gropius in Schlemmer et al., *Bühne*, 88–90 (quote); Schlemmer in Schneede, *Jahre*, 181–83; Föhl et al., *Bauhaus-Museum*, 74, 89; Wahl, *Meisterratsprotokolle*, 287; Droste, *Bauhaus*, 101–3; Karin von Maur in *Oxford Art Online*.

46. Neumann, *Bauhaus*, 53; Hans Haffenrichter ibid., 50–51; Schreyer, *Texte*, 63–108; Schreyer, *Erinnerungen*, 158; Muche, *Blickpunkt*, 129; Isaacs, *Gropius*, 294; Droste, *Bauhaus*, 101; Föhl et al., *Bauhaus-Museum*, 72–73, 90; Weber, "Totenbild," 94–95.

47. See Kandinsky, *Geistige*, 124, and reproductions opp. 98, 106, 122; Vivian Endicott Barnett in *Oxford Art Online* (quote); Julia Voss, "Die Thronstürmerin," *FAZ.NET*, April 16, 2011; Watson, *Genius*, 515–18.

48. Kandinsky in Kandinsky/Marc, *Reiter* (Munich, 1912), 130–31.

49. Kandinsky, *Geistige*, esp. 72–90, 100–5 (quotes 48, 72); Kandinsky (1923) in *Staatliches Bauhaus*, 26–28; Droste, *Bauhaus*, 66–67; Wick, "Itten," 116; Föhl et al., *Bauhaus-Museum*, 43–44.

50. Kandinsky, *Geistige*, 37.

51. Zimmermann, "Dispositionen," 118–22; Zimmermann, "Esoteriker," 50–54; Kandinsky, *Kandinsky*, 111–13, 236–37; Grohmann, *Kandinsky*, 174–75.

52. Föhl et al., *Bauhaus-Museum*, 59–60; Neumann, *Bauhaus*, 72; Muche, *Blickpunkt*, 145; Baumgartner, "Itten," 106; Anna Rowland in *Oxford Art Online*; Ackermann, "Leer," 119.

53. Anna Rowland in *Oxford Art Online*; Zimmermann, "Dispositionen," 118–22; Christoph Wagner in Uthemann, *Itten*, 34, 42–43.

54. Bruno Adler in Neumann, *Bauhaus*, 17; Felix Klee ibid., 23–24; Paul Citroen ibid., 29–34; Georg Muche ibid., 73–75; Droste, *Bauhaus*, 27 (quote 32); Anna Rowland in *Oxford Art Online*; Zimmermann, "Dispositionen," 132; Wahl, *Meisterratsprotokolle*, 103; Hünecke, *Schlemmer*, 79; Mahler-Werfel, *Bridge*, 143; Itten, *Design*, 6–9; Wagner, "Lebensreform," 65–66, 69–74; Felix Klee in Gradmann, *Itten*, n.p.

55. Droste, *Bauhaus*, 27 (quote); Föhl et al., *Bauhaus-Museum*, 35–38; Wick, "Itten," 113–16.

56. Föhl et al., *Bauhaus-Museum*, 42–44; Baumgartner, "Itten," 111.

57. See Wick, "Itten," 119–20.

58. Terence A. Senter in *Oxford Art Online* (quote); Stuckenschmidt, *Musik*, 7; Isaacs, *Gropius*, 295; Walter Gropius in Schlemmer et al., *Bühne*, 90; Föhl et al., *Bauhaus-Museum*, 40, 91; Passuth, *Moholy-Nagy*, 41–47.

59. Wahl, *Meisterratsprotokolle*, 69; Ute Ackermann ibid., 32; Preiss, "Hochschulen," 37 (quote); Scheidig, *Bauhaus*, 26; Hüter, *Bauhaus*, 21–23, 26–27, 217–18, 226–28; Ness, *Feininger*, 98; Hünecke, *Schlemmer*, 74, 119.

60. Wahl, *Meisterratsprotokolle*, 152, 176; Ute Ackermann ibid., 30; Hünecke, *Schlemmer*, 78; Alexander Bortnik in Neumann, *Bauhaus*, 69; Isaacs, *Gropius*, 259, 303–4; Föhl et al., *Bauhaus-Museum*, 77, 82; Schädlich, *Hochschule*, 27; de Fries, "Auflösung," 78; de Michelis, "Determann."

61. Wahl, *Meisterratsprotokolle*, 243–44; Isaacs, *Gropius*, 258–61; 302–3; Föhl et al., *Bauhaus-Museum*, 78, 81; Droste, *Bauhaus*, 105, 110; Muche, *Blickpunkt*, 128; Preiss, *Abschied*, 142–45; Winkler, *Baulehre*, 17–20.

62. Hüter, *Bauhaus*, 20, 225; Paul Teichgräber et al. to Weimarer Künstlerschaft, December 19, 1919, ibid., 213–14 (quote); Wahl, *Meisterratsprotokolle*, 50, 57–58, 61–62, 107–8; Ute Ackermann ibid., 31; Müller, *Women*, 44; Droste, *Bauhaus*, 50; Ulbricht, "Willkomm," 9, 12; Ness, *Feininger*, 108, 110; Hünecke, *Schlemmer*, 108.

63. Muche, *Blickpunkt*, 59.

64. Scheidig, *Bauhaus*, 20.

65. Oskar Schlemmer to Otto Meyer-Amden, December 7, 1921, in Hünecke, *Schlemmer*, 8 (quote); Wahl, *Meisterratsprotokolle*, 153; Wagner, "Lebensreform," 74.

66. Droste, *Bauhaus*, 46; Droste, "Aneignung," 12; Wagner in Uthemann, *Itten*, 47; Wick, "Itten," 121; Hünecke, *Schlemmer*, 93; Hüter, *Bauhaus*, 231; Rotzler, *Itten*, 72–73.

67. Allan Doig in *Oxford Art Online*.

68. Doesburg, "Will"; Scheidig, *Bauhaus*, 27; Droste, *Bauhaus*, 54 (quote); Droste "Aneignung," 14; Wagner in Uthemann, *Itten*, 47.

69. Droste, *Bauhaus*, 54, 57.

70. Ness, *Feininger*, 112; Hünecke, *Schlemmer*, 83; Adler, *Bauhaus*, [11]; Föhl et al., *Bauhaus-Museum*, 94–96; Droste, "Aneignung," 15–16, 26–28.

71. Gropius (February 3, 1922) in Hüter, *Bauhaus*, 231; Ute Ackermann in Wahl, *Meisterratsprotokolle*, 3, 40; Stenzel/Winkler, *Kontroversen*, 50; Droste, *Bauhaus*, 58; Ulbricht, "Willkomm," 8.

72. Lyonel to Julia Feininger, May 21, 1919, in Ness, *Feininger*, 99 (quote); Schreyer, *Erinnerungen*, 216–18; Tut Schlemmer in Neumann, *Bauhaus*, 122; Steinfeld, *Weimar*, 250; Isaacs, *Gropius*, 221; Ute Ackermann in Wahl, *Meisterratsprotokolle*, 30; Stenzel/Winkler, *Kontroversen*, 49–50; Felix Klee in Neumann, *Bauhaus*, 27.

73. Ulbricht, "Willkomm," 14; Herfurth, *Weimar* (quote 6); Hüter, *Bauhaus*, 19–25, 213, 217–20; Ziegler, *Kunst*, 272–73.

74. Schlemmer quoted in Droste, *Bauhaus*, 72, also 38, 40 (2nd quote), 73–74, 78; Ute Ackermann in Wahl, *Meisterratsprotokolle*, 40; Hüter, *Bauhaus*, 226; Müller, *Women*, 9–12, 25, 72, 84; Marianne Brandt in Neumann, *Bauhaus*, 78.

75. Gertrud Grunow (1923) in *Staatliches Bauhaus*, 20–21; Stadler-Stölzl, "Textilwerkstatt"; Droste, *Bauhaus*, 33, 72; Müller, *Women*, 7, 14–25.

76. Schreyer, *Erinnerungen*, 249–51.

77. Mahler-Werfel, *Bridge*, 135; Herbert Bayer in Neumann, *Bauhaus*, 108; Ness, *Feininger*, 125–26; Schreyer, *Erinnerungen*, 174; Hünecke, *Schlemmer*, 129; Stephan, "Bauhaus," 10.

78. See Ness, *Feininger*, 103; Isaacs, *Gropius*, 248.

79. See Isaacs, *Gropius*, 229, 290.

80. Ibid., 241–42.

81. Ibid., 304.

82. Henselmann, *Reisen*, 213.

83. Wahl, *Meisterratsprotokolle*, 244.

84. Ibid., 241–45, 258, 290, 326.

85. Meyer, *Briefe*, 110; Okrassa, *Raabe*, 80.

86. Schönberg, "Verhältnis."

87. Kandinsky, *Geistige*, 109.

88. Schoenberg to Kandinsky, April 19, 1923, in Hahl-Koch, *Arnold*, 76.

89. Kandinsky, *Kandinsky*, 193–95.

90. Kandinsky to Schoenberg, April; 24, 1923, in Hahl-Koch, *Arnold*, 77 (italics in the original).

91. Scheidig, *Bauhaus*, 38–41; Droste, *Bauhaus*, 71, 113–14, 120; Stenzel/Winkler, *Kontroversen*, 81–95; Hünecke, *Schlemmer*, 119–22, 127, 129; Winkler, "Dokumentation," 149; Isaacs, *Gropius*, 339.

92. *Staatliche Bauhochschule*; Nicolaisen, "Bartning," 11–39; Stenzel/Winkler, *Kontroversen*, 98–104; Winkler, "Dokumentation," 179–80.

Chapter Six: Weimar in the Weimar Republic, 1918 to 1933

1. Weber, *Villen*, vol. 2, 80–83.

2. Herwig, *Fleet*, 178–90, 194–98; Scheer, *Hochseeflotte*, 305–64.

3. Epkenhaus, *Schatz*, 53–54.

4. See Peters, *Schwester*, 284.

5. Isaacs, *Gropius*, 233–34; Naake, *Nietzsche*, 87.

6. Peters, *Schwester*, 290–97; Wollkopf, "Gremien," 232–33; Hoffmann, *Geschichte*, 102–5; Galindo, *Triumph*, 186–91; Naake, *Nietzsche*, 76, 85–86, 98–99, 103; Diethe, *Sister*, 143–47. Emge's admiration for Nietzsche, Hitler/National Socialism and hatred of Jews are evinced in *Mensch*.

7. Baeumler, "Nachwort," in Nietzsche, *Wille*, 699–709; Whyte, "Uses," 178–82; Riedel, *Nietzsche*, 99–108.

8. See Steinweis, "Culture."

9. Rosenberg, *Mythus*, 530.

10. Baeumler, *Nietzsche*, 90.

11. Erich F. Podach, "Die Schändung geht weiter," *Literarische Welt*, September 30, 1932; Diethe, *Sister*, 148. See e.g. Baeumler, *Briefen*, and Baeumler's "Einleitung" ibid., vii–xxvii.

12. Diethe, *Sister*, 142–43.

13. Oehler, *Manen*; Diethe, *Sister*, 141; Naake, *Nietzsche*, 78, 83, 87; Peters, *Schwester*, 282–83.

14. Diethe, *Sister*, 144–45; Hoffmann, *Geschichte*, 96, 99–100. See Bertram, *Nietzsche*.
15. Mann, *Betrachtungen*; Hoffmann, *Geschichte*, 98; Wollkopf, "Nietzsche-Archiv," 139; Peters, *Schwester*, 279.
16. Spengler, *Untergang*, 38–39, 536–37, 540–43, 545; Diethe, *Sister*, 143–44; Hoffmann, *Geschichte*, 97, 105; Naake, *Nietzsche*, 77, 93; Wollkopf, "Nietzsche-Archiv," 139.
17. Hoffmann, *Geschichte*, 97, 101; Naake, *Nietzsche*, 78–84, 107–9; Wollkopf, "Nietzsche-Archiv," 136–38, 140–41, 158.
18. Hoffmann, *Geschichte*, 97–98; Peters, *Schwester*, 283–84 (Förster-Nietzsche quoted 283).
19. Diethe, *Sister*, 148; Hoffmann, *Geschichte*, 92–93, 98–100, 107; Naake, *Nietzsche*, 82, 91–92; Wollkopf, "Nietzsche-Archiv," 229; Peters, *Schwester*, 280, 284–85, 287–88.
20. Diethe, *Sister*, 146; Hoffmann, *Geschichte*, 108.
21. Naake, *Nietzsche*, 75–77, 87–89; Wollkopf, "Nietzsche-Archiv," 230; Peters, *Schwester*, 280–83.
22. Diethe, *Sister*, 151; Hoffmann, *Geschichte*, 101–2, 107–8; Kirsten, *Weimar*, 133–35; Naake, *Nietzsche*, 94–110; Wollkopf, "Nietzsche-Archiv," 139–40; Wollkopf, "Gremien," 233–40; Peters, *Schwester*, 291–97.
23. Naake, *Nietzsche*, 88.
24. Wachler, *Heimat*, esp. 5–17, 20–21, 28–29, 40–42, 56, 61–62, 65 (quotes 7, 8, 17).
25. Langenbucher, *Lienhard*, 118, 127–29, 132–33; Châtellier, "Kreuz," 101, 104.
26. Schlösser, *Volk*, 44, 49; Bonn, *Jugend*, 132.
27. Schlaf, "Aufgabe," 1–3; Schlaf, *Krieg*, 21–22, 40–43; Schlaf, "Weltaufgabe"; Bäte, *Akte*, 39–40; Rudolf Borche in Bäte et al., *Schlaf-Buch*, 75–76; Kafitz, *Schlaf*, 174–78, 195–96; Erdmann, *Naturalismus*, 240–66.
28. Felix Klee in Neumann, *Bauhaus*, 25; Kafitz, *Schlaf*, 27–28; Winkler, "Dokumentation," 147–48; Schlaf, *Leben*, 58.
29. Bartels, *Verfall*, 15, 19, 24–28, 32, 36, 38–40 (quote 39); Bartels, *Weshalb*, 3, 8–12; Bartels, *Berechtigung*, 9, 16–17, 29, 32; Bartels, *Herkunft*, 30–31, 36, 147, 159–62, 165, 199–200, 216; Fuller, *Grandfather*, 178.
30. Schüssler, *Hardt*, 172; Okrassa, *Raabe*, 57.
31. Kirsten, *Weimar*, 98; Fuller, *Grandfather*, 153–55, 157–60.
32. Bartels, *Rettung*, 3–8, 20, 25–26; Bartels in *Deutsches Schrifttum* 16, no. 9 (1924): 2–3; Bartels, "Nationalsozialismus"; Loose, *Festgabe* (1944), 140–43; Naake, *Nietzsche*, 95; Fuller, *Grandfather*, 160–66.
33. Iain Boyd Whyte in *Oxford Art Online*; Borrmann, *Schultze-Naumburg*, 18, 29–30, 69–72, 104, 124; Bartning, *Schultze-Naumburg*, 9–19; 25–31; Pese, "Name," 387–88.
34. Schultze-Naumburg, *Dach*, esp. 9, 12 (1st quote), 30–32, 45, 56, 58–60, 64 (2nd quote); Borrmann, *Schultze-Naumburg*, 152.
35. Kaufmann, "Dach."
36. Steinweis, "Culture," 406, 414.
37. Pese, "Name," 388; Kirsten, *Weimar*, 126.
38. Schultze-Naumburg, "Kunstausstellung," quote 442; Schultze-Naumburg, *Kunst und Rasse*. For the pictures, see 90–97. Also Borrmann, *Schultze-Naumburg*, 217. Cf. [Kaiser], *Führer*; Bernhard Post in Dornheim et al., *Thüringen*, 13.
39. Neliba, "Frick," 90.
40. Weisenburger, "Günther," 161–66; Hossfeld, "Jahre," 54.
41. Saller, *Rassenlehre*, 19.
42. Fischer, *Bastards*, 294, 304 (quotes); *SZ*, September 27 and October 1–3, 2011. Thanking Fischer, Christian Fetzer mentions 17 "Hottentot heads" of prisoners – among them children aged one and three years, who after the 1904 rebellion died in a German concentration camp on Shark Island, allegedly of scurvy – which were prepared for scientific investigation: "Untersuchungen," esp. 95. Also see Wistrich, *Who*, 75–76; Macrakis, *Swastika*, 125–30; Schmuhl, *Grenzüberschreitungen*, 444–82.
43. See Weiss, *Symbiosis*, 20–59.
44. Weisenburger, "Günther," 171.
45. Günther, *Ritter*, esp. 17, 32, 56, 80–84, 123, 137–48; Lenz, "Berufung," 338; Weisenburger, "Günther," 166–70.
46. See Weisenburger, "Günther," 171.

47. Günther, *Rassenkunde deutschen*, 128–45.
48. Ibid., 120–21; Weisenburger, "Günther," 174.
49. Günther, *Rassenkunde deutschen*, 128–45 (quote 130).
50. Weisenburger, "Günther," 172–73.
51. Günther, *Rassenkunde deutschen*, 367–434.
52. Weisenburger, "Günther," 171.
53. Quote in Günther, *Rassenkunde jüdischen*, 218.
54. Quote ibid., 222.
55. Quotes ibid., 224, 250.
56. Quote ibid. 252.
57. Günther, *Rassenkunde jüdischen*, 217–25, 249–67, 303–26, 345–46.
58. Pioneering: Mosse, *Crisis*, 208 (quote). On pseudo-science, see Weinreich, *Professors*; Kater, *"Ahnenerbe"*.
59. See Darré, *Neuadel*, 190; Kershaw, *Opinion*, 224–77.
60. Bartels, *Verfall*, 35–37.
61. Günther, *Ritter*, 47, 123, 140 (first quote); Günther, *Rassenkunde deutschen*, 134 (second quote 37).
62. Tanzmann, "Bartels," esp. 150 (quote). Also see Bartels, *Bauer*. On Tanzmann, see Piefel, "Tanzmann," 255–71.
63. Kater, "Artamanen," 627; Field, "Racism," 528–29; Löwenberg, "Hentschel," 36–61.
64. Kater, "Artamanen," 577–78.
65. Himmler quoted in Longerich, *Himmler*, 87–88. On the Artam League see Kater, "Artamanen," 577–638 (Tanzmann's quote 604).
66. Wistrich, *Who*, 45; Kater, "Artamanen," 600.
67. Salomon, *Geächteten*, 312–27.
68. Kirsten, *Weimar*, 126.
69. Darré, *Neuadel*, esp. 6 (first two quotes), 171 (third quote), 7, 14, 157, 181, 188, 190, 193, 198, 220, 223–24, 226.
70. Kater, "Artamanen," 584, 622–37; Kater, *"Ahnenerbe"*, 147–69; Longerich, *Himmler*, 272–74, 375, 619–20; Gerwarth, *Heydrich*, 246–50.
71. Scholz, *Ilm*, 86; Buchwald, *Geschichte*, 368–69; Golz, "Goethe- und Schillerarchiv," 43.
72. "Goethe and Schiller Archive," *www.klassik-stiftung.de*; Golz, "Goethe- und Schillerarchiv," 40–48; Mauersberger, *Hitler*, 75; Ulbricht, "Erinnerung," 8; "Sein Forschen," *TLZ*, February 22, 1989.
73. Buchhorn, *Goethe*, 4; Nägele, "Goethefeiern," 108; Linden, *Goethe*, 35; Eduard Scheidemantel in Crodel, ed., *Goethe-Jahr*, 56–57; Mandelkow, "Goethe-Gesellschaft," 347; Ledebur, *Mythos*, 56. On Herder, see Becker, *Herder-Rezeption*, 129–32.
74. Chamberlain, *Goethe*, 688–93, 697, 715, 720–21. For an early postwar example, see Mauersberger, *Hitler*, 3, 70, 85–96.
75. Fischer, "'Zwischen,'" 15.
76. Buchhorn, *Goethe*, 5–6, 18–23.
77. Crommelin, "Goethe," 13, 19, 23; Mann, "Goethe," 244.
78. Wachler, *Heimat*, 21, 28–29; Günther, *Ritter*, 17, 25, 32, 44, 56, 80, 123, 145; Günther, *Rassenkunde deutschen*, 132, 141, 143, 418; Günther, *Rassenkunde jüdischen*, 317; Schrumpf, *Goethe*, 7; Mandelkow, *Urteil*, xxvii.
79. Friedenthal, *Goethe*, 555 (quote).
80. Norbert Oellers in König/Lämmert, *Literaturwissenschaft*, 357; Seemann, *Weimar*, 237–38.
81. Boden, *Petersen*, 82–96.
82. Mandelkow, *Rezeptionsgeschichte*, vol. 2, esp. 13, 19; Mandelkow, "Goethe-Gesellschaft," 347; Fischer, "Zwischen," 13–14; Boden/Fischer, *Petersen*, 31; Boden, "Petersen," 96.
83. Neumann, "Triebe," 186–210.
84. Roethe, *Reden*, 309–32.
85. Eberhard Lämmert in Lämmert et al., *Germanistik*, 13–15 (quote 14). Also see Jäger, *Seitenwechsel*, 42.
86. Neumann, "Zukunft," 61, 66–67; Neumann, "Triebe," 201, 209–10; Boden/Fischer, *Petersen*, 33–34; Bahr, "Petersen," 140–41. For Mann's metamorphosis, see Sprecher et al., *Briefe II*, esp. 9–10, 42–43, 45–50, 440–41, 450, 988–89; and Mann, *Republik*.

87. Mandelkow, "Restauration," 136. There were other Goethe festivities, e.g. in Frankfurt, not planned by the Goethe-Gesellschaft.
88. "Aufruf zum Goethe-Jahr" (1932) in Mandelkow, *Urteil*, 106–7. On Binding, see Baird, *Poets*, 32–65, on Kolbenheyer see Wistrich, *Who*, 177–78.
89. Petersen, *Lebensjahre*, 93; Zeller, *Klassiker*, vol. 1, 68–69.
90. Michalski/Steiner, *Weimarhalle*, 51; Wilderotter, "Symbolische," 115–16.
91. Petersen, "Erdentage"; Mandelkow, *Rezeptionsgeschichte*, vol. 2, 74.
92. Wilderotter, "Symbolische," 109–10.
93. Merseburger, *Mythos*, 332–33; Petersen, *Lebensjahre*, 95.
94. Mann, "Goethereise"; Sprecher et al., *Briefe III*, 611–12.
95. Mann, "Goethereise," 161.
96. [Vaget], "Vorwort," in Sprecher et al., *Briefe III*, 26 (quote 27); Mann, *Lotte in Weimar*.
97. Mann, "Goethe," esp. 55; Sprecher et al., *Briefe III*, 618–19.
98. Zeller, *Klassiker*, vol. 1, 67–68.
99. Hans Severus Ziegler, "Thomas Mann spricht," *VB*, March 27–29, 1932.
100. Halperin, *Germany*, 79–125; Large, *Berlin*, 158–64.
101. Baudert, *Ende*, 42.
102. Ibid., 42–45; Oehme, *Damals*, 333–52; Stenzel/Winkler, *Kontroversen*, 10–13; Müller-Seidel, *Geschichtlichkeit*, 3–4; Dorrmann, "Potsdam."
103. Baudert, *Ende*, 45–46; Oehme, *Nationalversammlung*, 68–69; Buchwald, *Geschichte*, 377; Rüss, *Dokumente*, 7–10; Wiesner, *Ernst*, 60–61; Ness, *Feininger*, 103, 105, 109; Mauersberger, *Hitler*, 104; Dorrmann, "Potsdam," 23.
104. Oehme, *Nationalversammlung*, 26, 68, 98, 263–64; Mauersberger, *Hitler*, 104–5; Okrassa, *Raabe*, 54; Dorrmann, "Potsdam," 27.
105. Horkenbach, *Reich*, 51–52; Meissner, *Staatssekretär*, 76–77; Baudert, *Ende*, 46; Winkler, *Revolution*, 227–42; Mauersberger, *Hitler*, 110; Stern, *Five*, 59 (quote).
106. Horkenbach, *Reich*, 48, 84–85; Heilfron, *Nationalversammlung*, 8–9; Mauersberger, *Hitler*, 107–9; Oehme, *Nationalversammlung*, 70–71; Mandelkow, *Rezeptionsgeschichte*, vol. 2, 9–10; Johannes Schlaf's reaction in Erdmann, *Naturalismus*, 242.
107. Horkenbach, *Reich*, 62, 66–81; MacMillan, *Paris*, 167–203, 459–83 (quote 460); Stern, *Five*, 57–58; Mauersberger, *Hitler*, 115–16; Oehme, *Nationalversammlung*, 301–2, 326, 331–33; Schlaf's reaction in Erdmann, *Naturalismus*, 243, Förster-Nietzsche's in Peters, *Schwester*, 279.
108. Details and dates for 1919 in Horkenbach, *Reich*, 48–93. For after 1919, see Mommsen, *Freiheit*, 141–547; Weitz, *Weimar*.
109. Horkenbach, *Reich*, 100–5; Baudert, *Ende*, 58–74; Wiesner, *Ernst*, 65–69; Rüss, *Dokumente*, 22–26; Witzmann, *Thüringen*, 13–14; Isaacs, *Gropius*, 264.
110. Göring, *Seite*, 23–26; Weber, *Villen*, vol. 2, 39–40.
111. Göring, *Seite*, 26–28.
112. Horkenbach, *Reich*, 61; Mai in Heiden/Mai, *Thüringen*, 17–18; Witzmann, *Thüringen*, 9–12, 48–51, 57; Post et al., *Thüringen-Handbuch*, 23–31; Overesch, *Brill*, 59; Mauersberger, *Hitler*, 81.
113. Overesch, *Brill*, 60–68, 111–13, 160–63; Witzmann, *Thüringen*, 41, 45, 55–56, 94–112; Post et al., *Thüringen-Handbuch*, 31; Mai in Heiden/Mai, *Thüringen*, 18–20; Stenzel/Winkler, *Kontroversen*, 15, 21, 27–31.
114. Size: 3,610 versus 11,724 square kilometers (letter Dr. Jens Riederer, Director, Stadtarchiv Weimar, to author, March 14, 2012). Also see Horkenbach, *Reich*, 604; Hille, "Beispiel," map at 204; Mai in Heiden/Mai, *Thüringen*, 18.
115. Hille, "Beispiel," 190.
116. For size: Keyser, *Städtebuch*, 389.
117. Overesch, *Brill*, 61–62, 120; Walter, *Thüringen*, 22–34; Bernhard Post in Dornheim et al., *Thüringen*, 10; Mai in Heiden/Mai, *Thüringen*, 21–26; Hüter, *Bauhaus*, 13–15.
118. Schilling, *Ende*, 44–46; Rassloff, *Sauckel*, 40–50; Piper, *Rosenberg*, 168–69; Heiden/Mai, *Thüringen*, 193–94; Dinter, *Sünde*; Dinter, *Ursprung*, 5, 14–16, 30–34.
119. Tracey, "Aufstieg," 49–58; Heiden/Mai, *Thüringen*, 195–98; Ziegler, *Hitler*, 31, 97, 107 (quote), 291–92; Ziegler, *Bartels*, 7, 12; Ziegler in Loose, *Festgabe* (1922), 129–35; Overesch, *Brill*, 195–97. On Bormann, see Lang, *Sekretär*, 29, 49–51.

120. Schaumburg-Lippe, *Pflicht*, 273–76; Ziegler, *Hitler*, 124–26; Tracey, "Aufstieg," 62.
121. Baudert, *Ende*, 43; Ledebur, *Mythos*, 53, 72, 74; Bernhard Post in Dornheim et al., *Thüringen*, 13.
122. Rassloff, *Sauckel*, 44; Ziegler, *Hitler*, 45–48; Tracey, "Aufstieg," 59.
123. Kirsten, *Weimar*, 10–13, 22–25, 109, 114–16, 120; Rassloff, *Sauckel*, 52; Tracey, "Aufstieg," 60–61; Schirach, *Ich glaubte*, 7–58.
124. Such as Annette Seemann, *Weimar*, 248, who also repeats that Schirach became Reichsjugendführer. She contradicts herself on p. 288. For the facts, see text on p. 203.
125. *VB*, July 3, 1926 (first quote); Kershaw, *Hubris*, 276–79 (second quote); Mauersberger, *Hitler*, 226–31; Tracey, "Aufstieg," 63–64; Kirsten, *Weimar*, 10–11, 26–33; Müller/Stein, *Familien*, 61. For the corrupted history of the HJ, see Bernhard Post in Dornheim et al., *Thüringen*, 13; Okrassa, *Raabe*, 132; Piper, *Rosenberg*, 234 and, correctly, *Nationalsozialistisches Jahrbuch* 5 (1931): 151; Evans, *Coming*, 214.
126. Kater, *Nazi Party*, 49, 263; Evans, *Coming*, 211, 230 (quote).
127. Kirsten, *Weimar*, 39 (Hitler quoted), 110, 120; Tracey, "Aufstieg," 68; Piper, *Rosenberg*, 169, 261; Longerich, *Himmler*, 102; Mauersberger, *Hitler*, 185; Ledebur, *Mythos*, 6–7.
128. Sauckel quoted in Schilling, "Ende," 48; also Hille, "Beispiel," 189–94; Tracey, "Aufstieg," 71; Piper, *Rosenberg*, 139, 232.
129. Hitler quoted in Dickmann, "Regierungsbildung," 461; Hille, "Beispiel," 194–96.
130. Hille, "Beispiel," 194; Post et al., *Thüringen-Handbuch*, 32 (quote). Qualifying: Neliba, "Frick," 93–94.
131. Hille, "Beispiel," 193–203; Brill, *Strom*, 7 (quote); Witzmann, *Thüringen*, 164.
132. Hille, "Beispiel," 204–7; Lenz, "Berufung"; Heiden/Mai, *Thüringen*, 228–30; Borrmann, *Schultze-Naumburg*, 192; Hossfeld, "Jahre," esp. 61 (quote); Kater, *Studentenschaft*, 112, 114, 124, 187, 215.
133. Hitler quoted in Dickmann, "Regierungsbildung," 463. Also Hille, "Beispiel," 211–15; Witzmann, *Thüringen*, 170–72; Mauersberger, *Hitler*, 272.
134. Hille, "Beispiel," 207–11.
135. Ibid., 211; Fabricius, *Frick*, 43; Neliba, "Frick", 87–88; Sauckel, *Kampf*, 18–22; Kirsten, *Weimar*, 111.
136. Brenner, *Kunstpolitik*, 17 (quote); Neliba, "Frick," 91; Borrmann, *Schultze-Naumburg*, 183; Overesch, *Brill*, 208–9; Ziegler, *Hitler*, 208; Kirsten, *Weimar*, 43.
137. Schilling, "Ende," 62; Stenzel/Winkler, *Kontroversen*, 182.
138. Evans, *Coming*, 259–65; Kershaw, *Hubris*, 333–36; Schilling, "Ende," 63.
139. Stenzel/Winkler, *Kontroversen*, 111; Bernhard Post in Dornheim et al., *Thüringen*, 18; Bernhard Post in Heiden/Mai, *Thüringen*, 152–54; Rassloff, *Sauckel*, 57; Kirsten, *Weimar*, 50.
140. Schilling, "Ende," 64; Bernhard Post in Dornheim et al., *Thüringen*, 19; Rassloff, *Sauckel*, 56.
141. Schilling, "Ende," 66–113; Bernhard Post in Dornheim et al., *Thüringen*, 335; Post et al., *Thüringen-Handbuch*, 33; Müller/Stein, *Familien*, 63; John, "NS-Gau," 29–30; Rassloff, *Sauckel*, 58; Göring, *Seite*, 29–31; Weber, *Villen*, vol. 2, 44.

Chapter Seven: Weimar in the Third Reich, 1933 to 1945

1. Mann, "Goethereise," 159.
2. Calculated according to figures in *Partei-Statistik*, 1, 10, 12, 20, 34, 36.
3. Calculated according to figures in letter Dr. Jens Riederer, Director, Stadtarchiv Weimar, to author, January 19, 2012; *Statistisches Jahrbuch* (1938), 27; Kater, *Nazi Party*, 263. Riederer's figures are corroborated in letter Dr. Frank Boblenz, Thüringisches Hauptstaatsarchiv Weimar, to author, May 17, 2012.
4. See the figures in Seela, *Ärzteschaft*, 202; Kater, *Doctors*, 56, 245.
5. Cohn quoted in Müller/Stein, *Familien*, 174.
6. "Zu Weihnachten 1943," *TLZ*, April 19, 1997.
7. Herbert, *Ausländerpolitik*, 124–89.
8. Post et al., *Thüringen-Handbuch*, 33–40; Schilling, "Ende," 118, 124, 132–35, 141–42; commentator: Schulze, *Thüringen*, 25 (quote).
9. Qualifying this point: Wehler, *Gesellschaftsgeschichte: Vierter Band*, 709–11.

10. Population figures from Müller/Stein, *Familien*, 51; letter Riederer to author, January 19, 2012. Also see Schulze, *Thüringen*, 6, 10, 12, 19, 22–23; Günther, *Weimar*, 164; Wallraf in Günther/Wallraf, *Geschichte*, 605–6, 627; Stutz, "Weimar," 96.

11. Günther, *Weimar*, 165; Wallraf in Günther/Wallraf, *Geschichte*, 607, 628; Rassloff, *Sauckel*, 70; Stutz, "Weimar," 97–99.

12. Kirsten, *Weimar*, 112–13; Okrassa, *Raabe*, 297.

13. Stenzel, "Kunst," 26–27; Burkhard Stenzel in Dornheim et al., *Thüringen*, 70, 73–77.

14. Ziegler, "Nationaltheater," 28–32; Schulze, *Thüringen*, 32–33; Wallraf in Günther/Wallraf, *Geschichte*, 611, 630; Kirsten, *Weimar*, 82–84, 112; Schilling, "Ende," 99; Burkhard Stenzel in Dornheim et al., *Thüringen*, 101–6; Huschke, *Glut*, 182–83.

15. Oberborbeck quoted in Kater, *Muse*, 151. Also see Oberborbeck, "Volkslied"; Wulf, *Musik*, 330–31; Hartwig et al., *Festschrift*, 63–64; Wallraf in Günther/Wallraf, *Geschichte*, 614; Messner, *Nationaltheater: Anfängen*, 85–86.

16. Ziegler, *Musik*, esp. 6–8 (quote 6); Günther, *Weimar*, 164; Wallraf in Günther/Wallraf, *Geschichte*, 613; Kater, *Muse*, 78–79.

17. [Kaiser], *Führer*; Pese, "Name," 396–98; Wendermann, "Weimar," 426, 431–32; Engelhardt, "Ausstellung," 136–37; Zuschlag, *Kunst*, 277–80.

18. Schulze, *Thüringen*, 31 (quote); Wallraf in Günther/Wallraf, *Geschichte*, 609; Günther, *Weimar*, 150.

19. Pfister, "Hochschule," 378–85; Winkler, "Dokumentation," 194–98; Offenberg, "Mosaik," 285, 293, 296; Schädlich, *Hochschule*, 42–43; Pese, "Name," 393; Borrmann, *Schultze-Naumburg*, 193.

20. Klee, *Personenlexikon*, 20, 151–52, 513.

21. Aly/Roth, *Erfassung*.

22. Hossfeld, "Wissenschaft," 85, 105, 109 (first quote); Astel, *Aufgabe*, 15 (second quote); Astel/Weber, *Kinderzahl*; Schulze, *Thüringen*, 6–7; Astel, *Rassekurs*, esp. 6–10; Weissbecker, "NSDAP," 75; Weiss, *Symbiosis*, 190–92; Rassloff, *Sauckel*, 79.

23. Fleischhauer, *Klassik*, 83–85 (Sauckel quoted 82); Burkhard Stenzel in Dornheim et al., *Thüringen*, 68; Hossfeld, "Jahre," 88; Hossfeld, "Wissenschaft," 1–3, 70, 79–88, 107–8; Kater, *"Ahnenerbe"*, 185–86. Short biographies in Klee, *Personenlexikon*, 161–62, 234, 308, 351–52, 361, 516, 601–2.

24. Ziegler, *Hitler*, 13.

25. Schaumburg-Lippe, *Pflicht*, 273; Hanfstaengl, *Haus*, 299.

26. Kirsten, *Weimar*, 72; Spotts, *Bayreuth*, 159–99; Hamann, *Wagner*, 270–507; Wagner, *Wagner Theater*.

27. Hitler quoted in Fest, *Speer*, 76. Also see ibid., 33, 49–51, 56–61, 64–65, 68–93; Speer to Schwarz, February 19, 1941, facsimiles in Korrek at al., *Gauforum*, 90–91; Speer, *Erinnerungen*, 67–69, 71–76, 87–94, 113, 147–59, 162–63; Kater, *Muse*, 49–51; Orth, *System*, 48–49; Spotts, *Hitler*, 351–78.

28. Full text in Dusik, *Hitler*, 17–25.

29. Wolf, *Gauforen*, 70–71, 105–19 (numbers: 106); Korrek et al., *Gauforum*, 35, 47, 55, 59, 63, 92; Kirsten, *Weimar*, 62–67; Loos, "Weimar," 335–41; Giesler, *Hitler*, 119–24; Köhler, *Weimar*, 44–45.

30. Sauckel, *Führer*, 18–19; Sauckel, "Weimar"; Korrek et al., *Gauforum*, 90–91; Giesler, *Hitler*, 124–27; Stutz, "Weimar," 94–95; Kirsten, *Weimar*, 68–71.

31. Kirsten, *Weimar*, 135–36; Peters, *Schwester*, 298–300 (Förster-Nietzsche quoted 299).

32. Kirsten, *Weimar*, 137; Peters, *Schwester*, 301–2; Hoffmann, *Geschichte*, 110; Naake, *Nietzsche*, 112–15.

33. *Ansprachen* (1935) (Oehler quoted ibid., n.p.); Peters, *Schwester*, 302–3; Kirsten, *Weimar*, 138–39.

34. Galindo, *Triumph*, 184, 185 (first two quotes), 191–94; Hoffmann, *Geschichte*, 105, 110–11, 114–15 (Spengler quoted 114). See Förster-Nietzsche, *Frauen*.

35. Rosenberg, *Nietzsche*, quotes 22; Whyte, "Uses," 192; Galindo, *Triumph*, 195–202, 205–6; Cancik, "Nietzsche-Kult . . . (II)," 87–91; Naake, *Nietzsche*, 116, 122–24, 131–33.

36. Riedel, *Nietzsche*, 127.

37. Aschheim, *Nietzsche*, 240–52, 255. A Nazi corroboration is in Härtle, *Nietzsche*, 45–57, 61, 64, 162–64.

38. Schmuhl, *Rassenhygiene*, 381, n. 1, 416, n. 60; Klee, *Personenlexikon*, 366–67, 466.
39. Goebbels, *Michael*, 242.
40. Galindo, *Triumph*, 207. On Frank, see Klee, *Personenlexikon*, 160.
41. Gd., "Unsere Härte," *SS-Leitheft* 9, no. 1 (January 1943): 3.
42. *SS-Leitheft* 9, no. 11 (November 1943): 15–18.
43. Horst Slesina, "Krieg ohne Gnade," *SS-Leitheft* 9, no. 12 (December 1943): 31–32.
44. Naake, *Nietzsche*, 131.
45. Härtle, *Nietzsche*, 44–47, 58–64, 162–63 (quote 60). Also see Aschheim, *Nietzsche*, 253–55; Riedel, *Nietzsche*, 124–26, 129–35. Short biographies in Klee, *Personenlexikon*, 125, 341; Bollmus, *Amt*, 259–60, n. 3; Heiber, *Frank*, 501–32.
46. Naake, *Nietzsche*, 125; Hoffmann, *Geschichte*, 112.
47. Galindo, *Triumph*, 202–4; Cancik, "Nietzsche-Kult (II)," 102–5; Kirsten, *Weimar*, 137–40; Riedel, *Nietzsche*, 143–44.
48. Thamer, "Geschichte," esp. 349 (quote), 367. Also see Spotts, *Hitler*.
49. Rassloff, *Sauckel*, 68; Günther, *Weimar*, 163; Burkhard Stenzel in Dornheim et al., *Thüringen*, 93; Kater, *Muse*, 20–21, 184.
50. "Programm für die zehnjährige Wiederkehr des 1. Reichsparteitages 1926 in Weimar am 3., 4. und 5. Juli 1936," in Voss, *Wiederkehr*, n.p.; Sauckel, *Führer*, 17; Kirsten, *Weimar*, 59–61; Kater, *Muse*, 13.
51. Schirach's sister was Rosalind von Schirach. Schirach, *Ich glaubte*, 24, 75; Goebbels, "Schütz"; Heiber, *Goebbels*, 30.
52. Günther et al., *Weimar*, 88.
53. Zander, *Weimar*, 83; Burkhard Stenzel in Dornheim at el., *Thüringen*, 92; Kühn, *Schreibtisch*. 59.
54. Zander, *Weimar-Festspiele*, n.p., esp. the stage programs. On social integration, also see "Der Dank des Arbeiters," in Zander, *Weimar*, 77–78. Cerff's biography in Stockhorst, *Köpfe*, 91.
55. Schirach, *Revolution*, 187.
56. Cerff quoted in Zander, *Weimar*, 47.
57. Geissler quoted ibid., 56.
58. Jutta Rüdiger ibid., 62–63. Also see Kater, *Hitler Youth*, 94–99.
59. *Weimar-Festspiele* (1939), n.p.
60. Zander, *Eröffnungsrede*, 10 (quote); Dennis, *Inhumanities*, 420–21.
61. Ziegler, *Bartels*.
62. Zeller, *Klassiker*, vol. 1, 155; Hausmann, "Intellektuelle," 400.
63. Trommler, "Performance," 125.
64. http://www.polunbi.de/pers/erckmann-01.html (April 2012).
65. Klee, *Personenlexikon*, 216.
66. Burkhard Stenzel in Dornheim et al., *Thüringen*, 100.
67. Erckmann in *Weimarer Reden . . . 1938*, 9–10.
68. Ibid., 13.
69. Hohlbaum in *Weimarer Reden . . . 1938*, esp. 22, 27–29. On Dwinger, Zöberlein, and Binding see Baird, *Poets*, 32–65, 96–164; on Beumelburg, Stockhorst, *Köpfe*, 57; Hillesheim/Michael, *Lexikon*, 53–59.
70. Zillich and Weinheber in *Weimarer Reden . . . 1938*, 55–69. Also see Totok, "Finger," 57–72; Berger, *Weinheber*, 260–340.
71. In *Die Dichtung . . . 1940*, 5.
72. Johst quoted in *Die Dichtung . . . 1940*, 13; also Düsterberg, *Johst*, 256–75. In his drama *Schlageter* (1933) Johst had literally referred to the unsecuring of a "Browning." See Albrecht et al., *Lexikon*, vol. 1, 428.
73. *Die Dichtung . . . 1940*, 15–97.
74. Renkewitz, cultural-political directive no. 9, September 29, 1941, cited in Wulf, *Literatur*, 250.
75. List of foreigners in *Die Dichtung . . . 1941*, 6–7.
76. Spotts, *Peace*.
77. On the subsequent fate of the collabos see Dufay, *Herbstreise*, 119–71.
78. For the actual tour, see Hausmann, *Dichte*, 143–78; Dufay, *Herbstreise*, 23–104.
79. Jouhandeau quoted in Spotts, *Peace*, 46.

80. In *Die Dichtung . . . 1941*, 7.
81. Goebbels, *Herz*, 69.
82. Brehm in *Die Dichtung . . . 1941*, 42–48; Jahn ibid., 53–55, 60, 64. See Hildebert Reinhardt, "Kämpfer und Dichter," in Schremmer, *Buch*, 14–20.
83. Spotts, *Peace*, 46–47.
84. Baird, *Poets*, 117–64; Düsterberg, *Johst*, 272.
85. Dwinger in Erckmann, *Dichter*, 15 (quote), 21.
86. Haegert in Cölln, *Bartels* (1942), 72–77 (quotes 73).
87. One may safely discard the mendacious, skin-saving, version in Carossa, *Welten*, 117–27. See, instead, Langenbucher, *Dichtung*, 306–7; Friedrich Mössinger, "Die Hausschlange," *SS-Leitheft* 9, no. 11 (November 1943): 18. Also see Zeller, *Klassiker*, vol. 1, 156–58; Piper, *Rosenberg*, 603; and Carossa's own homilies in "Beschaulichkeit," 48–50.
88. Hausmann, *Dichte*, 21–80.
89. Schlaf, "Aphorismen über das Wesen der Kunst," *Neue Literatur* 38 (July 1937): 329 (quote); Schlaf, *Leben*, 65–71; Zeller, *Klassiker*, vol. 1, 131–32; Kafitz, *Schlaf*, 29, 97–98, 120–21, 178, 195–97, 201; Erdmann, *Naturalismus*, 20–21, 266–74.
90. Fuller, *Grandfather*, 175–79; Kirsten, *Weimar*, 100–1; Ziegler, *Bartels*, 13–14; Kindermann in Cölln, *Bartels* (1942), 52 (quote); Loose, *Festgabe* (1944), 5, 143.
91. See, for example, Goebbels, *Michael*, 14, 21, 26, 71, 199; Rosenberg, *Mythus*, 121, 259–61, 429, 515, 684–85.
92. Kleinschmidt, "Goethe," 461, 465, 468; Mandelkow, *Rezeptionsgeschichte*, vol. 2, 78; Lepenies, *Kultur*, 386.
93. Mathieu, "Directive," 130–35 (quote 135).
94. Linden, *Leben*, 1–2; Halbach, "Eschenbach," 179, 182; Koch, *Geschichte*, 149; Schott, *Faust*, 8, 11. Critically: Mahal, *Faust*, 587; Vaget, "Faust," 148–49.
95. Linden, *Leben*, 24; Raabe, *Sendung*, 19.
96. As shown by Mahal, *Faust*, 584.
97. Schott, *Faust*, 29.
98. Fehse, *Goethe*, 37.
99. Engelbrecht, *Faust*, see 5–19, 112–13.
100. As explained in Mandelkow, *Rezeptionsgeschichte*, vol. 2, 34; Mandelkow, "Restauration," 136. Also see Fehse, *Goethe*, 14; Linden, *Aufgaben*, 57; Bertram, *Faust*, 42, 61, 65–66.
101. Ziegler quoted in Mandelkow, *Urteil*, 176; also Bertram, *Faust*, 92.
102. Schirach, *Revolution*, 169, 172; also Fehse, *Goethe*, 142.
103. Huber, "Goethe," 6; Linden, *Leben*, 100–1; Koch, *Geschichte*, 145; Dahmen, *Idee*, 17, 20.
104. Raabe, *Sendung*, 8–10, 14.
105. Srbik, "Goethe," 226; Huber, "Goethe," 1. Also see Linden, *Aufgaben*, 29–33.
106. Marcks according to Wichert, "Bismarck," 330.
107. Linden quoted in Mandelkow, *Rezeptionsgeschichte*, vol. 2, 92. Also see ibid., 93; Schirach, *Revolution*, 169, 171; Fechter, *Geschichte*, 300; Büttner, *Gedanken*, 116; Linden, *Aufgaben*, 31. Joining Mandelkow's critique are Zabka, "Mythus," 313, and Mahal, *Faust*, 588.
108. Koch, *Goethe*, 18–20, 34 (first quote); Raabe, *Sendung*, 52 (second quote), also 39–41; Büttner, *Gedanken*, 115; Srbik, "Goethe," 229; Fehse, *Goethe*, 52; Schott, *Faust*, 29. Critically: Dennis, *Inhumanities*, 96–99.
109. *Jahrbuch der Goethe-Gesellschaft* 19 (1933): 264 (first quote), 265 (second quote). Also see 266.
110. Petersen quoted in Hecker, *Jahrbuch* (1935), 23. Also see 217–41; Petersen, *Goethe-Reden*, 32, 42, 44–45, 51.
111. Hecker, *Jahrbuch* (1935), 225, 238; Bahr, "Petersen," 145–48.
112. Stenzel, "Pg. Goethe," 233–43; Ehrlich, "Goethe-Gesellschaft," 252–64; Seemann, *Weimar*, 318 (quote). Seemann in particular is contradicted by Stephan Speicher, "Die Bürger stossen alles ab, was von aussen kommt," *SZ*, March 13, 2012.
113. Petersen, *Sehnsucht* (quote 60). On Landauer and Mühsam, see Albrecht et al., *Lexikon*, vol. 2, 7, 109–10.
114. Boden, "Petersen," 97; Boden/Fischer, *Petersen*, 9–10, 23–34; Jäger, *Seitenwechsel*, 39; Mandelkow, *Rezeptionsgeschichte*, vol. 2, 89; Vosskamp, "Kontinuität," 142.
115. Fabricius, *Schiller*, 9; Ruppelt, *Schiller*, 10–12. On the Schiller Year in all of Germany, esp. Weimar, see Ruppelt, 33–38; Kirsten, *Weimar*, 54–57; Albert, "Schiller," 68–71.

116. Ruppelt, *Schiller*, 12–16; Maurer, "Schiller," 35–36.
117. Fabricius, *Schiller*, 13–16, 42–43, 104; Ruppelt, *Schiller*, 16–24; Maurer, "Schiller," 34; Pongs, *Urbilder*, 45; Kühn, *Schreibtisch*, 114–15.
118. Cysarz quoted in Zeller, *Klassiker*, vol. 1, 301. Also see Fabricius, *Schiller*, 24–25, 75–90, 126–28; Ruppelt, *Schiller*, 24–28; Bertram, "Schiller," esp. 216, 218, 221–22, 231–32; Pongs, *Urbilder*, 4, 20; Albert, "Schiller," 73–75.
119. Deubel, "Schiller," 497–99; Ruppelt, *Schiller*, 29–30.
120. Oellers, *Schiller*, L; Maurer, "Schiller," 31–33.
121. Wapnewski, *Auge*, 53; Ruppelt, *Schiller*, 41–44, 113–14.

Chapter Eight: Buchenwald, 1937 to 1945

1. Knigge/Stein, *Ehrlich*, 12–13, 16–20, 112–13; Megargee, *Encyclopedia*, 140–41.
2. Günther et al., *Weimar*, 233; Merseburger, *Mythos*, 29–31; Seemann, *Weimar*, 46.
3. Müller/Stein, *Familien*, 51.
4. Figures according to Müller/Stein, *Familien*, 51; Winkler, "Antisemitismus," 284.
5. Figures from Günther et al., *Weimar*, 234; Müller/Stein, *Familien*, 51.
6. Müller/Stein, *Familien*, 70–75.
7. Gibas, *Thüringen*, 150.
8. Müller/Stein, *Familien*, 101–5 (advertisement facsimile dated January 9, 1933: 104), 115–19. Other figures according to *Statistisches Jahrbuch* (1938), 332, 339.
9. Müller/Stein, *Familien*, 106–8.
10. Köhler, *Weimar*, 49; Günther, *Weimar*, 164; Wallraf in Günther/Wallraf, *Geschichte*, 612; Krakulec et al., *Buchenwald*, 118; Müller/Stein, *Familien*, 123, 131.
11. Ritscher, *Speziallager*, 233–34; Müller/Stein, *Familien*, 135, 154–61.
12. Bernhard Post in Dornheim et al., *Thüringen*, 37; Müller/Stein, *Familien*, 135–70.
13. Wohlfeld, *Buchenwald*, 44–46.
14. Müller/Stein, *Familien*, 95–98.
15. Ibid., 115–20.
16. Ibid., 147–53; Uecker, *Kulturverlust*, 52–56.
17. Müller/Stein, *Familien*, 136–42; Gibas, *Thüringen*, 251–53; Uecker, *Kulturverlust*, 37–39.
18. Müller/Stein, *Familien*, 84–89.
19. Gerwarth, *Heydrich*, 168–69; Bessel, *Germany*, 50; Schley, *Nachbar*, 22–24; Stein, "Juden," 102–3; Orth, *System*, 23–24, 33–39; 51–54; Wachsmann, "Dynamics," 21–23, 30–33.
20. Gerwarth, *Heydrich*, 68–69, 109; Hackett, *Report*, 56; Orth, *System*, 28–30; Wachsmann, "Dynamics," 21.
21. Gerwarth, *Heydrich*, 121; Longerich, *Himmler*, 498.
22. Kershaw, *End*, 331.
23. Rassloff, *Sauckel*, 84–85; Overesch, *Brill*, 288 (Eicke quoted ibid.); Stein, "Stadt," 30; Schley, *Nachbar*, 25–27.
24. Kogon, *SS-Staat*, 209; Günther, *Weimar*, 161; Hackett, *Report*, 23–24, 74–75; Niethammer, *Buchenwald*, 187.
25. Hackett, *Report*, 89–91; Overesch, *Buchenwald*, 164–65; Niethammer, *Buchenwald*, 188.
26. Overesch, *Buchenwald*, 172; Klee, *Personenlexikon*, 323–24, 463.
27. Rassloff, *Sauckel*, 86; Hackett, *Report*, 304–5; Overesch, *Buchenwald*, 52, 157–58; Greiser, *Todesmärsche*, 49–76; Schley, *Nachbar*, 28, 76; Günther Wallraf in Günther/Wallraf, *Geschichte*, 625; Orth, *System*, 224–27; Wachsmann, "Dynamics," 33–35; Kershaw, *End*, 330.
28. Steiner et al., *Weimar*, 14; Niven, *Child*, 48; Overesch, *Buchenwald*, 38–39, 70–71, 78–81, 154–56; Niethammer, *Buchenwald*, 45, 65; Post, "Nationalsozialismus," 233.
29. Kogon, *SS-Staat*. Also see Orth, *System*, 25; Prümm, *Dirks*, 17–120.
30. Hackett, *Report*, 33.
31. Ibid., 33, 36, 47, 51, 57, 58 (quote); Freund, *Buchenwald*, 136; Stein, "Juden," 92–93; Kogon, *SS-Staat*, 188.
32. Kowollik, *Buchenwald*, 17–18; D'Harcourt, *Enemy*, 123; Stein "Juden," 140; Freund, *Buchenwald*, 134–36; Hackett, *Report*, 51, 69.
33. Freund, *Buchenwald*, 124–25; Kowollik, *Buchenwald*, 22–23; Bunzol, *Erlebnisse*, 16; Fein/Flanner, *Buchenwald*, 92.

34. Freund, *Buchenwald*, 140–41; Fein/Flanner, *Buchenwald*, 95.
35. Snyder, *Bloodlands*, 183–84 (quotes); Hackett, *Report*, 70.
36. *Buchenwald: Mahnung*, 156–57; Overesch, *Buchenwald*, 172–73; Hackett, *Report*, 64, 71–73, 224.
37. Schley, *Nachbar*, 30, 100; Smith, Jr., *Koch*, 27, 87–88; Klee, *Personenlexikon*, 323–24; Kogon, *SS-Staat*, 290–307 (quote 299).
38. Kater, *Hitler Youth*, 70–71; Klee, *Personenlexikon*, 323; Overesch, *Buchenwald*, 172; Fein/ Flanner, *Buchenwald*, 95; Hackett, *Report*, 43; Smith, Jr., *Koch*, 28, 37, 85, 93.
39. Kogon, *SS-Staat*, 202–7 (quote 202); Sharples, *Legacy*, 53–56; Fein/Flanner, *Buchenwald*, 95–96.
40. Hackett, *Report*, 38, 50, 64, 69, 80–81, 84–87, 91; Vance, *Soldiers*, 251–59; Overesch, *Buchenwald*, 168–71, 219–21; Schley, *Nachbar*, 29–32; D'Harcourt, *Enemy*, 116–22, 139–41; Semprún, *Sonntag*, 204–50; Niethammer, *Buchenwald*, 49–50, 58, 188–90; Zimmermann/ Zimmermann, "Fakultät," 158–59; Kater, *"Ahnenerbe"*, 185–86.
41. See facsimiles of envelope addressed to Robert Zeiler, and postcard sent by Max Wandki, in Müller, *Recht*, 20; Fein/Flanner, *Buchenwald*, 85.
42. Richard Alewyn quoted in Mandelkow, *Urteil*, 335.
43. Vance, *Soldiers*, 257; Hackett, *Report*, 32.
44. See Semprún, *Sonntag*, 188–89; Kühn, *Schreibtisch*, 257.
45. Quote Eicke to Himmler, July 24, 1937, in Overesch, *Brill*, 288. Also see *Konzentrationslager Buchenwald*, 18; Schley, *Nachbar*, 21.
46. *Das Postleitzahlenbuch*, 926–27.
47. König, *Germanistenlexikon*, vol. 1, 18–21.
48. Schley, *Nachbar*, 1–5 (quotes 4–5); Mauersberger, *Hitler*, 295–96.
49. Quote from "Ein Leben in Weimar (I)," *TLZ*, April 30, 1991; Schley, *Nachbar*, 43–48, 60; Niethammer, *Buchenwald*, 45; Hackett, *Report*, 66; Kühn, *Schreibtisch*, 134–37; Günther, *Weimar*, 162.
50. Schley, *Nachbar*, 50–55; Zimmermann/Zimmermann, "Fakultät," 156.
51. Kowollik, *Buchenwald*, 27; Freund, *Buchenwald*, 75; Schley, *Nachbar*, 61.
52. Schley, *Nachbar*, 55–59.
53. Wohlfeld, *Buchenwald*, 65–66.
54. Schley, *Nachbar*, 53, 80–83.
55. On Tietz see p. 249. Also Schley, *Nachbar*, 79–80, 83–85, 137–44; Wohlfeld, *Buchenwald*, 124–26; Krakulec et al., *Buchenwald*, 82–83; Poller, *Arztschreiber*, 127.
56. Offenberg, "Mosaik," 292; Kühn, *Schreibtisch*, 138; Schley, *Nachbar*, 96, 103 (2nd quote), 104, 138.
57. Stein, "Juden," 152; Stein, "Stadt," 16–17; Schley, *Nachbar*, 35, 60–63, 93–98; Steiner et al., *Weimar*, 180; Poller, *Arztschreiber*, 125; Krakulec et al., *Buchenwald*, 85, 103; Semprún, *Sonntag*, 336; Mauersberger, *Hitler*, 298–99.
58. Köhler, *Weimar*, 48; Overesch, *Buchenwald*, 185–86; Schley, *Nachbar*, 33, 55, 70–80; Hackett, *Report*, 194; Rassloff, *Sauckel*, 86; Krakulec et al., *Buchenwald*, 93; Wohlfeld, *Buchenwald*, 126–27; Korrek et al., *Gauforum*, 65.
59. Schley, *Nachbar*, 113–16; Weber, *Villen*, vol. 4, 156–57; Müller/Stein, *Familien*, 93, 103, 125, 128, 161.
60. Freund, *Buchenwald*, 26–27, 184–85; Steiner et al., *Weimar*, 139, 163; Kowollik, *Buchenwald*, 7; Kühn, *Schreibtisch*, 131–32; Müller/Stein, *Familien*, 133; Overesch, *Buchenwald*, 82.
61. Schley, *Nachbar*, 63; Bernhard Post in Dornheim et al., *Thüringen*, 45; *Buchenwald: Mahnung*, 223–24; Vance, *Soldiers*, 255.
62. Mommsen, "Dissolution"; Kershaw, *End*, esp. 86–87, 135–40, 167, 190–91, 209–25, 256, 260–61, 323, 346.
63. Kershaw, *End*, 135, 190–91, 235–39; Bessel, *Germany*, 12; Feuchter, *Luftkrieg*, 255–57; Gregor, *Nuremberg*, 25.
64. Günther, *Weimar*, 165–67; Steiner et al., *Weimar*, 9–10, 105–7, 134, 181; Overesch, *Brill*, 315–16; Mandelkow, *Urteil*, 260–61; Köhler, *Weimar*, 66–67 (quote); "Das Ende eines Vorfrühlingstages," *TLZ.de*, February 8, 2008.
65. Steiner et al., *Weimar*, 12, 144; Bernhard Post in Dornheim et al., *Thüringen*, 46; Schneider, *Weimar*, 51; Günther Wallraf in Günther/Wallraf, *Geschichte*, 618–19; Offenberg, "Mosaik," 298–300; Rassloff, *Sauckel*, 103.

Chapter Nine: Weimar in East and West Germany, 1945 to 1990

1. Ritscher, *Speziallager*, 222–23; "Geschichten zwischen Gestapo-Keller und Buchenwald," *WeltOnline,* January 3, 1998.
2. Kielmansegg, *Katastrophe*, 73, 167, 224, 498–500, 518–20, 526–27, 533, 539–41, 551; Jarausch, *Hitler*, 67–68. See *A bis Z* (1969) for quote.
3. "Die Bestie vom Lager Buchenwald," *SZ,* June 23, 1958; "Ehe mit dem Satan," *Stern,* June 28, 1958; "Frau Sommer muss kündigen," *FAZ,* July 2, 1958. Critically reflective: Sharples, *Legacy*, 54–63, 71; Gregor, *Nuremberg*, 89–90, 253–55; Frei, *Germany*, 67–68.
4. Bollenbeck, "Weimar," 221 (quote). Also see Mandelkow, *Rezeptionsgeschichte*, vol. 2, 135–40.
5. Klee, *Personenlexikon*, 676; Walter Boehlich, "Die bedingte Karriere," *Der Spiegel* (June 28, 1982): 153–55; Bert-Oliver Manig, "Einer der bekanntesten Germanisten der frühen Bundesrepublik," www/dradio.de/kultur/sendungen/kalenderblatt/1664937.
6. Hans Joachim Schrimpf, "Vorwort," in Schrimpf, *Literatur*, n.p.
7. Meinecke to Siegfried A. Kaehler, July 4, 1940, in Dehio/Classen, *Meinecke*, 363 (quote); Meinecke, *Katastrophe*, 168–76; Wehler, *Gesellschaftsgeschichte: Vierter Band*, 718.
8. Von Wiese, *Leben*, 138–207, 350–64; Klessmann, *Staaten*, 263–85; Lepenies, *Kultur*, 393; Seeliger, *Universität*; Lämmert in Lämmert et al., *Germanistik*, esp. 32–35; Berghahn, "Andere," 3–4.
9. Jaspers, *Zukunft* (quote 34); Curtius, "Goethe oder Jaspers?" in Mandelkow, *Urteil*, 304–7; Klee, *Personenlexikon*, 285. Judiciously: Kleinschmidt, "Goethe," 470–71; Spitzer, "Goethekult," 582–91; Nägele, "Goethefeiern," 111–12; Mandelkow, *Rezeptionsgeschichte*, vol. 2, 140–42.
10. Richard Alewyn, "Goethe als Alibi," in Mandelkow, *Urteil*, 333–35. See Chapter Eight, pp. 263–65.
11. Hans-Dieter Roos, "Ulbricht hebt das Glas," *SZ*, November 14, 1959; Karl Korn, "Goethe drüben," *FAZ,* July 15, 1961; Gärtner, *Kultur*, 150–56; Ehrlich, "Goethe-Gesellschaft," 253; von Wiese, *Leben*, 335–38.
12. Kielmansegg, *Katastrophe*, 533–34; Gärtner, *Kultur*, 147–49.
13. Gärtner, "Weimar," 341.
14. Schröer/Lanfer, *Städte*, 11–25, 55–61.
15. "Hinterhöfe waren nicht tabu," *TLZ*, February 27, 1990.
16. Letter to the editor, *TAZ*, February 2, 1990.
17. Müller-Enbergs et al., *DDR*, vol. 1, 64–65, 198–99; vol. 2, 1062, 1220; Hackett, *Report*, 4; Niethammer, *Buchenwald*, 63–66, 73, 90, 102–3, 129–30.
18. Knigge, "Schatten," 167.
19. Mayer, *Deutscher*, vol. 2, 34; Müller-Enbergs et al., *DDR*, vol. 2, 858. On copy, see Kahler, "Jugend," 254; Marlies Menge in Sommer, *Reise*, 206–7; Edgar Hartwig and Wallraf in Günther/Wallraf, *Geschichte*, 632, 634; "Kränze für Opfer," *TLZ*, April 12, 1989.
20. Bartel as quoted in Overesch, *Buchenwald*, 254.
21. Knigge, "Schatten," 168; Overesch, *Buchenwald*, 235; Timpel/Schäfer, *dich*, 17; Günther et al., *Weimar*, 64–65.
22. "Thälmann-Ehrung," *TLZ*, April 15, 1989; "Konferenz in Buchenwald," *TLZ,* June 7, 1989; "Ehrendes Gedenken," *TLZ*, August 19, 1989.
23. *A bis Z*, 261; Müller-Enbergs et al., *DDR*, vol. 1, 64, 198–99; vol. 2, 1062–63; Niethammer, *Buchenwald*, 71–77, 90–92, 103–4, 111, 131–33; Overesch, *Buchenwald*, 218, 222–34, 291–94; Groehler, "Antifaschismus," 535–37.
24. "Keine pauschalen Urteile," *TAZ*, March 3, 1990; Müller-Enbergs et al., *DDR*, vol. 2, 985–86; Pätzold, *Geschichte*, 166–67, 185–89, 248–68.
25. "Buchenwalds Kreuz," *TAZ*, February 7, 1990; "Aufklärung zu Tabuthema," *TAZ*, June 7, 1990.
26. Ritscher, *Speziallager*, 7–8, 82, 167, 172, 176, 274–79, 284–85, 290, 295–99; Klotz, *Heimat*, 12–14, 86 (quote), 157, 163; Finn, *Häftlinge*, 207–9; Lenzer, *Frauen*, 97. On purge machinations, telling examples are in Figes, *Whisperers*, and Snyder, *Bloodlands*.
27. Ritscher, *Speziallager*, 84, 298–99; Müller, *Recht*, 49; Lenzer, *Frauen*, 151; Krypczik/Ritscher, *Krankheit*, 21, 35–38.
28. Ritscher, *Speziallager*, 8, 254; Klotz, *Heimat*, 43, 46–47, 88, 113, 134–36; Müller, *Recht*, 61–63.

29. Ritscher, *Speziallager*, 142; Klotz, *Heimat*, 22; Joachim Heyne in Müller, *Recht*, 41–43; Horst Kranich interview, "Ich war fünfzehn," *TLZ*, February 16, 1990; "Gefordert," *TLZ*, September 28, 1992. On Werwolf: Kater, *Hitler Youth*, 226–28.

30. Ritscher, *Speziallager*, 142; Lenzer, *Frauen*, 14, 40–49; Müller, *Recht*, 37–38, 46–47.

31. See Müller, *Recht*, 48; Klotz, *Heimat*, 80.

32. Ochs, *Zeit*, 204–5.

33. Ritscher, *Speziallager*, 138; Klotz, *Heimat*, 67–71, 121; Müller, *Recht*, 45; Finn, *Häftlinge*, 39; Lenzer, *Frauen*, 79–80; Krypczik/Ritscher, *Krankheit*, 12, 25–28, 73–81. On minimum calories, see Guradze/Freudenberg, "Existenzminimum," 328.

34. Krypczik/Ritscher, *Krankheit*, 13, 28–30, 66–81, 87–89 (Wagner quoted 74); Ritscher, *Speziallager*, 108–11, 138, 291; Klotz, *Heimat*, 64–65, 122, 141; Lenzer, *Frauen*, 90–91; Ochs, *Zeit*, 208–9.

35. Ritscher, *Speziallager*, 116, 124–25, 128; Klotz, *Heimat*, 75–78, 81, 84, 101, 104–7, 119–20; Lenzer, *Frauen*, 115–17; Ochs, *Zeit*, 196.

36. Ritscher, *Speziallager*, 128, 298; Klotz, *Heimat*, 109–11; Lenzer, *Frauen*, 124–25; Ochs, *Zeit*, 207, 210–19.

37. Ritscher, *Speziallager*, 232, 252, 261 (Soviet authorities' quote); Klotz, *Heimat*, 104, 109–11; Overesch, *Buchenwald*, 211–12; Ochs, *Zeit*, 184; Diethe, *Sister*, 142; "Häftling Nr. 10711," *TLZ*, February 16, 1990.

38. Quotes from Lepenies, *Kultur*, 393; Jarausch, *Hitler*, 137; Wehler, *Gesellschaftsgeschichte: Fünfter Band*, 23; Kielmansegg, *Katastrophe*, 603. A thoughtful consideration of the GDR's regime character is in Kocka, *Society*, 37–38, 40–41.

39. Stasi was short for [*Ministerium für*] *Staatssicherheit*. See Vollnhals, "Ministerium"; Schroeder, *SED-Staat*, 430–49; Fulbrook, *Anatomy*, esp. 46–56, 115–25; de Bruyn, *Jahre*, 238–41.

40. Plans graduated from one half to seven years, followed by a *Perspektivplan*, 1948–70 (*A bis Z*, 474–75). See "Wanzen lauschten," *TLZ*, January 12, 1990; Dönhoff et al., *Land*, 22.

41. NDPD stood for *Nationaldemokratische Partei Deutschlands*. See Steiner et al., *Weimar*, 26, 30, 34; Edgar Hartwig in Günther/Wallraf, *Geschichte*, 654, 673–75, 706, 721–22; Post et al., *Thüringen-Handbuch*, 21, 48–60.

42. Kocka, *Society*, 46, 48–49.

43. "Erika Benkowitz ist tot," *thüringer–allgemeine.de*, January 4, 2009; "Erinnerung an Weimars Ehrenbürger Erich Kranz," ibid., March 12, 2009; Victor, *Oktoberfrühling*, 153–54; Mühlen, *Aufbruch*, 187; Neubert/Auerbach, *kann*, 79–84, 117, 130, 166–68; 192; Haufe, *Staat*, esp. 10–13, 21–25, 33, 47, 61, 215.

44. Calculations according to figures in Henselmann, *Reisen*, 245; Steiner et al., *Weimar*, 36; Edgar Hartwig in Günther/Wallraf, *Geschichte*, 684–86; Eberhardt, *Umwelt*, 18; Strubelt, *Jena*, 199; *A bis Z*, 109–10, 173, 704; Kossert, *Heimat*, 193–228; Douglas, *Orderly*, esp. 308–9. Because of extreme population flux before and after the end of the war, none of the figures can be called reliable. The Thuringian State Archive Weimar indicates there were 64,741 persons in Weimar on October 23, 1945, including refugees and 9,051 Nazi Party members (Dr. Frank Boblenz to author, March 5, 2013).

45. Edgar Hartwig in Günther/Wallraf, *Geschichte*, 689–90, 703, 782, 819, 838; Hammer, *Zeit*, 194; Steiner et al., *Weimar*, 182; Ragwitz/Riederer, *Zwiebelmarkt*, 64; Schneider, *Weimar*, 64; Ritter, *Preis*, 176–79; "Guter Betreuungsgrad," *TLZ*, April 11, 1989.

46. Hildner quoted in "Noch ein paar Takte," *TLZ*, January 27, 1989; also see *TLZ*, January 25, February 4, 10, 24 and April 18, 1989; Edgar Hartwig in Günther/Wallraf, *Geschichte*, 684–86, 690–91, 783, 818–19; Kühnlenz/Messner, *Weimar*, 39; Korrek et al., *Gauforum*, 102.

47. Hinze-Reinhold, *Lebenserinnerungen*, 156; Abusch, *Visier*, 317; Rudolf Walter Leonhardt in Dönhoff et al., *Land*, 65; Schneider, *Weimar*, 66; "Baugerüst," *TLZ*, January 7, 1989; author's oberservation of Interhotels in Weimar, Leipzig, East Berlin, and Gera, September 1968.

48. Edgar Hartwig in Günther/Wallraf, *Geschichte*, 697–702, 737–40, 781–82, 806, 813; Steiner et al., *Weimar*, 121; Schneider, *Weimar*, 62–63; Schädlich, *Hochschule*, 85; Peter Christ in Sommer, *Reise*, 85; "Nicht nur Goethe," *TLZ*, April 25, 1989; "Verbrauch," *TLZ*, June 8, 1989; "Robotron," *TLZ*, February 28, 1990; Macrakis, *Secrets*, 112–40.

49. Steiner et al., *Weimar*, 164; Edgar Hartwig in Günther/Wallraf, *Geschichte*, 703; Sommer in Sommer, *Reise*, 24–25.

50. Sommer in Sommer, *Reise*, 34; Peter Christ ibid., 89; Ritter, *Preis*, 135; Edgar Hartwig in Günther/Wallraf, *Geschichte*, 819; Wolle, *Welt*, 217–18; "Rentner," *TLZ*, March 10, 1990; Frank Ellmers, "50 Jahre Trabi," June 11, 2007, *epochtimes.de*; "Automarkt," *TLZ*, January 13, 1990.

51. "PKW-Service-Station," *TLZ*, March 21, 1989; "Wo das Herz," *TLZ*, April 15, 1989; "Was unserem," *TLZ*, November 2, 1989; Steiner et al., *Weimar*, 26.

52. Gärtner, "Weimar," 86; Gärtner, *Kultur*, 99; "Im Linienbus," *TLZ*, January 10, 1989; "Diebstahl," *TLZ*, February 18, 1989.

53. Satjukow, *Besatzer*, 89.

54. Hinze-Reinhold, *Lebenserinnerungen*, 144–46; Steiner et al., *Weimar*, 140, 192; Köhler, *Weimar*, 76; Satjukow, *Besatzer*, 29, 314; Satjukow, *Erinnerungen*, 28, 116–17; Regwitz/Riederer, *Zwiebelmarkt*, 67; Allinson, *Politics*, 46; Weber, *Villen*, vol. 4, 133; vol. 5, 125.

55. The "Society for German–Soviet Friendship." See Edgar Hartwig in Günther/Wallraf, *Geschichte*, 671–72, 730; Satjukow, *Befreiung*, 191–96, 206–10; Satjukow, *Erinnerungen*, 29–34, 97–101; Satjukow, *Besatzer*, 52, 57, 101, 206–8.

56. Poutrus, "Massenvergewaltigungen," 176–77, 197–98, n. 38; Antony Beevor, "Introduction," in *A Woman*, 10.

57. Delank quoted in Steiner et al., *Weimar*, 109, also ibid., 141–42; Satjukow, *Besatzer*, 263–68.

58. Satjukow, *Besatzer*, 29–30, 57–59, 285–87.

59. Satjukow, *Befreiung*, 48–50, 112–15; Satjukow, *Erinnerungen*, 60–61, 98–101, 118, 153–54; Satjukow, *Besatzer*, 171–72, 249; Finn, *Häftlinge*, 210, 212–215, 217–18, 221; Merker, *Zensur*, 9; Neubert/Auerbach, *kann*, 19, 45–46; Köhler, *Weimar*, 79–80; "Russischunterricht," *TLZ*, January 24, 1989.

60. Otto Grotewohl in *Protokoll*, 21; *Arbeiterbewegung*, 226–32; *Um ein . . . Deutschland*, 145–48, 165–67; *Die SED*, 27, 37–41, 424. Critically: Gransow, *Kulturpolitik*, 50–52; Scharfschwerdt, "Klassik-Ideologie," 115; Hohendahl, "Theorie," 16–17; Dietrich, *Politik*, 14–15, 46.

61. Cf. Faust: "Auf freiem Grund mit freiem Volke stehn" (463, author's English translation). Also see: *Arbeiterbewegung*, 227, 245, 344; Abusch, *Visier*, 290; Günther Dahlke in Dahlke, *Menschheit*, 9–10; Schröder, "DDR," 61–62; Ernst, "Erbe," 16, 19, 25; Mandelkow, *Urteil*, xlvii, liii–liv, 290, 425–26; Mandelkow, "Bedeutung," 78–79; Lützeler, "Faust," 35–36; Trommler, "Kulturpolitik," 36; Lepenies, *Kultur*, 392 (quote).

62. Tjulpanow, *Deutschland*, 217 (quote); Abusch, *Visier*, 208; Ziermann, *Dymschitz*, esp. 15, 19–22; Heider, *Politik*, 45, 61–62; Dietrich, *Politik*, 14–17; Schulmeister, *Kulturbund*, 109.

63. *Arbeiterbewegung*, 236, 244–48; Schlenker, *Erbe*, 61, 97; Scharfschwerdt, "Klassik-Ideologie," 118–19; Mandelkow, *Rezeptionsgeschichte*, vol. 2, 161–63; Wehner, *Kulturpolitik*, 890–92; Dietrich, *Politik*, 182–86.

64. *Arbeiterbewegung*, 313–15; Trommler, "Kulturpolitik," 62 (quote), 63; Trommler, "Prosaentwicklung," 315–16; Jäger, *Kultur*, 87–89, 103; Gransow, *Kulturpolitik*, 90–91, 95–96; Ernst, "Erbe," 25–27.

65. *Arbeiterbewegung*, 36, 42, 47, 245, 315 (quote); Dahlke in Dahlke, *Menschheit*, 22, 24; "Beschluss des SED-Politbüros," January 25, 1955, ibid., 277; *Protokoll*, 37; Abusch, *Schiller*, 262; Abusch, "Faust," 185; Mayer, "Goethe," 31. Critically: Hinderer, "Universalideologie," 159–60; Heukenkamp, "Goethe-Rezeption," 285; Mandelkow, *Urteil*, lii–liii; Scharfschwerdt, "Klassik-Ideologie," 119; Wehner, *Kulturpolitik*, 894–96.

66. Professor Heinrich Deiters in *Protokoll*, 68, 83, 86, 90; *Um ein . . . Deutschland*, 736–39; Dietrich, *Politik*, 34, 303; Ernst, "Erbe," 21–22; Schlenker, *Erbe*, 49–50; Mandelkow, "Bedeutung," 97.

67. The full name was Kulturbund zur demokratischen Erneuerung Deutschlands.

68. Wegener quoted in *Die SED*, 76.

69. Becher, *Art*, 559; Becher, *Werke*, vol. 3, 236, 499–508; Bartels, *Herkunft*, 207–15; Klemperer, *Tagebücher*, vol. 1, 89–90; Staritz, *Geschichte*, 74–75; Heider, *Politik*, 33, 39, 45; Janka, *Spuren*, 285; Shirer, "Becher," 1; Albrecht et al., *Lexikon*, vol. 1, 52–54.

70. Lukács, *Goethe*, 7, 12, 14–15; Bronner, "Lukács," 13, 20–21, 26–27; Aschheim, *Nietzsche*, 4; Ehrlich et al., "Weimarer Klassik," 11–12.

71. Pike, *Politics*, 72–88; Segal, "Style," 237; Heider, *Politik*, 34–54, 81–83, 114–16; Jäger, *Kultur*, 12–15; Hartmann/Eggeling, *Präsenz*, 188–96; Wehner, *Kulturpolitik*, 138–44; Dietrich, *Politik*, 17–19, 27–35, 98, 216–18.

72. As in an address to the FDJ, March 21, 1949. See Mayer, "Goethe," 314, 318–19, 324, 326. Mayer had fluid loyalties. In the 1950s, he criticized the party line, fell into disfavor and in the early 1960s conveniently left the GDR for the FRG, to be placed on a pedestal by anti-GDR West Germans.

73. Erbe, *Moderne*, 56–87 (first quote 64); Ehrlich, "Faust" (Abusch quoted 335); Staritz, *Gründung*, 257–60; Schlenker, *Erbe*, 87–91; Dietrich, *Politik*, 162–65; Hartmann/Eggeling, *Präsenz*, 165–69; Heider, *Politik*, 90–92, 117–19, 129–32.

74. Schröder, "DDR," 63; Lützeler, "Faust," 44; Mandelkow, "Bedeutung," 99–100; Jäger, *Kultur*, 67–68; Vaget, "Faust" (quote 173); Abusch, "Faust," esp. 188–89 (quotes).

75. See Brecht's defense in Bunge, *Debatte*, 139–79. Also Mandelkow, "Bedeutung," 99–100 (quote); Lützeler, "Faust," 42–43.

76. Quotes: Honecker, *Leben*, 342; James, *Identity*, 175; Jarausch, *Hitler*, 200. Also Erbe, "Geschmack," 665–67; Bathrick, "Kultur," 67–70; Hohendahl, "Theorie," 15–47; Scharfschwerdt, "Klassik-Ideologie," 139–45; Mandelkow, *Rezeptionsgeschichte*, vol. 2, 230–33; Mandelkow, "Bedeutung," 104–15; Ehrlich et al., "Weimarer Klassik," 16–22.

77. Edgar Hartwig in Günther/Wallraf, *Geschichte*, 783–84.

78. *Arbeiterbewegung*, 220–21, 224–25; Edgar Hartwig in Günther/Wallraf, *Geschichte*, 679, 708–9, 788–89; Steiner et al., *Weimar*, 36; Dietrich, "Goethepächter," 167.

79. Hammer, *Zeit*, 157–58, 207–9; Heider, *Politik*, 51–53; Abusch, *Visier*, 305–7; "Weimars grüne Seite," *TLZ*, March 14, 198; "Dienst am Dichter," *SZ*, April 2, 2002. See Klee, *Kulturlexikon*, 368, 639.

80. Müller-Enbergs et al., *DDR*, vol. 2, 1171; Wahl, "Überwindung," 78–80; Krenzlin, *Scholz*, 198–215; Mandelkow, *Rezeptionsgeschichte*, vol. 2, 163–64.

81. The full German designation was Nationale Forschungs- und Gedenkstätten der klassischen deutschen Literatur in Weimar. Its founding charter dates from August 6, 1953. See Lübbe, *Dokumente*, 85–88.

82. *Arbeiterbewegung*, 316–27; Golz, "Goethe-und Schiller-Archiv," 54–60, 65; Edgar Hartwig in Günther/Wallraf, *Geschichte*, 787–90, 830–31; Wahl, "Überwindung," 75–102; Cleve, "Ideal," 343–57; Gärtner, *Kultur*, 172–73; Gärtner, "Weimar," 320–27; Mandelkow, *Rezeptionsgeschichte*, vol. 2, 167–68, 193; *Kolloquium...1960*, 921–23; Hinderer, "Universalideologie," 168–71; Kahler, "Jugend," 255–58; Ehrlich, "Sozialismus und Klassik," 14–19.

83. Müller-Enbergs et al., *DDR*, vol. 1, 16–17, 393–94, 475, 573–74; Ehrlich, "Goethe-Gesellschaft," 251–81; Mandelkow, *Rezeptionsgeschichte*, vol. 2, 165–71; Schultz, "Kultur," 157–81; Staadt, "Zinnen," 187–89, 201–2; Wahl, "Gesellschaften," 125–26, 130–31; "Goethe," *TLZ*, May 18, 1989, "Neue Sichten," *TLZ*, May 22, 1989.

84. See Edgar Hartwig in Günther/Wallraf, *Geschichte*, 716; Mandelkow, *Rezeptionsgeschichte*, vol. 2, 162.

85. Johannes R. Becher, "Der Befreier," in Becher, *Werke*, vol. 3, 391–431; Mann, *Ansprache*, 10 (quoting Alfred Kantorowicz); *Arbeiterbewegung*, 239–43; Wehner, *Kulturpolitik*, 905–13; Mandelkow, "Restauration," 142; *Die SED*, 117–20; Dietrich, *Politik*, 185–86.

86. Albrecht et al., *Lexikon*, vol. 1, 335–36; vol. 2, 98–99; Vaget, *Amerikaner*, 484–91; Abusch, *Visier*, 253–55; Merseburger, *Mythos*, 398; Mayer, *Deutscher*, vol. 2, 72–78; Reinhardt, *Zeitungen*, 61; Gärtner, *Kultur*, 38–44; Ritscher, *Speziallager*, 295; Klemperer, *Tagebücher*, vol. 1, 668–69; Mandelkow, *Rezeptionsgeschichte*, vol. 2, 154 (1st quote 55); Tjulpanow, *Deutschland*, 291; Edgar Hartwig in Günther/Wallraf, *Geschichte*, 717; Mann, *Ansprache*, esp. 4, 7, 16 (last quote); Strohmeyer, *Mitläufer*, 69–79; Hausmann in Bade/Haacke, *Jahr*, 159–63; Josef Marein, "Thomas Mann: Goethe-Preisträger östlich und westlich," *DZ*, June 23, 1949.

87. *Arbeiterbewegung*, 264–65, 280–84; Johannes R. Becher, "Denn er ist unser: Friedrich Schiller der Dichter der Freiheit" (May 9, 1955), in Dahlke, *Menschheit*, 298–315 (quotes 314).

88. Otto Grotewohl, "Wir sind ein Volk!" (April 3, 1955), in Dahlke, *Menschheit*, 281–97 (quotes 284, 286).

89. Mayer, *Deutscher*, vol. 2, 89; Thomas Mann, "Schiller-Rede" (May 14, 1955) in Oellers, *Schiller*, 389–401.

90. Thomas Mann to Hans Armin Peter, February 2, 1925, in Sprecher et al., *Briefe III*, 128.

91. Naake, *Nietzsche*, 141–54, 229–31; Gärtner, *Kultur*, 202; Hahn, "Nietzsche-Archiv," 18–19; Hoffmann, *Geschichte*, 121, 125–26, 131; Riedel, *Nietzsche*, 157–62; Jäger, *Kultur*, 248; Harich, "Revision," esp. 1020; "Nietzsche," *TAZ*, June 27, 1990.

92. Klee, *Kulturlexikon*, 9; John, *Musikstadt*, 111–12.

93. First quote Edgar Hartwig in Günther/Wallraf, *Geschichte*, 790 (also 709–10, 831, 791); second quote Busch in Hasche et al., *Theater*, 97; 3rd quote Rudolf Walter Leonhardt in Dönhoff et al., *Land*, 97. Also see Gülke, *Musik*, esp. 1; John, *Musikstadt*, 112–14; Huschke, *Glut*, 201, 203, 206–7, 211; Messner, *Nationaltheater: Zweiter Teil*, 3–8, 17–24, 33–40, 57–58, 62–64, 81–84; "Und Ostern," *TLZ*, February 23, 1989; "Das aktuelle Interview," *TLZ*, February 13, 1992.

94. Hartwig et al., *Festschrift*, 68–78, 87–109 (quote 81); John, *Musikstadt*, 107–9; Edgar Hartwig in Günther/Wallraf, *Geschichte*, 711, 796–97; Müller-Enbergs et al., *DDR*, vol. 1, 205, 385–86; Klee, *Kulturlexikon*, 98, 181.

95. Marie Torhorst, "Das Wandgemälde des Deutschen Nationaltheaters," *Das Volk*, July 27, 1950, quoted in Dollichon, *Dokumentation*, 91. Also see ibid., 84–85, 89; Dollichon, *Kunstpolitik*, 171–84, 202–6; Edgar Hartwig in Günther/Wallraf, *Geschichte*, 707, 794–95, 798, 832–33; Henselmann, *Reisen*, 225, 228–31, 259, 282–83, 302; Henselmann, *Familie*, 126, 130, 140; Schädlich, *Hochschule*, 45–69, 77–79, 87–88; Hoormann, "Bauhaus-Idee," 423–35; Winkler, "Dokumentation," 205–6, 209, 211, 224, 233, 238; Preiss, *Hochschulen*, 47–48; Kossel, "Modernerezeption," Webber, *Berlin*, 107, 120; Henselmann, "Brecht"; Jutta Wartewig-Hörning, in Wartewig-Hörning et al., *Weimar*, 17; "Ansteigende Wege," *TLZ*, January 24, 1989.

96. See Neubert/Auerbach, *kann*, 205; Jarausch, *Hitler*, 205.

97. "Unstimmigkeiten," *TLZ*, November 8, 1989; Neubert/Auerbach, *kann*, 199; Victor, *Oktoberfrühling*, 20–27.

98. Schmigalle quoted in "Verbrauch steigt," *TLZ*, June 8, 1989; "Tips zur Vorbereitung," *TLZ*, May 17, 1989; "Reges Bauen," *TLZ*, May 25, 1989; "Ende," *TLZ*, October 18, 1989; Victor, *Oktoberfrühling*, 28–36, 45–56; Uta Kühne in Hoffmeister/Hempel, *Wende*, 39–44; Borchert, *Derberes*, 66, 69–71, 75–76, 142; Haufe, *Staat*, 266–68, 277; Stein, *Sorgt*, 24–26.

99. Holm Kirsten to author, April 24, 2013.

100. Victor, *Oktoberfrühling*, 57–99 (quote 66); Uta Kühne in Hoffmeister/Hempel, *Wende*, 40–45; Haufe, *Staat*, 268, 272–78; Neubert/Auerbach, *kann*, 215, 225, 230, 234–35, 240, 251–52; Rassloff, *Revolution*, 46; Fascher, "Parteien," 43–48; "Tausende verlangen," *TLZ*, October 25, 1989; "Mit Kerzen," *TLZ*, October 26, 1989; "Die Patrioten," *TLZ*, February 6, 1990; also *TLZ*, October 28, November 9, December 8, 1989, and January 12, 1990.

101. Kielmansegg, *Katastrophe*, 622; Maier, *Dissolution*, 70–95, 230–43; "16 Konzerte," *TLZ*, November 3, 1989; "Bis an die Grenzen," *TLZ*, November 21, 1989; "Ex-Sicherheitsleute," *TLZ*, January 26, 1990; "Die Silvesterfeier 1991," *TLZ*, August 15, 1990; also *TLZ*, November 2 and 24, 1989, June 14, July 25, 1990.

102. "Skinhead-Szene," *TLZ*, February 1, 1990; "Skins und Rowdys," *TLZ*, April 3, 1990; "Der Bahnhof?" and "Das Schweigen," *TLZ*, April 19, 1990; also *TLZ*, April 24, July 28, September 20, 22, 26, 1990.

Chapter Ten: Weimar after the Fall of the Berlin Wall, 1990 to 2013

1. Hochhuth, *Wessis in Weimar*, 53–77.

2. "Verbitterung," *TLZ*, February 5, 1991.

3. Satjukow, *Besatzer*, 11–12; "Harte Bedingungen," *TLZ*, October 22, 1990; "Nicht," *TLZ*, April 11, 1991; "Soldaten gehen," *TLZ*, May 30, 1991; "Gedenken," *TLZ*, June 13, 1991; "Sieger," *TLZ*, September 25, 1991; "Die Panzer," *TLZ*, November 30, 1991; "Abschiedstränen," *TLZ*, November 23, 1992; "Die letzten," *TLZ*, March 16, 1993; "Millionenprojekt," *TLZ*, August 10, 1993.

4. Rassloff, *Revolution*, 63; Post et al., *Thüringen-Handbuch*, 61–68.

5. Müller-Enbergs et al., *DDR*, vol. 1, 259–60; Ditfurth, *Blockflöten*, 194–95; "Opposition," *TLZ*, November 29, 1991; "Die CDU," "Josef Duchac," *TLZ*, December 2, 1991; "Duchac synonym," *TLZ*, December 18, 1991; "Rücktritt," *TLZ*, January 25, 1992.

6. "Import, " *TLZ*, January 29, 1992.
7. "Späte Reaktion," *TLZ*, July 9, 1992; "Die Thüringer," *TLZ*, October 15, 1992; "Land," *TLZ*, November 16, 1992; "Neue Ideen," *TLZ*, December 22, 1992; "Thüringen," *TLZ*, July 24, 1993; "Zeh," *TLZ*, July 27, 1993; "Regierung," *TLZ*, July 29, 1993.
8. Müller-Enbergs et al., *DDR*, vol. 1, 32–33; "Gewendeter Minister," *TLZ*, June 11, 1993.
9. "Zweifelhafte Staatsschützer," *TLZ*, October 30, 1993.
10. "Polizei," *TLZ*, July 26, 1994; "Ermittlungsverfahren," *TLZ*, September 2, 1994; "Lernen mit Rudolf Hess," *SPIEGELONLINE*, November 11, 2011; "Die Pannen-Truppe," *SPIEGELONLINE*, November 14, 2011.
11. "Zweifel," *TLZ*, January 10, 1994; "Regierungschef," *TLZ*, January 13, 1994; "Gehalt," *TLZ*, January 14, 1994; "Gehälter-Affaire," *TLZ*, January 17, 1994.
12. "Minister," "Sklenar," *TLZ*, May 9, 1994; "Millionenloch," *TLZ*, May 24, 1995; "Wirtschaftsprüfer," *TLZ*, March 7, 1998; "Computer-Skandal," *TLZ*, March 23, 1998; "Die Dewes-Affaire," *TLZ*, March 25, 1998.
13. "Fiedler," *TLZ*, October 11, 1996.
14. "Vorwurf," *TLZ*, March 30, 1998; "Nächtlicher," *TLZ*, May 30, 1998 (quote).
15. Sinn, *Germany*, 140–44; Maier, *Dissolution*, 298–302 (quote 302).
16. See the recurring graphs "Arbeitslosenquote" and "Arbeitslosigkeit in Thüringen" and adjoining commentaries, *TLZ*, 1989–98; Ritter, *Preis*, 117.
17. Ritter, *Preis*, 110 (quote); "Selbst," *TLZ*, October 13, 1992.
18. "Gemässigte," *TLZ*, February 15, 1991; "Ein Handelsriese," *TLZ*, June 26, 1991; "Die Herzen," *TLZ*, June 29, 1991; "Verwaltung," *TLZ*, December 9, 1991 (quote).
19. "Herbe," *TLZ*, December 11, 1991; "Arbeitslosenquote," *TLZ*, January 6, 1994; "Mehr," *TLZ*, August 9, 1995; "Pendler," *TLZ*, May 7, 1997; Ritter, *Preis*, 118–19; Kocka, *Society*, 51, 57.
20. "Noch," *TLZ*, December 6, 1990; "Start," *TLZ*, March 8, 1995; "Lehrstellennot," *TLZ*, August 7, 1997.
21. "Wohnungsfrage," *TLZ*, January 12, 1991; "Grosse," *TLZ*, September 14, 1991; "Vermieter," *TLZ*, December 20, 1991; "Noch," *TLZ*, December 2, 1992; "700 neue," *TLZ*, January 20, 1993; "Wir," *TLZ*, April 17, 1993 (quote); "Statistiken," *TLZ*, October 13, 1993; "Wohnungsmangel," *TLZ*, March 17, 1994; "Ruhig," *TLZ*, January 27, 1996; Katja Rempel in Rasche, *Provinz*, 141–56. For GDR background see Schmidt, *Handeln*, 117–20. On the topography of the Weimar-Nord tenements see Czaja, "Weimar."
22. For regional background: Ritter, *Preis*, 140–49. See "Fachkräfte," *TLZ*, June 21, 1991; "Das Land," *TLZ*, September 19, 1991; "Westflucht," *TLZ*, January 6, 1992; "5000 Einwohner," *TLZ*, December 30, 1993; "Thüringer," *TLZ*, August 5, 1994; "Thüringer," *TLZ*, July 19, 1997; "Viele," *TLZ*, February 3, 1998; "Entwicklung der Geburten," Weimar 2005 (n.p.).
23. "Kleinod," *TLZ*, November 1, 1990; "Kulturstadt," *TLZ*, November 1, 1995.
24. "Eine Brücke," *TLZ*, December 23, 1991; "Goethe-Gäste," *TLZ*, January 17, 1995.
25. "Späte," *TLZ*, January 8, 1994; "Von sparsamer," *TLZ*, January 10, 1994.
26. "Umbau," *TLZ*, November 3, 1994; "Wallfahrt," *SZ*, December 30, 1994; "Beschränkung," *SZ*, August 21, 1996; "Das Haus," *SZ*, November 5, 1996.
27. Golz, "Goethe- und Schiller-Archiv," 65–67; "Goethe," *TLZ*, August 20, 1991; "Pantheon," *TLZ*, June 26, 1996; "Streit," *TLZ*, June 3, 1998.
28. "Nietzsche," *TLZ*, November 12, 1990; "Nietzsches Rückkehr," *TLZ*, May 21, 1991; "Nietzsche," *TLZ*, October 18, 1993; "Rederecht," *SZ*, October 8, 1994; "Ist denn," *TLZ*, February 25, 1996; "Drama," *TLZ*, June 19, 1997.
29. Thomas Steinfeld, "Fäulnis," *FAZ*, July 15, 1997. See "Heiterkeit," *TLZ*, September 18, 1991; "Handschriften," *SZ*, August 23, 1996; "Bilder," *FAZ*, February 1, 1997; "Extreme," *FAZ*, August 8, 1998.
30. "Prof. Ehrlich," *TLZ*, March 4, 1992; "Oh naht nie," *FAZ*, September 1, 2003.
31. Martin Doerry, "Die Maske des Dandys," *DS* (May 20, 1996): 230–32.
32. "Gespräch mit Bernd Kauffmann," *FAZ*, November 25, 1995.
33. Bernd Kauffmann, "Gelassen Neues wagen," *TLZ*, July 18, 1992. Also see "Keine," *TLZ*, April 2, 1992; "Ermöglicher," *TLZ*, July 4, 1992.
34. "Einzigartiger," *TLZ*, March 23, 1993.

35. "16 Millionen," *TLZ*, April 17, 1993; "Eine Uraufführung," *TLZ*, November 14, 1990 (quote). Böhme rates no mention in the authoritative *Oxford Music Online*. Frank garners a single mention alongside other Weimar conductors, including Peter Gülke.
36. "Zweimal," *TLZ*, February 12, 1991.
37. "Narkotische," *TLZ*, March 12, 1991.
38. "Ein verfrühter," *TLZ*, February 17, 1992.
39. "Konzentriertes," *TLZ*, December 5, 1992.
40. "Die kleine," *TLZ*, May 6, 1995.
41. Klaus Bennert, "Solistenglück nach Schiwago-Tändelei," *SZ*, January 24, 1995.
42. "Irrtum," *TLZ*, April 3, 1991.
43. "Walhall," *TLZ*, June 4, 1991.
44. "Rummelplatz," *TLZ*, September 14, 1992; "Bewegende," *TLZ*, December 21, 1993.
45. "Knisternd," *SZ*, January 19, 1996.
46. "Anders," *TLZ*, May 22, 1993; "Erregung," *SZ*, October 19, 1994; "Ich brauche Platz," *FAZ*, June 6, 1998.
47. "Ein neuer," *TLZ*, July 1, 1993; "Ein Wackeltanz," *TLZ*, July 17, 1993; "Klassische," *TLZ*, September 25, 1993; "Weimars Theater," *TLZ*, April 16, 1994; "Gartenzwerge," *SZ*, November 9, 1995; "Raum," *TLZ*, May 16/17, 1996; "Trumpf," *TLZ*, October 31, 1996; "Weimarer," *TLZ*, January 24, 1997; "Der Hilferuf," *TLZ*, January 28, 1997; "Es steht," *TLZ*, February 4, 1997; "Nationaltheater," *TLZ*, February 6, 1997; "Beelitz," *TLZ*, May 22, 1997; "Ein Ganzes," *FAZ*, June 6, 1997; "Die ideale," *TLZ*, September 9, 1997; "DNT-Sanierung," *TLZ*, January 27, 1998; "Vorhang," *TLZ*, September 10, 1998; "Die Stadt," *TLZ*, September 16, 1998; "Beelitz," *TLZ*, September 17, 1998.
48. "Die Drehscheibe," *TLZ*, December 4, 1990.
49. "Studenten," *TLZ*, March 8, 1991.
50. "Gedämpfter," *TLZ*, April 4, 1991; "Abschied," *TLZ*, July 27, 1991; "Ziel," *TLZ*, June 25, 1993 (quote); "Seminar," *TLZ*, July 13, 1993; "Krönungskonzert," *TLZ*, July 17, 1993; "Märchenaugen," *TLZ*, July 28, 1993; "Musikseminar," *TLZ*, July 30, 1993; "Flucht," *TLZ*, February 11, 1995; "So sind," *TLZ*, July 13, 1996.
51. "Neue Musik," *TLZ*, November 23, 1990.
52. "Bis die Noten," *TLZ*, February 4, 1993.
53. "Brahms," *TLZ*, January 24, 1995.
54. "Reparatur," *TLZ*, September 17, 1991; "Offener," *TLZ*, October 31, 1991; "Mann," *TLZ*, January 3, 1992; "Abberufung," January 4, 1992; "Anstand," *TLZ*, January 11, 1992; "Mönnig weist," "Erst," "Mönnig unter," *TLZ*, January 14, 1992; "Mönnig," *TLZ*, January 31, 1992; "HAB-Rektor," *TLZ*, February 1, 1992; "HAB," *TLZ*, June 6, 1992; "Mönnig," *TLZ*, July 31, 1992; "Bewegung," *SZ*, February 16, 1998.
55. "Weimarer," "HAB," "Die Klüfte," *TLZ*, October 31, 1992; "Bauhaus," *TLZ*, October 2, 1993; "Pluralen," *TLZ*, March 9, 1994; "Kreative," *TLZ*, October 15, 1994; "Diskussion," *TLZ*, February 2, 1995; "Kein," *TLZ*, June 1, 1995; "Gestalter," *TLZ*, July 12, 1995; "Fakultätsaustritt," *TLZ*, July 13, 1995; "Experimentelle," *TLZ*, June 27, 1996; "Alle," *TLZ*, November 7, 1996; "Das Erbe," *SZ*, January 3, 1994; Zimmermann's rectoral inauguration address, November 27, 1992, in Winkler, "Dokumentation," 272–73.
56. "Jeder," *TLZ*, June 18, 1993; "Hoch," *TLZ*, May 13, 1995; *DS* (December 23, 1996): 161.
57. "Ohne," *TLZ*, July 18, 1991; "Buchenwald," *TLZ*, February 17, 1992; "Angst," "Den Schwur," *TLZ*, April 13, 1992; "Gefordert," *TLZ*, September 28, 1992; "Das Gedenken," "Buchenwaldfeier," *TLZ*, April 13, 1993; "Gesellschaftliche," *TLZ*, December 29, 1993; "Hofmann," *TLZ*, February 23, 1994; "Streit," *SZ*, February 24, 1994; "Tempelwächter," *TLZ*, April 7, 1994; "Zwei," *TLZ*, April 18, 1994; "Ende," *BZ*, April 21, 1994; "Neue," *TLZ*, July 18, 1994; "Neuer," *TLZ*, July 21, 1994; "Knigge," *TLZ*, September 2, 1994; "Forscherstreit," *DS* (September 26, 1994): 61; "Buchenwald-Streit," *TLZ*, February 9, 1995.
58. "Buchenwald," *TLZ*, December 18, 1990; "Der verweigerte," *TLZ*, May 22, 1991; "Keine," *TLZ*, July 2, 1991; "Begegnen," *TLZ*, September 21, 1991; "Auf Spurensuche," *TLZ*, May 22, 1992; "Mahnmal," *TLZ*, July 14, 1992; "Neue," *TLZ*, April 20, 1994.
59. "Polizei," *SZ*, July 30, 1994; "Polizei," *TLZ*, July 30, 1994; "Buchenwald," *TLZ*, August 8, 1994; "Nazis," *TLZ*, August 17, 1994; "Deckerts," *SZ*, January 31, 1995; "Gedenken," *SZ*,

April 15, 1997; "Rechtsradikale," *SZ*, August 9, 1997; "KZ-Mahnmal," *SZ*, July 29, 1998; "Symbolischer," *TLZ*, November 13, 1998.

60. Kohl's television address, July 1, 1990, *Bulletin des Presse- und Informationsamtes der Bundesregierung* 86 (July 3, 1990): 741–42.

61. "Ein Festival," *TLZ*, April 11, 1990; "Weimarer Sommerloch," *TLZ*, June 9, 1990; "Kunst(-)fest," *TLZ*, June 16, 1990; "Das Eis," *TLZ*, May 17, 1991; Frank/Roth, "Säulen," 212–13. See the fundamental critique of the Kunstfest idea in Steinfeld, *Weimar*, 275–77.

62. "Kunst- und Gunstfest," *TLZ*, June 20, 1990; "Arts Festival," *Deseret News*, Salt Lake City, August 12, 1990; "Noch einmal," *ZEITONLINE*, May 24, 1991 (quote); "Mit Quadflieg," *TLZ*, February 27, 1991.

63. "Im Geist," *TLZ*, April 17, 1991; "Und vor allem," *TLZ*, April 22, 1991; "Im Geist," "Das Eis," "Marketenderin," *TLZ*, May 17, 1991; "Beseeltes," "Angst," *TLZ*, May 21, 1991; "Junges Ensemble," *TLZ*, May 30, 1991.

64. "Wir bauen," *ZEITONLINE*, May 24, 1991; "Mehrkampf," *TLZ*, June 1, 1991; "Es bleibt," *TLZ*, June 10, 1991; "Zukunft," *TLZ*, June 21, 1991; "Das dritte," *TLZ*, July 16, 1991; "Weimarer Künstler," *TLZ*, August 15, 1991.

65. See the complaints of ordinary Weimarers Eike Havenstein, Angela Priebst, Holger Höhne, Yvonne Strube, Dieter Herdrich, and Sylvia Reiber in "Drittes Kunstfest," *TLZ*, June 1, 1991. Also "Ein Spektakel," *TLZ*, June 6, 1992; "Halbvoll," *TLZ*, June 13, 1992 (quote); "Es hat," *TLZ*, September 21, 1992.

66. "Halbvoll," *TLZ*, June 13, 1992; "Politiker," *TLZ*, December 18, 1992; "Das Kunstfest," *TLZ*, December 19, 1992; "Das Erbe," *TLZ*, December 29, 1992; "Kunstfest," "Weimar Kunstfest," *TLZ*, January 27, 1993.

67. See "Faust und Übermensch," *FAZ*, April 24, 1993.

68. "Ein Kubus," *TLZ*, April 22, 1993; "Faust," *TLZ*, June 28, 1993.

69. "Nietzsche," *TLZ*, June 17, 1993; "Brillant," *TLZ*, July 12, 1993 (quote).

70. "Küss die Hand," *TLZ*, July 26, 1993.

71. "Im Zeichen," *TLZ*, July 27, 1993.

72. "Ein eigenes," *TLZ*, August 13, 1993; "Kulturelle," *TLZ*, January 28, 1994.

73. "Faustus," *SZ*, June 26, 1995.

74. "Kunstfest-Eklat," *TLZ*, June 21, 1994; "Eine Geschichte," *SZ*, June 21, 1994; "Dunst," *TLZ*, June 27, 1994; "Der Vater," *FAZ*, July 22, 1994; "Nicht," *SZ*, June 17, 1996; "Sandmann," *TLZ*, June 17, 1996; "Dichterraten," *FAZ*, June 17, 1996; "Keine weissen Socken" (quote), "Johann," *SZ*, July 1, 1996; "Vorbei," *TLZ*, July 1, 1996.

75. "Yfrah Neaman," *TLZ*, July 26, 1993; "Echter," *TLZ*, July 27, 1993; "Cello," *TLZ*, June 28, 1994.

76. "Friedhof," *SZ*, July 17, 1995; "Weimar," *TLZ*, July 19, 1995; "Nicht," *TLZ*, June 16, 1997; "Wie," *TLZ*, June 19, 1997.

77. "Ein eigenes," *TLZ*, August 13, 1993; "Bauen," *TLZ*, July 4, 1998.

78. Neugier," *TLZ*, July 31, 1993; "Viertes," *TLZ*, August 16, 1993; "Don Quichote," *FAZ*, June 26, 1996; "Telefondrähte," *TLZ*, June 23, 1996; "Bilanz," *TLZ*, June 20, 1998; "Weimars," *TLZ*, July 2, 1998.

79. Müller-Enbergs et al., *DDR*, vol. 1, 641–42; "Grosses Ziel," *TLZ*, February 14, 1990; "Votum," *TLZ*, February 28, 1992; "Weimar," *TLZ*, May 7, 1992; "Kulturstadt," *TLZ*, May 9, 1992; "Vielfalt," *TLZ*, July 31, 1992; "Kulturstadt '99," *TLZ*, August 28, 1992; "Weimars," *TLZ*, September 1, 1992; "Zuerst," *TLZ*, November 10, 1992; "Entscheidung," *TLZ*, November 4, 1993.

80. "Weimar," *TLZ*, November 6, 1993; "Was," *FAZ*, March 19, 1994; "Gestaffelter," *TLZ*, August 31, 1994; "Projekt," "Kulturstadt," *TLZ*, March 1, 1995; "Retter," *FAZ*, July 21, 1995.

81. "Kauffmann," *TLZ*, November 7, 1995; "Ereigniskultur," *SZ*, December 13, 1995; "Ich," *FAZ*, March 19, 1996; Doerry, as in n. 31 (quote 232).

82. "Appell," *TLZ*, May 10, 1997; "Ein ausgemachter Skandal," *TLZ*, May 15, 1997; "Verwirrung," *TLZ*, October 3, 1997; "Marketing," *FAZ*, October 6, 1997; "Weimar," *TLZ*, March 7, 1998; "Wie," *SZ*, January 7, 1998; "Minister," *TLZ*, March 5, 1998; "Den Stuhl," *TLZ*, May 8, 1998.

83. "Buren-Projekt," *TLZ*, April 30, 1998; "Tollplatz," *SZ*, May 11, 1998; "Eine blühende," *TLZ*, December 30, 1998.

84. "Das letzte," *TLZ*, November 3, 1999.
85. "Blitzstart," *SZ*, January 5, 1999.
86. "Konzert," *TLZ*, March 5, 1999; "Das Maximum," *TLZ*, August 10, 1999; "Der interkulturelle Küchendienst," *SZ*, August 17, 1999; "Das heikelste Orchester," *DW*, August 16, 1999; "Leitmotive," *WS*, August 22, 1999.
87. "Der Teufel," *FAZ*, April 8, 1999. From 1996 to 2000 Ivo was solo dancer and director of the dance theater at the DNT.
88. "Das Balletical," *SZ*, May 26, 1999.
89. "Jazz," *TLZ*, July 5, 1999.
90. "Dammbrüche," *TLZ*, July 9, 1999.
91. "Fast," *SZ*, May 5, 1999; "Matador," *DW*, July 17, 1999.
92. "Verspätung," *FAZ*, January 4, 1999; "Misstöne," *DS* (January 11, 1999): 163; "Ein Wessi," *FocusOnline*, March 8, 1999.
93. "Kulturkampf," *TLZ*, May 19, 1999.
94. *Die 7*, 63–66; *Der Weimarer Bilderstreit*, 39–133; Achim Preiss ibid., 9–14; Hanns Wershoven ibid., 27–35; "Im Schatten," *SZ*, May 6, 1999; "Kunst," *TLZ*, May 8, 1999; "Geisterparade," *TLZ*, May 10, 1999; "Autistisch," *TLZ*, May 15, 1999; "Rückfall," *TLZ*, May 18, 1999; "Inszenierung," *TLZ*, May 19, 1999; "Erstes Bild," *TLZ*, May 21, 1999; "Maler," *TLZ*, May 22, 1999; "Kesseltreiben," *ZEITONLINE*, May 27, 1999; "An die Wand," *SZ*, May 29, 1999; "Bildersturm," *TLZ*, May 31, 1999; Jürgen Hohmeyer, "Ich bin kein Terminator," *DS* (May 31, 1999): 210; "Feiges," *TLZ*, June 4, 1999; "Der Rechtsweg," *WS*, June 6, 1999; "Zwei," *DW*, June 19, 1999; "Wechsel," *TLZ*, June 23, 1999; "Herbst," *SZ*, September 8, 1999. For Sitte's art exhibited in Weimar, see Bothe/Föhl, *Aufstieg*, 451, 455, 460, 465 (Olsen's has been expunged).
95. Ad "Optik-Zopfs," *TLZ*, July 19, 1999; "Goethe," *TLZ*, August 20, 1999; "Der Geheimrat," *TLZ*, August 26, 1999; "Weimar," *SZ*, August 28, 1999; "Hauptsache," *DW*, August 30, 1999; "Verwurstet," *SZ*, August 30, 1999.
96. *NYT*, August 3, 1999.
97. "Mehrweggeschirr," *FAZ*, October 20, 1999; "Das kostet," *TLZ*, December 1, 1999; Gerd Zimmermann in conversation with author, Weimar, November 5, 2008.
98. "Tourismus," *TLZ*, July 3, 1999; "Weimar," *TLZ*, September 3, 1999; "7 gegen Kauffmann," *TLZ*, October 7, 1999; "Regierung," *TLZ*, November 20, 1999; "Der Lunaparkwächter," *FAZ*, November 23, 1999.
99. "Jahr 2000," *TLZ*, October 30, 1999; "Erfolgs-Duo," *TLZ*, February 15, 2000; "Das Ganze," *TLZ*, April 13, 2000; "Hymnen," *TLZ*, June 17, 2000; "Workshop," *TLZ*, July 15, 2000; "Halbvoll," *TLZ*, July 19, 2000; "Kunstfest," *TLZ*, September 1, 2000; "Kauffmann," *DW*, December 2, 2000; "Poetisch-intellektuelles," *TLZ*, August 9, 2001; "Von," *TLZ*, August 10, 2001; "Weimar-Eklat," *TLZ*, August 11, 2001; "Kulturdiktat," *TLZ*, August 16, 2001; "Hörbar," *TLZ*, August 24, 2001; "Augen," *DW*, August 28, 2001; Thomas Steinfeld, "Frauenplanlos," *SZ*, August 28, 2001 (quote).
100. "Weimar a.D.," *SZ*, September 1, 2001; "Klassik-Zirkus," *DW*, April 24, 2002; "Kunstfest-Zukunft," *TLZ*, July 25, 2002; "Der Anfang," *TLZ*, August 3, 2002; "Werbung," *DW*, August 13, 2002; "Kein Geld," *TLZ*, October 5, 2002; "Kunstfest," *FAZ*, October 9, 2002; "Weimarer," *TLZ*, December 18, 2002; "Nike," *SZ*, December 20, 2002.
101. Wagner, *Wagner Theater*; "Heimweh," *TLZ*, January 18, 2003; "Nikes Liszt," *FR*, January 20, 2003; Wagner quoted in "Anziehungskraft," *TLZ*, May 15, 2003.
102. "Viele," *TLZ*, September 9, 1999; "Intendant," *DW*, March 21, 2001.
103. "Der Haushalt," *TLZ*, November 7, 1998; "Jeder," *SZ*, January 22, 1999; "Märki," *TLZ*, August 31, 1999; "Keine," *DW*, September 10, 1999; "Gedanken," *TLZ*, November 20, 1999; "Die Fauste," *BZ*, March 31, 2000; "Theaterrenner," *SZ*, April 1, 2000, "Ein Neubeginn," *TLZ*, June 9, 2000; "Als," *TLZ*, February 20, 2001; "Theater," *TLZ*, February 2, 2002.
104. "Es wird," *TLZ*, August, 14, 2001; "Schöne," *SZ*, October 9, 2001; "Nein danke," *SZ*, February 21, 2002; "Ein DNT-Stuhl," *TLZ*, February 21, 2002; "Weimarer," *TLZ*, April 30, 2002; "Unerhörte," *SZ*, August 31, 2002; "Das Theatermodell," *TLZ*, September 26, 2002; "Man," *SZ*, December 16, 2002; "Ich," *SZ*, March 10, 2003; "Weimar," *TLZ*, September 17, 2003; "Die Schaubühne," *TLZ*, September 25, 2003.

105. "Bei Schiller," *TLZ*, August 28, 1999; "Rettung," *TLZ*, September 3, 1999; "Der gute Europäer," *SZ*, October 20, 1999; "Ein Festival," *FAZ*, December 30, 1999; "Dirigent," *TLZ*, April 15, 2000; "Letzte," *SZ*, April 17, 2000.

106. "Planungssicher," *FAZ*, April 17, 2000; "Keine Angelegenheit," *DW*, May 25, 2001; "Klassische," *SZ*, December 21, 2001; "Die Politik," *TLZ*, January 24, 2002; "Goethe," *SZ*, August 27, 2003.

107. See the monthly entries, "Arbeitslosigkeit in Thüringen," in *TLZ*, 1998–2003; "Mehr Arbeit," *TLZ*, April 6, 2000; "Überschuldung," *TLZ*, April 6, 2001; "Der Schuldenberg," *TLZ*, June 7, 2001; "Der Kuckuck," *TLZ*, June 15, 2001; "Thüringen," *TLZ*, June 23, 2001; "Mini-Lohn," *TLZ*, March 11, 2003.

108. "Schon," *TLZ*, February 10, 1999; "Osten," *TLZ*, March 9, 2000; "Mehr," *TLZ*, January 10, 2001; "Dem Osten," "Bremsspuren," *TLZ*, April 5, 2001; "Thüringens," "Pessimistische," *TLZ*, August 8, 2001; "Gegenseitige," *TLZ*, September 6, 2001; "Wirtschaft," *TLZ*, April 4, 2003.

109. "Winter," *TLZ*, March 10, 1999; "Mehr," *TLZ*, June 9, 2000; "Mehr," *TLZ*, January 10, 2001.

110. "Frühling," *TLZ*, April 9, 1999; "Ernüchternde," *TLZ*, February 7, 2001; "Jugendliche," *TLZ*, March 27, 2001; "Thüringen," *TLZ*, April 5, 2001.

111. "Talente," *TLZ*, August 26, 1999; "Junge," *TLZ*, July 21, 2000; "Junge," *TLZ*, August 31, 2000; "Abwanderung," *TLZ*, November 1, 2000; "Fachkräfte," *TLZ*, February 16, 2001, "Carolin," "Dem Osten," "Wenig," *TLZ*, April 5, 2001; "Mit," *TLZ*, April 6, 2001; "Abwanderung," *TLZ*, April 20, 2001; "Verdruss," *TLZ*, June 18, 2002; "Hoffnungslosigkeit," *TLZ*, July 22, 2002; "Die Frauen," *TLZ*, October 1, 2002; "Abwanderungswelle," *TLZ*, August 14, 2003.

112. "Lehrer," *TLZ*, June 24, 1999; "Eichel," *TLZ*, June 25, 1999; "Jahrgangs-Breite," *TLZ*, April 17, 2000.

113. "Ein Wackelkandidat," *TLZ*, July 8, 1999; "DGB," *TLZ*, July 15, 1999; "Thüringen," January 8, 2002; "Null," *TLZ*, January 10, 2002.

114. "Arbeitslosigkeit in Thüringen," *TLZ*, 1998–2003; "Fujitsu," *TLZ*, March 24, 1999; "Nur," *TLZ*, May 4, 2001; "Handwerkerschaft," *TLZ*, June 9, 2001; "Mehr," *TLZ*, January 5, 2002; "Mehr," *TLZ*, August 9, 2002; "Nie," *TLZ*, October 8, 2002; "Saller," *TLZ*, December 13, 2002; "Der Schuldenberg," *TLZ*, February 14, 2003; "Mehr," *TLZ*, September 30, 2003. On *Plattenbauten* in Weimar, see Eckardt, "Urban Myth," 125.

115. "Althaus," *TLZ*, September 8, 2000; "Unvermögen," *TLZ*, April 7, 2001.

116. "Sein," *TLZ*, October 26, 2002.

117. "Popularität," *TLZ*, June 3, 2004; "Minister," *TLZ*, September 6, 2006; "Krause," *SPIEGELONLINE*, May 5, 2008; "Der ewige Junge," *SPIEGELONLINE*, June 8, 2008; "Abgang," *SPIEGELONLINE*, September 3, 2009.

118. "Althaus," *SPIEGELONLINE*, September 11, 2008; "Ministerpräsident," *sueddeutsche.de*, January 1, 2009; "Althaus," *SPIEGELONLINE*, March 3, 2009; "Althaus," *sueddeutsche.de*, September 10, 2009; "Althaus," *SPIEGELONLINE*, March 5, 2009; "Solidarisch," *sueddeutsche.de*, March 14, 2009; "Thüringer CDU," *SPIEGELONLINE*, March 14, 2009; "Scharfe Kritik," *sueddeutsche.de*, August 20, 2009; "Althaus' Desaster," *sueddeutsche.de*, August 30, 2009; "Ein Gefühl," *sueddeutsche.de*, September 8, 2009; "Nach Machnig," *SPIEGELONLINE*, September 20, 2013.

119. "Viele," *TLZ*, January 9, 2004; "Junge," *TLZ*, January 26, 2004; "Die Thüringer," *TLZ*, Februay 19, 2004; "Vor," "Für," *TLZ*, April 23, 2004 (quote); "Trotz," *TLZ*, January 17, 2005; "Es fehlt," *TLZ*, May 31, 2005; "In Thüringen," *TLZ*, June 30, 2005; "Thüringens," *TLZ*, August 13, 2005; "Jugend," *TLZ*, September 29, 2005; "Entlastung," *TLZ*, April 28, 2006; "Land," *TLZ*, July 11, 2006; "In Thüringen," *SPIEGELONLINE*, September 8, 2008; "Die Umsätze," *TLZ*, October 24, 2008; "Ost," *SPIEGELONLINE*, August 27, 2009; "Der Osten," *FAZ.NET*, August 28, 2009; "Aufbau," *sueddeutsche.de*, August 30, 2009; "Lobbygruppe," *SPIEGELONLINE*, December 4, 2009.

120. "Bis," *TLZ*, May 20/21, 2004; "Insolvenzen," *TLZ*, July 9, 2004; "Weimar," *SPIEGELONLINE*, July 13, 2004; Ullrich Fichtner, "Leckere Luft," *DS* (September 27, 2004): 78–80; "Industrie," *TLZ*, September 7, 2005; "Ende," *TLZ*, November 25, 2005; "Unter," *TLZ*, December 23, 2005; "Jeder," *TLZ*, January 5, 2006; "Insel," *TLZ*, March 31,

2006; "Die Wirtschaft," *TLZ*, December 15, 2006; "Von," *BZ*, June 18, 2008; "Weimar," *TAZ*, September 17, 2008.

121. "Knigge," *TLZ*, October 23, 1999; also "Der Minister," *TLZ*, January 26, 2007.

122. See "Die Geschichte," *TLZ.de*, September 9, 2008.

123. "4500 Mark," *TLZ*, February 13, 1999; "Hakenkreuze," *TLZ*, October 4, 2000; "Verurteilungen," *SZ*, August 29, 2001; "Rechter," *TLZ*, May 13, 2003; "Jugendliche," *TLZ. de*, February 24, 2008; "Jenseits," *thueringer-allgemeine.de*, April 13, 2008.

124. "Nichts," *SZ*, October 26, 1999; "Endzeit," *SZ*, September 11, 2000; "Wir," *TLZ*, January 28, 2003; "Wir," *SZ*, April 11, 2005; "Appell," *SZ*, April 13, 2004; "Sandberg," *thueringer-allgemeine.de*, March 31, 2008; "Kunst-Exkurs," *thueringer-allgemeine.de*, April 4, 2008; "Schwierige," *thueringer-allgemeine.de*, December 10, 2008; "Dieser Ort," *SPIEGELONLINE*, June 5, 2009.

125. See "Gedenkstätte," *TLZ*, September 15, 2003; "Buchenwald," *SZ*, April 26, 2005; "Schulterschluss," *TLZ*, October 17, 2005.

126. Roth, "Goethe," 98.

127. Thomas Schmidt/Sophie-Thérèse Krempl in *Wer ist*, 10 (1st quote); "Wie klassische," *TLZ*, November 18, 2005 (2nd quote); "Abschied," *SZ*, April 15, 2004; "Vorteil Schiller," *SZ*, November 9, 2005; "Mit 196," *TLZ*, November 10, 2005; "Menschenwürde," "Die Grenzen," "Auf den Zeilen," *TLZ*, November 18, 2005; "Weimar," *TLZ.de*, April 20, 2008; Reinhard Wengierek, "Immer bloss Bratwürstelei," *DW* (September 9, 2005), 27 (3rd quote).

128. "Massiver Ärger," *TLZ*, July 7, 2006; "Massiver Protest," *TLZ*, September 12, 2006; "Noch," *TLZ*, January 18, 2007; "Ein Ruf," *TLZ*, February 7, 2007; "Weimar," *TLZ*, February 8, 2007.

129. "Märki," *TLZ.de*, July 13, 2008; "Das System," "Hasselmann," *TLZ.de*, July 21, 2008; "Eine Politik," *TLZ.de*, October 1, 2008; "Weimar," *WELTONLINE*, October 2, 2008; "Der Zorn," "Das Weimar-Spiel," "Meinungen," "Weimarer Modelle," *thueringer-allgemeine.de*, October 3, 2008; "Einmal Ungnade," *sueddeutsche.de*, October 6, 2008 (1st quote); "Provinzielles Weimar," *BZ*, October 4, 2008 (2nd quote); "Machtvolle," *TLZ.de*, October 7, 2008; "Investition," *TLZ*, October 17, 2008; "Weimar," *TLZ.de*, January 27, 2009; "Märki," *thueringer-allgemeine.de*, January 27, 2009.

130. Jens Bisky, "Methusalem in Weimar," *SZ*, July 21, 2004 (quote); "Kein Weg," *TLZ*, January 8, 2004; "Ein Seemann," *TLZ*, January 21, 2004; "Ja zu Maenz," *TLZ*, January 22, 2004; "Weimar," *TLZ*, February 27, 2004; "Um Goethe," *TLZ*, April 21, 2004; "Freigeist," *FAZ*, May 24, 2004; "Glückliche Wende," *FAZ*, June 9, 2004; "Schöne Schleife," *SZ*, June 11, 2004; "Grosse Defizite," *TLZ*, July 20, 2004; "Ein Klassiker," *TLZ*, July 20, 2004; "Seemanns," *TLZ*, August 11, 2004; "Heilige," *SZ*, August 11, 2004; "Nach," *SZ*, August 12, 2004; "Den Rest," *DZ*, September 16, 2004; "Weimar," *SZ*, October 20, 2004; "Filzpantoffeln," *SZ*, October, 21, 2004; "Paul Maenz," *TLZ*, September 8, 2005; "Immer," *DW*, September 9, 2005.

131. Knoche, *Bibliothek*, esp. 9–10, 16–17, 42–46, 86; "Jahresbericht 2006" in Seemann, *Anna Amalia*, 359; "Eine Million," *TLZ*, July 24, 2004; "Hier waren," *sueddeutsche.de*, September 4, 2004; "Unersetzlicher," *DW*, September 4, 2004; "Weimars," *FAZ*, September 4, 2004; "Keine Ursache," *SZ*, September 8, 2004; "Die Sammelbüchsen," *DW*, September 20, 2004; "Im Brandherd," *SZ*, October 15, 2004; "Komfortable," *SZ*, November 5, 2004; "Weimar II," *SZ*, November 15, 2004; "Aktualisierung," *SZ*, February 5, 2005; "Studienzentrum," *TLZ*, January 6, 2007; "1147 Tage," *SZ*, October 25, 2007.

132. "Ferdinand," *SZ*, June 20, 2005; "Aufbruch-Signal," *TLZ*, June 25, 2005; "Mehltau," *SZ*, June 25, 2005; "Weimars," *FAZ*, June 25, 2005; "Klassik-Stiftung," *TLZ*, July 6, 2005; "Die Not," *SZ*, March 25, 2006; "Inmitten," *SZ*, May 3, 2006; "Wer," *SZ*, May 3, 2006; "Mehr," *thueringer-allgemeine.de*, March 5, 2008; "Singuläre," *thueringer-allgemeine.de*, May 14, 2008; "Etiketten-Schwindel," *thueringer-allgemeine.de*, February 15, 2008; "Symbol," *TLZ. de*, May 15, 2008; "Ich," *thueringer-allgemeine.de*, August 5, 2008; "Schwer," *thueringer-allgemeine.de*, August 6, 2008; "Haus-Kauf," *thueringer-allgemeine.de*, August 7, 2008; "Stein-Haus," *thueringer-allgemeine.de*, August 14, 2008; "Paten," *TLZ.de*, September 9, 2008; "Bauhaus," *TLZ.de*, September 15, 2008; "Klassischer," *TLZ*, October 15, 2008; "Das Bauhaus," *DW*, October 22, 2008; "Ein Rat," *TLZ*, November 11, 2008; "Ein buntes," *TLZ. de*, December 10, 2009; "Archiv," *TLZ.de*, December 23, 2009; "Anhörung," *TLZ.de*, February 8, 2010; "Bauhausmuseum," *thueringer-allgemeine.de*, March 12, 2010;

"Bauhaus-Museum," *TLZ.de*, March 14, 2010; "Rückblick," *thueringer-allgemeine.de*, December 29, 2011; "Neue," *thueringer-allgemeine.de*, February 17, 2012.

133. "Klassikstiftung," *thueringer-allgemeine.de*, October 4, 2010; "Klassikpräsident," "Klassikstiftung," *thueringer allgemeine.de*, October 5, 2010; "Hellmut Seemann," *thueringer-allgemeine.de*, April 1, 2011; "Herr," *dradio.de*, April 7, 2011; Weimarer," *thueringer-allgemeine. de*, April 8, 2011; "Leid," *thueringer-allgemeine.de*, November 24, 2011; "2011," *thueringer-allgemeine.de*, December 31, 2011.

134. Castell interviewed in *TLZ*, September 10, 2004.

135. "Mehr," *HA*, March 27, 2004; "Nike," *TLZ*, April 2, 2004; "Kunstfest," *DW*, April 2, 2004.

136. "Schiff," *TLZ*, July 29, 2004; "Kunstfest," "Ein Kunstfest-Wein," *TLZ*, August 7, 2004; "Eine mutige," *TLZ*, August 21, 2004; "Sternstunden," *TLZ*, September 7, 2004; "Begegnung," *SZ*, September 14, 2004; "Vorfreude," "Über," *TLZ*, September 18, 2004; "Kunstfest," *TLZ*, September 22, 2004.

137. "Der Liebesbeweis," *TLZ*, August 22, 2005; "Weimarer," *TLZ*, August 23, 2005.

138. "Schmerzhafte," *TLZ*, August 20, 2005; "Eklat," *TLZ*, August 22, 2005; "Hüpfendes," *TLZ*, September 9, 2005; "Endspurt," *BM*, September 9, 2005.

139. "Die Causa," *TLZ*, August 16, 2006; Joachim Kronsbein, "Beckham des Pianos," *DS* (August 21, 2006), 156; "Leise," *FAZ*, August 30, 2006; "Die Schwerkraft," *FAZ*, September 11, 2007; "Weimar-Pilger," *TLZ.de*, August 21, 2008; "Buchenwald-Konzert," *TLZ.de*, August 22, 2008; "Fest," "Bananen," *thueringer-allgemeine.de*, August 24, 2008; "Ein Bad," *TLZ.de*, August 31, 2008; "Bilanz," *BM*, September 13, 2008; "Der ideale," *thueringer-allgemeine.de*, August 27, 2009; "Eine Séance," *TLZ.de*, September 3, 2009; "Bach," *thueringer-allgemeine.de*, September 3, 2009; "Stiller," *thueringer-allgemeine.de*, September 4, 2009; "Kunstfest," *TLZ.de*, September 11, 2009; "Mit," *thueringer-allgemeine.de*, March 25, 2010; "Nike," *thueringer-allgemeine.de*, August 18, 2010; "Künstler," *thueringer-allgemeine.de*, August 24, 2010.

140. "Gérard Mortier," *FAZ.NET*, August 24, 2008.

141. "Kunstfest-Debatte," *TLZ*, October 15, 2005; "Auftakt," "Kunstfest," *TLZ*, September 16, 2006; "Fehler," *TLZ.de*, September 23, 2009; Seiler quoted in *thueringer-allgemeine.de*, May 28, 2011.

142. Schäfer's address, "Den Opfern verpflichtet," printed in *TLZ*, November 28, 2006.

143. Wagner quoted in "Kulturpolitiker," *SPIEGELONLINE*, August 26, 2006. Also See "Kunstfest-Eklat," *TLZ*, August 26, 2006; "Heftiger," *WELTONLINE*, August 26, 2006; "Pfiffe, *SZ*, August 28, 2006; "Suppe," *TLZ*, August 28, 2006; "Schlaflos," *SZ*, August 29, 2006; "Gute," *FAZ*, August 30, 2006; Stefan Berg/Marcel Rosenbach, "Umtriebe eines Beamten," *DS* (September 4, 2006): 40.

144. For the controversial preliminaries, see "Germans Argue," *NYT*, May 15, 1988.

145. "Tränen," *FAZ*, December 5, 2005.

146. Wagner to Schäfer, March 8, 2006, facsimile in *TLZ*, August 30, 2006.

147. Malte Herwig/Hans Michael Kloth, "Eine Art Performance," *DS* (September 4, 2006): 41; "Nike Wagner," *FAZ*, September 6, 2006; "Rede," *TLZ*, November 28, 2006.

148. "Kunstfest," "Die Gräfin," *TLZ*, November 24, 2006.

149. "Ein energisch," *FAZ.NET*, August 25, 2008.

150. "Neumann und Schäfer," *TLZ*, August 31, 2006.

151. Wagner quoted in "Nike Wagner," *thueringer-allgemeine.de*, August 22, 2011; "Weimarer Kunstfest," *3sat.online*, October 18, 2012.

Epilogue

1. Schwerte, *Faust*, esp. 7–12, 148–55, 184–87, 238–46 (quotes 242), 266–78. On Mann's affinity with Dürer and in particular the engraving see Mann, *Doktor Faustus*; Ruehl, "Master."

2. See Chapter Eight at p. 262.

3. *Das Schwarze Korps*, March, 27, 1935 and August 7, 1935.

4. Wüst, *Bekenntnis*, 12; Hans Ernst Schneider, "Das Tragische," *DR*, February 7, 1943.

5. Corr. Kater-Zotz, March 5, 1963–August 31, 1964; minutes of Kater–Zotz conversation, March 18, 1963, both ZS/A25, Institut für Zeitgeschichte München.

6. Kater, "Artamanen," 627–29; Kater, *Ahnenerbe*, 174–78, 182–84, 188, 190, 306, 311–13, 342, 344–49, 404, 407; Jäger, *Seitenwechsel*, 11–44, 54–56, 126–27, 136–50, 266–80; Leggewie, *Schneider*, 54–65; Alan Cowell, "German Scholar Unmasked as former SS Officer," *NYT*, June 1, 1995; "Der Stich ins Wespennest," *DS* (September 14, 1998): 84–88; Hubert Winkels, "Vertuschte Vergangenheit," *dradio.de*, May 14, 1997; Ulrich Greiner, "Mein Name sei Schwerte," *ZEITONLINE*, May 12, 1995. German literature scholars who cited Schwerte, even after his discovery in 1995, include Müller-Seidel, *Geschichtlichkeit*, 7; Scholz, *Seele*, 44, 108; Mandelkow, *Urteil*, lvii; Mandelkow, *Rezeptionsgeschichte*, vol. 2, 196; also see Farrelly, *Goethe*, 153; Borchmeyer, "Goethe," 196.

7. Goethe, *Faust*, 90.

8. "Tanz den Goethe," *Zeitmagazin* (July 4, 1997): 36.

9. See "Weimarer Modelle," *thueringer-allgemeine.de*, October 3, 2008. For additional examples of a parallel between the twenty-first century and earlier times, see Knoche, *Bibliothek*, 53; Borchmeyer, *Klassik*, 45; Silke Feldhoff in Satjukow, "*Nach Drüben*," 131, 135; "Flurschaden," *TLZ*, October 15, 2008; "Weimar tanzen," *TLZ*, May 26, 2001; "Wir wollen," *TLZ*, March 9, 2001; "Weimar ohne Zirkus," *FAZ*, December 4, 200.

10. Falter, *Wähler*, 136–324; Kater, *Nazi Party*, 32–71.

11. Puttkamer, *Hof*, 126.

12. Hardt, "Rede"; "In Armut," *TLZ*, September 25, 2002; "Kostbare Schatulle," *TLZ*, November 29, 2002; Emmel, *Theater*, 7.

13. "Ost-Unis," *SPIEGELONLINE*, November 22, 2013. Schmidt, *Handeln*, 182–83; "Orientierungskrisen," *SZ*, April 26, 1996; *nationalstiftung.de*.

14. See Thomas Steinfeld, "Wer klein ist, muss frech sein," *SZ*, May 3, 2006.

15. Seemann interview in "Thüringen," *TLZ*, March 3, 2007.

Bibliography

A bis Z: Ein Taschen- und Nachschlagebuch über den anderen Teil Deutschlands, ed. Bundesministerium für gesamtdeutsche Fragen, 11th edn (Bonn, 1969)

A Woman in Berlin: Diary 20 April 1945 to 22 June 1945, intro. Antony Beevar (London, 2011)

Abusch, Alexander, "Faust – Held oder Renegat in der deutschen Nationalliteratur?" *Sinn und Form* 3–4 (1953): 179–94

Abusch, Alexander, *Mit offenem Visier: Memoiren* (Berlin, 1986)

Abusch, Alexander, *Schiller: Grösse und Tragik eines deutschen Genies* (Berlin, 1955)

Ackermann, Ute, "Sophie von Leer und Georg Muche: Eine 'missionarische Beziehung' zwischen Mazdaznan-Lehre, Mystik und Katholizismus," in Christoph Wagner, ed., *Johannes Itten, Wassily Kandinsky, Paul Klee: Das Bauhaus und die Esoterik* (Bielefeld, 2005), 115–22

Adler, Bruno, *Das Weimarer Bauhaus* (Darmstadt, n.d.)

Albert, Claudia, "Schiller als Kampfgenosse?" in Albert, ed., *Deutsche Klassiker im Nationalsozialismus: Schiller – Kleist – Hölderlin* (Stuttgart, 1994), 48–76

Albrecht, Günter/Kurt Böttcher/Herbert Greiner-Mai/Paul Günter Krohn, eds, *Lexikon deutschsprachiger Schriftsteller: Von den Anfängen bis zur Gegenwart*, vol. 1, 2nd edn (Leipzig, 1972)

Albrecht, Günter/Kurt Böttcher/Herbert Greiner-Mai/Paul Günter Krohn, eds, *Lexikon deutschsprachiger Schriftsteller: Von den Anfängen bis zur Gegenwart*, vol. 2, 2nd edn (Leipzig, 1974)

Allinson, Mark, *Politics and Popular Opinion in East Germany, 1945–68* (Manchester, 2000)

Altenburg, Detlef, "Franz Liszt und das Erbe der Klassik," in Altenburg, ed., *Liszt und die Weimarer Klassik* (Laaber, 1997), 9–32

Altenburg, Detlef/Britta Schilling-Wang, "Vorwort," in Altenburg/Schilling-Wang, eds, *Franz Liszt: Sämtliche Schriften*, vol. 3 (Wiesbaden, 1997), vii–xiii

Aly, Götz/Karl Heinz Roth, *Die restlose Erfassung: Volkszählen, Identifizieren, Aussondern im Nationalsozialismus* (Berlin, 1984)

Ansprachen zum Gedächtnis der Frau Dr. phil. h.c. Elisabeth Förster-Nietzsche bei den Trauerfeierlichkeiten in Weimar und Röcken am 11. und 12. November 1935 [Weimar, 1935]

Applegate, Celia, *A Nation of Provincials: The German Idea of Heimat* (Berkeley, 1990)

Arbeiterbewegung und Klassik: Ausstellung im Goethe- und Schiller-Archiv der Nationalen Forschungs- und Gedenkstätten der Klassischen Deutschen Literatur in Weimar, 1964–1966 (Weimar, 1964)

Argan, Giulio Carlo, *Gropius und das Bauhaus* (Reinbek, 1962)

Aschheim, Steven E., *The Nietzsche Legacy in Germany, 1890–1990* (Berkeley, 1992)

Astel, Karl, *Die Aufgabe: Rede zur Eröffnung des Winter-Semesters 1936/37 an der Thüringischen Landesuniversität Jena in Gegenwart des Reichsstatthalters und Gauleiters Fritz Sauckel gehalten am 6. November anlässlich der Einführung der neu berufenen Dozenten Dr. B. Kummer und Joh. von Leers* (Jena, 1937)

Astel, Karl, *Rassekurs in Egendorf: Ein rassehygienischer Lehrgang des Thüringischen Landesamts für Rassewesen* (Munich, 1935)

Astel, Karl/Erna Weber, *Die Kinderzahl der 29000 politischen Leiter des Gaues Thüringen der NSDAP und die Ursachen der ermittelten Fortpflanzungshäufigkeit* (Berlin, 1943)

Bade, Wilfrid and Wilmont Haacke, eds, *Das heldische Jahr: Front und Heimat berichten den Krieg* (Berlin, 1941)

Baeumer, Max L., "Der Begriff 'klassisch' bei Goethe und Schiller," in Reinhold Grimm/Jost Hermand, eds, *Die Klassik-Legende: Second Wisconsin Workshop* (Frankfurt am Main, 1971), 17–49

Baeumler, Alfred, *Nietzsche der Philosoph und Politiker* (Leipzig, 1931)

Baeumler, Alfred, *Nietzsche in seinen Briefen und Berichten der Zeitgenossen: Die Lebensgeschichte in Dokumenten* (Leipzig, 1932)

Bahr, Ehrhard, "Julius Petersen und die Goethe-Gesellschaft in Weimar zwischen 1926 und 1938," in Jochen Golz/Justus H. Ulbricht, eds, *Goethe in Gesellschaft: Zur Geschichte einer literarischen Vereinigung vom Kaiserreich bis zum geteilten Deutschland* (Cologne, 2005), 137–50

Bahr, Thomas, "Die Emanzipation der Juden in Sachsen-Weimar-Eisenach im 18. und in der ersten Hälfte des 19. Jh.," in Bahr, ed., *Beiträge zur Geschichte jüdischen Lebens in Thüringen* (Jena, 1996), 105–9

Baird, Jay W., *Hitler's War Poets: Literature and Politics in the Third Reich* (New York, 2008)

Bamberg, Eduard von, *Die Erinnerungen der Karoline Jagemann nebst zahlreichen unveröffentlichten Dokumenten aus der Goethezeit*, 2 vols (Dresden, 1926)

Barner, Wilfried, "Goethe und Schiller," in Jean-Marie Valentin, ed., *Johann Wolfgang Goethe zum 250. Geburtstag: Vorträge im Frankfurter Römer (April–Juli 1999)* (Paris, 1999), 75–91

Bartels, Adolf, *Der Bauer in der deutschen Vergangenheit* (Leipzig, 1900)

Bartels, Adolf, *Der deutsche Verfall und der Zusammenbruch*, 3rd edn (Zeitz, 1919)

Bartels, Adolf, *Der Nationalsozialismus: Deutschlands Rettung* (Leipzig, 1925; 1st edn 1924)

Bartels, Adolf, "Der Nationalsozialismus und die deutsche Kultur," *Deutsches Schrifttum* 22, no. 9 (1930): 1–2

Bartels, Adolf, *Deutschvölkische Gedichte* (Zeitz, 1918)

Bartels, Adolf, *Die Berechtigung des Antisemitismus: Eine Widerlegung der Schrift von Herrn von Oppeln-Bronikowski "Antisemitismus"?* (Leipzig, 1921)

Bartels, Adolf, *Die deutsche Dichtung der Gegenwart: Die Alten und die Jungen*, 6th edn (Leipzig, 1904)

Bartels, Adolf, *Die ersten Weimarer Nationalfestspiele für die deutsche Jugend: Berichte der führenden Lehrer* (Weimar, 1909)

Bartels, Adolf, *Geschichte der deutschen Literatur*, 7th/8th edn (Hamburg, 1919)

Bartels, Adolf, "Heimatkunst," *Deutsche Heimat* 1, no. 1 (1900): 1019

Bartels, Adolf, *Heine-Genossen: Zur Charakteristik der deutschen Presse und der deutschen Parteien* (Dresden, 1908)

Bartels, Adolf, *Heinrich Heine: Auch ein Denkmal* (Dresden, 1906)

Bartels, Adolf, *Judentum und deutsche Literatur: Vortrag, gehalten am 29. Juni 1910 im Deutschvölkischen Studentenverband, Berlin* (Berlin, 1912)

Bartels, Adolf, *Jüdische Herkunft und Literaturwissenschaft: Eine gründliche Erörterung* (Leipzig, 1925; 1st edn 1897)

Bartels, Adolf, *Meine Lebensarbeit* (Wesselburen, 1932)

Bartels, Adolf, *Rasse: Sechzehn Aufsätze zur nationalen Weltanschauung* (Hamburg, 1909)

Bartels, Adolf, *Weshalb ich die Juden bekämpfe: Eine deutliche Auskunft* (Hamburg, 1919)

Barthel, Ernst, *Friedrich Lienhard: Die Künstlerseele aus dem deutschen Elsass* (Kolmar, 1941)

Bartning, Otto, *Paul Schultze-Naumburg: Ein Pioneer deutscher Kulturarbeit* (Munich, 1929)

Bäte, Ludwig, ed., *Die Akte Johannes Schlaf* (Berlin, 1967)

Bäte, Ludwig/Kurt Meyer-Rotermund/Rudolf Borch, eds, *Das Johannes Schlaf-Buch: Zu seinem sechzigsten Geburtstag* (Rudolstadt, 1922)

Bathrick, David, "Kultur und Öffentlichkeit in der DDR," in Peter Uwe Hohendahl/Patricia Herminghouse, eds, *Literatur der DDR in den siebziger Jahren* (Frankfurt am Main, 1983), 53–81

Batts, Michael, "The Other (Non-Classical) Side of Weimar in Goethe's Time," in Peter M. Daly, ed., *Why Weimar? Questioning the Legacy of Weimar from Goethe to 1999* (New York, 2003), 23–38

Baudert, August, *Sachsen-Weimars Ende: Historische Tatsachen aus sturmbewegter Zeit* (Weimar, 1923)

Baumgartner, Michael, "Johannes Itten und Paul Klee: Aspekte einer Künstler-Begegnung," in Christa Lichtenstern/Christoph Wagner, eds, *Johannes Itten und die Moderne: Beiträge eines wissenschaftlichen Symposiums* (Ostfildern-Ruit, 2003), 101–15

Becher, Johannes R., *Auf andere Art so grosse Hoffnung: Tagebuch 1950, Eintragungen 1951* (Berlin, 1969)

Becher, Johannes Robert, *Werke in drei Bänden*, ed. Günther Deicke/Horst Hasse, 3 vols (Berlin, 1971)

Becker, Bernhard, *Herder-Rezeption in Deutschland: Eine ideologiekritische Untersuchung* (St. Ingbert, 1987)

Benz, Richard, *Heidelberg: Schicksal und Geist* (Konstanz, 1961)

Berger, Albert, *Josef Weinheber (1892–1945): Leben und Werk – Leben im Werk* (Salzburg, 1999)

Berger, Joachim, "'Tieffurth' oder 'Tibur'? Herzogin Anna Amalias Rückzug auf ihren 'Musensitz'," in Joachim Berger, ed., *Der "Musenhof" Anna Amalias: Geselligkeit, Mäzenatentum und Kunstliebhaberei im klassischen Weimar* (Cologne, 2001), 125–64

Berger, Leonie/Joachim Berger, *Anna Amalia von Weimar: Eine Biographie* (Munich, 2006)

Berghahn, Klaus L., "Das Andere der Klassik: Von der 'Klassik-Legende' zur jüngsten Klassik-Diskussion," *Goethe Yearbook* 6 (1992): 1–27

Berghahn, Klaus L., "Von Weimar nach Versailles: Zur Entstehung der Klassik-Legende im 19. Jahrhundert," in Reinhold Grimm/Jost Hermand, eds, *Die Klassik-Legende: Second Wisconsin Workshop* (Frankfurt am Main, 1971), 50–78

Bergmann, Klaus, *Agrarromantik und Grossstadtfeindschaft* (Meisenheim, 1970)

Bernstein, Susan, "Heine's Versatility," in E. Wellbery, ed., *A New History of German Literature* (Cambridge, MA, 2004), 526–31

Bertram, Ernst, *Nietzsche: Versuch einer Mythologie* (Berlin, 1918)

Bertram, Ernst, "Schiller: Festvortrag gehalten am 26. Mai 1934," *Jahrbuch der Goethe-Gesellschaft* 20 (1934): 215–49

Bertram, Johannes, *Goethes Faust im Blickfeld des XX. Jahrhunderts: Eine weltanschauliche Deutung*, 3rd edn (Hamburg-Garstedt, 1942)

Bessel, Richard, *Germany 1945: From War to Peace* (New York, 2009)

Biedermann, Karl, *Mein Leben und ein Stück Zeitgeschichte* (Breslau, 1886)

Binion, Rudolf, *Frau Lou: Nietzsche's Wayward Disciple* (Princeton, 1968)

Birkin, Kenneth, "Richard Strauss in Weimar: Part I: The Concert Hall," *Richard-Strauss-Blätter* (June 1995): 3–34

Birkin, Kenneth, "Richard Strauss in Weimar: Part II: The Opera House," *Richard-Strauss-Blätter* (December 1995): 3–56

Bismarck, Otto von, *Gedanken und Erinnerungen: Die drei Bände in einem Band* (Stuttgart, 1919)

Blumenthal, Paul, *Erinnerungen an Ernst von Wildenbruch* (Frankfurt an der Oder, 1924)

Bode, Wilhelm, *Der weimarische Musenhof, 1756–1781* (Berlin, 1920)

Boden, Petra, "Julius Petersen: Ein Wissenschaftsmanager auf dem Philologenthron," *Euphorion* 88 (1994): 82–102

Boden, Petra/Bernhard Fischer, *Der Germanist Julius Petersen (1878–1941): Bibliographie, systematisches Nachlassverzeichnis und Dokumentation* (Marbach, 1995)

Böhme, Helmut, "Was soll uns Goethe '82?" in Böhme/Hans-Jochen Gamm, eds, *Johann Wolfgang Goethe: Versuch einer Annäherung* (Darmstadt, 1984), 7–15

Bollenbeck, Georg, "Weimar," in Etienne François/Hagen Schulze, eds, *Deutsche Erinnerungs-Orte I*, 2nd edn (Munich, 2001), 206–24

Bollmus, Reinhard, *Das Amt Rosenberg und seine Gegner: Studien zum Machtkampf im national-sozialistischen Herrschaftssystem* (Stuttgart, 1970)

Bonn, Friedrich, *Jugend und Theater* (Emsdetten, 1939)

Borchert, Ralf, "*. . . bisschen was Derberes": Rechtsextremismus und Zivilgesellschaft – Das Beispiel Weimar* (Jena, 2004)

Borchmeyer, Dieter, "Goethe," in Etienne François/Hagen Schulze, eds, *Deutsche Erinnerungs-Orte I*, 2nd edn (Munich, 2001), 187–206

Borchmeyer, Dieter, *Goethe: Der Zeitbürger* (Munich, 1999)

Borchmeyer, Dieter, "Liszt und Wagner: Allianz in Goethes und Schillers Spuren," *Wagner Spectrum* 7, no. 1 (2011): 69–81

Borchmeyer, Dieter, *Weimarer Klassik: Portrait einer Epoche* (Weinheim, 1994)

Borodin, Alexander, "Meine Erinnerungen an Liszt," in Hedwig Weilguny, ed., *Das Liszthaus in Weimar*, 9th edn (Weimar, 1978), 21–48

Borrmann, Norbert, *Paul Schultze-Naumburg, 1869–1949: Maler, Publizist, Architekt: Vom Kulturreformer der Jahrhundertwende zum Kulturpolitiker im Dritten Reich: Ein Lebens- und Zeitdokument* (Essen, 1989)

Böttiger, Karl August, *Literarische Zustände und Zeitgenossen: Begegnungen und Gespräche im klassischen Weimar*, ed. Klaus Gerlach/Renè Sternke, 2nd edn (Berlin, 1998)

Boyle, Nicholas, *Goethe: The Poet and the Age*, vol. 1 (Oxford, 1992)

Boyle, Nicholas, *Goethe: The Poet and the Age*, vol. 2 (Oxford, 2000)

Brenner, Hildegard, *Die Kunstpolitik des Nationalsozialismus* (Reinbek, 1963)

Brockmann, Stephen, *A Critical History of German Film* (Rochester, NY, 2010)

Bronner, Stephen Eric, "Lukács and the Dialectic: Contributions to a Theory of Practice," in Michael J. Thompson, ed., *Georg Lukács Reconsidered: Critical Essays in Politics, Philosophy and Aesthetics* (New York, 2011), 13–32

Bruford, Walter H., *Germany in the Eighteenth Century: The Social Background of the Literary Revival* (Cambridge, 1965; 1st edn 1935)

Buchenwald: Mahnung und Verpflichtung: Dokumente und Berichte, 3rd edn (Berlin, 1961)

Buchhorn, Josef, *Zwischen Goethe und Scheidemann: Weimarer Eindrücke* (Berlin, 1919)

Buchwald, Reinhard, *Miterlebte Geschichte: Lebenserinnerungen* (Cologne, 1992)

Bülow, Hans von, *Briefe*, ed. Marie von Bülow, vol. 1, 2nd edn (Leipzig, 1896–1908)

Bunge, Hans, ed., *Die Debatte um Hanns Eislers "Johann Faustus": Eine Dokumentation* (Berlin, 1991)

Bunzol, Alfred, *Erlebnisse eines politischen Gefangenen im Konzentrationslager Buchenwald* (Weimar, 1946)

Büttner, Ludwig, *Gedanken zu einer biologischen Literaturbetrachtung* (Munich, 1939)

Cancik, Hubert A., "Der Nietzsche-Kult in Weimar (II): Ein Beitrag zur Religionsgeschichte der nationalsozialistischen Ära (1942–1944)," in Peter Antes/Donate Pahnke, eds, *Die Religion von Oberschichten: Religion – Profession – Intellektualismus* (Marburg, 1989), 87–116

Cancik, Hubert A., "Der Nietzsche-Kult in Weimar: Ein Beitrag zur Religionsgeschichte der wilhelminischen Ära," *Nietzsche-Studien* 16 (1987): 405–29

Carl Alexander, Grossherzog von Sachsen-Weimar-Eisenach, *Tagebuchblätter von einer Reise nach München und Tirol im Jahre 1858* (Eisenach, 1933)

Carossa, Hans, *Ungleiche Welten* (Wiesbaden, 1951)

Carossa, Hans, "Von der Beschaulichkeit des schöpferischen Schaffens," in Hans Hagemeyer, ed., *Einsamkeit und Gemeinschaft: Zehn Vorträge der 5. Arbeitstagung des Amtes Schrifttumspflege beim Beauftragten des Führers für die gesamte geistige und weltanschauliche Erziehung der NSDAP.* (Stuttgart, 1939), 46–51

Chamberlain, Houston Stewart, *Goethe* (Munich, 1912)

Champa, Kermit, ed., *German Painting of the 19th Century* (New Haven, 1970)

Châtellier, Hildegard, "Kreuz, Rosenkreuz und Hakenkreuz: Synkretismus in der Weimarer Zeit am Beispiel Friedrich Lienhards," in Manfred Gangl/Gérard Raulet, eds, *Intellektuellendiskurse in der Weimarer Republik: Zur politischen Kultur einer Gemengelage*, 2nd edn (Frankfurt am Main, 2007), 93–104

Clarkson, Jesse D., *A History of Russia* (New York, 1966)

Cleve, Ingeborg, "Zwischen Ideal und Wirklichkeit: Klassik in Weimar in der Ära Holtzhauer (1954–1973)," in Lothar Ehrlich/Gunther Mai, eds, *Weimarer Klassik in der Ära Ulbricht* (Cologne, 2000), 343–58

Coellen, Ludwig, "Lyonel Feininger," *Kunstblatt* 3, no. 5 (1919): 130–37

Cölln, Detlef, ed., *Adolf Bartels: Leben, Wesen, und Werk* (Heide, 1935)

Cölln, Detlef, *Adolf Bartels zum achtzigsten Geburtstag* (Heide, 1942)

Conrady, Karl Otto, *Goethe: Leben und Werk*, vol. 1 (Frankfurt am Main, 1992)

Conrady, Karl Otto, *Goethe: Leben und Werk*, vol. 2 (Frankfurt am Main, 1993)

Conze, Werner, "Mittelstand," in Otto Brunner/Conze/Reinhard Koselleck, eds, *Geschichtliche Grundbegriffe: Historisches Lexikon zur politisch-sozialen Sprache in Deutschland*, vol. 4 (Stuttgart, 1978), 54–62

Conze, Werner, "Vom 'Pöbel' zum 'Proletariat': Sozialgeschichtliche Voraussetzungen für den Sozialismus in Deutschland," in Hans-Ulrich Wehler, ed., *Moderne deutsche Sozialgeschichte* (Cologne, 1966), 112–28

Corinth, Lovis, *Selbstbiographie* (Leipzig, 1993)

Cornelius, Carl Maria, ed., Peter Cornelius: *Ausgewählte Briefe nebst Tagebuchblättern und Gelegenheitsgedichten*, vol. 1 (Leipzig, 1904)

Cornelius, Carl Maria, ed., *Peter Cornelius: Ausgewählte Briefe nebst Tagebuchblättern und Gelegenheitsgedichten*, vol. 2 (Leipzig, 1905)

Crodel, Richard, ed., *Das Goethe-Jahr in Weimar* (Munich, 1932)

Crommelin, Armand, "Goethe und Bismarck, die Staatskünstler," *Bayreuther Blätter* 42, no. 1 (1919): 11–23

Czaja, Tanja, "Magic Weimar in the North," in Frank Eckardt/Anna Karwińska, eds, *Kraków and Weimar: The Tale of Urban Magics* (Marburg, 2006), 138–49

Dahlke, Günther, ed., *Der Menschheit Würde: Dokumente zum Schiller-Bild der deutschen Arbeiterklasse* (Weimar, 1959)

Dahmen, Hans, *Die nationale Idee von Herder bis Hitler* (Cologne, 1934)

Damm, Sigrid, *Christiane und Goethe: Eine Recherche* (Frankfurt am Main, 1998)

Damm, Sigrid, *Das Leben des Friedrich Schiller: Eine Wanderung* (Frankfurt am Main, 2004)

Damrosch, Walter, *My Musical Life* (New York, 1923)

Darré, Richard Walther, *Neuadel aus Blut und Boden* (Munich, 1930)

Das Land Goethes, 1914–1916: Ein vaterländisches Gedenkbuch, ed. Berliner Goethebund (Stuttgart, 1916)

Das Postleitzahlenbuch: Alphabetisch Geordnet (Bonn, [1993])

De Bruyn, Günter, *Vierzig Jahre: Ein Lebensbericht* (Frankfurt am Main, 1996)

De Fries, H., "Die Auflösung des Staatlichen Bauhauses in Weimar und seine zukünftige Form," *Die Baugilde* (January 25, 1925): 77–79

De Michelis, Marco, "Walter Determann: Bauhaus Settlement Weimar, 1920," in Barry Bergdoll/Leah Dickerman, eds, *Bauhaus 1919–1933: Workshops for Modernity* (New York, 2009), 86–89.

De Staël, Baroness Anne-Louise-Germaine, *Germany*, vol. 1 (New York, 1814)

Dehio, Ludwig/Peter Classen, eds, *Friedrich Meinecke: Ausgewählter Briefwechsel*, vol. 6 (Stuttgart, 1962)

Dennis, David B., *Inhumanities: Nazi Interpretations of Western Culture* (New York, 2012)

Dent, Edward J., *Ferruccio Busoni: A Biography* (London, 1966)

Der Weimarer Bilderstreit: Szenen einer Ausstellung: Eine Dokumentation (Weimar, 2000)

Deubel, Werner, "Schiller und die deutsche Erneuerung," *Völkische Kultur* 2 (1934): 497–500

D'Harcourt, Pierre, *The Real Enemy* (London, 1967)

Dickmann, Fritz, "Die Regierungsbildung in Thüringen als Modell der Machtergreifung: Ein Brief Hitlers aus dem Jahre 1930," *Vierteljahrshefte für Zeitgeschichte* 14 (1966): 454–64

Die Dichtung im Kampf des Reiches: Weimarer Reden 1940, 2nd edn (Hamburg, 1943)

Die Dichtung im kommenden Europa: Weimarer Reden 1941 (Hamburg, 1942)

Die SED und das kulturelle Erbe: Orientierungen, Errungenschaften, Probleme (Berlin, 1986)

Die 7 für Weimar: Beiträge zum Programm Weimar 1999 – Kulturstadt Europas (Weimar, 1998)

Diethe, Carol, *Nietzsche's Sister and the Will to Power: A Biography of Elisabeth Förster-Nietzsche* (Urbana, IL, 2003)

Dietrich, Gerd, "'Die Goethepächter': Klassikmythos in der Politik der SED," in Lothar Ehrlich/Gunther Mai, eds, *Weimarer Klassik in der Ära Ulbricht* (Cologne, 2000), 151–74

Dietrich, Gerd, *Politik und Kultur in der Sowjetischen Besatzungszone Deutschlands (SBZ), 1945–1949* (Berne, 1993)

Dietrich, Marlene, *Nehmt nur mein Leben . . .: Reflexionen* (Munich, 1979)

Dinter, Artur, *Die Sünde wider das Blut: Ein Zeitroman*, 3rd edn (Leipzig, 1919)

Dinter, Artur, *Ursprung, Ziel und Weg der deutschvölkischen Freiheitsbewegung: Das völkisch-soziale Programm* (Weimar, 1924)

Ditfurth, Christian von, *Blockflöten: Wie die CDU ihre realsozialistische Vergangenheit verdrängt* (Cologne, 1991)

Doesburg, Theo van, "The Will to Style: The Reconstruction of Life, Art and Technology" (1922), in Hans L. C. Jaffé, ed., *De Stijl* (New York, 1967), 148–63

Dolgner, Dieter, *Henry van de Velde in Weimar, 1902–1917* (Weimar, 1996)

Dollichon, Elfi, *Kunstpolitik im östlichen Nachkriegsdeutschland mit besonderer Berücksichtigung des Landes Thüringen von 1945 bis 1952* (Hamburg, 1992)

Dollichon, Elfi, *Kunstpolitik im östlichen Nachkriegsdeutschland mit besonderer Berücksichtigung des Landes Thüringen von 1945 bis 1952: Dokumentation* (Hamburg, 1992)

Dömling, Wolfgang, *Franz Liszt und seine Zeit* (Laaber, 1985)

Dönhoff, Marion Gräfin/Rudolf Walter Leonhard/Theo Sommer, *Reise in ein fernes Land: Bericht über Kultur, Wirtschaft und Politik in der DDR* (Gütersloh, 1966)

Dornheim, Andreas/Bernhand Post/Burkhard Stenzel, *Thüringen, 1933–1945: Aspekte national-sozialistischer Herrschaft* (Erfurt, 1997)

Dorrmann, Michael, "'Aber nicht nach Potsdam sind wir ausgewandert, sondern nach Weimar': Die Nationalversammlung in Weimar, 1919," in Hans Wilderotter/Dorrmann, eds, *Wege nach Weimar: Auf der Suche nach der Einheit von Kunst und Politik* (Berlin, 1999), 21–26

Douglas, [Ray] M., *Orderly and Humane: The Expulsion of the Germans after the Second World War* (New Haven, 2012)

Dreise-Beckmann, Sandra, "Anna Amalia und das Musikleben am Weimarer Hof," in Joachim Berger, ed., *Der "Musenhof" Anna Amalias: Geselligkeit, Mäzenatentum und Kunstliebhaberei im klassischen Weimar* (Cologne, 2001), 53–79

Droste, Magdalena, "Aneignung und Abstossung: Expressive und konstruktive Tendenzen am Weimarer Bauhaus," in Brigitte Salmen, ed., *Bauhaus-Ideen um Itten, Feininger, Klee, Kandinsky: Vom Expressiven zum Konstruktiven* (Murnau, 2007), 11–29

Droste, Magdalena, *Bauhaus, 1919–1933* (Cologne, 1993)

Dufay, François, *Die Herbstreise französischer Schriftsteller im Oktober 1941 in Deutschland: Ein Bericht* (Berlin, 2001)

Dusik, Bärbel, ed., *Hitler: Reden, Schriften, Anordnungen, Februar 1925 bis Januar 1933*, vol. 2, part 1 (Munich, 1992)

Düsterberg, Rolf, *Hanns Johst: "Der Barde der SS"* (Paderborn, 2004)

Easton, Laird McLeod, *The Red Count: The Life and Times of Harry Kessler* (Berkeley, 2002)

Easton, Laird McLeod, "The Rise and Fall of the 'Third Weimar': Harry Graf Kessler and the Aesthetic State in Wilhelmian Germany, 1902–1906," *Central European History* 29 (1997): 495–532

Eberhardt, Hans, *Goethes Umwelt: Forschungen zur gesellschaftlichen Struktur Thüringens* (Weimar, 1951)

Eckardt, Frank, "Urban Myth: The Symbolic Sizing of Weimar, Germany," in David Bell/Mark Jayne, eds, *Small Cities: Urban Experience beyond the Metropolis* (New York, 2006), 121–32

Egloffstein, Hermann Freiherr von, *Das Weimar von Carl Alexander und Wilhelm Ernst: Erinnerungen* (Berlin, 1934)

Ehrlich, Lothar, "Die Goethe-Gesellschaft im Spanungsfeld der Deutschland- und Kulturpolitik der SED," in Ehrlich/Gunther Mai, eds, *Weimarer Klassik in der Ära Ulbricht* (Cologne, 2000), 251–81

Ehrlich, Lothar, "'Faust' im DDR-Sozialismus," in Frank Möbus et al., eds, *Faust: Annäherung an einen Mythos* (Göttingen, 1995), 332–42

Ehrlich, Lothar, "Liszt und Goethe," in Detlef Altenburg, ed., *Liszt und die Weimarer Klassik* (Laaber, 1997), 33–45

Ehrlich, Lothar, et al., "Weimarer Klassik in der Ära Honecker," in Ehrlich/Gunther Mai, eds, *Weimarer Klassik in der Ära Honecker* (Cologne, 2001), 7–28

Ehrlich, Willi, "Sozialismus und Klassik: Ansprache zur Festveranstaltung am 28. August 1964," in *Vom Werden und Wachsen der Weimarer Goethe-Institute: Ansprachen zur Festsitzung und Vorträge der wissenschaftlichen Konferenzen anlässlich der Feier des zehnjährigen Bestehens der Nationalen Forschungs- und Gedenkstätten der klassischen deutschen Literatur in Weimar, 27. bis 30. August 1964* (Weimar, 1965), 14–20

Eissler, Kurt Robert, *Goethe: A Psychoanalytic Study, 1775–1786*, 2 vols (Detroit, 1963)

Elster, Hanns Martin, *Ernst von Wildenbruch: Leben – Werk – Persönlichkeit* (Berlin, 1934)

Emge, Karl August, *Geistiger Mensch und Nationalsozialismus: Ein Interview für die Gebildeten unter seinen Gegnern* (Berlin, 1931)

Emmel, Felix, *Theater aus deutschem Wesen* (Berlin, 1937)

Engelbrecht, Kurt, *Faust im Braunhemd* (Leipzig, 1933)

Engelhardt, Katrin, "Die Ausstellung 'Entartete Kunst' in Berlin 1938," in Uwe Fleckner, ed., *Angriff auf die Avantgarde: Kunst und Kunstpolitik im Nationalsozialismus* (Berlin, 2007), 87–158

Epkenhaus, Michael, ed., *Mein lieber Schatz! Briefe von Admiral Reinhard Scheer an seine Ehefrau: August bis November 1918* (Bochum, 2006)

Erbe, Günter, *Die verfemte Moderne: Die Auseinandersetzung mit dem "Modernismus" in Kulturpolitik, Literaturwissenschaft und Literatur der DDR* (Opladen, 1993)

Erbe, Günter, "Geschmack an der 'Dekadenz': Wandlungen im literarischen und kulturellen Traditionsverständnis," in Gert-Joachim Glaessner, ed., *Die DDR in der Ära Honecker: Politik – Kultur – Gesellschaft* (Opladen, 1988), 656–73

Erckmann, Rudolf, ed., *Dichter und Krieger: Weimarer Reden 1942* (Hamburg, 1943)

Erdmann, Ulrich, *Vom Naturalismus zum Nationalsozialismus: Zeitgeschichtlich-biographische Studien zu Max Halbe, Gerhart Hauptmann, Johannes Schlaf und Hermann Stehr: Mit unbekannten Selbstzeugnissen* (Frankfurt am Main, 1997)

Ernst, Anna-Sabine, "Erbe und Hypothek: (Alltags-) kulturelle Leitbilder in der SBZ/DDR, 1945–1961," in *Kultur und Kulturträger in der DDR: Analysen* (Berlin, 1993), 9–132

Evans, Richard J., *The Coming of the Third Reich* (New York, 2004)

Fabricius, Hans, *Dr. Frick, der revolutionäre Staatsmann* (Berlin-Schöneberg, [1933])

Fabricius, Hans, *Schiller als Kampfgenosse Hitlers: Nationalsozialismus in Schillers Dramen*, 2nd edn (Berlin-Schöneberg, 1934)

Facius, Friedrich, "Carl Alexander von Weimar und die deutsche Kolonialpolitik, 1850–1901," *Koloniale Rundschau* 32, no. 6 (1941): 339–53

Falter, Jürgen W., *Hitlers Wähler* (Munich, 1991)

Farrelly, Daniel J., *Goethe in East-Germany, 1949–1989: Toward a History of Goethe Reception in the GDR* (Columbia, SC, 1998)

Fascher, Eckhard, "Politische Parteien und Stadtparlamente im heutigen Weimar: Eine Modellstudie zu Kontinuität und Wandel der politischen Kultur in den neuen Ländern," *Zeitschrift für Parlamentsfragen* 27, no. 1 (1996): 37–61

Fay, Amy, *Music-Study in Germany: The Classic Memoir of the Romantic Era* (New York, 1965)

Fechter, Paul, *Geschichte der deutschen Literatur: Von den Anfängen bis zur Gegenwart* (Berlin, 1941)

Fehse, Wilhelm, *Goethe im Lichte des neuen Werdens* (Brunswick, 1935)

Fein, Erich/Karl Flanner, *Rot-Weiss-Rot in Buchenwald: Die österreichischen politischen Häftlinge im Konzentrationslager am Ettersberg bei Weimar, 1938–1945* (Vienna, 1987)

Feininger, Lux, "Die Bauhauskapelle," in Peter Hahn/Rolf Bothe/Hans Christoph von Tavel, eds, *Das frühe Bauhaus und Johannes Itten: Katalogbuch anlässlich des 75. Gründungsjubiläums des Staatlichen Bauhauses in Weimar* (Berlin, 1994), 374–80

Fest, Joachim C., *Speer: The Final Verdict* (Orlando, FL, 2003)

Fetzer, Christian, "Rassenanatomische Untersuchungen an 17 Hottentottenköpfen," *Zeitschrift für Morphologie und Anthropologie* 16 (1914): 95–156

Feuchter, Georg W., *Der Luftkrieg*, 3rd edn (Frankfurt am Main, 1964)

Feuchter-Schawelka, Anne, "Der Kampf um das Tafelbild, 1900–1920," in Rolf Bothe/Thomas Föhl, eds, *Aufstieg und Fall der Moderne* (Ostfildern-Ruit, 1999), 216–28

Fiala, Claudia/Jens Riederer/Volker Wahl, eds, *Goethes Amtstätigkeit für den Ilmenauer Bergbau: Dokumentation zur Ausstellung: Eine Archivalienausstellung des Thüringischen Hauptstaatsarchivs Weimar in Verbindung mit dem Stadtmuseum in Ilmenau, 23. September bis 7. November 1998 im Technologie- und Gründerzentrum Ilmenau* (Ilmenau, 1998)

Fiedler, Theodore, "Weimar between Modernism and *Heimatkunst*: Contrary Visions of Cultural Renewal and National Identity at the Turn of the Century," in Peter M. Daly, ed., *Why Weimar? Questioning the Legacy of Weimar from Goethe to 1999* (New York, 2003), 133–62

Field, Geoffrey G., "Nordic Racism," *Journal of the History of Ideas* 38 (1977): 523–40

Figes, Orlando, *The Whisperers: Private Life in Stalin's Russia* (New York, 2007)

Findeli, Alain, "Goethe und das Bauhaus: An Epistemological Inquiry," in Peter M. Daly, ed., *Why Weimar? Questioning the Legacy of Weimar from Goethe to 1999* (New York, 2003), 109–32

Finn, Gerhard, *Die politischen Häftlinge der Sowjetzone, 1945–1959* (Pfaffenhofen, 1960)

Fischer, Eugen, *Die Rehobother Bastards und das Bastardierungsproblem beim Menschen: Anthropologische und ethnographische Studien am Rehobother Bastardvolk in Deutsch-Südwest-Afrika, ausgeführt mit Unterstützung der Kgl. preuss. Akademie der Wissenschaften* (Jena, 1913)

Fischer, Jens Malte, "'Zwischen uns und Weimar liegt Buchenwald': Germanisten im Dritten Reich," *Merkur* 41, no. 1 (January 1987): 12–25

Fleischhauer, Markus, "'Eine neue Klassik bauen': Kulturelle Konzepte Fritz Sauckels," in Justus H. Ulbricht, ed., *Klassikerstadt und Nationalsozialismus: Kultur und Politik in Weimar, 1933 bis 1945* (Weimar, 2002), 77–90

Föhl, Thomas, *Henry van de Velde: Architekt und Designer des Jugendstils* (Weimar, 2010)

Föhl, Thomas, "Kunstpolitik und Lebensentwurf: Das Neue Weimar im Spiegel der Beziehungen zwischen Henry van de Velde und Harry Graf Kessler," in Rolf Bothe/Föhl, eds, *Aufstieg und Fall der Moderne* (Ostfildern-Ruit, 1999), 60–89

Föhl, Thomas/Michael Siebenbrodt, et al., *Bauhaus-Museum*, 2nd edn (Munich, 1996)

Förster-Nietzsche, Elisabeth, *Das Leben Friedrich Nietzsche's*, vol. 1 (Leipzig, 1895)

Förster-Nietzsche, Elisabeth, *Das Leben Friedrich Nietzsche's*, vol. 2 (*Erste Abtheilung*, Leipzig, 1897)

Förster-Nietzsche, Elisabeth, *Das Leben Friedrich Nietzsche's*, vol. 2 (*Zweite Abtheilung*, Leipzig, 1904)

Förster-Nietzsche, Elisabeth, *Das Nietzsche-Archiv: Seine Freunde und seine Feinde* (Berlin, 1907)

Förster-Nietzsche, Elisabeth, *Der einsame Nietzsche* (Leipzig, 1914)

Förster-Nietzsche, Elisabeth, *Friedrich Nietzsche und die Frauen seiner Zeit* (Munich, 1935)

Francke, Otto, *Geschichte des Wilhelm-Ernst-Gymnasiums in Weimar* (Weimar, 1916)

Frank, Susanne/Silke Roth, "Die Säulen der Stadt: Festivalisierung, Partizipation und lokale Identität am Beispiel des Events 'Weimar 1999'," in Winfried Gebhardt/Ronald Hitzler/Michaela Pfadenhauer, eds, *Events: Soziologie des Aussergewöhnlichen* (Opladen, 2000), 203–21

Frede, Lothar, "Die Todesstrafe bei Goethe," *Zeitschrift für die gesamte Strafrechtswissenschaft* 80 (1968): 385–88

Frei, Norbert, *Adenauer's Germany and the Nazi Past: The Politics of Amnesty and Integration* (New York, 2002)

Freund, Julius, *O Buchenwald!* (Klagenfurt, [1946])

Friedenthal, Richard, *Goethe: Sein Leben und seine Zeit* (Munich, 1968)

Fritsch, Theodor, *Handbuch der Judenfrage: Die wichtigsten Tatsachen zur Beurteilung der Jüdischen Frage*, 49th edn (Leipzig, 1944)

Fulbrook, Mary, *Anatomy of a Dictatorship: Inside the GDR, 1949–1989* (Oxford, 1997)

Fuller, Steven Nyole, *The Nazis' Literary Grandfather: Adolf Bartels and Cultural Extremism, 1871–1945* (New York, 1996)

Gärtner, Marcus, "Weimar und Bitterfeld: Vom Umgang mit kulturellen Traditionen im technischen Zeitalter," in Lothar Ehrlich/Gunther Mai, eds, *Weimarer Klassik in der Ära Ulbricht* (Cologne, 2000), 319–41

Gärtner, Marcus, ed., *Kultur in Thüringen, 1949–1989* (Erfurt, 2000)

Galindo, Martha Zapata, *Triumph des Willens zur Macht: Zur Nietzsche-Rezeption im NS-Staat* (Hamburg, 1995)

Gall, Lothar, *Bismarck der Weisse Revolutionär*, 4th edn (Frankfurt am Main, 1980)

Gay, Peter, *Modernism: The Lure of Heresy from Baudelaire to Beckett and Beyond* (New York, 2007)

Gay, Peter, *Weinear Culture: The Outsider as Insider* (New York, 1968)

Gebhardt, Bruno, *Handbuch der Geschichte*, vol. 3, ed. Herbert Grundmann, 8th edn (Stuttgart, 1963)

Genast, Eduard, *Aus Weimars klassischer und nachklassischer Zeit: Erinnerungen eines alten Schauspielers*, ed. Robert Kohlrausch, 7th edn (Stuttgart, n.d.)

Gerstenberg, Heinrich, *Aus Weimars nachklassischer Zeit* (Hamburg, 1901)

Gerwarth, Robert, *Hitler's Hangman: The Life of Heydrich* (New Haven, 2011)

Gibas, Monika, ed., *"Arisierung" in Thüringen: Entrechtung, Enteignung und Vernichtung der jüdischen Bürger Thüringens, 1933–1945* (Erfurt, 2006)

Giesler, Hermann, *Ein anderer Hitler: Bericht seines Architekten: Erlebnisse, Gespräche, Reflexionen*, 3rd edn (Leoni, 1978)

Gillies, A., "Herder and Goethe," in J. Boyd, ed., *German Studies* (Oxford, 1952), 82–97

Goebbels, Joseph Paul, *Das eherne Herz: Reden und Aufsätze aus den Jahren 1941/42*, ed. M. A. von Schirmeister (Munich, 1943)

Goebbels, Joseph Paul, *Michael: Ein deutsches Schicksal in Tagebuchblättern* (Munich, 1931; 1st edn 1929)

Goebbels, Joseph Paul, "Wilhelm von Schütz als Dramatiker: Ein Beitrag zur Geschichte des Dramas der Romantischen Schule," PhD dissertation (Heidelberg, 1922)

Goeken, Walther, *Herder als Deutscher: Ein literarhistorischer Beitrag zur Entwicklung der deutschen Nationalidee* (Stuttgart, 1926)

Goethe, Johann Wolfgang von, *Faust* [=*Goethes Werke: Kleine Ausgabe*, ed. Robert Petsch, vol. 3 (Leipzig, n.d.)]

Goethe, Johann Wolfgang von, ed., *Winkelmann* [*sic*] *und sein Jahrhundert: In Briefen und Aufsätzen* (Vienna, 1811)

Goetz, Wolfgang, *Fünfzig Jahre Goethe-Gesellschaft* (Weimar, 1936)

Golz, Jochen, "Das Goethe- und Schiller-Archiv in Geschichte und Gegenwart," in Golz, ed., *Das Goethe- und Schiller-Archiv, 1896–1996: Beiträge aus dem ältesten deutschen Literaturarchiv* (Weimar, 1996), 13–70

Göring, Emmy, *An der Seite meines Mannes: Begebenheiten und Bekenntnisse* (Göttingen, 1967)

Gottschalg, Alexander Wilhelm, *Franz Liszt in Weimar und seine letzten Lebensjahre*, ed. Carl Alfred René (Berlin, 1910)

Gräbner, Karl, *Die Grossherzogliche Haupt- und Residenz-Stadt Weimar, nach ihrer Geschichte und ihren gegenwärtigen Verhältnissen dargestellt* (Leipzig, 1987; 1st edn 1830)

Gradmann, Erwin, et al., *Johannes Itten, 1888–1967* (n.p., [1967])

Grans, Heinrich, *Fünfzehn Jahre in Weimar: Erlebtes und Erlittenes* (Leipzig, 1889)

Gransow, Volker, *Kulturpolitik in der DDR* (Berlin, 1975)

Gregor, Neil, *Haunted City: Nuremberg and the Nazi Past* (New Haven, 2008)

Greiner-Mai, Herbert, ed., *Weimar im Urteil der Welt: Stimmen aus drei Jahrhunderten* (Berlin, 1977)

Greiser, Katrin, *Die Todesmärsche von Buchenwald: Räumung, Befreiung und Spuren der Erinnerung* (Göttingen, 2008)

Grimm, Herman Friedrich, *Goethe*, ed. Wilhelm Hansen (Detmold-Hiddesen, 1948)

Grimm, Reinhold/Jost Hermand, eds, *Die Klassik-Legende: Second Wisconsin Workshop* (Frankfurt am Main, 1971)

Groehler, Olaf, "Der verordnete Antifaschismus: Die Rezeption des thüringischen kommunistischen Widerstandes in der DDR," in Detlev Heiden/Gunther Mai, eds, *Nationalsozialismus in Thüringen* (Weimar, 1995), 531–50

Grohmann, Will, *Wassily Kandinsky: Leben und Werk* (Cologne, 1958)

Gronau, Dietrich, *Max Liebermann: Eine Biographie* (Frankfurt am Main, 2001)

Gülke, Peter, *Fluchtpunkt Musik: Reflexionen eines Dirigenten zwischen Ost und West* (Kassel, 1994)

Günther, Gitta, *Weimar: Eine Chronik* (Leipzig, 1996)

Günther, Gitta/Lothar Wallraf, eds, *Geschichte der Stadt Weimar* (Weimar, 1975)

Günther, Gitta/Wolfram Huschke/Walter Steiner, eds, *Weimar: Lexikon zur Stadtgeschichte* (Weimar, 1998)

Günther, Hans F. K., *Rassenkunde des deutschen Volkes* (Munich, 1922)

Günther, Hans F. K., *Rassenkunde des jüdischen Volkes*, 2nd edn (Munich, 1930)

Günther, Hans F. K., *Ritter, Tod und Teufel: Der heldische Gedanke* (Munich, 1920)

Günzel, Klaus, *Das Weimarer Fürstenhaus: Eine Dynastie schreibt Kulturgeschichte* (Cologne, 2001)

Guradze, Hans/Karl Freudenberg, "Das Existenzminimum des geistigen Arbeiters," *Jahrbücher für Nationalökonomie und Statistik* 120 (1923, I): 327–33

Gutheil-Schoder, Marie, *Erlebtes und Erstrebtes: Rolle und Gestaltung* (Vienna, 1937)

Hackett, David A., ed., *Der Buchenwald-Report: Bericht über das Konzentrationslager Buchenwald bei Weimar* (Munich, 1996)

Hahl-Koch, Jelena, ed., *Arnold Schoenberg, Wassily Kandinsky: Letters, Pictures, and Documents* (London, 1984)

Hahn, Karl-Heinz, "Das Nietzsche-Archiv," *Nietzsche-Studien* 18 (1989): 1–19

Halperin, S. William, *Germany Tried Democracy: A Political History of the Reich from 1918 to 1933* (New York, 1965)

Hamann, Brigitte, *Winifred Wagner oder Hitlers Bayreuth* (Munich, 2002)

Hammer, Franz, *Zeit der Bewährung: Ein Lebensbericht* (Berlin, 1984)

Hanfstaengl, Ernst, *Zwischen Weissem und Braunem Haus: Memoiren eines politischen Aussenseiters* (Munich, 1970)

Hardt, Ernst, "Rede zur Weihe des Nationaltheaters" (1919), in Thomas Neumann, ed., *Quellen zur Geschichte Thüringens: Kultur in Thüringen, 1919–1949* (Erfurt, 1998), 46–50

Harich, Wolfgang, "Revision des nazistischen Nietzschebildes?" *Sinn und Form* 39, no. 5 (1987): 1018–53

Härtle, Heinrich, *Nietzsche und der Nationalsozialismus* (Munich, 1937)

Hartmann, Anne/Wolfram Eggeling, *Sowjetische Präsenz im kulturellen Leben der SBZ und frühen DDR, 1945–1953* (Berlin, 1998)

Hartwig, Edgar, et al., eds, *Festschrift der Hochschule für Musik "Franz Liszt" Weimar zum hundertsten Jahrestag ihrer Gründung als Orchesterschule* [Weimar, 1972]

Hasche, Christa/Traute Schölling/Joachim Fiebach, *Theater in der DDR: Chronik und Positionen* (Berlin, 1994)

Haufe, Eberhard, ed., *Wilhelm von Humboldt über Schiller und Goethe: Aus den Briefen und Werken* (Weimar, 1963)

Haufe, Rüdiger, ed., *Macht aus dem Staat Gurkensalat: Eine andere Jugend: Weimar, 1979–1989* (Berlin, 2011)

Hausmann, Frank-Rutger, *"Dichte, Dichter, tage nicht!": Die Europäische Schriftsteller-Vereinigung in Weimar, 1941–1948* (Frankfurt am Main, 2004)

Hausmann, Frank-Rutger, "Kollaborierende Intellektuelle in Weimar – Die 'Europäische Schriftsteller-Vereinigung' als 'Anti-P.E.N.-Club'," in Hellmut Th. Seemann, ed., *Europa in Weimar: Visionen eines Kontinents* (Göttingen, 2008), 399–422

Hayman, Ronald, *Nietzsche: A Critical Life* (New York, 1980)

Hecht, Christian, *Streit um die richtige Moderne: Henry van de Velde, Max Littmann und der Neubau des Weimarer Hoftheaters* (Weimar, 2005)

Hecker, Bernhard, *In Weimar zu Gast: Gästebucher erzählen: Von der Klassik bis heute* (Stuttgart, 1998)

Hecker, Max, ed., *Jahrbuch der Goethe-Gesellschaft* 21 (1935)

Heftrich, Eckhard, "Nietzsches Goethe: Eine Annäherung," *Nietzsche-Studien* 16 (1987): 1–20

Heiber, Helmut, *Joseph Goebbels* (Munich, 1965)

Heiber, Helmut, *Walter Frank und sein Reichsinstitut für Geschichte des neuen Deutschlands* (Stuttgart, 1966)

Heiden, Detlev/Gunther Mai, eds, *Thüringen auf dem Weg ins "Dritte Reich"* (Erfurt, 1996)

Heider, Magdalena, *Politik, Kultur, Kulturbund: Zur Gründungs- und Frühgeschichte des Kulturbundes zur demokratischen Erneuerung Deutschlands, 1945–1954, in der SBZ/DDR* (Cologne, 1993)

Heilfron, Eduard, ed., *Die deutsche Nationalversammlung im Jahre 1919 in ihrer Arbeit für den Aufbau des neuen deutschen Volksstaates*, vol. 1 (Berlin, 1920)

Heintze, Else, ed., *Chronik des Geschlechts Heintze* (Hannover-Döhren, 1926)

Hellmuth, Edith/Wolfgang Mühlfriedel, *Zeiss 1846–1905: Vom Atelier für Mechanik zum führenden Unternehmen des optischen Gerätebaus* (Weimar, 1996)

Henselmann, Hermann, "Brecht und die Stadt," *Die Weltbühne* (September 25, 1973): 1225–27

Henselmann, Hermann, *Drei Reisen nach Berlin* (Berlin, 1981)

Henselmann, Irene, *Meine grosse Familie: An der Seite des Architekten: Lebenserinnerungen* (Berlin, 1995)

Herbert, Ulrich, *Geschichte der Ausländerpolitik in Deutschland: Saisonarbeiter, Zwangsarbeiter, Gastarbeiter, Flüchtlinge* (Munich, 2001)

Herfurth, Emil, *Weimar und das Staatliche Bauhaus* (Weimar, 1920)

Herold, J. Christopher, *Mistress to an Age* (New York, 1964)

Herwig, Holger H., *"Luxury" Fleet: The Imperial German Navy, 1888–1918* (London, 1980)

Heukenkamp, Ursula, "Goethe-Rezeption: Wandel von kulturellen Mustern in der DDR der sechziger Jahre," in Lothar Ehrlich/Gunther Mai, eds, *Weimarer Klassik in der Ära Ulbricht* (Cologne, 2000), 283–301

Hille, Karoline, "Beispiel Thüringen: Die 'Machtergreifung' auf der Probebühne 1930," in Dieter Ruckhaberle, ed., *1933 – Wege zur Diktatur: Staatliche Kunsthalle Berlin und Neue Gesellschaft für Bildende Kunst: Ausstellung im Rahmen der Projekte des Berliner Kulturrats vom 9.1. bis 10.2. 1983* (Berlin, 1983), 187–217

Hillesheim, Jürgen/Elisabeth Michael, *Lexikon nationalsozialistischer Dichter: Biographien, Analysen, Bibliographien* (Würzburg, 1993)

Hilmes, Oliver, *Herrin des Hügels: Das Leben der Cosima Wagner*, 4th edn (Munich, 2007)

Hilmes, Oliver, *Witwe im Wahn: Das Leben der Alma Mahler-Werfel* (Munich, 2004)

Hinderer, Walter, "Die regressive Universalideologie: Zum Klassikbild der marxistischen Literaturkritik von Franz Mehring bis zu den *Weimarer Beiträgen*," in Reinhold Grimm/Jost Hermand, eds, *Die Klassik-Legende: Second Wisconsin Workshop* (Frankfurt am Main, 1971), 141–75

Hinderer, Walter, "Wieland's Cosmopolitan Classicism," in David E. Wellbery, ed., *A New History of German Literature* (Cambridge, MA, 2004), 381–86

Hinze-Reinhold, Bruno, *Lebenserinnerungen*, ed. Michael Berg (Weimar, 1997)

Hobsbawm, Eric J./Terence Osborne Ranger, *The Invention of Tradition* (Cambridge, 1983)

Hochhuth, Rolf, *Wessis in Weimar: Szenen aus einem besetzten Land*, 2nd edn (Berlin, 1993)

Hoffmann, David Marc, *Zur Geschichte des Nietzsche-Archivs* (Berlin, 1991)

Hoffmann von Fallersleben, August Heinrich, *Mein Leben: Aufzeichnungen und Erinnerungen*, vols 5–6 (Hanover, 1868)

Hoffmeister, Hans/Mirko Hempel, eds, *Die Wende in Thüringen: Ein Rückblick*, 2nd edn (Arnstadt, 2000)

Hohendahl, Peter Uwe, "Theorie und Praxis des Erbes: Untersuchungen zum Problem der literarischen Tradition in der DDR," in Hohendahl/Patricia Herminghouse, eds, *Literatur der DDR in den siebziger Jahren* (Frankfurt am Main, 1983), 13–52

Holt, Elizabeth Gilmore, ed., *From the Classicists to the Impressionists: Art and Architecture in the Nineteenth Century* (Garden City, NY, 1966)

Honecker, Erich, *Aus meinem Leben*, 6th edn (Berlin, 1981)

Honegger, Marc/Günther Massenkeil, eds, *Das Grosse Lexikon der Musik in acht Bänden*, vol. 5 (Freiburg, 1981)

Honigmann, Liselotte, "Vorwort," in *Die Weimarer Kunstschule, 1860–1919* (Weimar, 1980)

Hoormann, Anne, "Von der Bauhaus-Idee zur Formalismus-Debatte: Kunstausbildung an der Staatlichen Hochschule für Baukunst und Bildende Kunst (1946–1951)," in Rolf Bothe/Thomas Föhl, eds, *Aufstieg und Fall der Moderne* (Ostfildern-Ruit, 1999), 422–35

Horkenbach, Cuno, ed., *Das Deutsche Reich von 1918 bis Heute* (Berlin, 1930)

Hossfeld, Uwe, "Die Jenaer Jahre des 'Rasse-Günther' von 1930 bis 1935: Zur Gründung des Lehrstuhls für Sozialanthropologie an der Universität Jena," *Medizinhistorisches Journal* 34 (1999): 47–103

Hossfeld, Uwe, "'Kämpferische Wissenschaft': Zum Profilwandel der Jenaer Universität im Nationalsozialismus," in Hossfeld, ed., *"Im Dienst an Volk und Vaterland": Die Jenaer Universität in der NS-Zeit* (Cologne, 2005), 1–126

Houben, Heinrich Hubert, ed., *Damals in Weimar: Erinnerungen und Briefe von und an Johanna Schopenhauer* (Leipzig, 1924)

Huber, Ernst Rudolf, "Goethe und der Staat," *Das Innere Reich* 11 (1944): 1–19

Hünecke, Andreas, ed., *Oskar Schlemmer: Idealist der Form: Briefe, Tagebücher, Schriften, 1912–1943* (Leipzig, 1990)

Hufeland, Christoph Wilhelm, *Leibarzt und Volkserzieher: Selbstbiographie* (Stuttgart, 1937)

Hunstock, Sebastian, *Die (gross-)herzogliche Residenzstadt Weimar um 1800: Städtische Entwicklungen im Übergang von der ständischen zur bürgerlichen Gesellschaft (1770–1830)* (Jena, 2011)

Huschke, Wolfgang, "Einige orts- und familiengeschichtliche Betrachtungen über Goethes Weimar," in Walter Schlesinger, ed., *Festschrift für Friedrich von Zahn*, vol. 1 (Cologne, 1968), 539–97

Huschke, Wolfram, *Musik im klassischen und nachklassischen Weimar, 1756–1861* (Weimar, 1982)

Huschke, Wolfram, . . . *von jener Glut beseelt: Geschichte der Staatskapelle Weimar* (Jena, 2002)

Hüter, Karl-Heinz, *Das Bauhaus in Weimar: Studie zur gesellschaftspolitischen Geschichte einer deutschen Kunstschule* (Berlin, 1976)

Huth, Franz, *Aus dem Skizzenbuch meines Lebens: Begegnungen und Begebenheiten* (Weimar, 1966)

Immermann, Karl Leberecht, *Zwischen Poesie und Wirklichkeit: Tagebücher, 1831–1840* (Munich, 1984)

Irmscher, Hans Dietrich, *Johann Gottfried Herder* (Stuttgart, 2001)

Isaacs, Reginald R., *Walter Gropius: Der Mensch und sein Werk* (Berlin, 1983)

Itten, Johannes, *Design and Form: The Basic Course at the Bauhaus and Later* (New York, 1975)

Jäger, Ludwig, *Seitenwechsel: Der Fall Schneider/Schwerte und die Diskretion der Germanistik* (Munich, 1998)

Jäger, Manfred, *Kultur und Politik in der DDR, 1945–1990* (Cologne, 1995)

Jaeggi, Annemarie, "Ein geheimnisvolles Mysterium: Bauhütten-Romantik und Freimaurerei am frühen Bauhaus," in Christoph Wagner, ed., *Johannes Itten, Wassily Kandinsky, Paul Klee: Das Bauhaus und die Esoterik* (Bielefeld, 2005), 37–45

Jakobson, Hans-Peter, "'In Dornburg hoffe ich auf ungestörte Arbeitsjahre': Gerhard Marcks als Formmeister der Keramischen Werkstatt des Staatlichen Bauhauses Weimar," in Erik Stephan, ed., *Gerhard Marcks: Zwischen Bauhaus und Dornburger Atelier* (Jena, 2004), 21–27

James, Harold, *A German Identity, 1770–1990* (London, 1989)

Janka, Walter, *Spuren eines Lebens* (Berlin, 1991)

Jarausch, Konrad H., *After Hitler: Recivilizing Germans, 1945–1995* (New York, 2006)

Jasper, Willi, "Faust and the Germans," in Peter M. Daly, ed., *Why Weimar? Questioning the Legacy of Weimar from Goethe to 1999* (New York, 2003): 179–88

Jaspers, Karl, "Goethes Menschlichkeit" (1949) in Jaspers, *Rechenschaft und Ausblick: Reden und Aufsätze* (Munich, 1958), 59–80

Jaspers, Karl, *Unsere Zukunft und Goethe* (Zurich, 1948)

Jena, Detlef, *Das Weimarer Quartett: Die Fürstinnen Anna Amalia, Louise, Maria Pawlowna, Sophie* (Regensburg, 2007)

Jerger, Wilhelm, *Franz Liszts Klavierunterricht von 1884–1886: Dargestellt an den Tagebuchaufzeichnungen von August Göllerich* (Regensburg, 1975)

Joachim, Johannes/Andreas Moser, eds, *Briefe von und an Joseph Joachim*, vol. 1 (Berlin, 1911)

John, Hans, *Musikstadt Weimar* (Leipzig, 1985)

John, Jürgen, "Der NS-Gau Thüringen 1933 bis 1945: Grundzüge seiner Struktur- und Funktionsgeschichte," in Justus H. Ulbricht, ed., *Klassikerstadt und Nationalsozialismus: Kultur und Politik in Weimar, 1933 bis 1945* (Weimar, 2002), 25–52

Jonscher, Reinhard, "Grossherzog Alexander von Sachsen-Weimar-Eisenach (1853–1901): Politische Konstanzen und Wandlungen in einer fast fünfzigjährigen Regierungszeit," in Lothar Ehrlich/Justus H. Ulbricht, eds, *Carl Alexander von Sachsen-Weimar-Eisenach: Erbe, Mäzen und Politiker* (Cologne, 2004), 15–31

Jung, Hans Rudolf, ed., *Franz Liszt in seinen Briefen: Eine Auswahl* (Berlin, 1988)

Kafitz, Dieter, *Johannes Schlaf – Weltanschauliche Totalität und Wirklichkeitsblindheit: Ein Beitrag zur Neubestimmung des Naturalismus-Begriffs und zur Herleitung totalitärer Denkformen* (Tübingen, 1992)

Kahler, Manfred, "Jugend und Klassik: Ergebnisse und Erfahrungen der 'Weimartage der Jugend'," *Neue Museumskunde* 16 (1973): 253–59

[Kaiser, Fritz], *Führer durch die Ausstellung Entartete Kunst* (Berlin, [1937])

Kalckreuth, Johannes Graf von, *Wesen und Werk meines Vaters: Lebensbild des Malers Graf Leopold von Kalckreuth* (Hamburg, 1967)

Kandinsky, Nina, *Kandinsky und ich* (Bergisch Gladbach, 1978)

Kandinsky, Wassily, *Über das Geistige in der Kunst, insbesondere in der Malerei*, 2nd edn (Munich, 1912)

Kandinsky, Wassily/Franz Marc, eds, *Der Blaue Reiter* (Munich, 1976, 1st edn 1912)

Kapp, Julius, *Franz Liszt und die Frauen* (Leipzig, 1911)

Kater, Michael H., *Composers of the Nazi Era: Twelve Portraits* (New York, 2000)

Kater, Michael H., *Das "Ahnenerbe" der SS, 1935–1945: Ein Beitrag zur Kulturpolitik des Dritten Reiches*, 4th edn (Munich, 2006)

Kater, Michael H., "Die Artamanen – Völkische Jugend in der Weimarer Republik," *Historische Zeitschrift* 213 (1971): 577–638

Kater, Michael H., *Doctors under Hitler* (Chapel Hill, 1989)

Kater, Michael H., *Hitler Youth* (Cambridge, MA, 2004)

Kater, Michael H., *Never Sang for Hitler: The Life and Times of Lotte Lehmann, 1888–1976* (New York, 2008)

Kater, Michael H., *Studentenschaft und Rechtsradikalismus in Deutschland, 1918–1933: Eine sozial-geschichtliche Studie zur Bildungskrise in der Weimarer Republic* (Hamburg, 1975)

Kater, Michael H., *The Nazi Party: A Social Profile of Members and Leaders, 1919–1945* (Cambridge, MA, 1983)

Kater, Michael H., *The Twisted Muse: Musicians and their Music in the Third Reich* (New York, 1997)

Kaufmann, E., "Das flache Dach in seiner konstruktiven und wirtschaftlichen Wertung," *Bauwelt* 33 (1927): 806–10

Kershaw, Ian, *Hitler, 1889–1936: Hubris* (New York, 1999)

Kershaw, Ian, *Popular Opinion and Political Dissent in the Third Reich: Bavaria, 1933–1945* (Oxford, 1983)

Kershaw, Ian, *The End: The Defiance and Destruction of Hitler's Germany, 1944–1945* (New York, 2011)

Kessler, Harry Graf, *Der deutsche Künstlerbund* (Berlin, [1904])

Keyser, Erich, ed., *Deutsches Städtebuch: Handbuch städtischer Geschichte*, vol. 2 (Stuttgart, 1941)

Kielmansegg, Peter Graf, *Nach der Katastrophe: Eine Geschichte des geteilten Deutschland* (Berlin, 2000)

Kirsten, Holm, "*Weimar im Banne des Führers": Die Besuche Adolf Hitlers, 1925–1940* (Cologne, 2001)

Klauss, Jochen, *Alltag im "klassischen" Weimar, 1750–1850* (Weimar, 1990)

Klee, Ernst, *Das Kulturlexikon zum Dritten Reich: Wer war was vor und nach 1945* (Frankfurt am Main, 2007)

Klee, Ernst, *Das Personenlexikon zum Dritten Reich: Wer war was vor und nach 1945*, 3rd edn (Frankfurt am Main, 2011)

Klee, Paul, *Über die moderne Kunst*, 2nd edn (Berne, 1979)

Kleinschmidt, Erich, "Der vereinnahmte Goethe: Irrwege im Umgang mit einem Klassiker, 1932–1949," *Jahrbuch der Deutschen Schillergesellschaft* 28 (1984): 461–82

Klemperer, Victor, *So sitze ich denn zwischen allen Stühlen: Tagebücher, 1950–1959*, ed. Walter Nowojski, 2 vols, 2nd edn (Berlin, 1999)

Klessmann, Christoph, *Zwei Staaten, eine Nation: Deutsche Geschichte, 1955–1970*, 2nd edn (Bonn, 1997)

Klotz, Ernst E., *So nah der Heimat: Gefangen in Buchenwald, 1945–1948* (Bonn, 1992)

Knigge, Volkhard, "Im Schatten des Ettersberges: Von den Schwierigkeiten der Vernunft – Unbefragte Traditionen und Geschichtsbilder," in Knigge/Imanuel Baumann, eds, ". . . mitten im deutschen Volke": Buchenwald, Weimar und die nationalsozialistische Volksgemeinschaft* (Göttingen, 2008), 151–75

Knigge, Volkhard/Harry Stein, eds, *Franz Ehrlich: Ein Bauhäusler in Widerstand und Konzentrationslager* (Weimar, 2009)

Knoche, Michael, *Die Bibliothek brennt: Ein Bericht aus Weimar* (Göttingen, 2006)

Koch, Franz, *Geschichte deutscher Dichtung*, 4th edn (Hamburg, 1941)

Koch, Franz, *Goethe und die Juden* (Hamburg, 1937)

Kocka, Jürgen, *Civil Society and Dictatorship in Modern German History* (Hanover, NH, 2010)

Kogon, Eugen, *Der SS-Staat: Das System der deutschen Konzentrationslager* (Munich, 1974)

Köhler, Margot, *Weimar: Meine Stadt, mein Leben* (Weimar, 2001)

Kolloquium über Probleme der Goetheforschung, 31. Oktober bis 4. November 1960 in Weimar: Vorträge und Diskussionen (Weimar, 1960)

König, Christoph, ed., *Internationales Germanistenlexikon, 1800–1950*, 3 vols (Berlin, 2003)

König, Christoph/Eberhard Lämmert, eds, *Literaturwissenschaft und Geistesgeschichte, 1910 bis 1925* (Frankfurt am Main, 1993)

Konzentrationslager Buchenwald Post Weimar/Thür.: Katalog zu der Ausstellung aus der Deutschen Demokratischen Republik im Martin-Gropius-Bau Berlin (West), April–Juni 1990 (Buchenwald, 1990)

Koopmann, Helmut, *Goethe und Frau von Stein: Geschichte einer Liebe* (Munich, 2002)

Korrek, Norbert/Justus H. Ulbricht/Christiane Wolf, *Das Gauforum in Weimar: Ein Erbe des Dritten Reiches* (Weimar, 2001)

Kossel, Elmar, "Modernerezeption in der frühen Sowjetischen Besatzungszone/DDR," in Klaus-Jürgen Winkler, ed., *Neubeginn: Die Weimarer Bauhochschule nach dem Zweiten Weltkrieg und Hermann Henselmann* (Weimar, 2005), 107–19

Kossert, Andreas, *Kalte Heimat: Die Geschichte der deutschen Vertriebenen nach 1945*, 3rd edn (Munich, 2008)

Kowollik, Paul, *Das war das Konzentrationslager Buchenwald*, 2nd edn (Waldkirch, [1945])

Krakulec, Peter/Roland Schopf/Siegfried Wolf, *Buchenwald – Weimar: April 1945: Wann lernt der Mensch?* (Münster, 1994)

Krell, Max, *Das alles gab es einmal* (Frankfurt am Main, 1961)

Krenzlin, Leonore, *Gerhard Scholz und sein Kreis: Zum 100. Geburtstag des Mitbegründers der Literaturwissenschaft in der DDR* (Berlin, 2004)

Kriesche [Oberbaudirektor], *Die Stadt Weimar zur Zeit Goethes* (Weimar, 1909)

Krypczik, Kathrin/Bodo Ritscher, *Jede Krankheit konnte tödlich sein: Medizinische Versorgung, Krankheiten und Sterblichkeit im sowjetischen Speziallager Buchenwald, 1945–1950* (Göttingen, 2005)

Kuhn, Karl, *Aus dem alten Weimar: Skizzen und Erinnerungen* (Wiesbaden, 1905)

Kühn, Dieter, *Schillers Schreibtisch in Buchenwald: Bericht* (Frankfurt am Main, 2005)

Kühn, Paul, *Weimar*, 3rd edn, ed. Hans Wahl (Leipzig, 1921)

Kühnlenz, Fritz/Paul Messner, *Weimar*, 2nd edn (Berlin, 1983)

Küster, Bernd, *Max Liebermann: Ein Maler-Leben* (Hamburg, 1988)

Lachmund, Carl, *Mein Leben mit Franz Liszt: Aus dem Tagebuch eines Liszt-Schülers* (Eschwege, 1970)

Lämmert, Eberhard, et al., *Germanistik – eine deutsche Wissenschaft: Beiträge* (Frankfurt am Main, 1967)

Lang, Jochen von, *Der Sekretär: Martin Bormann, der Mann, der Hitler beherrschte* (Stuttgart, 1977)

Langenbucher, Hellmuth, *Deutsche Dichtung in Vergangenheit und Gegenwart* (Berlin, 1937)

Langenbucher, Hellmuth, *Friedrich Lienhard und sein Anteil am Kampf um die deutsche Erneuerung* (Hamburg, 1935)

Large, David Clay, *Berlin* (New York, 2000)

Ledebur, Ruth Freifrau von, *Der Mythos vom deutschen Shakespeare: Die Deutsche Shakespeare-Gesellschaft zwischen Politik und Wissenschaft, 1918–1945* (Cologne, 2002)

Leggewie, Claus, *Von Schneider zu Schwerte: Das ungewöhnliche Leben eines Mannes, der aus der Geschichte lernen wollte* (Munich, 1998)

Lenz, Fritz, "Günthers Berufung nach Jena," *Archiv für Rassen- und Gesellschaftsbiologie* 23 (1931): 337–39

Lenzer, Gudrun, *Frauen im Speziallager Buchenwald, 1945–1950: Internierung und lebensgeschichtliche Einordnung* (Münster, 1996)

Lepenies, Wolf, *Kultur und Politik: Deutsche Geschichten* (Munich, 2006)

Lienhard, Friedrich, *Ahasver am Rhein: Trauerspiel aus der Gegenwart in drei Aufzügen* (Stuttgart, 1914)

Lienhard, Friedrich, *Die Vorherrschaft Berlins: Litterarische Anregungen* (Leipzig, 1900)

Lienhard, Friedrich, *Nordlandslieder* (Strasbourg, 1900)

Lienhard, Friedrich, *Oberflächen-Kultur* (Stuttgart, 1904)

Linden, Walther, *Goethe und die deutsche Gegenwart* (Berlin, 1932)

Linden, Walther, *Goethes Leben und Werk* (Bielefeld, 1937)

Liszt, Franz, *Gesammelte Schriften*, ed. Lina Ramann, vols 4, 5 (Leipzig, 1882)

Litzmann, Berthold, *Ernst von Wildenbruch*, vol. 2 (Berlin, 1916)

Löwenberg, Dieter, "Willibald Hentschel (1858–1947): Seine Pläne zur Menschenzüchtung, sein Biologismus und Antisemitismus," MD dissertation (Mainz, 1978)

Loewenberg, Peter, "The *Bauhaus* as a Creative Playspace: Weimar, Dessau, Berlin, 1919–1933," *Annual of Psychoanalysis* 33 (2005): 209–26.

Longerich, Peter, *Heinrich Himmler: Biographie* (Munich, 2010)

Loos, Karina, "Das 'Gauforum' in Weimar: Vom bewusstlosen Umgang mit nationalsozialistischer Geschichte," in Detlev Heiden/Gunther Mai, eds, *Nationalsozialismus in Thüringen*
(Weimar, 1995), 333–47

Loose, Walter, ed., *Adolf Bartels: Festgabe zum achtzigsten Geburtstag: Drittes Bartels-Jahrbuch 1942*
(Neumünster, 1944)

Loose, Walter, ed., *Festgabe zum sechzigsten Geburtstag von Adolf Bartels* (Leipzig, 1922)

Lübbe, Peter, ed., *Dokumente zur Kunst-, Literatur- und Kulturpolitik der SED, 1975–1980*
(Stuttgart, 1984)

Luckhardt, Ulrich, *Lyonel Feiniger* (Munich, 1989)

Lukács, Georg, *Goethe und seine Zeit* (Berne, 1947)

Lützeler, Paul Michael, "Goethes Faust und der Sozialismus: Zur Rezeption des klassischen
Erbes in der DDR," in Reinhold Grimm/Jost Hermand, eds, *Basis: Jahrbuch für deutsche
Gegenwartsliteratur* 5 (1975): 31–54

MacMillan, Margaret, *Paris 1919: Six Months that Changed the World* (New York, 2001)

Macrakis, Kristie, *Seduced by Secrets: Inside the Stasi's Spy-Tech World* (New York, 2008)

Macrakis, Kristie, *Surviving the Swastika: Scientific Research in Nazi Germany* (New York, 1993)

Mahal, Günther, *Faust: Untersuchungen zu einem zeitlosen Thema* (Neuried, 1998)

Mahler-Werfel, Alma, *And the Bridge is Love* (New York, 1958)

Maier, Charles S., *Dissolution: The Crisis of Communism and the End of East Germany*
(Princeton, 1997)

Mandelkow, Karl Robert, "Die Goethe-Gesellschaft in Weimar als literaturwissenschaftliche
Institution," in Christoph König/Eberhard Lämmert, eds, *Literaturwissenschaft und
Geistesgeschichte, 1910 bis 1925* (Frankfurt am Main, 1993), 340–55

Mandelkow, Karl Robert, "Die literarische und kulturpolitische Bedeutung des Erbes," in
Hans-Jürgen Schmitt, ed., *Die Literatur der DDR* (Munich, 1983), 78–119

Mandelkow, Karl Robert, ed., *Goethe im Urteil seiner Kritiker: Dokumente zur Wirkungsgeschichte
in Deutschland*, vol. 4: *1918–1982* (Munich, 1984)

Mandelkow, Karl Robert, *Goethe in Deutschland: Rezeptionsgeschichte eines Klassikers*, vol. 1
(Munich, 1980)

Mandelkow, Karl Robert, *Goethe in Deutschland: Rezeptionsgeschichte eines Klassikers*, vol. 2
(Munich, 1989)

Mandelkow, Karl Robert, "Restauration oder Neuanfang? West-östliche Konfigurationen der
Goetherezeption im ersten Nachkriegsjahrzehnt," in Lothar Ehrlich/Gunther Mai, eds,
Weimarer Klassik in der Ära Ulbricht (Cologne, 2000), 135–49

Mann, Thomas, *Ansprache im Goethejahr 1949* (Weimar, 1949)

Mann, Thomas, *Betrachtungen eines Unpolitischen* (Berlin, 1918)

Mann, Thomas, *Doktor Faustus: Das Leben des deutschen Tonsetzer Adrian Leverkühn erzählt von
einem Freunde* (Frankfurt am Main, 1967)

Mann, Thomas, "Goethe und Tolstoi: Vortrag," *Deutsche Rundschau* 48, no. 6 (1922): 225–46

Mann, Thomas, *Lotte in Weimar: Roman* (Frankfurt am Main, 2008; 1st edn 1939)

Mann, Thomas, "Meine Goethereise" [1932], in Thomas Neumann, ed., *Quellen zur Geschichte
Thüringens: Kultur in Thüringen, 1919–1949* (Erfurt, 1998), 159–63

Mann, Thomas, *Von deutscher Republik* (Berlin, 1923)

Marchand, Suzanne, "Becoming Greek," in David E. Wellbery, ed., *A New History of German
Literature* (Cambridge, MA, 2004), 376–81

Marggraf, Wolfgang, *Franz Liszt in Weimar* (Weimar, 1985)

März, Roland, "Portrait eines Weltmannes: Edvard Munch malt Harry Graf Kessler in Weimar,"
in Rolf Bothe/Thomas Föhl, eds, *Aufstieg und Fall der Moderne* (Ostfildern-Ruit, 1999),
182–93

Mathieu, Gustave, "A Nazi Propaganda Directive on Goethe," *Publications of the English Goethe
Society* 22 (1953): 129–37

Matthes, Paul, *Persönliche Erinnerungen an S. Kgl. Hoheit Grossherzog Carl Alexander von Sachsen*
(Weimar, [1912])

Mauersberger, Volker, *Hitler in Weimar: Der Fall einer deutschen Kulturstadt* (Berlin, 1999)

Maurer, Doris, "Schiller auf der Bühne des Dritten Reiches," in Horst Claussen/Norbert Oellers,
eds, *Beschädigtes Erbe: Beiträge zur Klassikerrezeption in finsterer Zeit* (Bonn, 1984), 31–44

Mayer, Hans, *Ein Deutscher auf Widerruf: Erinnerungen*, 2 vols (Frankfurt am Main, 1982–84)

Mayer, Hans, "Goethe in unserer Zeit" (1949), in Werner Schubert, ed., *Weimar: Einblicke in die Geschichte einer europäischen Kulturstadt* (Leipzig, 1999), 311–29

Megargee, Geoffrey P., ed., *Encyclopedia of Camps and Ghettos, 1933–1945*, vol. 1 (Bloomington, IN, 2009)

Meinecke, Friedrich, *Die deutsche Katastrophe: Betrachtungen und Erinnerungen* (Wiesbaden, 1946)

Meissner, Otto, *Staatssekretär unter Ebert – Hindenburg – Hitler: Der Schicksalsweg des deutschen Volkes von 1918–1945, wie ich ihn erlebte* (Hamburg, 1950)

Merker, Matthias, *Zensur und Gleichschaltung: Thüringer Zeitungen zwischen 1933–1993: Dokumentation auf der Grundlage der Tagung vom 19. Juni 1993 im Pavillon Scherfgasse Weimar* (Weimar, 1993)

Merseburger, Peter, *Mythos Weimar: Zwischen Geist und Macht* (Stuttgart, 1998)

Messner, Paul, *Das Deutsche Nationaltheater Weimar: Ein Abriss seiner Geschichte von den Anfängen bis Februar 1945* (Weimar, 1985)

Messner, Paul, *Das Deutsche Nationaltheater Weimar: Ein Abriss seiner Geschichte: Zweiter Teil, 1945 bis 1985* (Weimar, 1988)

Meyer, Jochen, ed., *Briefe an Ernst Hardt: Eine Auswahl aus den Jahren 1898–1947* (Marbach, 1975)

Michalski, Gundula/Walter Steiner, *Die Weimarhalle: Bau- und Wirkungsgeschichte* (Weimar, 1994)

Minor, Ryan, *Choral Fantasies: Music, Festivity, and Nationhood in Nineteenth-Century Germany* (New York, 2012)

Möbius, Paul Julius, *Über das Pathologische bei Nietzsche* (Wiesbaden, 1902)

Mommsen, Hans, *Die verspielte Freiheit: Der Weg der Republik von Weimar in den Untergang, 1918 bis 1933* (Frankfurt am Main, 1990)

Mommsen, Hans, "The Dissolution of the Third Reich," in Frank Biess/Mark Roseman/Hanna Schissler, eds, *Conflict, Catastrophe and Continuity: Essays on Modern German History* (New York, 2007), 104–16

Mommsen, Wolfgang J., *Bürgerliche Kultur und künstlerische Avantgarde: Kultur und Politik im deutschen Kaiserreich, 1870 bis 1918* (Frankfurt am Main, 1994)

Mommsen, Wolfgang J., *Bürgerliche Kultur und politische Ordnung: Künstler, Schriftsteller und Intellektuelle in der deutschen Geschichte, 1830–1933* (Frankfurt am Main, 2000)

Moser, Andreas, *Joseph Joachim: A Biography (1831–1899)* (London, 1901)

Moser, Andreas, ed., *Johannes Brahms in Briefwechsel mit Joseph Joachim*, 2 vols (Berlin, 1908)

Mosse, George L., *The Crisis of German Ideology: Intellectual Origins of the Third Reich* (New York, 1964)

Muche, Georg, *Blickpunkt: Sturm, Dada, Bauhaus, Gegenwart* (Munich, 1961)

Mühlen, Patrik von zur, *Aufbruch und Umbruch in der DDR: Bürgerbewegungen, kritische Öffentlichkeit und Niedergang der SED-Herrschaft* (Bonn, 2000)

Müller, Erika/Harry Stein, *Jüdische Familien in Weimar vom 19. Jahrhundert bis 1945: Ihre Verfolgung und Vernichtung* (Weimar, 1998)

Müller, Hanno, ed., *Recht oder Rache: Buchenwald 1945–1950: Betroffene erinnern sich* (Frankfurt am Main, 1991)

Müller, Ulrike, ed., *Bauhaus Women: Art, Handicraft, Design* (Paris, 2009)

Müller-Enbergs, Helmut Jan Wielgohs/Dieter Hoffmann/Andreas Herbst/Ingrid Kirschey-Feix, eds, *Wer war wer in der DDR? Ein Lexikon ostdeutscher Biographien*, 2 vols., 5th edn (Berlin, 2010)

Müller-Krumbach, Renate, "Kessler und die Tradition: Aspekte zur Abdankung 1906," in Gerhard Neumann/Günter Schnitzler, eds, *Harry Graf Kessler: Ein Wegbereiter der Moderne* (Freiburg, 1997), 205–25

Müller-Seidel, Walter, *Die Geschichtlichkeit der deutschen Klassik: Literatur und Denkformen um 1800* (Stuttgart, 1983)

Naake, Erhard, *Nietzsche und Weimar: Werk und Wirkung im 20. Jahrhundert* (Cologne, 2000)

Nabbe, Hildegard, "Im Zeichen von Apollo und Dionysos: Harry Graf Kesslers Pläne für eine Nietzsche-Gedenkstätte in Weimar," *Seminar: A Journal of Germanic Studies* 32 (November 1996): 306–24

Nägele, Rainer, "Die Goethefeiern von 1932 und 1949," in Reinhold Grimm/Jost Hermand, eds, *Deutsche Feiern* (Wiesbaden, 1977), 97–122

Neliba, Günter, "Wilhelm Frick und Thüringen als Experimentierfeld für die nationalsozialistische Machtergreifung," in Detlev Heiden/Gunther Mai, eds, *Nationalsozialismus in Thüringen* (Weimar, 1995), 75–94

Ness, June L., ed., *Lyonel Feininger* (New York, 1974)

Neubert, Ehrhart/Thomas Auerbach, *"Es kann anders werden": Opposition und Widerstand in Thüringen, 1945–1989* (Cologne, 2005)

Neumann, Eckhard, *Bauhaus und Bauhäusler* (Cologne, 1985)

Neumann, Thomas, "'... der die idealen Triebe Ihrer Vorschläge vollauf zu würdigen weiss': Friedrich Lienhard und die Goethe-Gesellschaft," in Lothar Ehrlich/Jürgen John, eds, *Weimar 1930: Politik und Kultur im Vorfeld der NS-Diktatur* (Cologne, 1998), 185–210

Neumann, Thomas, "'Die Zukunft der Goethe-Gesellschaft erfüllt mich mit Sorge': Anmerkungen zur Diskussion um die Nachfolge Gustav Roethes," in Wolfgang Bialas/ Burkhard Stenzel, eds, *Die Weimarer Republik zwischen Metropole und Provinz: Intellektuellendiskurse zur politischen Kultur* (Weimar, 1996), 57–70

Newman, Ernest, *The Man Liszt: A Study of the Tragi-Comedy of a Soul Divided against Itself* (London, 1970; 1st edn 1934)

Nicolaisen, Dörte, "Otto Bartning und die Staatliche Bauhochschule in Weimar, 1926–1930," in Nicolaisen, ed., *Das andere Bauhaus: Otto Bartning und die Staatliche Bauhochschule Weimar, 1926–1930* (Berlin, 1997), 11–44

Niethammer, Lutz, ed., *Der "gesäuberte" Antifaschismus: Die SED und die roten Kapos von Buchenwald: Dokumente* (Berlin, 1994)

Nietzsche, Friedrich, *Der Wille zur Macht: Versuch einer Umwertung aller Werte* (Leipzig, 1930)

Nietzsche, Friedrich, *Menschliches, Allzumenschliches: Ein Buch für freie Geister* (n.p., 1999)

Nipperdey, Thomas, "Nationalidee und Nationaldenkmal in Deutschland im 19. Jahrhundert," *Historische Zeitschrift* 206 (1968): 529–85

Nissen, Benedikt Momme, *Meine Seele in der Welt: Bekenntnisbuch* (Freiburg, 1940)

Niven, Bill, *The Buchenwald Child: Truth, Fiction, and Propaganda* (Rochester, NY, 2007)

Nostitz, Helene von, *Aus dem alten Europa: Menschen und Städte*, ed. Oswalt von Nostitz (Frankfurt am Main, 1978)

Oberborbeck, Felix, "Volkslied und Rasse," *Völkische Musikerziehung* 3 (1936): 56–59

Ochs, Günter, *Meine gestohlene Zeit ...: 50 Jahre danach! Erlebnisse eines Jugendlichen am Ende des Weltkrieges: Gefangenschaft – Gefängnis – Straflager II – KZ Buchenwald*, 3rd edn (Darmstadt, 1996)

Oehler, Max, ed., *Den Manen Friedrich Nietzsches: Weimarer Weihgeschenke zum 75. Geburtstag der Frau Elisabeth Förster-Nietzsche* (Munich, [1921])

Oehler, Richard, *Die Zukunft der Nietzsche-Bewegung: Vortrag* (Leipzig, 1938)

Oehme, Walter, *Damals in der Reichskanzlei: Erinnerungen aus den Jahren 1918/1919* (Berlin, 1958)

Oehme, Walter, *Die Weimarer Nationalversammlung, 1919: Erinnerungen* (Berlin, 1962)

Oellers, Norbert, "Die Sophienausgabe als nationales Projekt," in Jochen Golz/Justus H. Ulbricht, eds, *Goethe in Gesellschaft: Zur Geschichte einer literarischen Vereinigung vom Kaiserreich bis zum geteilten Deutschland* (Cologne, 2005), 104–12

Oellers, Norbert, ed., *Schiller – Zeitgenosse aller Epochen: Dokumente zur Wirkungsgeschichte Schillers in Deutschland, Teil II: 1860–1966* (Munich, 1976)

Oellers, Norbert/Robert Steeger, *Weimar: Literatur und Leben zur Zeit Goethes*, 2nd edn (Stuttgart, 2009)

Offenberg, Gerhard, "Mosaik meines Lebens" (manuscript, Universitätsbibliothek, Bauhaus-Universität, Weimar, [1973])

Okrassa, Nina, *Peter Raabe: Dirigent, Musikschriftsteller und Präsident der Reichsmusikkammer (1872–1945)* (Cologne, 2004)

Okuda, Osamu, "'Diesseitig bin ich gar nicht fassbar' – Paul Klee und die Esoterik," in Christoph Wagner, ed., *Johannes Itten, Wassily Kandinsky, Paul Klee: Das Bauhaus und die Esoterik* (Bielefeld, 2005), 57–63

Olhoff, Gerhard, "Richard Strauss' Berufung nach Weimar," *Schweizerische Musikzeitung* 104, no. 3 (May/June 1964): 155–64
Orth, Karin, *Das System der nationalsozialistischen Konzentrationslager: Eine politische Organisationsgeschichte* (Hamburg, 1999)
Osborne, Harold, ed., *The Oxford Companion to Art* (Oxford, 1975)
Otremba, Heinz, *15 Jahrhunderte Würzburg: Eine Stadt und ihre Geschichte* (Würzburg, 1979)
Otto, Regine, "Goethe in Weimar – Realitäten, Hoffnungen und Enttäuschungen," in Thomas Jung/Birgit Mühlhaus, eds, *Über die Grenzen Weimars hinaus – Goethes Werk in europäischem Licht: Beiträge zum Jubiläumsjahr 1999* (Frankfurt am Main, 2000), 11–22
Overesch, Manfred, *Buchenwald und die DDR: Oder die Suche nach Selbstlegitimation* (Göttingen, 1995)
Overesch, Manfred, *Hermann Brill in Thüringen, 1895–1946: Ein Kämpfer gegen Hitler und Ulbricht* (Bonn, 1992)

Paret, Peter, *Art as History: Episodes in the Culture and Politics of Nineteenth-Century Germany* (Princeton, 1988)
Paret, Peter, *The Berlin Secession: Modernism and its Enemies in Imperial Germany* (Cambridge, MA, 1980)
Partei-Statistik, ed. Reichsorganisationsleiter der NSDAP, vol. 1 (Munich, [1935])
Passuth, Krisztina, *Moholy-Nagy* (London, 1985)
Pätzold, Kurt, *Die Geschichte kennt kein Pardon: Erinnerungen eines deutschen Historikers* (Berlin, 2008)
Peillex, Georges, *Nineteenth-Century Painting* (New York, 1964)
Penzler, Johannes, ed., *Die Reden Kaiser Wilhelms II*, vol. 3 (Leipzig, [1907])
Pese, Claus, "'Der Name Schultze-Naumburg ist Programm genug!' Paul Schultze-Naumburg in Weimar," in Rolf Bothe/Thomas Föhl, eds, *Aufstieg und Fall der Moderne* (Ostfildern-Ruit, 1999), 386–98
Peters, Heinz Frederick, *Zarathustras Schwester: Fritz und Lieschen Nietzsche – Ein deutsches Trauerspiel* (Munich, 1983)
Petersen, Ella, *Reiche Lebensjahre an der Seite eines Goetheforschers* (n.p., n.d.)
Petersen, Julius, *Die Sehnsucht nach dem Dritten Reich in deutscher Sage und Dichtung* (Stuttgart, 1934)
Petersen, Julius, *Drei Goethe-Reden* (Leipzig, 1942)
Petersen, Julius, "Erdentage und Ewigkeit: Rede bei der Gedächtnisfeier in Weimar am 22. März 1932," *Jahrbuch der Goethe-Gesellschaft* 18 (1932): 3–22
Pfister, Rudolf, "Die Staatliche Hochschule für Baukunst in Weimar," *Baumeister* 31, no. 11 (November 1933): 378–85
Piefel, Matthias, "Bruno Tanzmann: Ein völkischer Agitator zwischen wilhelminischem Kaiserreich und nationalsozialistischem Führerstaat," in Walter Schmitz/Clemens Vollnhals, eds, *Völkische Bewegung – Konservative Revolution – Nationalsozialismus* (Dresden, 2005), 255–80
Pike, David, *The Politics of Culture in Soviet-Occupied Germany, 1945–1949* (Stanford, 1992)
Piper, Ernst, *Alfred Rosenberg: Hitlers Chefideologe* (Munich, 2005)
Pleticha, Heinrich, ed., *Das klassische Weimar: Texte und Zeugnisse* (Munich, 1983)
Pocknell, Pauline, ed., *Franz Liszt and Agnes Street-Klindworth: A Correspondence, 1854–1886* (Hillsdale, NY, 2000)
Poller, Walter, *Arztschreiber in Buchenwald: Bericht des Häftlings 996 aus Block 39* (Hamburg, 1946)
Pongs, Hermann, *Schillers Urbilder* (Stuttgart, 1935)
Post, Bernhard, "'Weimarer gegen Weimar': Der Nationalsozialismus in Weimar," in Hans Wilderotter/Michael Dorrmann, eds, *Wege nach Weimar: Auf der Suche nach der Einheit von Kunst und Politik* (Berlin, 1999), 219–42
Post, Bernhard/Dietrich Werner, *Herrscher in der Zeitenwende: Wilhelm-Ernst von Sachsen-Weimar-Eisenach, 1876–1923* (Jena, 2006)
Post, Bernhard/Volker Wahl/Dieter Marek, *Thüringen-Handbuch: Territorium, Verfassung, Parlament, Regierung und Verwaltung in Thüringen, 1920 bis 1995* (Weimar, 1999)
Pöthe, Angelika, *Carl Alexander: Mäzen in Weimars "Silberner Zeit"* (Cologne, 1998)

Pöthe, Angelika, *Fin de siècle in Weimar: Moderne und Antimoderne, 1885 bis 1918* (Cologne, 2011)
Pöthe, Angelika, *Schloss Ettersburg: Weimars Geselligkeit und kulturelles Leben im 19. Jahrhundert* (Cologne, 1995)
Poutrus, Kirsten, "Von den Massenvergewaltigungen zum Mutterschutzgesetz: Abtreibungspolitik und Abtreibungspraxis in Ostdeutschland, 1945–1950," in Richard Bessel/Ralph Jessen, eds, *Die Grenzen der Diktatur: Staat und Gesellschaft in der DDR* (Göttingen, 1996), 170–98
Preiss, Achim, *Abschied von der Kunst des 20. Jahrhunderts* (Weimar, 1999)
Preiss, Achim, "Hochschulen in Weimar," in Preiss/Klaus-Jürgen Winkler, *Weimarer Konzepte: Die Kunst- und Bauhochschule, 1860–1995* (Weimar, 1996), 13–54
Preller, Friedrich, *Tagebücher des Künstlers* (Munich, 1904)
Protokoll der Verhandlungen des Ersten Kulturtages der Sozialistischen Einheitspartei Deutschlands, 5. bis 7. Mai 1948 in der Deutschen Staatsoper zu Berlin (Berlin, 1948)
Prümm, Karl, *Walter Dirks und Eugen Kogon als katholische Publizisten der Weimarer Republik* (Heidelberg, 1984)
Puttkamer, Wanda von, *Der Hof zu Weimar unter Grossherzog Carl Alexander und Grossherzogin Sophie: Erinnerungen aus den Jahren 1893–97* (Berlin, 1932)

Raabe, August, *Goethes Sendung im Dritten Reich* (Bonn, 1934)
Raabe, Peter, *Franz Liszt*, vol. 1 (Stuttgart, 1931)
Raabe, Peter, *Grossherzog Carl Alexander und Liszt* (Leipzig, 1918)
Raabe, Peter, *Kulturwille im deutschen Musikleben: Kulturpolitische Reden und Aufsätze* (Regensburg, 1935)
Raeff, Marc, *Imperial Russia, 1682–1825: The Coming of the Age of Modern Russia* (New York, 1971)
Ragwitz, Renate/Jens Riederer, *350 Jahre Zwiebelmarkt: Von der Ersterwähnung 1653 bis 2003* (Weimar, 2003)
Ramann, Lina, *Lisztiana: Erinnerungen an Franz Liszt in Tagebuchblättern, Briefen und Dokumenten aus den Jahren 1873–1886/87*, ed. Arthur Seidl (Mainz, 1983)
Raschdau, Ludwig, *In Weimar als Preussischer Gesandter: Ein Buch der Erinnerungen an Deutsche Fürstenhöfe, 1894–1897* (Berlin, 1939)
Rasche, Rosalinde, ed., *Europäische Provinz Weimar: Stadtsoziologische Betrachtungen* (Weimar, 1992)
Rassloff, Steffen, *Friedliche Revolution und Landesgründung in Thüringen, 1989/90* (Erfurt, 2009)
Rassloff, Steffen, *Fritz Sauckel: Hitlers "Muster-Gauleiter" und "Sklavenhalter"* (Erfurt, 2007)
Raupp, Wilhelm, *Eugen d'Albert: Ein Künstler- und Menschenschicksal* (Leipzig, 1930)
Redslob, Edwin, *Von Weimar nach Europa: Erlebtes und Durchdachtes* (Jena, 1998)
Reif, Heinz, *Adel im 19. und 20. Jahrhundert* (Munich, 1999)
Reinhardt, Rudolf, *Zeitungen und Zeiten: Journalist im Berlin der Nachkriegszeit* (Cologne, 1988)
Reuter, Gabriele, *Vom Kinde zum Menschen: Die Geschichte meiner Jugend* (Berlin, 1921)
Richter, Lutz, ed., *Johann Gottfried Herder im Spiegel seiner Zeitgenossen: Briefe und Selbstzeugnisse* (Göttingen, 1978)
Riedel, Manfred, *Nietzsche in Weimar: Ein deutsches Drama* (Leipzig, 1997)
Riederer, Jens, "Weimars Grösse – statistisch: Eine quellenkritische Untersuchung zur Zahl seiner Einwohner zwischen 1640 und 1840," *Weimar-Jena: Die grosse Stadt* 3, no. 2 (2010): 87–116
Ritscher, Bodo, ed. *Das Sowjetische Speziallager Nr. 2 (1945–1950): Katalog zur ständigen historischen Ausstellung* (Göttingen, 1999)
Ritter, Gerhard A., *Der Preis der deutschen Einheit: Die Wiedervereinigung und die Krise des Sozialstaats* (Munich, 2006)
Roemer, Nils, *German City, Jewish Memory: the Story of Worms* (Waltham, MA, 2010)
Roethe, Gustav, *Deutsche Reden* (Leipzig, n.d.)
Roethe, Gustav, *Von deutscher Art und Kultur* (Berlin, 1915)
Rössner, Alf, "Weimar, Wartburg, Windhuk – Carl Alexanders 'warmes Herz' für die deutsche Kolonialpolitik," in Lothar Ehrlich/Justus H. Ulbricht, eds, *Carl Alexander von Sachsen-Weimar-Eisenach: Erbe, Mäzen und Politiker* (Cologne, 2004), 47–90
Rosenberg, Alfred, *Der Mythus des 20. Jahrhunderts: Eine Wertung der seelisch-geistigen Gestaltenkämpfe unserer Zeit*, 42nd edn (Munich, 1934; 1st edn 1930)

Rosenberg, Alfred, *Friedrich Nietzsche* (Munich, 1944)

Ross, Alex, *The Rest is Noise: Listening to the Twentieth Century* (New York, 2007)

Rost, Christine/Christiane Backhaus, "Die Stadt Weimar um 1800: Vitalstatistische Entwicklungen und demographische Trends zwischen 1770 und 1820," in Klaus Ries, ed., *Zwischen Hof und Stadt: Aspekte der kultur- und sozialgeschichtlichen Entwicklung der Residenzstadt Weimar um 1800* (Weimar, 2007), 27–57

Roth, Silke, "Goethe and Buchenwald: Re-Constructing German National Identity in the Weimar Year 1999," in Peter M. Daly, ed., *Why Weimar? Questioning the Legacy of Weimar from Goethe to 1999* (New York, 2003), 93–106

Rotzler, Willy, ed., *Johannes Itten: Werke und Schriften* (Zurich, 1972)

Ruehl, Martin A., "A Master from Germany: Thomas Mann, Albrecht Dürer, and the Making of a National Icon," *Oxford German Studies* 38 (2009): 61–106

Runkel, Ferdinand, ed., *Böcklin Memoiren: Tagebuchblätter von Böcklins Gattin Angela* (Berlin, 1910)

Ruppelt, Georg, *Schiller im nationalsozialistischen Deutschland: Der Versuch einer Gleichschaltung* (Stuttgart, 1979)

Rüss, Kurt, ed., *Dokumente und Materialien zur Geschichte der Arbeiterbewegung in Weimar* (Weimar, 1976)

Safranski, Rüdiger, *Friedrich Schiller, oder: Die Erfindung des Deutschen Idealismus* (Munich, 2004)

Safranski, Rüdiger, *Goethe und Schiller: Geschichte einer Freundschaft* (Munich, 2009)

Saller, Karl, *Die Rassenlehre des Nationalsozialismus in Wissenschaft und Propaganda* (Darmstadt, 1961)

Salomon, Franz von, *Die Geächteten* (Berlin, 1931)

Sangalli, Elisabeth, *Weimar* (Leipzig, 1855)

Satjukow, Silke, *Befreiung? Die Ostdeutschen und 1945* (Leipzig, 2009)

Satjukow, Silke, *Besatzer: "Die Russen" in Deutschland, 1945–1994* (Göttingen, 2008)

Satjukow, Silke, ed., *"Die Russen kommen!" Erinnerungen an sowjetische Soldaten, 1945–1992* (Erfurt, 2005)

Satjukow, Silke, ed., *"Nach Drüben": Deutsch-deutsche Alltagsgeschichten, 1989–2005* (Erfurt, 2006)

Sauckel, Fritz, "Das alte und das neue Weimar," *Der Deutsche Baumeister* 2, no. 4 (April 1940): 3–4

Sauckel, Fritz, ed., *Der Führer in Weimar, 1925–1938* (Leipzig, 1938)

Sauckel, Fritz, *Kampf und Sieg in Thüringen* (Weimar, 1934)

Schädlich, Christian, *Die Hochschule für Architektur und Bauwesen Weimar: Ein geschichtlicher Abriss* (Weimar, 1985)

Scharfschwerdt, Jürgen, "Die Klassik-Ideologie in der Kultur-, Wissenschafts- und Literaturpolitik," in Hans-Jürgen Schmitt, ed., *Einführung in Theorie, Geschichte und Funktion der DDR-Literatur* (Stuttgart, 1975), 109–63

Schaumburg-Lippe, Friedrich Christian Prinz zu, *Verdammte Pflicht und Schuldigkeit: Weg und Erlebnis, 1914–1933* (Leoni, 1966)

Scheer, [Reinhard], *Deutschlands Hochseeflotte im Weltkrieg: Persönliche Erinnerungen*, 3rd edn (Berlin, 1920)

Scheffler, Karl, *"Die fetten und die mageren Jahre": Ein Arbeits- und Lebensbericht* (Munich, 1946)

Scheidig, Walther, *Bauhaus Weimar, 1919–1924: Werkstattarbeiten* (Leipzig, 1966)

Scheidig, Walther, *Die Weimarer Malerschule, 1860–1900* (Leipzig, 1991)

Schilling, Willy, "Die Sauckel-Marschler-Regierung und das Ende des Parlamentarismus in Thüringen 1932/33," in *Zwischen Landesgründung und Gleichschaltung: Die Regierungsbildungen in Thüringen seit 1920 und das Ende der parlamentarischen Demokratie 1932/33* (Rudolstadt, 2001), 43–174

Schirach, Baldur von, *Ich glaubte an Hitler* (Hamburg, 1967)

Schirach, Baldur von, *Revolution der Erziehung: Reden aus den Jahren des Aufbaus*, 2nd edn (Munich, 1939)

Schlaf, Johannes, *Aus meinem Leben: Erinnerungen* (Halle, [1941])

Schlaf, Johannes, *Das dritte Reich: Ein Berliner Roman* (Berlin, 1900)

Schlaf, Johannes, *Der Kleine: Ein Berliner Roman in drei Büchern* (Stuttgart, 1904)

Schlaf, Johannes, "Deutschlands Weltaufgabe," *Der Hochwart* 2, no. 12 (1932): 233–37

Schlaf, Johannes, "Die deutsche Aufgabe," *Berliner Romantik* 1, no. 4 (1919): 1–4

Schlaf, Johannes, *Die Suchenden: Roman* (Berlin, 1902)

Schlaf, Johannes, *Mutter Lise: Roman* (Berlin, n.d.)

Schlaf, Johannes, *Vom Krieg, vom Frieden und dem Irrtum des Pazifismus* (Munich, 1918)

Schleif, Walter, *Goethes Diener* (Berlin, 1965)

Schlemmer, Oskar, et al., *Die Bühne im Bauhaus* (Mainz, 1965; 1st edn 1925)

Schlenker, Wolfram, *Das "Kulturelle Erbe" in der DDR: Gesellschaftliche Entwicklung und Kulturpolitik, 1945–1965* (Stuttgart, 1977)

Schley, Jens, *Nachbar Buchenwald: Die Stadt Weimar und ihr Konzentrationslager, 1937–1945* (Cologne, 1999)

Schlittgen, Hermann, *Erinnerungen* (Munich, 1926)

Schlösser, Rainer, *Das Volk und seine Bühne: Bemerkungen zum Aufbau des deutschen Theaters* (Berlin, 1935)

Schmidt, Eva, *Jüdische Familien im Weimar der Klassik und Nachklassik: In Memoriam Dr. Else Behrend-Rosenfeld* (Weimar, 1993)

Schmidt, Helmut, *Handeln für Deutschland: Wege aus der Krise* (Berlin, 1993)

Schmidt-Bergmann, Hansgeorg, "Stationen des Scheiterns: Joseph Victor von Scheffel, Carl Alexander und der 'Wartburg-Roman'," in Lothar Ehrlich/Justus H. Ulbricht, eds, *Carl Alexander von Sachsen-Weimar-Eisenach: Erbe, Mäzen und Politiker* (Cologne, 2004), 217–27

Schmidt-Möbus, Friederike/Frank Möbus, *Kleine Kulturgeschichte Weimars* (Cologne, 1998)

Schmuhl, Hans-Walter, *Grenzüberschreitungen: Das Kaiser-Wilhelm-Institut für Anthropologie, menschliche Erblehre und Eugenik, 1927–1945* (Göttingen, 2005)

Schmuhl, Hans-Walter, *Rassenhygiene, Nationalsozialismus, Euthanasie: Von der Verhütung zur Vernichtung "lebensunwerten Lebens," 1890–1945* (Göttingen, 1987)

Schneede, Uwe M., ed., *Die Zwanziger Jahre: Manifeste und Dokumente deutscher Künstler* (Cologne, 1979)

Schneider, Wolfgang, *Weimar: Historischer Überblick* (Weimar, 1976)

Scholz, Rüdiger, *Das kurze Leben der Johanna Catharina Höhn: Kindesmorde und Kindesmörderinnen im Weimar Carl Augusts und Goethes: Die Akten zu den Fällen Johanna Catharina Höhn, Sophia Rost und Margarethe Dorothea Altwein* (Würzburg, 2004)

Scholz, Rüdiger, *Die beschädigte Seele des grossen Mannes: Goethes "Faust" und die bürgerliche Gesellschaft*, 2nd edn (Rheinfelden, 1995)

Scholz, Wilhelm von, *An Ilm und Isar: Lebenserinnerungen* (Leipzig, 1939)

Scholz, Wilhelm von, *Der Jude von Konstanz: Tragödie in vier Aufzügen mit einem Nachspiel* (Munich, 1905)

Schönberg, Arnold, "Das Verhältnis zum Text," in Wassily Kandinsky/Franz Marc, eds, *Der Blaue Reiter* (Munich 1976; 1st edn 1912), 27–32

Schönberg, Arnold, *4 Lieder für eine Singstimme und Klavier, op. 2* (Berlin, n.d.)

Schorn, Adelheid von, *Das nachklassische Weimar unter der Regierungszeit Karl Friedrichs und Maria Pawlownas* (Weimar, 1911)

Schorn, Adelheid von, *Das nachklassische Weimar: Zweiter Teil: Unter der Regierungszeit von Karl Alexander und Sophie* (Weimar, 1912)

Schorn, Adelheid von, *Zwei Menschenalter* (Berlin, 1901)

Schott, Georg, *Goethes Faust in heutiger Schau* (Stuttgart, 1940)

Schremmer, Ernst, ed., *Buch des Dankes: Bruno Brehm zum fünfzigsten Geburtstag* (Karlsbad, 1942)

Schreyer, Lothar, *Erinnerungen an Sturm und Bauhaus: Was ist des Menschen Bild?* (Munich, 1956)

Schreyer, Lothar, *Texte des Glaubens* (Lewiston, NY, 2006)

Schrickel, Leonhard, *Geschichte des Weimarer Theaters von seinen Anfängen bis heute* (Weimar, 1928)

Schrimpf, Hans-Joachim, ed., *Literatur und Gesellschaft vom neunzehnten ins zwanzigste Jahrhundert* (Bonn, 1963)

Schröder, Jürgen, "Die DDR und die deutsche Klassik," in Jens Hacker/Horst Rögner-Francke, eds, *Die DDR und die Tradition* (Heidelberg, 1981), 57–78

Schroeder, Klaus, *Der SED-Staat: Partei, Staat und Gesellschaft, 1949–1990* (Munich, 1998)

Schröer, Helmut/Hans-Günther Lanfer, eds, *Ohne Städte ist kein Staat zu machen: Trier-Weimar, eine deutsche Partnerschaft* (Trier, 1992)

Schrul, Marco, "Die Umweltgeschichte der Stadt im Zeitalter der industriellen Revolution: Entwicklungen, Konflikte und Akteure in Apolda, Jena und Weimar, 1850–1905," PhD dissertation (Jena, 2008)

Schrumpf, Ernst, *Der nationale Goethe: Ein Wegweiser für unsere Tage* (Munich, 1927)

Schuh, Willi, ed., *Richard Strauss: Briefe an die Eltern, 1882–1906* (Zurich, 1954)

Schuh, Willi, *Richard Strauss: Jugend und frühe Meisterjahre: Lebenschronik, 1864–1898* (Zurich, 1976)

Schuh, Willi/Franz Trenner, eds, *Hans von Bülow and Richard Strauss: Correspondence* (London, 1953)

Schulmeister, Karl Heinz, *Begegnungen im Kulturbund* (Berlin, 2011)

Schultz, Maria, "Zwischen Kultur und Politik: Die Hauptversammlungen der Goethe-Gesellschaft in den Jahren 1954 bis 1960 als Orte deutsch-deutscher Auseinandersetzungen," in Jochen Golz/Justus H. Ulbricht, eds, *Goethe in Gesellschaft: Zur Geschichte einer literarischen Vereinigung vom Kaiserreich bis zum geteilten Deutschland* (Cologne, 2005), 157–81

Schultze-Naumburg, Paul, "Die internationale Kunstausstellung in Dresden in rassenhygienischer Betrachtung," *Archiv für Rassen- und Gesellschaftsbiologie* 18 (1926): 440–42

Schultze-Naumburg, Paul, *Flaches oder geneigtes Dach? Mit einer Rundfrage an deutsche Architekten und deren Antworten* (Berlin, 1927)

Schultze-Naumburg, Paul, *Kunst und Rasse*, 3rd edn (Munich, 1938; 1st edn 1928)

Schulze, Martin, *Nationalsozialistische Tätigkeit in Thüringen, 1932–1935* (Weimar, [1935])

Schüssler, Susanne, *Ernst Hardt: Eine monographische Studie* (Frankfurt am Main, 1994)

Schwabe, Johann Samuel Gottlob, *Selbstbiographie* (Weimar, [1820])

Schwerte, Hans, *Faust und das Faustische: Ein Kapitel deutscher Ideologie* (Stuttgart, 1962)

Seela, Reyk, *Die Ärzteschaft in Thüringen: Eine Vereins- und Standesgeschichte* (Jena, 2000)

Seeliger, Rolf, ed., *Braune Universität*, 6 vols (Munich, 1964–68)

Seemann, Annette, *Weimar: Eine Kulturgeschichte* (Munich, 2012)

Seemann, Hellmut Th., ed., *Anna Amalia, Carl August und das Ereignis Weimar* (Göttingen, 2007)

Segal, Joes, "Artistic Style, Canonization, and Idemnity Politics in Cold War Germany, 1947–1960," in Annette Vowinckel et al., eds, *Cold War Cultures: Perspectives on Eastern and Western European Societies* (New York, 2012), 235–53

Seibold, Wolfgang, *Robert und Clara Schumann in ihren Beziehungen zu Franz Liszt im Spiegel ihrer Korrespondenz und Schriften*, vol. 1 (Frankfurt am Main, 2005)

Seibt, Gustav, *Goethe und Napoleon: Eine historische Begegnung* (Munich, 2008)

Semprún, Jorge, *Was für ein schöner Sonntag!* (Frankfurt am Main, 1991)

Sengle, Friedrich, *Neues zu Goethe: Essays und Vorträge* (Stuttgart, 1989)

Sharples, Caroline, *West Germans and the Nazi Legacy* (New York, 2012)

Sheehan, James J., *German History, 1770–1866* (Oxford, 1989)

Shirer, Robert K., "Johannes R. Becher, 1891–1958," *German Language and Literature Papers* 3 (2000): 1–5

Simon, Hans-Ulrich, ed., *Eberhard von Bodenhausen Harry Graf Kessler: Ein Briefwechsel, 1894–1918* (Marbach, 1978)

Sinn, Hans-Werner, *Can Germany be Saved? The Malaise of the World's First Welfare State* (Cambridge, MA, 2007)

Smith, Arthur L., Jr., *Die "Hexe von Buchenwald": Der Fall Ilse Koch* (Cologne, 1983)

Snyder, Timothy, *Bloodlands: Europe between Hitler and Stalin* (New York, 2010)

Sommer, Theo, ed., *Reise ins andere Deutschland* (Reinbek, 1989)

Speer, Albert, *Erinnerungen*, 8th edn (Frankfurt am Main, 1970)

Spengler, Oswald, *Der Untergang des Abendlandes: Umrisse einer Morphologie der Weltgeschichte*, vol. 1 (Vienna, 1918)

Spitzer, Leo, "Zum Goethekult," *Die Wandlung* 4 (1949): 581–92

Spotts, Frederic, *Bayreuth: A History of the Wagner Festival* (New Haven, 1994)

Spotts, Frederic, *Hitler and the Power of Aesthetics* (Woodstock, NY, 2003)

Spotts, Frederic, *The Shameful Peace: How French Artists and Intellectuals survived the Nazi Occupation* (New Haven, 2008)

Sprecher, Thomas/Hans Rudolf Vaget/Cornelia Bernini, eds, *Thomas Mann: Briefe II, 1914–1923* (Frankfurt am Main, 2004)

Sprecher, Thomas/Hans Rudolf Vaget/Cornelia Bernini, eds, *Thomas Mann: Briefe III, 1924–1932* (Frankfurt am Main, 2011)

Srbik, Heinrich Ritter von, "Goethe und das Reich," *Goethea: Neue Folge des Jahrbuchs der Goethe-Gesellschaft* 4 (1939): 211–32

Staadt, Jochen, "'Auf den Zinnen der Partei': Die SED-Führung plante 1967 eine Spaltung der Goethe-Gesellschaft," in Jochen Golz/Justus H. Ulbricht, eds, *Goethe in Gesellschaft: Zur Geschichte einer literarischen Vereinigung vom Kaiserreich bis zum geteilten Deutschland* (Cologne, 2005), 183–202

Staatliche Bauhochschule Weimar: Aufbau und Ziel (Weimar, 1927)

Staatliches Bauhaus Weimar, 1919–1923, ed. Karl Nierendorf (Munich, 1980)

Stadler-Stölzl, Gunta, "In der Textilwerkstatt des Bauhauses, 1919 bis 1931," *Werk* 11 (1968): 744–46

Stahr, Adolf, *Weimar und Jena*, vol. 1, 3rd edn (Oldenburg, 1892)

Staritz, Dietrich, *Geschichte der DDR*, 2nd edn (Frankfurt am Main, 1996)

Statistisches Jahrbuch für das Deutsche Reich, ed. Statistisches Reichsamt (Berlin, 1923)

Statistisches Jahrbuch für das Deutsche Reich, ed. Statistisches Reichsamt (Berlin, 1938)

Steckner, Cornelius, *Der Bildhauer Adolf Brütt: Schleswig-Holstein, Berlin, Weimar: Autobiographie und Werkverzeichnis* (Heide, 1989)

Stein, Eberhard, *"Sorgt dafür, dass sie die Mehrheit nicht hinter sich kriegen!" MfS und SED im Bezirk Erfurt* (Berlin, 1999)

Stein, Harry, "Eine Stadt für die SS: Die Errichtung des Konzentrationslagers Buchenwald," in Volkhard Knigge/Imanuel Baumann, eds, *". . . mitten im deutschen Volke": Buchenwald, Weimar und die nationalsozialistische Volksgemeinschaft* (Göttingen, 2008), 12–32

Stein, Harry, "Juden im Konzentrationslager Buchenwald, 1938–1942," in Thomas Hofmann/ Hanno Loewy/Stein, eds, *Pogromnacht und Holocaust: Frankfurt, Weimar, Buchenwald. . .: Die schwierige Erinnerung an die Stationen der Vernichtung* (Weimar, 1994), 81–171

Steiner, Rudolf, *Friedrich Nietzsche: Ein Kämpfer gegen seine Zeit* (Dornach, 1963)

Steiner, Rudolf, *Mein Lebensgang: Eine nicht vollendete Autobiographie* (Dornach, 1990)

Steiner, Walter, et al., *Weimar 1945: Ein historisches Protokoll* (Weimar, 1997)

Steiner, Walter/Uta Kühn-Stillmark, *Friedrich Justin Bertuch: Ein Leben im klassischen Weimar zwischen Kultur und Kommerz* (Cologne, 2001)

Steinfeld, Thomas, *Weimar* (Stuttgart, 1998)

Steinweis, Alan E., "Weimar Culture and the Rise of National Socialism: The *Kampfbund für deutsche Kultur*," *Central European History* 24 (1991): 402–23

Stenzel, Burkhard, "'. . . Die deusche Kunst zu säubern'," *Weimar Kultur Journal* 4 (1996): 26–27

Stenzel, Burkhard, "'Pg. Goethe'? Vom politischen und philologischen Umgang mit einem Weimarer Klassiker," in Lothar Ehrlich/Jürgen John/Justus H. Ulbricht, eds, *Das Dritte Weimar: Klassik und Kultur im Nationalsozialismus* (Cologne, 1999), 219–43

Stenzel, Burkhard/Klaus-Jürgen Winkler, *Kontroversen und Kulturpolitik im Thüringer Landtag 1920–1933: Ein Beitrag des Thüringer Landtages zum Europäischen Kulturjahr 1999* (Weimar, 1999)

Stephan, Erik, "Zwischen Bauhaus und Dornberger Atelier: Gerhard Marcks in Thüringen," in Stephan, ed., *Gerhard Marcks: Zwischen Bauhaus und Dornburger Atelier* (Jena, 2004), 9–13

Stern, Fritz, *Five Germanys I Have Known* (New York, 2007)

Stern, Fritz, *The Politics of Cultural Despair: A Study in the Rise of the German Ideology* (Garden City, NY, 1965)

Stockhorst, Erich, *Fünftausend Köpfe: Wer war was im Dritten Reich* (Velbert, 1967)

Stradal, August, *Erinnerungen an Franz Liszt* (Berne, 1929)

Stravinsky, Igor, *An Autobiography* (New York, 1962; 1st edn 1936)

Strohmeyer, Arn, *Der Mitläufer: Manfred Hausmann und der Nationalsozialismus* (Bremen, 1999)

Strubelt, Wendelin, ed., *Jena, Dessau, Weimar: Städtebilder der Transformation, 1988–1990, 1995–1996* (Opladen, 1997)

Stuckenschmidt, Hans Heinz, *Musik am Bauhaus* (Berlin, 1978/79)

Stutz, Rüdiger, "Weimar als 'Stadt der Arbeit': Fritz Sauckel und die Gustloff-Werke," in Volkhard Knigge/Imanuel Baumann, eds, *". . . mitten im deutschen Volke": Buchenwald, Weimar und die nationalsozialistische Volksgemeinschaft* (Göttingen, 2008), 89–101

Tanzmann, Bruno, "Adolf Bartels und das Bauerntum," in Walter Loose, ed., *Festgabe zum sechzigsten Geburtstag von Adolf Bartels* (Leipzig, 1922)

Taube, Otto Freiherr von, *Wanderjahre: Erinnerungen aus meiner Jugendzeit* (Stuttgart, 1950)

Taylor, Ronald, *Robert Schumann: His Life and Work* (New York, 1982)

Thamer, Hans-Ulrich, "Geschichte und Propaganda: Kulturhistorische Ausstellungen in der NS-Zeit," *Geschichte und Gesellschaft* 24 (1998): 349–81

Thüna, Freiherr Lothar von, *Weimarische und andere Erinnerungen, 1868–1883, namentlich an Grossherzog Carl Alexander* (Weimar 1912)

Timpel, Claudia/Stefan Schäfer, ... *dich brenn' ich eigenhändig an ...: Buchenwald – Kristallisationspunkt für Extremisten?* (Erfurt, 1998)

Tjulpanow, Sergej, *Deutschland nach dem Kriege (1945–1949): Erinnerungen eines Offiziers der Sowjetarmee*, ed. Stefan Doernberg, 2nd edn (Berlin, 1987)

Totok, William, "'Die Finger zu rostigen Krallen gebogen': Heinrich Zillich und die Topographie der Verdrängung," *Halbjahresschrift für osteuropäische Geschichte, Literatur und Politik* 5, no. 1 (1993): 57–72

Tracey, Donald R., "Der Aufstieg der NSDAP bis 1930," in Detlev Heiden/Gunther Mai, eds, *Nationalsozialismus in Thüringen* (Weimar, 1995), 49–72

Trommler, Frank, "A Command Performance? The Many Faces of Literature under Nazism," in Jonathan Huener/Francis R. Nicosia, eds, *The Arts in Nazi Germany: Continuity, Conformity, Change* (New York, 2007), 111–33

Trommler, Frank, "Die Kulturpolitik der DDR und die kulturelle Tradition des deutschen Sozialismus," in Peter Uwe Hohendahl/Patricia Herminghouse, eds, *Literatur und Literaturtheorie in der DDR* (Frankfurt am Main, 1976), 13–72

Trommler, Frank, "Prosaentwicklung und Bitterfelder Weg," in Hans-Jürgen Schmitt, ed., *Einführung in Theorie, Geschichte und Funktion der DDR-Literatur* (Stuttgart, 1975), 293–327

Uecker, Günther, ed., *Kulturverlust: Ausstellung im Deutschen Nationaltheater Weimar, 11. Mai bis 7. Juli 2002: Die Vertreibung und Ermordung jüdischer Musiker des Deutschen Nationaltheaters Weimar während der NS-Zeit* (Weimar, 2002)

Ulbricht, Justus H., "'Deutsche Renaissance': Weimar und die Hoffnung auf die kulturelle Regeneration Deutschlands zwischen 1900 und 1933," in Jürgen John/Volker Wahl, eds, *Zwischen Konvention und Avantgarde: Doppelstadt Jena-Weimar* (Weimar, 1995), 191–208

Ulbricht, Justus H., "Fragmentarische Erinnerung – Weimar 1933 bis 1945," in Ulbricht, ed., *Klassikerstadt und Nationalsozialismus: Kultur und Politik in Weimar, 1933 bis 1945* (Weimar, 2002), 6–24

Ulbricht, Justus H., "'Goethe und Bismarck': Varianten eines deutschen Deutungsmusters," in Lothar Ehrlich/Ulbricht, eds, *Carl Alexander von Sachsen-Weimar-Eisenach: Erbe, Mäzen und Politiker* (Cologne, 2004), 91–128

Ulbricht, Justus H., "Kulturrevolution von rechts: Das völkische Netzwerk, 1900–1930," in Detlev Heiden/Gunther Mai, eds, *Nationalsozialismus in Thüringen* (Weimar, 1995), 29–48

Ulbricht, Justus H., "'Wege nach Weimar' und 'deutsche Wiedergeburt': Visionen kultureller Hegemonie im völkischen Netzwerk Thüringens zwischen Jahrhundertwende und 'Drittem Reich,'" in Wolfgang Bialas/Burkhard Stenzel, eds, *Die Weimarer Republik zwischen Metropole und Provinz: Intellektuellendiskurse zur politischen Kultur* (Weimar, 1996), 23–35

Ulbricht, Justus H., "Willkomm und Abschied des Bauhauses in Weimar: Eine Rekonstruktion," *Zeitschrift für Geschichtswissenschaft* 46 (1998): 5–27

Um ein antifaschistisch-demokratisches Deutschland: Dokumente aus den Jahren 1945–1949, ed. Gennadii Aleksandrovich Belov (Berlin, 1968)

Unseld, Siegfried, *Goethe und seine Verleger* (Frankfurt am Main, 1991)

Uthemann, Ernest W., ed., *Johannes Itten: Alles in Einem, alles in Sein* (Ostfildern-Ruit, 2003)

Vaget, Hans Rudolf, *Dilettantismus und Meisterschaft: Zum Problem des Dilettantismus bei Goethe: Praxis, Theorie, Zeitkritik* (Munich, 1971)

Vaget, Hans Rudolf, *Goethe: Der Mann von 60 Jahren* (Königstein, 1982)

Vaget, Hans Rudolf, "Introduction: The Poet as Liberator: Goethe's Priapean Project," in Johann Wolfgang von Goethe, *Erotic Poems* (Oxford, 1988), ix–xlvi

Vaget, Hans Rudolf, "The GDR Faust: A Literary Autopsy," *Oxford German Studies* 24 (1995): 145–74

Vaget, Hans Rudolf, *Thomas Mann, der Amerikaner: Leben und Werk im amerikanischen Exil, 1938–1952* (Frankfurt am Main, 2011)

Vaget, Hans Rudolf, "Who's Afraid of Daniel Wilson? Zum Stand der Diskussion über den politischen Goethe," *Monatshefte für deutschsprachige Literatur und Kunst* 98, no. 3 (2006): 333–48

Vance, Jonathan, *Unlikely Soldiers: How Two Canadians Fought against Nazi Occupation* (Toronto, 2008)

van de Velde, Henry, *Geschichte meines Lebens*, ed. Hans Curjel (Munich, 1962)

Vehse, Carl Eduard, *Der Hof zu Weimar* (Leipzig, 1991; 1st edn. 1854)

Ventzke, Marcus, "Hofökonomie und Mäzenatentum: Der Hof im Geflecht der weimarischen Staatsfinanzen zur Zeit der Regierungsübernahme Herzog Carl Augusts," in Joachim Berger, ed., *Der "Musenhof" Anna Amalias: Geselligkeit, Mäzenatentum und Kunstliebhaberei im klassischen Weimar* (Cologne, 2001), 19–52

Victor, Christoph, *Oktoberfrühling: Die Wende in Weimar 1989* (Weimar, 1992)

Vollnhals, Clemens, "Das Ministerium für Staatssicherheit: Ein Instrument totalitärer Herrschaftsausübung," in Hartmut Kaelble/Jürgen Kocka/Hartmut Zwahr, eds, *Sozialgeschichte der DDR* (Stuttgart, 1994), 498–518

Volz, Pia Daniela, *Nietzsche im Labyrinth seiner Krankheit: Eine medizinisch-biographische Untersuchung* (Würzburg, 1990)

Voss, Richard, *Aus einem phantastischen Leben: Erinnerungen* (Stuttgart, 1920)

Voss, Werner, *Zehnjährige Wiederkehr des Reichsparteitages Weimar, 3., 4., 5. Juli, 1926–1936* ([Weimar], 1936)

Vosskamp, Wilhelm, "Kontinuität und Diskontinuität: Zur deutschen Literaturwissenschaft im Dritten Reich," in Peter Lundgreen, ed., *Wissenschaft im Dritten Reich* (Frankfurt am Main, 1985), 140–62

Wachler, Ernst, *Die Freilichtbühne: Betrachtungen über das Problem des Volkstheaters unter freiem Himmel* (Leipzig, 1909)

Wachler, Ernst, *Heimat und Volksschauspiel* (Munich, 1904)

Wachler, Ernst, *Sommerspiele auf vaterländischer Grundlage* (Berlin, 1910)

Wachsmann, Nikolaus, "The Dynamics of Destruction: The Development of the Concentration Camps, 1933–1945," in Jane Caplan/Wachsmann, eds, *Concentration Camps in Nazi Germany: The New Histories* (London, 2010), 17–43

Wagner, Christoph, "Zwischen Lebensreform und Esoterik: Johannes Ittens Weg ans Bauhaus in Weimar," in Wagner, ed., *Johannes Itten, Wassily Kandinsky, Paul Klee: Das Bauhaus und die Esoterik* (Bielefeld, 2005), 65–77

Wagner, Nike, *Wagner Theater* (Frankfurt am Main, 1998)

Wagner, Richard, *Mein Leben*, 2 vols. (Munich, 1911)

Wahl, Hans Rudolf, *Die Religion des deutschen Nationalismus: Eine mentalitätsgeschichtliche Studie zur Literatur des Kaiserreichs: Felix Dahn, Ernst von Wildenbruch, Walter Flex* (Heidelberg, 2002)

Wahl, Volker, "Das Staatliche Bauhaus in Weimar, 1919 bis 1925: Zur Institutionsgeschichte und zur Überlieferung seiner Registratur," in Christoph Wagner ed., *Johannes Itten, Wassily Kandinsky, Paul Klee: Das Bauhaus und die Esoterik* (Bielefeld, 2005), 21–27

Wahl, Volker, "Die literarischen Gesellschaften in Weimar nach 1945: Eine Dokumentation zur Wiederaufnahme ihrer Tätigkeit unter der Besatzungsmacht 1945/46," *Mitteldeutsches Jahrbuch für Kultur und Geschichte*, 4 (1977): 123–41

Wahl, Volker, ed., *Die Meisterratsprotokolle des Staatlichen Bauhauses Weimar, 1919 bis 1925* (Weimar, 2001)

Wahl, Volker, "Die Überwindung des Labyrinths: Der Beginn der Reorganisation des Goethe- und Schiller-Archivs unter Willy Flach und die Vorgeschichte seines Direktorats," in Jochen Golz, ed., *Das Goethe- und Schiller-Archiv, 1896–1996: Beiträge aus dem ältesten deutschen Literaturarchiv* (Weimar, 1996), 71–103

Walden, Nell/Lothar Schreyer, eds, *Der Sturm: Ein Erinnerungsbuch an Herwarth Walden und die Künstler aus dem Sturmkreis* (Baden-Baden, 1954)

Walker, Alan, *Franz Liszt: The Final Years* (New York, 1996)

Walker, Alan, *Franz Liszt: The Virtuoso Years, 1811–1847* (London, 1983)

Walker, Alan, *Franz Liszt: The Weimar Years, 1848–1861* (Ithaca, NY, 1993)

Walter, Franz, "Thüringen – Einst Hochburg der sozialistischen Arbeiterbewegung," *Internationale Wissenschaftliche Korrespondenz zur Geschichte der deutschen Arbeiterbewegung* 28 (1992): 21–39

Walter, Karl, "Herder und Heintze: Aus der Geschichte des weimarischen Gymnasiums," *Neue Jahrbücher für das klassische Altertum, Geschichte und deutsche Literatur und für Pädagogik* 22/ II. Abteilung, no. 1 (1908): 36–59

Walter, Michael, *Richard Strauss und seine Zeit* (Laaber, 2000)

Walther, Emil, "Von Goethe zu Bismarck: Eine literarisch-politische Betrachtung," *Bismarck-Jahrbuch* 3 (1896): 362–89

Wapnewski, Peter, *Mit dem anderen Auge: Erinnerungen, 1922–1959* (Berlin, 2005)

Wartewig-Hörning, Jutta/Horst Daner/Klaus G. Beyer, *Weimar: Sozialistische Gegenwart und Tradition* [Weimar, 1975]

Watson, Peter, *The German Genius: Europe's Third Renaissance, the Second Scientific Revolution, and the Twentieth Century* (New York, 2010)

Watzdorf-Bachoff, Erika von, *Im Wandel und in der Verwandlung der Zeit: Ein Leben von 1878 bis 1963*, ed. Reinhard R. Doerries (Stuttgart, 1997)

Webber, Andrew J., *Berlin in the Twentieth Century: A Cultural Topography* (Cambridge, 2008)

Weber, Christiane, *Villen in Weimar*, vol. 2 (Arnstadt, 1997)

Weber, Christiane, *Villen in Weimar*, vol. 4 (Arnstadt, 2002)

Weber, Christiane, *Villen in Weimar*, vol. 5 (Arnstadt, 2005)

Weber, Klaus, "Totenbild, Lebensleib und Maske: Lothar Schreyers 'Totenhäuser'," in Christoph Wagner, ed., *Johannes Itten, Wassily Kandinsky, Paul Klee: Das Bauhaus und die Esoterik* (Bielefeld, 2005), 91–97

Weber, Nicholas Fox, *The Bauhaus Group: Six Masters of Modernism* (New York, 2009)

Wehler, Hans-Ulrich, *Das Deutsche Kaiserreich, 1871–1918*, 4th edn (Göttingen, 1980)

Wehler, Hans-Ulrich, *Deutsche Gesellschaftsgeschichte: Erster Band: Vom Feudalismus des Alten Reiches bis zur Defensiven Modernisierung der Reformära, 1700–1815* (Munich, 1987)

Wehler, Hans-Ulrich, *Deutsche Gesellschaftsgschichte: Zweiter Band: Von der Reformära bis zur industriellen und politischen "Deutschen Doppelrevolution," 1815–1845/49* (Munich, 1987)

Wehler, Hans-Ulrich, *Deutsche Gesellschaftsgeschichte: Dritter Band: Von der "Deutschen Doppelrevolution" bis zum Beginn des Ersten Weltkrieges, 1849–1914* (Munich, 1995)

Wehler, Hans-Ulrich, *Deutsche Gesellschaftsgeschichte: Vierter Band: Vom Beginn des Ersten Weltkriegs bis zur Gründung der beiden deutschen Staaten, 1914–1949* (Munich, 2003)

Wehler, Hans-Ulrich, *Deutsche Gesellschaftsgeschichte: Fünfter Band: Bundesrepublik und DDR, 1949–1990* (Munich, 2008)

Wehner, Jens, *Kulturpolitik und Volksfront: Ein Beitrag zur Geschichte der sowjetischen Besatzungszone Deutschlands, 1945–1949* (Frankfurt am Main, 1992)

Weimar-Festspiele der deutschen Jugend 1939, 10. bis 29. Juni im Deutschen Nationaltheater zu Weimar (Weimar, [1939])

Weimarer Reden des grossdeutschen Dichtertreffens 1938 (Hamburg, 1939)

Weinreich, Max, *Hitler's Professors: the Part of Scholarship in Hitler's Crimes against the Jewish People* (New York, 1946)

Weisenburger, Elvira, "Der 'Rassepapst': Hans Friedrich Karl Günther, Professor für Rassenkunde," in Michael Kissner/Joachim Scholtysack, eds, *Die Führer der Provinz: NS-Biographien aus Baden und Württemberg* (Konstanz, 1997), 161–99

Weiss, Sheila Faith, *The Nazi Symbiosis: Human Genetics and Politics in the Third Reich* (Chicago, 2010)

Weissbecker, Manfred, "Die NSDAP in Thüringen – Vom Experiment zum 'Schutz- und Trutzgau des Führers'," in Jens-F. Dwars/Mathias Günther, eds, *Das braune Herz Deutschlands? Rechtsextremismus in Thüringen* (Jena, 2001), 61–99

Weissheimer, Wendelin, *Erlebnisse mit Richard Wagner, Franz Liszt und vielen anderen Zeitgenossen nebst deren Briefen*, 2nd edn (Stuttgart, 1898)

Weitz, Eric D., *Weimar Germany: Promise and Tragedy* (Princeton, 2007)

Wendermann, Gerda, "Die 'entartete' Kunst und Weimar," in Cornelia Nowak/Kai Uwe Schierz/ Justus H. Ulbricht, eds, *Expressionismus in Thüringen: Facetten eines kulturellen Aufbruchs* (Jena, 1999), 426–33

"Wer ist so feig, der jetzt noch könnte zagen:" Deutsches Nationaltheater und Staatskapelle Weimar, *Intendanz Stephan Märki* (Berlin, 2012)

Whyte, Max, "The Uses and Abuses of Nietzsche in the Third Reich: Alfred Baeumler's 'Heroic Realism'," *Journal of Contemporary History* 43 (2008): 171–94

Wichert, Adalbert, "Bismarck und Goethe: Klassikrezeption der deutschen Geschichtswissenschaft zwischen Kaiserreich und Drittem Reich," in Karl Richter/Jörg Schönert, eds, *Klassik und Moderne: Die Weimarer Klassik als historisches Ereignis und Herausforderung im kulturgeschichtlichen Prozess* (Stuttgart, 1983), 321–39

Wick, Rainer, "Johannes Itten am Bauhaus: Ästhetische Erziehung als Ganzheitserziehung," in *Johannes Itten: Künstler und Lehrer* (Berne, 1984), 105–23

Wiese, Benno von, *Ich erzähle mein Leben: Erinnerungen* (Frankfurt am Main, 1982)

Wiesner, Erich, *Man nannte mich Ernst: Erlebnisse und Episoden aus der Geschichte der Arbeiterjugendbewegung*, 4th edn (Berlin, 1978)

Wildenbruch, Ernst von, *Ein Wort über Weimar* (Berlin, 1903)

Wildenbruch, Ernst von, *Gesammelte Werke: Dritte Reihe*, vol. 16 (Berlin, 1924)

Wildenbruch, Ernst von, *Grossherzog Carl Alexander: Ein Gedenkblatt zum 5. Januar 1901* (Weimar, 1901)

Wilderotter, Hans, "'Das Symbolische des deutschen Schicksals': Der politische Gehalt und der politische Kontext der Goethe-Gedächtniswoche 1932," in Wilderotter/Michael Dorrmann, eds, *Wege nach Weimar: Auf der Suche nach der Einheit von Kunst und Politik* (Berlin, 1999), 109–26

Wilson, Daniel, *Das Goethe-Tabu: Protest und Menschenrechte im klassischen Weimar* (Munich, 1999)

Winkler, Heinrich August, "Die deutsche Gesellschaft der Weimarer Republik und der Antisemitimus," in Bernd Martin/Ernst Schulin, eds, *Die Juden als Minderheit in der Geschichte*, 2nd edn (Munich, 1982), 271–89

Winkler, Heinrich August, *Von der Revolution zur Stabilisierung: Arbeiter und Arbeiterbewegung in der Weimarer Republik, 1918 bis 1924* (Berlin, 1984)

Winkler, Klaus-Jürgen, *Baulehre und Entwerfen am Bauhaus, 1919–1933* (Weimar, 2003)

Winkler, Klaus-Jürgen, "Kommentierte Dokumentation," in Achim Preiss/Winkler, *Weimarer Konzepte: Die Kunst- und Bauhochschule, 1860–1995* (Weimar, 1996), 57–280

Wistrich, Robert, *Who's Who in Nazi Germany* (New York, 1982)

Witzmann, Georg, *Thüringen von 1918–1933: Erinnerungen eines Politikers* (Meisenheim am Glan, 1958)

Wohlfeld, Udo, *". . . und unweigerlich führt der Weg nach Buchenwald": Der Geist von Weimar hinter Gittern* (Weimar, 1999)

Wolf, Christiane, *Gauforen: Zentren der Macht: Zur nationalsozialistischen Architektur und Stadtplanung* (Berlin, 1999)

Wolfradt, Willi, "Lyonel Feininger," *Cicerone* 16 (1924): 163–68

Wolle, Stefan, *Die heile Welt der Diktatur: Alltag und Herrschaft in der DDR, 1971–1989* (Berlin, 1998)

Wollkopf, Roswitha, "Das Nietzsche-Archiv im Spiegel der Beziehungen Elisabeth Förster-Nietzsches zu Harry Graf Kessler," *Jahrbuch der Deutschen Schillergesellschaft* 34 (1990): 125–67

Wollkopf, Roswitha, "Die Gremien des Nietzsche-Archivs und ihre Beziehungen zum Faschismus bis 1933," in Karl-Heinz Hahn, ed., *Im Vorfeld der Literatur: Vom Wert archivalischer Überlieferung für das Verständnis von Literatur und ihrer Geschichte* (Weimar, 1991), 227–41

Wulf, Joseph, ed., *Literatur und Dichtung im Dritten Reich: Eine Dokumentation* (Gütersloh, 1963)

Wulf, Joseph, ed., *Musik im Dritten Reich: Eine Dokumentation* (Gütersloh, 1963)

Wüst, Walther, *Indogermanisches Bekenntnis: Sechs Reden* (Berlin-Dahlem, 1942)

Zabka, Thomas, "Vom 'deutschen Mythus' zum 'Kriegshilfsdienst': 'Faust'-Aneignungen im nationalsozialistischen Deutschland," in Frank Möbus/Friederike Schmidt-Möbus/Gerd Unverfehrt, eds, *Faust: Annäherung an einen Mythos* (Göttingen, 1995), 313–31

Zander, Otto, *Eröffnungsrede von Oberbannführer Otto Zander, K.-Chef des Kulturamtes der Reichsjugendführung am 12. Juni 1941 in Weimar* ([Berlin], 1941)

Zander, Otto, ed., *Weimar: Bekenntnis und Tat: Kulturpolitisches Arbeitslager der Reichsjugendführung 1938* (Berlin, 1938)

Zander, Otto, ed., *Weimar-Festspiele der deutschen Jugend, 13. Juni bis 13. Juli 1938* (Weimar, [1938])

Zaremba, Michael, *Christoph Martin Wieland, Aufklärer und Poet: Eine Biographie* (Cologne, 2007)

Zaremba, Michael, *Johann Gottfried Herder, Prediger der Humanität: Eine Biographie* (Cologne, 2002)

Zeller, Bernhard, ed., *Klassiker in finsteren Zeiten, 1933–1945: Eine Ausstellung des Deutschen Literaturarchivs im Schiller-Nationalmuseum, Marbach am Neckar*, 2nd edn, 2 vols (Marbach, 1983)

Ziegler, Hans-Severus, *Adolf Bartels: Ein völkischer Vorkämpfer der deutschen Jugend* (Erfurt, 1942)

Ziegler, Hans Severus, *Adolf Hitler aus dem Erleben dargestellt* (Göttingen, 1964)

Ziegler, Hans Severus, "Das Deutsche Nationaltheater nach der Machtübernahme," in Otto zur Nedden, ed., *Festschrift zur feierlichen Wiedereröffnung des erneuerten Hauses, Mittwoch, 22. Mai 1940* ([Weimar], 1940), 28–32

Ziegler, Hans Severus, *Entartete Musik: Eine Abrechnung* (Düsseldorf, [1938])

Ziegler, Hendrik, "Carl Alexander und Wilhelm II: Fürstliches Kunstmäzenatentum im Vergleich," in Lothar Ehrlich/Justus H. Ulbricht, eds, *Carl Alexander von Sachsen-Weimar-Eisenach: Erbe, Mäzen und Politiker* (Cologne, 2004), 129–63

Ziegler, Hendrik, *Die Kunst der Weimarer Malerschule von der Pleinairmalerei zum Impressionismus* (Cologne, 2001)

Ziegler, Hendrik, "'Klein-Paris' in Weimar: Die Weimarer Malerschule und der französische Impressionismus," in Rolf Bothe/Thomas Föhl, eds, *Aufstieg und Fall der Moderne* (Ostfildern-Ruit, 1999), 14–25

Ziermann, Klaus, ed., *Alexander Dymschitz: Wissenschaftler, Soldat, Internationalist* (Berlin, 1977)

Zimmermann, Reinhard, "Der Bauhaus-Künstler Kandinsky – Ein Esoteriker?" in Christoph Wagner, ed., *Johannes Itten, Wassily Kandinsky, Paul Klee: Das Bauhaus und die Esoterik* (Bielefeld, 2005), 47–55

Zimmermann, Reinhard, "Von Kandinsky zu Itten: Dispositionen einer Kunsttheorie," in Christa Lichtenstern/Christoph Wagner, eds, *Johannes Itten und die Moderne: Beiträge eines wissenschaftlichen Symposiums* (Ostfildern-Ruit, 2003), 117–37

Zimmermann, Susanne/Thomas Zimmermann, "Die Medizinische Fakultät der Universität Jena im 'Dritten Reich'," in Uwe Hossfeld ed., *"Im Dienst an Volk und Vaterland": Die Jenaer Universität in der NS-Zeit* (Cologne, 2005), 127–64

Žmegač, Viktor, *Der historische und typologische Jude: Studien zu jüdischen Gestalten in der Literatur der Jahrhundertwende* (Tübingen, 1996)

Zur Nedden, Otto, ed., *Festschrift zur feierlichen Wiedereröffnung des erneuerten Hauses, Mittwoch, 22. Mai 1940* ([Weimar], 1940)

Zuschlag, Christoph, *"Entartete Kunst": Ausstellungsstrategien im Nazi-Deutschland* (Worms, 1995)

Index